THE EPIC OF MODERN MAN

THE EPIC OF

P R E N T I C E - H A L L ,   I N C .

EDITED BY

L. S. STAVRIANOS

MODERN MAN

A Collection of Readings

Englewood Cliffs, N.J.

THE EPIC OF MODERN MAN
A Collection of Readings

EDITED BY L. S. STAVRIANOS

Library of Congress Catalog Card No.: 66-10710

Printed in the United States of America

C-28334

Current printing (last digit):
10 9 8 7 6 5 4 3 2 1

PRENTICE-HALL OF CANADA, LTD., *Toronto*
PRENTICE-HALL OF INDIA (PRIVATE) LTD., *New Delhi*
PRENTICE-HALL OF JAPAN, INC., *Tokyo*
PRENTICE-HALL INTERNATIONAL, INC., *London*
PRENTICE-HALL OF AUSTRALIA, PTY., LTD., *Sydney*

Preface

The distinctive feature of this volume of readings in modern history is that it is globally oriented rather than West oriented. It reflects the viewpoint of an observer perched on the moon, surveying our planet as a whole, rather than one who is ensconced in London or Paris, or, for that matter, in Peking or Delhi. The guiding principle has been that no Western movement or institution be treated unless non-Western movements or institutions of similar magnitude or world significance also be treated. This rationale explains why certain familiar topics are considered here briefly or not at all. Conversely, it also explains why certain less familiar topics are considered at length. In the early modern period, for example, attention turns to not only the European discoveries, but also the conditions and institutions of the peoples being "discovered." For the nineteenth century, there are readings not only on Western imperialism but also on the manifold effects of that imperialism on the colonial territories. And although the contemporary period's crises, wars, and European alliances cannot be ignored, emphasis is placed on finding out why more than fifty countries have won their independence in the past two decades and why this is an era of Western decline and triumph.

One criterion made the choice of readings: their effectiveness in illuminating the subject under consideration. Short readings are sometimes more forceful than long ones, and secondary sources often provide more insight than primary ones. Accordingly, the following selections are of varied lengths and from diverse sources. The connective tissue of narrative introductions is designed to provide an integrated account of major trends and to relate the selections to those trends.

L. S. STAVRIANOS

OTHER BOOKS BY L. S. STAVRIANOS:

Contents

Part
III

WORLD OF WESTERN DOMINANCE, 1763-1914

Part
IV

WORLD OF WESTERN DECLINE AND TRIUMPH, 1914-

Chapter 30

EPILOGUE: OUR GOLDEN AGE? 518

*If we could first know
where we are and whither we
are tending, we could better judge
what to do and how to do it.*

ABRAHAM LINCOLN

*History, in order to become a
science of human growth, must be able
to make comparisons. It can only do so
by making itself more and more universal.*

JACQUES PIRENNE
The Tides of History

WORLD OF
ISOLATED REGIONS,
TO 1500

Chapter One

Introduction:
from regional to
global history

WORLD HISTORY IN MODERN EDUCATION 1

The teaching of history in the West has tended in the past to be West-oriented. This natural and understandable tendency has been accentuated by the predominant role of the West in world affairs in recent centuries. Since World War II, however, this emphasis on the West has been increasingly questioned, partly because the impact of two world wars and of the scientific-technological revolution has compelled general recognition of "One World." In the following selection, a historian stresses the need for teaching world history and, more specifically, world history that is taught as the interaction of civilizations rather than as an agglomeration of disparate civilizations.*

We are still so close to this dramatic transformation of world relationships that it is difficult to comprehend its full significance. "The rise to self-assertion of Asian and African peoples" (to borrow Rupert Emerson's expressive phrase) has come with dizzying suddenness, and we find ourselves ill-prepared to cope with the challenge it presents to our world outlook, to our foreign policy and, perhaps most important of all, to our concepts and methds of education.

· The liberal arts curriculum of the typical American college is overwhelmingly "Western" in orientation, in both the social sciences and the humanistic studies. In recent years there has been a growing

* M. D. Lewis, "How Many Histories Should We Teach? Asia and Africa in a Liberal Arts Education," *Liberal Education*, XLVIII (October, 1962), 1-8.

awareness of the limitations of this approach. Many questions come readily to mind. Will our present educational pattern offer students an adequate preparation for their future, or will it prove increasingly irrelevant to the problems of a rapidly changing world? Does our neglect of the peoples and cultures of the "non-Western world" reflect a considered judgment of relative importance or an outmoded ethnocentrism? Should education be a mirror of our own society or a window through which we can learn something of the dynamic forces affecting the vast majority of mankind? . . .

Historians, as specialists in the past, have good reason to resist suggestions that they tailor their academic interests to the seeming urgencies of the present day. Yet I venture the claim that there is more at stake than our manifest contemporary need for a wider acquaintance with the non-Western world. The real issue we face is the integrity of our discipline as a field of knowledge.

Our total historical outlook has been and to a large extent still is conditioned by a world that no longer exists. We have not yet come to grips with the implications of the post-colonial situation. Our historical emphases are derived from an age of Western domination that is as dead as the Ottoman Empire. As historians we take pride in our awareness of the social and cultural roots of ideas, yet we have been negligent in applying this insight to the intellectual content of our own professional discipline.

If this is true, what then should be done to correct the situation? Should we devote as much time and effort to the history of China as we do to the history of England? I will not argue this proposition, though I suspect that a strong case might be made for it. But even if we did give "equal time" to the world's oldest continuous historical civilization, then what of Japan, not to speak of India, Southeast Asia, the Middle East or Africa? The magnitude of the problem is staggering. Necessarily we find ourselves asking not only "how many histories should we teach," but also how many histories is it possible to teach? Specifically, we must ask what it is in the histories of the Asian and African areas that most urgently demands our attention.

Studies in the traditional civilizations of the non-Western world certainly deserve a place in our educational pattern. Nevertheless, there is a danger in over-emphasizing such studies as an answer to our problem. As John K. Fairbank has suggested, "to assume that mere knowledge and appreciation of the past is automatically an intellectual preparation for the current day may be a fatal *non sequitur*. . . . Preparing our students to answer Mao Tse-tung with the words of Confucius is not good enough."

If we take seriously the proposition that history is more than a grab-bag of unrelated facts, that it is a reasoned account of the evolution of human societies, we are challenged to seek an understanding of the forces which have brought forth not only Mao but also Nehru, and Nasser, and Nkrumah, and the other leaders whose names have suddenly become familiar terms. For those who take refuge in the dubious comforts of the conspiracy theory of history, there is of course no need to probe deeply into the roots of contemporary developments in Asia and Africa. If we take seriously our responsibility as scholars, however, we cannot be content with simplistic explanations. We have an obligation to use the techniques of our discipline to promote an understanding of the processes of social change which have created the world in which we live.

From this standpoint, the shortcomings of our present approach arise as much from our failure to realize the full significance of our own Western history as they do from our failure to be concerned with the histories of other cultures. In our concentration on the internal development of Western civilization, we have failed fully to appreciate its impact on the broader stream of world history.

In short, we need to comprehend as a major category within our discipline the historical process of interaction between Western civilization and the civilizations of Asia and Africa. This process, which began some five centuries ago, had reached an apparent climax at the beginning of the twentieth century with the establishment of a European world hegemony. When Ramsay Muir wrote in 1916 of *The Expansion of Europe,* he called it "the culmination of modern history." Half a century later we can see that appearances were deceiving.

The true product of this process has been the emergence of a world civilization in which the new states of Asia and Africa seek, not a return to their ancient patterns of life which prevailed before the Western intrusion, but the fulfilment of aspirations born in an era of European domination. We must revise Professor Muir's evaluation, but we must not forget the significance of his theme. "The imperial spread of Western European civilization over the face of the earth," Rupert Emerson reminds us in 1960, "has thrust elements of essential identity on peoples everywhere."

To say this in no way minimizes the vast differences that continue to divide the world's peoples. What it does do is emphasize the fact that the Asian and African societies of today are as much or more the product of the historical process of Western expansion, *and* of indigenous reaction and response, as they are of their own traditional civilizations. K. M. Panikkar, the Indian scholar and diplomat, has urged convincingly that the period of Western dominance "effected a transformation which touches practically every aspect of life" in the countries of Asia.

> The massiveness of the changes that have already taken place, the upsurges which have radically transformed their ancient societies, and the ideas that have modified their outlook, involve a qualitative break with the past which justly entitles the changes to be described as revolutionary.

In its main outlines, the same statement may be made for the emergent nations of Africa and the Middle East.

At this point we should inquire how these several non-Western regions have fared in American historiography and history teaching. Far Eastern history, encompassing China and Japan, has been an established field of interest for some time. It has a coherence derived both from geography and from common elements in the cultural tradition of the region. Nevertheless, it is hard to avoid the conclusion that its early recognition as an accepted area of historical study was in large part due to the circumstances that both countries remained independent throughout the modern period (however much China's independence may in fact have been impaired in the course of the nineteenth and early twentieth centuries).

India, on the other hand, has received far less attention from American historians than have the countries of East Asia. Until recently its history has been dealt with (if at all) primarily in connection with the history of the British Empire. And if India has been a "poor relation," Indonesia and the countries of Southeast Asia have been the orphans of history. It was difficult to ignore the British Empire (though India rarely received attention proportionate to its relative importance in that empire). The empires of the Dutch and French, however, were generally casualties to the pressure of other interests. The countries of the Middle East were viewed mainly as pawns in the "Eastern Question" of European politics, while Africa through the first half of the twentieth century remained as much a Dark Continent to historians as it had been to geographers at the beginning of the nineteenth. A modern student of African history has observed that it was "a cardinal premise of colonial rule" that "Africa has no history." An "uphill battle . . . had to be fought to demonstrate the very existence of the thing to be studied."

If we assume that it is a matter of some importance to introduce our students to the historical backgrounds of each of these regions—and that is hardly an unreasonable assumption—we must recognize that it is not feasible to approach our task in a geographically compartmentalized fashion. This is true for the practical reason that there are simply too many areas with which we must deal. It is equally true for an intellectual reason, however, and this is the one that should be most compelling.

The Portuguese voyages of exploration in the fifteenth century set in motion a process which has brought about a steadily growing degree of interaction between the world's peoples. As a result, it has become increasingly difficult to comprehend the determinants of historical change within a given society without reference to a broader framework. It is a commonplace that the rise of nationalist movements in colonial areas has been as much a product of Western influence as a reaction against it. But it is necessary to see not only the interaction of, let us say, England and India but also the role of Britain's Indian Empire as a factor in the nineteenth-century Western impact on China. At an earlier date, the foundations of Western influence in Asia cannot be divorced from the activities of the Portuguese, the Dutch and the English on the coasts of Africa. The penetration and partition of Africa in recent times drew heavily on the prior experience of European empire in Asia. Japan's nineteenth-century modernization—itself in considerable measure the result of Western pressure—made possible the critically important Japanese influence on the source of development of the Chinese revolution in the twentieth century, and ultimately on the collapse of European empire in Asia during and after World War II. This in turn has profoundly affected the course of events in the past decade in both the Middle East and Africa.

Obviously, no attempt to discuss in integrated fashion the interrelationships of Asia, Africa and the West can do full justice to the separate histories of the many distinct areas involved. What it does make possible, however, is an emphasis on those new elements of external influence and internal response which have had a determining effect in shaping the historical evolution of the Asian and African peoples in modern times. There is nothing unusual about focusing our attention as historians on a process rather than on a specific and limited geographical area. This is essentially what we do when we teach our survey courses on European history. We make no attempt to narrate in full the separate histories of Italy or Spain, France or Austria, the Netherlands or England, Germany or Russia. Instead, we seek to develop an understanding of a process in which first one and then another area stands forth, as each in turn comes to play a decisive role in the unfolding of a continental pattern. On a wider scale, such an approach affords the most meaningful way to introduce our students to the historical background of the Asian and African states of today.

In undertaking this approach, we must acknowledge the limitations of our present knowledge and the magnitude of the work which is still to be done in detailed investigation and broad interpretation. Yet we must recognize the true nature of the problem if we are to have an adequate theoretical framework within which to pursue our studies.

As we seek to analyze the sequence of events that brought about the establishment of Western world dominance, we may well begin by establishing for any particular area the point of intersection between the autonomous development of the indigenous culture and the impact of Western expansion. This point of intersection is by no means identical with the first appearance of venturesome Europeans coming from afar. In its earliest phase, the Europeans' role in Africa or Asia was less the determining element in the history of those regions than it was itself determined and limited by the existing indigenous societies. The presence of European traders on Indian shores was of little consequence in shaping the fortunes of the Mughal Empire in the sixteenth or seventeenth centuries. With the collapse of Mughal authority in the eighteenth century, however, an entirely new situation emerged in which the aspirations and rivalries of the European East India Companies came to have a controlling influence on the course of Indian historical development. In China, neither the seventeenth-century activity of the Jesuits nor the Old Canton Trade of the eighteenth century had a substantial impact on China's age-old civilization. Under the new conditions of the nineteenth century, the impact of the West was profound.

In our study of this process of interaction, it is obviously necessary to survey the development both of the indigenous society and of the expansive forces of European civilization prior to the decisive point of intersection. But our essential concern should be with the ensuing development, in which these two distinct influences blend and interact to produce our modern world.

The approach here proposed encompasses the historical categories summed up by the phrase "the expansion of Europe" and the word "imperialism," but it is of far wider scope. Neither term is adequate to describe the complexity of the historical process with which we are concerned. Both suggest a Europe-centered orientation. Our proper concern should be with the Asian and African societies themselves, as they are drawn into contact with a wider world.

Our subject demands a new and far more sophisticated analysis of the causative factors in historical development than we have been accustomed to make. In the era of European world hegemony, it was easy to assume that the dominant role of the West was the natural and inevitable result of Western "superiority"—material, technical, even moral. In retrospect, it should be apparent that no such simple answer will serve.

It would be well for us to approach our task without false pride. The transformation of traditional societies under the impact of Western expansion has been a many-sided phenomenon, destructive as well as creative. "The West," Arnold Toynbee reminds us, "has been the arch-aggressor of modern times" where Asia and Africa are concerned. Yet much of our writing of the history of empire has borne a mark of pious rectitude that does little credit to our scholarly pretensions. Lowell Ragatz has catalogued some recurring themes:

> The establishment of alien rule in any region is told in terms of grievous wrongs suffered there by honest traders and saintly church folk at the

hands of treacherous chieftains, ... of some insult to the flag demanding vengeance in the name of national honor, of gallant stands by small bodies of homeland troops against fantastic hordes of coloured men, of the outsiders' natural eventual triumph, of the blessings bestowed upon a wavering population by reforming governors, of the settlement of vacant lands and others made available through "purchase" or confiscation from "rebels," of amazing commercial development, of "rights graciously accorded the natives," and of the ultimate acceptance of a new and richer way of life ... by a regenerated and grateful body of dependent peoples.

The cruder manifestations of this outlook are happily disappearing, but in more subtle form the problem of bias is still with us. In analyzing the Western impact on Asia and Africa, can we honestly say that we have given due weight in our evaluations to the views of the Asians and Africans themselves? Two points in particular deserve careful scrutiny: the economic effects of Western dominance, and the nature and intent of Western political control over non-European peoples. On the first point, Jawaharlal Nehru has argued that "a great part of the costs of transition to industrialism in western Europe were paid for by India, China, and the other colonial countries whose economy was dominated by the European powers." On the second, Nehru has pointedly challenged the comforting view "that the British government through its higher services in India, was training us for the difficult and intricate art of self-government."

I do not suggest that the interpretations of nationalist writers should be accepted at face value. I do say that we shall do our students a disservice if we fail to acquaint them with the fact that the events of modern world history look different from an Asian or African perspective. I do insist that such nationalist interpretations deserve a more serious consideration than they have commonly received in the West. Needless to say, they also should be subjected to critical evaluation—the same critical evaluation which too often we have failed to give to imperialist apologetics.

The primary issue, however, is less the problem of bias in interpretation than it is our failure to accord to the Asian and African aspects of historical experience an emphasis commensurate with their relative importance. So long as we permit our students to consider themselves educated in the field of history when they have little or no knowledge of the process that has drastically reshaped the lives of the majority of mankind, we shall not have met our professional responsibility.

In seeking to rectify this situation, we shall encounter many difficult and complex problems. We shall also gain a new dimension to our view of historical change. Our studies of the interaction of Asia, Africa and the West will not only shed much-needed light on the transformation of traditional societies. They will enhance our understanding of the dynamics of Western civilization itself.

Chapter Two

Roots of
West European
expansion

Religion and the Expansion of Europe 2

The most important feature of modern world history is the over-seas expansion of Western Europe, leading eventually to European domi-nation of the entire globe. This fateful development has determined to a large degree the course of world history from 1500 to the present day. Yet European expansion and domination were by no means foreordained; rather, they were unexpected—particularly in view of the hitherto modest role played by Western Europe in world affairs. Why Western Europe rather than some other region of Eurasia took the lead in overseas enter-prise is, therefore, a question of fundamental significance for modern world history.

The expansion of Europe may be explained in part by the univer-salism and the militancy of the Christian church. From the beginning, Christianity asserted itself as a universal religion by its emphasis on the brotherhood of man. Missionary effort has characterized the church from the days of the apostles to the present; in the fifteenth century this mis-sionary spirit was particularly militant because of the centuries of armed conflict with Islam and because of repeated crusades to drive back the infidel from Europe. In contrast to Christianity's militancy and prose-lytism, Buddhism spread peacefully with the gradual diffusion of Indian culture by travelers and immigrants. Likewise, the Moslems, who had conquered a great empire by the sword, were not particularly concerned about the religion of their subjects so long as they paid tribute. But the Christian Europeans had an entirely different attitude, as is illustrated by the following selections. The first, by one of the conquistadors who

*took Mexico, relates how the Indians in the Spanish colonies were taught the
"true" faith.* The second, by an English promoter of overseas colonization, emphasizes the opportunity to convert the heathen as one of the reasons for planting
colonies in the New World.***

Teaching Christianity

After we had abolished idolatry and other abominations from among the
Indians, the Almighty blessed our endeavours and we baptized the men,
women, and all the children born after the conquest, whose souls would
otherwise have gone to the infernal regions. With the assistance of God, and
by a good regulation of our most Christian Monarch, of glorious memory,
Don Carlos, and of his excellent son Don Philip, our most happy and invincible king, to whom may God grant a long life and an increase of territory,
several pious monks of different orders arrived in New Spain, who travelled
from place to place, preached the gospel to the inhabitants, and baptized
new-born infants. By their unremitted exertions Christianity became planted
in their hearts, so that the inhabitants came to the confessional once every
year; and those who were better instructed in our Christian faith received
the holy communion. Their churches are very richly ornamented with altars,
crucifixes, candelabras, different-sized chalices, censers, and everything else
required in our religious ceremonies, all of pure silver. The more wealthy
townships have the vestments of choristers, the chasuble and the full canoni-
cals of a priest, mostly of velvet damask or silk, and of various colours and
manufacture. The flags which hang to the crosses are of silk, and richly
ornamented with gold and pearls. The funeral crosses are covered with satin,
and bear the figure of a death's head and cross bones; the funeral palls, in
some townships, are also more or less splendid. The churches are likewise
provided with a set of bells, have a regular band of choristers, besides flutes,
dulcimers, clarions, and sacbuts, and some have even organs. I do believe
there are more large and small trumpets in the province of Guatimala, where
I am writing this, than in my native country Old Castile. It is indeed wonderful, and we cannot thank God too much for it, to behold the Indians assisting
in the celebration of the holy mass, which they particularly do in those
places where the Franciscan friars or the Brothers of Charity officiate at
the altar.

It was also a great blessing for the Indians that the monks taught them to
say their prayers in their own language, and frequently to repeat them. The
monks have altogether so accustomed them to reverence everything relating
to religion, that they never pass by any altar or cross without falling down
on their knees and repeating a Pater Noster or an Ave Maria. We also taught
the Indians to make wax lights for the holy services, for, previous to our
arrival, they made no manner of use of their wax. We taught them to be so
obedient and respectful to the monks and priests, that whenever one of these

---

* *The Memoirs of the Conquistador Bernal Diaz Del Castillo . . . Containing a True
and Full Account of the Discovery and Conquest of Mexico and New Spain* (London:
J. Hatchard, 1844), II, 390-91.

** R. Hakluyt, "A Discourse on Western Planting," *Collections*, 2nd ser., *Documentary
History of the State of Maine* (Cambridge, Mass.: Maine Historical Society, 1877),
II, 7-10.

religious men approach a township the bells are rung, and the inhabitants go out to meet him with wax-lights in their hands; and they always give him a hospitable reception. On the day of Corpus Christi, the birth of Mary, and on other saint-days, when we are accustomed to form processions, the inhabitants of the districts surrounding Guatimala likewise march out in procession with crucifixes, lighted candles, and carry about their tutelar saint splendidly dressed up, all the time chanting hymns, accompanied by the sound of flutes and trumpets.

Colonizing for Conversion

Seinge that the people of that parte of America from 30. degrees in Florida northewarde unto 63. degrees (which ys yet in no Christian princes actuall possession) are idolaters; and that those which Stephen Gomes broughte from the coaste of NORUMBEGA in the yere 1524. worshipped the sonne, the moone, and the starres, and used other idolatrie, as it ys recorded in the historie of Gonsaluo de Ouiedo, in Italian, fol. 52. of the third volume of Ramusius; and that those of Canada and Hochelaga in 48. and 50. degrees worshippe a spirite which they call Cudruaigny, as we reade in the tenthe chapiter of the seconde relation of Jaques Cartier, whoe saieth: This people beleve not at all in God, but in one whome they call Cudruaigny; they say that often he speaketh with them, and telleth them what weather shall followe, whether goodd or badd, &c., and yet notwithstandinge they are very easie to be perswaded, and do all that they sawe the Christians doe in their devine service, with like imitation and devotion, and were very desirous to become Christians, and woulde faine have been baptized, as Verarsanus witnesseth in the laste wordes of his relation, and Jaques Cartier in the tenthe chapiter before recited—it remayneth to be thoroughly weyed and con-sidered by what meanes and by whome this moste godly and Christian work may be perfourmed of inlarginge the glorious gospell of Christe, and reducinge of infinite multitudes of these simple people that are in errour into the righte and perfecte way of their saluation. The blessed Apostle Paule, the converter of the Gentiles, Rom: 10. writeth in this manner: Whosoever shall call on the name of the Lorde shall be saved. But howe shall they call on him in whom they have not beleved? and howe shall they beleve in him of whom they have not hearde? and howe shall they heare withoute a preacher? and howe shall they preache excepte they be sente? Then it is necessary for the salvation of those poore people which have sitten so longe in darkenes and in the shadowe of deathe, that preachers should be sent unto them. But by whome shoulde these preachers be sente? By them no doubte which have taken upon them the protection and defence of the Christian faithe. Nowe the Kinges and Queenes of England have the name of Defendours of the Faithe. By which title I thinke they are not onely chardged to mayneteyne and patronize the faithe of Christe, but also to inlarge and advaunce the same. Neither oughte this to be their laste worke, but rather the principall and chefe of all others, accordinge to the comaundemente of our Saviour, Christe, Mathewe 6, Ffirste seeke the kingdome of God and the righteousness thereof, and all other thinges shalbe mynistred unto you.

Nowe the meanes to sende suche as shall labour effectually in this busi-ness ys, by plantinge one or twoo colonies of our nation upon that fyrme, where they may remaine in safetie, and firste learne the language of the people nere adjoyninge (the gifte of tongues beinge nowe taken awaye), and by little and little acquainte themselves with their manner, and so with discretion and myldenes distill into their purged myndes the swete and lively liquor of the gospel. Otherwise, for preachers to come unto them rashly with oute some suche preparation for their safetie, yt were nothinge els but to ronne to their apparaunte and certaine destruction, as yt happened unto those Spanishe ffryers, that, before any plantinge, withoute strengthe and company, landed in Fflorida, where they were miserablye massacred by the savages. On the other side, by meane of plantinge firste, the small nation of the Portingales towards the Southe and Easte have planted the Christian faithe accordinge to their manner, and have erected many bisshoprickes and colledges to traine upp the youthe of the infidells in the same, of which acte they more vaunte in all their histories and chronicles, then of anythinge els that ever they atchieved. And surely if they had planted the gospell of Christe purely, as they did not, they mighte justly have more rejoyced in that deede of theires, then in the conqueste of the whole contrie, or in any other thinge whatsoever. The like may be saied of the Spaniardes, whoe (as yt is in the preface of the last edition of Osorius de rebus gestis Emanuelis) have established in the West Indies three archebisshopricks, to witt, Mexico, Luna, and Onsco, and thirtene other bisshopricks there named, and have builte above CC. houses of relligion in the space of fyftie yeres or thereaboutes. Now yf they, in their superstition, by meanes of their plantinge in those partes, have don so greate thinges in so shorte space, what may wee hope for in our true and syncere relligion, proposinge unto ourselves in this action not filthie lucre nor vaine ostentation, as they in deede did, but principally the gayninge of the soules of millions of those wretched people, the reducinge of them from darkenes to lighte, from falsehodde to truthe, from dombe idolls to the lyvinge God, from the depe pitt of hell to the highest heavens.

3   TECHNOLOGY AND THE EXPANSION OF EUROPE

A basic factor in the overseas expansion of Western Europe in modern times is the technological progress achieved by that region during the medieval period. Medieval Europe is generally not associated with advanced technology. Instead, it brings to mind the Dark Ages when Western Europe retrogressed catastrophically from "the glory that was Greece and the grandeur that was Rome." It was an obvious and objective fact that medieval Europe was not as rich and luxurious as Byzantium, or the Moslem Near East, or India and China. But this ostentatious elegance was reserved for only the small ruling group, and was made possible by the exploitation of the masses who continued to practice their traditional crafts with the traditional techniques. Western Europe, being less wealthy and populous, was developing at the same time a labor-saving power technology and a new agriculture of unprecedented productivity. This, in turn, engendered an economic and technological dynamism that made the later overseas discoveries feasible. These developments, and their significance for European and world his-

*tory, are analyzed in the following study by Professor Lynn White, Jr., an out-standing American student of medieval technology.**

The Dark Ages doubtless deserve their name: political distintegration, economic depression, the debasement of religion and the collapse of litera-ture surely made the barbarian kingdoms in some ways unimaginably dismal. Yet because many aspects of civilization were in decay we should not assume too quickly that everything was back-sliding. Even an apparent coarsening may indicate merely a shift of interest: in modern painting we recognize that Van Gogh's technical methods were not those of David; so, when we contrast a Hellenistic carved gem with a Merovingian enamel, our judgement should be cautious. Few will dispute that the Irish illumination and the Scandinavian jewelry of the seventh and eighth centuries stand among the supreme arts of all time; yet they are far from classical canons of taste, being rooted in an ancient, and quite separate, tradition of Northern art. So in the history of technology we must be discriminating. Changing tastes and conditions may lead to the degeneration of one technique while the technology of the age as a whole is advancing. The technology of torture, for example, which achieved such hair-raising perfection during the Renaissance, is now happily in eclipse: viewed historically, our modern American "third degree" is bar-baric only in its simplicity.

Indeed, a dark age may stimulate rather than hinder technology. Economic catastrophe in the United States during the past decade has done nothing to halt invention—quite the contrary; and it is a commonplace that war en-courages technological advance. Confusion and depression, which bring havoc in so many areas of life, may have just the opposite effect on technics. And the chances of this are particularly good in a period of general migra-tion, when peoples of diverse backgrounds and inheritances are mixing.

There is, in fact, no proof that any important skills of the Graeco-Roman world were lost during the Dark Ages even in the unenlightened West, much less in the flourishing Byzantine and Saracenic Orient. To be sure, the di-minished wealth and power of the Germanic kings made engineering on the old Roman scale infrequent; yet the full technology of antiquity was avail-able when required: the 276-ton monolith which crowns the tomb of Theo-doric the Ostrogoth was brought to Ravenna from Istria; while more than two centuries later Charlemagne transported not only sizable columns but even a great equestrian statue of Zeno from Ravenna across the Alps to Aachen. Incidentally, we should do well to remember that the northern peoples from remote times were capable of managing great weights, as witness Stonehenge and the dolmens.

In military machines especially we might expect the barbarians to fall below the ancient standard; but at the siege of Paris in 886 we discover the Vikings, who presumably would be as untouched by Roman methods as any western people, using elaborate and powerful artillery; while the city itself was defended with catapults. However, the Dark Ages do not seem to have improved on ancient artillery: the Roman level was not surpassed until the twelfth century when the trebuchet, worked by counterweights, began to drive the less efficient tension and torsion engines from the field.

* L. White, Jr., "Technology and Invention in the Middle Ages," *Speculum*, XV (April, 1940), 149-56.

If the political and economic decay of the Dark Ages affected any technique adversely, it was that of road-building. Yet even here the case is not clear. For northern climates at least, the technical excellence of Roman roads has been exaggerated. They had massive foundations, which sometimes survive to the present day; but the surface, consisting of slabs of masonry cemented together, made no provision for contraction or expansion. Heat made the slabs buckle and crack; water seeped under them and froze, separating them from the foundation. Repairs were difficult and expensive: no modern roadbuilder would consider imitating Roman methods. It was the Middle Ages which developed the cheaper and more efficient method of laying cubes of stone in a loose bed of earth or sand which permitted expansion and made repairs easy: a type of paving still common.

Indeed, the technical skill of classical times was not simply maintained: it was considerably improved. Our view of history has been too top-lofty. We have been dazzled by aspects of civilization which are in every age the property of an elite, and in which the common man, with rare exceptions, has had little part. The so-called "higher" realms of culture might decay, government might fall into anarchy, and trade be reduced to a trickle, but through it all, in the face of turmoil and hard times, the peasant and artisan carried on, and even improved their lot. In technology, at least, the Dark Ages mark a steady and uninterrupted advance over the Roman Empire. Evidence is accumulating to show that a serf in the turbulent and insecure tenth century enjoyed a standard of living considerably higher than that of a proletarian in the reign of Augustus.

The basic occupation was, of course, agriculture. We have passed through at least two agricultural revolutions: that which began with "Turnip" Townshend and Jethro Tull in the early eighteenth century, and another, equally important, in the Dark Ages.

The problem of the development and diffusion of the northern wheeled plow, equipped with colter, horizontal share and moldboard, is too thorny to be discussed here. Experts seem generally agreed: (1) that the new plow greatly increased production by making possible the tillage of rich, heavy, badly-drained river-bottom soils; (2) that it saved labor by making crossplowing superfluous, and thus produced the typical northern strip-system of land division, as distinct from the older block-system dictated by the cross-plowing necessary with the lighter Mediterranean plow; (3) most important of all, that the heavy plow needed such power that peasants pooled their oxen and plowed together, thus laying the basis for the medieval cooperative agricultural community, the manor. But whatever may be the date and origin of the fully developed heavy plow, its effects were supplemented and greatly enhanced in the later eighth century by the invention of the three-field system, an improved rotation of crops and fallow which greatly increased the efficiency of agriculture labor. For example, by switching 600 acres from the two-field to the three-field system, a community of peasants could plant 100 acres more in crops each year with 100 acres less plowing. Since fallow land was plowed twice to keep down the weeds, the old plan required three acres of plowing for every acre of crops, whereas the new plan required only two acres of plowing for every productive acre.

In a society overwhelmingly agrarian, the result of such an innovation could be nothing less than revolutionary. Pirenne is only the most recent of many historians to speculate as to why the reign of Charlemagne witnesssed the shift of the center of European civilization, the change of the focus of history, from the Mediterranean to the plains of Northern Europe. The findings of agricultural history, it seems, have never been applied to this central problem in the study of the growth of the northern races. Since the spring sowing, which was the chief novelty of the three-field system, was unprofitable in the south because of the scarcity of summer rains, the three-field system did not spread below the Alps and the Loire. For obvious reasons of climate the agricultural revolution of the eighth century was confined to Northern Europe. It would appear, therefore, that it was this more efficient and productive use of land and labor which gave to the northern plains an economic advantage over the Mediterranean shores, and which, from Charlemagne's time onward, enabled the Northern Europeans in short order to surpass both in prosperity and in culture the peoples of an older inheritance.

In ways less immediately significant the Dark Ages likewise made ingenuous improvements. One of the most important of these was a contribution to practical mechanics. There are two basic forms of motion: reciprocal and rotary. The normal device for connecting these—a device without which our machine civilization is inconceivable—is the crank. The crank is an invention second in importance only to the wheel itself; yet the crank was unknown to the Greeks and Romans. It appears, even in rudimentary form, only after the Invasions: first, perhaps, in hand-querns, then on rotary grindstones. The later Middle Ages developed its application to all sorts of machinery.

Clearly there are nuggets in this stream for anyone to find. Perhaps the most successful amateur student of early mediaeval technology was the Commandant Lefebvre des Noëttes, who after his retirement from active service in the French cavalry, devoted himself to his hobby, the history of horses. He died in 1936 having made discoveries which must greatly modify our judgment of the Carolingian period. From his investigations Lefebvre des Noëttes concluded that the use of animal power in antiquity was unbelievably inefficient. The ancients did not use nailed shoes on their animals, and broken hooves often rendered beasts useless. Besides, they knew only the yoke-system of harness. While this was adequate for oxen, it was most unsatisfactory for the more rapid horse. The yoke rested on the withers of a team. From each end of the yoke ran two flexible straps: one a girth behind the forelegs, the other circling the horse's neck. As soon as the horse began to pull, the flexible front strap pressed on his windpipe, and the harder he pulled the closer he came to strangulation. Moreover, the ancient harness was mechanically defective: the yoke was too high to permit the horse to exert his full force in pulling by flinging his body-weight into the task. Finally, the ancients were unable to harness one animal in front of another. Thus all great weights had to be drawn by gangs of slaves; since animal power was not technically available in sufficient quantities.

According to Lefebvre des Noëttes this condition remained unchanged until the later ninth or early tenth century when, almost simultaneously, three major inventions appear: the modern horse-collar, the tandem harness, and the horseshoe. The modern harness, consisting of a rigid horse-collar resting on the shoulders of the beast, permitted him to breathe freely. This was connected to the load by lateral traces which enabled the horse to throw his whole body into pulling. It has been shown experimentally that this new apparatus so greatly increased the effective animal power that a team which can pull only about one thousand pounds with the antique yoke can pull three or four times that weight when equipped with the new harness. Equally important was the extension of the traces so that tandem harnessing was possible, thus providing an indefinite amount of animal power for the transport of great weights. Finally, the introduction of the nailed horseshoe improved traction and greatly increased the endurance of the newly available animal power. Taken together these three inventions suddenly gave Europe a new supply of non-human power, at no increase of expense or labor. They did for the eleventh and twelfth centuries what the steam-engine did for the nineteenth. Lefebvre des Noëttes has therefore offered an unexpected and plausible solution for the most puzzling problem of the Middle Ages: the sudden upswing of European vitality after the year 1000.

However, Lefebvre des Noëttes failed to point out the relation between this access of energy and the contemporary agricultural revolution. He noted that the new harness made the horse available for agricultural labor: the first picture of a horse so engaged is found in the Bayeux Tapestry. But while the horse is a rapid and efficient power-engine, it burns an expensive fuel—grain—as compared with the slower, but cheaper, hay-burning ox. Under the two-field system the peasant's margin of production was insufficient to support a workhorse; under the three-field system the horse gradually displaced the ox as the normal plow and draft animal of the northern plains. By the later Middle Ages there is a clear correlation on the one hand between the horse and the three-field system and on the other between the ox and the two-field system. The contrast is essentially one between the standards of living and of labor-productivity of the northern and the southern peasantry: the ox saves food; the horse saves man-hours. The new agriculture, therefore, enabled the north to exploit the new power more effectively than the Mediterranean regions could, and thereby the northerners increased their prosperity still further. . . .

These discoveries regarding the utilization of animal power illustrate the novel results which may be expected from the study of mediaeval technology. No less profitable is Marc Block's brilliant and thoroughly documented investigation of the origin and spread of the water-driven mill. His conclusion that, while it was invented in the first century before Christ, it did not become common until after the collapse of the Empire, confirms Lefebvre des Noëttes' contention that the technological position of the Dark Ages has been misunderstood.

The development of the windmill has not been so carefully sought out. Windmills are found in tenth-century Persia, but rotating on a vertical rather than on a horizontal axis. The first authenticated windmill in Europe turns up in Normandy *ca.* 1180. Twelve years later Jocelin of Brakelond mentions one near St. Edmundsbury and gives no indication that he considers it unusual. Within a generation this power-engine had become a typical part of the landscape on the plains of northwestern Europe. In such a region it was a great boon; for the fall of rivers was so gradual that expensive dams and mill-ponds often had to be constructed to run water-driven mills; likewise these mill-ponds must often have flooded good agricultural land which the windmill freed for production. The spread of the windmill into the more mountainous southern regions, which were better equipped with rapid streams, was slow. The first Italian reference to a windmill seems to be Dante's description (*ante* 1321) of Satan threshing his arms like "un molin che il vento gira" (*Inferno,* XXXIV, 6). This southward and eastward diffusion, together with the horizontal axis of the western mill, probably indicates that the windmill was not an importation from Islam.

The cumulative effect of the newly available animal, water, and wind power upon the culture of Europe has not been carefully studied. But from the twelfth and even from the eleventh, century there was a rapid replacement of human by non-human energy wherever great quantities of power were needed or where the required motion was so simple and monotonous that a man could be replaced by a mechanism. The chief glory of the later Middle Ages was not its cathedrals or its epics or its scholasticism: it was the building for the first time in history of a complex civilization which rested not on the backs of sweating slaves or coolies but primarily on non-human power.

ECONOMIC MOTIVE AND THE EXPANSION OF EUROPE   4

Promise of economic gain was a powerful stimulant to Europe's overseas expansion. It initiated the search for a route to the riches of the Spice Islands and then, with the discovery of the New World, led to ruthless looting and maximum exploitation of the Inca and Aztec empires. Northwest Europeans, envious of the riches that the Portuguese had come upon in the East Indies and the Spaniards had found in America, were eager to further their own economies through overseas enterprise. Their objective is made clear in the following selection from Richard Hakluyt, an English promoter for colonial expansion. Hakluyt urges the founding of colonies in America to absorb England's surplus population and to create markets for English manufacture.*

It is well worthe the observation to see and consider what the like voyadges of discoverye and plantinge in the Easte and Weste Indies hath wroughte in the kingdomes of Portingale and Spayne; bothe which realmes, beinge of themselves poore and barren and hardly able to susteine their inhabitaunts, by their discoveries have founde suche occasion of employmente, that these many yeres we have not herde scarcely of any pirate of those twoo nations; whereas wee and the Frenche are moste infamous for our outeragious, common, and daily piracies. Againe, when hearde wee almoste of one theefe amongest them? The reason is, that by these, their newe discoveries, they have so many honest wayes to set them on worke, as they rather wante men then meanes to ymploye them. But wee, for all the statutes that hitherto can be devised, and the sharpe execution of the same in poonishinge idle and lazye persons, for wante of sufficient occasion of honest employmente, cannot deliver our commonwealthe from multitudes of loyterers and idle vagabondes. Truthe it is, that through our longe peace and seldome sicknes (twoo singular blessinges of Almightie God) wee are growen more populous than

---

* R. Hakluyt, "A Discourse on Western Planting," *Collections*, 2nd ser., Documentary *History of the State of Maine* (Cambridge, Mass.: Maine Historical Society, 1877), II, 36-39.

ever heretofore; so that nowe there are of every arte and science so many, that they can hardly lyve one by another, nay rather they are readie to eate upp one another; yea many thousandes of idle persons are within this realme, which, havinge no way to be sett on worke, be either mutinous and seeke alteration in the state, or at leaste very burdensome to the common-wealthe, and often fall to pilferinge and thevinge and other lewdnes, whereby all the prisons of the lande are daily pestred and stuffed full of them, where either they pitifully pyne awaye, or els at lengthe are miserably hanged, even xx^ti. at a clappe oute of some one jayle. Whereas yf this voyadge were put in execution, these pety theves mighte be condempned for certen yeres in the westerne partes, expecially in Newefounde lande, in sawinge and fellinge of tymber for mastes of shippes, and deale boordes; in burninge of the firres and pine trees to make pitche, tarr, rosen, and sope ashes; in beatinge and workinge of hempe for cordage; and, in the more southerne partes, in settinge them to worke in mynes of golde, silver, copper, leade, and yron; in drag-ginge for perles and currall; in plantinge of sugar canes, as the Portingales have done in Madera; in mayneteynaunce and increasinge of silke wormes for silke, and in dressinge the same; in gatheringe of cotten whereof there is plentie; in tillinge of the soile there for graine; in dressinge of vines whereof there is greate aboundaunce for wyne; olyves, whereof the soile ys capable, for oyle; trees for oranges; lymons, almondes, figges, and other frutes, all which are founde to growe there already; in sowinge of woade and madder for diers, as the Portingales have don in the Azores; in dressinge of raw hides of divers kindes of beastes; in makinge and gatheringe of salte, as in Rochel and Bayon, which may serve for the newe lande fisshinge; in killinge the whale, seale, porpose, and whirlepoole for trayne oile; in fisshinge, saltinge, and dryenge of linge, codde, salmon, herringe; in makinge and gatheringe of hony, waxe, turpentine; in hewinge and shapinge of stone, as marble, jeate, christall, freestone, which will be goodd balaste for our shippes homewardes, and after serve for noble buildinges; in makinge of caske, oares, and all other manner of staves; in buildinge of fortes, townes, churches; in powdringe and barrellinge of fishe, fowles, and fleshe, which will be notable provision for sea and lande; in dryenge, sortinge, and packinge of fethers, whereof may be had there marvelous greate quantitie.

Besides this, such as by any kinde of infirmitie cannot passe the seas thither, and now are chardgeable to the realme at home, by this voyadge shal be made profitable members, by employinge them in England in makinge of a thousande triflinge thinges, which will be very goodd mar-chandize for those contries where wee shall have moste ample vente thereof.

And seinge the savages of the Graunde Baye, and all alonge the mightie ryver that ronneth upp to Canada and Hochelaga, are greately delighted with any cappe or garment made of course wollen clothe, their contrie beinge colde and sharpe in the winter, yt is manifeste wee shall finde great utter-aunce of our clothes, especially of our coursest and basest northerne doosens, and our Irishe and Welshe frizes and rugges; whereby all occupa-tions belonginge to clothinge and knittinge shal be freshly sett on worke, as cappers, knitters, clothiers, wollmen, carders, spynners, weavers, fullers, sheremen, dyers, drapers, hatters, and such like, whereby many decayed townes may be repaired.

In somme, this enterprice will mynister matter for all sortes and states of men to worke upon; namely, all severall kindes of artificers, husbandmen, seamen, marchauntes, souldiers, capitaines, phisitions, lawyers, devines, cosmographers, hidrographers, astronomers, historiographers; yea, olde folkes, lame persons, women, and younge children, by many meanes which hereby shall still be mynistred unto them, shalbe kepte from idlenes, and be made able by their owne honest and easie labour to finde themselves, withoute surchardginge others.

Social Organization and the Expansion of Europe

SOCIAL ORGANIZATION AND THE EXPANSION OF EUROPE 5

The Western Europeans were not pioneers or leaders so far as lengthy oceanic voyages were concerned. Between 1405 and 1443, the Ming emperors of China sent out seven great expeditions which visited the East Indies, Ceylon, India, the Persian Gulf, the Red Sea, and the eastern coast of Africa. At the same time, the Portuguese were merely beginning to inch their way southward along the African coast. Yet by the end of the century, the Portuguese had rounded Africa and reached India, while the Chinese had ceased their overseas enterprises and shut themselves off from the rest of the world. The following selection * indicates that one reason for this paradoxical outcome was the difference in the social organization of Western Europe and of China. This difference explains why cities and their merchant classes were dynamic and revolutionary forces in the West, while in the East they were subordinate to, and controlled by, the great imperial bureaucracies and the powerful landlord interests.

Every sedentary society has built cities, for even in a subsistence economy essential functions of exchange and of organization (both functions dealing with minds and ideas as much as with goods or with institutions) are most conveniently performed in a central location on behalf of a wider countryside. The industrial revolution has emphasized the economic advantages of concentration and centrality. But is it true to say that change, revolutionary change, has found an advantage in urbanization; in concentration and in numbers? The city has instigated or led most of the great changes in Western society, and has been the center of its violent and non-violent revolutions. In western Europe the city has been the base of an independent entrepreneur group which has successfully challenged and broken the authority of the traditional order. In China, while cities with the same universal economic functions arose, they tended until recently to have the opposite effect on the pattern of change. China has consistently reasserted itself as a single political unit, but it is otherwise the appropriate qualitative and quantitative counterpart of Europe, and provides a reasonable basis for comparison. China and Europe have been the two great poles of world civilization, and an examination of the different roles which their cities played may help to elucidate other differences between them. . . .

The cities of western Europe have been, at least since the high middle ages, centers of intellectual ferment; of economic change; and thus, in time, of

* R. Murphey, "The City as a Center of Change: Western Europe and China," *Annals of the Association of American Geographers,* XLIV (December, 1954), 349-58.

opposition to the central authority. They became rebels in nearly every aspect of their institutional life. It was trade (and to a somewhat lesser extent specialized manufacturing) which made them strong enough to maintain their challenge to the established order. Their spirit of ferment was the spirit of a new group, urban merchant-manufacturers, which could operate from a base large and rich enough to establish increasingly its own rules. This setting tended to ensure that the universities, which grew up in cities originally for convenience and centrality, would frequently nourish skepticism, heresy, and freedom of enquiry. Even where they did not overtly do so, the concentration of literacy and learning in the cities was a stimulus to dissent.

Most of the cities which rose out of the cultural and social chaos following the destruction of Roman unity and preceding the development of a new national unity grew in answer to new conditions, for northwest Europe was ideally situated for trade. Most of them were in their origins much older than this, and had begun as administrative, military, or ecclesiastical centers. But a score of major rivers, navigable and free from floods, silting, or ice throughout the year in this mild maritime climate, led across the great European plain to the open sea; the peninsular, indented nature of the coast critically heightened mobility. The invitation which this presented to inter-European trade furthered the ascendancy of the commercial function. The shift of commerce and associated urbanism from the Mediterranean to northwest Europe seems to have begun before the Age of the Discoveries, notably in the Hansa towns and in Flanders. This may be in part a reflection of the mobility inherent in the lands around the Baltic and North Seas, once they had learned from the Mediterranean the lessons of commerce and absorbed the civilizing influences of this earlier developed area. In any case, these northern cities came to be dominated by trader-manufacturers. Trade was a heady diet, and enabled urban merchants to command cities which had originally been administrative creations. While the cities did not alone destroy feudalism, they owed much of their prosperity and independence to its decline: freer trade, wider exchange, and failing power of the landed nobility. And their very growth as rival power bases accelerated the collapse of the old feudal order.

As the growth of national unity progressed, under the institutional and emotional leadership of monarchy, an alliance of convenience between king and city arose which met the crown's demands for funds and the city's demand for representation. Urban merchants had the money to support the king in his foreign wars and in his struggle with the divisive domestic ambitions of the nobility and the church. In return the city received an increasing voice in the affairs of state, through representation in parliaments, and indirectly through the making of policy in which the throne was obliged to follow. But while this alliance of revenue in exchange for concessions was one of mutual interest, its ultimate result was the strengthening of the urban commercial sector until it overthrew or emasculated the monarchy, and with it the traditional order as a whole. Having helped the king to power over the nobility, the city achieved a *modus vivendi* with him which left it in control of the affairs vital to it. As a current reminder of the development of urban independence, "the city" of London retains its originally hard-won privilege of excluding the reigning monarch, who is also excluded from the House of Commons, in part the city's creation and in part its weapon. To a certain extent the king, and even the nobility, were willing to go along with the process of economic change instigated by the city since they profited from it as the principal source of wealth in which they were often investors as well as tax collectors. But the new values which the city emphasized, and their institutional expression, were in direct conflict with the traditional society based on land; the city repeatedly bred overt revolutionary movements designed to establish its new order as the national way of life.

As centers of trade, the cities were free of the land and of its social and political limitations embodied in the institutions of post-Roman society. They developed their own law which was in differing degrees independent of the traditional, rural law. Their institutions were self-made, and they were not beholden to the traditional system which they challenged. The companies and corporations which the merchants organized went far beyond the scope of guilds in their successful attempt to order most of the social and economic fabric (instead of being limited to a trade-union function, as the guilds of China predominantly were). Traditional guilds were overlaid with new merchant organizations, or were clothed with new functions and powers, although some of the older guilds remained as conservative or retarding influences. The economic institutions which arose concurrently were also new-made sources of strength: banking, letters of credit, private property, interest, speculation and investment, representing needs and ideas which were almost wholly foreign to the traditional society of the countryside, and which were the accompaniment of an ever-widening trade. For the invitation to commercial expansion overseas was as strong in Europe's geography as the earlier invitation to trade among the lands surrounding the Baltic, Mediterranean, and North Seas. A leading agent of this process was necessarily the city, where trade flowed through break-in bulk points such as the mouths of the Rhine or the English ports facing the Channel. Merchant corporations for overseas trade became the strongest and most progressive, or revolutionary, of the city's agents. Interestingly, the original charter of the British East India Company stated that "gentlemen" (by which was meant the landed gentry) "shall be excluded" from membership.

The city was the natural center of political change as it had been of economic change. The growth of modern Europe may be regarded as the steady progress of a new class of urban traders and manufacturers toward a position of control in a society and economy which their own enterprise had largely created. It was they who had realized the potential of Europe's location for world trade, and they who had developed and applied the technological and economic tools which made Europe the center of the world. The destruction of the old pattern was implicit in this process, and also implicit was the revolutionary expression, by the cities, of their claim to political power . . .

The first great modern revolution, in seventeenth century England, was the work of a city-country alliance, but London was mainly Puritan, and the outcome might be regarded as the victory of urban merchants and their country confreres over the traditional authoritarian alliance of cavalier and peasant based on the land. . . .

In France the picture was less clear since urban merchant-manufacturers were less prominent in the national economy. Paris used peasant distress and rebellion, but was never dethroned by it. One may say that Paris later destroyed Charles X and Louis Philippe. . . . In eastern Europe it is difficult to draw distinctions between city and country, or to find an independent urban-based group living on trade and challenging the existing order. Nevertheless, even in twentieth century Russia, while the Soviet revolution was in part carried by peasant groups, leadership remained in the urban intellectual group which had instigated the change. . . .

In China, while the peasant and the countryside were in some respects like the West, the city's role was fundamentally different. Chinese cities were administrative centers. With few exceptions this function dominated their lives whatever their other bases in trade or manufacturing. Their remarkably consistent, uniform plan, square or rectangular walls surrounding a great cross with gates at each of the four arms, suggests their common administrative creation and their continued expression of this function. . . .

In China most cities or towns of 5,000 or more had well-defined commercial or manufacturing districts, and special areas for each important enterprise: banking, metal goods, food markets, textiles, woodwork, and so on. This pattern remains in most contemporary Chinese cities. But the cities were not decisive centers of change in a commercialized economy. They served as imperial or provincial capitals. . . . Their business was administration, and exploitation, of the countryside. . . .

Physically, China is built on a grander scale, but the landscape presents no such invitation to exchange as has sparked the development of Europe. Europe is multi-peninsular, each peninsula tending toward economic distinctiveness and political independence, but joined by cheap sea and river routes. This plethora of complementary areas and their transport links magnified the basis and the means of exchange. Although its early trade development was not larger than China's, by the middle of the eighteenth century commercial expansion overseas had joined and accelerated commercialization at home, and Europe stood in a class by itself. The cities of western Europe were both the creators and inheritors of this development. But in China the cities remained centers of the unitary national state and of the traditional order rather than its attackers, epitomes of the status quo. As direct links in the official hierarchy, they were the props of the empire. The universities were urban, for convenience, as in Europe, but they stimulated no dissent. Their accepted function was to train scholars who could staff the imperial civil service, and they fed their graduates into the imperial examination system. This, and the better economic and social position of scholars generally in China than in Europe, encouraged the universities and the literati to support the status quo; European intellectuals may have taken a vow of poverty, but they remained a dissident or discontented group.

Physically, China lacked Europe's outstanding advantages for trade, and on the other hand presented a base for highly productive agriculture, through irrigation. Wittvogel's revealing work on the organic connection between the need for mass organized water control and the growth of a monolithic bureaucratic state in China lends insight into the origins and pattern of the institutional structure. With China's environmental advantages, water control made agriculture the massive core of the economy, and at the same time left the bureaucracy in a position of ramified command. It was not possible for urban merchants to win independence from this system. They had less economic leverage than the rising European merchants because, with the preponderant position of agriculture, they never occupied proportionately as large a place in the economy. . . .

Where extra-agricultural opportunities for investment did exist, the individual entrepreneur was at the mercy of the bureaucratic state. Many of the major trade goods were government monopolies. Elsewhere the essentially

Western concepts of private property and due process of law, in a word, of the entrepreneur, were lacking in a society dominated by agriculture and officials. Extortion, forced levies, confiscation, and simple financial failure as the result of arbitrary government policies were the daily risk of the merchant. Some individuals did indeed become very rich, for example the famous *hong* merchants of Canton, but their wealth came necessarily through official connection: by possession of gentry status, by office holding or official favour, or by trading as part of a government monopoly (such as foreign trade under the Canton system and at most other periods was). Even so their gains were never secure. The greatest and richest of the *hong* merchants died in poverty, having lost official favour. While this also happened to many of the pre-eighteenth century European capitalists, it did not prevent the survival and growth of individual capitalist families or firms or of a moneyed group. The famous Ch'ing dynasty billionaire Ho Shen, said to have been worth the equivalent of nearly a billion and a half U.S. dollars, was not a merchant at all, but a favourite minister of the emperor Ch'ien Lung, which demonstrates the real source of wealth in traditional China. Yet he too died in poverty and disgrace (by suicide in place of a suspended death sentence in 1799) at the hands of Ch'ien Lung's successor.

In China merchant-capitalists did not use their money to establish their independence, as did the merchants of London or Antwerp, or to stimulate the growth of a new economic pattern. Unfortunately for the Chinese merchants, the imperial revenue was at most periods derived largely from the land tax and from the government trade monopolies. Agriculture was proportionately more productive than in Europe, and revenue from trade less necessary. Peking thus did not need the merchants as the king had needed them in Europe to finance the ascendancy of the national state, to pay for its wars with rival states, or to meet its normal bills. No concessions were necessary; the merchants could be squeezed dry, and were, with no harm to the state. The commanding position of the bureaucracy, and the fact of the bureaucratic state, are perhaps explainable by a similar process of default. Merchants were necessary or useful to perform essential (and, to the state, profitable) commercial functions; they were tolerated, but kept under strict control, and this was simpler and cheaper than for the state to manage all commercial dealings itself.

But the merchants were also identified with the state as well as being stifled by it. Their numbers were recruited largely from the gentry class, who had the capital and the official connections essential to commercial success. Gentry merchants worked willingly with gentry officials in the management of the state monopolies, including foreign trade. Outside the monopolies, the same partnership operated, as a matter of mutual interest. In addition, most gentry members, whether or not they were engaged in trade, also performed other semi-official functions, comparable in some degree to the British landed gentry. These "services" represented a considerable part of their income; they were not likely to attack the system which nourished them. In a more general sense, the tradition of revolt in this hierarchical society did not include the re-ordering of social or economic groups, but concentrated on the removal of bad government. Individual or group improvement was not to be won by destroying the fabric, but by making optimum use of one's position within it. . . .

The cities of China were consequently microcosms of the empire, not deviants. . . .

Westerners are prone to consider the dynamism of the West and the tradition-alism of the East as being natural, inevitable, and everlasting. Actually, this difference between East and West is of recent vintage and is today gradually disappearing before our eyes. The British economic historian R. H. Tawney has emphasized that the traditionalism which we consider to be peculiarly and dis-tinctively "Eastern" was indeed characteristic of the entire world until modern times. Then Western Europe assumed the role of maverick in expanding overseas and starting a chain reaction of events that has affected the world to the present day. The following selection from Tawney presents Europe's expansion and trans-formation in its proper historical perspective and also suggests some causes for the changes that Europe experienced.*

Such contrasts between the static civilisation of China—as it was formerly called—and the more mobile economy of the West are easily drawn and easily misinterpreted. They are misinterpreted when the differences which they emphasise are assumed to be the expression of permanent character-istics. History, with its record of the movement of leadership from region to region, lends little support to the theory that certain peoples are naturally qualified for success in the economic arts, and others unfitted for it, even were the criteria of such success less ambiguous than they are.

The traditionalism which has sometimes been described as a special mark of Chinese economic life is the characteristic, not of China, but of one phase of civilisation which Europe has shared with her. Rapid economic change as a fact, and continuous economic progress as an ideal, are the notes, not of the history of the West, but of little more than its last four centuries; and the European who is baffled by what appears to him the conservatism of China would be equally bewildered could he meet his own ancestors. During nearly a thousand years, the crafts of the husbandman, the weaver, the car-penter and the smith saw as little alteration in the West as they have seen in the East. In the former, as in the latter, common men looked to the good days of the past, not to the possibilities of the future, for a standard of conduct and criterion of the present; accepted the world, with plague, pestilence and famine, as heaven had made it; and were incurious as to the arts by which restless spirits would improve on nature, if not actually suspicious of them as smelling of complicity with malignant powers. In the former, as in the latter, political confusion, civil disturbance, brigandage and recurrent starvation were for generations the rule rather than the excep-tion. It is true, however, that, for wide ranges of Chinese life, the contrast is valid, though the area to which it applies is year by year contracting. In technological equipment and industrial organisation, as in the foundations of law, psychology and social habits, on which both ultimately rest, the greater part of the West lives on one plane, the greater part of China on another.

What is true to-day is less true than yesterday, and may be false to-morrow. The forces which have caused the economic development of China

---

* R. H. Tawney, *Land and Labour in China* (London: G. Allen, 1932), pp. 19-22.

and the West to flow in different channels are a fascinating theme for historical speculation, but they are one on which a layman is precluded from entering. Naturally, he will remind himself that the question is not merely why the economic life of China has not changed more, but why that of the West has changed so much. Naturally, certain commonplace considerations of geography, history, culture and social institutions will occur to his mind. Naturally, he will recall the position of China, with her vast and relatively homogeneous territory, isolated on the west by mountain barriers, and on the east in contact with civilisations inferior to her own, to whom she gave, and was conscious of giving, more than she received; her patriarchal family system which, far more than the state, has prevented the individual from being crushed by personal misfortune or social disorder, and has weakened the force of economic incentives by making his livelihood the concern and his earnings the property of the family group; the teeming population which that system encouraged and the obstacles to technical improvement offered by the cheapness of human labour; the influence of an educational policy devoted to the encouragement of academic culture and indifferent to the sciences by which man masters his environment; the philosophy of Chinese sages, with its scholastic contempt for the merchant and its idealisation of agriculture and the peasant; the small part played in the past by government and law, compared with personal relations, voluntary associations and local custom.

Naturally, he will compare these peculiarities with the characteristics of Europe. He will consider the significance of the long and deeply indented coastline of the latter, with its two inland seas in the south and north, which made foreign commerce possible for almost all her regions, and indispensable to some of them. He will recall her possession throughout history of numerous independent centres of economic energy, which fertilised each other by rivalry, imitation and actual migration, so that Italy, Spain and Portugal, France, Holland and England, not to mention, at a more recent date, Germany and the United States, became in turn her economic schoolmasters, and did for each other, though by different methods, what the West, as a whole, was to do later for China. He will ponder the impress stamped on her institutions by Roman law, and the ghost of past unity that, when anarchy was at its worst, still haunted her imagination. He will reflect on her early development of a powerful bourgeoisie based on trade and finance, which, first in Italy, then in Holland, and later in England, remade government, law and economic policy, and, when the scientific movement reborn at the Renaissance won its first great triumphs, was alert to turn them to practical account. He will remember the smallness, till recently, of the population of parts of the West in relation to its natural resources, and the consequent stimulus to technical invention.

Chapter Three

*Moslem world
at the time of
the West's expansion*

7   Ottoman Military Strength

*In order to understand both the course and the consequences of
Europe's expansion, it is necessary to understand the sort of world into
which the expansion took place. For convenience, this world can be divided into three broad regions: the Moslem world, the Confucian world,
and the non-Eurasian world. Each of these regions will be considered in
the following readings.*

*The Moslem world was dominated by three powerful empires, the
Safavid Empire in Persia, the Mogul Empire in India, and the Ottoman
Empire in North Africa, the Middle East, and the Balkans; all three of
these empires were militarily strong in the sixteenth century. Europeans
were most familiar with the military prowess of the Ottoman Empire,
with which they had much firsthand experience for obvious geographic
reasons. The following description of the Ottoman armed forces is by
Augier Ghislain de Busbecq, Hapsburg ambassador to Constantinople
from 1554 to 1562. Because Busbecq was a shrewd and intelligent observer, his description of a Turkish army camp is particularly revealing.**

. . . They considered it politic that I should pass some time in
their camp, and be treated courteously as the embassador of a
friendly prince. Accordingly, a very comfortable lodging was assigned me in a village adjoining the camp. The Turks were encamped

---

* C. T. Forster and F. H. B. Daniell, eds., *The Life and Letters of Ogier
Ghiselin de Busbecq* (London, 1881), I, 219-22, 243-45, 287-90, 293, 405-6.

in the neighbouring fields. As I stayed there three months, I had opportunities of visiting their camp, and making myself acquainted with their discipline. ... Having put on the dress usually worn by Christians in those parts, I used to sally out incognito with one or two companions. The first thing that struck me was that each corps had its proper quarters, from which the soldiers composing it were not allowed to move. Everywhere order prevailed, there was perfect silence, no disturbances, no quarrels, no bullying; a state of things which must seem well nigh incredible to those, whose experience is limited to Christian camps. You could not hear so much as a coarse word, or a syllable of drunken abuse. Besides, there was the greatest cleanliness, no dunghills, no heaps of refuse, nothing to offend the eyes or nose. Everything of the kind is either buried or removed out of sight. Holes are dug in the ground as occasion requires, for the use of the men, which are again filled in with earth. Thus the whole camp is free from dirt. Again, no drinking parties or banquets, and no sort of gambling, which is the great fault of our soldiers, are to be seen. The Turks are unacquainted with the art of losing their money at cards and dice. ...

I had a fancy also to be conducted through the shambles where the sheep were slaughtered, that I might see what meat there was for sale. I saw but four or five sheep at most, which had been flayed and hung up, although it was the slaughter-house of the Janissaries, of whom I think there were no fewer than four thousand in the camp. I expressed my astonishment that so little meat was sufficient for such a number of men, and was told in reply that few used it, for a great part of them had their victuals brought over from Constantinople. When I asked what they were, they pointed out to me a Janissary, who was engaged in eating his dinner; he was devouring, off a wooden or earthen trencher, a mess of turnips, onions, garlic, parsnips, and cucumbers, seasoned with salt and vinegar, though, for the matter of that, I fancy that hunger was the chief sauce that seasoned his dish, for, to all appearance, he enjoyed his vegetables as much as if he had been dining off pheasants and partridges. Water, that common beverage of men and animals, is their only drink. This abstemious diet is good both for their health and their pockets.

I was at the camp just before their fast, or Lent as we should call it, and thus was still more struck with the behaviour of the men. In Christian lands at this season, not only camps, but even orderly cities, ring with games and dances, songs and shouts; everywhere are heard the sounds of revelling, drunkenness, and delirium. In short, the world runs mad. It is not improbable that there is some foundation for the story, that a Turk, who happened to come to us on a diplomatic mission at one of these seasons, related on his return home, that the Christians, on certain days, go raving mad, and are restored to their senses and their health by a kind of ashes, which are sprinkled on them in their temples. He told his friends that it was quite remarkable to see the beneficial effects of this remedy; the change was so great that one would hardly imagine them to be the same people. He referred of course to Ash Wednesday and Shrove Tuesday. ...

So, drinking being prohibited, peace and silence reign in a Turkish camp, and this is more especially the case during their Lent. Such is the result produced by military discipline, and the stern laws bequeathed them by their ancestors. The Turks allow no crime and no disgraceful act to go unpunished. The penalties are degradation from office, loss of rank, confiscation of property, the bastinado, and death. ...

Against us stands Solyman, that foe whom his own and his ancestors' exploits have made so terrible; he tramples the soil of Hungary with 200,000 horse, he is at the very gates of Austria, threatens the rest of Germany, and brings in his train all the nations that extend from our borders to those of Persia. The army he leads is equipped with the wealth of many kingdoms. Of the three regions, into which the world is divided, there is not one that does not contribute its share toward our destruction. Like a thunderbolt he strikes, shivers, and destroys everything in his way. The troops he leads are trained veterans, accustomed to his command; he fills the world with the terror of his name. Like a raging lion he is always roaring around our borders, trying to break in, now in this place, now in that. . . .

It makes me shudder to think of what the result of a struggle between such different systems must be; one of us must prevail and the other be destroyed, at any rate we cannot both exist in safety. On their side is the vast wealth of their empire, unimpaired resources, experience and practice in arms, a veteran soldiery, an uninterrupted series of victories, readiness to endure hardships, union, order, discipline, thrift, and watchfulness. On ours are found an empty exchequer, luxurious habits, exhausted resources, broken spirits, a raw and insubordinate soldiery, and greedy generals; there is no regard for discipline, licence runs riot, the men indulge in drunkenness and debauchery, and, worst of all, the enemy are accustomed to victory, we, to defeat. Can we doubt what the result must be? . . .

8 Ottoman Administrative System

Busbecq was impressed not only by Ottoman military strength but also by Ottoman administrative efficiency, which he attributed to the strict merit system that determined appointments and promotions in the Ottoman bureaucracy. Busbecq describes this unique administrative service that surrounded Sultan Suleiman the Magnificent, and contrasts it with the nepotism and corruption prevailing in Christian Europe.*

. . . The Sultan was seated on a very low ottoman, not more than a foot from the ground, which was covered with a quantity of costly rugs and cushions of exquisite workmanship; near him lay his bow and arrows. His air, as I said, was by no means gracious, and his face wore a stern, though dignified, expression. . . .

The Sultan's hall was crowded with people, among whom were several officers of high rank. Besides these there were all the troopers of the Imperial guard, Spahis, Ghourebas, Ouloufedgis, and a large force of Janissaries; but there was not in all that great assembly a single man who owed his position to aught save valour and his merit. No distinction is attached to birth among the Turks; the deference to be paid to a man is measured by the position he holds in the public service. There is no fighting for precedence; a man's place is marked out by the duties he discharges. In making his appointments the

* *Ibid.,* pp. 152-55, 219-22.

Sultan pays no regard to any pretensions on the score of wealth or rank, nor does he take into consideration recommendations or popularity; he considers each case on its own merits, and examines carefully into the character, ability, and disposition of the man whose promotion is in question. It is by merit that men rise in the service, a system which ensures that posts should only be assigned to the competent. Each man in Turkey carries in his own hand his ancestry and his position in life, which he may make or mar as he will. Those who receive the highest offices from the Sultan are for the most part the sons of shepherds or herdsmen, and so far from being ashamed of their parentage, they actually glory in it, and consider it a matter of boasting that they owe nothing to the accident of birth; for they do not believe that high qualities are either natural or hereditary, nor do they think that they can be handed down from father to son, but that they are partly the gift of God, and partly the result of good training, great industry, and unwearied zeal; arguing that high qualities do not descend from a father to his son or heir, any more than a talent for music, mathematics, or the like; and that the mind does not derive its origin from the father, so that the son should necessarily be like the father in character, but emanates from heaven, and is thence infused into the human body. Among the Turks, therefore, honours, high posts, and judgeships are the rewards of great ability and good service. If a man be dishonest, or lazy, or careless, he remains at the bottom of the ladder, an object of contempt; for such qualities there are no honours in Turkey!

This is the reason that they are successful in their undertakings, that they lord it over others, and are daily extending the bounds of their empire. These are not our ideas, with us there is no opening left for merit; birth is the standard for everything; the prestige of birth is the sole key to advancement in the public service.

"THE GREAT MOGUL" 9

The three great Moslem empires were particularly impressive in the sixteenth century because of their unusually capable rulers; emperors such as the Ottoman Suleiman, the Safavid Abbas, and the Mogul Akbar would have been outstanding in any country and in any period. Their extraordinary talents were especially significant in view of the fact that their absolutist empires were peculiarly dependent on the quality of their leadership. The following portrait of Akbar is based on an account by the Portuguese Jesuit Father Monserrate, who, as tutor to Prince Murad, was able to observe Akbar at firsthand.*

It was in the year 1582 that his court was first visited by Fathers of the Company. He was then about forty years of age, of medium stature, and strongly built. He wore a turban on his head, and the fabric of his costume was interwoven with gold thread. His outer garment reached to his knees,

* P. Du Jarric, *Akbar and the Jesuits* (New York: Harper; London: Routledge, 1926), pp. 8-13.

and his breeches to his heels. His stockings were much like ours; but his shoes were of a peculiar pattern invented by himself. On his brow he wore several rows of pearls or precious stones. He had a great liking for European clothes; and sometimes it was his pleasure to dress himself in a costume of black velvet made after the Portuguese fashion; but this was only on private, not on public occasions. He had always a sword at his side, or at any rate so near by that he could lay his hand upon it in a moment. Those who guarded his person, and whom he kept constantly near him, were changed each day of the week, as were his other officers and attendants, but in such manner that the same persons came on duty every eighth day.

Echebar [Akbar] possessed an alert and discerning mind; he was a man of sound judgment, prudent in affairs, and, above all, kind, affable, and generous. With these qualities he combined the courage of those who undertake and carry out great enterprises. He could be friendly and genial in his intercourse with others, without losing the dignity befitting the person of a king. He seemed to appreciate virtue, and to be well disposed towards foreigners, particularly Christians, some of whom he always liked to have about him. He was interested in, and curious to learn about many things, and possessed an intimate knowledge not only of military and political matters, but of many of the mechanical arts. He took delight in watching the casting of pieces of artillery, and in his own palace kept workmen constantly employed in the manufacture of guns and arms of various descriptions. In short, he was well informed on a great variety of matters, and could discourse on the laws of many sects, for this was a subject of which he made a special study. Although he could neither read nor write, he enjoyed entering into debate with learned doctors. He always entertained at his court a dozen or so of such men, who propounded many questions in his presence. To their discussions, now on one subject, now on another, and particularly to the stories which they narrated, he was a willing listener, believing that by this means he could overcome the disadvantage of his illiteracy.

Echebar was by temperament melancholy, and he suffered from the falling-sickness; so that to divert his mind, he had recourse to various forms of amusement, such as watching elephants fight together, or camels, or buffaloes, or rams that butt and gore each other with their horns, or even two cocks. He was also fond of watching fencing bouts; and on certain occasions, after the manner of the ancient Romans, he made gladiators fight before him; or fencers were made to contend until one had killed the other. At other times, he amused himself with elephants and camels that had been trained to dance to the tune of certain musical instruments, and to perform other strange feats. But in the midst of all these diversions—and this is a very remarkable thing—he continued to give his attention to affairs of state, even to matters of grave importance.

Often he used to hunt the wild animals that abound in these regions. For this purpose he employed panthers instead of hunting-dogs; for in this country panthers are trained to the chase as we train dogs. He did not care much for hawking, though he had many well-trained falcons and other birds of prey; and there were some expert falconers amongst his retainers. Some of these were so skilful with the bow that they very rarely missed a bird at which they shot, even though it was on the wing, and though their arrows were unfeathered.

To catch wild deer he used other deer which had been trained for this purpose. These carried nets on their horns in which the wild deer that came to attack them became entangled, upon which they were seized by the hunters who had been lying in concealment near by. When on a military campaign, he used to hunt in the following manner. Four or five thousand men were made to join hands and form a ring round a piece of jungle. Others were then sent inside to drive the animals to the edge of the enclosure, where they were captured by those forming the ring. A fine was levied on those who allowed an animal to break through and escape.

So much for the king's recreations. We will now turn to more serious matters. That any person might be able to speak to him on business of importance, Echebar appeared twice daily in public, and gave audience to all classes of his subjects. For this purpose he made use of two large halls of his palace, in each of which was placed on a raised dais a splendid and costly throne. To the first of these halls all his subjects had access, and there he listened to all who sought speech with him. But to the second none was admitted but the captains and great nobles of his kingdom, and the ambassadors who came from foreign kings to confer with him on affairs of importance. Eight officers, men of experience and good judgment, were in constant attendance on him. Amongst these he apportioned the days of the week, so that each had his special day for introducing those who desired an audience. It was their duty to examine the credentials of all such persons, and to act as masters of ceremony, instructing them, more especially if they were foreigners, how to make reverence to the king, and how to comport themselves in his presence; for on these occasions much ceremony is observed, it being the custom, amongst other things, to kiss the feet of the king on saluting him. When giving audience, the king is also attended by a number of secretaries, whose duty is to record in writing every word that he speaks. This is a custom much practised by the princes of Persia, and other eastern countries.

For the administration of justice, there are magistrates whose judgement is final, and others from whom there is an appeal. In every case the proceedings are verbal, and are never committed to writing.

The king of whom we are speaking made it his particular care that in every case justice should be strictly enforced. He was, nevertheless, cautious in the infliction of punishment, especially the punishment of death. In no city where he resided could any person be put to death until the execution warrant had been submitted to him, some say, as many as three times. His punishments were not, ordinarily, cruel; though it is true that he caused some who had conspired against his life to be slain by elephants, and that he sometimes punished criminals by impalement after the Turkish fashion. A robber or sea-pirate, if he had killed no one, suffered the loss of a hand; but murderers, highwaymen, and adulterers were either strangled or crucified [attachez en croix], or their throats were cut, according to the gravity of their crimes. Lesser offenders were whipped and set free. In brief, the light of clemency and mildness shone forth from this prince, even upon those who offended against his own person. He twice pardoned an officer high in his service, who had been convicted of treason and conspiracy, graciously restoring him to favour and office. But when the same officer so far forgot himself as to repeat his offence a third time, he sentenced him to death by crucifixion.

Echebar seldom lost his temper. If he did so, he fell into a violent passion; but his wrath was never of long duration. Before engaging in any important undertaking, he used to consult the members of his council; but he made up his own mind, adopting whatever course seemed to him the best. Sometimes he communicated his intentions to his councillors, to ascertain their views. If they approved, they would answer with the words "Peace be to our lord the King." If anyone expressed an adverse opinion, he would listen patiently, answer his objections, and point out the reasons for his own decision. Sometimes, in view of the objections pointed out to him, he changed the plans he had made. Persian is the language usually spoken at his court, but learned men and the priests of Mahomet speak Arabic.

This is what we have been able to ascertain about the Great Mogor [Mogul] and his state.

10   MOSLEM TRADE AND PROSPERITY

*Fifteenth-century Europeans were impressed also by the wealth of the Moslem world, described in the following two selections. The first, by an American scholar, analyzes the Indian Ocean trade, controlled mostly by Moslem Arab merchants, and the prosperity resulting from this trade. The second account, by a French physician who lived and traveled widely in India between 1656 and 1668, describes, in his own words, "the fertility, wealth and beauty of the Kingdom of Bengale." ***

Moslem Arab Trade

For many centuries trade had been going on between the Orient and the West, overland and by water, but some time before the opening of the sixteenth century the overland routes had been reduced to little importance, and most of the traders went by sea from India along the coast of Arabia to Egypt and Syria, where their goods were exchanged for the products of the Middle East and of Europe. The center of most of the trade in India was Calicut, on the west coast of the peninsula. Diu also was a very important trading city. Many other towns in India, too, were engaged in this exchange of goods, all of which contributed to the prosperity of the Arabs. Indeed, frequently the galleys that went to Alexandria and Beirut from Venice returned with two hundred thousand ducats worth of cargo each, and since from four to nine ships left Syrian and Egyptian ports every year, a goodly sum was involved. At one Indian port as many as fifty ships were loaded annually with cotton and silk stuffs for the Indian, Levantine, and Chinese trade. Every monsoon ten to fifteen ships would leave Calicut for the Red Sea. Since some small fleets of Indian ships attained the value of two hundred thousand ducats, the total value of the trade may be estimated at a very high figure. The profits were very high, too, for the smallest figure of the merchants' profits is given at one hundred per cent. Many were not satisfied with such returns and managed to sell their wares at a difference of two thousand to ten thousand per cent.

* G. W. F. Stripling, "The Ottoman Turks and the Arabs 1511-1574," *Illinois Studies in the Social Sciences*, XXVI, No. 4 (Urbana: Univ. of Illinois, 1942), 19-21, 25, 26; and F. Bernier, *Travels in the Mogul Empire A.D. 1656-1668*, trans. A. Constable and V. A. Smith (London: Oxford Univ., 1916), pp. 437-40.

The culture and high civilization which prevailed among the Arabs in the years when they were prosperous would indicate that their decline after the commencement of the sixteenth century had for its cause the loss of the lucrative trade with the Far East and Europe. At any rate, the period of their holding the trade routes, both land and water, from India to Europe, coincided with the period of their greatness in the arts and in literature. . . .

The Mameluke Empire [comprising Egypt and Syria] was perhaps the most cultured land in all the world. Even Venice, the most powerful commercial and cultural center in Italy, owed much of its culture to the Arab world, and most of its prosperity to trade with the Mameluke Empire.

Cairo was an object of admiration to all European travelers. Reputedly there were two hundred merchants there each worth a million ducats (about $2,500,000) and two thousand more each worth one hundred thousand ducats ($250,000). A Jew in Cairo was so rich that although eight hundred thousand ducats ($2,000,000) were extorted from him on one occasion, he still remained rich.

The Mameluke court was maintained in luxury and pomp. Gold was used not only at the table but in the kitchen and throughout the palace. Poets, singers, musicians, and story-tellers flocked to the court to receive pensions. The grand palace was paved with marble, with gilded and painted roofs and gates of gold and azure, and was amply supplied with servants.

Cairo was said to extend over thirty-two miles in area, not including all its suburbs. At any rate, it was so large that a courier could not run around the town and suburbs in less than two days. One traveler believed it to be three times as large as Paris and to contain five times as many people. Far ahead of European cities, it was the custom in Cairo for each group of four or five houses to keep a light burning in the street every night. There were but few houses in which mosaics were not to be seen, and there were known to be three hundred homes with sculptures, ivory and ebony incrustations, and floors covered with very costly mosaics. There was a huge hospital in the town, maintained by a yearly endowment of two hundred thousand ducats ($500,000). Sick people were taken care of free of charge in that hospital, but if they died their property went to the institution. Although each street was paved only along the sides, all of them were daily watered to settle the dust. A rudimentary air-cooling system existed in many houses.

Situated between the Red Sea and the Mediterranean, Cairo drew merchants from India, Ethiopia, Italy, Greece, Nubia, Georgia, Bohemia, Turkey, Tartary, and North Africa, to sell their wares and buy others. At Bulaq, the port town of Cairo, there could be seen as many as a thousand barks along the wharves. The caravans from Arabia, Syria, and Iraq would stop there with their wares. But Bulaq was not entirely commercial, for it contained stately mosques, palaces, and colleges. . . .

And the [Mameluke] Sultans were not neglectful of their provincial towns, for in Mecca, Medina, and Jerusalem, and in many other towns, beautiful buildings were erected; charitable, pious, and literary endowments, schools, colleges of medicine, philosophy, art, and science, and homes for orphans were founded.

Prosperity of Bengal

Egypt has been represented in every age as the finest and most fruitful country in the world, and even our modern writers deny that there is any other land so peculiarly favoured by nature: but the knowledge I have acquired of *Bengale,* during two visits paid to that kingdom, inclines me to believe that the pre-eminence ascribed to *Egypt* is rather due to *Bengale.* The latter country produces rice in such abundance that it supplies not only the neighbouring but remote states. It is carried up the *Ganges* as far as *Patna,* and exported by sea to *Maslipatam* and many other ports on the coast of *Koromandel.* It is also sent to foreign kingdoms, principally to the island of *Ceylon* and the *Maldives. Bengale* abounds likewise in sugar, with which it supplies the kingdoms of *Golkonda* and the *Karnatic,* where very little is grown, *Arabia* and *Mesopotamia,* through the towns of *Moka* and *Bassora,* and even *Persia,* by way of *Bender-Abbasi. Bengale* likewise is celebrated for its sweetmeats, especially in places inhabited by *Portuguese,* who are skilful in the art of preparing them, and with whom they are an article of considerable trade. Among other fruits, they preserve large *citrons,* such as we have in *Europe,* a certain delicate root about the length of *sarsaparilla,* that common fruit of the *Indies* called *amba,* another called *ananas,* small *mirobolans,* which are excellent, *limes,* and *ginger.*

Bengale, it is true, yields not so much wheat as *Egypt;* but if this be a defect, it is attributable to the inhabitants, who live a great deal more upon rice than the *Egyptians,* and seldom taste bread. Nevertheless, wheat is cultivated in sufficient quantity for the consumption of the country, and for the making of excellent and cheap sea-biscuits, with which the crews of *European* ships, *English, Dutch* and *Portuguese,* are supplied. The three or four sorts of vegetables which, together with rice and butter, form the chief food of the common people, are purchased for the merest trifle, and for a single *roupie* twenty or more good fowls may be bought. Geese and ducks are proportionably cheap. There are also goats and sheep in abundance; and pigs are obtained at so low a price that the *Portuguese,* settled in the country, live almost entirely upon pork. This meat is salted at a cheap rate by the *Dutch* and *English,* for the supply of their vessels. Fish of every species, whether fresh or salt, is in the same profusion. In a word, *Bengale* abounds with every necessary of life. . . .

In regard to valuable commodities of a nature to attract foreign merchants, I am acquainted with no country where so great a variety is found. Besides the sugar I have spoken of, and which may be placed in the list of valuable commodities, there is in *Bengale* such a quantity of cotton and silks, that the kingdom may be called the common storehouse for those two kinds of merchandise, not of *Hindoustan* or the Empire of the *Great Mogol* only, but of all the neighbouring kingdoms, and even of *Europe.* I have been sometimes amazed at the vast quantity of cotton cloths, of every sort, fine and coarse, white and coloured, which the *Hollanders* alone export to different places, especially to *Japan* and *Europe.* The *English,* the *Portuguese,* and the native merchants deal also in these articles to a considerable extent. The same may be said of the silks and silk stuffs of all sorts. It is not possible to conceive the quantity drawn every year from *Bengale* for the supply of the whole of the *Mogol Empire,* as far as *Lahor* and *Cabol,* and generally of all those foreign nations to which the cotton cloths are sent. The silks are not certainly so fine as those of *Persia, Syria, Sayd,* and *Barut,* but they are of a much lower price; and I know from indisputable authority that, if they were well selected and wrought with care, they might be manufactured into most beautiful stuffs. The *Dutch* have sometimes seven or eight hundred natives employed in their silk factory at *Kassem-Bazar,* where, in like manner, the *English* and other merchants employ a proportionate number.

Bengale is also the principal emporium for *saltpetre.* A prodigious quantity is imported from *Patna.* It is carried down the *Ganges* with great facility, and the *Dutch* and *English* send large cargoes to many parts of the *Indies,* and to *Europe.*

Lastly, it is from this fruitful kingdom, that the best *lac, opium, wax, civet, long pepper,* and various drugs are obtained; and *butter,* which may appear to you an inconsiderable article, is in such plenty, that although it be a bulky article to export, yet it is sent by sea to numberless places.

RELIGIOUS TOLERATION IN THE OTTOMAN EMPIRE $\quad$ 11

Moslems popularly are associated with religious fanaticism, but in the sixteenth century, fanaticism was much more prevalent in the Christian than in the Moslem worlds. About the time that Christopher Columbus sailed westward from Spain to discover the New World, thousands of Jewish refugees were sailing eastward from the same country, bound for the Ottoman Empire; there they found the tolera-tion denied them throughout Christendom. The welcome they received stimulated further immigration, until approximately 100,000 found shelter under the star and crescent. The following selection describes the reception accorded to the Jews, the contributions that they made to their new homeland, and the general contrast, in this regard, between the Moslem and Christian worlds. *

... Even before the fall of Constantinople [to the Turks in 1453], an enthusiastic [Jewish] immigrant, newly-arrived in Turkey, sent a circular letter to the French and German communities, calling upon them to shake from their feet the dust of the cities of persecution and to emigrate with one accord to this new land of opportunity—not the least of the advantages of which was that it lay on the route to Palestine, the ultimate goal of every Jew's hopes and dreams. The reports of the last campaign [in 1453] against Constantinople were followed throughout the Jewish world with rapt atten-tion; for it seemed to be the veritable War of Gog and Magog which was to usher in the Messianic deliverance. Thereafter, the immigration increased, every new arrival attracting more and more to follow him. With the expulsion [of the Jews] from Spain in 1492, the settlement received a tremendous impetus. The Christian world, true to its record rather than its name, was with rare exceptions closed to the refugees. Only the Moslem world was open. To Africa, the unbelievers were admitted; to Turkey, they were avidly wel-comed. The reason for this was plain: they provided precisely that element which was most necessary to the ill-balanced state—a class of city-dwellers, merchants and craftsmen, who could practice the handicrafts that the Turks so painfully lacked and, moreover, prevent commerce from being entirely

* C. Roth, *The House of Nasi: Dona Gracia* (Philadelphia: Jewish Publication Society of America, 1948), pp. 83-91, 101-2.

in the hands of those whose interests were specifically anti-Turkish. ... When, in 1550, the handful of Jews left in Provence were threatened with expulsion and sent a deputation to the Levant to find a place of refuge, their compatriots wrote them an ecstatic letter describing in dithyrambic terms the amplitude of their life in that generous land. The wealthy could find lucrative outlet for their capital, the poor dignified employment, and all kindly treatment and complete freedom from physical attack and unjust accusations. "We have no words," they concluded, "to record the enlargement and deliverance that has been achieved by the Jews in this place."

Thus encouraged, more immigrants came and more, by every vessel that arrived from Western Europe. They settled by the score, the hundred, the thousand, in all the principal cities of the empire. They brought with them handicrafts and manufactures. They introduced the technical processes of the manufacture of firearms, gunpowder and cannon, which were used in battle against improvident rulers who had driven them out; and unwonted activity among the blacksmiths and the iron-foundries in the Jewish quarter was taken as a sign that the Grand Turk meditated a new military foray. They continued the professions of goldsmith, which they had practiced with such outstanding success in the Peninsula, and widely introduced the textile and dyeing industries in which they traditionally had such great ability. In many places, glass-making and even metal-working were Jewish monopolies. (Near Salonica, at a place called Sidroscapsi, there was a community almost entirely engaged in gold and silver mining.) With their knowledge of foreign languages and conditions, they were the greatest competitors of the Venetians in the import and export trade, notwithstanding the latter's strong political backing; and no foreign merchant could dispense with their services as interpreters. Jewish physicians from the school of Salamanca, or those brought up in the great tradition of Hispano-Arabic medicine, were generally sought after for their discretion as well as their skill, being employed in the service of the sultan, the imperial harem, the grand viziers, and even foreign embassies, not unwilling to forget at so great a distance from home the Church's prohibition of the employment of infidels in this capacity. In brief, just as the persecutions under the Cross reached their climax, a dazzling new world was opened up under the silvery radiance of the Crescent. The poet-chronicler Samuel Usque compared the country to the Red Sea, which the Lord divided for His people, when they went forth from Egypt, drowning their troubles in its broad expanse. ...

In order to appreciate the background of all this, it is necessary to rid one's mind of the nineteenth-century antithesis between the civilized West and the backward East, the amenities of the occidental world and the discomforts of the Levant, the humane environment of the Christendom and Moslem semi-barbarism. That, so far as it was ever true, belonged to the future. In the sixteenth century, Turkey was superior to the Occident in military power, equal in architecture and public works, hardly second as regards the amenities of life. What was more important, she was certainly not inferior in humanity. If the wars waged by the Grand Turk were cruel and barbaric, those waged by the Christian powers were no less so. When Charles V captured Tunis in 1535, thousands of men and women were killed or enslaved in an orgy of bloodshed. Nor was this the case only when infidels were in question; the sack of Rome in 1527 by the emperor's forces was hardly less appalling than the sack of Constantinople by the Turks in 1453.

The forays of the Knights of Malta and other Christian paladins, in the name of religion, were as pitiless and indiscriminate as those of the Corsairs (often in fact recent converts) who sailed under the Crescent. Nothing in Moslem annals of the time was as bloodthirsty as the Massacre of St. Bartholomew in France. Though the Turks did not always respect diplomatic immunities, they never perpetrated in this sphere any worse crime than the king of Hungary's barbarous butchery of the sultan's ambassador before the Battle of Mohacs in 1526, or for that matter that of the French envoys by the Spaniards in 1541 in Milan. The palace tragedies of Suleiman the Magnificent were no more gruesome than those at the court of his contemporary, King Henry VIII of England. The exaction of a tithe of their male children from the defeated Christians, to fill the ranks of the janissaries, was outdone in cruelty by kidnapping of Jewish children in Portugal a generation before to bring them up as Christians. Recruiting the imperial harem from captured Christian beauties was humanity itself if contrasted with the systematic dishonoring and then murder of beautiful Moslem captives by some of the Christian sea-captains of the time. No man was persecuted for his religion in sixteenth-century Turkey, when all over Europe—not only in Spain—Inquisitions were at work and the skies were reddened by the glare of the pyres in which thousands of unbelievers perished. In matters of personal hygiene, there was no question where the superiority lay: cleanliness in Constantinople was reckoned an integral part of godliness, and the Turks jeered unmercifully at their western European contemporaries who did not wash their bodies all over more than twice between birth and death. In transferring himself from West to East, a man hardly descended in the scale of material amenities, not at all in that of essential civilization.

PEACOCK THRONE OF THE GREAT MOGUL **12**

The Moslem world of the sixteenth and seventeenth centuries was outstanding for its achievements in culture as well as in other fields. In India, the Mogul Emperor Shah Jahan (1628–1658) built the famous Taj Mahal, still considered one of the most beautiful buildings in the world. The same emperor's magnificent Peacock Throne attracted international attention because of its fantastic ornamentation of diamonds, pearls, emeralds, and other precious stones. A French traveler observed this throne in 1665 and left the following description.*

...the Great Mogul has seven magnificent thrones, one wholly covered with diamonds, the others with rubies, emeralds, or pearls.

The principal throne, which is placed in the hall of the first court, is nearly of the form and size of our camp-beds; that is to say, it is about 6 feet long and 4 wide. Upon the four feet, which are very massive, and from 25 to 25 inches high, are fixed the four bars which support the base of the throne, and upon these bars are ranged twelve columns, which sustain the canopy on three sides, there not being any on that which faces the court. Both the feet and the bars, which are more than 18 inches long, are covered with gold inlaid and enriched with numerous diamonds, rubies, and emeralds. In the middle of each bar there is a large . . . ruby, . . . with four emeralds round it, which form a square cross. Next in succession, from one side to the other along the length of the bars there are similar crosses, arranged so that in one the ruby is in the middle of four emeralds, and in another the emerald is in the middle and four rubies surround it. The emeralds are table-cut, and the intervals between the rubies and emeralds are covered with diamonds, the largest of which do not exceed 10 to 12 carats in weight, all being showy stones, but very flat. There are also in some parts pearls set in gold, and upon one of the longer sides of the throne there are four steps to ascend it. . . . There is to be seen, moreover, a sword suspended from this throne, a mace, a round shield, a bow and quiver with arrows; and all these weapons, as also the cushions and steps, both of this throne and the other six, are covered over with stones which match those with which each of the thrones is respectively enriched. . . .

The underside of the canopy is covered with diamonds and pearls, with a fringe of pearls all round, and above the canopy, which is a quadrangular-shaped dome, there is to be seen a peacock with elevated tail made of blue sapphires and other coloured stones, the body being of gold inlaid with precious stones, having a large ruby in front of the breast, from whence hangs a pear-shaped pearl of 50 carats or thereabouts, and of a somewhat yellow water. On both sides of the peacock there is a large bouquet of the same height as the bird, and consisting of many kinds of flowers made of gold inlaid with precious stones. On the side of the throne which is opposite the court there is to be seen a jewel consisting of a diamond of from 80 to 90 carats weight, with rubies and emeralds round it, and when the King is seated he has this jewel in full view. But that which in my opinion is the most costly thing about this magnificent throne is, that the twelve columns supporting the canopy are surrounded with beautiful rows of pearls, which are round and of fine water, and weigh from 6 to 10 carats each. At 4 feet distance from the throne there are fixed, on either side, two umbrellas, the sticks of which for 7 or 8 feet in height are covered with diamonds, rubies, and pearls. The umbrellas are of red velvet, and are embroidered and fringed all round with pearls. . . .

13   Persian Miniature Painting

The Moslems also excelled in several minor fields of culture, such as carpet and textile weaving, porcelain, leather and jewelry work, and miniature painting. Most miniatures were painted for the purpose of illustrating costly manuscripts, and the art flourished especially in Persia between the fourteenth and sixteenth centuries. The following selection describes the subjects and the characteristics of this distinctive form of Moslem art.*

* "Persian Delight," *Aramco World,* IX (January, 1958), 22-24.

... Most Persian miniatures are not "miniature" in the sense of being very small; many were 8-by-12 and 9-by-11 inches. From early days the word "miniature" has had a confused meaning. It comes from the Latin "minimum" which means "red lead." Red lead pigment was used to "miniate" or portray initials and ornaments in early manuscripts. And because some of the early manuscript paintings were small, the word "minuteness" got mixed up with "miniated," and the word "miniature" came to be applied to small paintings. ...

Unlike Italian or Byzantine painters of the period, Persian artists could not turn to religion as a source of inspiration; for the world of Islam discourages the realistic representation of human forms in art. So miniature painting in Persia often portrayed incidents and scenes based on the country's folklore, literature, and social customs.

It was a joyous art which expressed the philosophy, "Live for today." Often it reflected a bright world of viziers and sultans, caliphs and shahs. Animals were very popular subjects and many beautiful miniatures of them remain to us. But usually the scenes were of man and his activities. He might be shown hunting, playing polo, philosophizing in a garden, listening to music, or poised at a dramatic moment in the heat of battle.

Persian miniatures were nearly always intended to illustrate manuscripts which were also illuminated by boxing the text and illustrations in richly embellished margins.

Today we take books as a matter of course. But in ancient days owning a book was a rare and cherished experience. Even a scholar was lucky if he owned six to twelve volumes. The illuminated manuscripts of Persia with their brightly colored miniatures and highly ornamented frames were especially treasured by their owners as works of art, and often carried on hunting expeditions, or even to war. To men who dwelt for a large part of the year amid deserts and arid steppe lands, the garden settings of Persian miniatures recalled nostalgically the spring time, the blooming of flowers, the songs of birds.

Some Persian manuscripts were about the size and shape of an old family Bible, about 15-by-17 inches, and three inches thick. The leather bindings were often tooled or embossed in geometric designs, and stamped with gold. The paper was handmade of linen rags and burnished to a glossy sheen with a crystal egg or mother-of-pearl. From ten to fifty-four miniatures, or sometimes more, would be included in a book, the number varying, perhaps, according to the purse of the patron.

The Persians were not the first to make picture books or miniature paintings. The Egyptian *Book of the Dead,* which dates back to at least 3000 B.C., was a papyrus-scroll book illustrated with paintings. And there are miniatures in existence today dating as far back as the third century. But Persian artists developed the art of miniature painting to its highest perfection and were masters of it for 300 years.

Combining the best features of Byzantine, Mesopotamian, and Seljuk art, learning all they could from the Chinese artists whom Genghis Khan brought into Persia in the thirteenth century, and borrowing from the art of their Mongol conquerors of the thirteenth and fourteenth centuries, Persian artists had synthesized all these outside influences into a truly great art of Persian miniature painting by the late 1400's.

Most Persian miniatures followed a set pattern. They showed a scene set within a frame, and painted as if the viewer were looking down from a slight elevation. There were no shadows, no contrast between dark and light, no tone gradations, nor any attempt at a third dimension. The artist started his painting with a sketch made by dipping his brush in water. Next the outline was drawn separately. The most amazing thing about a Persian miniature is its precision down to the tiniest margin.

Persian miniature painting, from beginning to end, was an expensive art, for only the wealthy and powerful could afford to finance the production of an illustrated book. It was a hand process from making the paper, grinding the pigments, beating in the gold, to the actual painting itself. In addition, the text had to be copied in fine calligraphy, and the book bound in tooled leather. A sultan of the seventeenth century is said to have paid eighteen purses of gold for the paper, the ornaments of gold, the salary of scribes, and to have rewarded the artist who made the miniatures for his book with a purse of 1,000 pieces of gold. To earn a living as an artist in those days required the support of a rich patron.

Creative ability was highly respected in Persia and many famous art patrons are remembered by history, among them, Mahmud of Ghazna, who founded an academy of painting in the eleventh century. Even the barbarous Tamerlane, who swept ruthlessly across Asia destroying populations and cities, showed his appreciation of art by sparing the lives of artists and shipping them off to Samarkand to work for him.

The most celebrated Persian miniature painter was Bihzad, described as the "marvel of the age," who lived in the fifteenth century and was particularly noted for his skill in capturing facial expression. He was so revered by Shah Ismail that once during a battle, the Shah ordered that Bihzad be hidden in a cave so no harm could come to him.

Unfortunately, many miniatures by Persia's best painters were destroyed before the art declined in the early seventeenth century. But enough examples survive to recall the artistic glory of an ancient land.

14 ROOTS OF MOSLEM DECLINE

From the seventeenth century onward, the Moslem world began to decline in every field, so that the Moslem states today are relatively underdeveloped. Whether in economic productivity, military power, or political efficiency, the Islamic world is lagging far behind the Western world—precisely the opposite of Busbecq's expectations and prophecies in the sixteenth century. Some of the reasons for this surprising outcome are given in the following penetrating analysis by a French physician who lived for several years in the mid-seventeenth century in Egypt, Persia, and India.*

... The king [of India], as proprietor of the land, makes over a certain quantity to military men [or timariots], as an equivalent for their pay. ... Similar grants are made to governors, in lieu of their salary, and also for the support of their troops, on condition that they pay a certain sum annually

* F. Bernier, *op. cit.,* pp. 224, 225, 227, 252-59.

to the king out of any surplus revenue that the land may yield. The lands not so granted are retained by the king as the peculiar domains of his house . . . and upon these domains he keeps farmers, who are also bound to pay him an annual rent.

The persons thus put in possession of the land, whether as timariots, governors or farmers, have an authority almost absolute over the peasantry, and nearly as much over the artisans and merchants of the towns and villages within their district; and nothing can be imagined more cruel and oppressive than the manner in which it is exercised. There is no one before whom the injured peasant, artisan or tradesman, can pour out his just complaints; no great lords, parliaments or judges of presidial courts exist, as in France, to restrain the wickedness of those merciless oppressors, and the cadis, or judges, are not invested with sufficient power to redress the wrongs of these unhappy people. This sad abuse of the royal authority may not be felt in the same degree near capital cities, such as Delhi and Agra, or in the vicinity of large towns and seaports, because in those places acts of gross injustice cannot easily be concealed from the court.

This debasing state of slavery obstructs the progress of trade and influences the manners and mode of life of every individual. There can be little encouragement to engage in commercial pursuits, when the success with which they may be attended, instead of adding to the enjoyment of life, provokes the cupidity of a neighbouring tyrant possessing both power and inclination to deprive any man of the fruits of his industry. When wealth is acquired, as must sometimes be the case, the possessor, so far from living with increased comfort and assuming an air of independence, studies the means by which he may appear indigent: his dress, lodging and furniture, continue to be mean, and he is careful, above all things, never to indulge in the pleasures of the table. In the mean time, his gold and silver remain buried at a great depth in the ground. . . .

The peasant cannot avoid asking himself this question: "Why should I toil for a tyrant who may come tomorrow and lay his rapacious hands upon all I possess and value, without leaving me the means to drag on my miserable existence?—The timariots, governors and farmers, on their part reason in this manner "why should the neglected state of this land create uneasiness in our minds? and why should we expend our own money and time to render it fruitful? we may be deprived of it in a single moment, and our exertions would benefit neither ourselves nor our children. Let us draw from the soil all the money we can, though the peasant should starve or abscond, and we should leave it, when commanded to quit, a dreary wilderness."

The facts I have mentioned are sufficient to account for the rapid declension of the Asiatic states. It is owing to this miserable system of government that most towns in Hindostan are made up of earth, mud, and other wretched materials; that there is no city or town which, if it be not already ruined and deserted, does not bear evident marks of approaching decay. Without confining our remarks to so distant a kingdom, we may judge of the effects of despotic power unrelentingly exercised, by the present condition of Mesopotamia, Anatolia, Palestine, the once wonderful plains of Antioch, and so many other regions anciently well cultivated, fertile and populous, but now desolate, and in many parts marshy, pestiferous, and unfit for human habitation. Egypt also exhibits a sad picture. . . .

A profound and universal ignorance is the natural consequence of such a state of society as I have endeavoured to describe. Is it possible to introduce in Hindostan academies and colleges properly endowed? Where shall we seek for founders? or, should they be found, where are the scholars? Where the individuals whose property is sufficient to support their children at college? or, if such individuals exist, who would venture to display so clear a proof of wealth?

15 RESULTS OF MOSLEM DECLINE

By the eighteenth century the Moslem empires had declined to the point where travelers invariably commented on the sad state of affairs. A good example is the following account by a British consul and merchant who lived for many years in the late eighteenth century in the Ottoman Empire. In sprightly manner, this observer describes the sterility in the arts and sciences, the suffocation of commerce and industry, and the breakdown of imperial authority.*

... General knowledge is little if at all cultivated; every man is supposed to know his own business or profession, with which it is esteemed foolish and improper for any other person to interfere. The man of general science, a character so frequent and so useful in Christian Europe, is unknown; and any one, but a mere artificer, who should concern himself with the founding of cannon, the building of ships, or the like, would be esteemed little better than a madman. The natural consequence of these narrow views is, that the professors of any art or science are themselves profoundly ignorant, and that the greatest absurdities are mixed with all their speculations.

I shall elucidate this by detailing the opinions received, not only by the populace, but even by the pretended *literati,* in various branches of knowledge.

From the mufti to the peasant it is generally believed, that there are seven heavens, from which the earth is immoveably suspended by a large chain; that the sun is an immense ball of fire, at least as big as a whole Ottoman province, formed for the sole purpose of giving light and heat to the earth; that eclipses of the moon are occasioned by a great dragon attempting to devour that luminary; that the fixed stars hang by chains from the highest heaven, etc., etc. These absurdities are in part supported by the testimony of the Koran; and the astronomers, as they are called, themselves all pretend to astrology, a profession so much esteemed, that an astrologer is kept in the pay of the court, as well as of most great men. ...

With regard to the general ideas entertained by all ranks in Turkey, relative to commerce, they are no less narrow and absurd than all their other opinions. "We should not trade," say they, "with those beggarly nations, who come to buy of us rich articles of merchandize, and rare commodities, which we ought not to sell to them, but we should trade with those who bring to us useful and valuable articles, without the labour of manufacturing, or the trouble of importing them on our part." Upon this principle it is that Mocha

* W. Eton, *A Survey of the Turkish Empire,* 4th ed. (London, 1809), pp. 190-93, 206-10, 231-33, 275, 278-81, 283-84.

coffee is prohibited to be sold to infidels. It is therefore no wonder that the foreign commerce of the Turks is comparatively trifling; their trade is mostly from province to province, and even this is inconceivably narrowed by the want of mutual confidence, and the ignorance and short-sightedness of their views. They have few bills of exchange, or any of those modes of transacting business which the ingenuity and enterprise of commercial nations have invented for the facilitation of commercial intercourse.

The effects which the insecurity of property, and the watchful avarice of the government produce upon commerce, are still more striking. In an extensive trade capital and credit must be alike great, but from both of these the Turk is cut off; he dares not make a display of wealth; and if he has been so fortunate as to accumulate a large sum of money, his first care is to conceal it from view, lest it should attract the bloodsuckers of power. The necessary consequence of this is, that credit, that vital spring of commerce, cannot be created, and instead of those commercial connections which in this part of Europe ramify so widely, and render commercial operations so easy, all business is transacted either by principals themselves, or their immediate factors, in a way little different from the barter of the rude ages. ...

The natural result of this combination of circumstances is, that commerce is every where checked; no emulation takes place, no communication of discoveries, no firm and solid association of interest; their mechanical arts are in many instances worse cultivated now than they were a century ago, particularly the tempering of sabres; and some of their manufactures have gone entirely to decay. ...

The relaxation of the bands of power has gone too far in the Turkish empire not to be, in some degree, perceived by the porte [central government]; it cannot but feel the weakness of its authority over most of the distant *pashaliks* [provinces]. ...

Casting our view over the pashaliks most immediately connected with the seat of empire, we shall find them distracted, disorganized, and scarcely yielding more than a nominal obedience to the sultan: such are the pashaliks of Asia Minor and Syria. With regard to the more distant provinces, they may be considered as connected with the porte rather by treaty than as integral parts of the empire. In this light I view Moldavia and Walachia on the north, and Egypt on the south.

Chapter Four

*Confucian world
at the time of
the West's expansion*

16 The Confucian Way of Life

On the eastern tip of Eurasia a highly sophisticated civilization developed that was comparable to those of India and the Middle East. A unique feature of this civilization is its persistence: it is today the oldest existing civilization. One reason for its durability is the moral code and the literary and intellectual heritage known as Confucianism, the bedrock of Chinese civilization for over two millennia. A practical moral system, it is concerned not with afterlife and the supernatural, but with the concrete problems of everyday living. Its aim is to make the human being good— a good father, a good mother, a good son, a good daughter, a good citizen. Confucius preached that the ideal society can be realized not through legislation, but by educating its citizens according to his principles. The following selections from his sayings present some of these principles.*

The Individual

It is by the rules of propriety that the character is established.

The rules of propriety serve as instruments to form men's characters. They remove from a man all perversity and increase what is beautiful in his nature. They make him correct, when employed in the ordering of himself; they ensure for him free course, when employed toward others.

* M. M. Dawson, *The Ethics of Confucius* (New York: Putnam, 1915), pp. 2 ff.

The Family

The superior man while his parents are alive, reverently nourishes them; and when they are dead, reverently sacrifices to them. His chief thought is how, to the end of life, not to disgrace them.

There are three degrees of filial piety. The highest is being a credit to our parents; the next is not disgracing them; and the lowest is merely being able to support them.

The services of love and reverence to parents when alive, and those of grief and sorrow for them when dead—these completely discharge the duty of living men.

Government

Good government obtains when those who are near are made happy, and those who are far are attracted.

The people are the most important element; ... the sovereign, least important.

If the people have plenty, their prince will not be left to want alone. If the people are in want, their prince will not be able to enjoy plenty alone.

When rulers love to observe the rules of propriety, these people respond readily to the calls upon them for service.

The superior man does not use rewards, yet the people are stimulated to virtue. He does not show wrath, yet the people are more awed than by hatchets and battle-axes.

The ruler must first himself be possessed of the qualities which he requires of the people; and must be free from the qualities which he requires the people to abjure.

Education and Arts

Even among the sons of the emperor, the princes and the great officials, if they were not qualified to rites and justice, they should be put down to the class of common people; even among the sons of the common people, if they have good education and character and are qualified to rites and justice, they should be elevated to the class of ministers and nobles.

In providing a system of education, one trouble is to secure proper respect for the teacher; when such is assured, what he teaches will also be regarded with respect; when that is done, the people will know how to respect learning.

Let relaxation and enjoyment be found in the polite arts!

A scholar should constantly pursue what is virtuous and find recreation in the arts.

Music produces pleasure which human nature cannot be without.

In music the sages found pleasure and that it could be used to make the hearts of the people good. Because of the deep influence which it exerts on a man and the change which it produces in manners and customs, the ancient kings appointed it as one of the subjects of instruction.

17 THE CIVIL SERVICE EXAMINATION

The unique longevity of Chinese civilization can be explained also by the stabilizing influence of the civil service examination system, which provided a trained bureaucracy based on merit rather than on family or political connections. This system lasted over two millennia—from 165 B.C. to A.D. 1905. Examinations were held at three levels: local county, provincial capital, and the imperial capital; the tests lasted for several days and were given in special walled enclosures which held rows on rows of small brick cells. The following account by a well-known modern Chinese scholar describes the examination he took at the county level.*

Early one morning, as the time for the civil examination drew near, I started for Shaoshing where the examination was to be held for our district. The luggage man slung his bamboo pole over his shoulder with my suitcase and bamboo basket roped to one end and bedding outfits balancing the other. I followed on his heels. As my luggage swung out of the college gate a teacher who happened to see me smiled and wished me good luck. . . .

The examination began with roll call at the entrance of the Examination Hall at about four o'clock in the morning. The early autumn morning was chilly. A large crowd of literati, several thousand strong and each wearing a red-tasseled hat—without a button—and carrying a lantern, gathered around the spacious courtyard. At the entrance to the hall the Prefect sat in stately dignity at a long desk. He wore a red-tasseled hat with a blue crystal button at the top, a black jacket over a deep blue gown, and a chain of beads around his neck. This was his full official attire. With a vermilion pen in his hand he began to call the roll. As he went down the list a man standing by him called out in long-drawn tones the name of each candidate, who promptly sang out at the top of his voice, "Here! So-and-so, the guarantor." Immediately the guarantor sang his own name in acknowledgement of the sponsorship. The Prefect then glanced about quickly to see if anything was wrong and made a red dot above the name with his vermilion pen.

The candidate was then let in. His hat and clothes were searched to see that he carried no notes with him. Anything found written on paper would be confiscated.

The candidates moved on in files to their respective seats, which were numbered, each finding his place accordingly. The names on the examination papers were written on detachable slips to be torn off before the papers were handed in. Each paper was also numbered in a sealed corner, which was not opened until the papers were marked and the successful candidates selected, so as to prevent any possible favoritism. Toward the end of the Manchu Dynasty, when corruption ran rampant in many branches of government office, the Imperial examination system remained independent and free alike of external interference and internal corruption. This was one reason why the degrees conferred were so much honored in China.

Questions were limited to the Confucian classics and this was why a candidate must commit to memory all the texts in the classics. This I had done through years of laborious conning in my country school and the Sino-

---

* Chiang Monlin, *Tides From the West* (New Haven: Yale Univ., 1947), pp. 54-57.

Occidental School in Shaoshing. Questions were shown to the candidates by means of cubic lanterns, on the screens of which the questions were written; they were lighted with candles so that the black letters on the white screens could be seen distinctly at a distance. Bearers raised the lanterns high above their heads and carried them up and down the aisles several times, so that none could miss them.

About noon officials went around to check on how far the candidates had gone with their essays and set on each paper a seal at the spot to which the lines had run. At about four in the afternoon cannon began to roar, marking the first call for the collection of papers. The gates were flung open and the band began to play. Candidates who were able to answer the first call handed in their papers and made their way out slowly through the gates with music playing and an anxious crowd waiting. After everyone had made his exit the gates were closed again. The second call was made about an hour later with the same ceremony. The third or final call was made about six, with both cannon and band remaining silent.

We had about a week or ten days to wait for the results of the examination. In the interim there was plenty of time for amusement. Bookstores, large and small, were found everywhere near the Examination Hall. There were chess stands, temporary restaurants with famous Shaoshing wines and delicious dishes at moderate prices, and traveling theatres where we could go and enjoy ourselves.

On the day when the results were to be made public a large crowd waited anxiously in front of a high, spacious wall opposite the entrance of the Examination Hall. Cannon and band announced the moment when the list of names, or rather numbers, of the successful candidates was issued. The numbers were set down in a circular formation instead of in a column, so as to avoid having a top and bottom to the list.

I was pleasantly surprised to find my own number in big black letters among the others in the circle on the enormous oblong paper posted on the wall. To make sure I rubbed my eyes and looked at it several times. When I was sure they had not deceived me, I elbowed through the packed crowd and hastened back to my lodginghouse. As I made my way out I noticed a man with an open umbrella which caught on a railing. When he jerked it off the umbrella went upward, looking like a giant artichoke, but in his excitement he kept on running and paid no attention to it.

The second session of the examination came within a few days. Everyone who had passed the first had reason to worry, since some would be eliminated. I was lucky in the second trial. In the list of names which was posted on the wall I found mine somewhere in the middle rows.

The third and final session was merely perfunctory. In addition to an essay we were supposed to write down from memory a section of the "Imperial Instructions in Morals"; in reality each of us had with us a copy of the text, which we were allowed to carry into the Examination Hall and which we copied outright. The Imperial Examiner appeared in person to supervise the final examination. His official title I learned from the inscription on two identical pennants about fifteen feet long which streamed in the air from flagpoles standing symmetrically at either side of the entrance. It read: "The Imperial Vice-Minister of Rites and Concurrently Imperial Examiner of Public Instruction for the Province of Chekiang, etc."

Early in the morning, some days later, I was awakened from slumber by the rapid beating of a tom-tom outside my window. It was an official reporter coming to announce the award of the First Degree—*Wu-shen,* popularly known as *Hsiu-tsai.* The official announcement, which was printed in bold block prints on a piece of red paper about six feet by four, read as follows:

> His Majesty's Imperial Vice-Minister of Rites and Concurrently Imperial Examiner of Public Instruction for the Province of Chekiang, etc., wishes to announce that your honorable person, Chiang Monlin, is awarded the Degree of Wu-shen and entitled to enjoy the privilege of entering the District Government School as a government scholar.

18 Jesuit Report on Sixteenth Century China

Direct contact between China and Western Europe was made when Portuguese merchants opened trade with Canton in 1514. Jesuit missionaries soon followed to convert the Chinese to Christianity. One of the outstanding pioneer Jesuit missionaries was Matteo Ricci, who labored in China from 1583 to 1610. In his diary, he left a glowing account of the strange civilization that he came to know well. The following excerpt from that record shows how impressive China appeared to the best European minds of the period.*

He whose authority extends over this immense kingdom is called Lord of the Universe, because the Chinese are of the opinion that the extent of their vast dominion is to all intents and purposes coterminous with the borders of the universe. The few kingdoms contiguous to their state, of which they had any knowledge before they learned of the existence of Europe, were, in their estimation, hardly worthy of consideration. If this idea of assumed jurisdiction should seem strange to a European, let him consider that it would have seemed equally strange to the Chinese, if they had known that so many of our own rulers applied this same title to themselves, without at the same time having any jurisdiction over the vast expanse of China. So much then for the name of the kingdom known as China.

Relative to the extent of China, it is not without good reason that the writers of all times have added the prefix great to its name. Considering its vast stretches and the boundaries of its lands, it would at present surpass all the kingdoms of the earth, taken as one, and as far as I am aware, it has surpassed them during all previous ages. . . .

Referring again to the enormous extent and renown of this empire, it should be observed that it is quite well protected on all sides, by defenses supplied by both nature and science. To the south and the east it is washed by the sea, and the coast is dotted with so many small islands that it would be difficult for a hostile fleet to approach the mainland. To the north the country is defended against hostile Tartar raids by precipitous hills, which are joined into an unbroken line of defense with a tremendous wall four

---

* *China in the Sixteenth Century: the Journals of Matthew Ricci,* trans. Louis J. Gallagher, S.J., pp. 7-11, 14, 54-56. Copyright 1942 by Louis J. Gallagher, S.J. Reprinted by permission of Random House, Inc.

hundred and five miles long. To the northwest it is flanked by a great desert of many days' march, which either deters an advancing army from attacking the Chinese border or becomes the burial place of those who attempt the attack. Beyond the mountain range which hems in the kingdom to the west, there exist only impoverished countries to which the Chinese pay little or no attention, as they neither fear them nor consider them worth while annexing.

Due to the great extent of this country north and south as well as east and west, it can be safely asserted that nowhere else in the world is found such a variety of plant and animal life within the confines of a single kingdom. The wide range of climatic conditions in China gives rise to a great diversity of vegetable products, some of which are most readily grown in tropical countries, others in arctic, and others again in the temperate zones. The Chinese themselves, in their geographies, give us detailed accounts of the fertility of the various provinces and of the variety of their products. It hardly falls within the scope of my present treatise to enter into a comprehensive discussion of these matters. Generally speaking, it may be said with truth that all of these writers are correct when they say that everything which the people need for their well-being and sustenance, whether it be for food or clothing or even delicacies and superfluities, is abundantly produced within the borders of the kingdom and not imported from foreign climes. I would even venture to say that practically everything which is grown in Europe is likewise found in China. If not, then what is missing here is abundantly supplied by various other products unknown to Europeans. To begin with, the soil of China supplies its people with every species of grain—barley, millet, winter wheat, and similar grains.

Rice, which is the staple article of Chinese diet, is produced here in far greater abundance than in Europe. Vegetables, especially beans, and the like, all of which are used not only as food for the people but also as fodder for cattle and beasts of burden, are grown in unlimited variety. The Chinese harvest two and sometimes three crops of such plants every year, owing not only to the fertility of the soil and the mildness of the climate but in great measure to the industry of the people. With the exception of olives and almonds, all the principal fruits known in Europe grow also in China, while the real fig tree, which, by the way, our Fathers introduced into China, yields in nothing to its European progenitors. The Chinese, moreover, possess a variety of fruits unknown in Europe which are found exclusively in the province of Canton and in the southern parts of China. These fruits are called licya and longana by the natives and for the most part they are very pleasing to the taste. The Indian nut-bearing palm tree and other Indian fruits are found here, and there is a species of fruit called the Chinese fig, a very sweet and appetizing fruit which the Portuguese call sucusina. This particular fruit can be eaten only after it is dried, hence the Portuguese call it a fig. It has nothing in common with the real fig, however, since it resembles a large Persian apple, [probably the peach] only it is red, and lacks the soft down and the pit. Here, too, we find oranges and other citrus fruits and every kind of fruit that grows on thornbushes, in a larger variety and possessing a finer flavor than the same fruits grown in other countries. . . .

All of the known metals without exception are to be found in China. Besides brass and ordinary copper alloys, the Chinese manufacture another metal which is an imitation silver but which costs no more than yellow brass. From molten iron they fashion many more articles than we do, for example, cauldrons, pots, bells, gongs, mortars, gratings, furnaces, martial weapons, instruments of torture, and a great number of other things, all but equal in workmanship to our own metal-craft. . . .

. . . it seems to be quite remarkable when we stop to consider it, that in a kingdom of almost limitless expanse and innumerable population, and abounding in copious supplies of every description, though they have a well-equipped army and navy that could easily conquer the neighboring nations, neither the King nor his people ever think of waging a war of aggression. They are quite content with what they have and are not ambitious of conquest. In this respect they are much different from the people of Europe, who are frequently discontent with their own governments and covetous of what others enjoy. While the nations of the West seem to be entirely consumed with the idea of supreme domination, they cannot even preserve what their ancestors have bequeathed them, as the Chinese have done through a period of some thousands of years. . . .

Another remarkable fact and quite worthy of note as marking a difference from the West, is that the entire kingdom is administered by the Order of the Learned, commonly known as The Philosophers. The responsibility for orderly management of the entire realm is wholly and completely committed to their charge and care. The army, both officers and soldiers, hold them in high respect and show them the promptest obedience and deference, and not infrequently the military are disciplined by them as a schoolboy might be punished by his master. Policies of war are formulated and military questions are decided by the Philosophers only, and their advice and counsel has more weight with the King than that of the military leaders. In fact very few of these, and only on rare occasions, are admitted to war consultations. Hence it follows that those who aspire to be cultured frown upon war and would prefer the lowest rank in the philosophical order to the highest in the military, realizing that the Philosophers far excel military leaders in the good will and the respect of the people and in opportunities of acquiring wealth. What is still more surprising to strangers is that these same Philosophers, as they are called, with respect to nobility of sentiment and in contempt of danger and death, where fidelity to King and country is concerned, surpass even those whose particular profession is the defense of the fatherland. Perhaps this sentiment has its origin in the fact that the mind of man is ennobled by the study of letters. Or again, it may have developed from the fact that from the beginning and foundation of this empire the study of letters was always more acceptable to the people than the profession of arms, as being more suitable to a people who had little or no interest in the extension of the empire.

The order and harmony that prevails among magistrates, both high and low, in the provinces and in the regal Curia is also worthy of admiration. Their attitude toward the King, in exact obedience and in external ceremony, is a cause of wonderment to a foreigner.

19 FAILURE OF JESUIT MISSION TO CHINA

European intellectuals of the seventeenth and eighteenth centuries admired and respected Chinese civilization, but the Chinese were not particularly impressed by *what they learned of European civilization. They noted the proficiency of the Jesuits in astronomy and mathematics, but this did not affect in the slightest their condescending attitude toward the outside world, including the West, and the Christian faith of the West. The Jesuit mission that labored in Peking from 1601 to 1775 ended in failure, despite the talents and persistence of its members. A British historian's account of this mission shows that the China of this period had a much greater impact on Europe than Europe had upon China.**

The obstacles to evangelizing China were indeed formidable, and they did not come from one side only. The pioneer Portuguese missionaries in the East knew no Chinese, and they had to depend upon interpreters, who were naturally better acquainted with market prices and bazaar gossip than with subtle theological arguments. For a long time the missionaries paid little or no attention to the basic beliefs and sacred books of those whom they were trying to convert, being content to dismiss them as the inventions of the devil. It remained for the Italian Jesuit Visitor-General, Alexandro Valignano, to establish the Far Eastern missions on a firm basis with their headquarters at Macao and a plan of action which included intensive study of their languages, literatures and religious beliefs, under the guidance of competent Chinese and Japanese teachers. But even this more intelligent method of approach did not necessarily get the missionaries very far.

No European could reside in China without official permission, and Chinese officialdom was intensely suspicious of the "foreign devils," who were strictly confined to Macao, apart from occasional and closely supervised trading-trips to Canton. Chinese civilization was based upon the "family system," with the veneration of ancestors as its core; and the worship of the dead was incompatible with Christianity in any of its forms. The traditional Chinese view of filial piety, which considers that children were born to nourish their parents and to perpetuate the family in their turn, ran counter to much Christian teaching, which places an exaggerated value on celibacy and virginity, and compels the parent to "lay up for the children." The practice of polygamy was another great obstacle, though not an insuperable one having regard to the Western practice (as opposed to theory) of keeping one wife and several mistresses. But ancestor-worship was first and last the main obstacle, since this was the keystone of the Confucian system; and it was from this system that the governing-class of China—the so-called *literati* or scholar-gentry—and the emperor ultimately derived their authority.

The establishment and maintenance of the Jesuit mission at Peking was primarily due to the tact, ability, and mathematical learning of three outstanding men: the Italian Matteo Ricci (1583-1610), the German Johann Adam Schall von Bell (1622-1666), and the Belgian Ferdinand Verbiest (1659-1688). "Oh rock, when wilt thou open?" Valignano used to exclaim while gazing from Macao towards the mainland, and it was Ricci who supplied the "open sesame." Briefly, his method was to identify the Jesuit missionaries as the cultural counterpart of the Chinese scholar-gentry, and to sugar the pill of Christian proselytism with the coating of Western science. Keeping religion at first in the background, and only unobtrusively introducing the topic when

* C. R. Boxer, "Jesuits at the Court of Peking 1601-1775," *History Today,* VII (September, 1957), 581-89.

he had got to know his visitors really well, Ricci aroused the curiosity of the Chinese officials by his Western books, maps, clocks and mathematical instruments, and he secured their respect by his zealous study of the Chinese classics. His gift of a chiming clock to the Emperor Wan-li, and its repair and maintenance in running order, tipped the balance in favour of his being allowed to stay at Peking in 1601, following an abortive visit there two years earlier. Ricci also strove to reconcile the Confucian classics with Christian doctrine; and he claimed that the compulsory ritual observances connected with the cult of the Sage's memory were purely secular and had no religious significance. He further argued from his study of the classics that the ancient Chinese had believed in the one universal God of the Christians, and that their so-called ancestor-worship was, if rightly understood, merely the formal token of respect paid to the illustrious dead. With a few exceptions . . . the Jesuit missionaries followed his lead and allowed their converts to participate in certain Confucian (but not Buddhist or Taoist) rites and ceremonies on this understanding. Ricci himself was never received by the emperor in person during his ten-year stay at Peking, but he made some influential friends. His outspoken denunciation of Buddhism and Taoism also made him some enemies; but as he himself said on his deathbed to his colleagues, "I leave you facing an open door."

The door was indeed open, or at least ajar, but not so much for the missionaries as sowers of the gospel seed, as in their capacity of mathematicians and technicians. Their position remained insecure until, at the prompting of a Christian high official, Hsü Kuang-ch'i, some of them were appointed as assistants in a newly established Calendrical Bureau in 1629, to help with the revision of the calendar. This Bureau was annexed to the Board of Astronomy or Mathematics which had for long been under the technical direction of Muslim mathematicians, who . . . were no longer so competent as their predecessors had been in the days of Kublai Khan and Marco Polo. This was a very serious matter in a country where the annual compilation of the imperial calendar formed an essential part of government. Apart from offering purely astronomical information, such as the days of the month, the moon's phases, the equinoxes, solstices, etc., the calendar contained a wealth of astrological lore about lucky and unlucky days on the lines of Old Moore's Almanack. Copies were circulated throughout the empire and were invariably consulted before birth, marriage, setting out on a journey, erecting a building, or other occasions of daily life. The calendar was used, in short, largely for astrological purposes, to determine the influence of the stars and planets on human destiny. The replacement of the discredited Muslim experts by the Jesuits was due to the technical abilities of Schall and Verbiest, although the Jesuits were not allowed by Rome to follow the theories of Galileo and were compelled to be content with those of Tycho Brahé and Kepler.

The Jesuits stationed at the court of Peking now formed an integral part of the imperial bureaucracy in a land that was largely governed by bureaucrats, and their position was immensely strengthened thereby. From 1644, when Schall was appointed director of the Board of Astronomy by the regents of the Manchu (or Ch'ing) dynasty which had just overthrown the Ming, one or another of the resident Peking Jesuits subsequently held this post, save for a brief interval in 1664-1688, when they were out of favour. He usually had one or two of his colleagues as subordinates, but not all of the missionaries were employed in this work. Some were given jobs as mechanics, musicians, instrument-makers, portrait-painters, and in other technical and artistic capacities, while Schall and Verbiest were also on occasion employed as gun-founders. But it was their official connection with the Board of Mathematics and Astronomy that gave the Jesuits their privileged position at Peking and afforded them the cover for their own missionary activities, and those of their colleagues in the provinces, which otherwise would not have been tolerated.

. . . . .

At the height of their influence in Peking, the Jesuits ran into increasing difficulties on what might be termed the "home front" over the problem of the Confucian Rites. After some abortive attempts in the sixteenth century, the Spanish friars from the Philippines succeeded in establishing themselves in the China missionfield in the wake of the Jesuits. Most of these friars were strongly opposed to Ricci's accommodating attitude towards Confucianism and favoured a much more direct approach. They regarded the Rites as pure idolatry and refused to allow their converts to participate in them, although some of them modified their attitude after years of experience. . . .

The Rites and related problems—such as the correct Chinese term for God —were repeatedly referred to Rome for a decision, and after a good deal of vacillation the Papacy finally condemned the disputed ceremonies as idolatrous. The Jesuits, on one pretext and another, evaded compliance with this decision; and they even appealed to K'ang-hsi himself for a ruling on the true nature of the Rites. The Emperor obligingly declared that they were indeed of a civil and not a religious nature; but the Pope sent a special Apostolic Legate out to Peking with the task of enforcing the papal decision on the recalcitrant missionaries, regardless of the decision handed down from the Dragon Throne. The Papal Legate, Maillard de Tournon, failed completely in his errand and was detained by the Emperor's orders at Macao, where he died in June 1710, after receiving a cardinal's biretta from Rome. K'ang-hsi gave formal permission for all those missionaries who accepted the Jesuit standpoint on the Rites to remain in China; and, although he ordered the expulsion of those who refused the imperial p'iaou as it was called, this was not strictly enforced in his lifetime.

. . . . .

. . . The breach between Rome and Peking was made irreparable by the papal constitution *Ex quo singulari* of 1742, which compelled all present and future missionaries to take an oath that they would not tolerate the practice of the Rites on any pretext whatsoever. The Vatican reversed this stand by abrogating the oath in December 1939; but this *volte face* came a couple of centuries too late.

Another serious handicap to the progress of the missionaries in China arose from the conflicting claims of European nationalism. The mission was originally founded under the patronage of the Portuguese Crown, which, in return for the privilege of deciding what missionaries should be allowed to work in most of Africa and Asia, was supposed to endow and maintain them there. The monopolistic claims of the *Padroado,* as it was called, in the Far East were soon challenged by the Spanish friars from the Philippines, who came under the control of the Spanish crown's ecclesiastical patronage (*Patronazgo* or *Patronato*) in America. A still more serious threat to the Portuguese position was posed by the arrival of a group of French Jesuits at

Peking in 1688. They came with the backing of Louis XIV, and with the obvious intention of forwarding French temporal, as well as spiritual, interests. The Holy See, moreover, repenting of its Renaissance policy in giving a virtual monopoly of evangelization in three continents to the Portuguese and Spanish crowns, founded the Congregation of the Propaganda Fide at Rome in 1622. The chief aim of this institution, and the missionaries dispatched under its auspices, was to free the foreign missions in countries not controlled by either of the two Iberian crowns from any dependence on their temporal power. The result was a three-cornered struggle. . . .

Nor did the close connection between European spiritual and temporal power go unremarked at the court of Peking. The position of Macao, as the headquarters of the church militant in East Asia, was a particularly invidious one. "From this royal fortress," wrote an enthusiastic Jesuit in 1650, "sally forth nearly every year the gospel preachers to make war on all the surrounding heathendom, hoisting the royal standard of the holy cross over the highest and strongest bulwarks of idolatry, preaching Christ crucified, and subjugating to the sweet yoke of his most holy law the proudest and most isolationist kingdoms and empires." Macao was also heavily fortified after the European fashion as the result of an abortive Dutch attack in 1622; and many Chinese considered that it might become not merely a religious and commercial, but also a military and political, bridgehead of European expansionism. All the tact and influence of the Peking Jesuits were needed to frustrate the periodic efforts made by xenophobic officials to induce the Emperor to ordain the destruction or evacuation of the City of the Name of God in China.

K'ang-hsi's successor, the emperor Yung-cheng, was not nearly so well disposed towards the Jesuits as was his illustrious father; and he was even more conscious of the dangers of Christianity as a religion at least potentially subversive of the established order. Discussing the matter one day with some of the Peking Jesuits, he observed:

> You say that your law is not a false law. I believe it. If I thought it were false what would prevent me from destroying your churches and driving you away from them? What would you say if I sent a troop of Bonzes and Lamas into your country to preach their doctrines? You want all Chinese to become Christians. Your law demands it, I know. But in that case what will become of us? Shall we become subjects of your king? The converts you make recognize only you in time of trouble. They will listen to no other voice but yours. I know that at the present time there is nothing to fear, but when your ships come by thousands then there will probably be great disorder. . . . The emperor, my father, lost a great deal of his reputation among scholars by the condescension with which he let you establish yourselves here. The laws of our ancient sages will permit no change and I will not allow my reign to be laid open to such a charge.

Yung-cheng permitted the Peking Jesuits to stay in the capital owing to the use that was made of their scientific and technical abilities; but he ordered that all missionaries in the provinces should be deported to Macao and that all Christian churches outside Peking should be put to other uses. Once again this edict was not rigorously enforced, and many of the provincial authorities turned a blind eye to the existence of the missionaries and their converts in the districts under their charge. . . .

The long-lived Emperor, Ch'ien-lung, who reigned for sixty years (1736-1796), continued his predecessor's policy of patronizing the twenty-two Jesuit missionaries at Court and intermittently persecuting their colleagues and converts in the provinces. In one way his reign formed the Indian Summer of the Jesuit mission, for its cultural prestige and achievements now reached their zenith. It was at Ch'ien-lung's command that the Jesuits designed and supervised the erection of a group of Western-style fountains, gardens, and buildings in the grounds of the imperial summer palace of Yuan Ming Yuan in the Western Hills near Peking. The buildings were mostly of white marble, constructed in a mixed Chinese-Rococo style with reminiscences of Versailles. In 1860 this palace was looted and destroyed by the British expeditionary force as a reprisal for the torture and killing of some defenceless envoys who had been seized under a flag of truce. This act of retribution was intended to hurt the imperial family without harming the common people; but the Chinese in general have come to resent the loss of this palace as a national disgrace and catastrophe.

Several of the Jesuits were employed on topographical surveys in the provinces; and the maps which they and their Chinese collaborators produced were not superseded until the second half of the nineteenth century. Of the Jesuit court painters, the most famous is the Milanese, Castiglione, who worked under three Manchu emperors from 1716 to 1766. He painted in both European and Chinese styles, and his admirers claim that his best works in the latter *genre* are indistinguishable from those of native artists. It was not, however, a Jesuit but an Italian Propaganda priest, Matteo Ripa (1710-1723), who introduced the art of copper-engraving into China.

More important than the Jesuits' work in introducing Western arts and techniques, which hardly spread beyond the environs of Peking, was their rôle in interpreting China to the West, although this ultimately had results that they did not foresee. Their researches into Chinese history disclosed the awkward fact that the apparently well-authenticated Chinese chronology could not be reconciled with that of the Christian Bible. Their enthusiastic accounts of Chinese civilization in general, and of Confucianism in particular, . . . supplied the source material for the *Rêve Chinois* of the Age of Enlightenment. Leibniz, Montesquieu, Voltaire and Gibbon were all profoundly influenced in their different ways by reading this Jesuit Sinophile literature, of which the deists and the rationalists made great use.

The leading Jesuits of Peking corresponded with the Royal Society of London, and with the Academics of Sciences at Paris and St. Petersburg. Antoine Gaubil (1733-1759), whom Humboldt called *"le plus grand savant des missionaires,"* sent Chinese books, astronomical observations and botanical specimens to London, where some of his papers were published in the *Philosophical Transactions*. In exchange, he received presents of scientific books, and, on one occasion at least, two barrels of sherry, a gift which he acknowledged in a charming letter of May 8th, 1755. He explained that the wine would be divided into three portions: one for use in celebrating mass, one for the sick, and the third to be enjoyed at some meals, *"que nous tacherons de faire de notre mieux à l'anglaise dans un pays à demi Tartare."* He added that he and his confrères would learn some English phrases from grammars and dictionaries, so that they could drink a toast to their benefactors in London.

. . . . .

From their own viewpoint it was primarily as missionaries and not as scientists or as sinologues that the Jesuits came to China; and, as Protestant Peter Mundy acknowledged in 1638, "to speak truly, they neither spare cost nor labour, diligence, nor danger, to attain their purpose." How far, then, it may be asked, had they attained it when the suppression of the Society of Jesus in 1773 led to their replacement by the Lazarists? Exact figures for the number of converts are lacking; but all reliable authorities agree that the total of native Christians never exceeded 300,000 for this period. This is a remarkable figure having regard to the paucity of the missionaries of all the religious orders in China, and the increasing dangers and difficulties under which they worked; but it is extremely small in relation to the total population, which was something in the nature of one hundred million in 1700 and twice that amount a century later. It became, moreover, virtually impossible to make converts in high places after the death of K'ang-hsi; and the missionaries' efforts were necessarily confined to the poor and lowly. This in turn handicapped the formation of a native clergy—to which some of the missionaries were opposed on principle anyway—and meant that Christianity made no significant impression on the Confucian mould of China. The Middle Flowery Kingdom faced an aggressive and industrialized Europe in the nineteenth century with a social structure and a mental outlook essentially unmodified since the crystallization of Chinese thought by the Sung school-men of the twelfth century.

20 CHRISTIAN MARTYRDOM IN JAPAN

In contrast to their experience in China, the Jesuits in Japan met with great success at the outset. Their effectiveness was due partly to the positive attitude of the Japanese authorities, who viewed the Christians as a useful counterweight to dangerously powerful Buddhist orders, and partly to the receptivity of the oppressed peasantry who found solace and hope in the new faith. By 1582 there were 150,000 converts, mostly in western Japan. But the more converts that were won, the more a feeling of apprehension grew in official quarters. Christian teachings came to be regarded as subversive of traditional Japanese society, and the missionaries were suspected as being the forerunners of foreign invasion. In 1614, it was decreed that all missionaries must leave, and their converts, who by now numbered 300,000, must renounce their faith. Descriptions of the martyrdom of five fathers and the apostasy of a Japanese Christian and his wife show how this order was enforced.*

Martyrdom

. . . finally order came from Nagasaki, that all the Religious should be put to death, who so soone as they had understood the certainty thereof, shewed extraordinary signes of joy. Upon the 25 of August [1624] they

* C. R. Boxer, *The Christian Century in Japan 1549-1650* (Berkeley: Univ. of California, 1951), pp. 436, 437, 441.

were led forth of prison all five, fast bound, with ropes about their necks, and accompanied with a band of soldiers. The Priests went each bearing a crosse in his hand, and continually fixed in prayers till such time as they came to shippe, whither they entered with some few of the officers, the rest continuing their journey by land. They arrived at the place appointed for their death, a field called Hokonohara, when giving thanks unto those who had conducted them, for the pains they had taken they went to land, and the Priests lifting on high the crosses which they bare in their hands, they began to recite psalms with a loud voice; when Father *Carvalho* perceiving now a great multitude to be assembled, turning unto them, *you must understand,* said he, *that we are Christians, and that we die of our free and voluntary accord, for the faith of Christ our Lord.* The admirable serenity of their countenances put their joy so clearly in view of the beholders, that amazed thereat they said, *these men seemed to go rather to some feast or banquet, than unto death.* Finally, their desired end approaching, the first who was tied unto a stake, was Father Miguel Carvalho, of our *Society,* the second Father Peter *Vasquez,* of the Order of Saint *Dominicke,* the third, Father *Luis Sotelo,* the fourth Father *Luis Sasada* both of the same Order of *Saint Francis.* The fifth, Brother *Luis,* Observant of the third Order, a *Japanese;* Being ranked in this order, they were bound in such sort that after the cords should be burned, they might yet be able to stirre themselves, to the end their troubled action and disordered motion, might incite the people to laughter. Every one was attired in his own habit, with his eyes fixed upon heaven. When the fire was kindled, which in regard of the small quantity of wood, burned very slowly, so that, the rope wherewith Brother *Luis* the Japanese was bound, being consumed, he might have departed at his pleasure. The rest of his valorous associates were jointly with loud voice reciting a certain devote prayer, and the fire grew to advance itselfe; when he departing from his stake, with noble contempt of those raging flames, made haste to do reverence, and kiss submissively the hands of the Priests his companions; then exhorting with a loud voice the standers by to embrace the faith of *Christ* in which alone is true safety and salvation, he returned generously unto the stake again, and leaning himself unto it, without any further tying (for he was already sufficiently bound in the bands of charity to *Christ* our Lord) he endured, without ever moving himself, the fury of those flames, until at length he rendered his invincible soul to God. The others were already so oppressed with the smoke and fire which had now taken possession of their mouths, that they could not as they wished, express themselves; yet should you hear them now and then break forth into those sovereigne names of *Iesus* and *Maria* whose aid the servants of God implored in their torments. Father *Miguel Carvalho,* for as much as there had been more wood, and a more vehement fire about him, was the second who died, after he had given diverse arguments of his stout courage and extraordinary constancy. Father *Luis Sasada,* a Japanese of the Order of Saint *Francis* died in the third place. . . .

The other two remained, the fire not well approaching to them, and in particular to Father *Luis Sotelo.* The executers of this cruelty resolved to take some quantity of straw and other dry litter, and setting it on fire, they devided it into two parts, and yet for all this their piles not burning very violently, gave matter of more irksome torment to these servants of God. They remained therefore 3 hours in the fire, ever immovable, consuming away in lingering slow flames; after which space of time they ended the course of a combat so much more glorious, as it was produced longer. . . .

The glorious champions of *Christ* being dead, that the *Christians* might not enjoy their blessed bodies, they burned them even to cinders; then putting the ashes into a sack, and advancing themselves into a wide sea, there did those impious officers cast them abroad; yea they set some to watch the place where they had suffered, lest any bone or small relic which might be left, should be taken away. Yet it hath pleased God, notwithstanding all the diligence of the *Paynims,* that the *Christians* found certain bones, and pieces of stakes to which they had been bound, which were taken up, and are conserved. ...

Apostasy

We have been Christian believers for many years. Yet we have found out that the Christian religion is an evil religion. It regards the next life as the most important. The threat of excommunication is held over those who disobey the padres' orders, whilst they are likewise kept from associating with the rest of humanity in the present world and doomed to be cast into Hell in the next. It further teaches that there is no salvation in the next life unless sinners confess their faults to the padres and receive their absolution. In this way, the people were led to place their trust in the padres. Yet all this was done with the design of taking the lands of others. When we learned this, I became an adherent of the Hokke sect and my wife of the Ikko sect.

We hereby witness this statement in writing before you, worshipful magistrate. Hereafter we shall never revoke our apostasy, not even in the secret places of the heart. Should we even entertain the slightest thought thereof, then let us be punished by God the Father, God the Son, and God the Holy Ghost, St. Mary, and all Angels and Saints. Let us forfeit all God's mercy, and all hope like Judas Iscariot, becoming a laughing-stock to all men, without thereby arousing the slightest pity, and finally die a violent death and suffer the torments of Hell without hope of salvation. This is our Christian Oath.

We tell you frankly that we have no belief whatsoever in Christianity in our hearts. Should we be guilty of any falsehood in this respect, now or in the future, then let each and both of us be divinely punished by Bonten, Taishaku, Shiten-daijo, the great and small deities of the sixty and more provinces of Japan, particularly Gongen and Mishima-daimyojin of the two regions of Idzu and Hakone, Hachiman-daibosatsu, Tenman-daijizai-Tenjin, especially our own tutelary deity Suwa-daimyojin, and all the minor deities. This is our formal oath.

Second year of Shoho [1645]

KYUSUKE, HIS WIFE

21   Edict Closing Japan

The decree proscribing Christianity was not altogether effective because it often proved difficult to distinguish between the commercial activities of merchants and the religious activities of missionaries. The Japanese, therefore, followed up with *orders banishing all Spaniards in 1624, and all Portuguese in 1637. The only Westerners left were the Dutch, and they were restricted to the Deshima islet in Nagasaki harbor. This isolationist policy was reinforced in 1636 by the following Sakoku, or "Closed Country" edict prohibiting Japanese subjects from going abroad. Thus Japan, like China, rejected the West and entered a long period of seclusion.**

1. No Japanese ships may leave for foreign countries.

2. No Japanese may go abroad secretly. If anybody tries to do this, he will be killed, and the ship and owner(s) will be placed under arrest whilst higher authority is informed.

3. Any Japanese now living abroad who tries to return to Japan will be put to death.

4. If any Kirishitan [Christian] believer is discovered, you two [Nagasaki governors] will make a full investigation.

5. Any informer(s) revealing the whereabouts of a bateren [Jesuit father] will be paid 200 or 300 pieces of silver. If any other categories of Kirishitans are discovered, the informer(s) will be paid at your discretion as hitherto.

6. On the arrival of foreign ships, arrangements will be made to have them guarded by ships provided by the Omura clan whilst report is being made to Yedo, as hitherto.

7. Any foreigners who help the bateren or other criminal foreigners will be imprisoned at Omura as hitherto.

8. Strict search will be made for bateren on all incoming ships.

9. No offspring of Southern Barbarians will be allowed to remain. Anyone violating this order will be killed, and all relatives punished according to the gravity of the offence.

10. If any Japanese have adopted the offspring of Southern Barbarians they deserve to die. Nevertheless, such adopted children and their foster-parents will be handed over to the Southern Barbarians for deportation.

11. If any deportees should try to return or to communicate with Japan by letter or otherwise, they will of course be killed if they are caught, whilst their relatives will be severely dealt with, according to the gravity of the offence.

12. Samurai are not allowed to have direct commercial dealings with either foreign or Chinese shipping at Nagasaki.

13. Nobody other than those of the five places (Yedo, Kyoto, Osaka, Sakai and Nagasaki) is allowed to participate in the allocation of *ito-wappu* [bulk marketing of silk imports from Macao] and the fixing of silk import prices.

14. Purchases can only be made after the *ito-wappu* is fixed. However, as the Chinese ships are small, you will not be too rigorous with them. Only twenty days are allowed for the sale.

15. The twentieth day of the ninth month is the deadline for the return of foreign ships, but latecomers will be allowed fifty days grace from the date of their arrival. Chinese ships will be allowed to leave a little after the departure of the [Portuguese] galliots.

16. Unsold goods cannot be left in charge of Japanese for storage or safe-keeping. . . .

* *Ibid.*, pp. 439, 440.

Chapter Five

*Non-Eurasian world
at the time of
the West's expansion*

22 THE NATURE OF AFRICAN HISTORY

Archaeologists and research scholars are now uncovering the errors in widely-held assumptions that the African Negro is incapable of progress and that his history is one of stagnation and savagery before the advent of the white man in the fifteenth century. Findings clearly demonstrate that the African Negro had reached a high level of political and cultural development before the appearance of the Europeans, and even of the Arabs before them. In fact, the more advanced indigenous Negro cultures were in many respects comparable to those of Europe until the past few centuries when the Europeans bounded ahead with their scientific, technological, and economic revolutions. "Allowing for the difference between the Moslem and the Christian intellectual climates," writes an English scholar, "a citizen of 14th century Timbuktu would have found himself reasonably at home in 14th century Oxford. In the 16th century he still would have found many points in common between the two university cities. By the 19th century the gulf had grown very deep." * The important point here is that the gulf had grown deep not only between the Europeans and the Africans, but also between the Europeans and all the other people of the world. For the Europeans were the mavericks—the deviants—while the Africans, together with the rest of humanity, represented the norm in continuing along the traditional channels. In the following selection, this new approach to African history is expounded, and its implications are analyzed.**

* T. Hodgkin, "Islam in West Africa," *Africa South,* II (April-June, 1958), 98.
** Basil Davidson, "The Fact of African History: An Introduction," *Africa South,* II (January-March, 1958), 44-49.

... just because various African peoples have known nothing of the industrial revolution in its later, urban, phases; have remembered orally and not literally; fought without chariots; and refrained from sailing across the seas that lapped their shores, there is no ground for saying that they are not inherently as capable as anyone else. ... But the fact remains that these African peculiarities are often used to buttress the general European belief that all was savage chaos before the Europeans came, and to suggest that the reason for this savage chaos lay not in a certain set of objective circumstances, but in African incapacity to emerge from them. "Their thinking," a South African publicist wrote lately, "was not concerned with objective validity and was pre-occupied by the mystic powers of persons and things. This centuries-long stagnation cannot be attributed to their isolation from the main stream of civilization"; the implication, of course, being that it must be attributed to an African inability to evolve and progress.

So it is a matter of quite unusual interest and importance that the last few years should have raised the whole subject of African history—pre-European history—to a new and academically respectable status. Many scholars are producing many new facts about it. Far from being unconcerned with "objective validity" or hypnotized by the "mystic powers of persons and things," Africans, it would appear, were engaged in a great many "civilized activities," of one kind and another, for many centuries before European settlement, or even before European discovery. At a time when European mariners had yet to reach the Indian Ocean, or even the Bight of Benin, the kings and counsellors of Central Africa were eating from Chinese porcelain, and when Mr. Strijdom's forebears drove their ox carts into the old Transvaal, they encountered men and women who were not at the beginning of a long period of civilized development, but, through times of painful dissolution, were perilously near the end of one. In this tide of new information, and of reassessment of old information, the study of humanity in Tropical and Southern Africa has really begun: even if it is still in its infancy, its findings are a long way beyond the point where any but the obsessively bigoted will care to ignore them. ...

Africans south of the Sahara were in fact evolving and progressing towards destinations recognizably the same as Europeans (or Asians)—at a time long before Europeans first came across them.

A gap in social and technical development may always have existed, no doubt, between those who lived close to the cradles of ancient civilization and those who lived far from them. There is no more sense in sentimentalizing about the misery and barbarism of much of the African past than there is in pretending that European history does not tell the same kind of story. The important point is the width of the gap at any one time. If, as people are fond of saying, the gap was *always* immensely wide, then something might well be missing from the African make-up. But if the gap, though wide to-day, had once been relatively narrow, then history will draw quite other conclusions. Now the main consequence of a good deal of recent research into Southern and Central and East African history—over the past thousand years or so—is precisely to suggest that the gap was once a relatively narrow one, and not always to Europe's advantage either.

Writing in 1067, the mediaeval Arab scholar El Bekri described the court of the king of Ghana such as the Arabs knew it from their penetration and eventual conquest of that country. "When he gives audience to his people," wrote El Bekri, "to listen to their complaints and set them to rights, he sits in a pavillion around which stand his horses caparisoned in cloth of gold; behind him stand ten pages holding shields and gold-mounted swords; on his right hand are the sons of the princes of his empire, splendidly clad and with gold plaited into their hair. . . ." A barbaric king and a barbaric kingdom? But were they more barbaric or less civilized than the king and kingdom that William of Normandy had conquered the year before? Were they not, conceivably, less barbaric and more civilized?

When the Portuguese adventurers first rounded the Cape of Good Hope they were certainly as much concerned with "the mystic powers of persons and things" as the most superstitious native of any part of Africa. Their ignorance of the Eastern world was no smaller than East Africa's ignorance of Europe and was quite possibly greater. They were astonished to find the harbours of the East Coast—of what are now Mozambique and Tanganyika and Kenya—the goal and shelter of long-range ocean shipping; and when they sailed for India it was with pilots whose navigational equipment was, in some ways, better than their own. The superiority of the society of Lisbon over the society of Kilwa and Mombasa was not, in those days, by any means obvious. The one certain superiority of those Europeans was in cruelty and aggressiveness.

Yet three hundred and fifty years later, in the hey-day of Victorian rediscovery, the gap had grown immensely wide—so wide, indeed, that it became easy for Europeans to wonder (as many still do) whether Negroes did not after all belong to an inferior species. There is little mystery about the reasons for this widening of the gap: while Europe, freeing itself from mediaeval limits, plunged into commercialism and industrialism and won its great technical superiority over the rest of the world, much of Africa lay fettered in the oversea slave trade. The one went forward, the other went back, and the gap, narrow enough in 1500, grew into a gulf.

Historians and archaeologists are now building new bridges of explanation across that gulf. . . .

What appears to emerge from the present state of knowledge is nothing like a state of savage chaos, but, on the contrary, the long-enduring growth and development of an African Metal Age—beginning over two thousand years ago and producing, for example, the Monomotapa culture of what were Rhodesia and Mozambique in the 15th century—that went through many phases and vicissitudes, but showed remarkable flexibility of invention and resource. It is certain that there developed down the East Coast, sometime after the discovery of the trading use of the monsoon winds in the first century A.D., a flourishing and stable African trade with Arabia, Persia, India, Indonesia and China. It is probable that while the Arabs became the intermediaries and chief carriers in this trade, they were no more the originators of it in Africa than they were in India or China. They established trading posts as far south as Sofala, at points where African kingdoms already existed or subsequently grew. Behind these coastal kingdoms, in the hinterland of Africa, there was meanwhile developing a network of Metal Age polities whose growth was increasingly stimulated by the coastal and oversea demand for gold, ivory and iron. These African goods were exchanged by Africans—through Arab and Indian intermediaries—for Indian textiles, Indonesian beads, and Chinese porcelain. Only when the Portuguese arrived to monopolize this trade, and rapidly destroy it, did these coastal and inland civilizations enter their decline. The hand of the European guided, as it came about, not away from chaos, but towards it.

And what continually surprizes, in reviewing the evidence so far available, is the *coherence* of these African cultures. Already it is possible to glimpse connexions, whether by cultural drift, migration, or trade, between the early kingdoms of Uganda, for example, and those of Rhodesia; between Zimbabwe and the coastal cities as far north as Gedi, sixty miles beyond Mombasa; between the wooden cities of West Africa and the stone cities of Monomotapa. All these links between African societies of the past, whether immediate or remote, have the same kind of coherence and suggestions of common origin, native origin, as those which gave the Indo-European tribes their historical affinity as they spread across the northern world. We are clearly in the presence of a large segment of the human story: of another contribution to the proof of that unity-in-diversity which scientists otherwise ascribe to all branches of *homo sapiens*.

Negro Empire in the Sudan 23

It is often assumed that when the Europeans began their epoch-making voyages of discovery in the fifteenth century, they encountered savage, or at least primitive, peoples in Africa, Australia, and the Americas. This is true up to a point, but it is by no means the whole story. In Mexico and Peru, for example, magnificent Indian civilizations existed until they were destroyed by ruthless Spanish adventurers who had the advantage of firearms and cavalry. In Negro Africa, large and powerful empires were also found, though they are even less known than those of the Americas. The greatest of these empires was the Songhai, which lasted for a little over a century, from 1448 to 1591—a much shorter time, incidentally, than other Negro kingdoms, which existed for several centuries. The outstanding Songhai ruler was Askia the Great, who appears to have been a remarkable administrator and patron of the arts, as well as a conqueror. The following description of Askia and his empire, which stretched 1,500 miles from the Sudan to the Atlantic,* makes particularly significant references to Eurasian influences—the commercial and banking activities of the Arabs, the intellectual impact of the Moslems expelled from Spain, and above all, the Moslem faith with all its cultural and political implications.

To cross the dominions of the Askia was, we are told, a six months' journey. Yet so effective were the measures taken by him for its administration, that before the end of his reign, the result is thus summarised by his historian: "He was obeyed with as much docility on the farthest limits of the empire as he was in his own palace, and there reigned everywhere great plenty and absolute peace."

He laboured unceasingly to introduce the reforms which he thought desirable, and to appoint to every position of importance men whom he could trust to supervise his measures. The reformation of the army and the church,

---

* Flora L. Shaw [Lady Lugard], *A Tropical Dependency* (London: J. Nisbet, 1905), pp. 199-209.

which had occupied the opening years of his reign, represented but the beginning of the care which he continued to bestow upon these two great institutions. The evolution of systems of government suitable to the widely differing peoples over whom he ruled, the development of trade, the protection of letters and the opening of communications, were among questions to which he gave much of his time. Moslem judges were appointed in the lesser towns, which up to this time had been content with the services of scribes or conciliators; and among the biographies of upright judges given to us by Ahmed Baba or Es Sadi, the comment is not infrequent: "He was one of those appointed by Askia the Great." There was a state prison for political offenders, which seems to have served a purpose similar to that of the Tower of London, and the courtyard of the prison of Kanato was no less famous in local annals than Tower Hill. The general rule would seem to have been a rule of mildness, but it is to be noted that inhuman punishments which, in their survival, shock the sentiment of the twentieth century, were used on occasions which called for exceptional severity. Among these, burying alive in bottle-shaped holes, which were closed over the head of the victim, and sewing up in the hides of oxen or wild beasts, are two which connect the criminal code of Songhay with the past and with the present. The sewing up of victims in the skins of wild beasts was, it may be remembered, practised in Rome under the Emperor Makrinus, and was still in use at a much later period. The practice of burying alive remained among the punishments of the Soudan, and was only abolished in the states acknowledging British rule by the expedition to Sokoto and Kano in 1903. Askia the Great does not seem to have gone the length of codifying the Songhay laws, but the attention which was given to the study of law, and the long lists of distinguished lawyers who are mentioned in the annals of this and the succeeding reigns, would seem to indicate that Mohammedan law was generally accepted and practised through the Songhay Empire, with only such local modification as experience may have suggested. . . .

Askia also introduced a reform of the markets. A unification of weights and measures was drawn up. Inspectors of the markets—an office which already existed under the Sultans of Melle—were selected with special care. They were enjoined to keep close watch over the introduction of the new system, and any falsification was severely punished. The markets were, it is said, rendered so honest, that a child might go into the marketplace and would bring back full value for value sent. The Niger was, of course, the great highway of commerce, and the towns situated upon it were the principal centres of trade. . . .

Systems of banking and credit, which seem to have existed under the kings of Melle, were improved. Banking remained chiefly in the hands of Arabs, from whom letters of credit could be procured, which were operative throughout the Soudan, and were used by the black travelling merchants as well as by Arab traders. Commerce, as was to be expected, developed greatly under the encouragement and security given to it by the Askia's measures.

With the increase of commerce and luxury came also the gradual refinement and softening of manners which accompany wealth in a community where military service is no longer a universal obligation. The reforms of the great Askia did not neglect the department of morals. The great freedom prevailing in the intercourse of men and women was among the scandals for which he would seem to have endeavoured, but without much success, to legislate. He seems to have instituted a body of correctional police, who were charged with the prevention of any infringement of the laws. Women were placed on the same footing as in the harems of the East, and obliged to veil themselves when they appeared in public. Nevertheless, Timbuctoo remained ever celebrated for the luxury of its habits and the gaiety and licence of its manners. Music, dress, dancing, and amusement formed, say its indignant chroniclers, the principal objects of life to a large portion of the population. The immense domestic establishments of the East would seem to have excited in the Askia no displeasure. He was himself the father of a hundred sons, of whom the youngest was born when he was ninety years of age. But his influence appears to have been strongly and indignantly excited against forms of licence which exceeded the bounds of this very liberal standard of morality. . . .

The first result of the expulsion of the Moors was to drive the more learned Arabs of Spain into the recesses of the University of Fez, . . . the life of Timbuctoo had probably received some stimulus from the influx of learning to Morocco. The historians of Timbuctoo distinctly state that civilisation and learning came to it from the West [from Morocco]. In the middle of the sixteenth century there existed in the town, side by side with the luxury of the court and the frivolity of fashion, a large and learned society, living at ease, and busily occupied with the elucidation of intellectual and religious problems. The town swarmed also with Soudanese students, of whom we are optimistically told that they "were filled with ardour for knowledge and virtue."

The more distinguished professors would seem to have had schools in which they gave courses of lectures, attended by students, who afterwards received diplomas from the hands of their masters. . . . A sketch which Ahmed Baba gives of one of the principal professors under whom he himself had studied, may serve to indicate the type of sage who was revered by the youth of Timbuctoo, and incidentally presents a picture of local scholastic life.

Mohammed Abou Bekr of Wankore, his pupil tells us, writing himself as an old man forty or fifty years later, was "one of the best of God's virtuous creatures. He was a working scholar, and a man instinct with goodness. His nature was as pure as it was upright. He was himself so strongly impelled towards virtue, and had so high an opinion of others, that he always considered them as being so to speak his equals, and as having no knowledge of evil. He did not believe in the bad faith of the world, but always thought well of his fellow-creatures until they had committed a fault, and even after they had committed a fault. Calm and dignified, with a natural distinction and a modesty that rendered intercourse with him easy, he captured all hearts. Every one who knew him loved him." He taught during the whole of a long life, while at the same time he continued to take an active interest, and even some part, in public affairs. The Sultan, who shared the general respect for him, offered him the lucrative appointment of Governor of the Palace, but he refused it—"God having," he said, "delivered him from such cares." He was also offered the appointment of principal preacher to the great mosque, but that also he prayed the Sultan to excuse him from accepting. He was apparently wealthy, and possessed a fine library. "His whole life was given," says Ahmed Baba, "to the service of others. He taught his pupils to love science, to follow its teachings, to devote their time to it, to associate with scholars, and to keep their minds in a state of docility. He lavishly lent his most precious books, rare copies, and the volumes that he most valued, and never asked for them again, no matter what was the subject of which they treated." Sometimes "a student would present himself at the door and ask for a book, and he would give it without even knowing who the man was." Ahmed Baba recalls with affection an instance when he himself wanted a rare work on grammar, and the master not only lent it, but spent a long time searching through his library for other works which might help to elucidate his pupil's difficulties. "It was astonishing to see him," says Ahmed Baba; "and he acted thus, notwithstanding the fact that he had a passion for books, and that he collected them with ardour, both buying and causing them to be copied." It is not, alas! surprising to hear that "in this way he lost a great quantity of his books."

His industry in teaching was equalled only by his patience. "When I knew him," says Ahmed Baba, "he used to begin his lectures after the first prayer, and continued them until the second prayer at half-past nine, varying the subjects of which he treated. He then returned home for the prayer, and after it usually went to the cadi to occupy himself with public affairs. After that he taught at his own house till mid-day. He joined the public mid-day prayers, and then continued his lectures at home till the fourth prayer. Then he went out and lectured in another place until twilight. After the sunset prayer, he taught in the mosque until the last night prayer, and then returned to his own house. No pupil was too stupid or too ignorant for him. He never allowed himself to be discouraged, or to despair of gaining an entrance into the understanding of his hearer. . . .

The study of law, literature, grammar, and theology would seem to have been more general at Timbuctoo than that of the natural sciences. We hear, however, of at least one distinguished geographer, and allusions to surgical science show that the old maxim of the Arabian schools, "He who studies anatomy pleases God," was not forgotten. At a later date (1618) the author of the *Tarikh* incidentally mentions that his brother came from Jenné to Timbuctoo to undergo an operation for cataract at the hands of a celebrated surgeon there—an operation which was wholly successful. The appearance of comets, so amazing to Europe of the Middle Ages, is also noted calmly, as a matter of scientific interest, at Timbuctoo. Earthquakes and eclipses excite no great surprise. . . .

Travellers give us a picture of the town as it existed in the early part of the sixteenth century. The houses, which would seem to have been fairly spacious, were built, some say of clay, and some of wood covered with plaster—the roofs, like the Dutch buildings of South Africa, being universally thatched. The mosques are described as stately buildings of cut stone and lime, and there was a "princely palace," of which the walls were also of cut stone and lime. There were a great many shops and factories, "especially," says Leo Africanus, who was there in 1526, "of such as weave linen and cotton cloth." The court maintained by the Askias is described by Marmol as being so well ordered that it yielded in nothing spiritual or temporal to the courts of Northern Africa. Under the successors of Askia the Great, the palace was enlarged and greatly embellished, the court being then thronged with courtiers in ever-increasing numbers. The habits of dress became sumptuous, and it would seem from incidental allusions that different functionaries had their different uniforms and insignia of office, to the wearing of which great value was attached. The dress and appointments of women became also extravagantly luxurious. They were served on gold. In full dress their persons were covered with jewels, and the wives of the rich when they went out were attended by well-dressed slaves. ....

Among the amusements of the town, music held always a high place, and under Askia the Great's successors, orchestras, provided with singers of both sexes, were much frequented. Of Askia the Great himself, it is said that "his mind was set towards none of these things." Chess-playing of a kind which is particularly described as "Soudanese chess," was sometimes carried to the extreme of a passion. We hear of a general in the reign of one of the succeeding Askias, who gave it as an excuse for allowing himself to be surprised by the enemy's cavalry, that he was so much absorbed in a game of chess as not to have paid attention to the reports of his scouts. The whole town in Askia the Great's day was very rich, the people living with great abundance, and trade was active. The currency was of gold, without any stamp or superscription, but for small objects in the native markets shells were still used. A very great trade was done both here and at Kagho in cotton, which was exchanged for European cloth.

PYGMIES OF THE BELGIAN CONGO 24

Very different from the high culture of the Songhai Empire is the Paleolithic culture of the Pygmies of the Ituri Forest in the Belgian Congo. Here are a people who are exclusively food gatherers, who do not know how to make fire, and who have no chiefs, councils, or any other formal governing bodies. Their retardation may be explained in part by their difficult rain-forest environment. But at least equally important is their isolation from the centers of civilization in Eurasia. We noted in the preceding selection that Askia's subjects felt the stimulating influence of Eurasia in every field—economic, religious, and cultural, but the Pygmies had no such advantage. Their only contact with the outside world was through their Negro neighbors who provided them with tools and plantains in return for the honey and meat that they collected in the forests. The contrast between the culture of the Songhai Empire and that of the Congo Pygmies illustrates strikingly the significance of the degree of accessibility to the Eurasian civilizations. With Patrick Putnam, who lived with the Pygmies for nearly two decades, we catch a glimpse of their way of life. *

The Ituri forest is rolling country, so densely covered with trees that the relief of the landscape is invisible except from the air. It is a primary rain forest; that is, in most of the region it rains every day or every other day, averaging about one half of the days, from four to six in the afternoon—some 180 days a year. ...

This forest is inhabited by two kinds of people, Negroes and pygmies, who maintain an almost symbiotic relationship, based on trade. A Negro village

* Cited by C. S. Coon, *A Reader in General Anthropology* (New York: Holt, 1948), pp. 322-34. Reprinted by permission.

may own approximately 100 square miles of forest territory. In this territory are the Negro village and the pygmy village. The former is permanent, in a clearing; the latter is temporary, under the forest trees. In maintaining their relationship, it is the pygmies' job to take in honey and meat, while the Negroes' obligation is to give them plantains. In addition, the pygmies may bring in a certain amount of wild baselli fruit in season, or roofing leaves, or rattan and fibers for net makng; in return they may acquire ax blades, knives, and arrowheads from the Negroes.

There is no strict process of barter involved, and no accounting kept, other than through general observation. If the pygmies are stingy, their Negroes will hold back their bananas. If the Negroes are stingy, the pygmies will leave the territory and go to live with other pygmies serving other Negro hosts.

This relationship is interfamilial, between a pygmy family and a Negro family. It is a matter of close personal relations, inherited, on both sides, from father to son. These alliances may change from time to time, but when they do there are usually hard feelings; if a man's pygmy leaves him to serve another host it is a kind of divorce. In the old days, a frequent cause of inter-village warfare among the Negroes was the luring away of each other's pygmies.

Before the Belgians stopped inter-village and intertribal warfare, the most important single duty of the pygmy was to act as scout and intelligence agent in the forest. As soon as he became aware of a raiding party crossing the boundary of his host's territory he would hotfoot it to the village to give warning. This eternal vigilance on the part of the pygmy was probably of more value to his hosts than the meat that he brought in. Now that the need of this has ceased he is fulfilling only half of his contract; the Negro, who still provides plantains and manufactured objects, is still fulfilling all of his. Still both are satisfied. . . .

BASIC TOOLS.   The keynote to the simple and specialized pygmy technology is the fact that they do not have to make any of their basic tools, but instead obtain effective iron cutting tools from their Negro hosts. This eliminates much work and the need for much skills in toolmaking, and provides them with more efficient instruments than they could possibly make for themselves at a food-gathering level of technology.

When a pygmy needs an ax he will beg one from his Negro host. Perhaps the Negro will give him a whole ax, haft and all. The blade is a triangular piece of iron, made locally by Negro smiths, and set in a solid wooden handle, adzed out of a larger piece of wood. The handle has a hole which has been burned through it from side to side with a hot iron. Through this hole goes the narrow end of the ax. This is essentially a Neolithic type of hafting.

Perhaps the Negro will give him only the ax head, without a haft. In this case the pygmy will cut down a thin sapling, or a tree branch, just the right thickness, and use it bark and all. He splits this with his knife, at one end. Then he wraps the split and the blade which he has thrust through it with twine or rattan. The pygmy will use the Negro-hafted ax on the ground, but if he is climbing a tree and needs an ax while up there, he will take along one of his own hafting by preference, because it is lighter. . . .

FIRE.   The pygmies do not know how to make fire, nor do many of the Negroes with whom they are associated. Throughout all this countryside people keep fires going, and when one fire dies out the people will borrow it from each other. While on the march the pygmies carry glowing embers with them; they can keep a brand lighted for ten miles during a rainstorm. They do this by wrapping the burning ends in green leaves, and swinging it up and down; every two or three minutes they uncover it a bit and blow on it. At night these brands serve as torches. The Negroes have special wood which they use for torches but the pygmies do not. Their firewood is always fallen wood, and therefore always somewhat rotten and punky. . . .

Hunting is the principal occupation of the pygmies; it is their principal reason for being able to maintain their relationship with their Negro hosts. Although between themselves the pygmies have little division of labor, in another sense they are all specialists in hunting, and the division of labor is between them and the Negroes. In this sense the pygmies form an ethnic caste, a genetically and occupationally segregated segment of a larger economic entity.

This does not mean that the Negro does no hunting. However, the pygmy spends all of his time hunting, the Negro only a portion of his. The pygmy depends largely on his ability to move noiselessly and swiftly about the forest, and to climb trees. The Negro depends on his greater patience and mechanical ingenuity, for he hunts largely by means of elaborate traps, deadfalls, pits, weighted spears dangled over elephant paths, and other deadly devices. The pygmy could never be induced to dig a pit; it is too much work, takes too long, and takes too much concentration and persistence. Nor do they ever use traps. . . .

BOW AND ARROW HUNTING. In bow and arrow hunting, the pygmy relies not on his endurance but on his ability to move through the forest silently; that is his greatest skill and greatest asset. He can track an antelope to a thicket where it has lain down to sleep, and shoot it from five yards' distance before it wakes up. He shoots machine-gun style; he will pump five arrows in rapid sequence in the antelope's direction, and probably but one will hit him. The pygmy can do just as well by leaping on the animal barehanded, and either strangle it or kill it with a knife, and he often does this.

In his quiver the pygmy usually carries two kinds of arrows, the first with iron tips, which he generally uses on the larger, antelope-size, animals, and wooden-tipped ones which are poisoned, and which he uses for monkeys. He rarely shoots a monkey with an iron-tipped arrow, through fear of losing it. Each man makes his own poison as well as his own darts. The plants from which the poison is made are well known, and there is neither ritual nor mystery attached to the process. The vital plant is a strophanthus; they will mix other plants with it, but they know which one does the trick.

The strophanthus poison is a heart stimulant. Its action is not immediate. The monkey runs along a bit, grows weaker, and urinates. The pygmies watch for this, for the moment of urinating is the fatal one. If the monkey is out on a limb where there are no other branches, he will fall off; if he is within reach of a lateral branch or one rising upward, he will clutch it, and the hunter will be obliged to climb the tree if he wants the monkey. . . .

GOVERNMENT. There are no chiefs, councils, or any other formal governing bodies in a pygmy camp. In making any decisions concerning the whole camp, two factors are involved. The first of these is respect for older people.

A pygmy will always, in addressing a man of an older age group in any formal situation, call him "senior"; he will listen respectfully to an older man and will always obey any reasonable orders he may give. If a younger man shows disrespect, the other members of the camp will gang up on him and berate him. This respect for age, and for the opinions of wise old men, is the basis of pygmy government.

Secondly, while the opinions of most of the old men are respected, every man in the camp is entitled to state his own views on any subject. Thus, during the evening talking time, the pygmies will discuss whether to move camp, where to move it, and why; or whether to go nut hunting, and where to hunt. The discussion has no leader and may go on for several evenings. Finally the men who are shouting out different opinions will come to an agreement and the decision will be acted upon.

In general it is the older and more experienced men who make the decision, but as some of the old men are considered eccentrics and freaks, little attention is paid to them. Rather, it is an oligarchy of the more respected among the old men, a body with no formal membership or specific composition. In their decisions the pungent remarks of the women also have a considerable influence.

25 AZTEC CIVILIZATION OF MEXICO

One of the most intriguing chapters of human history is the rise of a series of indigenous civilizations in the Americas. Comparatively little is known about them, because the conquering Spaniards destroyed books, temples, and art treasures, as well as the native ruling and priestly classes. One of the basic remaining sources is the account of Bernal Díaz, a conquistador who accompanied Cortez in the conquest of Mexico. Bernal Díaz was a gifted and objective observer. He describes with color and accuracy the religion and institutions of the Aztecs, their palaces, temples, and markets, and the character of their leader Montezuma. Here we see the high level of a civilization that had developed an elaborate court ceremonial and hierarchy, a treasury for collecting taxes, an armory to ensure uniform weapons of standard quality, and a large and prosperous capital city. Particularly interesting are the references to tobacco and chocolate, hitherto unknown to Europeans, and Díaz's proposal to build a church on the temple mound —a dramatic example of the clash of religions and cultures.*

When it was announced to Cortes that Motecusuma himself was approaching, he alighted from his horse and advanced to meet him. Many compliments were now passed on both sides. Motecusuma bid Cortes welcome, who, through Marina, said, in return, he hoped his majesty was in good health. If I still remember rightly, Cortes, who had Marina next to him, wished to concede the place of honour to the monarch, who, however, would not accept of it, but conceded it to Cortes, who now brought forth a necklace of precious stones, of the most beautiful colours and shapes, strung upon

* J. I. Lockhart, trans., *The Memoirs of the Conquistador Bernal Diaz de Castillo . . .* (London: J. Hatchard, 1844), I, 220-23, 228-41.

gold wire, and perfumed with musk, which he hung about the neck of Motecusuma. Our commander was then going to embrace him, but the grandees by whom he was surrounded held back his arms, as they considered it improper. Our general then desired Marina to tell the monarch how exceedingly he congratulated himself upon his good fortune of having seen such a powerful monarch face to face, and of the honour he had done us by coming out to meet us himself. To all this Motecusuma answered in very appropriate terms, and ordered his two nephews, the princes of Tetzuco and Cohohuacan, to conduct us to our quarters. He himself returned to the city, accompanied by his two other relatives, the princes of Cuitlahuac and Tlacupa, with the other grandees of his numerous suite. As they passed by, we perceived how all those who composed his majesty's retinue held their heads bent forward, no one daring to lift up his eyes in his presence; and altogether what deep veneration was paid him.

The road before us now became less crowded, and yet who would have been able to count the vast numbers of men, women, and children who filled the streets, crowded the balconies, and the canoes in the canals, merely to gaze upon us? . . .

We were quartered in a large building where there was room enough for us all, and which had been occupied by Axayacatl, father of Motecusuma, during his life-time. Here the latter had likewise a secret room full of treasures, and where the gold he had inherited from his father was hid, which he had never touched up to this moment. Near this building there were temples and Mexican idols, and this place had been purposely selected for us because we were termed teules, or were thought to be such, and that we might dwell among the latter as among our equals. The apartments and halls were very spacious, and those set apart for our general were furnished with carpets. There were separate beds for each of us, which could not have been better fitted up for a gentleman of the first rank. Every place was swept clean, and the walls had been newly plastered and decorated.

When we had arrived in the great court-yard adjoining this palace, Motecusuma came up to Cortes, and, taking him by the hand, conducted him himself into the apartments where he was to lodge, which had been beautifully decorated after the fashion of the country. He then hung about his neck a chaste necklace of gold, most curiously worked with figures all representing crabs. The Mexican grandees were greatly astonished at all these uncommon favours which their monarch bestowed upon our general.

Cortes returned the monarch many thanks for so much kindness, and the latter took leave of him with these words: "Malinche, you and your brothers must now do as if you were at home, and take some rest after the fatigues of the journey," then returned to his own palace, which was close at hand.

We allotted the apartments according to the several companies, placed our cannon in an advantageous position, and made such arrangements that our cavalry, as well as the infantry, might be ready at a moment's notice. We then sat down to a plentiful repast, which had been previously spread out for us, and made a sumptuous meal.

This our bold and memorable entry into the large city of Temixtitlan Mexico took place on the 8th of November, 1519. Praise be to the Lord Jesus Christ for all this. . . .

The mighty Motecusuma may have been about this time in the fortieth year of his age. He was tall of stature, of slender make, and rather thin, but the symmetry of his body was beautiful. His complexion was not very brown, merely approaching to that of the inhabitants in general. The hair of his head was not very long, excepting where it hung thickly down over his ears, which were quite hidden by it. His black beard, though thin, looked handsome. His countenance was rather of an elongated form, but cheerful; and his fine eyes had the expression of love or severity, at the proper moments. He was particularly clean in his person, and took a bath every evening. Besides a number of concubines, who were all daughters of persons of rank and quality, he had two lawful wives of royal extraction, whom, however, he visited secretly without any one daring to observe it, save his most confidential servants. He was perfectly innocent of any unnatural crimes. The dress he had on one day was not worn again until four days had elapsed. In the halls adjoining his own private apartments there was always a guard of 2000 men of quality, in waiting: with whom, however, he never held any conversation unless to give them orders or to receive some intelligence from them. Whenever for this purpose they entered his apartment, they had first to take off their rich costumes and put on meaner garments, though these were always neat and clean; and were only allowed to enter into his presence barefooted, with eyes cast down. No person durst look at him full in the face, and during the three prostrations which they were obliged to make before they could approach him, they pronounced these words: "Lord! my Lord! sublime Lord!" Everything that was communicated to him was to be said in few words, the eyes of the speaker being constantly cast down, and on leaving the monarch's presence he walked backwards out of the room. I also remarked that even princes and other great personages who come to Mexican respecting law-suits, or on other business from the interior of the country, always took off their shoes and changed their whole dress for one of a meaner appearance when they entered his palace. Neither were they allowed to enter the palace straightway, but had to show themselves for a considerable time outside the doors; as it would have been considered want of respect to the monarch if this had been omitted.

Above 300 kinds of dishes were served up for Motecusuma's dinner from his kitchen, underneath which were placed pans of porcelain filled with fire, to keep them warm. Three hundred dishes of various kinds were served up for him alone, and above 1000 for the persons in waiting. He sometimes, but very seldom, accompanied by the chief officers of his household, ordered the dinner himself, and desired that the best dishes and various kinds of birds should be called over to him. We were told that the flesh of young children as a very dainty bit, were also set before him sometimes by way of a relish. Whether there was any truth in this we could not possibly discover; on account of the great variety of dishes, consisting in fowls, turkeys, pheasants, partridges, quails, tame and wild geese, venison, musk swine, pigeons, hares, rabbits, and of numerous other birds and beasts; besides which there were various other kinds of provisions, indeed it would have been no easy task to call them all over by name.

. . . . .

I had almost forgotten to mention, that during dinner-time, two other young women of great beauty brought the monarch small cakes, as white as snow, made of eggs and other very nourishing ingredients, on plates covered with clean napkins; also a kind of long-shaped bread, likewise made of very substantial things, and some pachol, which is a kind of wafer-cake. They then presented him with three beautifully painted and gilt tubes, which were filled with liquid amber, and a herb called by the Indians tabaco. After the dinner had been cleared away and the singing and dancing done, one of these tubes was lighted, and the monarch took the smoke into his mouth, and after he had done this a short time, he fell asleep.

About this time a celebrated cazique, whom we called Tapia, was Motecusuma's chief steward: he kept an account of the whole of Motecusuma's revenue, in large books of paper which the Mexicans call *Amatl*. A whole house was filled with such large books of accounts.

Motecusuma had also two arsenals filled with arms of every description, of which many were ornamented with gold and precious stones. These arms consisted in shields of different sizes, sabres, and a species of broadsword, which is wielded with both hands, the edge furnished with flint stones, so extremely sharp that they cut much better than our Spanish swords: further, lances of greater length than ours, with spikes at their end, full one fathom in length, likewise furnished with several sharp flint stones. The pikes are so very sharp and hard that they will pierce the strongest shield, and cut like a razor; so that the Mexicans even shave themselves with these stones. Then there were excellent bows and arrows, pikes with single and double points, and the proper thongs to throw them with; slings with round stones purposely made for them; also a species of large shield, so ingeniously constructed that it could be rolled up when not wanted: they are only unrolled on the field of battle, and completely cover the whole body from the head to the feet. Further, we saw here a great variety of cuirasses made of quilted cotton, which were outwardly adorned with soft feathers of different colours, and looked like uniforms. . . .

I will now, however, turn to another subject, and rather acquaint my readers with the skilful arts practised among the Mexicans: among which I will first mention the sculptors, and the gold and silversmiths, who were clever in working and smelting gold, and would have astonished the most celebrated of our Spanish goldsmiths: the number of these was very great, and the most skilful lived at a place called Ezcapuzalco, about four miles from Mexico. After these came the very skilful masters in cutting and polishing precious stones, and the calchihuis, which resemble the emerald. Then follow the great masters in painting, and decorators in feathers, and the wonderful sculptors. Even at this day there are living in Mexico three Indian artists, named Marcos de Aguino, Juan de la Cruz, and El Crespello, who have severally reached to such great proficiency in the art of painting and sculpture, that they may be compared to an Apelles, or our contemporaries Michael Angelo and Berruguete. . . .

The powerful Motecusuma had also a number of dancers and clowns: some danced in stilts, tumbled, and performed a variety of other antics for the monarch's entertainment: a whole quarter of the city was inhabited by these performers, and their only occupation consisted in such like performances. Lastly, Motecusuma had in his service great numbers of stone-cutters, masons, and carpenters, who were solely employed in the royal palaces. Above all, I must not forget to mention here his gardens for the culture of flowers, trees, and vegetables, of which there were various kinds. In these gardens were also numerous baths, wells, basins, and ponds full of limpid water, which regularly ebbed and flowed. All this was enlivened by endless varieties of small birds, which sang among the trees. Also the plantations of medical plants and vegetables are well worthy of our notice: these were kept in proper order by a large body of gardeners. All the baths, wells, ponds, and buildings were substantially constructed of stonework, as also the theatres where the singers and dancers performed. There were upon the whole so many remarkable things for my observation in these gardens and throughout the whole town, that I can scarcely find words to express the astonishment I felt at the pomp and splendour of the Mexican monarch. ...

We had already been four days in the city of Mexico, and neither our commander nor any of us had, during that time, left our quarters, excepting to visit the gardens and buildings adjoining the palace. Cortes now, therefore, determined to view the city, and visit the great market, and the chief temple of Huitzilopochtli. ... The moment we arrived in this immense market, we were perfectly astonished at the vast numbers of people, the profusion of merchandise which was there exposed for sale, and at the good police and order that reigned throughout. The grandees who accompanied us drew our attention to the smallest circumstance, and gave us full explanation of all we saw. Every species of merchandise had a separate spot for its sale. We first of all visited those divisions of the market appropriated for the sale of gold and silver wares, of jewels, of cloths interwoven with feathers, and of other manufactured goods; besides slaves of both sexes. This slave market was upon as great a scale as the Portuguese market for negro slaves at Guinea. To prevent these from running away, they were fastened with halters about their neck, though some were allowed to walk at large. Next to these came the dealers in coarser wares—cotton, twisted thread, and cacao. In short, every species of goods which New Spain produces were here to be found; and everything put me in mind of my native town Medino del Campo during fair time, where every merchandise has a separate street assigned for its sale. In one place were sold the stuffs manufactured of nequen; ropes, and sandals; in another place, the sweet maguey root, ready cooked, and various other things made from this plant. In another division of the market were exposed the skins of tigers, lions, jackals, otters, red deer, wild cats, and of other beasts of prey, some of which were tanned. In another place were sold beans and sage, with other herbs and vegetables. A particular market was assigned for the merchants in fowls, turkeys, ducks, rabbits, hares, deer, and dogs; also for fruit-sellers, pastry-cooks, and tripe-sellers. Not far from these were exposed all manner of earthenware, from the large earthen cauldron to the smallest pitchers. Then came the dealers in honey and honey-cakes, and other sweetmeats. Next to these, the timber-merchants, furniture-dealers, with their stores of tables, benches, cradles, and all sorts of wooden implements, all separately arranged. What can I further add? If I am to note everything down, I must also mention human excrements, which were exposed for sale in canoes lying in the canals near this square, and is used for the tanning of leather; for, according to the assurances of the Mexicans, it is impossible to tan well without it. I can easily imagine that many of my readers will laugh at this; however, what I have stated is a fact, and, as further proof of this, I must acquaint the reader that along every road accommodations were built of reeds, straw, or grass, by which those who made use of them were hidden from the view of the passers-by, so that great care was taken that none of the last-mentioned treasures should be lost. But why should I so minutely detail every article exposed for sale in this great market? If I had to enumerate everything singly, I should not so easily get to the end. And yet I have not mentioned the paper, which in this country is called amatl; the tubes filled with liquid amber and tobacco; the various sweet-scented salves, and similar things; nor the various seeds which were exposed for sale in the porticoes of this market, nor the medicinal herbs.

In this market-place there were also courts of justice, to which three judges and several constables were appointed, who inspected the goods exposed for sale. I had almost forgotten to mention the salt, and those who made the flint knives; also the fish, and a species of bread made of a kind of mud or slime collected from the surface of this lake, and eaten in that form, and has a similar taste to our cheese. Further, instruments of brass, copper, and tin; cups, and painted pitchers of wood; indeed, I wish I had completed the enumeration of all this profusion of merchandize. The variety was so great that it would occupy more space than I can well spare to note them down in; besides which, the market was so crowded with people, and the thronging so excessive in the porticoes, that it was quite impossible to see all in one day. . . .

On quitting the market, we entered the spacious yards which surrounded the chief temple. These appeared to encompass more ground than the market-place at Salamanca, and were surrounded by a double wall, constructed of stone and lime: these yards were paved with large white flag-stones, extremely smooth; and where these were wanting, a kind of brown plaster had been used instead, and all was kept so very clean that there was not the smallest particle of dust or straw to be seen anywhere.

Before we mounted the steps of the great temple, Motecusuma, who was sacrificing on the top to his idols, sent six papas and two of his principal officers to conduct Cortes up the steps. There were 114 steps to the summit. . . . Indeed, this infernal temple, from its great height, commanded a view of the whole surrounding neighbourhood. From this place we could likewise see the three causeways which led into Mexico,—that from Iztapalapan, by which we had entered the city four days ago; that from Tlacupa, along which we took our flight eight months after, when we were beaten out of the city by the new monarch Cuitlahuatzin; the third was that of Tepeaquilla. We also observed the aqueduct which ran from Chapultepec, and provided the whole town with sweet water. We could also distinctly see the bridges across the openings, by which these causeways were intersected, and through which the waters of the lake ebbed and flowed. The lake itself was crowded with canoes, which were bringing provisions, manufactures, and other merchandize to the city. From here we also discovered that the only communication of the houses in this city, and of all the other towns built in the lake, was by means of drawbridges or canoes. In all these towns the beautiful white plastered temples rose above the smaller ones, like so many towers and castles in our Spanish towns, and this, it may be imagined, was a splendid sight.

After we had sufficiently gazed upon this magnificent picture, we again turned our eyes toward the great market, and beheld the vast numbers of buyers and sellers who thronged there. The bustle and noise occasioned by this multitude of human beings was so great that it could be heard at a distance of more than four miles. Some of our men, who had been at Constantinople and Rome, and travelled through the whole of Italy, said that they never had seen a marketplace of such large dimensions, or which was so well regulated, or so crowded with people as this one at Mexico.

On this occasion Cortes said to father Olmedo, who had accompanied us: "I have just been thinking that we should take this opportunity, and apply to Motecusuma for permission to build a church here."

To which father Olmedo replied, that it would, no doubt, be an excellent thing if the monarch would grant this; but that it would be acting overhasty to make a proposition of that nature to him now, whose consent would not easily be gained at any time.

Cortes then turned to Motecusuma, and said to him, by means of our interpretress, Doña Marina: "Your majesty is, indeed, a great monarch, and you merit to be still greater! It has been a real delight to us to view all your cities. I have now one favour to beg of you, that you would allow us to see your gods and teules."

To which Motecusuma answered, that he must first consult the chief papas, to whom he then addressed a few words. Upon this, we were led into a kind of small tower, with one room, in which we saw two basements resembling altars, decked with coverings of extreme beauty. On each of these basements stood a gigantic, fat-looking figure, of which the one on the right hand represented the god of war Huitzilopochtli. This idol had a very broad face, with distorted and furious-looking eyes, and was covered all over with jewels, gold, and pearls, which were stuck to it by means of a species of paste, which, in this country, is prepared from a certain root. Large serpents, likewise, covered with gold and precious stones, wound round the body of this monster, which held in one hand a bow, and in the other a bunch of arrows. Another small idol which stood by its side, representing its page, carried this monster's short spear, and it golden shield studded with precious stones. Around Huitzilopochtli's neck were figures representing human faces and hearts made of gold and silver, and decorated with blue stones. In front of him stood several perfuming pans with copal, the incense of the country; also the hearts of three Indians, who had that day been slaughtered, were now consuming before him as a burnt-offering. Every wall of this chapel and the whole floor had become almost black with human blood, and the stench was abominable.

. . . . .

Respecting the abominable human sacrifices of these people, the following was communicated to us: The breast of the unhappy victim destined to be sacrificed was ripped open with a knife made of sharp flint; the throbbing heart was then torn out, and immediately offered to the idol-god in whose honour the sacrifice had been instituted. After this, the head, arms, and legs were cut off and eaten at their banquets, with the exception of the head, which was saved, and hung to a beam appropriated for that purpose. No other part of the body was eaten, but the remainder was thrown to the beasts which were kept in those abominable dens, in which there were also vipers and other poisonous serpents, and, among the latter in particular, a species at the end of whose tail there was a kind of rattle. This last mentioned serpent, which is the most dangerous, was kept in a cabin of a diversified form, in which a quantity of feathers had been strewed: here it laid its eggs, and it was fed with the flesh of dogs and of human beings who had been sacrificed. We were positively told that, after we had been beaten out of the city of Mexico, and had lost 850 of our men, these horrible beasts were fed for many successive days with the bodies of our unfortunate countrymen. Indeed, when all the tigers and lions roared together, with the howlings of the jackals and foxes, and hissing of the serpents, it was quite fearful, and you could not suppose otherwise than that you were in hell.

. . . . .

Our commander here said smilingly, to Motecusuma: "I cannot imagine that such a powerful and wise monarch as you are, should not have yourself discovered by this time that these idols are not divinities, but evil spirits, called devils. In order that you may be convinced of this, and that your papas may satisfy themselves of this truth, allow me to erect a cross on the summit of this temple; and, in the chapel, where stand your Huitzilopochtli and Tetzcatlipuca, give us a small space that I may place there the image of the holy Virgin; then you will see what terror will seize these idols by which you have been so long deluded."

Motecusuma knew what the image of the Virgin Mary was, yet he was very much displeased with Cortes' offer, and replied, in presence of two papas, whose anger was not less conspicuous, "Malinche, could I have conjectured that you would have used such reviling language as you have just done, I would certainly not have shown you my gods. In our eyes these are good divinities: they preserve our lives, give us nourishment, water, and good harvests, healthy and growing weather, and victory whenever we pray to them for it. Therefore we offer up our prayers to them, and make them sacrifices. I earnestly beg of you not to say another word to insult the profound veneration in which we hold these gods."

As soon as Cortes heard these words and perceived the great excitement under which they were pronounced, he said nothing in return, but merely remarked to the monarch with a cheerful smile: "It is time for us both to depart hence." To which Motecusuma answered, that he would not detain him any longer, but he himself was now obliged to stay some time to atone to his gods by prayer and sacrifice for having committed *gratlatlacol,* by allowing us to ascend the great temple, and thereby occasioning the affronts which we had offered them.

INDIANS OF VIRGINIA **26**

Díaz wrote of a civilization that was the exception in the New World. In most of North and South America the Indians failed to attain the levels of the Aztecs in Mexico and the Incas in Peru. The levels they did reach varied enormously: in California and Patagonia they remained at a primitive food-gathering stage, while along the Atlantic seaboard they were agriculturists settled in relatively populous villages. Captain John Smith, leader of the English settlers who founded Jamestown in Virginia in 1607, knew the agriculturists and how they raised their mainstays: corn, beans, and squashes. He also saw that hunting, fishing, and plant-gathering still remained essential for the Virginia Indians, as it did for all except those settled in the most populous sections of the Aztec and Inca empires. Smith's account of native religion and government provides a revealing contrast with corresponding Aztec institutions.* In general, we may conclude that the Indians north of the Rio Grande lagged far behind those of Mexico and Peru; yet they were much more advanced than the Paleolithic aborigines of Australia, who are described in the next selection. These distinctions are noteworthy because they *explain in part why the Europeans occupied Australia with less difficulty than North America, and North America, in turn, with less trouble than Africa.*

Of their planted Fruits in Virginia, and how they use them. . . . The greatest labour they take is in planting their corn, for the country naturally is overgrown with wood. To prepare the ground, they bruise the bark of the trees near the root, then do they scorch the roots with fire that they grow no more. The next year with a crooked piece of wood they beat up the weeds by the roots, and in that mould they plant their corn. Their manner is this. They make a hole in the earth with a stick, and into it they put four grains of wheat and two of beans. These holes they make four feet one from another. Their women and children do continually keep it weeding, and when it is grown middle high, they hill it about like a hop-yard.

In April they begin to plant, but their chief plantation is in May, and so they continue till the midst of June. What they plant in April they reap in August, for May in September, for June in October. Every stalk of their corn commonly beareth two ears, some three, seldom any four, many but one, and some none. Every ear ordinarily hath between two hundred and five hundred grains. The stalk being green hath a sweet juice in it, somewhat like a sugar cane, which is the cause that when they gather their corn green, they suck the stalks: for as we gather green peas, so do they their corn being green, which excelleth their old. They plant also peas they call assentamens, which are the same they call in Italy fagioli. Their beans are the same the Turks call garnanses; but these they much esteem for dainties.

Their corn they roast in the ear green, and bruising it in a mortar of wood with a polt, lap it in rolls in the leaves of their corn, and so boil it for a dainty. They also reserve that corn late planted that will not ripe, by roasting it in hot ashes, the heat thereof drying it. In winter they esteem it being boiled with beans for a rare dish, they call pausarowmena. . . .

In May also amongst their corn they plant pumpions, and a fruit like unto a muskmelon, but less and worse, which they call macocks. These increase exceedingly, and ripen in the beginning of July, and continue until September. They plant also maracocks, a wild fruit like a lemon, which also increase infinitely. They begin to ripen in September, and continue till the end of October. When all their fruits be gathered, little else they plant, and this is done by their women and children; neither doth this long suffice them, for near three parts of the year they only observe times and seasons, and live of what the country naturally affordeth from hand to mouth, &c. . . .

Of the natural Inhabitants of Virginia. The land is not populous, for the men be few; their far greater number is of women and children. Within sixty miles of James Town, there are about some five thousand people, but of able men fit for their wars scarce fifteen hundred. To nourish so many together they have yet no means, because they make so small a benefit of their land, be it never so fertile. . . . Each houshold knoweth their own lands and gardens, and most live of their own labour. For their apparel, they are sometime covered with the skins of wild beasts, which in winter are dressed with the hair, but in summer without. . . .

Their buildings and habitations are for the most part by the rivers, or not

* Captain John Smith, "The General History of Virginia, New England, and the Summer Isles . . . ," in J. Pinkerton, *Voyages and Travels . . .* (London, 1812), XIII, 32-43.

far distant from some fresh spring; their houses are built like our arbours, of small young springs bowed and tied, and so close covered with mats, or the barks of trees very handsomely, that notwithstanding either wind, rain, or weather, they are as warm as stoves, but very smoky, yet at the top of the house there is a hole made for the smoke to go into right over the fire.

Against the fire they lie on little hurdles of reeds covered with a mat, borne from the ground a foot and more by a hurdle of wood, on these round about the house they lie heads and points one by the other against the fire, some covered with mats, some with skins, and some stark naked lie on the ground, from six to twenty in a house. Their houses are in the midst of their fields or gardens, which are small plots of ground, some twenty acres, some forty, some one hundred, some two hundred, some more, some less. In some places from two to fifty of those houses together, or but a little separated by groves of trees. Near their habitations is little small wood or old trees on the ground by reason of their burning of them for fire, so that a man may gallop a horse amongst these woods any way, but where the creeks or rivers shall hinder. . . .

Their fire they kindle presently by chafing a dry pointed stick in a hole of a little square piece of wood, that firing itself, will to fire moss, leaves, or any such like dry thing that will quickly burn. In March and April they live much upon their fishing wires, and feed on fish, turkies, and squirrels. In May and June they plant their fields, and live most of acorns, walnuts, and fish. But to amend their diet, some disperse themselves in small companies, and live upon fish, beasts, crabs, oysters, land-tortoises, strawberries, mulberries, and such like. In June, July, and August, they feed upon the roots of tocknough berries, fish, and green wheat. It is strange to see how their bodies alter with their diet, even as the deer and wild beasts they seem fat and lean, strong and weak. Powhatan, their great king, and some others, that are provident, roast their fish and flesh upon hurdles as before is expressed, and keep it till scarce times. . . .

In their hunting and fishing they take extreme pains, yet it being their ordinary exercise from their infancy, they esteem it a pleasure, and are very proud to be expert therein; and by their continual ranging and travel, they know all the advantages and places most frequented with deer, beasts, fish, fowl, roots, and berries. At their huntings they leave their habitations, and reduce themselves into companies, as the Tartars do, and go to the most desert places with their families, where they spend their time in hunting and fowling up towards the mountains, by the heads of their rivers, where there is plenty of game; for betwixt the rivers the grounds are so narrow, that little cometh here which they devour not: it is a marvel they can so directly pass these deserts, some three or four days journey, without habitation. Their hunting-houses are like unto arbours covered with mats; these their women bear after them, with corn, acorns, mortars, and all bag and baggage they use. When they come to the place of exercise, every man doth his best to shew his dexterity, for by their excelling in those qualities they get their wives. Forty yards will they shoot level, or very near the mark, and one hundred and twenty is their best at random. At their huntings in the deserts they are commonly two or three hundred together. Having found the deer, they environ them with many fires, and betwixt the fires they place themselves, and some take their stands in the midst. The deer being thus frightened by the fires and their voices, they chase them so long within that circle, that many times they kill six, eight, ten, or fifteen at a hunting. They use also to drive them into some narrow point of land, when they find that advantage, and so force them into the river, where, with their boats, they have ambuscadoes to kill them. ...

Of Their Religion

There is yet in Virginia no place discovered to be so savage in which they have not a religion, deer, and bow and arrows. All things that are able to do them hurt beyond their prevention, they adore with their kind of divine worship; as the fire, water, lightning, thunder, our ordnance, pieces, horses, &c. But their chief god they worship is the devil. Him they call Okee, and serve him more of fear than love. They say they have conference with him, and fashion themselves as near to his shape as they can imagine. In their temples they have his image evil favouredly carved, and then painted and adorned with chains of copper, and beads, and covered with a skin in such manner as the deformities may well suit with such a god. By him is commonly the sepulchre of their kings. Their bodies are first bowelled, then dried upon hurdles till they be very dry, and so about the most of their joints and neck they hang bracelets, or chains of copper, pearl, and such like, as they use to wear, their inwards they stuff with copper beads, hatchets, and such trash. Then lap they them very carefully in white skins, and so roll them in mats for their winding sheets. And in the tomb which is an arch made of mats, they lay them orderly. What remaineth of this kind of wealth their kings have, they set at their feet in baskets. These temples and bodies are kept by their priests.

For their ordinary burials they dig a deep hole in the earth with sharp stakes, and the corpse being lapped in skins and mats with their jewels, they lay them upon sticks in the ground, and so cover them with earth. The burial ended, the women, being painted all their faces with black coal and oil, do sit twenty-four hours in the houses mourning and lamenting by turns, with such yelling and howling, as may express their great passions. ...

Upon the top of certain red sandy hills in the woods, there are three great houses filled with images of their kings and devils, and tombs of their predecessors. Those houses are near sixty feet in length, built harbour-wise, after their building. This place they count so holy as that but the priests and kings dare come into them; nor the savages dare not go up the river in boats by it, but they solemnly cast some piece of copper, white beads, or pocones into the river, for fear their Okee should be offended and revenged of them.

. . . . .

Of the Manner of the Virginians' Government. Although the country people be very barbarous, yet have they amongst them such government as that their magistrates for good commanding, and their people for due subjection and obeying, excel many places that would be counted very civil. The form of their commonwealth is a monarchical government, one as emperor, ruleth over many kings or governors. Their chief ruler is called Powhatan; but his proper name is Wahunsonacock. Some countries he hath which have been his ancestors, and came unto him by inheritance, as the country called Powhatan, Arrohateck, Appamatuck, Pamaunkee, Youghtanund, and Mattapanient. All the rest of his territories expressed in the map, they report, have been his several conquests. In all his ancient inheritances he hath houses built after their manner, like arbours, some thirty, some forty yards long, and at every house provision for his entertainment, according to the time. At Werowcomoco, on the north side of the river Pamaunkee, was his residence, when I was delivered him prisoner, some fourteen miles from James Town, where, for the most part, he was resident; but at last he took so little pleasure in our near neighbourhood, that he retired himself to Orapakes, in the desert betwixt Chickahamanta and Youghtanund. He is of personage a tall-well-proportion man, with a sour look, his head somewhat grey, his beard so thin that it seemeth none at all, his age near sixty, of a very able and hardy body to endure any labour; about his person ordinarily attendeth a guard of forty or fifty of the tallest men his country doth afford. . . .

A mile from Orapakes, in a thicket of wood, he hath a house, in which he keepeth his kind of treasure, as skins, copper, pearl, and beads, which he storeth up against the time of his death and burial. Here also is his store of red paint, for ointment, bows and arrows, targets and clubs. This house is fifty or sixty yards in length, frequented only by priests. At the four corners of this house stand four images as sentinels, one of a dragon, another a bear, the third like a leopard, and the fourth like a giant-like man, all made evil favouredly, according to their best workmanship.

. . . . .

He nor any of his people understand any letters, whereby to write or read, only the laws whereby he ruleth is custom. Yet, when he listeth, his will is a law, and must be obeyed; not only as a king, but as half a god, they esteem him.

AUSTRALIAN ABORIGINES 27

Australia, the prime example of the effect of complete and prolonged geographic isolation on plants, animals, and humans, is the home of archaic plants such as the eucalyptus, archaic mammals such as the monotremes and marsupials, and archaic humans—the aborigines. Of the many books written about the aborigines, none has attained the fame of Spencer and Gillen's Native Tribes of Central Australia. *One of the authors was a trained scientist; the other, an Australian official who worked with the aborigines for twenty years. Both men were fully initiated members of the Arunta tribe, which they studied the most carefully. Their account of the aborigines is significant in revealing why the Europeans were able to occupy the continent of Australia with negligible resistance.**

The native tribes with which we are dealing occupy an area in the centre of the Australian continent which, roughly speaking, is not less than 700 miles in length from north to south, and stretches out east and west of the transcontinental telegraph line, covering an unknown extent of country in either direction. . . .

* B. S. Spencer and F. J. Gillen, *The Native Tribes of Central Australia* (London: Macmillan, 1899), pp. 1-54.

Each of the various tribes speaks a distinct dialect, and regards itself as the possessor of the country in which it lives. In the more southern parts, where they have been long in contact with the white man, not only have their numbers diminished rapidly, but the natives who still remain are but poor representatives of their race, having lost all or nearly all of their old customs and traditions. With the spread of the white man it can only be a matter of comparatively a few years before the same fate will befall the remaining tribes, which are as yet fortunately too far removed from white settlements of any size to have become degraded. However kindly disposed the white settler may be, his advent at once and of necessity introduces a disturbing element into the environment of the native, and from that moment degeneration sets in, no matter how friendly may be the relations between the Aborigine and the new-comers. The chance of securing cast-off clothing, food, tobacco, and perhaps also knives and tomahawks, in return for services rendered to the settler, at once attracts the native into the vicinity of any settlement however small. The young men, under the new influence, become freed from the wholesome restraint of the older men, who are all-powerful in the normal condition of the tribe. The strict moral code, which is certainly enforced in their natural state, is set on one side, and nothing is adopted in place of it. The old men see with sorrow that the younger ones do not care for the time-honoured traditions of their fathers, and refuse to hand them on to successors who, according to their ideas, are not worthy to be trusted with them; vice, disease, and difficulty in securing the natural food, which is driven away by the settlers, rapidly diminish their numbers, and when the remnant of the tribe is gathered into some mission station, under conditions as far removed as they can well be from their natural ones, it is too late to learn anything of the customs which once governed tribal life.

Fortunately from this point of view the interior of the continent is not easily accessible, or rather its climate is too dry and the water supply too meagre and untrustworthy, to admit as yet of rapid settlement, and therefore the natives, in many parts, are practically still left to wander over the land which the white man does not venture to inhabit, and amongst them may still be found tribes holding firmly to the beliefs and customs of their ancestors.

If now we take the Arunta tribe as an example, we find that the natives are distributed in a large number of small local groups, each of which occupies, and is supposed to possess, a given area of country, the boundaries of which are well known to the natives. In speaking of themselves, the natives will refer to these local groups by the name of the locality which each of them inhabits. . . .

Still further examination of each local group reveals the fact that it is composed largely, but not entirely, of individuals who describe themselves by the name of some one animal or plant. Thus there will be one area which belongs to a group of men who call themselves kangaroo men, another belonging to emu men, another to Hakea flower men, and so on, almost every animal and plant which is found in the country having its representative amongst the human inhabitants. The area of country which is occupied by each of these, which will be spoken of as local Totemic groups, varies to a considerable extent, but is never very large, the most extensive one with which we are acquainted being that of the witchetty grub people of the Alice Springs district. This group at the present time is represented by exactly forty individuals (men, women, and children), and the area of which they are recognised as the proprietors extends over about 100 square miles. In contrast to this, one particular group of "plum-tree" people is only, at the present day, represented by one solitary individual, and he is the proprietor of only a few square miles. . . .

As amongst all savage tribes the Australian native is bound hand and foot by custom. What his fathers did before him that he must do. If during the performance of a ceremony his ancestors painted a white line across the forehead, that line he must paint. Any infringement of custom, within certain limitations, is visited with sure and often severe punishment. At the same time, rigidly conservative as the native is, it is yet possible for changes to be introduced. We have already pointed out that there are certain men who are especially respected for their ability, and, after watching large numbers of the tribe, at a time when they were assembled together for months to perform certain of their most sacred ceremonies, we have come to the conclusion that at a time such as this, when the older and more powerful men from various groups are met together, and when day by day and night by night around their camp fires they discuss matters of tribal interest, it is quite possible for changes of custom to be introduced. . . . The only thing that we can say is that, after carefully watching the natives during the performance of their ceremonies and endeavouring as best we could to enter into their feelings, to think as they did, and to become for the time being one of themselves, we came to the conclusion that if one or two of the most powerful men settled upon the advisability of introducing some change, even an important one, it would be quite possible for this to be agreed upon and carried out. That changes have been introduced, in fact, are still being introduced, is a matter of certainty. . . .

Turning again to the group, we find that the members of this wander, perhaps in small parties of one or two families, often, for example, two or more brothers with their wives and children, over the land which they own, camping at favourite spots where the presence of waterholes, with their accompaniment of vegetable and animal food, enables them to supply their wants.

In their ordinary condition the natives are almost completely naked, which is all the more strange as kangaroo and wallaby are not by any means scarce, and one would think that their fur would be of no little use and comfort in the winter time, when, under the perfectly clear sky, which often remains cloudless for weeks together, the radiation is so great that at night-time the temperature falls several degrees below freezing point. The idea of making any kind of clothing as a protection against cold does not appear to have entered the native mind, though he is keen enough upon securing the Government blanket when he can get one, or, in fact, any stray cast-off clothing of the white man. The latter is however worn as much from motives of vanity as from a desire for warmth; a lubra [female aborigine] with nothing on except an ancient straw hat and an old pair of boots is perfectly happy. . . .

If, now, the reader can imagine himself transported to the side of some waterhole in the centre of Australia, he would probably find amongst the scrub and gum-trees surrounding it a small camp of natives. Each family, consisting of a man and one or more wives and children, accompanied always by dogs, occupies a *mia-mia,* which is merely a lean-to of shrubs so placed as to shield the occupants from the prevailing wind, which, if it be during the winter months, is sure to be from the south-east. In front of this, or inside if the weather be cold, will be a small fire of twigs, for the black fellow never makes a large fire as the white man does. In this respect he certainly regards the latter as a strange being, who makes a big fire and then finds it so hot that he cannot go anywhere near to it. The black fellow's idea is to make a small fire such that he can lie coiled round it and, during the night, supply it with small twigs so that he can keep it alight without making it so hot that he must go further away.

Early in the morning, if it be summer, and not until the sun be well up if it be winter, the occupants of the camp are astir. Time is no object to them, and, if there be no lack of food, the men and women all lounge about while the children laugh and play. If food be required, then the women will go out accompanied by the children and armed with digging sticks and *pitchis* [wooden troughs], and the day will be spent out in the bush in search of small burrowing animals such as lizards and small marsupials. The men will perhaps set off armed with spears, spear-throwers, boomerangs and shields in search of larger game such as emus and kangaroos. The latter are secured by stalking, when the native gradually approaches his prey with perfectly noiseless footsteps. Keeping a sharp watch on the animal, he remains absolutely still, if it should turn its head, until once more it resumes its feeding. Gradually, availing himself of the shelter of any bush or large tussock of grass, he approaches near enough to throw his spear. The end is fixed into the point of the spear thrower, and, aided by the leverage thus gained, he throws it forward with all his strength. Different men vary much in their skill in spear-throwing, but it takes an exceptionally good man to kill or disable at more than twenty yards. Sometimes two or three men will hunt in company, and then, while one remains in ambush, the others combine to drive the animals as close as possible to him. Euros are more easily caught than kangaroos, owing to the fact that they inhabit hilly and scrub country, across which they make "pads," by the side of which men will lie in ambush while parties of women go out and drive the animals towards them. On the ranges the rock-wallabies have definite runs, and close by one of these a native will sit patiently, waiting hour by hour, until some unfortunate beast comes by.

In some parts the leaves of the pituri plant are used to stupefy the emu. The plan adopted is to make a decoction in some small waterhole at which the animal is accustomed to drink. There, hidden by some bush, the native lies quietly in wait. After drinking the water the bird becomes stupefied, and easily falls a prey to the black fellow's spear. Sometimes a bush shelter is made, so as to look as natural as possible, close by a waterhole, and from behind this animals are speared as they come down to drink. It must be remembered that during the long dry seasons of Central Australia waterholes are few and far between, so that in this way the native is aided in his work of killing animals. In some parts advantage is taken of the inquisitive nature of the emu. A native will carry something which resembles the long neck and small head of the bird and will gradually approach his prey, stopping every now and then, and moving about in the aimless way of the bird itself. The emu, anxious to know what the thing really is, will often wait and watch it until the native has the chance of throwing his spear at close quarters. Sometimes a deep pit will be dug in a part which is known to be a feeding ground of the bird. In the bottom of this a short, sharply-pointed spear will be fixed upright, and then, on the top, bushes will be spread and earth scattered upon them. The inquisitive bird comes up to investigate the matter, and sooner or later ventures on the bushes, and, falling through, is transfixed by the spear. Smaller birds such as the rock pigeons, which assemble in flocks at any waterhole, are caught by throwing the boomerang amongst them, and larger birds, such as the eagle-hawk, the down of which is much valued for decorating the body during the performance of sacred ceremonies, are procured by the same weapon.

It may be said that with certain restrictions which apply partly to groups of individuals and partly to individuals at certain times of their lives, everything which is edible is used for food. . . .

As a general rule the natives are kindly disposed to one another, that is of course within the limits of their own tribe, and, where two tribes come into contact with one another on the border land of their respective territories, there the same amicable feelings are maintained between the members of the two. There is no such thing as one tribe being in a constant state of enmity with another so far as these Central tribes are concerned.

·　·　·　·　·

There is, however, in these, as in other savage tribes, an undercurrent of anxious feeling which, though it may be stilled and, indeed, forgotten for a time, is yet always present. In his natural state the native is often thinking that some enemy is attempting to harm him by means of evil magic, and, on the other hand, he never knows when a medicine man in some distant group may not point him out as guilty of killing some one else by magic. It is, however, easy to lay too much stress upon this, for here again we have to put ourselves into the mental attitude of the savage, and must not imagine simply what would be our own feelings under such circumstances. It is not right, by any means, to say that the Australian native lives in constant dread of the evil magic of an enemy. The feeling is always, as it were, lying dormant and ready to be at once called up by any strange or suspicious sound if he be alone, especially at night time, in the bush; but on the other hand, just like a child, he can with ease forget anything unpleasant and enter perfectly into the enjoyment of the present moment. Granted always that his food supply is abundant, it may be said that the life of the Australian native is, for the most part, a pleasant one.

WORLD OF
THE EMERGING WEST,
1500-1763

Chapter Six

West European expansion: Iberian phase, 1500-1600

The numerous, complex motives that led the Portuguese to under-take their epoch-making explorations down the coast of Africa are made clear in The Chronicle of the Discovery and Conquest of Guinea *by Gomez Eannes de Azurara, a contemporary Portuguese writer who was personally acquainted with many of the principal actors in the stirring incidents that he relates. In reciting the motives that impelled Prince Henry the Navigator to send out his expeditions, Azurara mentions, in order, Henry's zeal for knowledge, his desire for trade, his concern about the extent of Moslem power in Africa, his wish to find some Christian king as an ally against the Moslems, and his desire to extend the faith.* It is interesting to note that Azurara brings his* Chronicle *to a close in the year 1448. "For after this year," he writes, "the affairs of these parts were henceforth treated more by trafficking and bargaining of merchants than by bravery and toil in arms." ***

We imagine that we know a matter when we are acquainted with the doer of it and the end for which he did it. And since in former chapters we have set forth the Lord Infant [Prince Henry the Navigator] as the chief actor in these things, giving as clear an understanding of him as we could, it is meet that in this present

---

* G. E. de Azurara, *The Chronicle of the Discovery and Conquest of Guinea,* ed. C. R. Beazley and E. Prestage (London: Hakluyt Society, 1896), I, 27-29.

** *Ibid.,* II, 289.

chapter we should know his purpose in doing them. And you should note well that the noble spirit of this Prince, by a sort of natural constraint, was ever urging him both to begin and to carry out very great deeds. For which reason, after the taking of Ceuta he always kept ships well armed against the Infidel, both for war, and because he had also a wish to know the land that lay beyond the isles of Canary and that Cape called Bojador, for that up to his time, neither by writings nor by the memory of man, was known with any certainty the nature of the land beyond that Cape. Some said indeed that Saint Branden had passed that way; and there was another tale of two galleys rounding the Cape, which never returned. But this doth not appear at all likely to be true, for it is not to be presumed that if the said galleys went there, some other ships would not have endeavoured to learn what voyage they had made. And because the said Lord Infant wished to know the truth of this,—since it seemed to him that if he or some other lord did not endeavour to gain knowledge, no mariners or merchants would ever dare to attempt it—(for it is clear that none of them ever trouble themselves to sail to a place where there is not a sure and certain hope of profit)—and seeing also that no other prince took any pains in this matter, he sent out his own ships against those parts, to have manifest certainty of them all. And to this he was stirred up by his zeal for the service of God and of the King Edward his Lord and brother, who then reigned. And this was the first reason of his action.

The second reason was that if there chanced to be in those lands some population of Christians, or some havens, into which it would be possible to sail without peril, many kinds of merchandise might be brought to this realm, which would find a ready market, and reasonably so, because no other people of these parts traded with them, nor yet people of any other that were known; and also the products of this realm might be taken there, which traffic would bring great profit to our countrymen.

The third reason was that, as it was said that the power of the Moors in that land of Africa was very much greater than was commonly supposed, and that there were no Christians among them, nor any other race of men; and because every wise man is obliged by natural prudence to wish for a knowledge of the power of his enemy; therefore the said Lord Infant exerted himself to cause this to be fully discovered, and to make it known determinately how far the power of those infidels extended.

The fourth reason was because during the one and thirty years that he had warred against the Moors, he had never found a Christian king, nor a lord outside this land, who for the love of our Lord Jesus Christ would aid him in the said war. Therefore he sought to know if there were in those parts any Christian princes, in whom the charity and the love of Christ was so ingrained that they would aid him against those enemies of the faith.

The fifth reason was his great desire to make increase in the faith of our Lord Jesus Christ and to bring to him all the souls that should be saved,—understanding that all the mystery of the Incarnation, Death, and Passion of our Lord Jesus Christ was for this sole end—namely the salvation of lost souls—whom the said Lord Infant by his travail and spending would fain bring into the true path.

In 1492, a new era in world history was opened with the discovery of the New World by Christopher Columbus. Columbus kept two journals during his historic journey, one open and for the encouragement of his men, the other secret and for his own use. Both have been lost, though the story they told is known in outline. In March, 1493, upon his return from the voyage, Columbus summarized his discoveries in a letter to Gabriel Sanchez, an officer of the Spanish royal treasury. This letter is of particular interest because it reveals Columbus' belief that he had found a way to the East, it reflects his interest in saving the souls of the heathens, and it also shows how anxious he was to convince his supporters that he had discovered lands "abounding in various kinds of spices, gold, and metals." *

As I know that it will afford you pleasure that I have brought my undertaking to a successful result, I have determined to write you this letter to inform you of everything that has been done and discovered in this voyage of mine.

On the thirty-third day after leaving Cadiz I came into the Indian Sea, where I discovered many islands inhabited by numerous people. I took possession of all of them for our most fortunate King by making public proclamation and unfurling his standard, no one making any resistance. To the first of them I have given the name of our blessed Saviour, trusting in whose aid I had reached this and all the rest; but the Indians call it Guanahani. To each of the others also I gave a new name, ordering one to be called Sancta Maria de Concepcion, another Fernandina, another Hysabella, another Johana; and so with all the rest. ... From there I saw another island to the eastwards, distant 54 miles from this Johana, which I named Hispana, and proceeded to it. ...

In the island, which I have said before was called Hispana, there are very lofty and beautiful mountains, great farms, groves and fields, most fertile both for cultivation and for pasturage, and well adapted for constructing buildings. The convenience of the harbors in this island, and the excellence of the rivers, in volume and salubrity, surpass human belief, unless one should see them. In it the trees, pasture-lands, and fruits differ much from those of Johana. Besides, this Hispana abounds in various kinds of spices, gold, and metals. The inhabitants of both sexes of this and of all the other islands I have seen, or of which I have any knowledge, always go as naked as they came into the world, except that some of the women cover parts of their bodies with leaves or branches, or a veil of cotton, which they prepare themselves for this purpose. They are all, as I said before, unprovided with any sort of iron, and they are destitute of arms, which are entirely unknown to them, and for which they are not adapted; not on account of any bodily deformity, for they are well made, but because they are timid and full of terror. They carry, however, canes dried in the sun in place of weapons, upon whose roots they fix a wooden shaft, dried and sharpened to a point. But they never dare to make use of these, for it has often happened, when I have sent two or three of my men to some of their villages to speak with

* *Old South Leaflets,* Vol. II, No. 33 (Boston: Directors of the Old South Work, 1897).

the inhabitants, that a crowd of Indians has sallied forth; but, when they saw our men approaching, they speedily took to flight, parents abandoning their children, and children their parents. This happened not because any loss or injury had been inflicted upon any of them. On the contrary, I gave whatever I had, cloth and many other things, to whomsoever I approached, or with whom I could get speech, without any return being made to me; but they are by nature fearful and timid. But, when they see that they are safe, and all fear is banished, they are very guileless and honest, and very liberal of all they have. No one refuses the asker anything that he possesses; on the contrary, they themselves invite us to ask for it. They manifest the greatest affection toward all of us, exchanging valuable things for trifles, content with the very least thing or nothing at all. But I forbade giving them a very trifling thing and of no value, such as bits of plates, dishes, or glass, also nails and straps; although it seemed to them, if they could get such, that they had acquired the most beautiful jewels in the world. ...

They do not practise idolatry; on the contrary, they believe that all strength, all power, in short, all blessings, are from Heaven, and that I have come down from there with these ships and sailors; and in this spirit was I received everywhere, after they had got over their fear. They are neither lazy nor awkward, but, on the contrary, are of an excellent and acute understanding. Those who have sailed these seas give excellent accounts of everything; but they have never seen men wearing clothes, or ships like ours.

· · · · ·

In all these islands, as I understand, every man is satisfied with only one wife, except the princes or kings, who are permitted to have 20. The women appear to work more than the men, but I could not well understand whether they have private property or not; for I saw that what every one had was shared with the others, especially meals, provisions, and such things. I found among them no monsters, as very many expected, but men of great deference and kind; nor are they black like the Ethiopians, but they have long, straight hair. ...

I was informed that there is another island larger than the aforesaid Hispana, whose inhabitants have no hair; and that there is a greater abundance of gold in it than in any of the others. Some of the inhabitants of these islands and of the others I have seen I am bringing over with me to bear testimony to what I have reported. Finally, to sum up in a few words the chief results and advantages of our departure and speedy return, I make this promise to our most invincible Sovereigns, that, if I am supported by some little assistance from them, I will give them as much gold as they have need of, and in addition spices, cotton, and mastic, which is found only in Chios, and as much aloes-wood, and as many heathen slaves as their Majesties may choose to demand. ...

· · · · ·

Therefore let King and Queen and Princes, and their most fortunate realms, and all other Christian provinces, let us all return thanks to our Lord and Saviour Jesus Christ, who has bestowed so great a victory and reward upon us; let there be processions and solemn sacrifices prepared; let the churches be decked with festal boughs; let Christ rejoice upon earth as he rejoices in heaven, as he foresees that so many souls of so many people heretofore lost are to be saved; and let us be glad not only for the exaltation of our faith, but also for the increase of temporal prosperity, in which not only Spain, but all Christendom is about to share.

As these things have been accomplished, so have they been briefly narrated. Farewell.

Lisbon, March 14th.

CHRISTOPHER COLOM,
Admiral of the Ocean Fleet.

VASCO DA GAMA REACHES INDIA **30**

To the end of his days, Columbus insisted that he had reached the Indies; but before his death in 1506, it was generally realized that he had stumbled upon a vast and, what seemed to be then, unpromising and uninviting New World that blocked the road to the East. It was not Columbus that blazed the route to the coveted Spice Islands, but rather the Portuguese Vasco da Gama, who rounded the Cape of Good Hope in 1497 and arrived in Calicut, India. Da Gama's official report on the voyage has been lost, so we are dependent upon the account of an unknown member of the expedition to illustrate certain significant features of the expedition: the comparatively low culture of the Negro tribesmen; the Arab civilization on the east coat of Africa; the mutual enmity of the Moslem Arabs (or "Moors") and the Christian Portuguese; the friendliness of the King of Calicut; the hostility of the Arab merchants in Calicut; and the inadequacy of the gifts and merchandise of the Portuguese.*

In the name of God. Amen!

In the year 1497 King Dom Manuel, the first of that name in Portugal, despatched four vessels to make discoveries and go in search of spices. Vasco da Gama was the captain-major of these vessels; Paulo da Gama, his brother, commanded one of them, and Nicolau Coelho another. . . .

The Bay of St. Helena

On Saturday, the 4th of the same month, [November 1497] a couple of hours before break of day, we had soundings in 110 fathoms, and at nine o'clock we sighted the land. We then drew near to each other, and having put on our gala clothes, we saluted the captain-major by firing our bombards, and dressed the ships with flags and standards. In the course of the day we tacked so as to come close to the land, but as we failed to identify it, we again stood out to sea.

On Tuesday [November 7] we returned to the land, which we found to be low, with a broad bay opening into it. The captain-major sent Pero d'Alenquer in a boat to take soundings and to search for good anchoring ground. The bay was found to be very clean, and to afford shelter against all winds except those from the N.W. It extended east and west, and we named it Santa Helena.

* E. G. Ravenstein, ed. and trans., *A Journal of the First Voyage of Vasco da Gama 1497-1499* (London: Hakluyt Society, 1898), pp. 1-72.

On Wednesday [November 8] we cast anchor in this bay, and we remained there eight days, cleaning the ships, mending the sails, and taking in wood.

. . . . .

The inhabitants of this country are tawny-coloured. Their food is confined to the flesh of seals, whales and gazelles, and the roots of herbs. They are dressed in skins, and wear sheaths over their virile members. They are armed with poles of olive wood to which a horn, browned in the fire, is attached. Their numerous dogs resemble those of Portugal, and bark like them. The birds of the country, likewise, are the same as in Portugal, and include cormorants, gulls, turtle doves, crested larks, and many others. The climate is healthy and temperate, and produces good herbage.

On the day after we had cast anchor, that is to say on Thursday [November 9], we landed with the captain-major, and made captive one of the natives, who was small of stature like Sancho Mexia. This man had been gathering honey in the sandy waste, for in this country the bees deposit their honey at the foot of the mounds around the bushes. He was taken on board the captain-major's ship, and being placed at table he ate of all we ate. On the following day the captain-major had him well dressed and sent ashore.

On the following day [November 10] fourteen or fifteen natives came to where our ships lay. The captain-major landed and showed them a variety of merchandise, with the view of finding out whether such things were to be found in their country. This merchandise included cinnamon, cloves, seed-pearls, gold, and many other things, but it was evident that they had no knowledge whatever of such articles, and they were consequently given round bells and tin rings. This happened on Friday, and the like took place on Saturday.

. . . . .

On that day [November 12] Fernão Velloso, who was with the captain-major, expressed a great desire to be permitted to accompany the natives to their houses, so that he might find out how they lived and what they ate. The captain-major yielded to his importunities, and allowed him to accompany them, and when we returned to the captain-major's vessel to sup, he went away with the negroes. Soon after they had left us they caught a seal, and when they came to the foot of a hill in a barren place they roasted it, and gave some of it to Fernão Velloso, as also some of the roots which they eat. After this meal they expressed a desire that he should not accompany them any further, but return to the vessels. When Fernão Velloso came abreast of the vessels he began to shout, the negroes keeping in the bush.

We were still at supper; but when his shouts were heard the captain-major rose at once, and so did we others, and we entered a sailing boat. The negroes then began running along the beach, and they came as quickly up with Fernão Velloso as we did, and when we endeavoured to get him into the boat they threw their assegais, and wounded the captain-major and three or four others. All this happened because we looked upon these people as men of little spirit, quite incapable of violence, and had therefore landed without first arming ourselves. We then returned to the ships.

Rounding the Cape

At daybreak of Thursday the 16th of November, having careened our ships and taken in wood, we set sail. ... Late on Saturday [November 18] we beheld the Cape. On that same day we again stood out to sea, returning to the land in the course of the night. On Sunday morning, November 19, we once more made for the Cape, but were again unable to round it, for the wind blew from the S.S.W., whilst the Cape juts out towards the S.W. We then again stood out to sea, returning to the land on Monday night. At last, on Wednesday [November 22], at noon, having the wind astern, we succeeded in doubling the Cape, and then ran along the coast.

To the south of this Cape of Good Hope, and close to it, a vast bay, six leagues broad at its mouth, enters about six leagues into the land. . . .

Mozambique

The people of this country [Mozambique] are of a ruddy complexion and well made. They are Mohammedans, and their language is the same as that of the Moors.* Their dresses are of fine linen or cotton stuffs, with variously coloured stripes, and of rich and elaborate workmanship. They all wear *toucas* with borders of silk embroidered in gold. They are merchants, and have transactions with white Moors, four of whose vessels were at the time in port, laden with gold, silver, cloves, pepper, ginger, and silver rings, as also with quantities of pearls, jewels, and rubies, all of which articles are used by the people of this country. . . .

In this place and island of Moncobiquy [Mozambique] there resided a chief [senhor] who had the title of Sultan, and was like a vice-roy. He often came aboard our ships attended by some of his people. The captain-major gave him many good things to eat, and made him a present of hats, *marlotas* [short dresses of silk or wool, worn in Persia and India], corals and many other articles. He was, however, so proud that he treated all we gave him with contempt, and asked for scarlet cloth, of which we had none. We gave him, however, of all the things we had.

One day the captain-major invited him to a repast, when there was an abundance of figs and comfits, and begged him for two pilots to go with us. He at once granted this request, subject to our coming to terms with them. The captain-major gave each of them thirty mitkals [coins reckoned at about $1.68 each] in gold and two *marlotas,* on condition that from the day on which they received this payment one of them should always remain on board if the other desired to go on land. With these terms they were well satisfied.

On Saturday, March 10, we set sail and anchored one league out at sea, close to an island, where mass was said on Sunday, when those who wished to do so confessed and joined in the communion.

One of our pilots lived on the island, and when we had anchored we armed two boats to go in search of him. The captain-major went in one boat and Nicolau Coelho in the other. They were met by five or six boats (barcas) coming from the island, and crowded with people armed with bows and long arrows and bucklers, who gave them to understand by signs that they were to return to the town. When the captain saw this he secured the pilot whom he had taken with him, and ordered the bombards to fire upon the boats. Paulo

* That is, Arabic. The "Moors" of the author are, in fact, either pure Arabs (white Moors) or Swahilis speaking Arabic.

da Gama, who had remained with the ships, so as to be prepared to render succour in case of need, no sooner heard the reports of the bombards than he started in the *Berrio*. The Moors, who were already flying, fled still faster, and gained the land before the *Berrio* was able to come up with them. We then returned to our anchorage.

· · · · ·

Mombasa

On Saturday [April 7] we cast anchor off Mombasa. . . . At midnight there approached us a *zavra* [small open vessel] with about a hundred men, all armed with cutlasses and bucklers. When they came to the vessel of the captain-major they attempted to board her, armed as they were, but this was not permitted, only four or five of the most distinguished men among them being allowed on board. They remained about a couple of hours, and it seemed to us that they paid us this visit merely to find out whether they might not capture one or the other of our vessels.

· · · · ·

At night the captain-major "questioned" two Moors [from Mozambique] whom we had on board, by dropping boiling oil upon their skin, so that they might confess any treachery intended against us. They said that orders had been given to capture us as soon as we entered the port, and thus to avenge what we had done at Mozambique. And when this torture was being applied a second time, one of the Moors, although his hands were tied, threw himself into the sea, whilst the other did so during the morning watch.

About midnight two *almadias* [ferry-boats] with many men in them, approached. The *almadias* stood off whilst the men entered the water, some swimming in the direction of the *Berrio,* others in that of the *Raphael*. Those who swam to the *Berrio* began to cut the cable. The men on watch thought at first that they were tunny fish, but when they perceived their mistake they shouted to the other vessels. The other swimmers had already got hold of the rigging of the mizzen-mast. Seeing themselves discovered, they silently slipped down and fled. These and other wicked tricks were practised upon us by these dogs, but our Lord did not allow them to succeed, because they were unbelievers. . . .

Across the Arabian Sea

We left Malindi on Tuesday, the 24th of the month [of April] for a city called Qualecut [Calicut], with the pilot whom the king [of Malindi] had given us. . . .

On Friday, the 18th of May, after having seen no land for twenty-three days, we sighted lofty mountains, and having all this time sailed before the wind we could not have made less than 600 leagues. . . . On Sunday [May 20] we found ourselves close to some mountains, and when we were near enough for the pilot to recognise them he told us that they were above Calicut, and that this was the country we desired to go to. . . .

When we arrived at Calicut the king was fifteen leagues away. The captain-major sent two men to him with a message, informing him that an ambassador had arrived from the King of Portugal with letters, and that if he desired it he would take them to where the king then was.

The king presented the bearers of this message with much fine cloth. He sent word to the captain bidding him welcome, saying that he was about to proceed to Qualecut (Calicut). As a matter of fact, he started at once with a large retinue. . . .

The king was in a small court, reclining upon a couch covered with a cloth of green velvet, above which was a good mattress, and upon this again a sheet of cotton stuff, very white and fine, more so than any linen. The cushions were after the same fashion. In his left hand the king held a very large golden cup [spittoon], having a capacity of half an almude [8 pints]. At its mouth this cup was two palmas [16 inches] wide, and apparently it was massive. Into this cup the king threw the husks of a certain herb which is chewed by the people of this country because of its soothing effects, and which they call *atambor* [betel nut]. On the right side of the king stood a basin of gold, so large that a man might just encircle it with his arms: this contained the herbs. There were likewise many silver jugs. The canopy above the couch was all gilt.

The captain, on entering, saluted in the manner of the country: by putting the hands together, then raising them towards Heaven, as is done by Christians when addressing God, and immediately afterwards opening them and shutting the fists quickly. The king beckoned to the captain with his right hand to come nearer, but the captain did not approach him, for it is the custom of the country for no man to approach the king except only the servant who hands him the herbs, and when anyone addresses the king he holds his hand before the mouth, and remains at a distance. When the king beckoned to the captain he looked at us others, and ordered us to be seated on a stone bench near him, where he could see us. He ordered that water for our hands should be given us, as also some fruit, one kind of which resembled a melon, except that its outside was rough and the inside sweet, whilst another kind of fruit resembled a fig, and tasted very nice. There were men who prepared these fruits for us; and the king looked at us eating, and smiled; and talked to the servant who stood near him supplying him with the herbs referred to.

And the captain told him he was the ambassador of a King of Portugal, who was Lord of many countries and the possessor of great wealth of every description, exceeding that of any king of these parts; that for a period of sixty years his ancestors had annually sent out vessels to make discoveries in the direction of India, as they knew that there were Christian kings there like themselves. This, he said, was the reason which induced them to order this country to be discovered, not because they sought for gold or silver, for of this they had such abundance that they needed not what was to be found in this country. He further stated that the captains sent out travelled for a year or two, until their provisions were exhausted, and then returned to Portugal, without having succeeded in making the desired discovery. There reigned a king now whose name was Dom Manuel, who had ordered him to build three vessels, of which he had been appointed captain-major, and who had ordered him not to return to Portugal until he should have discovered this King of the Christians, on pain of having his head cut off. That two letters had been intrusted to him to be presented in case he succeeded in discovering him, and that he would do so on the ensuing day; and, finally, he had been instructed to say by word of mouth that he [the King of Portugal] desired to be his friend and brother.

In reply to this the king said that he was welcome; that, on his part, he held him as a friend and brother, and would send ambassadors with him to Portugal. This latter had been asked as a favour, the captain pretending that he would not dare to present himself before his king and master unless he was able to present, at the same time, some men of this country.

. . . . .

On Tuesday [May 29] the captain got ready the following things to be sent to the king, viz., twelve pieces of *lambel* [striped cloth], four scarlet hoods, six hats, four strings of coral, a case containing six wash-hand basins, a case of sugar, two casks of oil, and two of honey. And as it is the custom not to send anything to the king without the knowledge of the Moor, his factor, and of the *bale* [Governor] the captain informed them of his intention. They came, and when they saw the present they laughed at it, saying that it was not a thing to offer to a king, that the poorest merchant from Mecca, or any other part of India, gave more, and that if he wanted to make a present it should be in gold, as the king would not accept such things. When the captain heard this he grew sad, and said that he had brought no gold, that, moreover, he was no merchant, but an ambassador; that he gave of that which he had, which was his own [private gift] and not the king's; that if the King of Portugal ordered him to return he would intrust him with far richer presents; and that if King Camolim would not accept these things he would send them back to the ships. Upon this they declared that they would not forward his presents, nor consent to his forwarding them himself. When they had gone there came certain Moorish merchants, and they all depreciated the present which the captain desired to be sent to the king.

When the captain saw that they were determined not to forward his present, he said, that as they would not allow him to send his present to the palace he would go to speak to the king, and would then return to the ships. They approved of this, and told him that if he would wait a short time they would return and accompany him to the palace. The captain waited all day, but they never came back. The captain was very wroth at being among so phlegmatic and unreliable a people, and intended, at first, to go to the palace without them. On further consideration, however, he thought it best to wait until the following day. As to us others, we diverted ourselves, singing and dancing to the sound of trumpets, and enjoyed ourselves much.

On Wednesday morning the Moors returned, and took the captain to the palace, and us others with him. The palace was crowded with armed men. Our captain was kept waiting with his conductors for fully four long hours, outside a door, which was only opened when the king sent word to admit him, attended by two men only, whom he might select. The captain said that he desired to have Fernão Martins with him, who could interpret, and his secretary. It seemed to him, as it did to us, that this separation portended no good.

When he had entered, the king said that he had expected him on Tuesday. The captain said that the long road had tired him, and that for this reason he had not come to see him. The king then said that he had told him that he came from a very rich kingdom, and yet had brought him nothing; that he had also told him that he was the bearer of a letter, which had not yet been delivered. To this the captain rejoined that he had brought nothing, because the object of his voyage was merely to make discoveries, but that when other ships came he would then see what they brought him; as to the letter, it was true that he had brought one, and would deliver it immediately.

The king then asked what it was he had come to discover: stones or men? If he came to discover men, as he said, why had he brought nothing? Moreover, he had been told that he carried with him the golden image of a Santa Maria. The captain said that the Santa Maria was not of gold, and that even if she were he would not part with her, as she had guided him across the ocean, and would guide him back to his own country. The king then asked for the letter. The captain said that he begged as a favour, that as the Moors wished him ill and might misinterpret him, a Christian able to speak Arabic should be sent for. The king said this was well, and at once sent for a young man, of small stature, whose name was Quaram. The captain then said that he had two letters, one written in his own language and the other in that of the Moors; that he was able to read the former, and knew that it contained nothing but what would prove acceptable; but that as to the other he was unable to read it, and it might be good, or contain something that was erroneous. As the Christian was unable to *read* Moorish, four Moors took the letter and read it between them, after which they translated it to the king, who was well satisfied with its contents.

The king then asked what kind of merchandise was to be found in his country. The captain said there was much corn, cloth, iron, bronze, and many other things. The king asked whether he had any merchandise with him. The captain replied that he had a little of each sort, as samples, and that if permitted to return to the ships he would order it to be landed, and that meantime four or five men would remain at the lodgings assigned them. The king said no! He might take all his people with him, securely moor his ships, land his merchandise, and sell it to the best advantage. Having taken leave of the king the captain returned to his lodgings, and we with him. . . .

Trade Difficulties

Five days afterwards [on June 7] the captain sent word to the king that, although . . . he had landed his merchandise as he had been ordered, . . . the Moors only came to depreciate it. . . . The Moors no longer visited the house where the merchandise was, but they bore us no good-will, and when one of us landed they spat on the ground, saying: "Portugal, Portugal." Indeed from the very first they had sought means to take and kill us.

When the captain found that the merchandise found no buyers at that place, he applied to the king for permission to forward it to Calicut. The king at once ordered the *bale* to get a sufficient number of men who were to carry the whole on their backs to Calicut. . . .

On Sunday, the 24th of June, being the day of St. John the Baptist, the merchandise left for Calicut. . . . We did not, however, effect these sales at the prices hoped for when we arrived at Moncobiquy [Mozambique], for a very fine shirt which in Portugal fetches 300 reis, was worth here only two fanôes, which is equivalent only to 30 reis, for 30 reis in this country is a big sum. And just as we sold shirts cheaply so we sold other things, in order to take some things away from this country, if only for samples. . . .

Departure

When the time arrived for our departure the captain-major sent a present to the king, consisting of amber, corals, and many other things. At the same time he ordered the king to be informed that he desired to leave for Portugal, and that if the king would send some people with him to the King of Portugal, he would leave behind him a factor, a clerk and some other men, in charge of the merchandise. In return for the present he begged on behalf of his lord [the King of Portugal] for a bahar of cinnamon, a bahar of cloves, as also samples of such other spices as he thought proper, saying that the factor would pay for them, if he desired it.

Four days were allowed to pass after the dispatch of this message before speech could be had with the king. And when the bearer of it entered the place where the king was, he (the king) looked at him with a "bad face," and asked what he wanted. The bearer then delivered his message, as explained above, and then referred to the present which had been sent. The king said that what he brought ought to have been sent to his factor, and that he did not want to look at it. He then desired the captain to be informed that as he wished to depart he should pay him 600 xerafins [about $625], and that then he might go: this was the custom of the country and of those who came to it. . . .

We . . . felt grieved that a Christian king, to whom we had given of ours, should do us such an ill turn. At the same time we did not hold him as culpable as he seemed to be, for we were well aware that the Moors of the place, who were merchants from Mecca and elsewhere, and who knew us, could ill digest us. They had told the king that we were thieves, and that if once we navigated to his country, no more ships from Mecca, nor from Quambaye [Cambay], nor from Ingros, nor from any other part, would visit him. They added that he would derive no profit from this [trade with Portugal] as we had nothing to give, but would rather take away, and that thus his country would be ruined. They, moreover, offered rich bribes to the king to capture and kill us, so that we should not return to Portugal.

31 Spanish Conquest of the Inca Empire

For two decades following Columbus' expeditions it seemed that Spain was destined to rank a poor second in overseas enterprise. Portugal was reaping handsome profits from the spice-laden ships that plied the Cape route, while Spain was receiving disappointingly small returns from her New World possessions. Then came fabulous windfalls of accumulated treasures in the Aztec Empire of Mexico and the Inca Empire of Peru. The story of the conquest of these empires by swashbuckling Spanish adventurers constitutes one of the most colorful, if not the most edifying, chapters of Western history. The classic histories of these freebooting expeditions were written by the nineteenth-century American historian

William H. Prescott. Here he tells how the Inca ruler, Atahualpa, was treacherously captured when he visited the Spanish commander Francisco Pizarro, in November, 1532, and how the Inca Empire was then stripped of its treasures.*

101

Elevated high above his vassals came the Inca Atahuallpa, borne on a sedan or open litter, on which was a sort of throne made of massive gold of inestimable value. The palanquin was lined with the richly-colored plumes of tropical birds and studded with shining plates of gold and silver. The monarch's attire was much richer than on the preceding evening. Round his neck was suspended a collar of emeralds of uncommon size and brilliancy. His short hair was decorated with golden ornaments, and the imperial *borla* [silk diadem] encircled his temples. The bearing of the Inca was sedate and dignified; and from his lofty station he looked down on the multitudes below with an air of composure, like one accustomed to command.

As the leading files of the procession entered the great square, larger says an old chronicler, than any square in Spain, they opened to the right and left for the royal retinue to pass. Every thing was conducted with admirable order. The monarch was permitted to traverse the *plaza* in silence, and not a Spaniard was to be seen. When some five or six thousand of his people had entered the place, Atahuallpa halted, and, turning round with an inquiring look, demanded, "Where are the strangers?"

At this moment Fray Vicente de Valverde, a Dominican friar, Pizarro's chaplain, and afterwards Bishop of Cuzco, came forward with his breviary, or, as other accounts say, a Bible, in one hand, and a crucifix in the other, and, approaching the Inca, told him that he came by order of his commander to expound to him the doctrines of the true faith, for which purpose the Spaniards had come from a great distance to his country. ... The friar concluded with beseeching the Peruvian monarch to receive him kindly, to abjure the errors of his own faith, and embrace that of the Christians now proffered to him, the only one by which he could hope for salvation, and, furthermore, to acknowledge himself a tributary of the Emperor Charles the Fifth, who, in that event, would aid and protect him as his loyal vassal.

.   .   .   .   .

The eyes of the Indian monarch flashed fire, and his dark brow grew darker, as he replied, "I will be no man's tributary. I am greater than any prince upon earth. Your emperor may be a great prince; I do not doubt it, when I see that he has sent his subjects so far across the waters; and I am willing to hold him as a brother. As for the Pope of whom you speak, he must be crazy to talk of giving away countries which do not belong to him. For my faith," he continued, "I will not change it. Your own God, as you say, was put to death by the very men whom he created. But mine," he concluded, pointing to his Deity,—then, alas! sinking in glory behind the mountains,—"my God still lives in the heavens and looks down on his children."

He then demanded of Valverde by what authority he had said these things. The friar pointed to the book which he held, as his authority. Atahuallpa, taking it, turned over the pages a moment, then, as the insult he had received probably flashed across his mind, he threw it down with vehemence, and ex-

* W. H. Prescott, *History of the Conquest of Peru* (Philadelphia: Lippincott, 1874), I, 402-13, 420-23, 428, 450-51, 453-55.

claimed, "Tell your comrades that they shall give me an account of their doings in my land. I will not go from here till they have made me full satisfaction for all the wrongs they have committed."

The friar, greatly scandalized by the indignity offered to the sacred volume, stayed only to pick it up, and, hastening to Pizarro, informed him of what had been done, exclaiming, at the same time, "Do you not see that while we stand here wasting our breath in talking with this dog, full of pride as he is, the fields are filling with Indians? Set on, at once; I absolve you." Pizarro saw that the hour had come. He waved a white scarf in the air, the appointed signal. The fatal gun was fired from the fortress. Then, springing into the square, the Spanish captain and his followers shouted the old war-cry of "St. Jago and at them." It was answered by the battle-cry of every Spaniard in the city, as, rushing from the avenues of the great halls in which they were concealed, they poured into the *plaza,* horse and foot, each in his own dark column, and threw themselves into the midst of the Indian crowd. The latter, taken by surprise, stunned by the report of artillery and muskets, the echoes of which reverberated like thunder from the surrounding buildings, and blinded by the smoke which rolled in sulphurous volumes along the square, were seized with a panic. They knew not whither to fly for refuge from the coming ruin. Nobles and commoners,—all were trampled down under the fierce charge of the cavalry, who dealt their blows, right and left, without sparing; while their swords, flashing through the thick gloom, carried dismay into the hearts of the wretched natives, who now for the first time saw the horse and his rider in all their terrors. They made no resistance,—as, indeed, they had no weapons with which to make it. Every avenue to escape was closed, for the entrance to the square was choked up with the dead bodies of men who had perished in vain efforts to fly. . . .

. . . . .

The Indian monarch, stunned and bewildered, saw his faithful subjects falling around him without fully comprehending his situation. The litter on which he rode heaved to and fro, as the mighty press swayed backwards and forwards; and he gazed on the overwhelming ruin, like some forlorn mariner, who, tossed about in his bark by the furious elements, sees the lightning's flash and hears the thunder bursting around him with the consciousness that he can do nothing to avert his fate. At length, weary with the work of destruction, the Spaniards, as the shades of evening grew deeper, felt afraid that the royal prize might, after all, elude them; and some of the cavaliers made a desperate attempt to end the affray at once by taking Atahuallpa's life. But Pizarro, who was nearest his person, called out, with stentorian voice, "Let no one who values his life strike at the Inca;" and, stretching out his arm to shield him, received a wound on the hand from one of his own men,—the only wound received by a Spaniard in the action.

The struggle now became fiercer than ever round the royal litter. It reeled more and more, and at length, several of the nobles who supported it having been slain, it was overturned, and the Indian prince would have come with violence to the ground, had not his fall been broken by the efforts of Pizarro and some other of the cavaliers, who caught him in their arms. The imperial *borla* was instantly snatched from his temples by a soldier named Estete, and the unhappy monarch, strongly secured, was removed to a neighboring building, where he was carefully guarded.

All attempt at resistance now ceased. The fate of the Inca soon spread over town and country. The charm which might have held the Peruvians together was dissolved. Every man thought only of his own safety. Even the soldiery encamped on the adjacent fields took the alarm, and, learning the fatal tidings, were seen flying in every direction before their pursuers, who in the heat of triumph showed no touch of mercy. At length night, more pitiful than man, threw her friendly mantle over the fugitives, and the scattered troops of Pizarro rallied once more at the sound of the trumpet in the bloody square of Caxamalca.

. . . . .

It was not long before Atahuallpa discovered, amidst all the show of religious zeal in his Conquerors, a lurking appetite more potent in most of their bosoms than either religion or ambition. This was the love of gold. He determined to avail himself of it to procure his own freedom. . . .

In the hope, therefore, to effect his purpose by appealing to the avarice of his keepers, he one day told Pizarro that if he would set him free he would engage to cover the floor of the apartment on which they stood with gold. Those present listened with an incredulous smile; and, as the Inca received no answer, he said, with some emphasis, that "he would not merely cover the floor, but would fill the room with gold as high as he could reach;" and, standing on tiptoe, he stretched out his hand against the wall. All stared with amazement; while they regarded it as the insane boast of a man too eager to procure his liberty to weigh the meaning of his words. Yet Pizarro was sorely perplexed. As he had advanced into the country, much that he had seen, and all that he had heard, had confirmed the dazzling reports first received of the riches of Peru. Atahuallpa himself had given him the most glowing picture of the wealth of the capital, where the roofs of the temples were plated with gold, while the walls were hung with tapestry and the floors inlaid with tiles of the same precious metal. There must be some foundation for all this. At all events, it was safe to accede to the Inca's proposition; since by so doing he could collect at once all the gold at his disposal, and thus prevent its being purloined or secreted by the natives. He therefore acquiesced in Atahuallpa's offer, and, drawing a red line along the wall at the height which the Inca had indicated, he caused the terms of the proposal to be duly recorded by the notary. The apartment was about seventeen feet broad, by twenty-two feet long, and the line round the walls was nine feet from the floor. This space was to be filled with gold; but it was understood that the gold was not to be melted down into ingots, but to retain the original form of the articles into which it was manufactured, that the Inca might have the benefit of the space which they occupied. He further agreed to fill an adjoining room of smaller dimensions twice full with silver, in like manner; and he demanded two months to accomplish all this.

No sooner was this arrangement made than the Inca despatched couriers to Cuzco and the other principal places in the kingdom, with orders that the gold ornaments and utensils should be removed from the royal palaces, and from the temples and other public buildings, and transported without loss of time to Caxamalca. . . .

But the distances were great, and the returns came in slowly. They consisted, for the most part, of massive pieces of plate, some of which weighed two or three *arrobas,*—a Spanish weight of twenty-five pounds. On some days, articles of the value of thirty or forty thousand *pesos de oro* were brought in, and, occasionally, of the value of fifty or even sixty thousand *pesos*. The greedy eyes of the Conquerors gloated on the shining heaps of treasure, which were transported on the shoulders of the Indian porters, and, after being carefully registered, were placed in safe deposit under a strong guard.

· · · · ·

... Without further delay, the division of the treasure was agreed upon. Yet, before making this, it was necessary to reduce the whole to ingots of a uniform standard, for the spoil was composed of an infinite variety of articles, in which the gold was of very different degrees of purity. These articles consisted of goblets, ewers, salvers, vases of every shape and size, ornaments and utensils for the temples and the royal palaces, tiles and plates for the decoration of the public edifices, curious imitations of different plants and animals. Among the plants, the most beautiful was the Indian corn, in which the golden ear was sheathed in its broad leaves of silver, from which hung a rich tassel of threads of the same precious metal. A fountain was also much admired, which sent up a sparkling jet of gold, while birds and animals of the same material played in the waters at its base. ...

The business of melting down the plate was intrusted to the Indian goldsmiths, who were thus required to undo the work of their own hands. They toiled day and night, but such was the quantity to be recast that it consumed a full month. When the whole was reduced to bars of a uniform standard, they were nicely weighed, under the superintendence of the royal inspectors. The total amount of the gold was found to be one million three hundred and twenty-six thousand five hundred and thirty-nine *pesos de oro,* which, allowing for the greater value of money in the sixteenth century, would be equivalent, probably, at the present time, to near *three millions and a half of pounds sterling,* or somewhat less than *fifteen millions and a half of dollars* [worth approximately 40 million dollars in 1960]. The quantity of silver was estimated at fifty-one thousand six hundred and ten marks. History affords no parallel of such a booty—and that, too, in the most convertible form, in ready money, as it were—having fallen to the lot of a little band of military adventurers, like the Conquerors of Peru.

32 SPANISH COLONIAL POLICY IN THE NEW WORLD

After an initial period of conquest and pillage, the Spaniards had to face the practical problem of administering their vast possessions in the New World. Having no precedent to guide them, they debated lengthily and conscientiously the problem of how to treat the Indians. All agreed that the Indians should be converted to the Catholic faith; but should they be granted legal and political rights? And should the Spanish settlers be allowed to collect tribute and labor service from the Indians? The following selection analyzes the policy that was finally adopted—a policy that made Indian labor available to the Spanish ruling class but also sought to erect safeguards against excessive exploitation. The final outcome was the hybridization of the native and the intruding cultures and the creation of a new Hispano-Indian society.*

* F. V. Scholes, "The Beginnings of Hispano-Indian Society in Yucatan," *Scientific Monthly,* XLIV (June, 1937), 530-38.

FACTORS AFFECTING COLONIAL POLICY.   Spanish colonial policy in America developed naturally from two basic factors: (1) conditions within the areas that were conquered and (2) the ideals and aims of the Spanish monarchy in the sixteenth century.

Although the Spanish colonies were for the most part within the tropical and sub-tropical zones, they contained large areas suitable for European settlement. Colonists in considerable numbers migrated to specially favored regions in New Spain and Peru, where they engaged in farming, stock raising, mining and trade. But the Spaniards found most of these areas already occupied by a numerous aboriginal population with highly developed civilizations based on an advanced agricultural economy. In this respect Hispanic America contrasted rather sharply with the temperate zones in which the British colonies in North America were founded, for the vast expanse of what is now the United States was lightly populated and the Indians were much less strongly rooted to the soil than those of Mexico, Guatemala and Peru. The British were able, therefore, to deal with the Indian tribes as independent units, as nations outside their own colonial system, whereas Spain was forced to incorporate them as an integral part of colonial society. Thus social evolution in Hispanic America has been characterized by the interaction and partial fusion of two races, and two sets of culture patterns, European and aboriginal.

The forces which influenced the formulation of policy dealing with the aborigines and their relations with the Spanish colonists were economic and religious, selfish and humanitarian. The original impelling motive of discovery and colonization was economic, and the exploitation of the resources of the colonies for the benefit of the Crown and of the colonists who supported the imperial system always remained the paramount factor in determining the character of administration. But the long crusade against the Moors had identified the cause of Catholic orthodoxy with national interests, and a militant zeal for the faith inspired the Spanish nation. It was inevitable, therefore, that when the Indies were conquered, the conversion of the aborigines and the extirpation of the older pagan religion and ceremonial should become one of the dominant aims of empire. Moreover, the Spanish jurists of the sixteenth century were inspired by a broad humanitarianism and an increasing interest in the relations between nations and peoples. The question of the aborigines raised important problems of theoretical and practical justice and the influence of the jurists contributed much to the formulation of legislation for the preservation of the liberties of the Indians within the limits imposed by the introduction of a new faith and the maintenance of Spanish supremacy.

The attempt to combine the economic and the ecclesiastico-humanitarian motives of empire created problems of tremendous historical significance. The Crown was obliged to recognize the demands of the colonists for the right to exploit Indian lands and labor, but it sought to limit abuses by protective legislation that would preserve at least the legal status of the Indians as free beings and prevent the total expropriation of Indian property. It sought also to ensure the conversion of the Indians to the Christian faith, at the same time preserving the traditional folk culture in so far as it did not conflict with Christian standards of morals and orthodoxy. Hispanic America became in effect a sociological laboratory where experiments in human relationships were made on a vast scale. The final result was the creation of a Hispano-Indian society characterized by the domination of the masses by a small privileged minority, the hybridization of culture and the existence of unsolved problems of land and labor. . . .

The basic pattern of Hispano-Indian society in Yucatan was clearly marked out by the end of the sixteenth century or about sixty years after the conquest. By that time a new ruling caste of foreign origin, extremely jealous of its privileges, had obtained firm control over the destinies of the Maya race; the exploitation of Indian labor for the benefit of this caste had become an important problem of interracial relations; and a considerable amount of fusion of culture, especially in the realm of religion, had taken place. During the remainder of the colonial period these basic problems of provincial society remained essentially the same. The methods of exploitation of Indian labor changed according to the needs of the ruling class. The proportion of Christian and pagan elements in the total content of belief and ceremonial by which the Indians made their adjustments with the invisible world varied from place to place and from time to time. But there was no essential change in the fundamental character of Hispano-Indian society.

Several centuries prior to the Spanish conquest the Maya of Yucatan had established a measure of political unity. However, rivalry between the chieftains had caused the disintegration of central authority, and at the opening of the sixteenth century Yucatan was divided into a number of petty states or cacicazgos which frequently engaged in interstate warfare. Political leadership within each state tended to be concentrated in the hands of a ruling family, such as the Xius in Mani or the Cocoms in Sotuta. The unifying forces were cultural rather than political—a common language and a common fund of folk tradition.

The Spanish conquest destroyed the independence of these states and re-established territorial and political unity within Yucatan, but the reins of government were held henceforth by an alien race. Supreme political and military authority was exercised by the Spanish governors appointed by the Crown. Subordinate to the governors were various local officers and the governing councils of the Spanish towns.

A measure of self-government was retained by the Maya in the Indian villages where local affairs continued to be controlled by native officers. In the beginning the Spanish authorities recognized the claims of former native lords and lesser nobles, and retained them as governors and principals of the pueblos. Moreover, during the sixteenth century certain chieftains even continued to exercise some leadership over areas that approximated the former petty states. But in the course of time the old rulers and their direct descendants were gradually removed from positions of influence and leadership.

This does not mean that the former ruling families lost all their old prestige. The Xius, for example, were recognized as having noble rank, and they obtained certain concessions and privileges, such as exemption from tribute, free labor on their farms and the right to possess firearms. They were also able to retain considerable holdings of land. But their influence as political and cultural leaders of the race was at an end.

THE RULING CASTE. The real governing class in Yucatan subsequent to the conquest was a group of about 125 families, made up of conquerors, first settlers and their descendants. Members of this group held most of the subordinate provincial offices, and they dominated the city councils of Merida, Campeche and Valladolid, membership in which could be purchased and held for life. Control of the local councils gave the conquerors and their descendants the means for resisting measures limiting their vested rights. They were frequently able also to force the provincial governor or the defender of the Indians to abandon policies for the amelioration of abuses of native labor and other reforms detrimental to the interests of the ruling caste. Occasionally a provincial governor would try to strengthen his own position by the appointment of relations or personal retainers to local offices, but the conquistador caste would immediately present a forceful protest to the Crown and would usually be upheld. Special claims were also made on behalf of younger sons for preference in appointments to curacies in Indian towns and to offices in the cathedral of Merida.

In so far as possible the conquistadores sought to keep their blood clean, at least the line which inherited property. A few formally contracted marriage with Indian women, but most of the unions between the two races were extra-marital. Mestizo children born out of wedlock were sometimes legitimized, but the ruling caste used all its influence to prevent them from holding office.

ENCOMIENDAS.   The most important privilege granted to the conquerors and their descendants in all parts of the Indies was preference in appointment to encomiendas. During the first half of the sixteenth century an encomienda grant was essentially the right to use the labor of a stated group of Indians without pay. But this led to such abuses that a fixed tribute usually payable in kind was introduced in lieu of service, with the result that the encomiendas became a form of pension. The encomenderos were always able, of course, to obtain a considerable amount of labor from their Indians by extra-legal means, but subsequent to 1550 the essence of the system was tribute.

In return for the tribute payments the encomenderos were supposed to assume responsibility for the indoctrination of their Indians, but this obligation became a mere formality in so far as personal assistance in the missionary program was concerned. The most important obligation imposed by a grant of encomienda was military service, and in Yucatan the encomenderos were frequently called upon to defend the coasts or the port of Campeche against foreign corsairs. Grants of encomienda were made for two lives or generations, but a third life was usually permitted by dissimulation on the part of the governing officials.

In Mexico proper, *i.e.,* in the area northwest of the Isthmus of Tehuantepec, about 55 per cent. of the Indian pueblos were held in encomienda, the remaining 45 per cent. paying tribute to the Crown. In Yucatan more than 90 per cent. of the towns were granted as encomiendas. This fact may be explained by the limited resources of Yucatan and the lack of opportunity for profitable enterprise other than agriculture. There were no mines; trade was limited mostly to dealings in those very native products of which the tribute payments were comprised, *viz.,* cotton cloth, maize, poultry and wax. In the sixteenth century grants of encomienda were practically the only means available for gratifying services performed during the conquest or for attracting new settlers to the province.

It is not surprising, therefore, that there was keen rivalry for appointments to encomiendas, that the tendency of a governor to fill vacancies by choosing new arrivals in preference to members of the old families was always bitterly resisted, or that protests were made against every attempt by the Crown to bring the system to an end. Grants of encomienda continued to be made until 1785, when the Crown finally ordered all tributes to be paid into the treasury, but even then payments continued to be made to former holders of encomiendas during the remainder of their lives. . . .

SYSTEM OF FORCED LABOR.   When the Crown ordered the abolition of the labor phases of the encomienda system, it had to provide some substitute, as the colonists were dependent on the natives for house servants, unskilled laborers for various services, burden bearers and semi-skilled artisans for house building and public works. The Spaniards were free to employ all the labor they needed at the current rate of wages, but the supply of Indians willing to work, even for pay, was often inadequate. Consequently, the Crown found it necessary to authorize a system of forced labor by which quotas of workers were summoned periodically from the Indian pueblos to serve in the mines, on farms, on building operations or in workshops of various kinds. For this labor they received wages at a fixed rate. This system of forced labor was generally applied in all parts of the Indies.

·   ·   ·   ·   ·

EFFECT OF CHRISTIAN RELIGION.   The introduction of the Christian religion had just as profound effects on the traditional folk culture as the loss of political independence or the imposition of a system of tribute and labor which made the Maya "hewers of wood and drawers of water" for an alien race. It may have required an even greater degree of adjustment for the Maya to accept a new religious faith than to change political rulers.

The temple worship with its traditional ritual was the most highly formalized part of native religion, and the priestly class, as custodians of that knowledge which enabled them to perform the traditional ceremonies at proper intervals and to mediate between the people and the powers of the invisible world, exercised tremendous influence. But every individual, as he followed the daily round of life, planted his milpa, shared in the communal hunt, tended his bees and faced the crises of life, performed a series of acts that were religious or had implications of a religious character. The old tradition provided him with explanations for the phenomena of nature and the means of propitiating supernatural powers. It gave him standards of conduct and answers to the riddle of life.

And now, suddenly, he was informed that these traditional modes of life were wrong. A new God, new ceremonial practices, a new priesthood and new standards of conduct were offered to him—indeed forced upon him. That the new faith brought to the Maya definite benefits is too self-evident to require discussion. But it also had powerful repercussions on Maya life and folk achievement which we are likely to forget.

THE MISSIONARY PROGRAM.   The missionary program had two phases— the positive and the negative. The positive phase included the teaching of a few essential elements of Christian faith and ceremonial; the negative consisted of measures to destroy the old cult, and, in so far as possible, the confidence of the Indians in the efficacy of the old ways.

The diocesan instructions of the first bishop, Fray Francisco de Toral, set forth the essential aims of the mission program in this early period. The Indians were to be baptized as rapidly as possible after receiving some instruction in the new faith. This instruction should emphasize such fundamental concepts as the belief in one God, the nature of the Trinity, the Incarnation and the Virgin Birth. A few prayers were to be taught, such as the Pater Noster and the Ave Maria, and these were to be followed by the Creed. Reverence for the Cross, respect for the clergy and punctual attendance at mass were stressed. Persons in danger of death were to be given general con-

fession and called upon to renounce the devil and the idols by which he deceived men. Especial care was to be exercised in teaching the true character
of the sacrament of marriage, and the degrees of carnal and spiritual relationship within which marriage was prohibited.

But even these few essentials involved a drastic change in the religious life
of the natives, and the Spanish authorities, secular as well as ecclesiastical,
realized that only by utmost vigilance could this minimum program succeed.
The greatest threat to the new ways was the influence of the native priests
and caciques and the continued practice of pagan ritual. Consequently the
negative phase of the missionary program was hardly less important than the
positive. The celebration of Indian festivals at night was expressly forbidden,
those performed during the day were carefully supervised and the wearing of
old ceremonial costumes prohibited. Secret gatherings in the houses of caciques
were not permitted, lest these meetings be made a means of perpetuating the
knowledge of the old ways and the influence of the native leaders. The custom of employing a casamentero, or native marriage maker, was forbidden,
as a means of ensuring the free character of Christian marriage. Body painting and the use of ear-plugs and nose ornaments were prohibited.

Enforcement of mission discipline required constant vigilance and effective
disciplinary measures. The form often employed for serious offenses was corporal punishment. Persistent offenders were frequently banished from the
pueblos, and from time to time the clergy, in conjunction with civil authority,
exacted even more stringent punishment, especially for cases involving practice of the forms of idolatry.

. . . . .

By discrediting the former political and religious officers the authorities
were attacking the intellectual leaders of the race. These men were the custodians of the complicated chronology and hieroglyphic writing which were
such essential elements of the whole body of folk tradition. By holding them
up to public humiliation, by a definite process of eliminating them from positions of influence and authority, by banishing them from their traditional
haunts, by forcing them to practice their profession in secret, if at all, the civil
and ecclesiastical authorities were striking a serious blow at some of the greatest achievements of the race. . . .

OLD FAITH NOT WHOLLY DESTROYED. But despite the stern measures for
the punishment of idolatry taken in 1562 and on other occasions later in the
century, a considerable amount of folk religion survived as part of the everyday life of the people. What was lost was the temple ritual and the learning
of the caciques and priests. The net result was to impose a veneer of Christian
practice without wholly destroying the old faith.

The reasons for the failure completely to substitute the new faith for the
old are numerous. During the first century after the conquest there was a
lack of clergy. A single friar or secular priest sometimes administered a parish
of several thousand. Moreover, the language problem was never surmounted.
The village schools did not succeed in teaching Spanish to more than a small
proportion of the Maya. Many of the clergy, it is true, learned the native language, but due to the fact that a large number of priests, especially in the
Franciscan Order, were recruited in Spain, it may be doubted whether more
than 60 per cent. of the clergy were proficient in Maya at any given time.
Frequent petitions were made asking the Crown to order preference for clergy

born in Yucatan in appointments to curacies, but during the first two centuries these petitions had little effect. Rivalry between the secular and regular clergy also reduced the effectiveness of the small and inadequately trained group available for the missions. Moreover, the lack of cooperation on the part of the civil authorities and the eager desire of officials and colonists alike to exploit Indian labor hindered the progress of the missionary program from the beginning. Finally, we must not forget that there was always a means of escape for the Indian who refused to accept the new regime. Hundreds escaped into the central part of Yucatan, where they could practice the old religion without interference from the Spanish clergy or civil authorities. And these settlements in the bush became in turn centers from which the folk religion could be "bootlegged" back into the conquered area.

The fate of the Maya was essentially the same as that of other aboriginal populations which have been brought into contact with a more advanced civilization. The influence of the intellectual leaders was gradually lessened. But everyday elements of culture, the language, the simple agricultural economy and a body of superstition that was preserved under the surface of a new cult remained, due largely to the inertia and powers of resistance of the masses.

Chapter Seven

West European expansion:
Dutch, French, British phase, 1600-1763

AMERICAN TREASURE AND THE
RISE OF NORTHWESTERN EUROPE 33

The sixteenth was the Iberian century. Spain and Portugal domi-
nated overseas enterprise and received vast profits from the spice trade
with the East and from the silver mines of the New World. But Iberian
predominance did not endure. Spain and Portugal gave way to Holland,
France, and Britain. Why northwestern Europe rose to a position of
leadership is an intriguing, basic question, answered in part by Professor
Hamilton's study * of the effects of American bullion on Europe's econ-
omy. The influx of treasure is shown to be a stimulant to capital accumu-
lation in northwestern Europe and a financial basis for economic growth.

The present paper purposes to examine the effects of the discovery of an all-water route to the East Indies, the opening of extensive markets in the New World, and above all the heavy European
imports of Mexican and Peruvian treasure upon the rise of modern
capitalism. For two reasons the study is confined to the sixteenth
and seventeenth centuries. First, during this period American gold
and silver and the markets of the East and West Indies exerted
their greatest influence upon the progress of capitalism. Second,
there was a significant development of capitalism in England, France,
and the Low Countries. In fact, the progress of capitalism during
the sixteenth and seventeenth centuries prepared the way for the
Industrial Revolution. Significant experiments with the factory sys-

---

* E. J. Hamilton, "American Treasure and the Rise of Capitalism (1500-
1700)," *Economica* (November, 1929), pp. 338-56.

tem were carried out in England in the sixteenth century and in France during the seventeenth. There is abundant evidence of a groping toward the factory system before the great inventions of the eighteenth century made such a course inevitable. ...

Capitalism did not develop out of a void during the early modern period. There were traces of it in the great nations of antiquity, and near the end of the Middle Ages it played an important role in the economy of Flanders, the Italian city states, and certain French cities. In these oases, especially in the great industrial, commercial, and financial centres of Italy—Amalfi, Pisa, Genoa, Florence, and Venice—many of the characteristic features of modern capitalism evolved. Arabic notation, destined to supersede cumbersome Roman numerals in accounting, was introduced. Double-entry bookkeeping, an indispensable instrument for the rational conduct of business, was developed. The mariner's compass, invaluable to ocean shipping, was introduced into the Western World. Portolan charts, later to be combined with the resuscitated theoretical geography of Ptolemy and Strabo to give birth to modern geography, arose to meet the needs of navigation in the Mediterranean. Important advances were achieved in naval architecture and in the art of navigation. Oriental arts and products were diffused through the trading centres of Italy. In the great seaports and in the fairs arose the law merchant—flexible, expeditious, and fashioned to meet the needs of trade. As a concomitant development, negotiable instruments originated or were popularised. Perhaps the development of organised dealings in foreign exchange and advances in the technique of banking by houses located in Genoa, Venice, and Florence—with agents scattered to the utmost confines of Europe—represented the greatest contribution of the Middle Ages to the rise of modern capitalism. These great banking houses aided materially in the perfection of banking and in the spread of the institution into countries where a fully developed species of capitalism was destined to emerge.

Although, as has been shown, many other forces contributed to the rise of modern capitalism, the phenomena associated with the discoveries of America and of the passage around the Cape of Good Hope to the East Indies were the principal factors in this development. Long distance voyages led to increases in the size of vessels and improvements in the instruments and technique of navigation analogous to the recent advances in aviation stimulated by transatlantic flying. As Adam Smith pointed out, the widening of the market facilitated division of labour and led to technological improvements. The introduction of new agricultural commodities from America and of new agricultural and manufactured goods, especially luxury products, from the East stimulated greater industrial activity to provide the wherewithal to pay for them. Emigration to colonies in the New World and to settlements in the East lessened the pressure of population upon the soil of the mother countries and thus enhanced the surplus—the excess of national production over national subsistence—from which savings could be drawn. The opening of distant markets and sources of supply for raw materials was a significant factor in the transfer of the control of industry and commerce from the guilds to capitalist employers. The old guild organisation—unable to cope with the new problems in purchasing, production, and marketing—commenced to disintegrate and finally gave way to the capitalist employer, a more efficient medium of control.

Let us turn to the greatest influence that the discovery of America had upon the progress of capitalism, to the vast influx of gold and silver from American mines. . . .

All the great colonising powers of the early modern period sought gold and silver. Greed for treasure was one of the greatest stimuli to colonisation, but Spain alone was successful in her quest. As early as 1503 Spain commenced to receive gold from Hispaniola with surprising regularity and shortly afterwards from Cuba and Porto Rico as well. Bating the driblets of gold from the region around Panama after 1513, no treasure came from the American continent before November 5th, 1519, when the first Aztec spoils reached Spain. Some fifteen years later the motherland began to enjoy Incan booty sent by Pizarro. Though the conquests of Mexico and Peru, with the resultant robbery, are among the most dramatic episodes in human history, the treasure obtained in this way was—contrary to general opinion—a mere bagatelle in comparison with the receipts from mining at a later date, especially after the discoveries of the renowned silver mines at Potosí, Guanajuato, and Zacatecas and the perfection of the amalgamation process for extracting silver, all of which occurred between 1545 and 1560. From the middle of the sixteenth century to the 'thirties of the seventeenth the treasure of the Indies poured into the motherland at a rate that exceeded the most fantastic dreams of the *conquistadores*. Thereafter the stream of gold and silver lessened considerably, but did not cease entirely. . . .

Undoubtedly the discovery of the Good Hope passage to the fabled Spice Islands would have stimulated trade in any event, but the physical barriers to transportation and the political throttling of trade along former routes by the Ottoman Turk were not the only obstacles to be overcome. For some inexplicable reason Orientals have always had a penchant for hoarding treasure. Hence, even in response to a protracted inflow of specie, Oriental prices, unlike those of the Western World, did not rise sufficiently to induce a counter flow. For more than two thousand years the East has proved a necropolis for European gold and silver. The seventeenth-century pamphleteers who in tract after tract denounced the English East India Company for draining away the country's treasure were not mistaken as to the facts. European products were carried to the East, but silver was the commodity that could be exchanged for Oriental goods on the most advantageous terms. So treasure flowed from Portugal, Holland, England, and France to the Orient in exchange for the eagerly sought spices and luxury goods of that region. Notwithstanding the enormous profits obtained in the East India trade, the passage around the Cape of Good Hope might have been rendered nugatory by a dearth of specie but for the vast streams of Mexican and Peruvian silver flowing into Europe. The voyage of Columbus was an imperative supplement to that of da Gama.

For about two thousand years monopoly of the East India trade—a trade that has always enriched the nations able to control it—has been an object of policy and a prize of diplomacy. But in the first two and a half centuries after the voyages of da Gama and Columbus the struggle for hegemony in the East Indies was intensified manyfold. Not only did statesmen precipitate or sanction sanguinary wars, but writers counselled aggression as a means of achieving political and economic ascendancy. Did the profits of the trade justify this rivalry?

From the very beginning of the modern era trade with the East Indies by the Cape route was almost incredibly lucrative. It is difficult to find in the annals of business either greater profits that those obtained on some of the early voyages to the Spice Islands or records of sustained earnings that surpass those of the English and Dutch East India Companies during the seventeenth century. "Da Gama returned to Lisbon in 1499 with a cargo which repaid sixty times the cost of the expedition," affording a profit of about 6,000 per cent. The Victoria, sole survivor of the memorable fleet of Magellan, brought back to Spain 556.72 quintals of spice, of which 501.35 were sold in Seville at 42 ducats per quintal. If we assume that the remaining 55.37 quintals were saleable—and at the same price—, the cargo was worth 23,382.24 ducats, a sum comparable to the value of the specie borne by the average treasure ship at that time. I know of no satisfactory account of the profits Portugal obtained from commerce with the East in the sixteenth century, during most of which she was in the ascendency; but such figures are not wanting for Holland—the nation upon which the Portuguese mantle fell in the seventeenth century. The Dutch East India Company, organised in 1602, was a highly successful enterprise until the close of the seventeenth century. "For nearly two hundred years it declared dividends ranging from 12½ per cent. to 20, 40, or even 50 per cent.; the average dividend from 1602 to 1796 was over 18 per cent." The earnings of the English East India Company were stupendous. On some of the early voyages profits of 195, 221, 311, 318, and 334 per cent. were realised. During the seventeenth century dividends averaged about 100:21 per cent. . . .

The enormous profits obtained from the East India trade doubtless contributed powerfully to capital formation and thus to the rise of modern capitalism. The bulk of savings at the present time come directly or indirectly from individuals with high incomes, and presumably this has always been true. Therefore the profits of the Dutch and English East India Companies, not to mention those of interlopers engaged in the same trade, must have afforded considerable stimulus to saving. Bating loans to Governments and ecclesiastical organisations, most of the savings were invested in commercial, industrial, or financial enterprises. . . .

The price revolution set in motion by American gold and silver contributed directly to the progress of capitalism. . . .

In England and France the vast discrepancy between prices and wages, born of the price revolution, deprived labourers of a large part of the incomes they had hitherto enjoyed, and diverted this wealth to the recipients of other distributive shares. As has been shown, rents, as well as wages, lagged behind prices, so landlords gained nothing from labour's loss. For a period of almost two hundred years English and French capitalists—and presumably those of other economically advanced countries—must have enjoyed incomes analogous to those American profiteers reaped from a similar divergence between prices and wages from 1916 to 1919. . . .

The windfalls thus received, along with gains from the East India trade, furnished the means to build up capital equipment, and the stupendous profits obtainable supplied an incentive for the feverish pursuit of capitalistic enterprise. We find, as might be expected, that during the seventeenth and latter part of the sixteenth centuries England, France, and the Low Countries were seething with such genuinely capitalistic phenomena as systematic mechanical invention, company formation, and speculation in the shares of financial and trading concerns. The developments of this period, accelerated and fructified by the important series of mechanical inventions in the last half of the eighteenth century, were a significant step in the direction of the modern factory system, with the concomitant developments in commerce and finance.

The riches won by the Spaniards in America and by the Portuguese in the East Indies encouraged other Europeans to seek new routes to Cathay. The English sent out several expeditions in search of a northwest or a northeast passage to the East; all these attempts failed, for the navigators of that period were unable, with their equipment, to find the way through the ice-dotted seas capping North America and Russia. One of these expeditions, however, did yield practical results when it reached the kingdom of Muscovy and established for the first time direct relations between that kingdom and Western Europe. The commander of the expedition, Richard Chancellor, narrated his experiences to a certain Clement Adams, from whose account the following selections are taken. They reveal the motives behind the expedition, the manner in which Muscovy was found, the nature of the court and the ruler in Moscow, and the endurance of the Russian soldiers.*

At what time our Marchants perceived the commodities and wares of England to bee in small request with the countreys and people about us, and neere unto us, and that those Marchandizes which strangers in the time and memorie of our auncesters did earnestly seeke and desire, were nowe neglected, and the price thereof abated, although by us carried to their owne portes, and all forreine Marchandises in great accompt, and their prises wonderfully raised: certaine grave Citizens of London, and men of great wisedome, and carefull for the good of their Countrey, began to thinke with themselves, howe this mischiefe might bee remedied. Neither was a remedie (as it then appeared) wanting to their desires, for the avoyding of so great an inconvenience: for seeing that the wealth of the Spaniards and Portingales, by the discoverie and search of newe trades and Countreys was marveilously increased, supposing the same to be a course and meane for them also to obteine the like, they thereupon resolved upon a newe and strange Navigation. And whereas at the same time one Sebastian Cabota, a man in those dayes very renowned, happened to bee in London, they began first of all to deale and consult diligently with him, and after much speech and conference together, it was at last concluded that three shippes should bee prepared and furnished out, for the search and discoverie of the Northerne part of the world, to open a way and passage to our men for travaile to newe and unknowen kingdomes. ...

To conclude, when they sawe their desire and hope of the arrivall of the rest of the shippes to be every day more and more frustrated, they provided to sea againe, and Master Chanceler held on his course towards that un-

* R. Hakluyt, *The Principal Navigations, Voyages, Traffiques and Discoveries of the English Nation* (Glasgow: J. MacLehose, 1903), II, 239-59.

knowen part of the world, and sailed so farre, that hee came at last to the place where hee found no night at all, but a continuall light and brightnesse of the Sunne shining clerely upon the huge and mightie Sea. And having the benefite of this perpetuall light for certaine dayes, at the length it pleased God to bring them into a certaine great Bay, which was of one hundreth miles or thereabout over. Whereinto they entered, and somewhat farre within it cast ancre, and looking every way about them, it happened that they espied a farre off a certaine fisher boate, which Master Chanceler, accompanied with a fewe of his men, went towards to common with the fishermen that were in it, and to knowe of them what Countrey it was, and what people, and of what maner of living they were: but they being amazed with the strange greatnesse of his shippe, (for in those partes before that time they had never seene the like) beganne presently to avoyde and to flee: but hee still following them at last overtooke them, and being come to them, they (being in great feare, as men halfe dead) prostrated themselves before him, offering to kisse his feete: but hee (according to his great and singular courtesie,) looked pleasantly upon them, comforting them by signes and gestures, refusing those dueties and reverences of theirs, and taking them up in all loving sort from the ground. And it is strange to consider howe much favour afterwards in that place, this humanitie of his did purchase to himselfe. For they being dismissed spread by and by a report abroad of the arrivall of a strange nation, of a singular gentlenesse and courtesie: whereupon the common people came together offering to these newe-come ghests victuals freely, and not refusing to traffique with them, except they had bene bound by a certaine religious use and custome, not to buy any forreine commodities, without the knowledge and consent of the king.

By this time our men had learned that this Countrey was called Russia, or Moscovie, and that Ivan Vasiliwich (which was at that time their Kings name) ruled and governed farre and wide in those places. . . .

Nowe while these things were a doing, they secretly sent a messenger unto the Emperour, to certifie him of the arrivall of a strange nation, and withall to knowe his pleasure concerning them. Which message was very welcome unto him, insomuch that voluntarily hee invited them to come to his Court. . . .

The Empire and government of the King is very large, and his wealth at this time exceeding great. And because the citie of Mosco is the chiefest of al the rest, it seemeth of it selfe to challenge the first place in this discourse. Our men say, that in bignesse it is as great as the Cities of London, with the suburbes thereof. There are many and great buildings in it, but for beautie and fairenesse, nothing comparable to ours. There are many Townes and Villages also, but built out of order, and with no hansomnesse: their streetes and wayes are not paved with stone as ours are: the walles of their houses are of wood: the roofes for the most part are covered with shingle boords. There is hard by the Citie a very faire Castle, [the Kremlin] strong, and furnished with artillerie, whereunto the Citie is joyned directly towards the North, with a bricke wall: the walles also of Castle are built with bricke, and are in breadth or thickenesse eighteene foote. This Castle hath on the one side a drie ditch, on the other side the river Moscua, whereby it is made almost inexpugnable. The same Moscua trending towards the East doth admit into it the companie of the river Occa.

In the Castle aforesaide, there are in number nine Churches, or Chappels, not altogether unhansome, which are used and kept by certaine religious men, over whom there is after a sort, a Patriarke, or Governour, and with him other reverend Fathers, all which for the greater part, dwell within the Castle. . . .

Nowe after that they had remained about twelve dayes in the Cities, there was then a Messenger sent unto them, to bring them to the Kings house: and they being after a sort wearied with their long stay, were very ready, and willing so to doe: and being entred within the gates of the Court, there sate a very honorable companie of Courtiers, to the number of one hundred, all apparelled in cloth of golde, downe to their ankles: and therehence being conducted into the chamber of presence, our men beganne to wonder at the Majestie of the Emperour: his seate was aloft, in a very royall throne, having on his head a Diademe, or Crowne of golde, apparelled with a robe all of Goldsmiths worke, and in his hand he held a Scepter garnished, and beset with precious stones: and besides all other notes and apparances of honour, there was a Majestie in his countenance proportionable with the excellencie of his estate: on the one side of him stood his chiefe Secretarie, on the other side, the great Commander of silence, both of them arayed also in cloth of gold: and then there sate the Counsel of one hundred and fiftie in number, all in like sort arayed, and of great state. This so honorable an assemblie, so great a Majestie of the Emperour, and of the place might very well have amazed our men, and have dasht them out of countenance: but notwithstanding Master Chanceler being therewithall nothing dismaied saluted, and did his duetie to the Emperour, after the maner of England, and withall, delivered unto him the letters of our king, Edward the sixt. The Emperour having taken, & read the letters, began a litle to question with them, and to aske them of the welfare of our king: whereunto our men answered him directly, & in few words: hereupon our men presented some thing to the Emperour. . . .

They are a kinde of people most sparing in diet, and most patient in extremitie of cold, above all others. For when the ground is covered with snowe, and is growen terrible and hard with the frost, this Russe hangs up his mantle, or souldiers coate, against that part from whence the winde and Snowe drives, and so making a little fire, lieth downe with his backe towards the weather: this mantle of his serves him for his bed, wall, house and all: his drinke is colde water of the river, mingled with oatemeale, and this is all his good cheere, and he thinketh himselfe well, and daintily fedde therewith, and so sitteth downe by his fire, and upon the hard ground, rosteth as it were his wearie sides thus daintily stuffed: the hard ground is his feather bed, & some blocke or stone his pillow: and as for his horse, he is as it were a chamberfellow with his master, faring both alike. How justly may this barbarous, and rude Russe condemne the daintinesse and nicenesse of our Captaines, who living in a soile & aire much more temperate, yet commonly use furred boots, and clokes?

Britain's American Colonies and Their Independent Spirit 35

Britain's American colonies were unique in that they had vigorous representative institutions; England, unlike France and the Iberian countries, had embarked upon the settlement of colonies in a period when representative government was flourishing in the mother country. As the colonies grew in strength, their repre-

sentative assemblies asserted with increasing boldness their demand for autonomy, especially in trade matters. British imperial legislation required that virtually all colonial produce be exported to England in English ships. The colonists ignored this and sent their produce wherever it fetched the highest prices in whatever ships (usually Dutch) charged the lowest rates. The following "Remonstrance to the Board of Trade," * passed by the Rhode Island legislature on January 24, 1764, expresses the colonial views on these matters, and illustrates the strength and assertiveness of representative institutions in Britain's American colonies.

The colony of Rhode Island included not a much larger extent of territory than about thirty miles square; and of this, a great part is a barren soil, not worth the expense of cultivation; the number of souls in it, amount to forty-eight thousand, of which the two sea-port towns of Newport and Providence, contain near one-third. The colony hath no staple commodity for exportation, and does not raise provisions sufficient for its own consumption; yet, the goodness of its harbors, and its convenient situation for trade, agreeing with the spirit and industry of the people, hath in some measure supplied the deficiency of its natural produce, and provided the means of subsistence to its inhabitants.

By a moderate calculation, the quantity of British manufactures and other goods of every kind imported from Great Britain, and annually consumed in this colony, amount at least to £120,000, sterling, part of which is imported directly into the colony; but as remittances are more easily made to the neighboring provinces of the Massachusetts Bay, Pennsylvania and New York, than to Great Britain, a considerable part is purchased from them.

This sum of £120,000, sterling, may be considered as a debt due from the colony, the payment of which is the great object of every branch of commerce, carried on by its inhabitants, and exercises the skill and invention of every trader.

The only articles produced in the colony, suitable for a remittance to Europe, consist of some flax seed and oil, and some few ships built for sale; the whole amounting to about £5,000, sterling, per annum. The other articles furnished by the colony for exportation, are some lumber, cheese and horses; the whole amount of all which together bears but a very inconsiderable proportion to the debt contracted for British goods. It can therefore be nothing but commerce which enables us to pay it.

As there is no commodity raised in the colony suitable for the European market, but the few articles aforementioned; and as the other goods raised for exportation, will answer at no market but in the West Indies, it necessarily follows that the trade thither must be the foundation of all our commerce; and it is undoubtedly true, that solely from the prosecution of this trade with the other branches that are pursued in consequence of it, arises the ability to pay for such quantities of British goods.

It appears from the custom house books, in Newport, that from January, 1763, to January, 1764, there were one hundred and eighty-four sail of vessels bound on foreign voyages; that is, to Europe, Africa and the West Indies; and three hundred and fifty-two sail of vessels employed in the coast-

---

* *Records of the Colony of Rhode Island and Providence Plantations, in New England* (Providence, 1861), VI, 379-80.

ing trade; that is, between Georgia and Newfoundland, inclusive; which, with the fishing vessels, are navigated by at least twenty-two hundred seamen.

Of these foreign vessels, about one hundred and fifty are annually employed in the West India trade, which import into this colony about fourteen thousand hogsheads of molasses; whereof, a quantity, not exceeding twenty-five hundred hogsheads, come from all the English islands together.

It is this quantity of molasses which serves as an engine in the hands of the merchant to effect the great purpose of paying the British manufactures; for part of it is exported to the Massachusetts Bay, to New York and Pennsylvania, to pay for British goods, for provisions and for many articles which compose our West India cargoes; and part to the other colonies, southward of these last mentioned, for such commodities as serve for a remittance immediately to Europe; such as rice, naval stores &c., or such as are necessary to enable us to carry on our commerce; the remainder (besides what is consumed by the inhabitants), is distilled into rum, and exported to the coast of Africa; nor will this trade to Africa appear to be of little consequence, if the following account of it be considered.

Formerly, the negroes upon the coast were supplied with large quantities of French brandies; but in the year 1723, some merchants in this colony first introduced the use of rum there, which, from small beginnings soon increased to the consumption of several thousand hogsheads yearly; by which the French are deprived of the sale of an equal quantity of brandy; and as the demand for rum is annually increasing upon the coast, there is the greatest reason to think, that in a few years, if this trade be not discouraged, the sale of French brandies there will be entirely destroyed. This little colony, only, for more than thirty years past, have annually sent about eighteen sail of vessels to the coast, which have carried about eighteen hundred hogsheads of rum, together with a small quantity of provisions and some other articles, which have been sold for slaves, gold dust, elephants' teeth, camwood, &c. The slaves have been sold in the English islands, in Carolina and Virginia, for bills of exchange, and the other articles have been sent to Europe; and by this trade alone, remittances have been made from this colony to Great Britain, to the value of about £ 40,000, yearly; and this rum, carried to the coast, is so far from prejudicing the British trade thither, that it may be said rather to promote it; for as soon as our rum vessels arrive, they exchange away some of the rum with the traders from Britain, for a quantity of dry goods, with which each of them sort their cargoes to their mutual advantage.

Besides this method of remittance by the African trade, we often get bills of exchange from the Dutch colonies of Surinam, Barbice, &c.; and this happens when the sales of our cargoes amount to more than a sufficiency to load with molasses; so that, in this particular, a considerable benefit arises from the molasses trade, for these bills being paid in Holland, are the means of drawing from that republic so much cash yearly, into Great Britain, as these bills amount to.

From this deduction of the course of our trade, which is founded in exact truth, it appears that the whole trading stock of this colony, in its beginning, progress and end is uniformly directed to the payment of the debt contracted by the importation of British goods; and it also clearly appears, that without this trade, it would have been and always will be, utterly impossible for the inhabitants of this colony to subsist themselves, or to pay for any considerable quantity of British goods.

*The eighteenth-century Anglo-French wars for the control of North America
ended with the complete triumph of Britain, an outcome that may be explained
in large part by the superiority of the British navy and the manpower preponderance of Britain's American colonies. At the outset the French enjoyed a great
strategic advantage; French voyageurs discovered the incomparable water route
from the Gulf of St. Lawrence to the Gulf of Mexico. The French government
followed up by building a string of forts along the St. Lawrence River, the Great
Lakes, and the Ohio and Mississippi rivers. The effect of this grand strategy was
to hem in the English colonies along the Atlantic seaboard. Alexander Spotswood,
the expansionist governor of Virginia, perceived the implications of this encircle-
ment and pointed out its dangers in a letter to his English superiors in 1718.**

. . . having of a long time endeavour'd to informe myself of ye scituation
of the French to the Westward of Us, and the Advantages they Reap by an
uninterrupted Communication along ye Lake, I shall here take the Liberty
of communicating my thoughts to Yo'r Lord'ps, both of the dangers to
w'ch his Majesty's Plantations may be exposed by this new Acquisition of
our Neighbours, and how the same may be best prevented. I have often
regretted that after so many Years as these Countrys have been Seated, no
Attempts have been made to dicover the Sources of Our Rivers, nor to
Establishing Correspondence w'th those Nations of Indians to ye Westw'd
of Us, even after the certain Knowledge of the Progress made by French in
Surrounding us w'th their Settlements. . . .

Having also informed myself of that extensive Communication w'ch the
French maintain by means of their water Carriage from the River St. Lawrence
to the mouth of Mississippi, I shall here set down the route from Montreal,
(a place well known and distinguished in ye ordinary Mapps,) to Maville,
their Chief Town in their New Settlement of Louisiana, according to the
account given me by three Fr. Men, who had often Travelled that way, and
were taken in a late Expedition under the Command of the Gov'r and
L't-Gov'r's Sons, of Montreal, and is as follows:

	French Leages.
From Montreal up St. Lawrence River, to Fort, Frontenac, at the Entrace of Lac Ontario, is	60
The Length of Lac Ontario, which is Navigable,	60
Up the River to the Falls of Niagara, where there is a necessity of Land Carriage,	3
From Niagara to the Lake Erie,	100
Up the River Mic., w'ch falls into Lake Erie,	60
From the River Mic. to the River Occabacke, a Land Carriage of	3
Down the River Occaback till it falls into the River Mississippi	200
Thence down Mississippi to Maville,	360

* R. A. Brock, ed., "The Official Letters of Alexander Spotswood," *Collections,* new
ser. (Richmond: Virginia Historical Society, 1885), II, 295-97.

By this Communication and the forts they have already built, the British Plantations are in a manner Surrounded by their Commerce w'th the numerous Nations of Indians seated on both sides of the Lakes; they may not only Engross the whole Skin Trade, but may, when they please, Send out such Bodys of Indians on the back of these Plantations as may greatly distress his Maj'ty's Subjects here, And should they multiply their Settlem'ts along these Lakes, so as to joyn their Dominions of Canada to their new Colony of Louisiana, they might even possess themselves of any of these Plantations they pleased. Nature, 'tis true, has formed a Barrier for us by that long Chain of Mountains w'ch run from the back of South Carolina as far as New York, and w'ch are only passable in some few places, but even that Natural Defence may prove rather destructive to us, if they are not possessed by us before they are known to them. to prevent the dangers w'ch Threaten his Maj'ty's Dominions here from the growing power of these Neighbours, nothing seems to me of more consequence than that now while the Nations are at peace, and while the French are yet uncapable of possessing all that vast Tract w'ch lies on the back of these Plantations, we should attempt to make some Settlements on ye Lakes, and at the same time possess our selves of those passes of the great Mountains, w'ch are necessary to preserve a Communication w'th such Settlements.

As the Lake Erie lyes almost in the Center of the French Communication, and, as I observed before, not above 5 days' March from the late discovered passage of Our great Mountains, That seems the most proper for forming a Settlement on, by w'ch we shall not only share w'th the French in the Commerce and friendship of those Indians inhabiting the banks of the Lakes, but may be able to cutt off or disturb the communication between Canada and Louisiana, if a War should happen to break out. If such a Settlement were once made, I can't see how the French could dispute our Right of Possession, the Law of Nations giving a Title to the first Occupant, and should they think fitt to dispossess us by force, We are nearer to Support than they to attack.

ENGLAND'S TRIUMPH IN NORTH AMERICA **37**

Between 1689 and 1763, England and France fought four colonial wars for the mastery of North America, the decisive struggle being the Seven Years' War, or the French and Indian War, as it was known in the colonies. The dramatic climax of this war was the fateful battle between the Marquis de Montcalm and General James Wolfe at Quebec in 1759. One of General Wolfe's officers, Captain John Knox, has left the following account * of the desperate and hazardous operation that brought victory. Frontal assault of the sheer cliffs of the Quebec fortress was out of the question, so General Wolfe ferried his men down the river to a point above the fortress. There they disembarked under cover of night and climbed up a precipitous path to the high Plains of Abraham overlooking the fortress. On these plains was fought the decisive battle that settled the fate of New France.

* Captain John Knox, *An Historical Journal of the Campaigns in North America for the Years, 1757, 1758, 1759, and 1760*, A. G. Doughty, ed. (Toronto: The Champlain Society, 1914), II, 94-103.

Before day-break this morning [September 13, 1759] we made a descent upon the north shore, about half a quarter of a mile to the eastward of Sillery; and the light troops were fortunately, by the rapidity of the current, carried lower down, between us and Cape Diamond; we had, in this debarkation, thirty flat-bottomed boats, containing about sixteen hundred men. This was a great surprise on the enemy, who, from the natural strength of the place, did not suspect, and consequently were not prepared against, so bold an attempt. The chain of centries, which they had posted along the summit of the heights, galled us a little, and picked off several men, and some Officers, before our light infantry got up to dislodge them. This grand enterprise was conducted, and executed with great good order and discretion; as fast as we landed, the boats put off for reinforcements, and the troops formed with much regularity: the General, with Brigadiers Monckton and Murray, were a-shore with the first division. We lost no time here, but clamoured up one of the steepest precipices that can be conceived, being almost a perpendicular, and of an incredible height. As soon as we gained the summitt, all was quiet, and not a shot was heard, owing to the excellent conduct of the light infantry under Colonel Howe; it was by this time clear day-light. Here we formed again, the river and the south country in our rear, our right extending to the town, our left to Sillery, and halted a few minutes. The General then detached the light troops to our left to route the enemy from their battery, and to disable their guns, except they could be rendered serviceable to the party who were to remain there; and this service was soon performed. We then faced to the right, and marched towards the town by files, till we came to the plains of Abraham; an even piece of ground which Mr. Wolfe had made choice of, while we stood forming upon the hill. Weather showery: about six o'clock the enemy first made their appearance upon the heights, between us and the town; whereupon we halted, and wheeled to the right, thereby forming the line of battle. ... The enemy had now likewise formed the line of battle, and got some cannon to play on us, with round and canistershot; but what galled us most was a body of Indians and other marksmen they had concealed in the corn opposite to the front of our right wing, and a coppice that stood opposite to our center, inclining towards our left; but the Colonel Hale, by Brigadier Monckton's orders, advanced some platoons, alternately, from the forty-seventh regiment, which, after a few rounds, obliged these sculkers to retire; we were now ordered to lie down, and remained some time in this position. About eight o'clock we had two pieces of short brass six-pounders playing on the enemy, which threw them into some confusion, and obliged them to alter their disposition, and Montcalm formed them into three large columns; about nine the two armies moved a little nearer each other. The light cavalry made a faint attempt upon our parties at the battery of Sillery, but were soon beat off, and Monsieur de Bougainville, with his troops from Cape Rouge, came down to attack the flank of our second line, hoping to penetrate there, but, by a masterly disposition of Brigadier Townshend, they were forced to desist, and the third battalion of Royal Americans was then detached to the first ground we had formed on after we gained the heights, to preserve the communication with the beach and our boats. About ten o'clock the enemy began to advance briskly in three columns, with loud shouts and recovered arms, two of them inclining to the left of our army, and the third towards our right, firing obliquely at the two extremities of our line, from the distance of one hundred and thirty—, until they came within forty yards; which our troops withstood with the greatest intrepidity and firmness, still reserving their fire, and paying the strictest obedience to their Officers: this uncommon steadiness, together with the havoc which the grape-shot from our field-pieces made among them, threw them into some disorder, and was most critically maintained by a well-timed, regular, and heavy discharge of our small arms, such as they could no longer oppose; hereupon they gave way, and fled with precipitation, so that, by the time the cloud of smoke was vanished, our men were again loaded, and, profiting by the advantage we had over them, pursued them almost to the gates of the town, and the bridge over the little river, redoubling our fire with great eagerness, making many Officers and men prisoners. The weather cleared up, with a comfortably warm sun-shine: the Highlanders chaced them vigorously toward Charles's river, and the fifty-eight to the suburb close to John's gate, until they were checked by the cannon from the two hulks; at the same time a gun, which the town had brought to bear upon us with grape-shot, galled the progress of the regiments to the right, who were likewise pursuing with equal ardour, while Colonel Hunt Walsh, by a very judicious movement, wheeled the battalions of Bragg and Kennedy to the left, and flanked the coppice where a body of the enemy made a stand, as if willing to renew the action; but a few platoons from these corps completed our victory. Then it was that Brigadier Townshend came up, called off the pursuers, ordered the whole line to dress, and recover their former ground. Our joy at this success is inexpressibly damped by the loss we sustained of one of the greatest heroes which this or any other age can boast of,—GENERAL JAMES WOLFE, who received his mortal wound, as he was exerting himself at the head of the grenadiers of Louis-bourg. ... Thus has our late renowned Commander, by his superior eminence in the art of war, and a most judicious *coup d'etat,* made a conquest of this fertile, healthy, and hitherto formidable country, with a handful of troops only, in spite of the political schemes, and most vigorous efforts, of the famous Montcalm, and many other Officers of rank and experience, at the head of an army considerably more numerous. My pen is too feeble to draw the character of this *British Achilles.*

Chapter Eight

Russian expansion in Asia

38 RUSSIAN CONQUEST AND EXPLOITATION OF SIBERIA

*At the same time that the Western European peoples were discovering and occupying new continents overseas, the Russian peoples were expanding overland and winning equally extensive territories in Siberia. The Russian eastward expansion to the Pacific is an epic story comparable to the American westward expansion to the same ocean. Its long-range implications were equally significant: Just as the Western European overseas enterprise ensured that the New World would become primarily Caucasoid in ethnic composition and European in culture, so the Russian conquest of Siberia made certain a similar outcome in that vast area. The policies of the Russians in conquering and exploiting Siberia are analyzed in the following account by an American authority on this topic.**

Ostrogs.—The conquest of the khanate of Sibir during the latter part of the sixteenth century, first undertaken by the Volga pirate, Ermak, and completed by the tsar's voevodas, laid the foundation for the Russian Empire in Asia. After defeating the khan Kuchum, the Russians continued their eastward advance until the whole of Siberia became the possession of the Muscovite sovereign.

The Siberian natives, politically disunited, backward, and unfamiliar with firearms, were invariably defeated whenever they dared

* G. V. Lantzeff, *Siberia in the Seventeenth Century: A Study of the Colonial Administration,* Univ. of California Publications in History, XXX (Berkeley: Univ. of California, 1940), 87-115.

offer open resistance to the military organization and superior military equipment of the Russians. The latter, however, were handicapped by inferiority in numbers and by the fact that they had to scatter their forces over such a vast territory. These unfavorable circumstances the Russians overcame by building a well-planned system of forts and blockhouses, generally referred to as *ostrogs*.

To control the chief means of communication and transportation, the Russians chose the sites for ostrogs along important waterways. By virtue of their location, ostrogs prevented any organized hostile action on the part of the natives in whose territory they were erected. In time of peace the ostrogs were administrative centers; in time of war they became bases for military operations.

The main feature of an ostrog was a stockade made of large timber; the tops of the stocks were sharpened, and along the stockade at certain intervals there were embrasures for marksmen. On the corners of the stockade and above the gates towers equipped with artillery were erected. The largest ostrogs were built in western Siberia. The towns there were fenced off by one or two lines of the stockade which protected the town population; within the stockade stood a wooden citadel, which contained the government buildings and storehouses. The walls of the citadel were surmounted by towers, twenty to thirty feet high, parapets and *gorodni* (places for marksmen). Sometimes a moat was dug along the walls of the citadel and stockade. Special care was taken to safeguard the landing place on the river with two or three rows of *nadolby* (palisades), so that during a siege communication with other towns would not be interrupted. . . .

Application of "Divide et empera."—Once an ostrog was established, the immediate problem of providing for the safety of the Russian expeditionary force was solved, and the local voevodas could proceed with subduing the natives within the vicinity of the ostrog and imposing upon them delivery of the *iasak* (fur tribute). For such purposes military prowess alone was not sufficient; the voevodas had to be diplomats as well as warriors. I.M. Trotskii, in his preface to the recently published collection of Siberian documents, remarks with surprise that

> . . . it is curious to note that the hostility among the natives themselves, apparently, increased with the advent of the conquerors: the iasak-paying natives helped to impose iasak on their neighbors, while the hostile natives chose as their victims those who accepted the domination.

As a matter of fact, it seems to have been a deliberate policy of the Russians to isolate the tribes by building ostrogs and fomenting intertribal hostility in the Russian interest. There are abundant proofs that such a policy bore fruit. . . .

In eastern Siberia there was continuous hostility between the Tungus and the Iukagirs, both sides appealing to the Russians for help. The Iukagirs were also having trouble with the Chukchis, and the Russian expeditionary force against the latter in 1659 consisted largely of Iukagirs, who in 1678-1679 again asked Russian protection against the Chukchis. The Tungus chief, Mozheul, offered his services in leading the Russians against his enemies, the Buriats, who had not as yet paid the iasak. . . .

RUSSIAN TREATMENT OF THE NATIVE UPPER CLASS. As soon as the natives in the newly acquired territory became more or less reconciled to Russian domination, the Russian administration, in order to establish regular and uninterrupted delivery of the iasak, tried to introduce peace and order among them.

The government sought especially to win the favor of the wealthy and influential natives. This policy was pursued from the very beginning of the Siberian occupation. Captured members of the native nobility were treated with consideration and sometimes released in the hope that they would bring their relatives and supporters to the Russian side. Mametkul, a relative of Kuchum, was taken prisoner by Ermak's cossacks and sent to Moscow, where he was well received and later given a military rank in the Russian service. As a voevoda he participated in the Swedish war of 1590 and in the Crimean expedition of 1598. Other members of Kuchum's family were treated in Moscow with the courtesy due their rank. . . .

The good will and support of the native chiefs was a weighty factor in the country, where the natives greatly outnumbered their conquerors. To win them over to the Russian side, special methods were used. Whenever a new voevoda was appointed, one of the first things he had to do was to invite the native chiefs and the "best men" from the surrounding territory to the ostrog, and to meet them in an impressive fashion, appealing to the natives' psychology. A solemn "reception" was held, with the voevoda and the serving men garbed in gala "colored dress." The chiefs passed between the ranks of serving men standing in military formation, while cannon and muskets were discharged in salute. The voevoda delivered a speech, emphasizing the power and benevolence of the government, enumerating the injustices from which the natives suffered, and promising, in the future, new favors and the elimination of evil practices. The procedure ended with a feast, where the natives were given an opportunity to gorge themselves with food and drink. Strong drinks were especially popular, and a petition has been preserved in which the natives complained that they were served beer instead of strong liquor. Similar feasts were held on the occasions when the chiefs arrived in town with the iasak from their volosts and were rewarded with various gifts in the form of cloth, metal tools, and brightly colored beads.

Some of the native chiefs, however, did not respond to the inducements offered by the Russians and remained stubborn in their resistance to the invaders. Toward them the government used ruthless and unscrupulous methods, quite in keeping with the times. There was no room for sentimentality, and treachery as a political weapon was lauded. . . .

GOVERNMENT POLICIES TOWARD THE NATIVES IN GENERAL. Once the government felt confident that the loyalty of the natives was reasonably assured, it prescribed that local officials use kindness and consideration in their treatment of them. The general tendency was to regard the natives as special wards of the state who needed supervision and protection. It was considered necessary to keep arms from reaching the natives, who might be tempted into some mischief, and to prevent, as far as possible, their demoralization by vices imported by the Russians, because it would affect their economic welfare and their ability to deliver the iasak. Therefore, in spite of protests from the natives, the merchants were forbidden to sell them axes, knives, or any arms or objects which could be converted into arms, as well as wine, tobacco, or any gambling devices. . . .

The government had shown considerable leniency toward the natives even in the matter of fur collection, which was its chief concern. In 1599 the natives of Siberia were informed with all due pomp and ceremony that the tsar, Boris Godunov, on account of his ascension to the throne, had released them from the delivery of iasak for one year. In general the voevodas were instructed not to require the delivery of iasak from poor, old, sick, or crippled natives. If, for some good reason, the iasak men could not deliver furs on time, the voevodas were to extend the date of delivery. Collection of the iasak had to be made with "kindness and not by cruelty and flogging . . . corporal punishment was not to be used . . . so as not to insult the natives and drive them away. . . ."

In accordance with its policy of preserving native tribal organization and native customs, the Muscovite government did not interfere with the religious beliefs of the natives. However, the conversion of the natives to Christianity had certain advantages. The baptized men, alienated by the change of religion from their kinsmen and former associates, were enlisted into Russian service and thus strengthened the garrisons. The baptized women solved the problem of the shortage of women in Siberia because they might marry serving men, as well as baptized natives. Therefore the government had reason to encourage somewhat the spread of Christianity and it did so by making gifts to those who embraced the new faith. As the Russians had no race prejudice and regarded religion as the only barrier separating them from the natives, the newly baptized were treated on equal terms with the Russians.

Nevertheless, in spite of the proselyting zeal of the churchmen, the government was not at all eager to baptize large numbers of natives. The advantages gained by their conversion were more than overbalanced by the financial losses, as the baptized natives, in effect, received Russian citizenship and ceased to pay iasak. Consequently, both the clergy and the local officials were repeatedly and explicitly forbidden to use any coercion in converting the natives. Christianity, if introduced at all, should prevail by "love and not by cruelty." For each baptism it became necessary to ask special permission from the administration. . . .

OBLIGATIONS AND GRIEVANCES OF THE NATIVES. The delivery of the iasak was the most important obligation the natives had toward the government. In addition to this the natives were called upon to perform other duties in connection with the various problems which confronted the colonial administration. . . .

The shortage of food supplies was one of the greatest difficulties which the Russians had to face in Siberia. At the beginning of the conquest, the grain had to be brought at considerable expense from European Russia. Therefore, one of the first tasks of the Siberian administration was to develop the local cultivation of land, and in an attempt to do this the voevodas of several uezds (Pelym, Verkhoturie, Turinsk, Tiumen, and later Eniseisk) tried to organize state farms operated by native labor. For the most part such enterprises were unsuccessful; the natives made poor farmers and repeatedly complained that they were not accustomed to agriculture. Fortunately, the gradual arrival of Russian colonists made further encouragement of farming among the natives unnecessary.

The natives were also used for other purposes. Shortage of guides and interpreters among the serving men necessitated the employment of natives in these roles, and the shortage of labor led to the use of them in the building and repairing of town fortifications and roads. For transportation, the Russians had to use natives as rowers of boats and drivers of carts. This caused a great deal of dissatisfaction among the natives, who were forced to provide horses, oxen, dogs, and even reindeer to carry men, supplies, and furs. They disliked the transportation service so much that in exchange for release from it some of them offered to pay triple the required amount of iasak. Frequently, the natives, besides their iasak obligation, had to catch fish, gather berries, bring wood for fuel or for building purposes, furnish hunting hawks, and, in general, "to serve the sovereign's service at the orders of the voevodas." Some of the voevodas interpreted this as justification for using natives for all kinds of personal service as well.

Imposition of the iasak delivery and of other forms of service constituted a heavy burden for the natives, who, because of their cultural backwardness and their inability to cope with the severe climate, already led a wretched and precarious existence. They needed all the "clemency and kindness" which were mentioned so often in the government instructions. The same instructions, however, demanded that the voevodas "seek profit for the sovereign with zeal." It is hardly surprising that the local officials, eager to win a reputation for financial efficiency (which might lead to another lucrative appointment) and more than anxious to fill their own pockets, were likely to forget all about "clemency" and to concentrate on "profit"—especially to themselves. . . .

The natives suffered from the Russian rule in many other ways. The government imported a number of colonists from Russia and a great many other Russian colonists came on their own initiative. In order to give room to these settlers, the natives often had to abandon their hunting grounds and fishing places, although some were able to recover at least a part of their land through appeals to Moscow. On several occasions, because of the lack of Russian women in Siberia, both colonists and serving men abducted native women, especially when their fathers and husbands were away hunting. In general, the conduct of the Russian settlers, as well as of numerous promyshlenniks [private Russian traders and hunters], was frequently such that, . . . the government had to issue special instructions to the local officers demanding protection for the natives. Instead of following the government instructions, the local administrators themselves often mistreated the natives. The voevoda of Narym kidnapped a son of the local chief and kept him until a ransom of one hundred rubles was paid. An official of Okhotsk gathered together all the children of the local tribe of Tungus and required the natives to bring a sable in return for each child. The officials of Tomsk, traveling in 1606 along the Ob' River, "tortured the natives and extorted exorbitant gifts." The voevoda of Tobolsk reported that in Pelym the local voevoda had flogged many Ostiaks to death. Golovin, the notorious voevoda of Iakutsk, "hanged 23 of the best men" and "flogged many Iakuts to death, used torture, and starved others to death in a dungeon." The boiar son Pushkin, in charge of the ostrog of Olekminsk, in order "to satisfy his greed, flogged the natives with rods and kept them in irons." The stolnik Bibikov in Okhotsk, repeating the methods of his predecessor, Krizhanovskii, hanged a number of Tungus, flogged others with a knout or mutilated them by cutting off their ears and noses. The golova Poiarkov, who was sent on an expedition to subdue a hostile chief, Kamuk, not only drove away the cattle belonging to the natives and appropriated all their possessions, but also burned the native town with its three hundred inhabitants, including the chief and his family. . . .

In response to oppression, the natives tried to protest to Moscow, to refuse the delivery of the iasak, to move to other lands, and, finally, to oppose the Russians with arms. Continual murders of the iasak collectors and attacks upon shipments of furs and food seriously hampered the collection of furs, and required constant military vigilance, while some of the largest uprisings even threatened the towns and centers of the administration.

Chapter Nine

*Significance
of the period
for world history*

DEMOGRAPHIC IMPACT OF EUROPEAN EXPANSION   39

One of the major repercussions of European expansion was a new global distribution of races. Prior to 1500 the Negroids had been concentrated largely in sub-Saharan Africa; the Mongoloids, in Central Asia, Siberia, East Asia, and the Americas; the Caucasoids, in Europe, North Africa, the Middle East, and India. By 1763 this racial segregation had been substantially modified. About fifteen million Africans were transported as slaves to the New World, affecting fundamentally the racial composition of that area to the present day. More massive was the large-scale emigration of Europeans to underpopulated regions such as Siberia, the Americas, and eventually Australia. These population shifts, quite unprecedented in volume, were accompanied in most cases by a drastic decline in the numbers of the indigenous peoples. This fateful demographic impact of European expansion is the subject of a paper in which an American historian concludes that diseases carried by Europeans were a primary factor in the decimation of isolated peoples who had not developed immunities.* This conclusion is particularly significant today, when scientists are concerned lest astronauts returning from the moon or planets bring back with them organisms harmful to the earth and its inhabitants. In exploring the universe, man may be exposed to medical hazards comparable to those encountered in exploring his own planet.

* Woodrow Borah, "America as Model: The Demographic Impact of European Expansion upon the Non-European World." This paper was read at the XXXV International Congress of Americanists at Mexico City, 1962, and is published in *Actas y Memorias del XXXV Congresso Internacional de Americanistas*, III (Mexico City, 1964), 379-87.

In this paper I propose to explore the demographic impact of European expansion upon the non-European world since the fifteenth century, a significant aspect of the period of political dominance of the globe by Europe, which today comes to a close. Any such exploration, within the time possible here, must consist of a series of speculations and suggestions, if only because there are as yet too few studies for well-based generalizations covering large portions of the planet. Yet a number of studies have begun to appear and permit at least a conjecture upon the probable form of the pattern that will be found.

The controversy over the size of the aboriginal population of America at the time of the voyages of Columbus is well known. The first European explorers and writers reported very dense American populations. Fray Bartolomé de las Casas calculated the aboriginal population of the island of Hispaniola alone at three million souls. Even the reduction of this calculation to two million by Fray Tomás de Angulo leaves an estimate that is very high indeed. Gonzalo Fernández de Oviedo's discussion of the havoc wrought by Pedrarias Dávila in Castilla del Oro and Nicaragua would suggest an initial Indian population of several millions for that part of Central America alone. For the Inca Empire and Central Mexico the testimony of the earliest conquerors and writers indicates comparably great densities. Such testimony points to a very large population for the whole of the New World, although all would agree that the densities varied greatly from region to region in accordance with climate, flora and fauna, soil, topography, and the technology known to the human inhabitants. Later discussion of these early reports has tended to divide scholars into two schools. In the first group are those who accept them as factual or have arrived at essentially corroborative results through other approaches. Spinden, on the basis of his archeological experience, arrived at a maximum New World population of fifty to seventy-five millions for the year 1200, and a population of perhaps forty to fifty millions at the close of the fifteenth century. Karl Sapper, whose knowledge of Mexico and Central America was especially profound, suggested, on the basis of a study of climate, resources, and technology, the same overall total of forty to fifty millions, of which present-day Mexico and the Andean zone of the Incan Empire and Chiboha culture would each have had from twelve to fifteen millions, whereas the region north of the Great Lakes would have had no more than half a million. Sapper expressly pointed out that at Los Altos in Guatemala in his day agricultural techniques essentially similar to pre-Conquest ones, except for the use of a rude plow, supported a density of one hundred persons per square kilometer. Such densities thus were possible before the Conquest—exactly as reported by the earliest writers.

The second group of writers has tended to reject early testimony and declare that Indian technology could not support the densities indicated. A. L. Kroeber has made as careful a study as Sapper's using the same technique of estimate on the basis of technology and resources, but applying also experience gained in the areas of relatively sparse settlement of western Anglo-America. He arrived at a total for the New World of 8.4 millions, of which three millions were in the Incan Empire, another three millions in Meso-America, and only 200,000 in all of the West Indies. Angel Rosenblat would raise these estimates to a total of 13.4 million for America in 1492. I should emphasize the point that in the long series of discussions during nearly five centuries and especially since the writings of Robertson and Humboldt there has been a great range of estimates for the Hemisphere and for various regions, of which I have merely given samples. In general, those who uphold large initial estimates have accepted the idea of a catastrophic drop in the aboriginal population whereas the upholders of the smallest estimates have tended to minimize the probable degree of such a drop or even to deny that a substantial one took place.

In recent years there has been a new approach to the problem, one based upon examination of materials capable of statistical treatment, mainly European fiscal records and missionary reports. For Mexico, one may mention the work of Miguel Othón Mendizábal, Sherburne Cook, Lesley Byrd Simpson, and myself. The Cook-Simpson study of 1948 arrived at an estimate for Central Mexico of approximately eleven millions. Since then further studies by Cook and myself, based upon a larger mass of fiscal information that has become available, have led to even higher estimates. For the population of Central Mexico on the eve of the European invasion, we estimate approximately twenty-five millions, essentially the mid-point of a range. Between 1519 and 1568 this population fell to less than three millions and continued to decline until some time between 1580 and 1620, when after a period of stability it began recovery, largely at first through the appearance and multiplication of non-Indian and mixed groups, and then through increase of the Indians. Only in our own day has the population returned to the densities of the early sixteenth century. Destruction was most rapid on the coasts, which became virtually depopulated within a generation of the coming of the Europeans, and much slower upon the plateau, where a greater part of the aboriginal mass was able to maintain itself.

These studies for Central Mexico have been paralleled by a few tentative studies for other areas of America. Especially suggestive are those of Rolando Mellafe, which would show for the region of Huánuco a comparable initial density of population and a depletion by the late sixteenth century of approximately ninety per cent. Mellafe would suggest further that depopulation for Central and Southern Chile was similar.

Obviously these studies are a narrow base from which to infer a pattern for all of America. Nevertheless, they do indicate directly a very great density of aboriginal population for Meso-America, and corroborate the statements of the earliest conquerors and writers. The *caveat* in Sapper's statement about the density that could be supported by aboriginal agriculture thus has meaning, as do Paul Kirchhoff's remarks that it is absurd to estimate the population of two continents on the basis of the technology and culture of its northern fringe, as absurd as would be estimates of the nature of the cultures and the population of Eurasia derived from examination of the technology of the tribes of Siberia. There emerges from these studies, then, the very real possibility that the Indian population of the New World at the end of the fifteenth century may well have been even greater than Sapper's estimates and indeed may have reached upwards of one hundred million. Such a total postulates that the population had bred well toward the limit of the food supply available to it under its technology. In Central Mexico, as is shown by massive erosion, it had even passed the long-term carrying capacity of its land.

Under the impact of lethal factors unleashed or given especially virulent force by the coming of the Europeans, the enormous aboriginal population of America shrank by perhaps ninety to ninety-five per cent in the relatively brief period of several decades or a century. The depopulation was most marked in the islands of the Caribbean and the tropical coasts of the continents where, in many areas, the aboriginal population disappeared within a generation. Demographic recovery has been a relatively slow process, marked often by the development of new non-Indian populations. Most of these new populations have come into being in the temperate zones, which were most attractive for direct rural settlement by Europeans, and in the islands and on the coasts, where Negro or mixed populations have become dominant. In the upland regions of the tropics, seats of the most highly developed aboriginal cultures, and in such lowland interior areas as those of Brazil and Paraguay, the original population, although taking very heavy loss, has been able to recover, and has supplied the bulk of the present-day population, although it has grown more slowly than new or mixed groups elsewhere. Only in the last decades, in all probability, has the population of America in the tropics returned to something like its previous size, especially in those areas which were most heavily settled in pre-Columbian times. Destruction and recovery thus constitute a cycle of perhaps four centuries.

The European conquest of America has been part of the general expansion of Europe since the fifteenth century. It has been a period in which Europe, having gained technological superiority over the rest of the world, made use of its advantage for exploration of the entire globe, for conquest of a large part of it, and settlement of areas that were either vacant at the time of discovery or made so through factors set in motion by discovery and conquest. (Let me state explicitly that I make no moral judgments since there is scant evidence that other peoples then or in other times have behaved differently, or indeed that the Europeans were more than unconscious agents in unleashing the most lethal factors.) We live now in the end of the period, for Europe has lost political control of the rest of the world, and we witness the opening of an interesting new period in which the extra-European regions have indeed saved themselves from European political control, but only by progressively deeper and more rapid adoption of the substance and forms of European technology and civilization. In effect, the entire globe is rapidly becoming Europeanized, and giant states that have developed outside the older confines of Europe now dispute the mastery of Europe and of the planet.

I have made a tentative formulation of pattern for America of the demographic impact of this period of European expansion just ended. To what extent can a similar pattern be detected in other major areas of the extra-European world? In the next pages I shall attempt tentative assessment for the islands of the Pacific, for Africa south of the Sahara, and for parts of the Far East. I exclude North Africa and the Middle East because they have been so continuously and closely in contact with Europe that they have really been part of it. Obviously the assessment must be a summary one and can deal only with samples.

For the islands of the Pacific, including Australia, the evidence is remarkably clear. Australia at the time of the first English settlement at Botany Bay is estimated to have had an aboriginal population of perhaps 300,000, which in 1937, after some recovery, numbered approximately 80,000 pure and mixed bloods, by then a small group in a large new population of European origin. In Tasmania, an aboriginal population of at least 2,000 disappeared completely by 1876. New Zealand, which was estimated by Capt. Cook in the 1770's to have perhaps 100,000 Maoris, is now thought on the basis of archeological and historical studies more probably to have had at that time a Maori population of from 300,000 to 500,000. The Maori population fell to 40,000 by 1900 and is now slowly rising. Meantime, New Zealand has become the seat of new settlement from Europe. The experience of Australia and New Zealand thus parallels that of temperate America. The New Hebrides are estimated to have had a dense aboriginal population, perhaps as great as a million, which by 1939 fell to 40,000. The Hawaiian Islands were estimated by the Cook expedition in 1778 to have a population of 400,000. Later estimates by missionaries show a steady decrease to 71,019 in 1853, the year of the first census. The native population reached a low of about 40,000 in the 1890's and is now slowly increasing. According to the census of 1950 there were 86,091 pure and partial Hawaiians in a total multi-racial population of approximately half a million. There has thus been some recovery of the aboriginal people, but predominantly the formation of a new population. Perhaps the most striking examples of population decline—next to Tasmania —are the island of Kusaie, estimated to have a population of 1,500 in 1855 and only 400 in 1895; the Marquesas, estimated to have had more than 80,000 native inhabitants before the Europeans and in 1939 barely 2,000; and Guam, where the Chamarros, estimated at from 70,000 to 100,000 in 1668, when the Spanish began occupation, fell to 1,654 by 1733. By 1939 they had recovered to approximately 22,000. The islands least affected by European contact have been Tonga, which, despite some decline, recovered so rapidly that the present population descended from aboriginal stock is thought to be larger than that existing at the time of European discovery, and Fiji, where an aboriginal population of perhaps 200,000 suffered a relatively small decline to 105,800 by 1891. The small proportion of loss in Fiji may have been due to the division of the island among actively warring tribes, who resisted European penetration and slowed it down. Fiji, like Hawaii, has had new settlement, here largely Hindu.

On the whole, then, the experience of Oceania has paralleled that of America: a relatively dense aboriginal population that seems to breed to the limits of the food resources available under the existing technology, precipitous demographic loss following European discovery and the opening of commercial relations or occupation as colonies, and demographic restoration after perhaps a century, both through recovery of the aboriginal stock and new settlement from Europe or Asia.

Africa, I have defined as Africa south of the Sahara. But even Africa south of the Sahara, Black Africa, must be understood for our purposes to consist of two different zones: one, the area draining into the Indian Ocean and into the Mediterranean through the Nile, which participated in the commerce and cultural interchanges taking place through millennia along the axis of the Mediterranean-Indian Ocean-Far East trade routes, and two, the area of drainage into the Atlantic Ocean, which remained all but isolated from extra-African influences until the Portuguese began exploration of the West Coast.

The evidence available at this time on the extent and movement of population in Black Africa since the fifteenth century is scanty and conflicting. Such estimates as exist are based upon sheer guesswork and supposition. One suspects that in the end much demographic evidence will be found through archeological investigation and in the writings of Arabic, Asiatic, and European travelers and chroniclers, although the difficulty of locating, let alone using, such diverse sources, thus far has impeded scholarly study. The difficulty of determining population movement is made much worse by the problem of the impact of the Atlantic slave trade, which may have brought as many as fifteen million Negroes to America between 1500 and 1850, most of them between 1650 and 1850. If one estimates that for each slave landed alive in America, at least two Negroes were killed in securing the slaves or died in transit, and makes allowance for slaves moved to areas other than America, it would seem likely that the slave trade of the years 1500-1850 caused the death or removal from Africa of perhaps fifty million persons, most of the loss being concentrated in the last two centuries of the period when the traffic was at its height. The dimension of the African slave trade was unparalleled in other non-European areas, but its effect upon African population was far less than the total would imply, for the annual removal of persons from a population of perhaps seventy to eighty millions was proportionately small and in many areas did no more than dispose of what would have been excees population. Since most of the slaves came from the forest lands of the Atlantic drainage, loss was concentrated in a relatively small part of Black Africa, but even in this area powerful states flourished because of the trade, and in such regions as Nigeria population remained dense despite losses to slavers. If one compares the slave trade with the steady and heavy emigration from western and central Europe in the nineteenth century, which merely drained off some of a rapidly increasing population, it becomes likely that except for limited areas and periods there was little substantial demographic effect in terms of numbers. . . .

For the Far East, information on historical demography is relatively good for the five centuries that we are interested in. Chinese population increased rather steadily until the middle of the nineteenth century, when civil disorders induced in part by overpopulation brought a halt that lasted perhaps half a century. European influence has been relatively slight and has tended to increase rather than decrease the population: new crops such as maize, peanuts, sweet potatoes, and Irish potatoes made possible a remarkable three-fold increase in the number of Chinese between 1650 and 1850. For Japan, the five centuries have, on the whole, witnessed a steady increase, although between about 1720 and 1868 population was stabilized at approximately 26 millions, a stabilization that was a result of local causes and deliberate limitation and in no way due to European influence. In India, although it is difficult to estimate the population prior to the nineteenth century, there is no evidence of decrease in the past five centuries and clear evidence of very rapid increase under British political rule, which brought peace, control of disease, and some diminution of famine. Similarly, for Indonesia, despite discrepancies in early estimates, the evidence would indicate very rapid increase in Java in the first centuries of Dutch rule and a truly enormous increase throughout the archipelago in the nineteenth and twentieth centuries. Finally, for the Philippines, the estimates assembled by John L. Phelan indicate some decrease in the Spanish-controlled area in the seventeenth century, but that decrease, which took place when labor and food were requisitioned during the wars with the Dutch, probably represented flight to areas outside Spanish control rather than a genuine decline in the population of the islands. Since the middle of the seventeenth century there has been a sustained increase in the island population that still continues. For the Far East, then, the pattern that emerges is one of steady population increase in the past five centuries, aided by the introduction of new crops, in some countries by long periods of peace and orderly administration brought by European political control, and by reduction of the death rate through diminution of famine and improvements in sanitation and medicine.

Our brief survey thus indicates that the pattern found in America applies fully to the islands of the Pacific, only in small measure to Black Africa, and not at all to the countries of the Far East, where there has been a relatively steady increase in population during the centuries of European domination —partly because of it. Our survey and comparison also afford some insight into the factors responsible. Many factors have been listed as responsible in part for the demographic destruction accompanying European expansion: the physical destruction of conquest, the disruption of existing systems of production and distribution (a category that would include changes to more oppressive systems of labor and taxation and the psychological impact of subjugation), depopulation through the slave trade and such parallel forms as blackbirding, the introduction of alcoholic beverages, and finally the introduction of diseases. It has been held that these factors operated much more strongly among those peoples who were classed as primitive than among those classed as advanced, but this division into primitive and civilized does not hold up since there is little evidence that the peoples of sub-Saharan Africa or of the Philippines should be held to be more advanced than those of America. In the Philippines, especially, the evidence indicates no serious demographic damage. The key would seem to be that the Philippines, although inhabited by tribes hardly more advanced in culture than those of Peru or Central Mexico, were in intermittent contact with the mainland of Asia and nearby islands, which in turn were linked to the long-distance lines of trade of the Old World, just as the Indian Ocean drainage of Africa was similarly so linked. Even the Atlantic Coast of Africa had some contact with the eastern areas of that continent and so some relation with long distance routes of trade. America and the Pacific islands had no such contact until it was suddenly thrust upon them. There is thus a high degree of positive correlation between previous isolation and the extent of demographic destruction consequent upon the opening of relations with Europe. That correlation further suggests that the most important factor in the destruction has been the spread of diseases. Regions linked with the long-distance lines of trade from Europe to the Far East absorbed the impact of various diseases over long periods of time and had opportunity to recover and develop resistance. Regions living in virtually complete isolation received within a few decades the united impact of all diseases that could be spread, for the movement of European ships and their cargoes and passengers quickly delivered to all parts of the globe most of the diseases that could flourish in them. They took in a few decades a series of blows that Europe and the Far East had been able to take over millennia. In effect, bacteria and viruses recognized the unity of the planet long before men.

ADAM SMITH ON THE EXPANSION OF EUROPE 40

The Scottish economist, Adam Smith, first published his world-famous Wealth of Nations *in 1778, in which he analyzed the contemporary economic situation and considered the motives and conditions that, in his opinion, were conducive to the production of wealth. Of necessity he paid considerable attention to overseas colonies which were affecting fundamentally the economy of Europe. Most of his references to colonies were in theoretical terms, since he was concerned not with colonies per se but rather with the restrictive system of tariffs, embargoes, monopolies, and navigation laws that controlled the trade relations be-*

tween colonies and mother countries. Typical is the following passage in which Adam Smith analyzed briefly the worldwide economic repercussions of the expansion of Europe.*

The discovery of America, and that of a passage to the East Indies by the Cape of Good Hope, are the two greatest and most important events recorded in the history of mankind. Their consequences have already been very great: but, in the short period of between two and three centuries which has elapsed since these discoveries were made, it is impossible that the whole extent of their consequences can have been seen. What benefits or what misfortunes to mankind may hereafter result from those great events, no human wisdom can foresee. By uniting, in some measure, the most distant parts of the world, by enabling them to relieve one another's wants, to increase one another's enjoyments, and to encourage one another's industry, their general tendency would seem to be beneficial. To the natives, however, both of the East and West Indies, all the commercial benefits which can have resulted from those events have been sunk and lost in the dreadful misfortunes which they have occasioned. These misfortunes, however, seem to have arisen rather from accident than from any thing in the nature of those events themselves. At the particular time when these discoveries were made, the superiority of force happened to be so great on the side of the Europeans, that they were enabled to commit with impunity every sort of injustice in those remote countries. Hereafter, perhaps, the natives of those countries may grow stronger, or those of Europe may grow weaker, and the inhabitants of all the different quarters of the world may arrive at that equality of courage and force which, by inspiring mutual fear, can alone overawe the injustice of independent nations into some sort of respect for the rights of one another. But nothing seems more likely to establish this equality of force than that mutual communication of knowledge and of all sorts of improvements which an extensive commerce from all countries to all countries naturally, or rather necessarily, carries along with it.

In the mean time, one of the principal effects of those discoveries has been to raise the mercantile system to a degree of splendour and glory which it could never otherwise have attained to. It is the object of that system to enrich a great nation rather by trade and manufactures than by the improvement and cultivation of land, rather by the industry of the towns than by that of the country. But, in consequence of those discoveries, the commercial towns of Europe, instead of being the manufacturers and carriers for but a very small part of the world, (that part of Europe which is washed by the Atlantic ocean, and the countries which lie round the Baltic and Mediterranean seas), have now become the manufacturers for the numerous and thriving cultivators of America, and the carriers, and in some respects the manufacturers too, for almost all the different nations of Asia, Africa, and America. Two new worlds have been opened to their industry, each of them much greater and more extensive than the old one, and the market of one of them growing still greater and greater every day.

The countries which possess the colonies of America, and which trade directly to the East Indies, enjoy, indeed, the whole show and splendour of this great commerce. Other countries, however, notwithstanding all the

---

* Adam Smith, *Wealth of Nations* (Edinburgh, 1838), p. 282.

invidious restraints by which it is meant to exclude them, frequently enjoy a greater share of the real benefit of it. The colonies of Spain and Portugal, for example, give more real encouragement to the industry of other countries than to that of Spain and Portugal. In the single article of linen alone the consumption of those colonies amounts, it is said, but I do not pretend to warrant the quantity, to more than three millions sterling a year. But this great consumption is almost entirely supplied by France, Flanders, Holland, and Germany. Spain and Portugal furnish but a small part of it. The capital which supplies the colonies with this great quantity of linen is annually distributed among, and furnishes a revenue to, the inhabitants of those other countries. The profits of it only are spent in Spain and Portugal, where they help to support the sumptuous profusion of the merchants of Cadiz and Lisbon.

INDIAN INFLUENCE ON AMERICAN CIVILIZATION 41

*The settlement of Europeans in relatively underpopulated territories led to the development of new overseas nations and cultures. These new societies have been studied largely from a European point of view, most scholars having been concerned with tracing the transplanting of European culture to new continents and with the displacement of the native cultures. Few attempts have been made to analyze the opposite process—the impact of the native cultures upon the new overseas societies. The following selection * is one of the earliest, and still one of the best, efforts along these lines.*

... I would seek to tell, in brief terms, the world's debt to the Red Man, what we owe to the race from whom we have snatched a continent. And the debt is, indeed, great. First our language owes him much. Though our unskilled tongues have all-too-often sorely marred them, the whole land is still dotted over with the names he gave. Republic, state, province, county, township, city, town, hamlet, mountain, valley, island, cape, gulf, bay, lake, river, and streamlet are his eternal remembrancers: Mexico, Alabama, Ontario, Multnomah, Muskoka, Lima, Parahiba, Kiowa, Managua, Kootenay, Yosemite, Chonos, Campeche, Panama, hail from as many distinct linguistic stocks as there are individual names in the list. ...

Of the states and territories of the Union, Alabama, Alaska, Arkansas, Arizona, Connecticut, the Dakotas, Idaho, Illinois, Iowa, Kansas, Kentucky, Massachusetts, (New) Mexico, Michigan, Minnesota, Mississippi, Missouri, Nebraska, Oklahoma, Tennessee, Texas, Utah, Wisconsin, Wyoming, derive their appellations from the Indian languages of the country. North of us Canada, and nine of her provinces and territories, Assiniboia, Athabasca, Keewatin, Manitoba, Ontario, Quebec, Saskatchewan, Ungava, Yukon, have been named from like sources. To the south the aborigines are remembered

* A. F. Chamberlain, "The Contributions of the American Indian to Civilization," *Proceedings of the American Antiquarian Society*, new ser., XVI (October, 1903-October, 1904), 93-119.

in Mexico, Nicaragua, Guatemala, Peru, Chile, Guiana, Uruguay, Paraguay, and in innumerable lesser divisions of these and the other Spanish-American republics and in Portuguese Brazil. . . .

But it is not place-names alone that have come to us from the Indians' store of speech. The languages of all sections of the peoples of European stock dwelling in the New World preserve scores and hundreds of words derived from one or another of the many tongues spoken by the aborigines. This debt to the Indian is, of course, greatest in Mexico, Central and South America, where the natives still exist in very large numbers, and where they have intermixed considerably with the white population, giving rise to millions of *mestizos* and mixed-bloods of various degrees.

To the English spoken and written in the United States and Canada one stock alone, the Algonkian, has furnished at least (according to the investigations of the present writer) one hundred and ninety words meriting record in our dictionaries; and a rough count of the words contributed to American English by all the Indian languages north of the Mexican boundary line makes the number about three hundred. The words adopted from the Indian tongues of Mexico, Central and South American would add some two hundred more. Thus, a fair estimate of the total contributions of the American Indian to English speech in America, spoken and written, literary, provincial and colloquial, would be, say five hundred words, which is under rather than above the mark. Some sixty selected from this long list will show the character of this aboriginal element in our modern English:

Alpaca, axolotl, barbecue, bayou, buccaneer, cannibal, canoe, caucus, Chautauqua, chipmunk, chocolate, condor, coyote, curari, guano, hammock, hickory, hominy, hurricane, ipecacuanha, jaguar, jalap, jerked (beef), Klondike, llama, mahogany, maize, manito, moccasin, moose, mugwump, ocelot, opossum, pampas, papoose, peccary, pemmican, persimmon, petunia, potato, powow, puma, quinine, raccoon, Saratoga, sequoia, skunk, squaw, Tammany, tapir, tarpon, terrapin, tobacco, toboggan, tomahawk, tomato, totem, tuxedo, vicuna, wahoo, wampum, wigwam, woodchuck, Wyandotte. . . .

When we turn to fiction and romance we find, again, that the American Indian has well served the white race. Defoe, Cooper, Chateaubriand, Marmontel, Mayne Reid, Rider Haggard, Robertson and many others have found inspiration in his history and achievements. In spite of inaccuracy of detail and too frequent and too extensive Anglification and Gallicization, the aboriginal characters of some of these writers stand firmly rooted in our literary memories. We cannot easily forget "Friday," "the last of the Mohicans," "the white God." . . .

Let us now turn from language and literature to more material things. How readily many of the natives of the New World consented to become guides and porters for the first European travellers and adventurers has been recorded by several of the chroniclers of early colonial days. Roger Williams was particularly cordial in this regard:

> The wilderness, being so vast, it is a mercy that for hire a Man shall never want guides, who will carry provisions and such as hire them over Rivers and Brookes, and find out oftentimes hunting houses or other lodgings at night. I have heard of many English lost and have often been lost myselfe, and myselfe and others have been often found and succoured by the Indians.

Exploration of the New World was all the easier because almost everywhere, missionary, soldier, adventurer, trader, trapper and hunter followed Indian guides over the old trails. . . .

Professor Turner does not exaggerate when he says:

> The buffalo-trail became the Indian trail, and this became the trader's "trace"; the trails widened into roads, and the roads into turnpikes, and these, in turn, were transformed into railroads. The same origin can be shown for the railroads of the South, the far West and the Dominion of Canada. The trading-posts reached by these trails were on the sites of Indian villages which had been placed in positions suggested by nature; and these trading-posts, situated so as to command the water-systems of the country, have grown into such cities as Albany, Pittsburgh, Detroit, Chicago, St. Louis, Council Bluffs, and Kansas City.

The very latest railroad to be born, the Crow's Nest Railroad in the Canadian Northwest, climbs the Rockies by an Indian trail, and the towns springing up beside it but occupy the abandoned camping-places of the "disappearing" Red Men. . . .

From the Indians the early settlers all over America, very naturally, borrowed many ideas and devices relating to hunting and fishing. Hence the fish-weirs of Virginia in the sixteenth and Brazil in the twentieth century; the use of narcotic poisons for killing fish; the employment of the blow-gun for obtaining animals and birds without injuring the skins; catching fish, especially eels and salmon, by torch-light; the "call" for deceiving the moose; methods of trailing and capturing the larger game and wild animals, etc. Also ways of rendering palatable or innocuous many of the plants and vegetables of the tropics in particular.

From the primitive agricultural processes of the American Indians not a little was transferred to the whites, particularly in the way of preparing the ground and cultivating the native plants and vegetables,—the New Englanders, e.g., learned from the aborigines how to treat corn in all its stages. The use of guano in Peru and of fish-manure (menhaden) in northeastern North America, like the burning over of the fields as a preparation for planting, was adopted by the whites from the Indians. From the same source they came to plant corn in hills and pumpkins or beans and corn together. Governor Bradford, in 1621, tells how Squanto, the Indian, came to the relief of the colonists at Plymouth, "showing them both the manner how to set it and after how to dress and tend it. Also he told them, except they got fish and set with it (in these old grounds) it would come to nothing." And Morton, in 1632, informs us how extensively the white inhabitants of Virginia were in the habit of "doing their grounds with fish."

Besides llama wool and alpaca (from Peru) several varieties of cotton (the chief is "Barbados cotton" of which the famous "Sea Island cotton" is the best known type) were known to the aborigines of the warmer parts of America and cultivated by them in pre-Columbian times. Also several kinds of hemps and fibres. Those of the maguey (*Agave americana*) and the *Agave mexicana,* now used to make many things, from rope to imitation haircloth; sisal hemp from Central America; the piassava of the Amazon; and the fibre of the pineapple, the *istle* of the ancient Mexican, which, under the name of *pita,* has become famous through its extensive production in the Philippine Islands. . . .

Of Indian inventions and devices for increasing the comfort of man the whites have adopted many,—some temporarily, others permanently. The infant of the Hudson's Bay factor in the far north, sleeps safe in the warm moss-bag of the Athapascans, and at the seashore the offspring of the New Englander toddles about in moccasins borrowed from the Iroquois or the Algonkin. The whaler and the Arctic adventurer adapted for their own uses the snow goggles and the dog-sled of the Eskimo. . . .

The third day after landing in the New World Columbus saw on the Bahamas the hamacas, or net-swings, which as hammocks are now in use all over the civilized world. This may be counted the first gift of the aborigines to the strange race that came to them from over-sea. . . .

Recreations, also, the Indian has furnished the white man. The canoe and the toboggan enter largely into American pleasures and sports,—and to the aboriginal ideas have been added the "water-toboggan" and light canoes for women. In Canada and parts of northeastern North America, the healthful game of lacrosse, known of old to the Indians, ranks among our best sports, and among the creoles of Louisiana still survives raquette, the southern variety of the same invention. The invigorating exercise of snowshoeing comes also from the Indian.

But it is on the food supply of the world that the American Indian has exerted the greatest influence. In his address before the German Geographical Congress at Stuttgart, in 1893, Dr. Rein said:

> The influence of the New World upon the material conditions of life in the Old World has been very varied. For most inhabitants of Europe, and even for the Maoris in far off New Zealand, potatoes have become an everyday food; Indian corn is even more widespread, and tobacco has conquered the whole world.

Coming not all of them directly through the Indian, but in most cases, largely through his mediation, "Cacao, vanilla, logwood, mahogany, and other useful or decorative timbers, as well as the many ornamental plants of our houses and gardens, have introduced considerable changes in our manners of life."

Tobacco,—noxious weed, or soothing panacea,—

> "Sublime tobacco! which, from East to West,
> Cheers the tar's labor, or the Turkman's rest,"

as Byron called it; tobacco, for whose sake Charles Lamb said he "would do anything but die"; tobacco, solace of old England's fox-hunting clerics; tobacco, safe refuge of American tariff-tinkers; tobacco, with all it brings of good and of evil, we owe to the Arawaks of the Caribbean. . . .

Concerning another gift we have received from the Red Man there has not been such divergence of opinion. The potato has been little sung by inspired bards or glorified by bishops of a great church,—its humbler task has been to furnish food to the world's hungry millions, and its duty in that respect has been well done. Disastrous, indeed, would be the result were the potato for but a single year to disappear from the food supply of man. . . .

Another food-plant that has travelled far from its original home in America is manioc, from which is obtained the tapioca of commerce (other than the variety of sago which goes also by that name). Manioc or cassava, in pre-Columbian days, was exploited, as a cultivated plant, by the aborigines of Brazil, Guiana, Mexico, etc. . . .

That very useful vegetable, the tomato, was cultivated in Mexico (its name is Aztec) and Peru prior to the European discovery. Since then it has extended even to the Malay Archipelago and the gardens of China and Japan. . . .

The New Englander dinner of today is incomplete, for a large part of the year, without squash in some form or other; and time was when pumpkin-pie was almost a sacred dish,—there were also pumpkin sauce, pumpkin bread, etc. . . .

Some of our "Boston baked beans," too, had their start from the Red Man, for the common haricot kidney bean, according to De Candolle, was cultivated in America in pre-Columbian times. The Lima bean, as its name indicates, is also American,—and antedates the coming of the whites. The use of these two kinds of beans (and they are employed in a variety of ways) was made possible by pre-Columbian horticulture. And baked beans on Saturday night is almost a religious observance with some New Englanders even in the twentieth century. . . .

The luscious pineapple, the pawpaw, the persimmon, the agave, the chirimoya, the guava, the sapodilla, the soursop, the starapple, the mammee, the marmalade plum, the custard-apple, the chayote, the cashew, the alligator-pear, etc., are all natives of the New World, and have had their virtues ascertained by the Indians before the discovery, or pointed out by them to the European since.

The artichoke, oca, quinoa, the cacao-bean, arracacha, arrow-root, and red peppers (whence paprika, tabasco sauce and the like), etc., are other gifts of the American aborigines to those who conquered them.

Besides all these mentioned, in Mexico, Central and South America there are hundreds of fruits and plant-foods, in more or less local use, which have not extended their influence much if any beyond the limits of the continent,—all having been made known to the whites by the Indians directly or indirectly. The "folk-foods" of Spanish America are largely of aboriginal origin. North America, however, has its succotash, pone, hominy, sagamity, suppawn, etc., name and thing alike adopted from the Indians. Nor must we forget the pemmican of the Canadian Northwest ("pemmican" is now made to order for Arctic expeditions in Europe and America) and the *"jerked* beef," representing the *charqui* of the Peruvian neighbors of the great plains of the Chaco. Indian ways of cooking clams ("Indian bed," e.g.), of preparing fish for eating ("planked shad," etc.), and, in the more southern regions, of boiling, roasting and otherwise cooking and making palatable fruits, roots and herbs, small animals, etc., deserve mention. In many parts of Spanish-America the methods of cooking are much after the aboriginal fashion. . . .

The primitive home of maize was probably in some portion of the Mexico-Isthmian region, whence it has spread wherever man will use or the climate tolerate. Says Mrs. Earle of Old New England:

> Next to fish, the early colonists found in Indian corn, or Guinny wheat, —Turkie wheat one traveller called it,—their most unfailing food supply.
> Our first poet wrote in 1675, of what he called early days:
> The dainty Indian maize
> Was eat in clamp-shells out of wooden trays.

142

Its abundance and adaptability did much to change the nature of their diet, as well as to save them from starvation. The colonists learned from the Indians how to plant, nourish, harvest, grind and cook it in many forms and in each way it formed a palatable food.

Take from the New England table during the time that has elapsed since the Indians welcomed the first settlers not merely by word of mouth, but also with agreeable food, its memories of "rye and Indian," with "Boston brown bread," yo-cake, johnny-cake, pone, suppawn, "Indian pudding," succotash, hulled corn, hominy, mush, and all the other concoctions of "Indian meal," rude and refined, and what a void there would be! And it startles us to think that the American child owes his popcorn to the Indian, to whom must be traced back ultimately such diversified application of the virtues of maize, as is represented by the innumerable uses which the white man has found for the cornstarch extracted from this American plant. Almost every part of the corn plant has been made use of by man for one purpose or another: the boy has his corn-stalk fiddle and his beard of corn-silk; the stalks are employed to make various things, from fuel to baskets; and from them in the green and soft state have been extracted syrup, sugar, brandy, etc.; the husks are used for packing, to stuff mattresses and chairs, to wrap cigarettes, to make paper; ...

Medicine owes much to the American Indian. In the early history of the European colonies the "Indian doctor" played a not unimportant *role* in stanching the wounds and alleviating the pains and aches of the pioneer. ... Dr. Bard, in 1894, credited the Indians of California with furnishing "three of the most valuable additions which have been made to the pharmacopaeia during the last twenty years." Two of these are the "yerba santa" (holy plant), Eriodyction glutinosum, used for affections of the respiratory tract; and the cascara sagrada (sacred bark), Rhamnus purshiana, a good laxative. In northeastern North America the lobelia was once the watchword of a local medical school and had an extended vogue as an emetic and cure for asthma. Mexico has furnished jalap, the well-known purgative. The Indians of South America have given the world jaborandi leaves (for dropsy, uraemia, snake-bite), the balsams capaiba, tolu, etc., ipecacuanha, quinine and copalchi, guaiacum (once a famous remedy for syphilis) coca, curari, etc. In this list quinine, coca, and curari deserve more particular mention.

42 EARLY EUROPEANS IN INDIA

The life and the occupations of the Europeans who migrated overseas depended upon the nature of the indigenous societies in which they found themselves. The French and the English, who settled in North America, were forced to farm and fish and trade in order to support themselves because the native Indians were too few and intractable to exploit. The Spaniards and the Portuguese, by contrast, took advantage of the numerous and settled Indian peoples in their colonies to establish large estates that were worked by native labor. In India, the position of the Europeans was entirely different from what it was anywhere in the Americas. The *density of the population, the sophistication of the ancient civilization, and the power of the Mogul compelled the Europeans at first to behave circumspectly in the few ports in which they were allowed to conduct their mercantile operations. The following selection describes the life led by the English merchants in Calcutta in the early eighteenth century—the obsequious deference to the Mogul emperor, the rigid discipline imposed by the East India Company, and the effort to preserve and display their "civilized" and "Christian" origins at the same time that they were taking native wives and adopting the native dress and cuisine and other features of everyday life.**

The power of the Moghul Emperor was more than enough to discourage any attempt on the part of the European traders to imitate the conquests of Cortez in the New World. All commercial rights in India were conceived as privileges awarded by the benefaction of the Moghul or one of his deputies, and it was therefore the constant endeavour of the Europeans to retain his favour. At sea they engaged frequently in open battle, but on Indian soil, although their Ambassadors to the Imperial Court were known to poison each other in their competition for Royal favour, they lived ostensibly as subjects of the Moghul and were rarely permitted to disturb the peace of his domains. As his dependents they commonly appealed for his intervention and protection in their petty disputes, and they relied upon the strength and stability of his government for the security of their settlements. . . .

The Bengal factories of the English were straight-forward business-like units set up and organised solely in accordance with the demands of commerce. The European staff of each was small and was appointed by the Court of Directors from their offices in Leadenhall Street. At Madras there was a President and Council, who communicated direct with the Court of Directors, to whose jurisdiction the settlements in Bengal were at first subordinated, and all decisions of importance concerning the Bengal trade were referred to the Madras Council by the "Agent and Council of the Bay."

Beneath the Agent of the Bay there was in every factory a Chief or No. 1, who was assisted by three or four less senior officers each with a specific duty to perform. Service in the Company was divided into three distinct grades, the lowest being that of the Writer, in which rank a recruit was apprenticed for the first five or six years of his service in the East. As a Writer his activities were confined to the transcription of accounts and the copying of confidential letters or such documents as could not safely be entrusted to locally recruited Indian and Eurasian clerks, but when his apprenticeship was finished, he was promoted to Factor, from which grade appointments to the executive posts of 2nd, 3rd or 4th officer in a settlement were generally made. Eventually, if he survived ten or twelve years service in the East, he might join the ranks of the Senior Merchants, and serve as a Chief Member of the Council, or even, perhaps, be appointed Agent to the Company. . . .

In these early days the Court of Directors set their faces rigidly against recruitment from outside the mercantile English middle-classes. In a far flung enterprise such as they controlled they rightly feared the more fiery nature and militaristic inclinations of the gentry, believing that young recruits from the cavalier class would be far too ready to dispute over small

* R. Pearson, *Eastern Interlude. A Social History of the European Community in Calcutta* (Calcutta: Thacker, 1954), pp. 5, 8-13, 55-57.

points of honour to live peaceably in the isolation of an East Indian factory. To maintain the efficiency of the eastern settlements the Court rightly insisted upon strict compliance with its instructions, and it was only the middle-class recruit who was generally prepared to accept the rigid self-discipline entailed by service in their distant trading-posts. Life in the settlements was therefore precisely ordered, and closely regulated, somewhat upon the corporate or communal lines which still characterise life in the older universities of England today. The chapel and dining hall formed the pivot of all social activity, and morning prayers, mid-day dinner and the evening supper were each communal functions, attendance at which was compulsory. Absence from meals or from daily prayers was punishable by a fine—as also was indiscretion. Swearing was rigidly banned and oaths involving blasphemy cost a Rupee a time, at more or less the same rate as that which had been laid down in Cromwell's New Model Army, for the attitude of the Court was strongly set against all forms of licence and frivolity, and frequently inclined in the direction of Puritanism.

Seniority played an important role in the maintenance of discipline, and largely determined both salary and promotion. At communal meals the order of precedence was strictly observed, and in the larger factories, such as that at Hooghly, the members of the Council sat on "high table," while the factors and writers took their seats, still in order of seniority, at the benches and tables set in the lower part of the hall. The observance of the rules of precedence was considered the elementary basis of discipline and was rigidly enforced. It found expression even in such matters as the size of the roundel or umbrella that servants of the Company were permitted to have carried over their heads when walking abroad in the heat of the day, and when a representative of the Madras Council arrived to inspect the Bengal Factories and reported that Bengal Factors were exceeding the specified limits in this respect, a severe letter of censure arrived from the Madras President by return ship.

Permission had been obtained in most settlements to fence off the bounds of the factory as a protection against thieves and dacoits, and the factory gates would in these cases be locked promptly at nine every evening. All factors were required to be in their quarters by that hour, and the young writer who returning late to the factory found the gates already closed could expect a sure penalty—often the loss of five weeks' pay. This particular offence was punished rigorously since the Company had in mind not only the moral character of its employees but also the cost of their replacement. Experienced writers, brought out at great expense from England, succumbed only too easily to the rigours of the climate to permit a further wastage of life in the dark alleys of the bazaar at night time.

Work began at nine or ten in the morning and finished at twelve. Only if some urgent necessity arose, such as the need to prepare a cargo for an unexpected ship, did labour continue beyond midday, and the afternoon was normally spent in sleep during the hot season and in out-door recreation in cool weather. Shooting at the butts with bow and arrow was a common pastime, and where local conditions permitted, hunting with cumbersome flint lock guns was popular. But the personal expenditure of the factors was subject to close criticism and control, and when one of the factors at Hooghly fenced off a corner of his compound the Court promptly wrote to him: "The Tayger (tiger) you keep at the expense of a goat a day, we look upon as a superfluous vain charge," and instructed him to dispose of it forthwith. Nor were their wishes to be treated lightly, despite the fact that letters to and from London might be delayed a year or more in transit if the vessel carrying them met with inclement weather.

Usually some attempt was made to cultivate an "English Garden" even though land could not always be procured in the immediate neighbourhood of the warehouses and factors' quarters. As a pleasant change from strolling in the bazaars and from constant contact with persons of an alien culture, the factors would often choose to spend an evening in these gardens, maintained at the expense of the Company, amongst surroundings reminiscent of their own homeland, and such communion with the characteristic elements of their own culture was considered a necessary antidote to the more exotic influence of the Indian city.

For the same reason most factors seem to have possessed a small library of English and Latin books to which they turned to combat the tedium and mental stagnation that constantly threatened their small communities. For their reading they chose Religio Medici and Eikon Basilike, and they took pleasure in filling their letters with pompous Latin phrases and quotations, and in debating, as was the fashion of the time, the finer points of current theological doctrines. Their ample leisure lent itself to philosophy and to the development of theosophical arguments, yet the blood-letting ceremonies and rituals of the Hindu religion they despised as unworthy of serious study, and few of them troubled to put on record any detailed description of the intricate pattern of contemporary Indian life.

It was largely because they felt superior to the "moors"—as they dubbed Moslems the world over—and to the Hindu "pagans," that they felt little inclination to adopt India as their permanent home. Nevertheless, being without women of their own nation, they either married Indian women or cohabited with them, and Indian habits and practices came easier to them than they perhaps would have been prepared to admit. Breakfast and the odd meals of the day were often taken lying on a carpet, dressed in nothing more than a 'dhoti' or loin cloth. In Bengal, the 'hooka' became popular with the English at an early date, and 'pan' was sometimes eaten, a habit that shocked new arrivals because of the unpleasant discolouration of the mouth and teeth which was caused by it. . . .

When engaged in office work it was customary to wear only thin, loose clothes so as to be at ease, but for all formal occasions, and for public appearances in the streets, there seems to have been no inclination to discard or even modify the style of contemporary costume as worn in England. Little or no concession was made to the heat of the Indian climate, and although unable to compete with their hosts in the display of jewelled ornaments and precious metals, the English who visited the Courts of native rulers were nevertheless the object of admiration on account of the quantities of exquisite lace and beautiful embroidery which they wore. Dress became a badge of which in their own hearts they were proud, and it gave them pleasure to display their "Christian" origin by adhering courageously to their heavy finery throughout even the hottest season of the year. The natives of Bengal were notable for the practical unostentation of their national costume, which comprised simply the dhoti or loin cloth, and in front of them the English paraded complete in every detail of their own unhealthy fripperies. Pride, which nevertheless served a useful purpose at times when unyielding courage was required, made them blind to the absurdity of their heavy broadcloth breeches and jackets and of their gallant but unsuitable headwear, which earned for them the nickname of "hatmen"; amongst the unsophisticated peasantry.

This adherence to the fashions of their homeland reveals a strong association with the mother country from which they never tried, as did the later American colonists, to break away and build up a separate culture of their own. The Englishman in the Americas and West Indies found himself in contact with a simple and primitive indigenous people over whom he was able rapidly to assert himself, and once having gained the Americas for himself, he set about declaring his own independence from the political authority of the European homeland. In the East Indies, however, the opposite was the case. The Indian adventure had begun neither as an attempt at colonisation nor as a revolt against dictatorship or social rigidity in the homeland: it was not an attempt to build a new life, but was merely an undertaking aimed at the accumulation of sufficient private wealth to make possible the fuller enjoyment of the amenities which the home country had to offer its richer citizens. Also, the Englishman in India found himself face to face with a highly complex and advanced culture, and the retention of the traditional costume of his homeland therefore became to him a gesture of defiance offered to the strange, exotic and somewhat cruel civilisation in which he found himself. A rigid adherence to the sartorial vagaries of Western Europe was consequently considered by him to be a vital point in the battle to preserve a standard of "civilized" conduct.

PART III

WORLD OF
WESTERN DOMINANCE,
1763-1914

Chapter Ten

Basis of dominance:
the scientific revolution

GALILEO GALILEI 43

The century-and-a-half between 1763 and 1914 stands out in world history as the period of European domination over a large part of the globe, when Europe extended its control from underpopulated territories such as Siberia and the Americas to ancient centers of civilization in Asia as well as to Africa. This unprecedented global domination was made possible by three great revolutions—scientific, industrial, and political—which gave Europe irresistible dynamism and power. This part of the readings will consider first the origin and nature of these revolutions, and then the impact Europe made upon the various regions of the world.

*Taking first the scientific revolution, Galileo Galilei, the Italian astronomer, physicist, and mathematician, is noteworthy as marking the transition from medieval to modern science. By his persistent investigation of natural laws he laid the foundation for modern experimental science, and by the construction of astronomical telescopes he greatly enlarged man's vision and conception of the universe. In the following selection an American authority on the history of science describes the nature of Galileo's work and its significance for the development of science.**

Probably no single name in the annals of science is as well known as that of Galileo. Yet so conflicting are the opinions in the literature on his work that it is difficult for the average scientist to

* I. Bernard Cohen, "Galileo," *Scientific American*, CXXCI (August, 1949), 40-47. Reprinted with permission. Copyright © 1949 in the U.S. and Berne Convention countries by Scientific American, Inc. All rights reserved.

find out exactly what Galileo did. Some writers tell us that Galileo was an empiricist who inaugurated the "scientific method" of learning "general truths of nature," and they illustrate by citing his supposed discovery of the laws of falling bodies by patient observation of what happened when balls of unequal weight were dropped from the Leaning Tower of Pisa. Others say that, on the contrary, Galileo never learned anything by making experiments; he used them only to check results which he had already obtained by mathematical reasoning and deductions from *a priori* assumptions. Many writers hail Galileo as the father of modern science. Others argue that almost everything Galileo did in science had been begun in the late Middle Ages. Many commentators agree with Sir David Brewster, who wrote of Galileo as one of the "martyrs of science." Others accept A. N. Whitehead's remark that Galileo's punishment by the Roman Inquisition was only "an honorable detention and a mild reproof before dying peaceably in bed."

What shall a scientist do when he is faced with making a choice between diametrically opposed points of view held by such respected writers? The example of Galileo provides one of the best possible arguments for the need of a continuing and increasing scholarship in the history of science. For if we are to understand the true significance of what Galileo did in physics and astronomy, obviously we must first have a clear picture of the scope and nature of the science that existed at the time he did his work, and next a knowledge of the history of physical science since his time, so that we may evaluate those elements which have proved most fruitful for the development of science.

The difficulty in interpreting Galileo stems in large part from the nature of his own thought and writings. He lived in that fertile period which marks the end of the Middle Ages and Renaissance and the beginning of the era of modern science. Thus he was a transitional figure with one foot in the past and the other striding into the future. Considering this state of affairs, one would need an unwarranted vanity to attempt to patch up all the contradictions in the various interpretations that have been made during the last hundred years. Yet certain clearly marked aspects of Galileo's achievement do emerge.

Galileo was a physicist, an astronomer and a mathematician. The first significant contribution to astronomy by Galileo occurred in 1604 while he was a professor in Padua, a post he had received in 1592 at the age of 28. The occasion was a new star seen in the heavens, a nova, which had aroused great interest among scientists, students and laymen everywhere. In a public lecture Galileo demonstrated, on the basis of careful observation, that the new star was truly a star. It could not be a mere meteor in the Earth's atmosphere, for it had no parallax and must be very distant, among the fixed stars well beyond our solar system. Galileo predicted that the nova would be visible for a short while and then would vanish into obscurity.

The boldness of this assertion is difficult to realize today. The outlook on the external world then was largely Aristotelian; it was generally believed that the heavens were perfect and unchangeable and subject neither to growth nor to decay. Only the Earth, the center of the universe, could change. The laws of physics on Earth were essentially different from those in the celestial beyond.

Galileo's assertion that the perfect and unchangeable heavens might witness growth and decay brought him into immediate conflict with the Aristotelians. The latter, as one of Galileo's biographers, J. J. Fahie, puts it, were probably as much "annoyed at the appearance of the star" as at Galileo's "calling attention to it so publicly and forcibly." In any event, Galileo was a better target than the star. Galileo was never one to shrink from controversy, and he seized the opportunity to repudiate the old physics of Aristotle, which he held to be inadequate, and with it the Ptolemaic, or geocentric, system of the universe.

Galileo had already been a confirmed Copernican for some time, although he had not dared to publish his arguments, "fearing," as he said in a letter to Johann Kepler, "the fate of our master, Copernicus." Soon after his studies of the new star, however, Galileo was provided with an extraordinary opportunity to vindicate the Copernican idea. This occasion was the most important event in Galileo's career as an astronomer. He wrote:

"About ten months ago a rumor came to our ears that an optical instrument had been elaborated by a Dutchman, by the aid of which visible objects, even though far distant from the eye of the observer, were distinctly seen as if near at hand; and some stories of this marvelous effect were bandied about, to which some gave credence and which others denied. The same was confirmed to me a few days after by a letter sent from Paris by the noble Frenchman Jacob Badovere, which at length was the reason that I applied myself entirely to seeking out the theory and discovering the means by which I might arrive at the invention of a similar instrument, an end which I attained a little later, from considerations of the theory of refraction; and I first prepared a tube of lead, in the ends of which I fitted two glass lenses, both plane on one side, one being spherically convex, the other concave, on the other side."

Thus in his great book *The Sidereal Messenger,* which he published in Venice in 1610, did Galileo describe his introduction to the telescope. There are several independent claimants to the invention, but there is no doubt that Galileo was the first to turn the telescope to observation of the heavenly bodies. It was an experience unique in the history of man. For millennia the heavens had been viewed only by the naked eye, and no one knew what glories might exist beyond the range of man's unaided vision. Wherever Galileo pointed his telescope he found extraordinary and astonishing new facts.

Galileo first examined the Moon. His conclusion was "that the surface of the Moon is not perfectly smooth, free from inequalities and exactly spherical, as a large school of philosophers considers with regard to the Moon and the other heavenly bodies, but . . . on the contrary, it is full of inequalities, uneven, full of hollows and protuberances, just like the surface of the Earth itself, which is varied everywhere by lofty mountains and deep valleys." Galileo even determined the height of the mountains on the Moon, and his results agree with modern determinations in order of magnitude. He believed at first that the dark and light areas on the Moon's surface represented land and water, but we must remember that even today beginning students of astronomy, on first looking at the Moon or at a photograph of it, have the same impression.

Next Galileo turned to the stars, and at once discovered a difference between the fixed stars and the planets, or wanderers. "The planets present their discs perfectly round, just as if described with a pair of compasses, and appear as so many little moons, completely illuminated and of a globular shape;

but the fixed stars do not look to the naked eye [as if they were] bounded by a circular circumference, but rather like blazes of light shooting out beams on all sides and very sparkling, and with the telescope they appear of the same shape as when they were viewed by simply looking at them. . . ." Galileo also noted that the telescope brought within the range of vision "a host of other stars, which escape the unassisted sight, so numerous as to be almost beyond belief. . . ."

The next subject of his observation was the Milky Way, which, to his astonishment, he found to be "nothing else but a mass of innumerable stars planted together in clusters." Furthermore, all of the "nebulosities," whose nature had long been a topic of dispute, also proved to be masses of stars.

Galileo reserved for last in his account "the matter, which seems to me to deserve to be considered the most important in this work, namely, that I should disclose and publish to the world the occasion of discovering and observing four PLANETS, never seen from the very beginning of the world up to our own times. . . ."

He had been examining the planet Jupiter on the seventh day of January in 1610 when he noticed "that three little stars, small but very bright, were near the planet; and although I believed them to belong to the number of the fixed stars, yet they made me somewhat wonder, because they seemed to be arranged exactly in a straight line, parallel to the ecliptic, and to be brighter than the rest of the stars, equal to them in magnitude. . . . On the east side [of Jupiter] there were two stars, and a single one towards the west. . . . But when on January 8th, led by some fatality, I turned again to look at the same part of the heavens, I found a very different state of things, for there were three little stars all west of Jupiter, and nearer together than on the previous night, and they were separated from one another by equal intervals, as the accompanying illustration shows."

Night after night Galileo continued to observe this group of "stars," and finally he "decided unhesitatingly, that there are three stars in the heavens moving about Jupiter, as Venus and Mercury round the Sun; which at length was established as clear as daylight by numerous other subsequent observations. These observations also established that there are not only three, but four erratic sidereal bodies performing their revolutions round Jupiter. . . ."

Galileo wrote that the discovery of Jupiter's four moons, which he called "planets," provided "a notable and splendid argument to remove the scruples of those who can tolerate the revolution of the planets round the Sun in the Copernican system, yet are so disturbed by the motion of one Moon about the Earth . . . for now we have not one planet only revolving about another . . . but four satellites circling about Jupiter, like the Moon about the Earth, while the whole system travels over a mighty orbit about the Sun in the space of twelve years." Galileo discovered another important fact: that the planet Venus has phases like those of the Moon; it waxes and wanes from a full orb to a thin crescent. "From the observation of these wonderful phenomena," wrote Galileo, "we are supplied with a determination most conclusive, and appealing to the evidence of our senses, of two very important problems, which up to this day were discussed by the greatest intellects with different conclusions. One is that the planets are bodies not self-luminous (if we may entertain the same views about Mercury as we do about Venus). . . . The second [is] that we are absolutely compelled to say that Venus (and Mercury also) revolves round the Sun, as do also all the rest of the planets. A truth believed indeed by the Pythagorean school, by Copernicus, and by Kepler, but never proved by the evidence of our senses, as it is now proved in the case of Venus and Mercury."

The discovery of the phases of Venus directly challenged the accepted Ptolemaic system. According to this system, Venus moved in an epicycle, a circular orbit whose center always lay between the Earth and the Sun. If this were true, then Venus, shining, as Galileo showed, by reflected light from the Sun, might be seen in some of its crescent phases, but we would never expect to scc Venus as a half circle, a full circle, or any phases between. Yet Galileo observed all these phases.

Galileo's discoveries made the Copernican system "philosophically rea-sonable" by showing that the Earth was like the other planets and the Moon. By observing the dark half of the quarter moon, faintly illuminated by earth-shine, he demonstrated that the Earth shone just like the planets. If observed through a telescope located on the Moon or on Venus, the Earth would exhibit phases like theirs. As Galileo put it, "The Earth, with fair and grateful ex-change, pays back to the Moon an illumination like that which it receives from the Moon nearly the whole time during the darkest gloom of night."

The Sun, by contrast, was self-luminous and thus set apart from the Earth, the Moon and the planets. If any single body was especially constituted to be at the center of the universe, surely it was the Sun and not the Earth! And as a model for this picture of the solar system, with the Sun at the center and its attendant planets circling it, there was Jupiter with its four satellites revolving about it in the same way.

Galileo's lifework shows a unity of purpose and achievement that is rare among men of science. His work in mechanics fitted in with his work in as-tronomy like an adjacent piece of a jig-saw puzzle. It is clear from his writ-ings that Galileo was at heart a gadgeteer with true mechanical feeling and inventive genius. One of his earliest discoveries was that a pendulum always makes a complete swing in the same period of time, no matter what the length of thc swing. IIe speedily applied this discovery to the invention of the "pulsi-logium," a device for mechanically recording and comparing pulse rates. Aside from his natural bent for mechanics, however, Galileo was strongly attracted to this subject because, in part at least, he thought of it as a cosmo-logical science, the link between earthly and celestial phenomena. If he could find the laws of motion on Earth, he could apply them to the motions of the planets and thc stars. It was thus his ambition to show that if one adopted the Copernican system, the planets followcd their patterns in the heavens by regular and simple laws, and not, as in the older theory, because each was guided by a "special intelligence."

In seeking a universal science of mechanics that would apply equally to the heavens and the Earth, Galileo was, of course, flying directly in the face of the contemporary point of view. The Aristotelian conception made a sharp distinction between motion on the Earth and Moon and motion in the trans-lunar, "celestial" universe. In the sublunar world, "natural motion" occurred in a straight line. An apple fell downward from the tree because it was "heavy" and its natural place was "down"; to make it go in any other direc-tion contrary to its nature required a "violent motion." In the translunar world, by contrast, the natural motion was circular, as befitted the perfect material out of which the celestial bodies were made.

By showing the similarity between the Earth, Moon and planets, which indicated that they must obey the same laws, Galileo brought terrestrial and celestial phenomena within one universal physics. The revolution in physical thinking effected by Galileo may be thought of as concentrating men's attention on change and on motion. He próved that even the Sun, that most "perfect" of all heavenly bodies, was subject to change, for when viewed by Galileo's telescope it showed changing spots! Anyhow, as Galileo put the matter, it was no "great honor" for bodies to be immutable and unalterable, nor was the Earth "corrupt" because it changed.

"It is my opinion," he asserted, "that the earth is very noble, and admirable, by reason of so many and so different alterations, mutations, generations, etc., which are incessantly made therein; and if without being subject to any alteration, it had been all one vast heap of sand, or a masse of jasper, or that . . . it had continued an immense globe of christal, wherein nothing had ever grown, altered, or changed, I should have esteemed it a lump of no benefit to the world, full of idlenesses, and in a word superfluous. . . . What greater folly can there be imagined, than to call jems, silver and gold pretious; and earth and dirt vile? For do not these persons consider, that if there should be as great a scarcity of earth, as there is of jewels and pretious metals, there would be no prince, but would gladly give a heap of diamonds and rubies, and many wedges of gold, to purchase onely so much earth as should suffice to plant a Gessemine in a little pot, or to set therein a China Orange [tangerine], that he might see it sprout, grow up, and bring forth so goodly leaves, so odoriferous flowers, and so delicate fruit? It is therefore scarcity and plenty that makes things esteemed and contemned by the vulgar. . . ."

We shall consider here only three aspects of Galileo's mechanics: the law of falling bodies, the principle of inertia, and the resolution and composition of independent motions. The law of falling bodies is the most celebrated of Galileo's discoveries. Modern scholarship has shown that Galileo's work on falling bodies was original not so much in his own statement of the law as in the particular use he made of it. Aristotle had said that the speed of a given falling body depended on the resistance of the medium in which it fell, *e.g.,* a stone obviously will fall faster in air than in water. He had also said that if two bodies were to fall in a resistant medium like air, their speed would depend on their weight. Even before Galileo, many writers had expressed their doubts concerning this dictum. In the sixth century, John Philoponos had demonstrated by an experiment that the contrary was true. Galileo approached the problem by using the principles of deductive reasoning and mathematics rather than by direct experiment.

He considered two possibilities in the case of a uniformly accelerated motion starting from rest: 1) that the speed was proportional to the distance fallen, 2) that it was proportional to the elapsed time. The first led to an apparent contradiction, so he accepted the second, the now familiar law that the velocity equals the acceleration times the time—$v = At$. Then, making use of the well-known proof that a uniformly accelerated body moves through a distance s in any time t equal to the distance it would have fallen in the same time t with the average velocity, he derived the equivalent of the law: $s = \frac{1}{2}At^2$.

As a check, Galileo proposed an experiment on an inclined plane. This test was a means of "diluting gravity," so that one could study the relatively slow rolling motion by timing it with a water clock. The test depended on Galileo's important theorem of the composition of motions. A body moving down an inclined plane, in the Galilean scheme, has two components: a horizontal or forward motion, and a vertical or falling motion. Each is independent of the other. By making a rough check with an inclined plane, he demonstrated that the law $s = \frac{1}{2}At^2$ seemed to hold along the inclined plane. From this he inferred that it also held for freely falling bodies.

Here we have a typical example of Galileo's method in physics: Imagine the conditions of a given situation, make a mathematical formulation and derive the reasonable consequences, then make a rough check, if it seems necessary, to be sure that the result is correct. His experimental test involved a brass ball rolling in a groove. He measured the time for different distances, at varying angles of inclination of the grooved board. In "experiments near an hundred times repeated," Galileo found that the times agreed with the law, with no differences "worth mentioning." His conclusion that the differences were not "worth mentioning" only shows how firmly he had made up his mind beforehand, for the rough conditions of the experiment would never have yielded an exact law. Actually the discrepancies were so great that a contemporary worker, Père Mersenne, could not reproduce the results described by Galileo, and even doubted that he had ever made the experiment.

Once Galileo had satisfied himself that he knew the law of falling bodies, he wished to apply it. He knew full well that the law would work precisely only in an ideal situation—one in which there was no resisting medium—but he nevertheless decided to apply it to falling bodies in air, since he observed that the effect of the air resistance was small for a heavy body such as a cannon ball.

Keeping in mind that motion in air departs slightly from the ideal case, Galileo next applied his principles to the problem of determining the trajectory of a projectile. According to the Galilean analysis, a projectile has two independent components of motion, horizontal and vertical, like the ball on the inclined plane. If fired horizontally from a gun, it moves forward the same distance in every second if we disregard the small factor of air resistance. As it emerges from the barrel it also begins to fall toward the earth. During the first second it will fall 16 feet; during the second second, 48 feet; during the third, 80 feet, and so on. Hence the path of the shell will be a parabola. Here was a brand new discovery that was of the utmost practical importance in the new science of artillery-ranging.

Implicit in Galileo's analysis was another brand new idea: the principle of inertia. While he did not state it explicitly, in his assumptions about the movement of the projectile he made use of the theorem that a body will continue in uniform motion in a straight line unless acted on by an outside force. Galileo introduced the revolutionary concept, contrary to all older physics, that uniform motion in a straight line is physically equivalent to a state of rest, thereby transforming the science of mechanics from a static to a kinematic basis.

These new principles gave the first complete explanation of the mechanics of the Copernican universe. Now one could explain why a stone dropped from a tower would fall at the base of the tower even though the Earth had moved while the ball fell. One could also understand for the first time why a stone dropped from the masthead of a moving ship would fall at the foot of the mast in spite of the movement of the ship. Galileo pointed out that the stone partakes of the ship's forward motion before it is dropped, and this forward motion continues unchanged while the stone falls because the forward and the downward motions are independent. Consequently an observer on such a boat could not tell from this experiment whether the boat was at rest or in uniform motion. In other words, an observer cannot distinguish between a state of rest and of uniform motion save with regard to an observable external system of reference. This is the principle of Galilean relativity. He observed: "In respect to the Earth, to the Tower, and to our selves, which all as one piece move with the diurnal motion together with the stone, the diurnal motion is as if it had never been."

At this point the reader may ask: What about the story of the famous experiment in which Galileo dropped two balls of unequal size and weight from the Leaning Tower of Pisa? At some time and place, he did drop two unequal weights and found that they did not hit the ground with the great difference that Aristotle had predicted. But it appears from modern scholarship that he never did so, at least publicly, from the Pisan tower.

Galileo worked out his physics by thought, by correct reasoning and mathematics, not by induction from experiments. During his days at Pisa, before he went to Padua, he wrote: "But, as ever, we employ reason more than examples (for we seek the causes of effects, and they are not revealed by experiment)." Galileo liked to use what we may call "thought experiments," imagining the consequences rather than observing them directly. Indeed, when he described the motion of a ball dropped from the mast of a moving ship, in his *Dialogue on the Two Great Systems of the World,* he then had the Aristotelian, Simplicio, ask whether he had made an experiment, to which Galileo replied: "No, and I do not need it, as without any experience I can affirm that it is so, because it cannot be otherwise."

To confute the supposed results of Aristotelian logic Galileo made a frontal attack on Aristotelians. For example, he pointed out that "it may be possible, that an artist may be excellent in making organs, but unlearned in playing on them, thus he might be a great logician, but unexpert in making use of logick; like as we have many that theorically understand the whole art of poetry, and yet are unfortunate in composing but mere four verses; others enjoy all the precepts of Cinci, and yet know not how to paint a stoole. The playing on the organs is not taught by them who know how to make organs, but by him that knows how to play on them; poetry is learnt by continual reading of poets: limning is learnt by continual painting and designing: demonstration from the reading of books full of demonstrations, which are the mathematical onely, and not the logical."

As for Aristotle's appeal to the experience of the senses, Galileo asks: "And doth he not likewise affirm, that we ought to prefer that which sense demonstrates, before all arguments, though in appearance never so well grounded? and saith he not this without the least doubt or hesitation?" To which Simplicio, the Aristotelian, replies, "He doth so." Then, says Galileo, ". . . you shall argue more Aristotelically, saying, the heavens are alterable, for that so my sense telleth me, than if you should say, the heavens are unalterable, for that logick so perswaded Aristotle. Furthermore, we may discourse of coelestial matters much better than Aristotle; because, he confessing the knowledg thereof to be difficult to him, by reason of their remoteness from the senses, he thereby acknowledgeth, that one to whom the senses can better represent the same, may philosophate upon them with more certainty. Now we by help of the telescope, are brought thirty or forty times nearer to the heavens, than ever Aristotle came; so that we may discover in them an hundred things, which he could not see, and amongst the rest, these spots in the Sun, which were to him absolutely invisible; therefore we may discourse of the heavens and Sun, with more certainty than Aristotle."

Galileo's writings abound with references to the facts of experience, of direct observation. In this sense, Galileo built his science on a somewhat empirical basis. But he was in no sense such an empiricist as the 19th-century writers attempted to make him out. He was not a careful experimenter, though he was a keen observer, and it is only the fallacy of writing history backwards that has made us visualize him as the patient investigator who only reluctantly drew conclusions after long test. The latter picture describes a much later kind of scientific man, of whom the prototype may well have been Robert Boyle.

Galileo's greatest general contribution was the idea that mathematics was the language of motion, and that change was to be described mathematically, in a way that would express both its complete generality and necessity, as well as its universality and applicability to the real world of experience. While Galileo ridiculed the numerology aspect of Platonism, he declared in the opening pages of the *Dialogue:* "I know perfectly well that the Pythagoreans had the highest esteem for the science of number and that Plato himself admired the human intellect and believed that it participates in divinity solely because it is able to understand the nature of numbers. And I myself am well inclined to make the same judgment." That nature herself "loves the integers" was shown in Galileo's discovery that a falling body moves so that its speeds after successive seconds are in the ratio of whole numbers 1, 2, 3. . . . The distances fallen in successive seconds are in the ratio of the odd numbers 1, 3, 5. . . . The most important influence on Galileo's thinking undoubtedly was Archimedes, but whereas the latter had constructed a geometry of rest, Galileo built a geometry of motion.

The net result of Galileo's lifework was to adduce new evidence for the Copernican theory of the solar system, and to provide the mechanical rationale of its operation. One evidence of the success of this activity was the hostility his work aroused. In the evening of his life he was brought into conflict with the Roman Inquisition. Galileo took the point of view, as expressed in his famous letter to the Grand Duchess Cristina, that the Holy Scriptures did not have the teaching of science as their ultimate aim. He argued that the language of the Bible was not to be taken literally. Thus when the Sun was described as moving around the Earth, this did not imply the truth of the geocentric system, but was merely an expression in everyday language. (In the same way we still speak of the Sun rising and setting.) From this point of view, Galileo held that one could accept the Copernican system while remaining a good Catholic and without in any way impugning the Scriptures.

Had Galileo remained at Padua under the rule of Venice, which held herself independent of papal jurisdiction, he would never have had to face the Inquisition. But with the fame attendant on his initial discoveries with the telescope, he chose to move to Florence. There is a vast and readily available literature on Galileo's trial and condemnation, which will not be discussed in this article confined to his scientific work. It is true that Galileo was never put to torture during his stay in the prison of the Inquisition. But the knowledge that others had been tortured there, and that not too long before Giordano Bruno had been burned alive, surely had their effects upon him. He was a man of 69 in poor health. Three physicians attempting to avert the trial had testified in 1633: "All these symptoms are worthy of notice, as under the least aggravation they might become dangerous to his life." The poor man, formerly eager for combat with those who would deny the new truths, was now crushed by the action of the Holy Office of the Church to which he had ever been faithful. Upon repeated examination, he "confessed":

"I, Galileo Galilei, son of the late Vincenzio Galilei of Florence, aged seventy years, being brought personally to judgment, and kneeling before you, Most Eminent and Most Reverend Lords Cardinals, General Inquisitors of the Universal Christian Commonwealth against heretical depravity, having before my eyes the Holy Gospels which I touch with my own hands, swear that I have always believed, and, with the help of God, will in future believe, every article which the Holy Catholic and Apostolic Church of Rome holds, teaches, and preaches. But because I have been enjoined, by this Holy Office, altogether to abandon the false opinion which maintains that the Sun is the centre and immovable, and forbidden to hold, defend, or teach, the said false doctrine in any manner ... I am willing to remove from the minds of your Eminences, and of every Catholic Christian, this vehement suspicion rightly entertained towards me, therefore, with a sincere heart and unfeigned faith, I abjure, curse, and detest the said errors and heresies, and generally every other error and sect contrary to the said Holy Church; and I swear that I will never more in future say, or assert anything, verbally or in writing, which may give rise to a similar suspicion of me; but that if I shall know any heretic, or any one suspected of heresy, I will denounce him to this Holy Office, or to the Inquisitor and Ordinary of the place in which I may be. I swear, moreover, and promise that I will fulfil and observe fully all the penances which have been or shall be laid on me by this Holy Office. But if it shall happen that I violate any of my said promises, oaths, and protestations (which God avert!), I subject myself to all the pains and punishments which have been decreed and promulgated by the sacred canons and other general and particular constitutions against delinquents of this description. So, may God help me, and His Holy Gospels, which I touch with my own hands, I, the above named Galileo Galilei, have abjured, sworn, promised, and bound myself as above; and, in witness thereof, with my own hand have subscribed this present writing of my abjuration, which I have recited word for word.

One can only wonder at the indomitable spirit that enabled Galileo—shamed, confined, ill, his major work placed on the Index of Prohibited Books—to complete his last major work, *The New Sciences,* the publication of which had to be arranged surreptitiously. And today we may also wonder whether the fight for freedom of belief has yet been truly won. For we can repeat Galileo's tragic declaration: "Philosophy wants to be free!"

44 THE ROYAL SOCIETY

During the seventeenth century several scientific societies were founded, outstanding ones being the Accademia del Cimento *at Florence (1661), the Royal Society at London (1662), the* Académie des Sciences *at Paris (1666), and the Berlin Academy (1700). These societies reflected the interest of the intellectuals and upper classes in the "new philosophy," as science was then called. The extent of their interest is indicated in the following account of the Royal Society written by Thomas Sprat, Bishop of Rochester, in 1667. Following a brief survey of an-*

There first Purpose was no more than only the Satisfaction of breathing a freer Air, and of conversing in Quiet one with another, without being ingag'd in the Passions and Madness of that dismal Age. And from the Institution of that *Assembly,* it had been enough if no other Advantage had come but this: That by this means there was a Race of young Men provided against the next Age, whose Minds receiving from them their first Impressions of *Sober* and *generous Knowledge,* were invincibly arm'd against all the Inchantments of *Enthusiasm.* . . .

For such a candid and unpassionate Company, as that was, and for such a gloomy Season, what could have been a fitter Subject to pitch upon than *Natural Philosophy?* To have been always tossing about some *Theological Question,* would have been, to have made that their private Diversion, the Excess of which they themselves dislik'd in the publick: To have been eternally musing on *Civil Business,* and the Distresses of their Country, was too melancholy a Reflexion: It was *Nature* alone, which could pleasantly entertain them in that Estate. The Contemplation of that, draws our Minds off from past, or present Misfortunes, and makes them Conquerors over Things, in the greatest publick Unhappiness: while the Consideration of *Men,* and *human Affairs,* may affect us with a thousand various Disquiets; *that* never separates us into moral Factions; that gives us room to differ, without Animosity; and permits us to raise contrary Imaginations upon it, without any Danger of a *Civil War.*

Their *Meetings* were as frequent, as their Affairs permitted: their Proceedings rather by Action, than Discourse; chiefly attending some particular Trials, in *Chymistry* or *Mechanicks:* they had no Rules nor Method fix'd: their Intention was more to communicate to each other their Discoveries, which they could make in so narrow a Compass, than an united, constant, or regular Inquisition. . . .

Their Purpose is, in short, to make faithful *Records* of all the Works of *Nature,* or *Art,* which can come within their Reach; that so the present Age, and Posterity, may be able to put a Mark on the Errors, which have been strengthened by long Prescription; to restore the Truths, that have lain neglected; to push on those, which are already known, to more various Uses; and to make the way more passable, to what remains unrevealed. This is the Compass of their Design. And to accomplish this, they have endeavoured, to separate the Knowledge of *Nature,* from the Colours of *Rhetorick,* the Devices of *Fancy,* or the delightful Deceit of *Fables.* They have labour'd to enlarge it, from being confined to the Custody of a few, or from Servitude to private Interests. They have striven to preserve it from being over-press'd by a confus'd Heap of vain and useless Particulars; or from being straightned and bound too much up by general Doctrines. They have tried to put into a Condition of perpetual Increasing; by settling an inviolable Correspondence between the Hand and the Brain. They have studied to make it not only an Enterprise of one Season, or of some lucky Opportunity; but a Business of Time; a steady, a lasting, a popular, an uninterrupted Work. They have attempted, to free it

* T. Sprat, *The History of the Royal Society of London, for the Improving of Natural Knowledge* (London, 1734), pp. 53, 55-56, 61-63, 71-73, 125-28.

from the Artifice, and Humours, and Passions of Sects: to render it an Instrument, whereby Mankind may obtain a Dominion over *Things,* and not only over one another's *Judgments:* And lastly, they have begun to establish these Reformations in Philosophy, not so much, by any solemnity of Laws, or Ostentation of Ceremonies, as by solid Practice and Examples; not by a glorious Pomp of Words; but by the silent, effectual, and unanswerable Arguments of real Productions. . . .

As for what belongs to the *Members* themselves that are to constitute the *Society:* It is to be noted, that they have freely admitted Men of different Religions, Countries, and Professions of Life. This they were obliged to do, or else they would come far short of the Largeness of their own Declarations. For they openly profess, not to lay the Foundation of an *English, Scotch, Irish, Popish,* or *Protestant* Philosophy; but a Philosophy of *Mankind.* . . .

All Places and Corners are now busy and warm about this Work: and we find many noble Rarities to be every Day given in not only by the Hands of learned and professed Philosophers; but from the Shops of *Mechanicks;* from the Voyages of *Merchants;* from the Ploughs of *Husbandmen;* from the Sports, the Fishponds, the Gardens of *Gentlemen;* . . . Men did generally think, that no Man was fit to meddle in Matters of this Consequence, but he that had bred himself up in a long Course of Discipline for that Purpose; that had the Habit, the Gesture, the Look of a Philosopher: Whereas Experience, on the contrary, tells us, that greater Things are produc'd by the *free* way, than the *formal.* This Mistake may well be compar'd to the Conceit we had of *Soldiers,* in the beginning of the civil Wars. None was thought worthy of that Name, but he that could shew his Wounds, and talk aloud of his Exploits in the *Low Countries:* Whereas the whole Business of fighting, was afterwards chiefly perform'd by *untravel'd Gentlemen, raw Citizens,* and *Generals* that had scarce ever before seen a Battle. But to say no more, it is so far from being a Blemish, that it is rather the Excellency of this Institution that *Men of various Studies* are introduced. For so there will be always many sincere Witnesses standing by, whom Self-love will not persuade to report falsly. . . .

It is evident, that this *searching Spirit,* and this Affection to *sensible Knowledge,* does prevail in most Countries round about us. . . .

The Country; that lyes next to *England* in its Situation is *France;* and that is also the nearest to it, in its Zeal for the Promotion of *Experiments.* In that Kingdom, the *Royal Society* has maintained a perpetual Intercourse, with the most eminent Men of *Art* of all Conditions; and has obtained from them, all the Help which might justly be hoped for, from the *Vigour,* and *Activity,* and *Readiness* of Mind, which is natural to that People. From their *Physicians, Chirurgeons,* and *Anatomists,* it has receiv'd many faithful *Relations* of extraordinary *Cures;* from their most judicious *Travellers* the Fruits of their *Voyages;* from their most famous *Mathematicians,* diverse *Problems,* which have been solved many different ways; from their *Chymists* the effects of their *Fires;* and from others of their best *Observers,* many Rarities, and Discourses of their *Fruits, Silk, Wine, Bread, Plants, Salt,* and such natural Productions of their Soil. And to instance once for all, it has been affectionately invited to a mutual Correspondence by the *French Academy* of *Paris.* . . .

In Italy the *Royal Society* has an excellent Privilege of receiving and imparting *Experiments,* by the Help of one of their own *Fellows,* who has the Opportunity of being *Resident* there for them, as well as for the *King.* From thence they have been earnestly invited to a mutual Intelligence, by many of their most noble Wits, but chiefly by the Prince *Leopoldo,* Brother to the

Great Duke of *Tuscany;* who is the Patron of all the *inquisitive Philosophers* of *Florence;* from whom there is coming out under his Name an Account of their Proceedings called *Ducal Experiments.* This Application to the *Royal Society* I have mention'd, because it comes from that Country, which is seldom wont to have any great Regard to the *Arts* of these Nations, that lye on this side of their Mountains.

In *Germany,* and its neighbouring Kingdoms, the *Royal Society* has met with great Veneration; as appears by several Testimonies in their late *printed Books,* which have been submitted to its Censure; by many Curiosities of *Mechanick Instruments,* that have been transmitted to it; and by the *Addresses* which have been sent from their *Philosophical Inquirers.* For which Kinds of Enterprizes the Temper of the *German* Nation is admirably fit, both in respect of their peculiar Dexterity in all Sorts of manual *Arts,* and also in Regard of the plain and unaffected Sincerity of their *Manners;* wherein they so much resemble the *English,* that we seem to have deriv'd from them the Composition of our *Minds,* as well as to have descended from their *Race.*

In the *Low-Countries,* their Interest, and Reputation has been established, by the Friendship of some of their chief learned Men, and principally of *Hugenius.* This Gentleman has bestowed his Pains, on many Parts of the *speculative* and *practical Mathematicks,* with wonderful Successes. And particularly his applying the Motion of *Pendulums* to Clocks, and Watches, was an excellent *Invention.* For thereby there may be a Means found out of bringing the *Measures* of *Time,* to an exact *Regulation;* of which the Benefits are infinite. In the Prosecution of such *Discoveries,* he has often required the Aid of this *Society;* he has receiv'd the Light of their *Trials,* and a Confirmation of his own, and has freely admitted their *Alterations* or *Amendments.* And this learned Correspondence with him, and many others, is still continued, even at this present Time, in the Breach between our *Countries:* Their great Founder, and Patron still permitting them to maintain the Traffick of Sciences, when all other *Commerce* is intercepted. Whence we may guess, what may be expected from the peaceful Part of our King's Reign, when his very Wars are managed without Injury to the Arts of *Civil Knowledge.*

But not to wander any farther in *Particulars,* it may perhaps in *general* be safely computed, that there has been as large a Communication of Foreign *Arts,* and *Inventions* to the *Royal Society,* within this small Compass of Time, as ever before did pass over the *English* Channel, since the very first Transportation of Arts into our *Island.* And that this Benefit will still increase by the Length of Time is indubitable.

NEWTON, THE MAN **45**

From time to time in the history of mankind a man appears whose work is of such significance that it leaves its imprint on all that comes after him. Such a man was Sir Isaac Newton. In his lifetime, his achievements were celebrated throughout Europe. He served as President of the Royal Society from 1703 until his death in 1727. This same society organized an international celebration of the 300th anniversary of Newton's birth, which should have been held in 1942 but was postponed to 1946 because of World War II. The proceedings of the celebra-

tion included the following study of Newton's personality which had been pre-pared some years earlier by the famous economist, John Maynard, Lord Keynes.*

In the eighteenth century and since, Newton came to be thought of as the first and greatest of the modern age of scientists, a rationalist, one who taught us to think on the lines of cold and untinctured reason.

I do not see him in this light. I do not think that any one who has pored over the contents of that box which he packed up when he finally left Cambridge in 1696 and which, though partly dispersed, have come down to us, can see him like that. Newton was not the first of the age of reason. He was the last of the magicians, the last of the Babylonians and Sumerians, the last great mind which looked out on the visible and intellectual world with the same eyes as those who began to build our intellectual inheritance rather less than 10,000 years ago. Isaac Newton, a posthumous child born with no father on Christmas Day, 1642, was the last wonder-child to whom the Magi could do sincere and appropriate homage.

Had there been time, I should have liked to read to you the contemporary record of the child Newton. For, though it is well known to his biographers, it has never been published *in extenso,* without comment, just as it stands. Here, indeed, is the makings of a legend of the young magician, a most joyous picture of the opening mind of genius free from the uneasiness, the melancholy and nervous agitation of the young man and student.

For in vulgar modern terms Newton was profoundly neurotic of a not un-familiar type, but—I should say from the records—a most extreme example. His deepest instincts were occult, esoteric, semantic—with profound shrinking from the world, a paralyzing fear of exposing his thoughts, his beliefs, his discoveries in all nakedness to the inspection and criticism of the world. 'Of the most fearful, cautious and suspicious temper that I ever knew,' said Whiston, his successor in the Lucasian Chair. The too well-known conflicts and ignoble quarrels with Hooke, Flamsteed, Leibnitz are only too clear an evidence of this. Like all his type he was wholly aloof from women. He parted with and published nothing except under the extreme pressure of friends. Until the second phase of his life, he was a wrapt, consecrated solitary, pursuing his studies by intense introspection with a mental endurance perhaps never equalled.

I believe that the clue to his mind is to be found in his unusual powers of continuous concentrated introspection. A case can be made out, as it also can with Descartes, for regarding him as an accomplished experimentalist. Nothing can be more charming than the tales of his mechanical contrivances when he was a boy. There are his telescopes and his optical experiments. These were essential accomplishments, part of his unequalled all-round technique, but not, I am sure, his *peculiar* gift, especially amongst his contemporaries. His peculiar gift was the power of holding continuously in his mind a purely mental problem until he had seen straight through it. I fancy his pre-eminence is due to his muscles of intuition being the strongest and most enduring with which a man has ever been gifted. Anyone who has ever attempted pure scientific or philosophical thought knows how one can hold a problem momentarily in one's mind and apply all one's powers of concentration to piercing through it, and how it will dissolve and escape and you find that what you are surveying

* Lord Keynes, "Newton, the Man," *Royal Society Newton Tercentenary Celebrations* (London: Cambridge Univ., 1947), pp. 27-34.

is a blank. I believe that Newton could hold a problem in his mind for hours and days and weeks until it surrendered to him its secret. Then being a supreme mathematical technician he could dress it up, how you will, for purposes of exposition, but it was his intuition which was pre-eminently extraordinary —"so happy in his conjectures," said de Morgan, "as to seem to know more than he could possibly have any means of proving." The proofs, for what they are worth, were, as I have said, dressed up afterwards—they were not the instrument of discovery.

There is the story of how he informed Halley of one of his most fundamental discoveries of planetary motion. "Yes," replied Halley, "but how do you know that? Have you proved it?" Newton was taken aback—"Why, I've known it for years," he replied. "If you'll give me a few days, I'll certainly find you a proof of it"—as in due course he did.

Again, there is some evidence that Newton in preparing the *Principia* was held up almost to the last moment by lack of proof that you could treat a solid sphere as though all its mass was concentrated at the centre, and only hit on the proof a year before publication. But this was a truth which he had known for certain and had always assumed for many years.

Certainly there can be no doubt that the peculiar geometrical form in which the exposition of the *Principia* is dressed up bears no resemblance at all to the mental processes by which Newton actually arrived at his conclusions.

His experiments were always, I suspect, a means, not of discovery, but always of verifying what he knew already.

Why do I call him a magician? Because he looked on the whole universe and all that is in it *as a riddle,* as a secret which could be read by applying pure thought to certain evidence, certain mystic clues which God had laid about the world to allow a sort of philosopher's treasure hunt to the esoteric brotherhood. He believed that these clues were to be found partly in the evidence of the heavens and in the constitution of elements (and that is what gives the false suggestion of his being an experimental natural philosopher), but also partly in certain papers and traditions handed down by the brethren in an unbroken chain back to the original cryptic revelation in Babylonia. He regarded the universe as a cryptogram set by the Almighty—just as he himself wrapt the discovery of the calculus in a cryptogram when he communicated with Leibnitz. By pure thought, by concentration of mind, the riddle, he believed, would be revealed to the initiate.

He *did* read the riddle of the heavens. And he believed that by the same powers of his introspective imagination he would read the riddle of the Godhead, the riddle of past and future events divinely fore-ordained, the riddle of the elements and their constitution from an original undifferentiated first matter, the riddle of health and of immortality. All would be revealed to him if only he could persevere to the end, uninterrupted, by himself, no one coming into the room, reading, copying, testing—all by himself, no interruption for God's sake, no disclosure, no discordant breakings in or criticism, with fear and shrinking as he assailed these half-ordained, half-forbidden things, creeping back into the bosom of the God head as into his mother's womb. 'Voyaging through strange seas of thought *alone',* not as Charles Lamb 'a fellow who believed nothing unless it was as clear as the three sides of a triangle'.

And so he continued for some twenty-five years. In 1687, when he was forty-five years old, the *Principia* was published. . . .

During these twenty-five years of intense study mathematics and astronomy were only a part, and perhaps not the most absorbing, of his occupations. Our record of these is almost wholly confined to the papers which he kept and put in his box when he left Trinity for London.

Let me give some brief indications of their subject. They are enormously voluminous—I should say that upwards of 1,000,000 words in his handwriting still survive. They have, beyond doubt, no substantial value whatever except as a fascinating sidelight on the mind of our greatest genius.

Let me not exaggerate through reaction against the other Newton myth which has been so sedulously created for the last two hundred years. There was extreme method in his madness. All his unpublished works on esoteric and theological matters are marked by careful learning, accurate method and extreme sobriety of statement. They are just as *sane* as the *Principia,* if their whole matter and purpose were not magical. They were nearly all composed during the same twenty-five years of his mathematical studies. They fall into several groups.

Very early in life Newton abandoned orthodox belief in the Trinity. . . . He was persuaded that the revealed documents give no support to the Trinitarian doctrines which were due to late falsifications. The revealed God was one God.

But this was a dreadful secret which Newton was at desperate pains to conceal all his life. . . . In the main the secret died with him. But it was revealed in many writings in his big box. After his death Bishop Horsley was asked to inspect the box with a view to publication. He saw the contents with horror and slammed the lid. A hundred years later Sir David Drewster looked into the box. He covered up the traces with carefully selected extracts and some straight fibbing. His latest biographer, Mr. More, has been more candid. Newton's extensive anti-Trinitarian pamphlets are, in my judgment, the most interesting of his unpublished papers. . . . It is a blot on Newton's record that he did not murmur a word when Whiston, his successor in the Lucasian Chair, was thrown out of his professorship and out of the University for publicly avowing opinions which Newton himself had secretly held for upwards of fifty years past. . . .

Another large section is concerned with all branches of apocalyptic writings from which he sought to deduce the secret truths of the Universe—the measurements of Solomon's Temple, the Book of David, the Book of Revelations, an enormous volume of work of which some part was published in his later days. Along with this are hundreds of pages of Church History and the like, designed to discover the truth of tradition.

A large section, judging by the handwriting amongst the earliest, relates to alchemy—transmutation, the philosopher's stone, the elixir of life. The scope and character of these papers have been hushed up, or at least minimized, by nearly all those who have inspected them. . . .

In these mixed and extraordinary studies, with one foot in the Middle Ages and one foot treading a path for modern science, Newton spent the first phase of his life, the period of life in Trinity when he did all his real work. Now let me pass to the second phase. . . .

In 1696 his friends were finally successful in digging him out of Cambridge, and for more than another twenty years he reigned in London as the most famous man of his age, of Europe, and—as his powers gradually waned and his affability increased—perhaps of all time, so it seemed to his contemporaries.

He set up house with his niece Catharine Barton. . . . Newton puts on rather too much weight for his moderate height. "When he rode in his coach one arm would be out of his coach on one side and the other on the other." His pink face, beneath a mass of snow-white hair, which "when his peruke was off was a venerable sight," is increasingly both benevolent and majestic. One night in Trinity after Hall he is knighted by Queen Anne. For nearly twenty-four years he reigns as President of the Royal Society. He becomes one of the principal sights of London for all visiting intellectual foreigners, whom he entertains handsomely. He liked to have clever young men about him to edit new editions of the *Principia*—and sometimes merely plausible ones as in the case of Facio de Duillier.

Magic was quite forgotten. He has become the Sage and Monarch of the Age of Reason. The Sir Isaac Newton of orthodox tradition—the eighteenth-century Sir Isaac, so remote from the child magician born in the first half of the seventeenth century—was being built up. Voltaire returning from his trip to London was able to report of Sir Isaac—"twas his peculiar felicity, not only to be born in a country of liberty, but in an Age when all scholastic impertinences were banished from the World. Reason alone was cultivated and Mankind cou'd only be his Pupil, not his Enemy." Newton, whose secret heresies and scholastic superstitions it had been the study of a lifetime to conceal!

But he never concentrated, never recovered "the former consistency of his mind." "He spoke very little in company." "He had something rather languid in his look and manner."

And he looked very seldom, I expect, into the chest where, when he left Cambridge, he had packed all the evidences of what had occupied and so absorbed his intense and flaming spirit. . . .

But he did not destroy them. They remained in the box to shock profoundly any eighteenth- or nineteenth-century prying eyes. . . .

As one broods over these queer collections, it seems easier to understand —with an understanding which is not, I hope, distorted in the other direction —this strange spirit, who was tempted by the Devil to believe at the time when within these walls he was solving so much, that he could reach *all* the secrets of God and Nature by the pure power of mind—Copernicus and Faustus in one.

DARWIN ON EVOLUTION 46

The most influential idea in nineteenth century science was the theory of evolution. Its author, Charles Darwin, studied medicine and theology before being encouraged by his Cambridge tutor to pursue his interest in natural history. While serving as naturalist aboard the ship Beagle *during its five-year cruise to South America and the Pacific, Darwin observed plant and animal life in widely scattered areas and gathered the evidence on which he based his theory of evolution. The following selections are taken from Darwin's two principal works,* The Origin of Species *(1859), his concept of biological evolution, and* The Descent of Man *(1871), which fits man into the evolutionary process.**

* Charles Darwin, *The Origin of Species, by Means of Natural Selection or the Preservation of Favoured Races in the Struggle for Life,* 6th ed. (London, 1872), I, 47, 48, 100-102; II, 186; and *The Descent of Man, and Selection in Relation to Sex* (New York, 1874), pp. 630-31, 633-34, 637, 643-44.

Nothing is easier than to admit in words the truth of the universal struggle for life, or more difficult—at least I have found it so—than constantly to bear this conclusion in mind. Yet unless it be thoroughly engrained in the mind, the whole economy of nature, with every fact on distribution, rarity, abundance, extinction, and variation, will be dimly seen or quite misunderstood. We behold the face of nature bright with gladness, we often see superabundance of food; we do not see or we forget, that the birds which are idly singing round us mostly live on insects or seeds, and are thus constantly destroying life; or we forget how largely these songsters, or their eggs, or their nestlings, are destroyed by birds and beasts of prey; we do not always bear in mind, that, though food may be now superabundant, it is not so at all seasons of each recurring year. . . .

A struggle for existence inevitably follows from the high rate at which all organic beings tend to increase. Every being, which during its natural lifetime produces several eggs or seeds, must suffer destruction during some period of its life, and during some season or occasional year, otherwise, on the principle of geometrical increase, its numbers would quickly become so inordinately great that no country could support the product. Hence, as more individuals are produced than can possibly survive, there must in every case be a struggle for existence, either one individual with another of the same species, or with the individuals of distinct species, or with the physical conditions of life. It is the doctrine of Malthus applied with manifold force to the whole animal and vegetable kingdoms; for in this case there can be no artificial increase of food, and no prudential restraint from marriage. Although some species may be now increasing, more or less rapidly, in numbers, all cannot do so, for the world would not hold them.

There is no exception to the rule that every organic being naturally increases at so high a rate, that, if not destroyed, the earth would soon be covered by the progeny of a single pair. Even slow-breeding man has doubled in twenty-five years, and at this rate, in less than a thousand years, there would literally not be standing-room for his progeny. . . .

But we have better evidence on this subject than mere theoretical calculations, namely, the numerous recorded cases of the astonishingly rapid increase of various animals in a state of nature, when circumstances have been favourable to them during two or three following seasons. Still more striking is the evidence from our domestic animals of many kinds which have run wild in several parts of the world; if the statements of the rate of increase of slow-breeding cattle and horses in South America, and latterly in Australia, had not been well authenticated, they would have been incredible. So it is with plants; cases could be given of introduced plants which have become common throughout whole islands in a period of less than ten years.

. . . . .

If under changing conditions of life organic beings present individual differences in almost every part of their structure, and this cannot be disputed; if there be, owing to their geometrical rate of increase, a severe struggle for life at some age, season, or year, and this certainly cannot be disputed; then, considering the infinite complexity of the relations of all organic beings to each other and to their conditions of life, causing an infinite diversity in structure, constitution, and habits, to be advantageous to them, it would be a most extraordinary fact if no variations had ever occurred useful to each being's own welfare, in the same manner as so many variations have occurred useful to man. But if variations useful to any organic being ever do occur, assuredly individuals thus characterised will have the best chance of being preserved in the struggle for life; and from the strong principle of inheritance, these will tend to produce offspring similarly characterised. This principle of preservation, or the survival of the fittest, I have called Natural Selection. . . . Amongst many animals, sexual selection will have given its aid to ordinary selection, by assuring to the most vigorous and best adapted males the greatest number of offspring.

. . . . .

The affinities of all the beings of the same class have sometimes been represented by a great tree. I believe this simile largely speaks the truth. The green and budding twigs may represent existing species; and those produced during former years may represent the long succession of extinct species. At each period of growth all the growing twigs have tried to branch out on all sides, and to overtop and kill the surrounding twigs and branches, in the same manner as species and groups of species have at all times overmastered other species in the great battle for life. The limbs divided into great branches, and these into lesser and lesser branches, were themselves once, when the tree was young, budding twigs; and this connection of the former and present buds by ramifying branches may well represent the classification of all extinct and living species in groups subordinate to groups. Of the many twigs which flourished when the tree was a mere bush, only two or three, now grown into great branches, yet survive and bear the other branches; so with the species which lived during long-past geological periods, very few have left living and modified descendants. From the first growth of the tree, many a limb and branch has decayed and dropped off; and these fallen branches of various sizes may represent those whole orders, families, and genera which have now no living representatives, and which are known to us only in a fossil state.

. . . . .

The Descent of Man

The main conclusion here arrived at, and now held by many naturalists who are well competent to form a sound judgment, is that man is descended from some less highly organized form. The grounds upon which this conclusion rests will never be shaken, for the close similarity between man and the lower animals in embryonic development, as well as in innumerable points of structure and constitution, both of high and of the most trifling importance—the rudiments which he retains, and the abnormal reversions to which he is occasionally liable—are facts which cannot be disputed. They have long been known, but until recently they told us nothing with respect to the origin of man. Now when viewed by the light of our knowledge of the whole organic world, their meaning is unmistakable. The great principle of evolution stands up clear and firm, when these groups of facts are considered in connection with others, such as the mutual affinities of the members of the same group, their geographical distribution in past and present times, and their geological succession. It is incredible that all these facts should speak falsely. He who is not content to look, like a savage, at the phenomena of nature as disconnected, cannot any longer believe that man is the work of a separate act of creation. He will be forced to admit that the close resemblance of the embryo of man to that, for instance, of a dog—the construction of his skull, limbs, and whole frame on the same plan with that of other mammals, independently of the uses to which the parts may be put—the occasional reappearance of various structures, for instance of several muscles, which man does not normally possess, but which are common to the Quadrumana—and a crowd of analogous facts—all point in the plainest manner to the conclusion that man is the co-descendant with other mammals of a common progenitor. . . .

The high standard of our intellectual powers and moral disposition is the greatest difficulty which presents itself, after we have been driven to this conclusion on the origin of man. But everyone who admits the principle of evolution must see that the mental powers of the higher animals, which are the same in kind with those of man, though so different in degree, are capable of advancement. Thus the interval between the mental powers of one of the higher apes and of a fish, or between those of an ant and scale-insect, is immense; yet their development does not offer any special difficulty; for, with our domesticated animals, the mental faculties are certainly variable, and the variations are inherited. No one doubts that they are of the utmost importance to animals in a state of nature. Therefore the conditions are favorable for their development through natural selection. The same conclusion may be extended to man; the intellect must have been all-important to him, even at a very remote period, as enabling him to invent and use language, to make weapons, tools, traps, etc., whereby, with the aid of his social habits, he long ago became the most dominant of all living creatures. . . .

I am aware that the conclusions arrived at in this work will be denounced by some as highly irreligious; but he who denounces them is bound to show why it is more irreligious to explain the origin of man as a distinct species by descent from some lower form, through the laws of variation and natural selection, than to explain the birth of the individual through the laws of ordinary reproduction. The birth both of the species and of the individual are equally parts of that grand sequence of events which our minds refuse to accept as the result of blind chance. . . .

The main conclusion arrived at in this work, namely, that man is descended from some lowly organized form, will, I regret to think, be highly distasteful to many. But there can hardly be a doubt that we are descended from barbarians. The astonishment which I felt on first seeing a party of Fuegians on a wild and broken shore will never be forgotten by me, for the reflection at once rushed into my mind—such were our ancestors. These men were absolutely naked and bedaubed with paint, their long hair was tangled, their mouths frothed with excitement, and their expression was wild, startled, and distrustful. They possessed hardly any arts, and, like wild animals, lived on what they could catch; they had no government, and were merciless to everyone not of their own small tribe. He who has seen a savage in his native land will not feel much shame if forced to acknowledge that the blood of some more humble creature flows in his veins. For my own part, I would as soon be descended from that heroic little monkey who braved his dreaded enemy in order to save the life of his keeper, or from that old baboon, who, descending from the mountains, carried away in triumph his young comrade from a crowd of astonished dogs—as from a savage who delights to torture his enemies, offers up bloody sacrifices, practises infanticide without remorse, treats his wives like slaves, knows no decency, and is haunted by the grossest superstitions.

Man may be excused for feeling some pride at having risen, though not through his own exertions, to the very summit of the organic scale; and the fact of his having thus risen, . . . may give him hope for a still higher destiny in the distant future. But we are not here concerned with hopes or fears, only with the truth as far as our reason permits us to discover it; and I have given the evidence to the best of my ability. We must, however, acknowledge, as it seems to me, that man, with all his noble qualities, with sympathy which feels for the most debased, with benevolence which extends not only to other men but to the humblest living creature, with his godlike intellect which has penetrated into the movements and constitution of the solar system—with all these exalted powers—Man still bears in his bodily frame the indelible stamp of his lowly origin.

Social Darwinism 47

Darwin's ideas of the struggle for survival and the survival of the fittest were taken over from biology into the political arena, where they were used to support a variety of positions, including the subjugation of native peoples, the exploitation of workers, and the glorification of the state. This application of Darwin's theories to the social scene is known as Social Darwinism, a good example of which is to be found in the following lecture by Karl Pierson, Professor of applied mathematics at University College, London. Speaking in 1900, when England was having difficulty in subduing the Boers in South Africa, Pierson boldly proclaimed the need for a powerful state and continual warfare in order to ensure the predominance of the superior races of the earth.*

History shows me one way, and one way only, in which a high state of civilization has been produced, namely, the struggle of race with race, and the survival of the physically and mentally fitter race. If you want to know whether the lower races of man can evolve a higher type, I fear the only course is to leave them to fight it out among themselves. . . .

The struggle means suffering, intense suffering, while it is in progress; but that struggle and that suffering have been the stages by which the white man has reached his present stage of development, and they account for the fact that he no longer lives in caves and feeds on roots and nuts. This dependence of progress on the survival of the fitter race, terribly black as it may seem to some of you, gives the struggle for existence its redeeming features; it is the fiery crucible out of which comes the finer metal. You may hope for a time when the sword shall be turned into the ploughshare, when American and German and English traders shall no longer compete in the markets of the world for their raw material and for their food supply, when the white man and the dark shall share the soil between them, and each till it as he lists. But, believe me, when that day comes, mankind will no longer progress; there will

* K. Pierson, *National Life from the Standpoint of Science* (London: A. & C. Black, 1901), pp. 19-20, 24-25, 34-35, 41-46, 60-62.

be nothing to check the fertility of inferior stock; the relentless law of heredity will not be controlled and guided by natural selection. Man will stagnate; and unless he ceases to multiply, the catastrophe will come again; famine and pestilence, as we see them in the East, physical selection instead of the struggle of race against race, will do the work more relentlessly, and, to judge from India and China, far less efficiently than of old. . . .

The first function [of science in national life] is to show us what national life means, and how the nation is a vast organism subject as much to the great forces of evolution as any other gregarious type of life. There is a struggle of race against race and of nation against nation. In the early days of that struggle it was a blind, unconscious struggle of barbaric tribes. At the present day, in the case of the civilized white man, it has become more and more the conscious, carefully directed attempt of the nation to fit itself to a continuously changing environment. The nation has to foresee how and where the struggle will be carried on; the maintenance of national position is becoming more and more a conscious preparation for changing conditions, an insight into the needs of coming environments.

This is the second important duty of science in relation to national life. It has to develop our brain-power by providing a training in method and by exercising our powers of cautious observation. It has to teach not only the leaders of our national life, but the people at large, to prepare for and meet the difficulties of new environments. . . .

I have asked you to look upon the nation as an organized whole in continual struggle with other nations, whether by force of arms or by force of trade and economic processes. I have asked you to look upon this struggle of either kind as a not wholly bad thing; it is the source of human progress throughout the world's history. But if a nation is to maintain its position in this struggle, it must be fully provided with trained brains in every department of national activity, from the government to the factory, and have, if possible, a *reserve of brain and physique* to fall back upon in times of national crisis. . . .

You will see that my view—and I think it may be called the scientific view of a nation—is that of an organized whole, kept up to a high pitch of internal efficiency by insuring that its numbers are substantially recruited from the better stocks, and kept up to a high pitch of external efficiency by contest, chiefly by way of war with inferior races, and with equal races by the struggle for trade-routes and for the sources of raw material and of food supply. This is the natural history view of mankind, and I do not think you can in its main features subvert it. Some of you may refuse to acknowledge it, but you cannot really study history and refuse to see its force. . . .

. . . . .

Science is not a dogma; it has no infallible popes to pronounce authoritatively what its teaching is. I can only say how it seems to one individual scientific worker that the doctrine of evolution applies to the history of nations. My interpretation may be wrong, but of the true method I am sure: a community of men is as subject as a community of ants or as a herd of buffaloes to the laws which rule all organic nature. We cannot escape from them; it serves no purpose to protest at what some term their cruelty and their bloodthirstiness. We can only study these laws, recognise what of gain they have brought to man, and urge the statesman and the thinker to regard and use them, as the engineer and inventor regard and then turn to human profit the equally unchangeable laws of physical nature. . . .

Mankind as a whole, like the individual man, advances through pain and suffering only. The path of progress is strewn with the wreck of nations; traces are everywhere to be seen of the hecatombs of inferior races, and of victims who found not the narrow way to the greater perfection. Yet these dead peoples are, in very truth, the stepping-stones on which mankind has arisen to the higher intellectual and deeper emotional life of to-day.

WESTERN SCIENCE AND TECHNOLOGY IN THE NEAR EAST 48

*One reason why non-Western peoples found Western civilization so fascinating and impressive was its scientific and technological achievements. This is made strikingly clear in the following passage from the autobiography of a Christian Arab, Edward Atiyah, who was born in Lebanon and spent his childhood in Lebanon, Egypt, and the Sudan. Educated in an English school in Alexandria and later at Oxford University, he had roots in two very different societies; this, together with his sensitive perceptiveness and his writing talents, makes his autobiography an unusually revealing document.**

The mechanical inventions of the West were beginning to invade the Near East about that time [the early twentieth century]. The telegraph and the railway had been there for some time. They were familiar to my generation, but not to the extent that breeds contempt. Now new wonders were appearing. The electric tram, electric light, motor-cars and gramophones. Miracle after miracle, and all invented by Europeans. When you first heard of these strange things you perhaps doubted, but then the miracles arrived and you saw and heard them. There were, too, rumours of stranger, more incredible miracles, of motor-cars that could fly, ships that went under the sea, and telegraphy without wire; and all, all invented by the extremely clever Europeans. Surely the cleverest people in the world, much cleverer than the Orientals who had never invented anything.

Among the factors that wrought for the apotheosis of the West in Eastern minds, the mechanical aspect of European civilization—inventions and scientific appliances—was beyond doubt the most potent. For there was not and never had been anything corresponding to it in the East. Oriental genius had produced great religions, achieved great triumphs in art and literature, constructed colossal empires, but it had never tamed and canned the elements, packed scientific principles into little mechanical parcels. And it happened that while the intellect of awaking Europe was ferreting out and applying the secrets of nature, the East was passing through a phase of decline and somnolence. When therefore this flood of mechanical inventions burst in upon the Near East towards the end of the 19th and the beginning of the 20th century, Easterners were completely dazzled and fascinated by these undreamt-of wonders and the mysterious power that lay behind them.

I was eleven when I saw the first aeroplane. It was 1914 (just before the war) and we were living at Omdurman. Early in the winter rumours began to go round that a French aviator was coming to Khartoum. No aeroplane had

* E. Atiyah, *An Arab Tells His Story* (London: J. Murray, 1946), pp. 29-32.

yet visited the Sudan, and so everybody was tremendously excited about it, especially the natives, most of whom at first would not believe that there were such things as aeroplanes. Then the rumours became more and more definite; the name of the aviator was given, the route he was following, the approximate date of his arrival, the place of landing. It was becoming real, imminent. At last the day and the hour were announced; and the whole population of Khartoum, from the Governor-General to street boys, assembled to see the miracle. The landing-place was in a stretch of sand some way outside the town, and we went there by cab. I was consumed with excitement. A good many of the natives were still sceptical, thought that there must be some trick afoot, some huge jest. Impossible that a man, a real man, should come in a machine flying like a bird. Impossible.

2 o'clock . . . 2.15 . . . 2.30 . . . Excitement, impatience, doubt. And then a low distant drone, and a black speck in the sky, there, coming from the north. A hush for a second . . . exclamations, jabberings, strained necks, stretched arms. There he is, there he is! Yes . . . No . . . yes . . . no . . . yes, yes, yes. The noise is louder, the speck is bigger. "What? that thing," said a doubting Sudanese standing next to us. "Why it is a vulture, and the noise is coming from the Power Station." But soon all doubt, all argument ceased. The vulture was above our heads, huge as ten eagles, filling the air with its deafening drone, and as it circled down, a human arm stretched out of it and waved to the crowd. The miracle had come off. Several Sudanese falling on their knees with upstretched arms exclaimed: "There is no god but Allah; the Resurrection Day has come."

Before the machine reached the ground, the seething crowd, beyond itself with excitement, had broken through the police cordon, and rushed towards the landing spot. The Governor-General, who according to plan was to advance with becoming dignity towards the machine, and welcome the distinguished aviator, while the watching crowd watched from a respectful distance, had to forget his dignity and advance with hurried steps to be able to get there at all, while the crowd pushed and jostled in its mad eagerness to see this huge artificial bird, and especially the man in it. Was it really a man, this weird-looking creature with its leather head and huge protruding oval eyes, stepping down on to the ground? See, see, he's waving his arm again, he is shaking hands with the Governor-General. *Wallahi zol, zol sahih.* (By God it's a man, a real man!) But even after this, our old Sudanese woman-servant had still some lingering doubts. "Really, Ya Sitt," she asked my mother when we had gone back home, "is it a real man, a *zol* like us, who eats and drinks and gets married?"

The cinema in its early days produced some curious reactions in the more primitive parts of the Sudan. An English friend of mine took with him a film-projector and some films to an out-station in Kordofan. One day he gathered several hundred tribesmen, and treated them to a performance. They squatted out on the sand before the screen, and shouted in great excitement at every picture. One of the films was an animated-drawings story, in which a man attacks a dog with an axe and splits him into two, after which the severed hind part runs along its legs until it catches up the front part, and the dog is thus reintegrated. "By the living God," said one of the spectators of this miracle, "if I hadn't seen it with my own eyes, I should never have believed it." This, of course, was an extreme case of unquestioning credulity in a primitive African. But even in Syria and Egypt, on sophisticated minds with a great civilization in their cultural background, these inventions made a profound impression.

Here was something uncanny, apparently supernatural, and it was entirely the product of Western minds. No conjurer producing rabbits from a hat could have more impressed an assembly of unsophisticated children. The children had yet to learn that the conjurer was no god, and that they too when they grew up, could, if they took the trouble, learn to produce rabbits from a hat. . . .

True, the older and more fanatical Moslems disapproved of these inventions. They looked upon them with aversion and suspicion, as the diabolical contrivances of the Kuffar, [Unbelievers], as something alien to Islam and the Koran, since they did not exist when the Prophet of God walked the earth. They scented in them half consciously the coming of a new world, mysterious, pregnant with alarming possibilities, hostile to them because incompatible with their old world, in which they and their ancestors have lived, secure in their faith, untroubled in their beliefs and prejudices. They saw this new world coming, and had the first premonition that their old world, which they had hitherto thought eternal, would soon begin to slip away from under their feet.

Chapter Eleven

Basis of dominance: the Industrial Revolution

49 THE INDUSTRIAL REVOLUTION RECONSIDERED

Europe was transformed by the Industrial Revolution as well as by the scientific. Although the term "Industrial Revolution" has been popular since the late nineteenth century, economic historians increasingly feel that it is a misnomer for what actually occurred. The reasons for their misgivings are set forth in the following article by a distinguished scholar in this field.*

The editor's letter asked for an article on the industrial revolution, "with the view to bringing teachers up to date on newer scholarship and interpretations." So I spent the morning of Thanksgiving Day examining several recent high school or university history or social science texts to see how they handled economic developments. I soon found I had a new reason for being thankful. One *History of Europe* gives 102 pages out of 845 to economic conditions and trends, and another gives 136 pages out of 1024. This is a mighty advance since the 'eighties, when Fyffe wrote over a thousand pages and never mentioned a machine or a railroad. It is even better than conditions were thirty years ago, when the *Cambridge Modern History* included only three economic chapters in its fourteen volumes. The "Manor," the "Commercial Revolution," "Mercantilism," and the "Industrial Revolution" have definitely been admitted to the texts. My daughter tells me she has heard the manor described in five different lecture

* Herbert Heaton, "The Industrial Revolution," *Social Education*, II (March, 1938), 159-65.

courses, and I notice that in her prescribed books the famous plan of a "typical manor" has been improved: a stork stands forlornly in the swamp, and the landlord is hunting a deer and a boar—simultaneously—in the Woodland.

This flush of gratitude for the many crumbs that are now falling from the general historian's table is, however, tempered a little by the staleness of some of the crumbs. Even the best of the university texts have provoked me to make several query marks in the margin; and some of the high school books ought to have whole paragraphs or even pages torn out.

. . . . .

Of the "Industrial Revolution," the sharp lines and strong colors—chiefly rose and black—of the old picture have become so blurred that some of us now put the title in quotation marks or avoid using it.

That old picture, painted about 1880 by Arnold Toynbee, is a triptych, or a melodrama in three acts. First there is "The Eve," still, placid, quiet, at the end of a long day that reaches back to the Normans, Nero, or even Noah. The methods of agriculture, industry, and transportation have changed little in a thousand years. Production is carried on by small manufacturers or farmers. The former, like the latter, live in the country, combine industry and agriculture, and supplement the family labor supply by training an apprentice and perhaps employing a journeyman or two. The wage earner usually works, aided by his family, in his own home on materials put out to him by his employer; but he may work under his master's roof. Between master and man is a "warm attachment"; they call each other by their Christian nicknames. The class of capitalist employers is still "in its infancy"; some merchant-employers put out material to be processed in the homes of their employees or of small masters, and a few factories or central workshops exist. But in general the family firm and the family farm prevail. Division of class and of labor is slight. The worker can express his personality in his work, though what happens if it is crooked is not clear. Production is for local markets or for the producer's larder and wardrobe, since defective means of transportation and mercantilistic policies shut off distant consumers. No one earns great rewards, but the domestic system insures on the whole a sound and healthy life under conditions favorable to the development of mind, body, and personal dignity. Contentment spins at the cottage door; there is plenty of honeysuckle, ivy, and good ale in this "quiet world" of "scarcely perceptible movement." A comprehensive code of state regulation of production and trade combines with technical inertia to prevent anything from changing.

Then, with a rapidity known in the tropics, "The Night" falls, a night full of noise and action. Seven men—four Lancashire men (Kay, Hargreaves, Arkwright, and Crompton), two Scots (Adam Smith and James Watt), and one Episcopalian parson (Cartwright)—invent some textile machines, improve the steam engine, or write *The Wealth of Nations*. Meanwhile other men revolutionize agriculture and redraw the village map, while others improve roads and rivers or cut canals. But it is the seven men who get their names on the record, for their actions or thoughts "destroyed the old world and built a new one." And what they did was crowded into a brief night that lasted from about 1760 to 1780.

Act Three is "The Murky Dawn," in which the effects become visible. It is a period of "economic revolution and anarchy," as machinery and steam overrun industry, and Smith's plea for laissez faire sweeps the statute book clear of the mercantilistic devil. Population is "torn up by the roots" and dragged "from cottages in distant valleys into factories and cities"; independent farmers, expelled from their lands and impoverished by the extension of sheep raising and the inclosure movement, join the small manufacturing master or journeymen in this rural exodus. In the towns a landless propertyless proletariat is the victim of the seven deadly sins of unrestrained inhuman industrial capitalists. The sins are the factory system, long hours, child labor, the exploitation of women, low wages, periodical or chronic unemployment, and slums. If the victims dislike the contrast between their deplorable lot and the fortunes made by fat factory owners; if they object, riot, join labor unions, or become chartists or socialists, they are shot down, put in jail, or sent to Botany Bay. Their economic masters become their political lords by displacing the landowners in the seats of government, and then legislate—or refuse to do so—with one eye on the cashbox and the other on some page of Smith, Ricardo, or Malthus. A dreary, tragic, selfish, sordid dawn! But by lunch time the weather is improving. The exploited grow class-conscious and organized, some employers grow softhearted, laws are passed to permit unions, to regulate child labor, or to provide a better water supply. Mass production makes goods cheaper, the corn laws are repealed, Victoria becomes queen, Albert the Good builds the Crystal Palace, and by the time it is opened in 1851 the grim tragedy is promising to turn into whatever the urban counterpart of a pastoral should be called.

This story has got into the general books, and the title for it has become so widely accepted that some wit has said all college courses now begin with the amoeba, Aristotle, or the industrial revolution. That is—all courses except those given by the economic historian, for he is getting more and more suspicious of the name and of the crisp dramatic conception. In the great university schools of economic history, Manchester admits that the name was useful when first adopted but thinks it has now served its turn and can scarcely be applied aptly to a movement which was in preparation for two centuries and then occupied at least one more. Oxford finds there is "no hiatus in economic development, but always a constant tide of progress and change, in which the old is blended almost imperceptibly with the new." Edinburgh chimes in with the remark that "sudden catastrophic change is inconsistent with the slow gradual process of human evolution." Harvard insists that the technological changes of the eighteenth century were "only the completion of tendencies which had been significantly evident since Leonardo da Vinci." Birmingham reinforces this by asserting that the developments between 1760 and 1830 "did but carry further, though on a far greater scale and with far greater rapidity, changes which had been proceeding long before." Cambridge finds the period presents a study in slow motion, and in London they tell the pass students there was an industrial revolution, but tell the honors students there never was any such thing.

These quotations give a composite picture of the revised view of the industrial revolution. Let me put it in three generalizations. (1) Steam and the textile machines did not break in on an almost unchanging world of smallscale slightly capitalistic enterprise. (2) The rate of technical change was *lento* rather than *allegro* for a long time; it took decades or even generations to transform old industries and build up new ones. (3) The social and economic "evils" were not new; they were not as black or as widespread as is usually asserted; their causes were often due to special or non-economic factors; and they were in no small measure offset by a substantial improvement in the real wages and living standards of a large part of the wage-earning population.

Sentimental unhistorical hysteria is not a good approach to a problem, whether present or past, but it dominated much of the discussion a hundred years ago and the description of a hundred years ago.

Let me elaborate these three contentions. In Toynbee's day little was known of sixteenth-century economic life, and little of any eighteenth-century industry except textiles. Now we know that during this period there were important changes in methods of production, and a quickening spirit of scientific inquiry and of inventive curiosity. New methods of extracting and refining metals were discovered; the preparation of silk yarn, the knitting of hose, the weaving or ribbons, the making of clocks, the finishing of cloth, all obtained new or improved equipment, as did shipbuilding, brewing, mining, sugar refining, and the manufacture of chemicals. The harnessing of wind, water, and animal power was made more efficient, and coal was used in increasing quantities by industries which needed heat. Professor Nef has shown that England had an industrial revolution between 1540 and 1640, and that the rate of technical change was possibly as striking during the age of Shakespeare as during that of Wordsworth or Byron. Holland, Sweden, France, and England alike contributed to technical progress, and by 1700 scientists, especially physicists, had learned enough to be able to answer some questions asked by industrialists. True, some industries or processes stood still, and spinning and weaving did not change much; but many were on the march.

At the same time the organization of production was changing. Small craftsmen did not have the capital necessary for some of the new equipment, or for bridging the long gap between buying raw material and getting paid for the finished article by a dilatory or distant customer. Hence where materials were costly or came from afar, where equipment was expensive, where the market was large or distant, the initiative had to be taken by merchants or large producers. Some of them bought the raw materials and put them out to be processed by small masters or by wage earners. Sometimes they supplied the equipment as well and paid the master only for his labor, just as he in turn might pay wages to his journeymen. Some of them gathered workers in, because the material could not be put out. You could not put out coal mining, smelting, sugar refining, building, cloth finishing, shipbuilding, calico printing, or the making of glass, bricks, paper, leather, or gunpowder. As these industries grew, so did the number of persons working for wages in their employer's plant; and the combined expansion of putting out and gathering in had created a large propertyless proletariat long before 1760. It may be true that in 1640 the great majority of industrial workers "laboured in their homes, in town cellars or garrets, or in village cottages. But that majority was by no means so overwhelming as has been supposed" (Nef) and was declining rapidly before a flying shuttle flew or a spinning jenny was devised, even in Lancashire cotton production. Wherever men worked, many of them were wage earners.

If they were, their wages tended to be low; but so were all returns in an age of low productivity. Their hours were long—twelve or more a day—but so were those of their employers and of independent workers, since the rate of production was so slow. Their children and their wives had to work, for every scrap of labor was needed; but so did all children and wives, except those of the rich. Unemployment was frequent and severe, industrial diseases and accidents were common, living and working conditions were often dank, unhealthy, and malodorous, whether in town or village. Labor unions were formed, class conflicts occurred, and the state usually took the employers' side.

This sketch of the period before 1760 takes much of the melodrama out of the next seventy years. Some of the remainder disappears, when we examine the pace at which the textile machines and the improved steam engines were adopted. The cotton industry, which was the scene of the famous inventions, has been used as a sample case. But it was not typical; various factors, such as the newness of the industry, the suitability of the cotton fiber for mechanical treatment, and the great market existing for cheap cotton cloth, prevent the story of cotton from being typical of the changes in industry at large. The transfer from domestic hand spinning of cotton to factory machine spinning was rapid—a matter of about twenty years. By 1815 "the power loom was entering into effective rivalry with the hand loom in the cotton industry, though another generation was to elapse before the battle was finally decided" (Redford, *post,* p. 20). But cotton was a lonely hare in an industrial world of tortoises. It loomed far less large in that world than it has done in the textbooks, for even in the 1830's the number of its employees was only two-thirds that of the number of female domestic servants.

When we get our eyes off this exception, we find the pace of change in the rest of industry much more sedate. Wool spinning, on hand jennies instead of on wheels, was still being done in Yorkshire homes in 1850. Power looms had not seriously threatened the woolen hand weaver at that date; the transfer from hand to power weaving came quietly during the next twenty-five years, but even in 1877 I find one manufacturer contending that the old method was as cheap as the new. As for steam power, Watt had only 320 of his engines at work in England in 1800, and in 1830 a quarter of the power used by cotton mills was still drawn from waterwheels. Mining had no great technical change, but a series of little ones. Building remained a manual industry until the concrete mixer came. The pottery industry relied less on machinery than on other factors. Clothes making, glass blowing, and printing were late in getting mechanical equipment, while mechanical engineering only slowly developed the tools it needed for shaping metal parts cheaply and accurately. In 1850 everything was not over except the shouting. Cheap steel, cheap lubricants, industrial chemistry, and cheap electricity were still to come. The railroad had won its battle, but the steamship was still fighting its sailing rival, even on the North Atlantic. Away from Lancashire and the railroad tracks, technical change between 1760 and 1850 had been gradual, slow, and unspectacular.

What then of the social and economic consequences and of the seven deadly sins? In the first place, if we leave out one or two exceptional industries or areas, people were not torn loose from a rural life of pleasant and virtually independent enterprise and plunged almost overnight into the horrible existence of an urban factory slumdwelling proletariat. Many of them were already proletarian; many of them already lived in industrial towns which now grew large or in villages which grew into towns; and some of them already worked under the employer's roof. For them there was not much shift of habitat or of economic class. There was little mass migration, and little long distance movement, except by the Irish, who swarmed into England before they swarmed into North America, and who made many labor and urban problems much more acute than they would otherwise have been.

In the second place, before we beat our anger to white heat in describing the slums, the foul streets, the smoke-laden atmosphere, the lack of water or sanitation, the ravages of disease, etc., let us remember three controlling considerations. (a) Technical. Cheap bricks, cheap sewer or water pipes, and cheap house fixtures were not available till at least 1840, and knowledge concerning public health was still scanty. Compare conditions in the industrial towns with those of non-industrial communities or with rural housing facilities; then it is evident that the housing and sanitary short-comings of the the manufacturing districts were not wholly due to the new machinery and the factory system. (b) Constitutional. Until 1835 no town government had adequate powers to cope with the new urban problems. (c) Economic. The provision of houses was never, until recent years, regarded as a public duty. It was left to private enterprise and the stimulus of investment or speculation. The potential builder considered whether his capital would yield a better return in houses than in the many other fields that were thirsty for capital; and the amount he put into a dwelling was limited by what the tenant could afford to pay. In one English town 76 per cent of the houses were rented at a dollar a week or less in 1839; the total capital outlay for one house could not be more than six hundred dollars. In view of the western world's housing impasse since 1914, we must speak more kindly of the builder who a century ago put a roof over the head of the poor, without the aid of mass-produced materials, machinery, or government subsidies.

In the third place, few of the factory working conditions were new. Not even the discipline of fixed hours of work was new to industries which had been conducted in central workshops. Night work may have been new, but long and late hours were not. The cruel treatment of some children by foremen was a personal matter; parents had not been free from it in the domestic workshop, and it was part of that streak of cruelty common in prisons, the army and navy, schools, and homes. The thing that was new and revolutionary was not the "evils," but the discovery that they were evils. For that we have to thank those employers who were heartless. We have to thank the factory for making noticeable in the mass what had been ignored in scattered small instances. We can thank onlookers, whether lay or ecclesiastic, and even Tory politicians who saw in factory conditions a new whip with which to flog their Whig industrial opponents. Finally, much credit must go to those employers—and they were many—who treated their workers decently. These men belonged to that growing army of humanitarians who cleaned up slavery, made the penal code less fierce, welcomed the attack on excessive drinking, pushed the cause of education, built hospitals, dispensaries, and charitable institutions, organized the relief of the unemployed in depressed days, established good working conditions, and fought for better factory laws and better town government.

One final comment may help us to understand better the years between 1760 and 1830. Twenty-six of those years (1789-1815) were dominated by the emotions and strain of the French Revolution and the Napoleonic war, and sixteen of them (1815-1830) were filled with the task of readjustment after a generation of war. The first period was torn by the fear of Jacobinism and the stress of war and famine. There could be little tolerance of mutterings of social discontent or of organized protest during those years; and there was little time to think of domestic problems. The second period we understand better because we have lived through a similar one. The legacies of war were high prices which collapsed, high interest rates and taxes which did not, a scarcity of houses, wide agrarian distress, a disarranged currency, a chaotic credit system, economic nationalism, choked trade channels, prohibitive tariffs, demobilized soldiers without jobs, and so forth. Much that has been blamed on the economic transition was not new, and much of the rest has to be put on the shoulders of the war. The remarkable thing is that by 1830 British opinion had got rid of most of its war phobias and was tackling its problems realistically and constructively by a combination of voluntary organization and state action. If anything was rapid and revolutionary in this whole period it was the change in outlook that between 1824 and 1835 removed the ban on labor organization, passed an effective factory act, reformed the poor law, lowered the tariff wall, made a hole in the navigation laws, remodelled urban government, reformed the House of Commons, liberated the slaves, emancipated Roman Catholics, fashioned a good banking system, and sowed the seeds of national education, trade unionism, and the cooperative movement.

Behind all this was the intense energy of manufacturers and merchants who, either with old equipment or new, enterprised and adventured. This energy is denounced by some as "an orgy of soulless cupidity," and praised by others as "a triumph of the spirit of enterprise." In general it was a bit of both. Cupidity, yes, as in all ages and occupations. Enterprise, yes, but not always triumphant, for the field was strewn with the wreckage of men who failed. When the classical economists said profit was the reward of risk and interest the reward of abstinence, they meant it. Not the abstinence that today would lead a man to pick a Buick for his twelfth car instead of a Rolls Royce, but one which meant meager living and the ploughing back of every spare penny into the business. As for risk, some day somebody will study the industrial revolution through the bankruptcy records; but we know enough to realize on what a treacherous sea the entrepreneur launched his tiny bark.

How does all this affect the teacher's presentation of economic aspects of modern Europe? It takes out some of the heroics—and the villainics, if I can coin a word—it cuts down the pace, and leaves the tale that of a trend rather than of a tumult. But there is enough left, and space has been made available for more that is of first class importance. Any survey of the making of modern Europe should have something to say about the gradual industrialization of parts of the continent, including the effect of hydro-electricity, industrial chemistry, and post-Bessemer metallurgical developments; the emergence of intensive agriculture; the effect of good roads, canals, railroads, steamships, and refrigeration; the end of serfdom in other countries than Russia and the evolution of an efficient peasant proprietor economy; the growing need for more capital and better banking; the unprecedented growth of population and the mass migration of 50,000,000 Europeans to other continents in a century; the steady advance of voluntary association and the influence of the social conscience in producing the social service state; the instability of a complex capitalistic system in a world economy; the twentyfold increase in the value of world trade; the impact of the new world on the old; and the ability of Europe to raise greatly the standard of living of an expanding population, thanks to better technique, better organization, and freedom for a hundred years from Armageddon. And if textbooks must have illustrations, I would dispense with pictures of the spinning jenny, Louis Blanc, and even Karl Marx, if thereby I had room for two graphs, one of the movement of general prices and one of the business cycle. These two would explain a lot of social, political, and even diplomatic history.

The fact that England led the world in industrialization is of first-rate historical significance. It explains in large part England's primacy in world affairs in the nineteenth century. Contemporary observers were aware of the importance of the industrialization process and a few of them speculated as to why it occurred first in England. One of the shrewdest analyses is contained in the following selection, found in a history of the British cotton industry published in 1835.* This analysis does not deal with all the factors that we are aware of today with the advantage of historical insight. Yet it is a shrewd interpretation which reveals a thorough understanding of current developments in England and on the continent.

The natural and physical advantages of England for manufacturing industry are probably superior to those of every other country on the globe. The district where those advantages are found in the most favourable combination, is the southern part of Lancashire, and the south-western part of Yorkshire, the former of which has become the principal seat of the manufacture of cotton. In the counties of Cheshire, Derbyshire, and Nottinghamshire, and in Renfrewshire and Lanarkshire, in Scotland, all of which districts are likewise seats of this branch of industry, advantages of a similar nature are found, though not in such close concentration as in Lancashire.

Three things may be regarded as of primary importance for the successful prosecution of manufactures, namely, water-power, fuel, and iron. Wherever these exist in combination, and where they are abundant and cheap, machinery may be manufactured and put in motion at small cost; and most of the processes of making and finishing cloth, whether chemical or mechanical, depending, as they do, mainly on the two great agents of water and heat, may likewise be performed with advantage.

The tract lying between the Ribble and the Mersey is surrounded on the east and north by high ranges of hills, and has also hills of some magnitude in the hundreds of Blackburn and Salford; owing to which cause the district is intersected by a great number of streams, which descend rapidly from their sources towards the level tract in the west. In the early part of their course, these streams and streamlets furnish water-power adequate to turn many hundred mills: they afford the element of water, indispensable for scouring, bleaching, printing, dyeing, and other processes of manufacture: and when collected in their larger channels, or employed to feed canals, they supply a superior inland navigation, so important for the transit of raw materials and merchandise.

Not less important for manufactures than the copious supply of good water, is the great abundance of coal found in the very same district. Beds of this invaluable mineral lie beneath almost the whole surface of Blackburn and Salford hundreds, and run into West Derby to within a few miles of Liverpool; and being near the surface, so as to yield their treasures easily, they are incomparably more fertile sources of wealth than mines of silver and gold. It is superfluous to remark that this mineral fuel animates the thousand arms

---

* Edward Baines, *History of the Cotton Manufactures in Great Britain* (London, 1835), pp. 85-89.

of the steam-engine, and furnishes the most powerful agent in all chemical and mechanical operations.

Of the equally indispensable metal, iron, the southern part of Lancashire is nearly destitute; but being at no great distance from the iron districts of Staffordshire, Warwickshire, Yorkshire, Furness, and Wales, with all of which it has ready communication by inland or coasting navigation, it is as abundantly and almost as cheaply supplied with this material, as if the iron was got within its own boundaries.

In mentioning the advantages which Lancashire possesses as a seat of manufactures, we must not omit its ready communication with the sea by means of its well-situated port, Liverpool, through the medium of which it receives, from Ireland, a large proportion of the food that supports its population, and whose commerce brings from distant shores the raw materials of its manufactures, and again distributes them, converted into useful and elegant clothing, amongst all the nations of the earth. Through the same means a plentiful supply of timber is obtained, so needful for building purposes.

To the above natural advantage of a canal communication, which ramifies itself through all the populous parts of this county, and connects it with the inland counties, the seats of other flourishing manufactures, and the sources whence iron, lime, salt, stone, and other articles in which Lancashire is deficient, are obtained. By this means Lancashire, being already possessed of the primary requisites for manufactures, is enabled, at a very small expense, to command things of secondary importance, and to appropriate to its use the natural advantages of the whole kingdom. The canals, having been accomplished by individual enterprise, not by national funds, were constructed to supply a want already existing: they were not, therefore, original sources of the manufactures, but have extended together with them, and are to be considered as having essentially aided and accelerated that prosperity from whose beginnings they themselves arose. The recent introduction of railways will have a great effect in making the operations of trade more intensely active, and perfecting the division of labour, already carried to so high a point. By the railway and the locomotive engine, the extremities of the land will, for every beneficial purpose, be united.

In comparing the advantages of England for manufactures with those of other countries, we can by no means overlook the excellent commercial position of the country—intermediate between the north and south of Europe; and its insular situation, which, combined with the command of the seas, secures our territory from invasion or annoyance. The German ocean, the Baltic, and the Mediterranean are the regular highways for our ships; and our western ports command an unobstructed passage to the Atlantic, and to every quarter of the world.

A temperate climate, and a hardy race of men, have also greatly contributed to promote the manufacturing industry of England.

The political and moral advantages of this country, as a seat of manufactures, are not less remarkable than its physical advantages. The arts are the daughters of peace and liberty. In no country have these blessings been enjoyed in so high a degree, or for so long a continuance, as in England. Under the reign of just laws, personal liberty and property have been secure; mercantile enterprise has been allowed to reap its reward; capital has accumulated in safety; the workman has "gone forth to his work and to his labour until the evening;" and, thus protected and favoured, the manufacturing prosperity of the country has struck its roots deep, and spread forth its branches to the ends of the earth.

England has also gained by the calamities of other countries, and the intolerance of other governments. At different periods, the Flemish and French protestants, expelled from their native lands, have taken refuge in England, and have repaid the protection given them by practising and teaching branches of industry, in which the English were then less expert than their neighbours. The wars which have at different times desolated the rest of Europe, and especially those which followed the French revolution, (when mechanical invention was producing the most wonderful effects in England,) checked the progress of manufacturing improvement on the continent, and left England for many years without a competitor. At the same time, the English navy held the sovereignty of the ocean, and under its protection the commerce of this country extended beyond all former bounds, and established a firm connexion between the manufacturers of Lancashire and their customers in the most distant lands.

When the natural, political, and adventitious causes, thus enumerated, are viewed together, it cannot be matter of surprise that England has obtained a preeminence over the rest of the world in manufactures.

MECHANIZATION OF THE ENGLISH COTTON INDUSTRY 51

The cotton industry was the first English industry to be mechanized. Mechanical techniques for making cloth had already advanced to a point where relatively minor changes could make them automatic or semiautomatic, and they could be propelled by power. A big domestic and overseas demand for cotton goods provided an incentive for the invention of devices to increase productivity. And the relatively new cotton industry was readier to adopt new methods and devices than the older tradition-bound woolen industry was. Thus by 1830 the English cotton industry was completely mechanized. Five years later a book was published in London entitled History of the Cotton Manufacture in Great Britain. *The following selection from this book shows the author's keen awareness of the historical significance of the mechanization of the cotton industry that was taking place in his time.**

The history of civilization consists greatly in the history of the USEFUL ARTS. These arts form the basis of social improvement. By their means men are raised above abject want, become possessed of comforts and luxuries, and acquire the leisure necessary to cultivate the higher departments of knowledge. There is also an intimate connexion between the arts and natural science. Mutually aiding each other, they go hand in hand in the course of improvement. The manufactory, the laboratory, and the study of the natural philosopher, are in close practical conjunction. Without the aid of science,

* *Ibid.,* pp. 5-7.

the arts would be contemptible: without practical application, science would consist only of barren theories, which men would have no motive to pursue.

These remarks apply with peculiar force to the arts by which clothing is produced, and, above all, to the Cotton Manufacture of England, which is the very creature of mechanical invention and chemical discovery, and which has, in its turn, rendered the most important service to science, as well as increased the wealth and power of the country.

The subject of this volume may therefore claim attention from the man of science and the political philosopher, as well as from the manufacturer and merchant. To trace the origin and progress of so great a manufacture, with the causes of that progress, is more worthy the pains of the student, than to make himself acquainted with the annals of wars and dynasties, or with nineteen-twentieths of the matters which fill the pages of history.

The Cotton Manufacture of England presents a spectacle unparalleled in the annals of industry, whether we regard the suddenness of its growth, the magnitude which it has attained, or the wonderful inventions to which its progress is to be ascribed. Within the memory of many now living, those machines have been brought into use, which have made as great a revolution in manufactures as the art of printing effected in literature. Within the same period, the Cotton Manufacture of this country has sprung up from insignificance, and has attained a greater extent than the manufactures of wool and linen combined, though these have existed for centuries.

Sixty years since, our manufacturers consumed little more than THREE millions lbs. of raw cotton annually; the annual consumption is now TWO HUNDRED AND EIGHTY million lbs. In 1750 the county of Lancaster, the chief seat of the trade, had a population of only 297,400; in 1831, the number of its inhabitants had swelled to 1,336,854. A similar increase has taken place in Lanarkshire, the principal seat of the manufacture in Scotland. The families supported by this branch of industry are estimated to comprise A MILLION AND A HALF of individuals; and the goods produced not only furnish a large part of the clothing consumed in this kingdom, but supply nearly one-half of the immense export trade of Britain, find their way into all the markets of the world, and are even destroying in the Indian market the competition of the ancient manufacture of India itself, the native country of the raw material, and the earliest seat of the art.

The causes of this unexampled extension of manufacturing industry are to be found in a series of splendid inventions and discoveries, by the combined effect of which a spinner now produces as much yarn in a day, as by the old processes he could have produced in a year; and cloth, which formerly required six or eight months to bleach, is now bleached in a few hours.

It is the object of this volume to record the rise, progress, and present state of this great manufacture;—briefly to notice its ancient history in the East, and its sluggish and feeble progress in other countries, until the era of invention in England. . . .

The appearance of the power loom illustrates well that necessity is the mother of invention, or to put it more precisely, social need rather than genius is usually responsible for invention. When the need for a certain machine is felt simultaneously in several places, a number of varieties are evolved independently of one another. And so when there was a need during the Industrial Revolution for a machine to perform a certain function, it was soon forthcoming. A series of spinning machines had been developed which had enormously speeded up the output of thread. The weavers were not able to keep up with the pace, but to export the yarn would have encouraged foreign competition and endangered the British weaving industry. The dilemma was resolved by Edmund Cartwright, a minister of the Church of England, who invented the power loom in 1785; according to his own testimony, he had never seen cloth woven before it was brought to his attention that his country needed a power loom.*

Happening to be at Matlock in the summer of 1784, I fell in company with some gentlemen of Manchester, when the conversation turned on Arkwright's spinning machinery. One of the company observed, that as soon as Arkwright's patent expired, so many mills would be erected, and so much cotton spun, that hands never could be found to weave it. To this observation I replied, that Arkwright must then set his wits to work to invent a weaving mill. This brought on a conversation on the subject, in which the Manchester gentlemen unanimously agreed that the thing was impracticable; and, in defence of their opinion, they adduced arguments which I certainly was incompetent to answer, or even to comprehend, being totally ignorant of the subject, having never at that time seen a person weave. I controverted however, the impracticability of the thing by remarking, that there had lately been exhibited in London an automaton figure which played at chess. Now you will not assert, gentlemen, said I, that it is more difficult to construct a machine that shall weave, than one which shall make all the variety of moves which are required in that complicated game.

Some little time afterwards, a particular circumstance recalling this conversation to my mind, it struck me that, as in plain weaving, according to the conception I then had of the business, there could only be three movements, which were to follow each other in succession, there would be little difficulty in producing and repeating them. Full of these ideas, I immediately employed a carpenter and smith to carry them into effect. As soon as the machine was finished, I got a weaver to put in the warp, which was of such materials as sail-cloth is usually made of. To my great delight, a piece of cloth, such as it was, was the produce. As I had never before turned my thoughts to any thing mechanical, either in theory or practice, nor had ever seen a loom at work, or knew any thing of its construction, you will readily suppose that my first loom was a most rude piece of machinery. The warp was placed perpendicularly, the reed fell with the weight of at least half a hundred-weight, and the springs which threw the shuttle were strong enough to have thrown a Congreve rocket. In short, it required the strength of two powerful men to

* *Ibid.,* pp. 229-30.

work the machine at a slow rate, and only for a short time. Conceiving, in my great simplicity, that I had accomplished all that was required, I then secured what I thought a most valuable property, by a patent, 4th of April, 1785. This being done, I then condescended to see how other people wove; and you will guess my astonishment, when I compared their easy modes of operation with mine. Availing myself, however, of what I then saw, I made a loom, in its general principles nearly as they are now made. But it was not till the year 1787 that I completed my invention, when I took out my last weaving patent, August 1st of that year.

53   MASS PRODUCTION BY ELI WHITNEY

One of the basic features of modern mass production is the making of standard interchangeable parts and the assembling of these parts into the completed unit with a minimum of handicraft labor. The American inventor Eli Whitney devised this system while filling a government contract for muskets, although the basic concept of interchangeable parts did not originate with Whitney alone; others in England and France also conceived the idea. But Whitney hit upon it independently, and he was the first in the United States to actually put the idea into practice. After his success others adapted his technique to various industries—Isaac M. Singer in sewing machines, Cyrus H. McCormick in agricultural implements, Lyman Blake in shoe machinery, and best known, Henry Ford in automobiles. Thus Eli Whitney contributed basically to the industrial supremacy that the United States attained by World War I.

*The following letter which Eli Whitney sent to a friend on July 30, 1779 sets forth his conception of the principle of standard interchangeable parts.**

My general plan does not consist in one great complicated machine, wherever one small part being out of order or not answering to the purpose expected, the whole must stop & be considered useless. If the mode in which I propose to make one part of the musket should prove by experiment not to answer, it will in no way affect my mode of making any other part. *One of my primary objects is to form the tools so the tools themselves shall fashion the work and give to every part its just proportion—which when once accomplished, will give expedition, uniformity, and exactness to the whole.*

If each individual workman must form and fashion every part according to his own fancy & regulate the size & proportion by his own Eye or even by a measure, I should have as many varieties as I have members of each part —many of them would require an inscription upon them to point out the use for which they were designed, & it would require treble the number of hands to do the same work. By long practice and many trials mere Mechanics who have no correct taste, acquire the art of giving a particular uniformity, I hope, to particular substances. But very few really good experienced workmen in

* J. Mirsky and Allan Nevins, *The World of Eli Whitney* (New York: Macmillan, 1952), pp. 201-2.

this branch of business are to be had in this country. In order to supply ourselves in the course of the next few years with any considerable number of really good muskets, such means must be devised as will preclude the necessity of every workman's being bred to the business. An accurate Eye, close attention and much time are necessary (where experience is wanting) to form things rightly; but few among the great mass can proportion things accurately.

In short, the tools which I contemplate are similar to an engraving on copper plate from which may be taken a great number of impressions perceptibly alike.

DYNAMICS OF MODERN IMPERIALISM   54

Modern imperialism has profoundly affected the entire world and has aroused strong feelings both for and against it. Some have hailed it as the beneficent expansion of the superior European race, bringing civilization and progress to the inferior subject peoples. Others have denounced it as an abominable system by which a few Europeans made fortunes by ruthlessly exploiting millions of helpless natives. In the following selection, the well-known American publicist, Walter Lippmann, objectively analyzes the factors explaining the appearance of modern imperialism and also the relations and attitudes of the average citizen toward imperialism. It should be noted that this analysis was written in 1915 and therefore refers to the imperialism of the pre-World War I period.*

Missionaries, explorers, adventurers, prospectors come back home with tales of unbounded wealth. The tales are told to merchants with goods to sell, to capitalists with money to invest, to church congresses with a gospel to spread. Private companies are formed to exploit the new market and the new riches. Their directors at home consult with the colonial officials and receive what are rather vague promises of support. The news of the venture spreads to the trading and financial centers of other nations; they too begin to form companies and send out capital and goods.

Trouble appears in the country which is being opened. It may be that the natives put exorbitant custom duties on merchandise; it may be that in transacting business the invading business men outrage local superstitions; it may be that an insolent missionary is killed in a riot; it may be that business rivals stir up the natives against one another. The newspapers at home are furnished with lurid accounts of anarchy and of the danger to their "nationals." At the same time some concessionaire company may be working on the feeling of the bureaucracy at home with the object of securing some important monopoly—perhaps an exclusive franchise, perhaps the control of mines, perhaps harbor rights or navigation facilities on a river. The anarchy in the country furnishes not only a justification but a pretext, too,

---

* Walter Lippmann, *The Stakes of Diplomacy* (New York: Holt, 1915), pp. 76-78, 87-91, 93-96, 98, 151-53. Copyright 1915, 1917 by Walter Lippmann, renewed 1943 by Walter Lippmann. Reprinted by permission of The Macmillan Company.

and some kind of intervention takes place. There are visions of manifest destiny and the white man's burden among those who have read too much Kipling or smoked too many cigarettes in their editorial careers. The other Powers, also having manifest destinies and ambitious financiers, protest at the intervention and ask an accounting. Then, after much gnashing of teeth and an unlimited outflow of careless patriotism, a European conference meets to deal with the situation.

The well-known psychology of a horse deal is naive and trusting compared to the state of mind in which the diplomats take up the international task. They bristle with dignity, they are explosive with prestige, they are rigid with notions of sovereignty. The problem before them is not treated on its merits. It is set in magnificent and indefinite theories of world politics, and practically every judgment is based by the grand strategy of international diplomacy. Between intrigue, secret understandings, and a morbid national vanity, the negotiations are carried on and an act is framed. The act is passed by the conference either in the name of humanity or, as at Algeciras, "in the name of God Almighty." . . .

This whole business of jockeying for position is at first glance so incredibly silly that many liberals regard diplomacy as a cross between sinister conspiracy and a meaningless etiquette. It would be all of that if the stakes of diplomacy were not real. Those stakes have to be understood, for without such understanding diplomacy is incomprehensible and any scheme of world peace an idle fancy.

The chief, the overwhelming problem of diplomacy seems to be the weak state—the Balkans, the African sultanates, Turkey, China, and Latin America, with the possible exception of the Argentine, Chile, and Brazil. These states are "weak" because they are industrially backward and at present politically incompetent. They are rich in resources and cheap labor, poor in capital, poor in political experience, poor in the power of defense. The government of these states is the supreme problem of diplomacy. Just as the chief task of American politics to the Civil War was the organization of the unexploited West, so the chief task of world diplomacy to-day is the organization of virgin territory and backward peoples. I use backward in the conventional sense to mean a people unaccustomed to modern commerce and modern political administration. . . .

To the dogmatic anti-imperialist it seems absurd that white people do not stay at home and civilize themselves, leaving the Indians and Moors and Hottentots and Yaquis to work out their own salvation. The whole business of expansion by the western peoples is hateful to these liberals. They remember the caste system, the arrogance, the unspeakable horrors of the Congo and Putomayo, the ravishing and despoiling and debauching of natives by the European. It is a hideous story. And yet the plain fact is that the interrelation of peoples has gone so far that to advocate international laissez-faire now is to speak a counsel of despair. Commercial cunning, lust of conquest, rum, bibles, rifles, missionaries, traders, concessionaires have brought the two civilizations into contact, and the problem created must be solved, not evaded.

The great African empires, for example, were not created deliberately by theoretical imperialists. Explorers, missionaries, and traders penetrated these countries. They found rubber, oil, cocoa, tin; they could sell cotton goods, rifles, liquor. The native rulers bartered away enormous riches at trivial prices. But the trading-posts and the concessions were insecure. There were raids and massacres. No public works existed, no administrative machinery. The Europeans exploited the natives cruelly, and the natives retaliated. Concession hunters and merchants from other nations began to come in. They bribed and bullied the chiefs, and created still greater insecurity. An appeal would be made to the home government for help, which generally meant declaring a protectorate of the country. Armed forces were sent in to pacify, and civil servants to administer the country. These protectorates were generally sanctioned by the other European governments on the proviso that trade should be free to all. . . .

It is essential to remember that what turns a territory into a diplomatic "problem" is the combination of natural resources, cheap labor, markets, defenselessness, corrupt and inefficient government. The desert of Sahara is no "problem," except where there are oases and trade routes. Switzerland is no "problem," for Switzerland is a highly organized modern state. But Mexico is a problem, and Haiti, and Turkey, and Persia. They have the pretension of political independence which they do not fulfill. They are seething with corruption, eaten up with "foreign" concessions, and unable to control the adventurers they attract or safeguard the rights which these adventurers claim. More foreign capital is invested in the United States than in Mexico, but the United States is not a "problem" and Mexico is. . . . Foreigners invest in the United States, and they are assured that life will be reasonably safe and that titles to property are secured by orderly legal means. But in Mexico they are given "concessions," which means that they secure extra privileges and run greater risks, and they count upon the support of European governments or of the United States to protect them and their property.

The weak states, in other words, are those which lack the political development that modern commerce requires. To take an extreme case which brings out the real nature of the "problem," suppose that the United States was organized politically as England was in the time of William the Conqueror. Would it not be impossible to do business in the United States? There would be an everlasting clash between an impossible legal system and a growing commercial development. And the internal affairs of the United States would constitute a diplomatic "problem."

This, it seems to me, is the reason behind the outburst of modern imperialism among the Great Powers. It is not enough to say that they are "expanding" or "seeking markets" or "grabbing resources." They are doing all these things, of course. But if the world into which they are expanding were not politically archaic, the growth of foreign trade would not be accompanied by political imperialism. Germany has "expanded" wonderfully in the British Empire, in Russia, in the United States, but no German is silly enough to insist on planting his flag wherever he sells his dyestuffs, or stoves. It is only when his expansion is into weak states—into China, Morocco, Turkey, or elsewhere that foreign trade is imperialistic. This imperialism is actuated by many motives—by a feeling that political control insures special privileges, by a desire to play a large part in the world, by national vanity, by a passion for "ownership," but none of these motives would come into play if countries like China or Turkey were not politically backward.

Imperialism in our day begins generally as an attempt to police and pacify. This attempt stimulates national pride, it creates bureaucrats with a vested interest in imperialism, it sucks in and receives added strength from concessionaries and traders who are looking for economic privileges. There is no doubt that certain classes in a nation gain by imperialism, though to the people as a whole the adventure may mean nothing more than an increased burden of taxes. ...

The whole situation might be summed up by saying that the commercial development of the world will not wait until each territory has created for itself a stable and fairly modern political system. By some means or other the weak states have to be brought within the framework of commercial administration. Their independence and integrity, so-called, are dependent upon their creating conditions under which world-wide business can be conducted. The pressure to organize the globe is enormous. ...

How does it happen, though, that the people not concerned in a special interest are so ready to defend it against the world? Plain men who have no financial interest in copper will feel aggrieved if American copper interests in a foreign land are attacked. The German people felt "humiliated" because German trade was thwarted in Morocco.

The most obvious reason for this is that the private citizens are in the main abysmally ignorant of what the real stakes of diplomacy are. They do not think in terms of railroad concessions, mines, banking, and trade. When they envisage Morocco they do not think of the Mannesmann Brothers, but of "German prestige" and "French influence." When the Triple Entente compelled Germany to recede in the Moroccan affair of 1911, the rage of the German people was not due to a counting of their economic losses. They were furious, not that they had lost Morocco, but that they had lost the dispute. There is small doubt that the masses of people in no country would risk war to secure mining concessions in Africa. But the choice is never presented to them that way. Each contest for economic privileges appears to the public as a kind of sporting event with loaded weapons. The people wish their team, that is, their country, to win. Just as strong men will weep because the second baseman fumbles at the crucial moment, so they will go into tantrums of rage because corporations of their own nationality are thwarted in a commercial ambition.

They may have nothing tangible to gain or lose by the transaction; certainly they do not know whether they have. But they feel that "our" trade is their own, and though they share few of its profits they watch its career with tender solicitude.

Chapter Twelve

Basis of dominance:
the political revolution

In addition to the scientific and industrial revolutions, Europe was transformed in modern times by the political revolution. By this is meant the ending of the assumption of a divinely ordained division of mankind into rulers and ruled. Instead, the masses of the people gradually awakened and increasingly participated in governmental processes. One of the earliest manifestations of this political revolution was the English Revolution of the seventeenth century.

The significance of the English Revolution is that it defined and implemented the principles of liberalism, which were, at that time, primarily freedom of religion and security of person and of property. But the English Revolution, like the French, witnessed a split between moderate and radical elements. The latter, known as the Levellers, wished to democratize liberalism by basing it on the principle of the inherently equal rights of all individuals, regardless of birth or property, and they prepared the document An Agreement of the People *(1647) which represents the first systematic exposition of democratic liberalism. This type of liberalism was resolutely opposed by Cromwell and his followers, who were willing to accept equality before the law but not before the ballot box. What lay behind this conflict is apparent in the following selections, the first being the text of* An Agreement of the People, *and the second, a sampling of the debate over the* Agreement.**

* A. S. P. Woodhouse, *Puritanism and Liberty* (London: Dent, 1938), pp. 53-59, 63, 69-70, 443-45. By permission of The University of Chicago Press.

192   I. That the people of England, being at this day very unequally distributed by counties, cities, and boroughs, for the election of their deputies in Parliament, ought to be more indifferently proportioned, according to the number of the inhabitants; the circumstances whereof, for number, place, and manner, are to be set down before the end of this present Parliament.

II. That to prevent the many inconveniences apparently arising from the long continuance of the same persons in authority, this present Parliament be dissolved upon the last day of September, which shall be in the year of our Lord 1648.

III. That the people do of course choose themselves a Parliament once in two years, *viz.,* upon the first Thursday in every second March, after the manner as shall be prescribed before the end of this Parliament, to begin to sit upon the first Thursday in April following, at Westminster (or such other place as shall be appointed from time to time by the preceding representatives), and to continue till the last day of September then next ensuing, and no longer.

IV. That the power of this, and all future Representatives of this nation is inferior only to theirs who choose them, and doth extend, without the consent or concurrence of any other person or persons, to the enacting, altering, and repealing of laws; to the erecting and abolishing of offices and courts; to the appointing, removing, and calling to account magistrates and officers of all degrees; to the making war and peace; to the treating with foreign states; and generally to whatsoever is not expressly or impliedly served by the represented to themselves.

Which are as followeth:

1. That matters of religion, and the ways of God's worship, are not at all entrusted by us to any human power, because therein we cannot remit or exceed a title of what our consciences dictate to be the mind of God, without wilful sin; nevertheless the public way of instructing the nation (so it be not compulsive) is referred to their discretion.

2. That the matter of impressing and constraining any of us to serve in the wars is against our freedom, and therefore we do not allow it in our representatives; the rather because money (the sinews of war) being always at their disposal, they can never want numbers of men apt enough to engage in any just cause.

3. That after the dissolution of this present Parliament, no person be at any time questioned for anything said or done in reference to the late public differences, otherwise than in execution of the judgments of the present representatives, or House of Commons.

4. That in all laws made, or to be made, every person may be bound alike, and that no tenure, estate, charter, degree, birth, or place, do confer any exemption from the ordinary course of legal proceedings, whereunto others are subjected.

5. That as the laws ought to be equal, so they must be good, and not evidently destructive to the safety and well-being of the people.

These things we declare to be our native rights, and therefore are agreed and resolved to maintain them with our utmost possibilities against all opposition whatsoever, being compelled thereunto not only by the examples of our ancestors, whose blood was often spent in vain for the recovery of their freedoms, suffering themselves, through fraudulent accommodations, to be still deluded of the fruit of their victories, but also by our own woeful experience, who, having long expected, and dearly earned, the establishment of these certain rules of government, are yet made to depend for the settlement of our peace and freedom upon him that intended our bondage and brought a cruel war upon us.

Debates

MAJOR RAINBOROUGH (Leveller). ... I think that the poorest he that is in England hath a life to live, as the greatest he; and therefore truly, sir, I think it's clear, that every man that is to live under a government ought first by his own consent to put himself under that government; and I do think that the poorest man in England is not at all bound in a strict sense to that government that he hath not had a voice to put himself under; and I am confident that, when I have heard the reasons against it, something will be said to answer those reasons, insomuch that I should doubt whether he was an Englishman or no, that should doubt of these things.

GENERAL HENRY IRETON (Cromwell's son-in-law). ... Give me leave to tell you, that if you make this the rule I think you must fly for refuge to an absolute natural right, and you must deny all civil right; and I am sure it will come to that in the consequence. This, I perceive, is pressed as that which is so essential and due: the right of the people of this kingdom, and as they are the people of this kingdom, distinct and divided from other people, and that we must for this right lay aside all other considerations; this is so just, this is so due, this is so right to them. ... For my part, I think it is no right at all. I think that no person hath a right to an interest or share in the disposing of the affairs of the kingdom, and in determining or choosing those that shall determine what laws we shall be ruled by here—no person hath a right to this, that hath not a permanent fixed interest in this kingdom, and those persons together are properly the represented of this kingdom, and consequently are [also] to make up the representers of this kingdom, who taken together do comprehend whatsoever is of real or permanent interest in the kingdom. And I am sure otherwise I cannot tell what any man can say why a foreigner coming in amongst us—or as many as will coming in amongst us, or by force or otherwise settling themselves here, or at least by our permission having a being here—why they should not as well lay claim to it as any other. We talk of birthright. Truly [by] birthright there is thus much claim. Men may justly have by birthright, by their very being born in England, that we should not seclude them out of England, that we should not refuse to give them air and place and ground, and the freedom of the highways and other things, to live amongst us—not any man that is born here, though by his birth there come nothing at all (that is part of the permanent interest of this kingdom) to him. That I think is due to a man by birth. But that by a man's being born here he shall have a share in that power that shall dispose of the lands here, and of all things here, I do not think it a sufficient ground. I am sure if we look upon that which is the utmost (within [any] man's view) of what was originally the constitution of this kingdom, upon that which is most radical and fundamental, and which if you take away, there is no man hath any land, any goods, [or] any civil interest, that is this: that those that choose the representers for the making of laws by which this state and kingdom are to be governed, are the persons who, taken together, do comprehend the local interest of this kingdom; that is, the persons in whom all land lies, and those in corporations in whom all trading lies. This is the most fundamental constitution of this kingdom and [that] which if you do not allow, you allow none at all. ...

RAINBOROUGH.   ... I do hear nothing at all that can convince me, why any man that is born in England ought not to have his voice in election of burgesses. It is said that if a man have not a permanent interest, he can have no claim; and [that] we must be no freer than the laws will let us be, and that there is no [law in any] chronicle will let us be freer than that we [now] enjoy. Something was said to this yesterday. I do think that the main cause why Almighty God gave men reason, it was that they should make use of that reason, and that they should improve it for that end and purpose that God gave it them. And truly, I think that half a loaf is better than none if a man be an hungry: [this gift of reason without other property may seem a small thing], yet I think there is nothing that God hath given a man that any [one] else can take from him. And therefore I say, that either it must be the Law of God or the law of man that must prohibit the meanest man in the kingdom to have this benefit as well as the greatest. I do not find anything in the Law of God, that a lord shall choose twenty burgesses, and a gentleman but two, or a poor man shall choose none: I find no such thing in the Law of Nature, nor in the Law of Nations. But I do find that all Englishmen must be subject to English laws, and I do verily believe that there is no man but will say that the foundation of all law lies in the people. ...

IRETON.   ... Now I wish we may all consider of what right you will challenge that all the people should have right to elections. Is it by the right of nature? If you will hold forth that as your ground, then I think you must deny all property too, and this is my reason. For thus: by that same right of nature (whatever it be) that you pretend, by which you can say, one man hath an equal right with another to the choosing of him that shall govern him—by the same right of nature, he hath the same [equal] right in any goods he sees—meat, drink, clothes—to take and use them for his sustenance. He hath a freedom to the land, [to take] the ground, to exercise it, till it; he hath the [same] freedom to anything that any one doth account himself to have any propriety in. Why now I say then, if you, against the most funda-mental part of [the] civil constitution (which I have now declared), will plead the Law of Nature, that a man should (paramount [to] this, and con-trary to this) have a power of choosing those men that shall determine what shall be law in this state, though he himself have no permanent interest in the state, [but] whatever interest he hath he may carry about with him—if this be allowed, [because by the right of nature] we are free, we are equal, one man must have as much voice as another, then show me what step or dif-ference [there is], why [I may not] by the same right [take your property, though not] of necessity to sustain nature. ...

RAINBOROUGH.   ... For my part, as I think, *you* forgot something that was in *my* speech, and you do not only yourselves believe that [some] men are inclining to anarchy, but you would make all men believe that. And, sir, to say because a man pleads that every man hath a voice [by right of nature], that therefore it destroys [by] the same [argument all property—this is to forget the Law of God]. That there's a property, the Law of God says it; else why [hath] God made that law, *Thou shalt not steal?* ... And therefore I think that to that it is fully answered: God hath set down that thing as to propriety with this law of his, *Thou shalt not steal.* And for my part I am against any such thought, and, as for yourselves, I wish you would not make the world believe that we are for anarchy.

CROMWELL.   I know nothing but this, that they that are the most yielding have the greatest wisdom; but really, sir, this is not right as it should be. No man says that you have a mind to anarchy, but [that] the consequence of this rule tends to anarchy, must end in anarchy; for where is there any bound or limit set if you take away this [limit], that men that have no interest but the interest of breathing [shall have no voice in elections]? Therefore I am confident on't, we should not be so hot one with another.

RAINBOROUGH.   I know that some particular men we debate with [believe we] are for anarchy.

COLONEL NATHANIEL RICH.   I confess [there is weight in] that objection that the Commissary-General last insisted upon; for you have five to one in this kingdom that have no permanent interest. Some men [have] ten, some twenty servants, some more, some less. If the master and servant shall be equal electors, then clearly those that have no interest in the kingdom will make it their interest to choose those that have no interest. It may happen, that the majority may by law, not in a confusion, destroy property; there may be a law enacted, that there shall be an equality of goods and estate. ...

SEXBY (Leveller).   I see that though liberty were our end, there is a degeneration from it. We have engaged in this kingdom and ventured our lives, and it was all for this: to recover our birthrights and privileges as Englishmen; and by the arguments urged there is none. There are many thousands of us soldiers that have ventured our lives; we have had little propriety in the kingdom as to our estates, yet we have had a birthright. But it seems now, except a man hath a fixed estate in this kingdom, he hath no right in this kingdom. I wonder we were so much deceived. If we had not a right to the kingdom, we were mere mercenary soldiers. There are many in my condition, that have as good a condition [as I have]; it may be little estate they have at present, and yet they have as much a [birth] right as those two who are their lawgivers, as any in this place. I shall tell you in a word my resolution. I am resolved to give my birthright to none. Whatsoever may come in the way, and [whatsoever may] be thought, I will give it to none. If this thing [be denied the poor], that with so much pressing after [they have sought, it will be the greatest scandal]. There was one thing spoken to this effect; that if the poor and those in low condition [were given their birthright it would be the destruction of this kingdom]. I think this was but a distrust of Providence. I do think the poor and meaner of this kingdom—I speak as in relation [to the condition of soldiers], in which we are—have been the means of the preservation of this kingdom. I say, in their stations, and really I think to their utmost possibility; and their lives have not been [held] dear for purchasing the good of the kingdom. [And now they demand the birthright for which they fought.] Those that act to this end are as free from anarchy or confusion as those that oppose it, and they have the Law of God and the law of their conscience [with them]. . . .

56 SIGNIFICANCE OF THE AMERICAN REVOLUTION

A stirring appraisal of the American Revolution is found in Thomas Paine's Rights of Man *(1791), written in reply to Edmund Burke's denunciatory* Reflections on the French Revolution. *Paine's work was immediately accepted as a veritable declaration of the rights of man rather than as a mere rejoinder to Burke. The English political philosopher William Godwin, who had secured an early copy, exclaimed enthusiastically: "I have got it! If this do not cure my cough, it is a damned perverse mule of a cough." Paine had had similar success with his earlier work,* Common Sense, *which had contributed appreciably to the outbreak of the American Revolution. His extraordinary effectiveness as a polemicist stemmed from the fact that he made preaching democracy democratic. He shunned the sonorous language of Parliament and affected no refinements of scholarship, as is evident in the following passages from his* Rights of Man.*

What Archimedes said of the mechanical powers, may be applied to Reason and Liberty: "Had we," said he, "a place to stand upon, we might raise the world."

The revolution of America presented in politics what was only theory in mechanics. So deeply rooted were all the governments of the old world, and so effectually had the tyranny and the antiquity of habit established itself over the mind, that no beginning could be made in Asia, Africa, or Europe, to reform the political condition of man. Freedom had been hunted round the globe; reason was considered as rebellion; and the slavery of fear had made men afraid to think.

But such is the irresistible nature of truth, that all it asks, and all it wants, is the liberty of appearing. The sun needs no inscription to distinguish him from darkness; and no sooner did the American governments display themselves to the world, than despotism felt a shock, and man begin to contemplate redress.

The independence of America, considered merely as a separation from England, would have been a matter but of little importance, had it not been accompanied by a revolution in the principles and practice of governments. She made a stand, not for herself only, but for the world, and looked beyond the advantages herself could receive. Even the Hessian, though hired to fight against her, may live to bless his defeat; and England, condemning the viciousness of its government, rejoice in its miscarriage.

As America was the only spot in the political world, where the principles of universal reformation could begin, so also was it the best in the natural

* Thomas Paine, *Rights of Man, Part the Second Combining Principle and Practice* (London, 1792), pp. 1-5.

world. An assemblage of circumstances conspired, not only to give birth, but to add gigantic maturity to its principles. The scene which that country presents to the eye of a spectator, has something in it which generates and encourages great ideas. Nature appears to him in magnitude. The mighty objects he beholds, act upon his mind by enlarging it, and he partakes of the greatness he contemplates.—Its first settlers were emigrants from different European nations, and of diversified professions of religion, retiring from the governmental persecutions of the old world, and meeting in the new, not as enemies, but as brothers. The wants which necessarily accompany the cultivation of a wilderness produced among them a state of society, which countries, long harassed by the quarrels and intrigues of governments, had neglected to cherish. In such a situation man becomes what he ought. He sees his species, not with the inhuman idea of a natural enemy, but as kindred; and the example shews to the artificial world, that man must go back to Nature for information.

From the rapid progress which America makes in every species of improvement, it is rational to conclude, that if the governments of Asia, Africa, and Europe, had begun on a principle similar to that of America, or had not been very early corrupted therefrom, that those countries must, by this time, have been in a far superior condition to what they are. Age after age has passed away, for no other purpose than to behold their wretchedness.—Could we suppose a spectator who knew nothing of the world, and who was put into it merely to make his observations, he would take a great part of the old world to be new, just struggling with the difficulties and hardships of an infant settlement. He could not suppose that the hordes of miserable poor, with which old countries abound, could be any other than those who had not yet had time to provide for themselves. Little would he think they were the consequence of what in such countries is called government.

If from the more wretched parts of the old world, we look at those which are in an advanced stage of improvement, we still find the greedy hand of government thrusting itself into every corner and crevice of industry, and grasping the spoil of the multitude. Invention is continually exercised, to furnish new pretences for revenue and taxation. It watches prosperity as its prey, and permits none to escape without a tribute.

As revolutions have begun, (and as the probability is always greater against a thing beginning, than of proceeding after it has begun), it is natural to expect that other revolutions will follow. The amazing and still increasing expences with which old governments are conducted, the numerous wars they engage in or provoke, the embarrassments they throw in the way of universal civilization and commerce, and the oppression and usurpation they practice at home, have wearied out the patience, and exhausted the property of the world. In such a situation, and with the examples already existing, revolutions are to be looked for. They are become subjects of universal conversation, and may be considered as the Order of the day.

If systems of government can be introduced, less expensive, and more productive of general happiness, than those which have existed, all attempts to oppose their progress will in the end be fruitless. Reason, like time, will make its own way, and prejudice will fall in a combat with interest. If universal peace, civilization, and commerce, are ever to be the happy lot of man, it cannot be accomplished but by a revolution in the system of governments. All the monarchical governments are military. War is their trade, plunder and revenue their objects. While such governments continue, peace has not the absolute security of a day. What is the history of all monarchical governments, but a disgustful picture of human wretchedness, and the accidental respite of a few years repose? Wearied with war, and tired with human butchery, they sat down to rest, and called it peace. This certainly is not the condition that Heaven intended for man; and if *this be monarchy,* well might monarchy be reckoned among the sins of the Jews.

The revolutions which formerly took place in the world, had nothing in them that interested the bulk of mankind. They extended only to a change of persons and measures, but not of principles, and rose or fell among the common transactions of the moment. What we now behold, may not improperly be called a *"counter revolution."* Conquest and tyranny, at some early period, dispossessed man of his rights, and he is now recovering them. And as the tide of all human affairs has its ebb and flow in directions contrary to each other, so also is it in this. Government founded on a *moral theory, on a system of universal peace, on the indefeasible hereditary Rights of Man,* is now revolving from west to east, by a stronger impulse than the government of the sword revolved from east to west. It interests not particular individuals, but nations, in its progress, and promises a new era to the human race.

57 SIGNIFICANCE OF THE FRENCH REVOLUTION

The essence of the French Revolution is summarized in the Declaration of the Rights of Man and the Citizen,* *a statement of principles, or a bill of rights, adopted on August 26, 1789 as a preamble to a new constitution that was being drawn up by the National Assembly. The* Declaration, *with its ringing proclamation of the rights of the individual, reflects the influence of the English and the American revolutions, but it also reflects the dominant role of the bourgeoisie in its explicit enunciation of the rights of property. Robespierre, the Jacobin leader, observed, "You have . . . afford[ed] the largest possible latitude to the right to use one's property, and yet you have not added a word in limitation of this right, with the result that your* Declaration of the Rights of Man *might make the impression of having been created not for the poor, but for the rich, the speculators, for the stock exchange jobbers." Nevertheless, the* Declaration *was, in the words of a French historian, "the death certificate of the old regime." It was even more than this, for the document was translated into dozens of languages and it propagated the principles of the French Revolution throughout Europe, and eventually throughout the world.*

The Representatives of the people of France, formed into a National Assembly, considering that ignorance, neglect, or contempt of human rights, are the sole causes of public misfortunes and corruptions of Government, have resolved to set forth, in a solemn declaration, these natural, imprescriptible,

---

* Cited in Thomas Paine, *Rights of Man: Being an Answer to Mr. Burke's Attack on the French Revolution* (London, 1791), pp. 116-19.

and unalienable rights: that this declaration being constantly present to the minds of the members of the body social, they may be ever kept attentive to their rights and their duties: that the acts of the legislative and executive powers of Government, being capable of being every moment compared with the end of political institutions, may be more respected: and also, that the future claims of the citizens, being directed by simple and incontestible principles, may always tend to the maintenance of the Constitution, and the general happiness.

For these reasons, the National Assembly doth recognize and declare, in the presence of the Supreme Being, and with the hope of his blessing and favour, the following sacred rights of men and of citizens:

I. Men are born, and always continue, free, and equal in respect of their rights. Civil distinctions, therefore, can be founded only on public utility.

II. The end of all political associations is the preservation of the natural and imprescriptible rights of man; and these rights are liberty, property, security, and resistance of oppression.

III. The nation is essentially the source of all sovereignty; nor can any Individual, or Any Body of Men, be entitled to any authority which is not expressly derived from it.

IV. Political Liberty consists in the power of doing whatever does not injure another. The exercise of the natural rights of every man, has no other limits than those which are necessary to secure to every other man the free exercise of the same rights; and these limits are determinable only by the law.

V. The law ought to prohibit only actions hurtful to society. What is not prohibited by the law, should not be hindered; nor should any one be compelled to that which the law does not require.

VI. The law is an expression of the will of the community. All citizens have a right to concur, either personally, or by their representatives, in its formation. It should be the same to all, whether it protects or punishes; and all being equal in its sight, are equally eligible to all honours, places, and employments, according to their different abilities, without any other distinction than that created by their virtues and talents.

VII. No man should be accused, arrested, or held in confinement, except in cases determined by the law, and according to the forms which it has prescribed. All who promote, solicit, execute, or cause to be executed, arbitrary orders, ought to be punished, and every citizen called upon, or apprehended by virtue of the law, ought immediately to obey, and renders himself culpable by resistance.

VIII. The law ought to impose no other penalties but such as are absolutely and evidently necessary: and no one ought to be punished, but in virtue of a law promulgated before the offence, and legally applied.

IX. Every man being presumed innocent till he has been convicted, whenever his detention becomes indispensable, all rigour to him, more than is necessary to secure his person, ought to be provided against by the law.

X. No man ought to be molested on account of his opinions, not even on account of his religious opinions, provided his avowal of them does not disturb the public order established by the law.

XI. The unrestrained communication of thoughts and opinions being one of the most precious rights of man, every citizen may speak, write, and publish freely, provided he is responsible for the abuse of this liberty in cases determined by the law.

XII. A public force being necessary to give security to the rights of men and of citizens, that force is instituted for the benefit of the community, and not for the particular benefit of the persons with whom it is entrusted.

XIII. A common contribution being necessary for the support of the public force, and for defraying the other expenses of government, it ought to be divided equally among the members of the community, according to their abilities.

XIV. Every citizen has a right, either by himself or his representative, to a free voice in determining the necessity of public contributions, the appropriation of them, and their amount, mode of assessment, and duration.

XV. Every community has a right to demand of all its agents, an account of their conduct.

XVI. Every community in which a separation of powers and a security of rights is not provided for, wants a constitution.

XVII. The right to property being inviolable and sacred, no one ought to be deprived of it, except in cases of evident public necessity, legally ascertained, and on condition of a previous just indemnity.

58 EVOLUTION OF NATIONALISM

Europe's impact on the rest of the world in the nineteenth century was ideological in nature as well as economic and military, the three ideologies that had the greatest worldwide influence being nationalism, liberalism, and socialism. The following selections from the writings of the Italian revolutionary leader Giuseppe Mazzini,* and of the German historian Heinrich von Treitschke,** illustrate the transformation of nationalism from a liberal and tolerant ideology to a militaristic and chauvinistic one. Mazzini, despite the failure of his uprisings in 1830 and 1848, retained to the end of his days a passionate faith in humanity, in the brotherhood of all nationalist movements. But after the mid-nineteenth century, nationalism changed in character, becoming exclusive and antiforeign, basing itself on military power and narrow state interests. This change is best exemplified by the career and writings of Treitschke, who started as a liberal and ended as an eloquent apologist of Prussian militarism.

Life and Writings of Joseph Mazzini

Love your country. Your country is the land where your parents sleep, where is spoken that language in which the chosen of your heart blushing whispered the first word of love; it is the home that God has given you, that by striving to perfect yourselves therein, you may prepare to ascend to him. It is your name, your glory, your sign among the people. Give to it your thoughts, your counsels, your blood. Raise it up, great and beautiful as it

* *Life and Writings of Joseph Mazzini* (London: Smith, Elder, 1891), V, 163-65. Reprinted by permission of J. Murray (Publishers) Ltd.
** Adam L. Gowans, trans., *Selections from Treitschke's Lectures on Politics* (New York: F. Stokes, 1914), pp. 12, 14-17, 10-11.

was foretold by our great men. And see that you leave it uncontaminated by any trace of falsehood or of servitude; unprofaned by dismemberment. Let it be one, as the thought of God. You are twenty-five millions of men, endowed with active, splendid faculties; possessing a tradition of glory the envy of the nations of Europe; an immense future is before you; you lift your eyes to the loveliest heaven, and around you smiles the loveliest land in Europe; you are encircled by the Alps and the sea, boundaries traced out by the finger of God for a people of giants—you are bound to be such, or nothing. Let not a man of that twenty-five millions remain excluded from the fraternal bond destined to join you together; let not a glance be raised to that heaven which is not that of a free man. Let Rome be the ark of your redemption, the temple of your nation. Has she not twice been the temple of the destinies of Europe? In Rome two extinct worlds, the Pagan and the Papal, are super-posed like the double jewels of a diadem; draw from these a third world greater than the two. From Rome, the holy city, the city of love (Amor) the purest and wisest among you, elected by the vote and fortified by the inspira-tion of a whole people, shall dictate the Pact that shall make us one, and represent us in the future alliance of the peoples. Until then you will either have no country, or have her contaminated and profaned.

Love Humanity. You can only ascertain your own mission from the aim set by God before humanity at large. God has given you your country as cradle, and humanity as mother; you cannot rightly love your brethren of the cradle if you love not the common mother. Beyond the Alps, beyond the sea, are other peoples now fighting or preparing to fight the holy fight of independence, of nationality, of liberty; other peoples striving by different routes to reach the same goal,—improvement, association, and the founda-tion of an Authority which shall put an end to moral anarchy and re-link earth to heaven; an authority which mankind may love and obey without remorse or shame. Unite with them; they will unite with you. Do not invoke their aid where your single arm can suffice to conquer; but say to them that the hour will shortly sound for a terrible struggle between right and blind force, and that in that hour you will ever be found with those who have raised the same banner as yourselves.

Selections from Treitschke's Lectures on Politics

The State is in the first instance power, that it may maintain itself; it is not the totality of the people itself, as Hegel assumed in his deification of the State—the people is not altogether amalgamated with it; but the State pro-tects and embraces the life of the people, regulating it externally in all di-rections. On principle it does not ask how the people is disposed; it demands obedience: its laws must be kept, whether willingly or unwillingly. It is a step in advance when the silent obedience of the citizens becomes an inward, rational consent, but this consent is not absolutely necessary. Kingdoms have lasted for centuries as powerful, highly-developed States, without this inward consent of their citizens. What the State needs, is in the first place what is external; it wills that it be obeyed, its nature is to execute what it chooses. ... When the State can no longer carry out what it wills, it perishes in anarchy. ...

This truth remains: the essence of the State consists in this, that it can suffer no higher power above itself. How proud and truly worthy of a State was Gustavus Adolphus's declaration when he said: "I recognize no one above me but God and the sword of the victor." ...

Every State will for its own sake in a certain respect limit its sovereignty by treaties. If States conclude treaties with one another, their completeness as powers is to some extent restricted. But that does not invalidate the rule, for every treaty is a voluntary limitation of the individual power, and all international treaties are written with the stipulation: *rebus sic stantibus*. A State cannot possibly bind its will for the future in respect to another State. The State has no higher judge above it, and will therefore conclude all its treaties with that silent reservation. This is vouched for by the truth, that, so long as there has been a law of nations, at the moment that war was declared between the contending States all treaties ceased; but every State has as sovereign the undoubted right to declare war when it chooses, consequently every State is in the position of being able to cancel any treaties which have been concluded. ...

If we apply the standard of self-government, it is to be observed, how in the company of States of Europe the larger States are gaining an ever more pronounced predominance. ... It is not yet so very long since that States like Piedmont-Savoy could actually turn the scale in a coalition by their adhesion or desertion. No one will consider that possible nowadays. Since the Seven Years' War the ascendency of the Five Great Powers has developed itself, having proved itself necessary. Great European questions are discussed in that circle only. Italy is nearly on the point of entering it; but neither Belgium nor Sweden nor Switzerland may join in the discussion if they are not themselves directly concerned.

The whole development of our company of States aims unmistakably at ousting the States of the second rank. ...

Yet how tragic is the fate of Spain, which discovered the New World and has preserved for itself to-day in a direct way nothing whatever of that great achievement of civilization! The Spanish have only the one advantage still left, that so many millions of Spanish-speaking people live across the sea. Other nations have come to wrest from the Iberian nations the fruits of their labour; first Holland and then the English. History wears thoroughly masculine features; it is not for sentimental natures or for women. Only brave nations have a secure existence, a future, a development; weak and cowardly nations go to the wall, and rightly so.

59   EVOLUTION OF LIBERALISM

An outstanding exponent of liberalism, the second creed comprising modern Europe's political evolution, was John Stuart Mill, whose essay, On Liberty, *is the most famous presentation of classic liberalism. Mill's chief concern in this essay was to find an adequate basis for limiting the power of government over individual liberties. But liberalism, like nationalism, changed during the course of the nineteenth century. The manifold pressures of modern industrial society compelled liberals to recognize the need for government legislation that would correct social injustice or maladjustment. Thus a new democratic liberalism evolved which insisted on the responsibility of the state for the welfare of all its citizens. An elo-*

quent spokesman of this new liberalism was the English statesman Joseph Chamberlain, who finally left the Liberal party when it refused to support adequately his social reform program. The following selections from Mill's On Liberty * and from Chamberlain's Speeches ** illustrate the early political liberalism and the later democratic or social liberalism.

On Liberty

The subject of this Essay is . . . the nature and limits of the power which can be legitimately exercised by society over the individual. A question seldom stated, and hardly ever discussed, in general terms, but which profoundly influences the practical controversies of the age by its latent presence, and is likely soon to make itself recognized as the vital question of the future. It is so far from being new, that, in a certain sense, it has divided mankind, almost from the remotest ages, but in the stage of progress into which the more civilized portions of the species have now entered, it presents itself under new conditions, and requires a different and more fundamental treatment.

The struggle between Liberty and Authority is the most conspicuous feature in the portions of history with which we are earliest familiar, particularly in that of Greece, Rome, and England. . . .

The object of this Essay is to assert one very simple principle, . . . That principle is, that the sole end for which mankind are warranted, individually or collectively, in interfering with the liberty of action of any of their number, is self-protection. That the only purpose for which power can be rightfully exercised over any member of a civilized community, against his will, is to prevent harm to others. His own good, either physical or moral, is not a sufficient warrant. He cannot rightfully be compelled to do or forbear because it will be better for him to do so, because it will make him happier, because, in the opinions of others, to do so would be wise, or even right. These are good reasons for remonstrating with him, or reasoning with him, or persuading him or entreating him, but not for compelling him, or visiting him with any evil, in case he do otherwise. To justify that, the conduct from which it is desired to deter him must be calculated to produce evil to some one else. The only part of the conduct of any one, for which he is amenable to society, is that which concerns others. In the part which merely concerns himself, his independence is, of right, absolute. Over himself, over his own body and mind, the individual is sovereign. . . .

This, then, is the appropriate region of human liberty. It comprises, first, the inward domain of consciousness; demanding liberty of conscience, in the most comprehensive sense; liberty of thought and feeling; absolute freedom of opinion and sentiment on all subjects, practical or speculative, scientific, moral or theological. The liberty of expressing and publishing opinions may seem to fall under a different principle, since it belongs to that part of the conduct of an individual which concerns other people; but, being almost of as much importance as the liberty of thought itself, and resting in great part on the same reasons, is practically inseparable from it. Secondly, the prin-

* John Stuart Mill, *On Liberty* (New York: Holt, 1874), pp. 1-2, 23-24, 27-29.
** C. W. Boyd, ed., *Mr. Chamberlain's Speeches* (London: Constable, 1914), I, 166, 168-70, 218-19.

ciple requires liberty of tastes and pursuits; of framing the plan of our life to suit our own character; of doing as we like, subject to such consequences as may follow; without impediment from our fellow-creatures, so long as what we do does not harm them even though they should think our conduct foolish, perverse, or wrong. Thirdly, from this liberty of each individual, follows the liberty, within the same limits, of combination among individuals; freedom to unite, for any purpose not involving harm to others: the persons combining being supposed to be of full age, and not forced or deceived.

No society in which these liberties are not, on the whole, respected, is free, whatever may be its form of government; and none is completely free in which they do not exist absolute and unqualified. The only freedom which deserves the name, is that of pursuing our own good in our own way, so long as we do not attempt to deprive others of theirs, or impede their efforts to obtain it. Each is the proper guardian of his own health, whether bodily, or mental and spiritual. Mankind are greater gainers by suffering each other to live as seems good to themselves, than by compelling each to live as seems good to the rest.

Mr. Chamberlain's Speeches

It is not desirable, even if it were possible, that all Liberals should think exactly alike, and that every candidate should be cut to precisely the same pattern. In the Liberal army there must be pioneers to clear the way, and there must be men who watch the rear. Some may always be in advance, others may occasionally lag behind; but the only thing we have a right to demand is, that no one shall stand still. . . .

I do not want you to think that I suggest to you that legislation can accomplish all that we desire, and, above all, I would not lead you into wild and revolutionary projects, which would upset unnecessarily the existing order of things. But, on the other hand, I want you not to accept as final or as perfect, arrangements under which hundreds of thousands, nay, millions, of your fellow-country-men are subjected to untold privations and misery, with the evidence all around them of accumulated wealth and unbounded luxury. The extremes of wealth and of poverty are alike the sources of great temptation. I believe that the great evil with which we have to deal is the excessive inequality in the distribution of riches. Ignorance, intemperance, immorality, and disease—these things are all interdependent and closely connected; and although they are often the cause of poverty, they are still more frequently the consequence of destitution, and if we can do anything to raise the condition of the poor in this country, to elevate the masses of the people, and give them the means of enjoyment and recreation, to afford to them opportunities of improvement, we should do more for the prosperity, ay, for the morality of this country than anything we can do by laws, however stringent, for the prevention of excess, or the prevention of crime. I want you to make this the first object in the Liberal programme for the reformed Parliament. It is not our duty, it is not our wish, to pull down and abase the rich, although I do not think that the excessive aggregation of wealth in a few hands is any advantage to anybody; but our object is to raise the general condition of the people. The other day I was present at a meeting, when a labourer was called upon suddenly to speak. He got up, and in his rude dialect, without any rhetorical flourish, said something to this effect. He said, "Neighbours and friends, you have known me for forty years. I have lived among you, and worked among you. I am not a drunkard; I am a steady man; I am an industrious man; I am not a spending man. I have worked and laboured for forty years; it has been a weary task, and I ain't any forwarder now than I was when I began. What is the reason of it? What is the remedy?" Gentlemen, believe me, the questions of the poor labourer cannot be put aside. Our ideal, I think, should be that in this rich country, where everything seems to be in profusion, an honest, a decent, and an industrious man should be able to earn a livelihood for himself and his family, should have access to some means of self-improvement and enjoyment, and should be able to lay aside something for sickness and old age. Is that unreasonable? Is it impossible? ... I am not a Communist, although some people will have it that I am. Considering the difference in the character and the capacity of men, I do not believe that there can ever be an absolute equality of conditions, and I think that nothing would be more undesirable than that we should remove the stimulus to industry and thrift and exertion which is afforded by the security given to every man in the enjoyment of the fruits of his own individual exertions. I am opposed to confiscation in every shape or form, because I believe that it would destroy that security, and lessen that stimulus. But, on the other hand, I am in favour of accompanying the protection which is afforded to property with a large and stringent interpretation of the obligations of property. ...

I ask you to believe that I have never been presumptuous enough to imagine that I had found any complete or sufficient remedy for all the evils of our social system, neither have I been indifferent to the work which is being done in every direction by many reformers. On the contrary, I have welcomed their co-operation. I have, for instance, always attached the greatest importance and value to the services of those able and devoted men who have given themselves to the temperance cause. ... Then, I have always supported the great trade union movement, and I have never failed to acknowledge the services that it has rendered to the working classes, whose independence it has done much to secure, and whose material progress it has greatly advanced. I approved the principle, even while I was a manufacturer myself, of all the measures for the protection of the working classes in our factories and in our shops, of the Mines Regulation Act, and of the Employers' Liability Act. I have advocated, and I shall continue to advocate, the claims of our seamen, and to attempt to give them some greater protection against the avoidable risks of their dangerous profession. I see with great pleasure that Lord Rosebery the other night spoke eloquently and well of the necessity for some arrangement whereby the hours of labour may be shortened, especially in the case of railway servants and assistants in shops. I am very glad this cause should have so powerful a champion. In the fifteenth century we are told that the ordinary duration of a day's work was eight hours, and I am convinced from my own experience, which is not a small one, that nine hours, at all events, is as much as either man or woman can give to continuous employment of the same kind without injury to themselves or with satisfaction to their employers. But all these things, and others I could name to you, are so many branches of the same great subject. It is from many directions and from many quarters that we must seek for assistance. The harvest is plentiful; it is the labourers who are too few. There is room for all. Let us mutually assist each other.

The third of the great "isms" comprising modern Europe's political revolution is socialism, or communism. (These two terms were generally used interchangeably until the 1917 Bolshevik Revolution in Russia which led to the establishment of the Communist International.) The early nineteenth century socialists are commonly known as utopian socialists because of their penchant for devising detailed plans for model societies without seriously considering how these societies were to be established. The following selection from the American socialist Albert Brisbane,* is, in effect, a paraphrasing of the work of the famous French utopian socialist, Charles Fourier (1772–1837), whom Brisbane rated as a genius, comparable to "Columbus, Copernicus and Newton." In this selection, Brisbane faithfully reproduces Fourier's specifications for a "phalanx" or "association," the model community which Fourier believed would form the basis of future society. Completely different from this fanciful fabricating is the selection from the Principles of Communism, *written in 1847 by Friedrich Engels,** who, together with Karl Marx, founded "scientific" socialism. Marx and Engels viewed the socialist society of the future as the inevitable outcome of class struggle and the unfolding of historical forces rather than as the brainchild of a thinker in an ivory tower.*

Brisbane

For an Association of eighteen hundred to two thousand persons a tract of land three miles square, say in round numbers six thousand acres, will be necessary. A fine stream of water should flow through it. Its surface should be undulating and its soil adapted to a varied cultivation. It should be adjoining a forest, and situated in the vicinity of a large city, which would afford a convenient market for its products.

The first Phalanx being alone and without the aid of neighboring Associations, will have, in consequence of its isolated position, so many voids in attraction, so many passional calms to fear, that it will be necessary to select a fine position adapted to all varieties of cultivation and occupations. . . .

Two thousand persons of different degrees of fortune, of different ages and characters, of varied theoretical and practical knowledge, should be associated. The greatest diversity possible should exist, for the greater the diversity of passions, talents, fortunes, etc., of the members, the easier it will be to harmonize them. . . .

Every possible variety of agricultural pursuits should be carried on in the Association. Three branches of manufactures at least should be organized to afford occupation during rainy days and the winter months; besides various practical branches of the arts and sciences, without including those pursued in the schools.

Seven-eighths of the members should be agriculturalists and manufacturers; the balance capitalists, men of science and artists. . . .

* Albert Brisbane, *Association and Reorganization of Industry* (Philadelphia: C. F. Stollmeyer, 1840), pp. 350-51, 353-54, 366-69.
** Friedrich Engels, *Principles of Communism,* trans. Paul M. Sweezy, Monthly Review Pamphlet Series, No. 4 (New York: Monthly Review, 1952), pp. 5-15.

The internal organization of the Phalanx will, *in the commencement,* be under the direction of a Council, composed of stockholders, distinguished for their wealth or their industrial and scientific acquirements. Women, if there be any capable, will take part with the men; they will in Association be upon a level with them in all business matters, provided they possess the necessary knowledge.

In Association no community of property can exist, nor can any *collective* payments to whole families take place. An account is kept with every member individually, even with children over four and a half years of age; and every person is remunerated according to LABOR, CAPITAL and SKILL. . . .

All lands, machines furniture, or other objects, brought by members into the Association, are appraised at their cash value, and represented, as well as the monied capital paid in, by transferable shares, which are secured upon the personal and real estate of the Phalanx, that is upon its domain, edifices, flocks, manufactories, etc. The Council transfers to each person the value in shares of the objects, which he has furnished. A person may be a member without being a stockholder, or a stockholder without being a member. In the latter case, he receives no part of the profits, which are awarded to *Labor* and *Skill.*

The annual profits of the Association are, after taking an inventory, divided into three unequal portions, and paid as follows:

Five twelfths *to Labor.*

Four twelfths *to Capital.*

Three twelfths *to Practical and theoretical knowledge.*

Every person may, according to circumstances, receive a part of the three classes of profit, or of any one separately.

The Council, which has charge of the financial department, advances to the poorer members, clothing, food and lodging for a year. . . .

The edifice, outhouses and the distribution of the grounds of a Society, whose operations and industry are regulated by Series of groups, must differ prodigiously from the constructions of civilization, from its isolated dwellings and villages, which are adapted to families, between whom very few social relations, and no combination of action, exist. Instead of the confused mass of small houses, which compose our towns and villages, and which vie with each other in dirt and ugliness, a Phalanx builds a regular edifice, as far as the land permits. We will add a general description, supposing the location to be a favorable one.

The centre of the Palace should be reserved for quiet occupations; it will contain the dining halls, council rooms, the exchange, library, reading-rooms, etc. In it will also be placed the observatory, the telegraph, the chime of bells and the tower of observation, which overlooks the domain, and from which orders can be issued; the range of buildings, which form the centre, will enclose a winter garden and promenade, ornamented with evergreens.

In one of the wings should be located all manufactories and workshops of a noisy nature, like those of carpenters and blacksmith; in it also should be held assemblages of children engaged in industrial pursuits, who are generally very noisy. Association will avoid by this means a great inconvenience of our cities in almost every street of which some tin or blacksmith, or some learner of the clarionet stuns the ears of fifty families around. . . .

Besides the private rooms and apartments, the Palace must contain a great many public halls and saloons for social relations, and for the meetings, occupations and pleasures of the Series. . . .

The store-houses, granaries and stables must be placed, if possible, opposite the Palace. The space between the two will form the grand square, where parades and important festivities will be held. . . .

The gardens should be placed, as far as practicable, behind the Palace, and not behind the stables and granaries, near which the wheat and other fields would be better located. This distribution, however, will be regulated by localities; but we are now speculating upon a choice location.

Engels

QUESTION: What is communism?

Answer. Communism is the doctrine of the conditions of the liberation of the proletariat.

QUESTION: What is the proletariat?

Answer. The proletariat is that class in society which lives entirely from the sale of its labor and does not draw profit from any kind of capital; whose weal and woe, whose life and death, whose whole existence depends on the demand for labor, hence on the changing state of business, on the vagaries of unbridled competition. The proletariat, or the class of proletarians, is, in a word, the working class of the nineteenth century.

QUESTION: Proletarians, then, have not always existed?

Answer. No, there have always been poor and working classes; and the working classes have mostly been poor. But there have not always been workers and poor people living under conditions as they are today; in other words, there have not always been proletarians, any more than there has always been free unbridled competition.

QUESTION: How did the proletariat originate?

Answer. The proletariat originated in the industrial revolution which took place in England in the last half of the last [eighteenth] century, and which has since then been repeated in all the civilized countries of the world. This industrial revolution was precipitated by the discovery of the steam engine, various spinning machines, the mechanical loom, and a whole series of other mechanical devices. These machines, which were very expensive and hence could be bought only by big capitalists, altered the whole mode of production and displaced the former workers, because the machines turned out cheaper and better commodities than the workers could produce with their inefficient spinning wheels and handlooms. The machines delivered industry wholly into the hands of the big capitalists and rendered entirely worthless the meager property of the workers (tools, looms, etc.). The result was that the capitalists soon had everything in their hands and nothing remained to the workers. This marked the introduction of the factory system into the textile industry.

Once the impulse to the introduction of machinery and the factory system had been given, this system spread quickly to all other branches of industry. . . .

This is how it has come about that in civilized countries at the present time nearly all kinds of labor are performed in factories, and in nearly all, branches of work handicrafts and manufacture have been superseded. This process has to an ever greater degree ruined the old middle class, especially the small handicraftsmen; it has entirely transformed the condition of the workers; and two new classes have been created which are gradually swallowing up all the others.

These are:

(1) The class of big capitalists, who in all civilized countries are already in almost exclusive possession of all the means of subsistence and of the instruments (machines, factories) and materials necessary for the production of the means of subsistence. This is the bourgeois class, or the bourgeoisie.

(2) The class of the wholly propertyless, who are obliged to sell their labor to the bourgeoisie in order to get in exchange the means of subsistence necessary for their support. This is called the class of proletarians, or the proletariat. . . .

QUESTION: What were the immediate consequences of the industrial revolution and of the division of society into bourgeoisie and proletariat?

Answer. First, the lower and lower prices of industrial products brought about by machine labor totally destroyed in all countries of the world the old system of manufacture or industry based upon hand labor. In this way, all semi-barbarian countries, which had hitherto been more or less strangers to historical development and whose industry had been based on manufacture, were violently forced out of their isolation. They bought the cheaper commodities of the English and allowed their own manufacturing workers to be ruined. Countries which had known no progress for thousands of years, for example India, were thoroughly revolutionized, and even China is now on the way to a revolution. We have come to the point where a new machine invented in England deprives millions of Chinese workers of their livelihood within a year's time. In this way big industry has brought all the people of the earth into contact with each other, has merged all local markets into one world market, has spread civilization and progress everywhere and has thus ensured that whatever happens in the civilized countries will have repercussions in all other countries. It follows that if the workers in England or France now liberate themselves, this must set off revolutions in all other countries—revolutions which sooner or later must accomplish the liberation of their respective working classes.

Second, wherever big industries displaced manufacture, the bourgeoisie developed in wealth and power to the utmost and made itself the first class of the country. The result was that wherever this happened the bourgeoisie took political power into its own hands and displaced the hitherto ruling classes, the aristocracy, the guildmasters, and their representative, the absolute monarchy. The bourgeoisie annihilated the power of the aristocracy, the nobility, by abolishing the entailment of estates, in other words by making landed property subject to purchase and sale, and by doing away with the special privileges of the nobility. It destroyed the power of the guildmasters by abolishing guilds and handicraft privileges. In their place, it put competition, that is, a state of society in which everyone has the right to enter into any branch of industry, the only obstacle being a lack of the necessary capital. The introduction of free competition is thus a public declaration that from now on the members of society are unequal only to the extent that their capitals are unequal, that capital is the decisive power, and that therefore the capitalists, the bourgeoisie, have become the first class in society. ... Having raised itself to the actual position of first class in society, it proclaims itself to be also the dominant political class. This it does through the introduction of the representative system which rests on bourgeois equality before the law and the recognition of free competition, and in European countries takes the form of constitutional monarchy. In these constitutional monarchies only those who possess a certain capital are voters, that is to say, only members of the bourgeoisie. These bourgeois voters choose the deputies, and these bourgeois deputies, by using their right to refuse to vote taxes, choose a bourgeois government.

Third, everywhere the proletariat develops in step with the bourgeoisie. In proportion as the bourgeoisie grows in wealth the proletariat grows in numbers. For, since proletarians can be employed only by capital, and since capital expands only through employing labor, it follows that the growth of the proletariat proceeds at precisely the same pace as the growth of capital. Simultaneously, this process draws members of the bourgeoisie and proletarians together into the great cities where industry can be carried on most profitably, and by thus throwing great masses in one spot it gives to the proletarians a consciousness of their own strength. Moreover, the further this process advances, the more new labor-saving machines are invented, the greater is the pressure exercised by big industry on wages, which, as we have seen, sink to their minimum and therewith render the condition of the proletariat increasingly unbearable. The growing dissatisfaction of the proletariat thus joins with its rising power to prepare a proletarian social revolution.

QUESTION: What will this new social order have to be like?

Answer. Above all, it will have to take the control of industry and of all branches of production out of the hands of mutually competing individuals, and instead institute a system in which all these branches of production are operated by society as a whole, that is, for the common account, according to a common plan, and with the participation of all members of society. It will, in other words, abolish competition and replace it with association. Moreover, since the management of industry by individuals necessarily implies private property, and since competition is in reality merely the manner and form in which the control of industry by private property owners expresses itself, it follows that private property cannot be separated from competition and the individual management of industry. Private property must therefore be abolished and in its place must come the common utilization of all instruments of production and the distribution of all products according to common agreement—in a word, what is called the communal ownership of goods. In fact, the abolition of private property is doubtless the shortest and most significant way to characterize the revolution in the whole social order which has been made necessary by the development of industry, and for this reason it is rightly advanced by communists as their main demand.

Chapter Thirteen

Impact of dominance: Russia

Because of her location, Russia has been deeply affected by both European and Asian influences. Consequently, Russian thinkers for long have debated the relations of their country with Europe: Is Russia European? Are the differences between Russia and Europe to be deplored as an indication of Russian backwardness or to be hailed as signs of a distinctive and superior civilization?

Tsar Peter the Great (1689–1725) contributed greatly to this debate by using his imperial authority and Herculean energy to Westernize Russia as rapidly as possible. He reorganized his army and bureacracy, founded industries, established schools, and forced his subjects to shave their beards, wear Western clothes, drink coffee, and smoke tobacco. His violent measures of enforcement left an indelible imprint on the country, and also left it divided between the Westerners and the Slavophils—between those who hailed Peter as the great innovator and regenerator, and those who denounced him as the corruptor of Russia's Slavic spirit and culture. The conflicting views of these two groups are set forth in the following selections. The first * is from a book review written in 1841 by the famous literary critic and spokesman for the Westerners, V. G. Belinsky. Especially revealing is his low opinion of the Chinese and

* V. G. Belinsky, *Selected Philosophical Works* (Moscow: Foreign Languages Publishing House, 1948), pp. 107, 114-15, 128-29, 133-40.

Japanese societies because they had not yet been galvanized by Europe's dynamism, and also his reference to the subject status of India. The second selection * is from a speech delivered by the Slavophil poet Ivan Aksakov on the occasion of the assassination of Alexander II in 1881.

Belinsky

Russia was covered in darkness for many years:
God said: let there be Peter—and there was
light in Russia!

Russia, ... before Peter the Great was only a people and became a nation as a result of the *motion* given to it by the reformer.

From nothing, nothing is made, and a great man does not create of his own, but merely gives actual being to what existed in potentiality before him. That all Peter's efforts were aimed against ancient Russian usage is as clear as daylight, but the idea that he endeavoured to destroy our substantial spirit, our nationality, is more than ungrounded: it is simply absurd! ...

In pre-Petrine Russia there was no trade, no industry, no police, no civil security, no diversity of wants and demands, no military organization, for this was all poor and insignificant, since it was not law but custom. And morals? —What a sad spectacle! How much there was that was Asiatic, barbaric, Tataric! How many rites degrading to human dignity there were, *e.g.,* in marriage, and not only practised by the common people, but by the highest personages in the realm! How much was there that was vulgar and coarse in feasting! Compare those heavy repasts, those incredible beverages, those gross kissings, those frequent knockings of the forehead on the floor, those grovellings on the ground, those Chinese ceremonies—compare them with the tournaments of the Middle Ages, the European fetes of the seventeenth century. ... Remember what our long-bearded knights and chevaliers were like! Think of our gay ladies lapping up vodka! Men married they knew not whom! Deluded, they beat and tormented their wives in order to raise them by brute force to angelic status—and if that did not work, poisoned them with philters; they ate Homerically, drank almost in tubfuls, kept their wives out of sight, and only when flushed after having eaten several score peppery dishes and drunk several buckets of wine and mead would they call them out for a kiss. ... All this is as *moral* as it is aesthetic. ... But, for all that, this has not the slightest bearing on a nation's degradation either morally or philosophically: for it was all the result of isolated historical growth and Tatar influence. No sooner did Peter open his nation's door to the light of the world than the darkness of ignorance was gradually dispersed—the nation did not degenerate, did not yield its native soil to another tribe, but it became something it had not been before. ... Yes, gentlemen, defenders of ancient custom, say what you will, but the horse statue to Peter the Great on St. Isaac's Square is not enough: altars should be put up to him in all the squares and streets of the great kingdom of Russia! ...

If Russia was to learn the military art of Europe of the seventeenth century she had to study mathematics, fortification, the artillery and engineering arts and navigation, and she could not, consequently, take up geometry before

* O. Novikov, *Skobelleff and the Slavonic Cause* (London: Longmans, 1883), pp. 354-62.

she had thoroughly mastered arithmetic and algebra, the study of which would have had to make complete and equal progress among all estates of the nation. Uniformity of soldiers' clothes is not a whim but a necessity. Russian costume was not suited for soldiers' uniforms; consequently the European uniform had to be adopted; and how could that be done with the soldiers, alone, unless the repugnance to foreign clothes was overcome in the whole nation? And what sort of separate nation within a nation would the soldiery have presented if all the rest of menfolk went about in beards, long and flowing *balakhons* and huge ugly boots? To clothe the soldiers, mills were needed (and, thanks to patriarchal crudities there weren't any); was one to wait for the free and natural development of industry? Soldiers must have officers (is that not so, Messieurs Old Believers and Anti-Europeans?), and the officers had to be from a higher stratum of society than those from which the soldiers were recruited, and their uniforms had to be of finer cloth than those of the soldiers: was that cloth then to be purchased from foreigners with Russian money, or was the country to bide its time until (in perhaps 50 years) the soldiers' cloth mills were brought to perfection and evolved into fine-cloth mills? It is preposterous! No, everything had to be begun in Russia at a leap. ... Whatever you may say about the poverty of our literature and the paucity of our book trade, we do have books that enjoy a ready sale, and bookdealers who have made an annual turnover of a quarter of a million rubles on periodical publications alone! How is that? Because our great Empress, our Little Mother Catherine II, was solicitous about creating a literature and a reading public, compelled her court to read, and from them the appetite passed on through the higher nobility to the lower and thence to officialdom, and now it is beginning to pass to the merchantry. ...

True, Russia would probably have linked herself with Europe and adopted its civilization without the reforms of Peter, but in the same fashion as India did with England. ...

Some people impute to Peter the Great's reforms the mischievous effect of having placed the nation in a singular position by divorcing it from its native sphere and throwing it off its ground of innate horse sense without having inoculated real Europeanism. Despite the fallacy of this view, it possesses a foundation and is at least worthy of being refuted. ... Naturally, the old boyars, ... looked with profound contempt on those new-fledged and home-bred Europeans who, through lack of practice, got their legs entangled in their sword, dropped their cocked hat from under their arm, trod on the ladies' toes when coming up to kiss their hand, needlessly, parrot-fashion, employed foreign words, substituted for courtesy rude and impudent gallantry and, as sometimes happened, put their clothes on the wrong way. Even today, though in another shape, vestiges of this sham, distorted Europeanism still survive: these forms sans ideas, that courtesy sans respect to self and others, that urbanity sans aesthetics, that foppery and *lionhood* sans elegance. ... Yes, that is all true, but it would be as absurd to blame Peter for it as it would be to blame the physician who, in order to cure a sick man of the fever, first weakens and utterly debilitates him by bloodletting and plagues him when convalescent by a strict diet. The point is not whether Peter made us half-Europeans and half-Russians, consequently neither Europeans nor Russians: the point is are we always to remain in this characterless condition? If not, if we are destined to become European Russians and Russian Europeans, we should not reproach Peter, but rather wonder how he could have accomplished such a gigantic, such an unprecedented task! And so the crux of the matter consists in the words, "shall we"—and we can answer firmly and explicitly that we not only *shall be,* but are already *becoming* European Russians and Russian Europeans, that we have been becoming so since the reign of Catherine II, and are making progress therein day by day. We are today the pupils and no longer the zealots of Europeanism, we no longer wish to be either Frenchmen, or Englishmen or Germans, we want to be Russians in the European spirit. . . .

The building of St. Petersburg is also placed by many to the discredit of its great founder. It is said: on the margin of a vast realm, on swamps, in a terrible climate, with the sacrifice of many workmen's lives, many were forced against their wishes to build their homes there and so on and so forth; but the question is, was it necessary, and was it avoidable? Peter had to abandon Moscow—the beards hissed at him there; he had to secure a safe haven for Europeanism, make the visitor welcome in the bosom of the family, so that he may quietly and unobtrusively influence Russia and act as the lightning conductor for ignorance and bigotry. For such a haven he required an entirely new and traditionless soil, where his Russians would find themselves in an utterly new environment in which they could not help but recast their customs and habits of their own accord. . . .

There are only two tranquil states in the world—China and Japan; but the best the former produces is tea, and the latter, I believe, lacquer: nothing else can be said of them.

Aksakov

Gentlemen,—I came from Moscow to take part in your assembly, and to join my Moscow voice to yours. I should greatly like to convey to you what is said and thought at Moscow, but it is beyond expression by spoken word. How, indeed, are we to define the impressions which fill our souls at this moment? . . .

The Emperor is murdered; the same Emperor who was the greatest benefactor to his country, who emancipated, bestowing upon them human and civil rights, tens of millions of Russian peasants. He is murdered; not from personal vengeance, not for booty, but precisely because he is the Emperor, the crowned head, the representative, the first man of his country, that vital, single man, who personified the very essence, the whole image, the whole strength and power, of Russia. From time immemorial that power constituted the strength of the country. The attempt directed against the person of the Tzar is always directed against the whole people; but in this case the whole historical principle of the national life has been attacked, the autocratic power bestowed upon the Emperor by the country itself. Who are those who dared to bring that awful shame upon the people, and, as if by mockery, in the name of the people? Who are they? Is it merely a handful of criminals, blood-thirsty blockheads, enslaved by the demon of destruction? Where did they come from? Let us address that question sternly to ourselves. Is it not the product of our moral treason, of which is guilty almost all the so-called liberal press? Can it be anything else but the logical, extreme expression of that Westernism which, since the time of Peter the Great, demoralised both our government and our society, and has already marred all the spiritual manifestations of our national life? Not content to profit by all the riches of European thought and knowledge, we borrowed her spirit, developed by a foreign history and foreign religion. We began idolising Europe, worshipping her gods and her idols! Who is to be blamed? Some forty years ago has not Khomiakoff warned us, threatening us with Divine punishment for "deserting all that is sacred to our hearts"? But really, what are these "Anarchists," "Social Democrats," and Revolutionists, as they call themselves? Have they the smallest particle of Russian spirit in all their aspirations and aims? Is there the slightest shade in their teachings of a protest against the real shortcomings of which Russia is suffering? Just the opposite; what they despise most is precisely the Russian people. In their servile imitation of foreign teaching and foreign idols, they only borrow what can easily be explained, if not excused, in Western Europe by historical and social conditions. There, results of that kind are the natural protest caused by unequal partition of land, the unjust reign of the *bourgeoisie* over the fourth class—deprived of all civil organisation and political rights—a protest, therefore, against the present constitutional forms.

But that injustice is exactly what we do not possess. Thank God, and thanks to that very martyr-Emperor so brutally murdered, our "fourth class," or our peasantry, forming almost eighty per cent, of the whole realm, now possess land, organisation, and the most complete self-government. To this very day, that fourth class is the keeper of our historical instinct, of our religion, and of the whole element of our political organism. They, and not the so-called "Intelligencia," are the real supporters of our country. ...

. . . . .

The time is come for us to bethink ourselves. The time is come to fix our mobile heart, our mobile thoughts, on the rock of Divine and national truth. I am happy to have been able to express aloud, in the name of the Slavonic society, the civil and moral aims and ideals of the Russian people. But that is not sufficient. It is necessary—it is absolutely necessary—for us to implore our Emperor to allow us, the whole country, the whole nation, to surround his throne and to express fearlessly, openly to the whole world, our horror and indignation to all who dare to make any attempt against what is most sacred to our national feeling, the historical principle of the autocracy, which constitutes the very foundation of our political life. Yes; let us implore that the old union between the Emperor and the country shall be revived, based upon reciprocal, sincere confidence, love, and union of souls.

CRIMEAN WAR: REPERCUSSIONS IN RUSSIA   62

The debate between the Westerners and the Slavophils was greatly influenced by the Crimean War, in which Russia was defeated by Britain and France. The Slavophils had boasted that the war would demonstrate the superiority of Russia's autocratic tsardom over the democratic institutions of the West. Actually, the war demonstrated the exact opposite: the corruption and general backwardness of the Tsarist regime. Accordingly, a strong reaction was leveled against the old order— a reaction illustrated in the following tirade that was circulated in manuscript form.*

... "God has placed me over Russia," said the Tsar to us, "and you must bow down before me, for my throne is His altar. Trouble not yourselves with

* D. M. Wallace, *Russia,* rev. ed. (London: Cassell, 1912), pp. 446-49.

public affairs, for I think for you and watch over you every hour. My watchful eye detects internal evils and the machinations of foreign enemies; and I have no need of counsel, for God inspires me with wisdom. Be proud, therefore, of being my slaves, O Russians, and regard my will as your law."

We listened to these words with deep reverence, and gave a tacit consent; and what was the result? Under mountains of official papers real interests were forgotten. The letter of the law was observed, but negligence and crime were allowed to go unpunished. While grovelling in the dust before ministers and directors of departments, in the hope of receiving *tchins* and decorations, the officials stole unblushingly; and theft became so common that he who stole the most was the most respected. The merits of officers were decided at reviews; and he who obtained the rank of General was supposed capable of becoming at once an able governor, an excellent engineer, or a most wise senator. Those who were appointed governors were for the most part genuine satraps, the scourges of the provinces entrusted to their care. The other offices were filled up with as little attention to the merits of the candidates. A stable-boy became Press Censor! an Imperial fool became admiral! ! Kleinmichel became a count! ! ! In a word, the country was handed over to the tender mercies of a band of robbers.

And what did we Russians do all this time?

We Russians slept! With groans the peasant paid his yearly dues; with groans the proprietor mortgaged the second half of his estate; groaning, we all paid our heavy tribute to the officials. Occasionally, with a grave shaking of the head, we remarked in a whisper that it was a shame and a disgrace—that there was no justice in the courts—that millions were squandered on Imperial tours, kiosks, and pavilions—that everything was wrong; and then, with an easy conscience, we sat down to our rubber, praised the acting of Rachel, criticised the singing of Frezzolini, bowed low to venal magnates, and squabbled with each other for advancement in the very service which we so severely condemned. If we did not obtain the place we wished we retired to our ancestral estates, where we talked of the crops, fattened in indolence and gluttony, and lived a genuine animal life. If anyone, amidst the general lethargy, suddenly called upon us to rise and fight for the truth and for Russia, how ridiculous did he appear! How cleverly the Pharisaical official ridiculed him, and how quickly the friends of yesterday showed him the cold shoulder! Under the anathema of public opinion, in some distant Siberian mine he recognised what a heinous sin it was to disturb the heavy sleep of apathetic slaves. Soon he was forgotten, or remembered as an unfortunate madman; and the few who said, "Perhaps after all he was right," hastened to add, "but that is none of our business."

But amidst all this we had at least one consolation, one thing to be proud of—the might of Russia in the assembly of kings. "What need we care," we said, "for the reproaches of foreign nations? We are stronger than those who reproach us." And when at great reviews the stately regiments marched past with waving standards, glittering helmets, and sparkling bayonets, when we heard the loud hurrah with which the troops greeted the Emperor, then our hearts swelled with patriotic pride, and we were ready to repeat the words of the poet—

"Strong is our native country, and great the Russian Tsar!" Then British statesmen, in company with the crowned conspirator of France, and with treacherous Austria, raised Western Europe against us, but we laughed scornfully at the coming storm. "Let the nations rave," we said; "we have no cause to be afraid. The Tsar doubtless foresaw all, and has long since made the necessary preparations." Boldly we went forth to fight, and confidently awaited the moment of the struggle.

And lo! after all our boasting we were taken by surprise, and caught un- awares, as by a robber in the dark. The sleep of innate stupidity blinded our Ambassadors, and our Foreign Minister sold us to our enemies. Where were our millions of soldiers? Where was the well-considered plan of defence? One courier brought the order to advance; another brought the order to retreat; and the army wandered about without definite aim or purpose. With loss and shame we retreated from the forts of Silistria, and the pride of Russia was humbled before the Habsburg eagle. The soldiers fought well, but the parade-admiral (Menshikov)—the amphibious hero of lost battles—did not know the geography of his own country, and sent his troops to certain destruction.

Awake, O Russia! Devoured by foreign enemies, crushed by slavery, shamefully oppressed by stupid authorities and spies, awaken from your long sleep of ignorance and apathy! You have been long enough held in bondage by the successors of the Mongol Khan. Stand forward calmly before the throne of the despot, and demand from him an account of the national disaster. Say to him boldly that his throne is not the altar of God, and that God did not condemn us to be slaves.

Peasant Unrest after Emancipation 63

The general discontent following the Crimean defeat compelled Tsar Alexander II to introduce many far-reaching reforms, the most significant being the emancipation of the serfs in 1861. The Emancipation Manifesto *liberated the serfs by granting them the civil rights of free peasants. It also gave them a portion of the nobles' lands which they had tilled, though the nobles were indemnified with government treasury bonds and the government, in turn, was repaid by annual "redemption" dues collected from the peasants. This* Emancipation Manifesto *marked a major turning point in modern Russian history, yet it did not satisfy the peasants. The causes for their continued discontent are described in the following account by Donald Mackenzie Wallace, a British observer who traveled widely in Russia before and after the emancipation.* *

. . . In reality the Manifesto created among the peasantry a feeling of disappointment rather than delight. To understand this strange fact we must endeavour to place ourselves at the peasant's point of view.

In the first place it must be remarked that all vague, rhetorical phrases about free labour, human dignity, national progress, and the like, which may readily produce among educated men a certain amount of temporary enthusiasm, fall on the ears of the Russian peasant like drops of rain on a granite rock. The fashionable rhetoric of philosophical liberalism is as incomprehensible to him as the flowery circumlocutionary style of an Oriental scribe would be to a keen City merchant. The idea of liberty in the abstract and the mention of rights which lie beyond the sphere of his ordinary everyday life awaken no enthusiasm in his breast. And for mere names he has a profound indifference.

* *Ibid.,* pp. 504-6, 547, 550.

What matters it to him that he is officially called, not a "serf," but a "free village-inhabitant," if the change in official terminology is not accompanied by some immediate material advantage? What he wants is a house to live in, food to eat, and raiment wherewithal to be clothed, and to gain these first necessaries of life with as little labour as possible.

He looked at the question exclusively from two points of view—that of historical right and that of material advantage—and from both of these the Emancipation Law seemed to him very unsatisfactory.

On the subject of historical right the peasantry had their own traditional conceptions, which were completely at variance with the written law. According to the positive legislation the Communal land formed part of the estate, and consequently belonged to the proprietor; but according to the conceptions of the peasantry it belonged to the Commune, and the right of the proprietor consisted merely in that personal authority over the serfs which had been conferred on him by the Tsar. The peasants could not, of course, put these conceptions into a strict legal form, but they often expressed them in their own homely laconic way by saying to their master, "Mui vashi no zemlyá nasha"— that is to say, "We are yours, but the land is ours." And it must be admitted that this view, though legally untenable, had a certain historical justification. In old times the nobles had held their land by feudal tenure, and were liable to be ejected as soon as they did not fulfill their obligations to the State. These obligations had long since been abolished, and the feudal tenure transformed into an unconditional right of property, but the peasants clung to the old ideas in a way that strikingly illustrates the vitality of deep-rooted popular conceptions. In their minds the proprietors were merely temporary occupants, who were allowed by the Tsar to exact labour and dues from the serfs. What, then, was Emancipation? Certainly the abolition of all obligatory labour and money dues, and perhaps the complete ejectment of the proprietors. On this latter point there was a difference of opinion. All assumed, as a matter of course, that the Communal land would remain the property of the Commune, but it was not so clear what would be done with the rest of the estate. Some thought that it would be retained by the proprietor, but very many believed that *all* the land would be given to the Communes. In this way the Emancipation would be in accordance with historical right and with the material advantage of the peasantry, for whose exclusive benefit, it was assumed, the reform had been undertaken.

Instead of this the peasants found that they were still to pay dues, even for the Communal land which they regarded as unquestionably their own! . . . Briefly, then, the emancipated serf had to pay three kinds of direct taxation: Imperial to the Central Government, local to the Zemstvo, [provincial assembly] and Communal to the Mir [village organization]; and besides these he had to pay a yearly sum for the redemption of the land allotment which he received at the time of the Emancipation. Taken together, these sums formed a heavy burden. . . .

The last cause of peasant impoverishment that I have to mention is perhaps the most important of all: I mean the natural increase of population without a corresponding increase in the means of subsistence. Since the Emancipation in 1861 the population has nearly doubled, whilst the amount of Communal land, in the great majority of Communes, has remained the same. It is not surprising, therefore, that when talking with peasants about their actual condition, one constantly hears the despairing cry, *"Zemli malo!"* ("There is not enough land"); and one notices that those who look a little ahead ask anxiously: "What is to become of our children?"

TERRORIST STRATEGY OF THE SOCIALIST REVOLUTIONARIES 64

The Socialist Revolutionary party, organized in 1898, sought to use the peasant unrest to overthrow the Tsarist regime. The two distinctive characteristics of the Socialist Revolutionaries were a belief that the peasants rather than the city workers were the chief revolutionary force in Russia, and a readiness to resort to terrorist acts against the government. Their justification for the use of terrorism is set forth in the following selection from one of their pamphlets, Nasha Zadatcha (Our Task), *published in 1902.**

One of the powerful means of struggle, dictated by our revolutionary past and present, is political Terrorism, consisting of the annihilation of the most injurious and influential personages of Russian autocracy. ... Systematic Terrorism, in conjunction with other forms of open mass-struggle (industrial riots and agrarian risings, demonstrations, etc.) which receive from Terrorism an enormous, decisive significance, will lead to the disorganisation of the enemy. Terrorist activity will cease only with the victory over autocracy and the complete attainment of political liberty. Besides its chief significance as a means of disorganising, Terrorist activity will serve at the same time as a means of propaganda and agitation, a form of open struggle taking place before the eyes of the whole people, undermining the prestige of Government authority, and calling into life new revolutionary forces, while the oral and literary propaganda is being continued without interruption. Lastly, the Terrorist activity serves for the whole secret revolutionary party as a means of self-defence and of protecting the organisation against the injurious elements of spies and treachery.

LENIN'S STRATEGY FOR REVOLUTION 65

Just as the Socialist Revolutionaries sought to organize the discontented peasants, so the Social Democrats sought to organize the dissatisfied city workers. Established in 1898, the Social Democratic party split in 1903 into two factions— the moderate Mensheviks and the radical Bolsheviks. The leader of the Bolsheviks was V. I. Lenin, who maintained that a socialist party could not function effectively in autocratic Tsarist Russia unless it was led by a small group of well-trained and fully discipline professional revolutionaries. This proposition is set forth in the following selection from Lenin's work, What Is to Be Done?, *written in 1902. Other members of the Social Democratic party opposed Lenin's proposals*

* *Ibid.,* p. 685.

because they feared it would lead to undemocratic control by a handful of people. This dispute led to a split in the party the following year.*

I assert: 1. That no movement can be durable without a stable organisation of leaders to maintain continuity; 2. that the more widely the masses are drawn into the struggle and form the basis of the movement, the more necessary is it to have such an organisation and the more stable must it be (for it is much easier then for demagogues to side-track the more backward sections of the masses); 3. that the organisation must consist chiefly of persons engaged in revolution as a profession; 4. that in a country with a despotic government, the more we restrict the membership of this organisation to persons who are engaged in revolution as a profession and who have been professionally trained in the art of combating the political police, the more difficult will it be to catch the organisation; and 5. the *wider* will be the circle of men and women of the working class or of other classes of society able to join the movement and perform active work in it. . . .

The centralisation of the secret functions of the *organisation* does not mean the concentration of all the functions of the *movement*. The active participation of the greatest masses in the dissemination of illegal literature will not diminish because a dozen professional revolutionists concentrate in their hands the secret part of the work; on the contrary, it will *increase tenfold*. Only in this way will the reading of illegal literature, the contribution to illegal literature almost *cease to be secret work,* for the police will soon come to realise the folly and futility of setting the whole judicial and administrative machine into motion to intercept every copy of a publication that is being broadcast in thousands. This applies not only to the press, but to every function of the movement, even to demonstrations. The active and wide-spread participation of the masses will not suffer; on the contrary, it will benefit by the fact that a "dozen" experienced revolutionists, no less professionally trained than the police, will concentrate all the secret side of the work in their hands—prepare leaflets, work out approximate plans and appoint bodies of leaders for each town district, for each factory district, and for each educational institution. . . . The centralisation of the more secret functions in an organisation of revolutionists will not diminish, but rather increase the extent and the quality of the activity of a large number of other organisations intended for wide membership and which, therefore, can be as loose and as public as possible, for example, trade unions, workers' circles for self-education, and the reading of illegal literature. . . .

A man who is weak and vacillating on theoretical questions, who has a narrow outlook, who makes excuses for his own slackness on the ground that the masses are awakening spontaneously, who resembles a trade-union secretary more than a people's tribune, who is unable to conceive a broad and bold plan, who is incapable of inspiring even his enemies with respect for himself, and who is inexperienced and clumsy in his own professional art—the art of combating the political police—such a man is not a revolutionist but a hopeless amateur!

Let no active worker take offence at these frank remarks, for as far as insufficient training is concerned, I apply them first and foremost to myself. I used to work in a circle that set itself a great and all-embracing task: and every member of that circle suffered to the point of torture from the realisation that we were proving ourselves to be amateurs at a moment in history when we

* V. I. Lenin, *What Is to Be Done?* (London: M. Lawrence, n.d.), pp. 116-19.

might have been able to say—paraphrasing a well-known epigram: "Give us an organisation of revolutionists, and we shall overturn the whole of Russia!" And the more I recall the burning sense of shame I then experienced, the more bitter are my feelings towards those pseudo-Social-Democrats whose teachings bring disgrace on the calling of a revolutionist, who fail to understand that our task is not to degrade the revolutionist to the level of an amateur, but to *exalt* the amateur to the level of a revolutionist.

CONSTITUTIONAL DEMOCRATS AND THE RUSSIAN PEOPLE 66

In addition to the Social Democrats and Socialist Revolutionaries, there were the Constitutional Democrats, or Cadets, who represented primarily the small Russian middle class. The Cadets never won a mass following, and the reasons for this are set forth in the following analysis by an American journalist who is of Russian origin and who lived in Russia during these pre-World War I years.*

The party was founded in 1905 by [Professor] Milyukov. Originally it was made up of college professors, publicists, lawyers, *zemstvo*-workers, liberal noblemen, small shopkeepers, business-men and all other elements to whom autocracy was either economically or intellectually intolerable, and to whom the radicalism of the other opposition parties, all socialist of various shades, was repugnant. . . .

The outstanding feature of the Cadet philosophy of government—parliamentarism—is the political expression of the economic interests and the social ideology of the elements that make up the party. On the one hand are the intellectuals—teachers, publicists, lawyers, men of an academic stamp of mind, students of parliamentary institutions and constitutional forms of government, and by traditions, habits of thought, temperament and training, averse to violent changes in government. They are not of the masses, nor even in close contact with them, but are earnestly interested in their welfare. In a parliamentary form of government, preferably a constitutional monarchy, in the slow solid development of a parliamentary state, patterned more or less after the Anglo-Saxon model, they see a panacea for all Russia's ills. They are sticklers for legality and regularity. Though they advocate many advanced social measures such as an eight-hour labor day, social insurance, progressive inheritance and income taxes, and other measures of a similar nature, they insist that these must be inaugurated only in a legal manner, after a constitution has been adopted and government machinery set up. In other words, they condition the fulfillment of their social reforms upon the attainment of their political goal. Direct action of any nature, they deprecate. . . .

Whatever, therefore, one may think of the Cadet political program, the indisputable fact is, that there is almost an unbridgeable chasm between the Cadets and the masses. The Cadets are scholars, saturated with western political thought and tradition, advocates of western especially Anglo-Saxon political institutions, averse to revolutionary tactics under all circumstances, bent upon subjecting the evolution of Russia to their formulas, whereas the masses do

* M. G. Hindus, *The Russian Peasant and the Revolution* (New York: Holt, 1920), pp. 207-8, 214.

not even understand the language of the Cadets, have as yet cultivated no regard for constitutional formalities, are impelled in their thoughts and actions
by their immediate wants, and are ready to resort to any method available,
however desperate, to attain their goal.

67 RUSSIAN EXPANSION IN CENTRAL ASIA

*Between the sixteenth and eighteenth centuries Russia expanded across Siberia
and annexed relatively empty territories that were comparable to the New-World
acquisitions of the western powers. But in the nineteenth century, Russia overran
Central Asia and won colonial possessions that had denser populations and more
highly developed civilizations, similar to the colonies that the Western European
states carved out in South and East Asia; and the Russians used largely the same
arguments as the West Europeans did to justify their conquests. This is evident in
the following memorandum * issued on November 21, 1864 by Prince Gorchakov,
the Russian foreign minister. Gorchakov referred to his country's security requirements, trade interests, and civilizing mission, but he made the error of pledging
that Russia would not advance beyond a certain line. He was unaware at the
time that several weeks earlier a Russian general had besieged Tashkent, a city
far outside the designated line. Gorchakov had overlooked his basically sound
premise that one annexation was likely to lead to another.*

The position of Russia in Central Asia is that of all civilised states which
are brought into contact with half-savage nomad populations possessing no
fixed social organisation.

In such cases, the more civilised state is forced in the interest of the security
of its frontier, and its commercial relations, to exercise a certain ascendancy
over their turbulent and undesirable neighbours. Raids and acts of pillage must
be put down. To do this, the tribes on the frontier must be reduced to a state
of submission. This result once attained, these tribes take to more peaceful
habits, but are in turn exposed to the attacks of the more distant tribes against
whom the State is bound to protect them. Hence the necessity of distant, costly,
and periodically recurring expeditions against an enemy whom his social organisation makes it impossible to seize. If, the robbers once punished, the expedition is withdrawn, the lesson is soon forgotten; its withdrawal is put down to
weakness. It is a peculiarity of Asiatics to respect nothing but visible and palpable force. The moral force of reasoning has no hold on them.

In order to put a stop to this state of permanent disorder, fortified posts are
established in the midst of these hostile tribes, and an influence is brought
to bear upon them which reduces them by degrees to a state of submission.
But other more distant tribes beyond this outer line come in turn to threaten
the same dangers, and necessitate the same measures of repression. The State
is thus forced to choose between two alternatives—either to give up this endless labour, and to abandon its frontier to perpetual disturbance, or to plunge

---

* A. Krause, *Russia in Asia: A Record and a Study 1558-1899* (New York: Holt, 1901),
pp. 224-25.

deeper and deeper into barbarous countries, when the difficulties and expenses increase with every step in advance.

Such has been the fate of every country which has found itself in a similar position. The United States in America, France in Algeria, Holland in her Colonies, England in India; all have been forced by imperious necessity into this onward march, where the greatest difficulty is to know where to stop.

Such have been the reasons which have led the Imperial Government to take up, first, a position resting, on one side, on the Sir Daria, on the other, the Lake of Issik Kul, and to strengthen these lines by advanced forts.

It has been judged indispensable that our two fortified lines, one extending from China to the Lake of Issik Kul, the other from the Sea of Aral, along the Sir Daria, should be united by fortified points, so that all posts should be in a position of mutual support leaving no gap through which nomad tribes might make their inroads and depredations with impunity.

Our original frontier line along the Sir Daria to Fort Perovski, on the one side, and on the other, to Lake Issik Kul, had the drawback of being almost on the verge of the desert. It was broken by a wide gap between the two extreme points; it did not offer sufficient resources to our troops, and left unsettled tribes over the back with which any settled arrangement became impossible.

In spite of our unwillingness to extend our frontier, these motives had been powerful enough to induce the Imperial Government to establish this line between Issik Kul and the Sir Daria by fortifying the town of Chemkend, lately occupied by us. This line gives us a fertile country, partly inhabited by Kirghis tribes, which have already accepted our rule, and it therefore offers favourable conditions for colonization, and the supply of provisions to our garrisons. In the second place, it puts us in the neighbourhood of the agricultural and commercial population of Khokand.

Such are the interests which inspire the policy of our august master in Central Asia.

It is needless for me to lay stress on the interest which Russia evidently has not to increase her territory, and, above all, to avoid raising complications on her frontiers, which can but delay and paralyse her domestic development. Very frequently of late years the civilisation of these countries, which are her neighbours on the Continent of Asia, has been assigned to Russia as her special mission.

RUSSIA DEFEATED BY JAPAN **68**

By the 1890's Russia had completed her expansion in Central Asia and was turning her attention to the Far East. Rich prizes were thought to be available there owing to the steady disintegration of the decrepit Chinese Empire. But as the Russians began to push across the Amur River into Manchuria and Korea, they encountered the Japanese, who were now expanding outside of their home islands; the outcome of this clash was the Russo-Japanese War of 1904–1905. Contrary to general expectation, the Japanese emerged triumphant, defeating the Russians in a series of land battles in Manchuria and also in a naval engagement *in the Tsushima Strait between Korea and Japan. The following account of the sea battle is from the report prepared by Admiral Togo.**

. . . By the help of Heaven our united squadron fought with the enemy's Second and Third Squadrons on May 27 and 28, and succeeded in almost annihilating him.

When the enemy's fleet first appeared in the south seas, our squadrons, in obedience to Imperial command, adopted the strategy of awaiting him and striking at him in our home waters. We therefore concentrated our strength at the Korean Straits, and there abode his coming north. After touching for a time on the coast of Annam, he gradually moved northward, and some days before the time when he should arrive in our waters several of our guard-ships were distributed on watch in a south-easterly direction, according to plan, while the fighting squadrons made ready for battle, each anchoring at its base so as to be ready to set out immediately.

Thus it fell out that on the 27th, at 5 a.m., the southern guard-ship *Shinano Maru* reported by wireless telegraphy, "Enemy's fleet sighted in No. 203 section. He seems to be steering for the east channel."

The whole crews of our fleet leaped to their posts; the ships weighed at once, and each squadron, proceeding in order to its appointed place, made its dispositions to receive the enemy. . . . Thus, though a heavy fog covered the sea, making it impossible to observe anything at a distance of over five miles, all the conditions of the enemy were as clear to us, who were thirty or forty miles distant, as though they had been under our very eyes. Long before we came in sight of him we knew that his fighting force comprised the Second and Third Baltic Squadrons, that he had seven special service ships with him, that he was marshalled in two columns line ahead, that his strongest vessels were at the head of the right column, that his special service craft followed in the rear, that his speed was about twelve knots, and that he was still advancing to the north-east. . . .

At 1.45 p.m. we sighted the enemy for the first time at a distance of several miles south on our port bow. . . .

I now ordered the whole fleet to go into action, and at 1.55 p.m. I ran up this signal for all the ships in sight: "The fate of the Empire depends upon the event. Let every man do his utmost." . . .

The head of the enemy's column, when our main squadron bore down on it, changed its course a little to starboard, and at eight minutes past two o'clock he opened fire. We did not reply for some time, but when we came within 6,000 mètres' range we concentrated a heavy fire on two of his battleships. This seemed to force him more than ever to the south-east, and his two columns simultaneously changed their course by degrees to the east, thus falling into irregular columns line ahead, and moving parallel to us. The *Oslyabya,* which headed the left column, was soon heavily injured, burst into a strong conflagration, and left the fighting line. The whole of the armoured cruiser squadron was now steaming behind the main squadron in line, and, the fire of both squadrons becoming more and more effective as the range decreased, the flagship *Kniaz Suvaroff* and the *Imperator Alexander III.,* which was the second in the line, burst heavily into flames and left the fighting line, so that the

* C. A. Repington, *The War in the Far East 1904-1905* (London: J. Murray, 1905), pp. 580-83.

enemy's order became more deranged. Several of the ships following also took fire, and the smoke, carried by the westerly wind, quickly swept over the face of the sea, combining with the fog to envelop the enemy's fleet, so that our principal fighting squadrons ceased firing for a time. . . .

Such was the state of the main fighting forces on each side at 2.45 p.m. Already the result of the battle had been decided in this interval.

PETITION TO THE TSAR **69**

The war with Japan was extremely unpopular with the Russian people who saw no reason why they should be fighting thousands of miles away in the Far East. The humiliating defeats inflicted by the Japanese increased the discontent, which was further aggravated by the chronic grievances of the peasants over land-hunger, and the workers over conditions of labor. These circumstances prompted a socially-minded priest, Father George Gapon, to organize in St. Petersburg a peaceful demonstration to submit to the Tsar a petition requesting certain reforms. The text of this petition is given below.*

SIRE!

We, the workers and residents of the city of St. Petersburg, of various ranks and stations, our wives, children, and helpless old people—our parents, have come to you, Sire, to seek justice and protection. We have become destitute, we are being persecuted, we are overburdened with work, we are being insulted, we are not regarded as human beings, we are treated as slaves who must endure their bitter fate in silence. We have suffered, but even so we are being pushed more and more into the pool of poverty, disfranchisement, and ignorance. We are being stifled by despotism and arbitrary rule, and we are gasping for breath. We have no strength left, Sire. We have reached the limit of endurance. For us that terrible moment has arrived, when death is preferable to the continuance of unbearable torture.

And so we stopped work and declared to our bosses that we will not resume work until our demands are met. We have not asked for much. We only want what is indispensable to life, without which there is nothing but hard labor and eternal torture. Our first request was that our bosses should discuss our needs with us. But this they refused to do—they denied us the right to speak about our needs, saying that, according to the law, we had no such right. Our requests likewise were considered unlawful: the reduction of the working day to eight hours; the establishment of wage levels in consultation with us and with our consent; the investigation of our misunderstandings with the lower echelons of factory administration; wage increases for unskilled laborers and women up to one ruble per day; the abolition of overtime; provision for medical aid, administered attentively, carefully, and without abuse; the construction of factories so that it is possible to work in them without dying from horrible drafts, rain, and snow.

* I. Spector, *The First Russian Revolution: Its Impact on Asia* (Englewood Cliffs: Prentice-Hall, 1962; A Spectrum Book), pp. 117-21.

All this seemed, according to our bosses in the factory and foundry administration to be unlawful, every one of our requests is regarded as a crime, and our desire to improve our plight is interpreted as outrageous insolence.

Sire, we are many thousands here; but all of us merely resemble human beings—in reality, however, not only we, but the entire Russian people, enjoy not a single human right, not even the right to speak, to think, to assemble, to discuss our needs, to take measures to improve our plight.

We have been enslaved, and enslaved under the auspices of your officials, with their aid, and with their cooperation. Every one of us who has the temerity to raise his voice in defence of the interests of the working class and the people is thrown into jail and sent into exile. We are punished for a good heart and for a sympathetic soul as we would be for a crime. To feel compassion for an oppressed, disfranchised, tortured man—this is tantamount to a flagrant crime. All the working people and the peasants are at the mercy of the bureaucratic government, comprised of embezzlers of public funds and thieves, who not only disregard the interests of the people, but defy these interests. The bureaucratic government has brought the country to complete ruin, has imposed upon it a disgraceful war, and leads Russia on and on to destruction. We, the workers and the people, have no voice whatsoever in the expenditure of the huge sums extorted from us. We do not even know whither and for what the money collected from the impoverished people goes. The people are deprived of the opportunity to express their wishes and demands, to take part in levying taxes and their expenditure. The workers are deprived of the possibility of organizing unions for the protection of their interests.

Sire! Is this in accordance with God's law, by the grace of which you reign? Is it possible to live under such laws? Isn't it better to die—for all of us, the toiling people of all Russia, to die? Let the capitalist-exploiters of the working class, the bureaucratic embezzlers, and the plunderers of the Russian people live and enjoy life. This is the dilemma before us, Sire, and this is why we have assembled before the walls of your palace. This is our last resort. Don't refuse to help your people, lead them out of the grave of disfranchisement, poverty, and ignorance, give them an opportunity to determine their own fate, and cast off the unbearable yoke of the bureaucrats. Tear down the wall between you and your people, and let them rule the country with you. You have been placed on the throne for the happiness of the people, but the bureaucrats snatch this happiness from our hands, and it never reaches us. All we get is grief and humiliation. Look without anger, attentively, at our requests; they are not intended for an evil, but for a good cause, for both of us, Sire. We do not talk arrogantly, but from a realization of the necessity to extricate ourselves from a plight unbearable to all of us. Russia is too vast, her needs too diverse and numerous to be run only by bureaucrats. It is necessary to have popular representation, it is necessary that the people help themselves and govern themselves. Only they know their real needs. Do not reject their help; take it; command at once, forthwith, that there be summoned the representatives of the land of Russia from all classes, all strata, including also the representatives of the workers. Let there be a capitalist, a worker, a bureaucrat, a priest, a doctor, and a teacher—let them all, whoever they are, elect their own representatives. Let everyone be equal and free in the matter of suffrage, and for that purpose command that the elections for the Constituent Assembly be carried out on the basis of universal, secret, and equal suffrage.

This is our chief request; in it and upon it everything else is based; this is the main and sole bandage for our painful wounds, without which these wounds will bleed badly and will soon bring us to our death.

But one measure cannot heal our wounds. Still others are necessary, and, directly and frankly, as to a father, we tell you, Sire, in the name of all the toiling masses of Russia what they are.

The following measures are indispensable:

I. Measures to eliminate the Ignorance and Disfranchisement of the Russian People.

1. The immediate release and return of all those who have suffered for their political and religious convictions, for strikes, and peasant disorders.

2. An immediate declaration of personal freedom and inviolability, freedom of speech and the press, freedom of assembly, and freedom of conscience in regard to religion.

3. Universal and compulsory popular education financed by the state.

4. Responsibility of the Ministers to the people and a guarantee of rule by law.

5. Equality of everyone, without exception, before the law.

6. Separation of church and state.

II. Measures to eliminate the Poverty of the People.

1. Abolition of indirect taxation and the substitution of direct, progressive income taxes.

2. Abolition of redemption payments, low interest rates, and the gradual transfer of the land to the people.

3. Procurement orders for the Navy Department must be placed in Russia and not abroad.

4. Termination of the war by the will of the people.

III. Measures to eliminate the Yoke of Capital over Labor.

1. Abolition of the institution of factory inspectors.

2. Establishment at the factories and foundries of permanent committees chosen by the workers, which, together with the administration, would examine all claims of individual workers. The discharge of a worker cannot take place other than by the decision of this committee.

3. Immediate freedom for consumer and trade unions.

4. An eight-hour working day and standardization of overtime.

5. Immediate freedom for the struggle between labor and capital.

6. Immediate introduction of a minimum wage.

7. Immediate participation of representatives of the working classes in the drafting of a bill for state insurance of workers.

These, Sire, are our chief needs, concerning which we have come to you. Only by their satisfaction will the liberation of our Motherland from slavery and poverty be possible; only thus can it flourish; only this will make it possible for the workers to organize for the protection of their interests from the brazen exploitation of the capitalists and government bureaucrats, who plunder and choke the people. Issue decrees for this purpose and swear to carry them out, and you will make Russia both happy and famous, and your name will be engraved in our hearts and in those of our posterity forever. And if you do not so decree, and do not respond to our supplication, we will die here, in this square, in front of your palace. We have nowhere else to go and it is useless to go. There are only two roads open to us: one toward freedom and happiness, the other toward the grave. Let our lives be the sacrifice for suffering Russia. We do not regret this sacrifice. We are glad to make it.

The peaceful demonstration organized by Father Gapon was met by gunfire from the imperial guards of the winter palace. Many of the unarmed men, women, and children were killed or wounded. "Bloody Sunday," as it was popularly called, served as a spark to set off the long-smoldering discontent of workers, peasants, and veterans returned from the Far East. The result was an empire-wide revolution which came very close to overthrowing the Tsarist regime. The following account describes the violence of the land-hungry peasants during this 1905 revolution.*

When the pillage began [during the 1905 revolution] and there appeared "the redness in the sky," the sign of the burning of landowners' property, "unknown persons," made their appearance in the villages and took the leadership of the movement upon themselves. Before an attack began the peasants sometimes went to the landowner and demanded "keys, money, and arms"; sometimes they demanded the books of the estate, in order that the records of their indebtedness might be destroyed. In other cases no warning was given.

One purpose alone animated the peasants—"to smoke out" the landowners, to force them to leave their estates, so that the peasants might obtain the land for nothing or for a low price. "If we pillage the landowners they will the sooner give up their land. Land is the gift of God. It must belong to the labouring people."

All classes of the peasantry joined in the pillage—poor, middleclass rich, and even very rich peasants. Each took his turn and carried off as much as he could. In all villages, however, the poor peasants gave direction to the movement. In some they forced the rich peasants to join in the pillage under threats of turning upon them; in others they prevented the rich from engaging in the pillage on the ground that they would be inclined to take too much for themselves. "There were cases in which the rich peasants who were on a pillaging expedition found, on their return, that their own property had been pillaged by poorer peasants." Some rich peasants neither joined in the movement nor allowed themselves to be pillaged; they collected their families and friends and defended their property against the pillagers. In general, the rich peasants, whether they took part in the movement by compulsion or not, were opposed to it. They spoke contemptuously of the *agrarnēkē,* in whose ranks were the idle and the poverty-stricken.

The village youth was everywhere in the front of the movement. The older men at the beginning tried to impede the movement—"to keep their sons from sin"; but later they were drawn into the current. They saw enviously their neighbours enriching themselves, and they could not withstand the temptation. In some cases the old men succeeded in stopping the movement. The women in general were sympathetic, and occasionally were even more active in pillage than their husbands.

Soldiers returning from Manchuria found, in frequent cases, that their households had been impoverished by external economic causes or by bad manage-

* J. Mavor, *An Economic History of Russia,* 2nd rev. ed. (New York: Dutton, 1925), II, 330-31, 331-38. By permission of J. M. Dent & Sons, Ltd.

ment during their absence. They had nothing to eat, and no fuel to heat their houses with; they found that their families were getting no regular assistance or no assistance at all. Such men threw themselves into the pillaging movement and increased the general excitement. "For what," they said, "did we shed our blood, when we have no land?" . . .

A general review of the evidence suggests that everywhere the peasants were animated by the same general idea—viz. that the land must be obtained somehow. They seemed to think that they must secure possession of the land, and that they were being unjustly deprived of this possession by the existing owners, whether these were private owners, or whether, as State lands, the lands were in the hands of the Treasury. In either case, they thought that the lands should be transferred to them, in order that they might cultivate them. . . . They knew nothing of constitutional procedure. It was enough that they knew what they wanted. The only solution of the land question which they could recognize as effectual was to give the land to them, or to give at least as much of it as they could cultivate. Endless time might be consumed in debating about the terms of transference. These terms could be discussed afterwards. The important thing was to get the land at once into their hands. *L'action directe* was the simplest and speediest method. If they had force enough to take the land, the transference might be accomplished in that way; if they had not force enough to take the land, they had enough at least to make occupation of the land by anyone but themselves exceedingly uncomfortable and even dangerous. Landowner and State alike might be compelled to surrender the land to the peasants by making ownership of it by anyone else impracticable. So far as the peasants were concerned, there is no evidence of wider political ideas. The supreme question for them was the question of the land. Their demands were concentrated upon possession of land, without payment, if possible, but in any case, possession. . . .

While in some cases the influence of the propaganda of the socialist revolutionary party is apparent, it must be realized that almost everywhere the movement in its essential features was spontaneous. Indeed, the peasants were "more advanced" than the revolutionists. Although they did not work out the implications of their movement, it meant in effect that the land was to be given to them, and that they were to be allowed to cultivate it without State taxes. They might collect taxes from themselves, but the funds produced by these taxes were to be expended locally. Under these conditions, of course, the State as such must disappear, and the nation must dissolve into loosely-connected groups of independent and autonomous communities.

RUSSIA AND THE WEST: UNRESOLVED ISSUE   71

Throughout the nineteenth century, Russia was profoundly influenced by the West. The Crimean defeat, the industrialization of the country, the various revolutionary ideologies, and the constitutional arrangements begun in 1905 were all inspired either directly or indirectly by the West. Yet the debate raged on as to whether this Western influence was a curse or a blessing; whether Europe offered a model to be imitated or an object lesson to be avoided. The basic issue of Russia's relations with the West was as unresolved at the beginning of the twentieth *century as it had been at the beginning of the nineteenth. This is apparent in the following analysis written in 1906 by an informed British observer in Russia,* which should be compared with an earlier reading,* Russia and the West.

... In Russia the two classes are the defenders and the opponents of the Government, or rather of the autocracy. The former base their arguments on the affirmation that Russia is an Oriental country and that Western institutions are unsuited to the Russian people. Parenthetically, I must mention that I am not alluding to the extreme reactionaries—to those people who wish to go back to institutions which existed before the time of Peter the Great. I am referring to intelligent people who, while belonging to no political parties, simply disbelieve in the Liberal movement in Russia, consider it to be the hysterical cackling of an unimportant minority, and think that the whole matter is mere stuff and nonsense. The opinion of these people is certainly worth considering, not because they are more impartial than others who belong to parties, since their ideas are equally based upon prejudice, but because they may be right. These people say that all talk of a Constitution is beside the mark. They argue thus:

"We must have a Constitution, just as we have an Army and a Navy, because the idea soothes the revolution-haunted breasts of foreign financiers, but we shall never have a real Constitution because we don't want one. Reforms? Oh, yes, as many as you please, on paper, signed and countersigned, but they will remain a dead letter, because they are not adapted to the character and the spirit of the nation. You cannot force Russian peasants to own land in the way Western peasants do. You can make laws telling them to do so, but if you force them you will only drive them to rebellion. Russia is like China; you can draw up a Constitution for Russia, but when it is carried out you will find that the only practical difference between the old state of affairs and the new is that the writing-table of the Minister of Foreign Affairs is to be oblong instead of round. People say that the Russian people is good and that its Government is bad, but the faults of the people are not the result of the inherent vices of the Government; the vices of the Government are the logical result of the faults, which in their turn are the inevitable complement of the good qualities, of the people. The desire for Liberal reforms based on Western examples is merely a fictitious agitation of a minority, namely, the 'Intelligentsia' or middle class, who have forgotten and lost their native traditions and instincts and have adopted and not properly assimilated the traditions and instincts of Western Europe. They have ceased to be Russian, and they have not become European. They have taken the European banner of ideals, but they do not know what to do with it; they cannot hold it up in their weak Slav hands. The result is words, words. This chatter will continue for a time, and when people get tired of listening, it will cease. As for the people, the real people, they will settle their affairs with those immediately connected with them, with their landlords, etc. The Government will make plenty of reforms on paper and have a Duma; but everything will go on exactly as it was before. Because you cannot change the character of a people, and the form of government they enjoy is the result and the expression of their qualities and of their defects."

Such are the arguments I have often heard advanced by these people, and

* M. Baring, *A Year in Russia,* rev. ed. (New York: Dutton, 1917), pp. 281-84.

I say once more that they may be right. Three years ago I was firmly convinced that they were right, and even now I have an open mind on the subject, although two years of close contact with Russians of all classes have led me to change my own opinion, and to agree with the other equally impartial people, who are just as Russian and have just as much knowledge of the country and experience of their fellow-countrymen, and who flatly deny the whole thing. According to this school, . . . the present *régime* in Russia is not the natural expression of national characteristics, but a fortuitous disease which has been allowed to spread without ever having been radically treated. Neither Autocracy nor Bureaucracy is a thing which has grown out of the immemorial traditions and habits of the Russian people; Autocracy was the product of a comparatively recent change in Russian history, and Bureaucracy the accidental result of the further changes introduced by a man of genius. The Government made certain things impossible: such as education for the peasants, laws for the peasants, justice, etc.; then, when the results of these prohibitions began to make themselves felt, turned round and said: "You see what these men are like; it is no use giving them anything because they are hopeless; they are like niggers and must be treated as such." This has been the proceeding of the Government: to prevent, prevent, and prevent again; and then, when the explosion resulting from the prevention occurred, to observe how right they had been in preventing, and how necessary it was to prevent more and more, because it was the only thing the people understood. In this blindness and obstinacy, year after year deferring the payment of their debt, they have let the interest accumulate; and when they eventually have to pay, far more will be required of them than they need originally have surrendered.

The people who represent these two schools of thought both say that they are Russia. . . . Which really represents Russia, we shall know perhaps in ten years' time.

Chapter Fourteen

Impact of dominance:
the Middle East

72 DIMITRIJE OBRADOVIĆ: BALKAN DISCIPLE OF THE WEST'S ENLIGHTENMENT

The next area after Russia to feel the impact of the West was the *Middle East, a region with a great variety of peoples, religions, and cultures. Furthermore, it was a loosely organized region, since the Ottoman Empire was a ramshackle imperial structure. Accordingly, the response to Western intrusion varied greatly from one part of the Middle East to the other. The following readings will deal, therefore, with the response of Balkan Christians, Moslem Turks, Arabs, and Persians.*

An outstanding example of the West's influence on the Balkans is found in the work of Serbian leader Dimitrije Obradović. He was born in 1743 at a time when the Serbians had no literature of any sort in their spoken language—other than ecclesiastical literature in the artificial Church Slavonic. Obradović became a monk, but being restless, he set forth in 1760 on travels that were to take him to Germany, England, France, and Russia. His observations and experiences transformed him from a monk with an intellectual outlook that was essentially Byzantine into an enthusiastic champion of the current rationalism and enlightenment. He now found it intolerable that his people should have no literature in their own language. So he proceeded to write about his adventures and his new secular ideas in the unaffected spoken language of his country-men. The following passages reflect his militant rationalism, his critical *attitude toward superstition and traditional religious practices, and his nationalistic objectives in writing in "our common Serbian language."* *

233

I have learned to think and to pass judgment in a better and more rational manner on my religious beliefs and my faith. The books of learned men have given me the means to distinguish orthodoxy from superstition and the pure teaching of the Gospels from all manner of human traditions and additions. ... I am no longer deceived by any gay colors, by gilding and by external glitter: I recognize what is necessary and fundamental and what is accidental and superfluous; what is true and internal reverence and piety and what are external customs, ritual, and ceremonies. ...

You ask me why I have rebelled against fasts, long prayers, and the great number of holidays; and wherein they offend me and make me take up arms against them. Read the Holy Gospel and you will see that the same things offended our Savior, so that he cried out against them and on that account rebuked the Pharisees, saying: "Woe unto you, scribes and Pharisees, hypocrites, who by fasting make pale and sad your faces and pray in the streets and byways, that men may see you." The abuses that were committed in those times by those acts are committed also today; and whoever receives, recognizes, and loves the teaching of Christ must hate all that Christ hated and against which he cried out. I have spent twenty-five years with various peoples of our faith in Greece, Albania, Bosnia, Herzegovina, Moldavia, and other regions: practically the entire population are conscious of being Christians of the Eastern Church only through its fasts and its holidays. And how do they fast? Ah, my brethren, God sees and hears all things; we must tell the truth! No one fasts except such as are extremely poor, people who live on sterile soil and who during several months of the year would think that they sat at royal tables if they merely had bread of wheat or of maize. These poor people fast the greater part of their lives, but by grim necessity. But those who have various fasting foods, as we term them, including olive oil and wine, never fast at any time whatever. (You should know that I do not regard it as fasting when a man has no dinner but at supper eats enough for both dinner and supper, nor when a man eats no meat but stuffs himself with beans and sauerkraut till his belly rumbles and sweat comes out on his brow.) But you will say: "The custom is old, let it be kept up! If it does no good, neither does it do harm!" Ha, I too want to speak about that! That it does no good, sensible men recognized long, long ago, but here is the trouble: it does much harm! You know well that an Albanian or a Montenegrin will kill a man like a wild goat and then atone for his act by fasting. Theft, lying, and every sort of injury and injustice he is confident of blowing away by peppered beans and of scattering it as if by a thunderbolt. There is no stench or impurity that he is not confident of washing away with sorrel and vinegar, of driving off with leeks and onions. If people only fasted as the divine Apostle Paul bids them, as a restraint on themselves, of their own free will, and not by compulsion, then who would be foolish enough to cry out against fasting? "Let not him that fasteth not blame him that fasteth; and let not him which fasteth condemn him that fasteth not." ...

You ask me who I am and who gave me authority to assume the tone of

* G. R. Noyes, *The Life and Adventures of Dimitrije Obradović* (Berkeley: Univ. of California, 1953), pp. 99-100, 107, 133-35.

a teacher. Among so large a multitude of Serbs God willed that I be born; being a rational man, I have a God-given and natural authority to communicate my thoughts to my fellow men and to tell them whatever good and sensible things I have heard and learned from others. In every nation and society there must be men of all sorts of callings and occupations, and among them there should be firm cooperation and harmony: it is not right for one man to say to another, "You are not needed." ... Man is not only carnal but also rational. Therefore, as many trades and inventions are required for our bodily needs, it is just and proper that there be some trade which will serve our rational qualities; and this is the more needful since man surpasses all other animals solely through his superiority in intellect and reason. Consequently, since so many men work and strive in behalf of various needs of mine—some bear arms in order to defend my peace and security; others till the soil that they may give me bread to eat; some men clothe me and provide me with footwear; others bring me from distant provinces all manner of necessary things,—therefore it is right that I by my trade do something in their behalf: that I compose and write something that will be necessary and useful for their more noble parts; that is to say, for the heart, intellect, and reason. That is my trade! ...

Here [in Leipzig] I purpose to remain for at least a year, and with the help of God and of some kind Serbian I intend to publish in our common Serbian language a book printed in the civil alphabet that shall be called *Counsels of Sound Reason,* for the benefit of my nation, that my toil and my long wanderings may not be all in vain. My book will be written in pure Serbian, just as is this letter, that all Serbian sons and daughters may understand it, from Montenegro to Smederevo and the Banat. So for all the Serbian race I shall translate the thoughts and counsels of famous and wise men, desiring that all of us may profit by them. My book will be intended for every person who understands our language and who with a pure and honest heart desires to enlighten his mind and to improve his character. I shall pay no heed whatever to what religion and faith any man belongs, nor is that a matter for consideration in the present enlightened age. ...

Let us cast a brief glance at the enlightened nations of all Europe. At the present time every one of those nations is striving to perfect its own dialect. This is a very useful object, seeing that when learned men write their thoughts in the general language of the whole nation, then the enlightenment of the intellect and the light of learning are not confined to persons who understand the old literary language, but are spread abroad and reach even the villagers, being taught to the humblest peasants and to the shepherds, provided only that they know how to read. And how easy it is to teach a child how to read his own language! ... I am aware that someone may reply to me that if we begin to write in the common dialect the old language will be neglected and will gradually disappear. I answer: "What profit have we from a language which, taking our nation as a whole, not one person in ten thousand understands properly and which is foreign to my mother and my sisters?" ... "Then let them learn it!" you may object. That is easier said than done. How many people have the time and means to learn the old literary language? Very few! But everybody knows the general, common dialect; and in it all who can read may enlighten their minds, improve their hearts, and adorn their manners. A language derives its value from the good that it does. And what language can do more good than the general language of the whole nation? The French and the Italians had no fears that the Latin language would perish if they began to write their own languages, and indeed learned men of our nation will always know it.

The first of the Balkan peoples to feel the impact of the West, the Greeks were, consequently, the first to experience an awakening that ultimately led to revolution and independence. The following selection analyzes the varied aspects of the impact—economic, political, and intellectual—and the manifold repercussions in the Greek world. It is significant in that the same forces, with regional variations, awakened the other Balkan peoples—Serbs, Bulgars, Rumanians, and Albanians.*

. . . Of all the Balkan peoples the Greeks were the most advanced in practically every respect, and in the eighteenth and early nineteenth centuries they were the most influential of the subject races of the Ottoman Empire. During the earlier centuries the position of the Greeks was by no means outstanding. At that time the church was the centre of their national life and it maintained a press and schools at Constantinople. But this church was obscurantist and concerned itself only with strictly religious matters. The church writings of the sixteenth and seventeenth centuries are uniformly unimpressive and uninfluenced by current forces. In the eighteenth century, however, a remarkable renaissance occurred in the Greek world, and this renaissance was independent of, and not infrequently antagonistic to, the Patriarchate.

The most important single factor in the Greek awakening was the great revival of commerce. . . . Economic progress in Greece [in the eighteenth century] was both rapid and widespread, and was due primarily to three factors: the Greek commercial colonies abroad, Russian diplomacy, and the French Revolution.

The largest and wealthiest Greek colonies were to be found in the Hapsburg Empire where Turkish subjects were granted trading rights by the Treaty of Karlovitz [1699], and in Russia where the Greeks were attracted by the purposeful hospitality of Catherine the Great and by the opportunities for profit following the opening of the Black Sea trade routes. Moreover emigration from Greece was greatly stimulated by the slaughter and destruction resulting from the Morean revolt [1769], so that by 1821 numerous and prosperous Greek colonies dotted the map of Europe.

The oldest of these communities, that of Venice, dating from the Turkish invasions of the fifteenth century, carried on a flourishing commerce with the western provinces of European Turkey. At Trieste the Greek community was engaged in commerce, shipping, and manufacturing, and by 1821 it numbered fifteen hundred souls. The outstanding Greek colony was in Vienna, where such men as Baron Sinas and the Zosimades brothers ac-

* L. S. Stavrianos, *Balkan Federation. A History of the Movement Toward Balkan Unity in Modern Times* (Northampton: Smith College Studies in History, 1944), pp. 28-33.

cumulated tremendous fortunes and played a prominent role in the economy of the Hapsburg Empire. In the Hungarian cities also the Greeks were prominent, especially because of the lack of economic enterprise on the part of the court and the land magnates. The situation was very similar in the Danubian Principalities [of Rumania] and the Greeks were able to gain control of a large percentage of the trade and to retain their position until well into the nineteenth century. In Russia the Greeks carried on much of the profitable Black Sea trade, and in addition, great commercial houses were established by Varvakes in Astrakhan, Balanos in Nizhni-Novgorod, Kaplanes in Moscow and others. By 1821 one could even find a prosperous Greek colony in Calcutta, many Greek merchants engaged in the trade between Russia and China, while in England, the famous firm, Ralli Brothers, had just gotten under way.

The existence of these colonies abroad was of the utmost significance. Apart from the profound political, social and cultural repercussions, it should be noted at this point that these merchant princes usually established commercial relations with their homeland and thus stimulated its economic life. The English traveller, Dr. Holland, who associated mostly with merchants while travelling in Greece in 1812, wrote in this connection that:

> The active spirit of the Greeks, deprived in great measure of political or national objects, has taken a general direction towards commerce. But, fettered in this respect also, by their condition on the continent of Greece, they emigrate in considerable numbers to the adjacent countries, where their activity can have more scope. ... Some branches of the migrating families, however, are always left in Turkey, either from necessity, from the possession of property in the country, or from the convenience to both parties in a commercial point of view. Thus by far the greater part of the exterior trade of Turkey, in the exchange of commodities, is carried on by Greek houses, which have residents at home, and branches in various cities of Europe, mutually aiding each other, extending their concerns much more variously than could be done in Turkey alone.

An even more important factor in Greek economic activity during this period was the encouragement and protection afforded by Russia. By the treaties of Kuchuk-Kainardji (1774), Jassy (1792), and the supplementary conventions of 1779 and 1789, Russia was able to extract from Turkey various concessions which, directly and indirectly, stimulated Greek commerce. The opening of the Black Sea and the Straits to Russian and Austrian commerce revived the ancient trade routes between the Mediterranean and the Black Sea and provided a valuable new market for Greek products. In addition the Greek subjects of the Sultan were given the privilege of flying the Russian flag on their ships, thus safeguarding themselves against the arbitrary exactions and restrictions of the Turkish officials. Finally the newly acquired Russian privilege of consular representation in the Ottoman Empire aided the Greeks because many of them were appointed consuls and still more of them obtained patents which removed them from Turkish jurisdiction and enabled them to trade free of all taxation excepting the three percent paid by all "Franks [Europeans]." As a result of these various privileges an important new market was opened for Greek products which consequently rose in value; hundreds of Greek ships, most of them flying the Russian flag, obtained a virtual monopoly of the Black Sea trade; and Greek merchants and marines everywhere were protected and aided in their activities by Russian consuls and patents.

The final and most spectacular factor in this Greek commercial renaissance was the French Revolution. With the outbreak of the Anglo-French wars the French merchantmen, which hitherto had first place in the carrying trade of the Levant, were swept off the seas by the English navy. The Greeks at once seized the golden opportunity. Wherever profits were to be made, Greek mariners were present, fighting off pirates, running blockades, slipping into harbors on dark nights with their eagerly awaited cargoes which they sold for fabulous profits. By 1813 the Greek merchant marine had increased to the phenomenal figure of 615 ships totalling 153,580 tons, equipped with 5,878 cannon and manned by 37,526 seamen. In addition to the impetus it gave to the development of the merchant marine, the French Revolution also enabled the Greek merchants to drive the French from the dominant position which they had hitherto held in the commerce of the Greek lands. During the revolutionary wars the French merchants throughout the Levant were left stranded as the routes to Marseilles were cut. The number of French trading establishments throughout the Levant was drastically reduced, and as one contemporary observed, this enabled the Greeks ". . . to drive the Frank merchants from the fairs of Greece, to obtain a great part of the internal maritime commerce of Turkey, and at length to share very largely in the exchange of the corn, oil, silk and other products of Greece for the manufactured goods and colonial produce of the European nations." Finally the French Revolution affected the economic development of Greece by increasing the demand and, therefore, the price of wheat, silk, cotton, grain, and other Greek products. One authority has estimated that the general price level of Morean products in 1794 compared to that of 1815 was in the proportion of 1:3.2.

Such were the causes of the revolution which was taking place in Greek economic life during these years. The results of these economic changes were far-reaching and varied. In the first place the intellectual atmosphere was completely changed. Students now began to go to foreign universities to complete their studies. Educational institutions multiplied by leaps and bounds, both within Greece and in the communities abroad. The Greek merchants, especially those of Vienna, stimulated the progress of education in Greece proper by bestowing lavish gifts of books, equipment and money. All this meant not only more education but a new type of education. It was no longer primarily religious. Instead it was profoundly influenced by the current Enlightenment in western Europe. For the first time the works of Locke, Descartes, Leibnitz and others were translated into Greek, and the students who studied abroad returned with a first hand knowledge of the new body of thought. Thus education and learning in the Greek world gradually broke with the traditional clericalism and scholastic pedantry, although only in the face of bitter opposition from the church which frequently denounced the "atheistic" and "immoral" nature of the new theories. In this way the Greeks were prepared intellectually for the French Revolution and were much influenced by it. Merchants, mariners, students, and the numerous French agents, all enthusiastically propagated the revolutionary principles throughout Greece. . . .

As might be expected, the new middle class in Greece, as elsewhere, was the class which was the most receptive to the new principles and which assumed the leadership of the revolutionary movement. ... Moreover it was the wealth of the merchants and ship-owners which made it economically possible for the Greeks to strike for independence and to finance the revolution with practically no outside aid during the first three years. Similarly it was the large, well-armed, and skilfully-manned merchant marine which gave the Greeks command of the sea and made it impossible for the Turks to transport their armies across the Aegean. In short, the Greece of the early nineteenth century was entirely different from that of the early eighteenth century. A decade before the outbreak of the revolution Dr. Holland sensed this process of change which was taking place. "Of late years the Greeks, considering them in their whole extent as a people, have been making progress in population, in commerce, in education, and literature; and above all, as it would seem, in that independent consciousness of power which is necessary as a step to their future liberation."

74 EARLY NINETEENTH CENTURY TURKEY

We noted earlier that the Ottoman Empire, at its height, was impressive in many respects and commanded the admiration and fear of Westerners (see Ottoman Military Strength, Ottoman Administrative System, *and* Religious Toleration in the Ottoman Empire). *By the nineteenth century, however, it had declined to the point where it was commonly termed "the sick man of Europe." The following selections by English travelers who visited the Ottoman Empire about 1800, describe its economic retardation and its decline in learning.**

Economic Retardation

Suppose a stranger to arrive from a long journey, in want of clothes for his body; furniture for his lodgings; books or maps for his instruction and amusement; paper, pens, ink, cutlery, shoes, hats; in short those articles which are found in almost every city of the world; he will find few or none of them in Constantinople; except of a quality so inferior as to render them incapable of answering any purpose for which they were intended. The few commodities exposed for sale are either exports from England, unfit for any other market, or, which is worse, German and Dutch imitations of English manufacture. ... Let a foreigner visit the bazars ... he will see nothing but slippers, clumsy boots of bad leather, coarse muslins, pipes, tobacco, coffee, cooks' shops, drugs, flower-roots, second-hand pistols, poignards, and the worst manufactured wares in the world. ... View the exterior of Constantinople, and it seems the most opulent and flourishing city in Europe; examine its interior, and its miseries and deficiencies are so striking that it must be considered the meanest and poorest metropolis of the world. The ships which crowd its ports have no connection with its welfare: they are for the most part French, Venetian, Ragusan, Slavonian, and Grecian ves-

* E. D. Clarke, *Travels in Various Countries of Europe, Asia and Africa* (Cambridge, England, 1810), I, 689-91; W. Eton, *A Survey of the Turkish Empire,* 4th ed. (London, 1809), pp. 190 ff.

sels, to or from the Mediterranean, exchanging the produce of their own countries for the rich harvests of Poland; the salt, honey, and butter of the Ukraine; the hides, tallow, hemp, furs, and metals of Russia and Siberia; the whole of which exchange is transacted in other ports without any interference on the part of Turkey. Never was there a people in possession of such advantages, who either knew or cared so little for their enjoyment.

Decline in Learning

Few are the inducements which the torpid Turk has to apply himself to science, and those few are annihilated by the fear of exciting distrust in the government. Travelling, that great source of expansion and improvement to the mind, is entirely checked by the arrogant spirit of his religion. . . .

The present sultan is the first Turkish sovereign who has condescended to send ministers to reside at foreign courts. . . .

Of the relative situation of countries they are ridiculously ignorant, and all their accounts of foreign nations are mixed with superstitious fables. . . .

Before the Russian fleet came into the Mediterranean, the ministers of the porte would not believe it possible for them to approach Constantinople but from the Black Sea. The captain pasha (great admiral) affirmed, that their fleet might come by the way of Venice. From this, and a thousand similar and authentic anecdotes, their ignorance of the situation of countries is evident. . . .

It is a certain fact, that a few years ago a learned man of the law having lost an eye, and being informed that there was then at Constantinople an European who made false eyes, not to be distinguished from the natural, he immediately procured one; but when it was placed in the socket, he flew into a violent passion with the eye-maker, abusing him as an impostor, because he could not see with it. The man, fearing he should lose his pay, assured him that in time he would see as well with that eye as with the other. The effendi was appeased, and the artist liberally rewarded, who having soon disposed of the remainder of his eyes, left the Turks in expectation of seeing with them.

WESTERNIZED EDUCATION IN TURKEY *75*

The retarded Turkey described in the above selection was substantially changed during the course of the nineteenth century, the most important factor behind this change being the influence of the West, which manifested itself in virtually every field. The following account by an American historian analyzes the nature and extent of Western influence in the field of education.*

Into Muslim Turkish society came Western educational influences, beginning in a trickle in the later eighteenth century, and growing into a flood

* R. H. Davison, "Westernized Education in Ottoman Turkey," *The Middle East Journal* (Summer, 1961), pp. 290-91, 294-99.

by the early twentieth. All parts of the Ottoman Empire were affected, Egypt and the Balkan areas in some ways more profoundly than the rest. Our concern here, however, is with the Turkish portions of the empire in particular. Turks were affected by Western educational influences which came through six channels. The most important of these is too broad to deal with in brief compass, and will have to be dismissed with only a mention of its significance. This channel is education in its truest sense—the totality of life-long individual experience, gained on the job, in travel, through private reading, and in discussions with others, often in the salons and coteries of learning that congregated about one or another of the leading statesmen, poets or writers of Istanbul. Suffice it to note here that those nineteenth-century Turks who were best educated and who best absorbed Western learning were essentially autodidacts, whatever their formal schooling—Ahmed Vefik Paşa, a voracious reader, who was nicknamed an "upset library" by his contemporaries; Ali Paşa, who learned his French under a tree in the Ottoman embassy garden in Vienna; Münif Paşa, whose private studies far eclipsed his three years at the University of Berlin; Ziya Gökalp, who studied French philosophy and sociology by himself in nine years of Anatolian exile. Each took from the Islamic past and from the West what suited his intellectual needs. Each was a decided individual, yet all realized the advantages of borrowing from Western education. These men and others like them were the first real leaders for the Westernization of education in the empire.

The other five channels through which Western educational influences flowed into the empire were those of formal schools or school systems. The most obvious channel was the large group of schools in the Ottoman Empire which were supported and operated by Westerners. Almost all were mission schools. Although some foreign Catholic schools, in particular French, had existed for many years in the empire, the rapid growth of mission schools came in the nineteenth and earlier twentieth centuries. These were the years of the great flowering of Protestant oversea missions, of Catholic reaction in kind, and of the new imperialism which led governments and peoples of several European powers to support in the Near East schools purveying their own brand of culture. By the eve of World War I an unofficial count put French Catholic schools in the Ottoman Empire at 500, American schools at 675, British at 178. The French schools enrolled 59,414 students, the American schools 34,317, and the British 12,800. There were also German, Italian, Austro-Hungarian and Russian schools in lesser numbers. Most of these schools were elementary, though there were among them some excellent secondary schools and a few collegiate level. It looks as if, in the century before 1914, the Ottoman Empire had received a massive infusion of Western education. What impact had this on the Turks?

To the extent that the impact is measurable, it was slim. This is in part because the figures for schools are deceptive. Many of the foreign schools were located in the Arab portions of the empire, where few Turks lived; and the Arabs who attended such schools were largely Christians, of whatever communion. Many of the schools were in fact run by native Christians, with a bit of foreign support and supervision. But the major reason for the lack of influence on the Turks was that, even in the Turkish-populated areas, very few of them attended such schools. In part this was owing to suspicion of things foreign, but even more the suspicion of things Christian, coupled with the tradition that each millet, or religious community, should provide its own schools for its own communicants. . . .

Far more important in total impact on Turks were the specialized higher schools set up by the Ottoman government itself. These provided what was probably the major educational channel for the introduction of Western ideas into the empire. The need for such schools was felt when defeat in eighteenth century wars brought home the lesson of Ottoman military backwardness in relation to Europe. Army and navy schools for mathematics and engineering were created in the later eighteenth century, with the aid of European renegades and translated textbooks. More such special higher schools were established in the nineteenth century, including a school of military medicine and a military academy. Civil schools of public affairs, of medicine, of languages, of law, and others were added. Though designated "higher" schools, most began at quite an elementary level, or confounded in themselves all grades from primary years to technical college. In the naval academy in the 1830's, for instance, half of the 200 students were just learning to read and write; only 30 were advanced enough to study navigation.

Until past mid-century these schools provided little of the leadership needed for modernizing the Ottoman Empire. Such leadership still came largely from the self-taught. Graduates of the military schools did, however, sometimes become teachers and so exercised influence in the secular lower and middle schools which the government began to institute in the 1860's. And from about 1875 on the higher schools were producing a significant portion of the leadership of the empire. The great advantage of these schools was to teach French, which opened up a new world of ideas, and to bring Western concepts of mathematics, science, geography, history, politics. . . .

Another method by which Westernized schooling was introduced into the Ottoman Empire was the creation of a whole system of elementary and secondary education and of a university, all under government auspices. A proclamation made in the mosques by Sultan Abdülmecid on March 7, 1845, started this development off with the assertion that "the Will of the Padishah is that ignorance, the source of much evil, should vanish from among the people." A commission of able men was appointed to work out educational reform, and shortly a ministry of education was created. Kemal Efendi, inspector-general of schools, was sent to study the systems of England, France and Germany. The very fact of government initiative, of governmental assumption of responsibility for education, was a step toward Westernization. Sultans and officials had long supported educational institutions with their personal gifts, but the government as such had not heretofore planned or financed a school system. Except for the higher special schools, state-supported because they were directly training officials, education had been left to private charity and religious foundations.

While governmental responsibility for education was an accepted fact after the 1840's, the start toward creating the new system was fitful, and characteristic of the reform from the top down that has so often taken place in the Near East. A university was thrice still-born—in 1846, 1870 and 1879—and did not become firmly established until 1900. . . . Some progress in reforming the primary schools was achieved after 1870, but it was painfully slow. Until the end of the Ottoman Empire there remained many examples of the traditional primary school in which "the main duty of the teacher was to see that each child shouted, and that the accent and enunciation were passable." Ömer Seyfeddin, a writer who had his primary education in the 1890's, describes his experience in "Falaka," one of his popular short stories: "We were forty youngsters in the school. . . . We had no division into grades. In chorus we learned the alphabet and texts from the Koran, in chorus we learned the multiplication table by repetition, in chorus we chanted the prayers. So all our lessons went along in an endless learning by rote of things, the meaning of which we never were able to comprehend." But Westernized education had at least added the chant of the multiplication table to the chorus of Quranic passages. . . .

The other two educational channels which brought Western influence to the Turks may be mentioned briefly. One was the schooling of Turks abroad. From 1834 on the government sent, at irregular intervals, groups of young Turks to Western Europe for study. At the start, most of these were graduates of the military schools. Later more civilians went, and more Turks went to Europe as individuals to study. Some returned home quite well educated, and fairly Westernized; others did not. Some on return became leaders in reform efforts; others became cynical or disillusioned when they compared conditions at home to those they had known in Europe. The wife of one of the empire's grand viziers said her husband got in Europe a veneer of knowledge over a mass of ignorance, like "the greater number of those who have been sent to Europe to be educated." Mehmed Said Paşa, educated in Britain at Edinburg and at Woolwich, said in 1877, "I had lived abroad till I fancied I had made myself a man, and when I came back to my country I saw about me merely brutes . . ." Some acquired only expensive Western tastes and vices: in the acid jest of an Ottoman statesman, they were "syphilized, not civilized." But by the early twentieth century those Turks who had studied abroad probably exercised, as a group, considerable influence on Ottoman development. . . .

The final channel of Westernized educational influence was indirect. This influence came from the non-Turkish minorities—principally Greeks, Armenians and Jews—who in somes cases were getting education abroad, but in most cases were getting a more modernized education in the schools maintained within the empire by each of these millets. Such schools grew rapidly in the later nineteenth century, and often had some significant foreign financial and educational support—from the *Alliance Israélite* for Jewish schools, from Greeks abroad and the University of Athens for Greek schools, and a little Armenian support from Russia for Armenian schools. Turks did not attend these schools, but the progress in non-Muslim education was a spur to the Turks. . . . Ziya Bey complained bitterly that the Turks were far behind in promoting literacy: ten-year-old boys in a Greek or Armenian school could read newspapers in their own languages, while it was rare that a Turkish boy of fifteen could do so, or could write a short letter. The conservative Istanbul newspaper *Basiret* in the 1870's demanded as a remedy that the government severely control the Greek and Armenian schools. But the actual result of improved Westernized schools among the non-Muslim millets seems to have been to prod the Turks to greater efforts.

76   Turkish Attempts at Westernization

Following their period of greatness between the fifteenth and seventeenth centuries, the Turks suffered repeated defeats at the hands of the Austrians and the

Russians. A few forward-looking Turkish leaders sensed that these defeats re-
flected their failure to keep up with the West's economic and technological ad-
vances. They realized that survival depended upon ability to transform their
empire along Western lines; this was the objective of the reform movement com-
monly referred to as the Tanzimat, *as it is called in Turkish. One of the landmarks*
of the Tanzimat *was the* Hatti-Humayun *reform edict issued on February 18, 1856,*
the following passages from which * reveal the aspirations and objectives of the
Turkish reforms, and indicate by inference the shortcomings and injustices that
needed correction.

All the Privileges and Spiritual Immunities granted by my ancestors *ab antiquo,* and at subsequent dates, to all Christian communities or other non-Mussulman persuasions established in my Empire under my protection, shall be confirmed and maintained. . . .

Every distinction or designation tending to make any class whatever of the subjects of my Empire inferior to another class, on account of their Religion, Language, or Race, shall be for ever effaced from the Administrative Protocol. The laws shall be put in force against the use of any injurious or offensive term, either among private individuals or on the part of the authorities.

As all forms of Religion are and shall be freely professed in my dominions, no subject of my Empire shall be hindered in the exercise of the Religion that he professes, nor shall be in any way annoyed on this account. No one shall be compelled to change their Religion.

The nomination and choice of all Functionaries and other Employees of my Empire being wholly dependent upon my Sovereign will, all the subjects of my Empire, without distinction of nationality, shall be admissible to public employments, and qualified to fill them according to their capacity and merit, and conformably with rules to be generally applied.

All the subjects of my Empire, without distinction, shall be received into the Civil and Military Schools of the Government, if they otherwise satisfy the conditions as to age and examination which are specified in the Organic Regulations of the said Schools. Moreover, every community is authorized to establish Public Schools of Science, Art, and Industry. Only the method of instruction and the choice of Professors in schools of this class shall be under the control of a Mixed Council of Public Instruction, the members of which shall be named by my Sovereign command.

All Commercial, Correctional, and Criminal Suits between Mussulmans and Christian or other non-Mussulman subjects, or between Christians or other non-Mussulmans of different sects, shall be referred to Mixed Tribunals.

The proceedings of these Tribunals shall be public: the parties shall be confronted, and shall produce their witnesses, whose testimony shall be received, without distinction, upon an oath taken according to the religious law of each sect. . . .

The Laws against Corruption, Extortion, or Malversation shall apply, according to the legal forms, to all the subjects of my Empire, whatever may be their class and the nature of their duties.

Steps shall be taken for the formation of Banks and other similar Institu-

* E. Hertslet, *The Map of Europe by Treaty* (London, 1875-1891), II, 1243-49. 4 vols.

tions, so as to effect a reform in the monetary and financial system, as well as to create Funds to be employed in augmenting the sources of the material wealth of my Empire.

Steps shall also be taken for the formation of Roads and Canals to increase the facilities of communication and increase the sources of the wealth of the country. Everything that can impede commerce or agriculture shall be abolished. To accomplish these objects means shall be sought to profit by the science, the art, and the funds of Europe, and thus gradually to execute them.

Such being my wishes and my commands, you, who are my Grand Vizier, will, according to custom, cause this Imperial Firman to be published in my capital and in all parts of my Empire: and you will watch attentively, and take all the necessary measures that all the orders which it contains be henceforth carried out with the most rigorous punctuality.

10 Dzemaziul, 1272 (18th February, 1856).

77 FAILURE OF TURKISH WESTERNIZATION

The Turkish reform movement was partly successful in that it did result in an appreciable improvement of the position of the Christian subjects in the Otto-man Empire. Yet the empire was doomed to extinction because it had proved basically incapable of adjusting and responding to the challenge of the West. This failure to adapt is made clear in the following passages from a famous descrip-tion of the Ottoman Empire on the eve of its dissolution. The author, a gifted linguist who knew Turkish, Arabic, and several other oriental languages, entered the British diplomatic service in 1887 and filled several posts in the Near East. With this background, he wrote in 1900 his Turkey in Europe, *an authoritative and engagingly written work from which the following selections are taken.**

. . . Yet clearly there must be something Turkish, and that something a force of no mean magnitude, seeing the part that Turks and Turkey still play in the history of the world. The something in question is the Turkish nation itself, as seen best in the provinces of Anatolia, but also in some parts of Turkey in Europe. And here let me say, if I seem to have had little praise for the Turks up to now, that the reason why most people blame them is because they know so little of them. As already explained, the ruling classes of Constantinople are one of the most mixed breeds in the world. The true Turk must be sought in the provinces. Those who have passed even one night in a Turkish village cannot but have been struck by many character-istics of the inhabitants. One is their dignified courtesy and beautiful manners, due no doubt to the consciousness that every Turk, as a member of the ruling race, is an aristocrat. Ragged soldiers and rough shepherds have often an air which makes it impossible for the stranger to feel that they are socially his inferiors. Another characteristic is their hospitality: they will rarely accept

* C. Eliot, *Turkey in Europe,* 2nd ed. (London: E. Arnold, 1908), pp. 94-96, 153-54.

money, and when it is proffered merely reply, "I am not an innkeeper." The Eastern Christian, on the contrary, after receiving his guest with effusion, and dwelling on their common religion, often presents an exorbitant bill. In industry, honesty, and truthfulness the country Turk usually compares favourably with his Christian neighbours, and may be trusted implicitly when he has given his word. Alas! that one must add another salient characteristic—his extraordinary stupidity, or rather the extraordinary limitation of his knowledge and interests. Even this expression is not quite accurate, for the Turk has no interests in our sense of the word. Few things throw a more instructive light on the character of a nation than an examination of the ideas which cannot be expressed in its language. Now the Turkish language, copious as it is, contains no equivalent for "interesting." You can say this is a useful book, or a funny book, or a learned book, or a book which attracts attention, but you cannot precisely translate our expression, "This is an interesting book." Similarly you cannot render in Turkish the precise shade of meaning conveyed by the phrase, "I take an interest in the Eastern question or the Mohammedan religion." The various approximate equivalents imply either a more active and less intellectual participation than that denoted by interest, or else suggest that these serious subjects are something queer and funny which it is amusing to hear about.

This *lacuna* in the language has its counterpart in the brain. The ordinary Turk does not take an interest in anything, and his intelligence seems incapable of grappling with any problem more complex than his immediate daily needs. A natural want of curiosity, and a conviction that their own religion contains all that man knows or needs to know, keep the provincial population in a state of ignorance which seems incredible and fantastic. There are thousands, perhaps millions, of people in the Ottoman Empire who believe that the Sultan is suzerain of Europe, and that all other monarchs pay him tribute. There were people in the time of the last Russo-Turkish war who, when they saw shells falling and bursting, thought they were stars brought down from heaven by enchantment. There are Mollahs and Kadis who seriously discuss how near to a mosque a telegraph wire can properly pass, seeing that it is a means of conveying the voice of Satan from one place to another. Most extraordinary of all, there are people who have never seen gold coins, and refuse to accept them in payment. It is well to remember the existence of such people when one hears allusions to the influence and effects of European public opinion in Turkey. But perhaps the characteristic which has been of most vital importance in forming the destiny of the Ottoman race, and has raised to the status of a great nation a Siberian tribe which might otherwise have remained as obscure as the Tunguses, is the feature which was noticed by the old Chinese chroniclers, and which can be observed to-day—the innate sense of discipline. It is the only cement which keeps together the apparently tottering fabric of the Turkish Empire. It makes the half-fed, half-clothed soldiers ready to endure every privation, and prevents the corruption and incapacity of the officers from producing the anarchy which would be inevitable in any other country. Probably the lot of the Mussulman peasant is in ordinary times worse than that of the Christian, Armenian or other, yet anything like sedition is unknown, and even complaints are rare. Were a holy war proclaimed, not a man but would be prepared to die in defence of the system of extortion which grinds him down.

Perhaps I ought to allude to another characteristic of the Turk—his laziness. In some ways the popular European idea of Oriental indolence is unjust; for the Turk, as a peasant, is the most laborious and industrious of men, and as a soldier the most enterprising. But clearly many of the qualities which we have already reviewed tend to produce inertia. The Turk is too proud to do many things; too stupid to do others. His religion . . . inculcates a fatalism which leads to a conviction that effort is useless. But perhaps what gives more than anything else the impression that the Turk is fundamentally indolent is the fact that all his recreations consist of repose. When the nomad halts, he does not wish to sing, or dance, or distract himself with games after the European fashion, but merely to rest quietly. He has a power of sitting still, of doing nothing, and wanting to do nothing, which seems to us animal rather than human. His idea of bliss—what he calls *keif*—is to recline in the shade, smoking and listening to the soothing murmur of running water. . . .

If we assume that it is desirable to continue the Ottoman Government— an assumption which no one but a Turk need make—we must admit that this implies the superiority of Turks to Christians. It does not mean the equality of Turks and Christians; that is a thing which is talked of but never realised, for the very good reason that it is impossible. As long as force rules, the Turks are superior to the Christians. They are stronger, braver, and more united. But when force does not rule, when progress, commerce, finance, and law give the mixed population of the Empire a chance of redistributing themselves according to their wits, the Turk and the Christian are not equal; the Christian is superior. He acquires the money and land of the Turk, and proves in a law-court that he is right in so doing. One may criticise the Turkish character, but given their idiosyncrasies, one must admit that they derive little profit from such blessings of civilization as are introduced into the country. Foreign syndicates profit most, and after them native Christians, but not the Osmanli, except in so far as he can make them disgorge their gains. . . .

The Turk has a dim perception that even in military matters he cannot understand and practise European methods. If he tries to do so, the control will pass out of his hands into those of people who are cleverer than himself. But though he may think them clever, he does not on that account feel any respect for them. He regards them as conjurors who can perform a variety of tricks, which may be, according to circumstances, useful, amusing, or dangerous; but for all Christendom he has a brutal, unreasoning contempt —the contempt of the sword for everything that can be cut, and to-day the stupid contempt of a blunt sword.

78   Napoleon and the Arab World

The first major intrusion of the West into the Arab world in modern times was Napoleon's invasion of Egypt in 1798. The purpose of the expedition was to undermine Britain's position in the East, a plan that was not carried out because Lord Nelson destroyed Napoleon's fleet near Alexandria and compelled the French invader to return home. However, the fourteen months that Napoleon spent in Egypt left a marked imprint on the country: he destroyed the ruling Mamluk class and thus paved the way for the rise to power of Mehemet Ali a few years later. (See the following introductory passage and reading.) His contingent of *scientists, engineers, and educators introduced new ideas and techniques into the stagnant Arab society. Important in this respect was Napoleon's proclamation upon his landing on July 1, 1798. Distributed widely in Arabic, this proclamation informed Egyptians about such novel concepts and institutions as "republic," "liberty and equality," and the right of anyone to advancement on the basis of ability and performance.**

... In the name of God, the Merciful and Compassionate; there is no God but God;

In the name of the French Republic, based upon the foundations of Liberty and Equality, Bonaparte, the Commander-in-Chief of the French Forces, informs all the population of Egypt:

For a long time, those in power in Egypt have insulted the French Nation and unfairly treated her merchants by various deceitful and aggressive tactics. Now, the hour of their punishment has arrived.

For many decades, these Mamluks, who were brought in from the Caucasus and Georgia, have been corrupting the best region of the whole world. But God, the Omnipotent, the Master of the Universe, has now made the destruction of their state imperative.

People of Egypt, some may say to you that I did not come except to obliterate your religion. That is an outright lie; do not believe it. Tell those fabricators that I came only to rescue your rights from the oppressors. And that I worship Almighty God, and respect his Prophet Muhammad and the glorious *Qur'an* more than the Mamluks do. Tell them also that all people are equal before God.

The only grounds for distinctions among them are reason, virtue and knowledge. [But] what virtue, reason and knowledge distinguish the Mamluks from others which would give them exclusive rights over everything that makes life sweet? Wherever there is fertile land, it belongs to the Mamluks; so also do they exclusively possess the most beautiful maids, horses and houses.

If the Egyptian land has been bestowed on them, let them produce the Title which God wrote for them. But God, the Master of the Universe, is compassionate and just with his people. With God's help, from now on, no Egyptian will be barred from entering the highest positions [of the State] and from acquiring the most elevated status. The intelligent, virtuous and learned men will take charge of affairs and thus the plight of the entire nation will improve.

Formerly, there were great cities, wide canals, and thriving commerce in Egypt, all of which have disappeared as a result of the Mamluks' greed and oppression.

Judges, Shaykhs, Imams, officers and notables of the country, inform your people that the French are also faithful Muslims. As proof of this, they attacked Great Rome, where they destroyed the Papal Throne, which was always urging the Christians to fight the Muslims. Then they went to Malta from which they expelled the Knights who allege that Almighty God asked them to fight the Muslims. In addition, the French at every time have been the most faithful friend of the Ottoman Sultan and the enemy of his enemies,

* Ilbrahim A. Abu-Lughod, *Arab Rediscovery of Europe 1800-1870* (Princeton: Princeton Univ., 1963), pp. 13-15.

may God preserve his reign, and destroy the Mamluks who refused to obey him and heed his orders. They [Mamluks] only obeyed him originally to advance their personal greed.

Blessings and happiness to the Egyptian people who agree with us promptly, thus improving their own condition and elevating their status. Happiness also to those who remain at home, taking no side in the fighting; they will hasten to our side when they know us better.

But woe to those who join the Mamluks and aid them in the war against us; they will find no way to escape and no trace of them will be left.

79 MEHEMET ALI ATTEMPTS TO INDUSTRIALIZE EGYPT

Mehemet Ali, an adventurer of Albanian origin, took advantage of the power vacuum created by Napoleon's expedition to seize power in Egypt and become the de facto ruler of the country, though he continued to recognize the nominal suzerainty of the Sultan in Constantinople. Unlike other potentates in the Near East, Mehemet Ali recognized the significance of Europe's technological achievements and made an extraordinary effort to industrialize his country. The following analysis of his policies and his final failure clearly reveals the obstacles that prevented the Near East and other non-Western regions from keeping pace with Europe in economic development.*

Conditions of industrial production in the Middle East at the turn of the eighteenth and during the first third of the nineteenth century were determined by

1. The predominantly agrarian character of the population in general.
2. The widespread custom amongst the agricultural and, to a certain extent, the urban population also, of providing itself with consumer goods of its own.
3. The gradual shrinking of local handicrafts in line with the general economic decline of the Middle East as a result of
   (a) the diversion of traffic routes (new sea route to India, growing importance of the Western Hemisphere).
   (b) the increasing competition from European production.
4. The stagnation and alienation of production technique and loss of initiative in trade and handicrafts.
5. The decay of vocational organisations (guilds and the like).

It is only when this background is clearly visualised that the approach and achievement of Mohammed Ali can be duly appreciated. . . .

In view of the general stagnation and the improbability that the Egyptians would of their own accord make profitable use of the ideas infiltrating from Europe, the conviction grew in Mohammed Ali that active intervention on the part of Government in the sphere of industry and education was im-

---

* A. Bonné, *State and Economics in the Middle East* (New York: Humanities Press, 1948; London: Routledge, 1955), pp. 238-39, 241-46.

perative. The mentality of the Oriental at that time did not hold out much hope that he would be able to overcome all the difficulties confronting the revival of industrial initiative, let alone the introduction of European production methods on his own account. This could be achieved only by some dominant body invested with extensive powers. Thus, the State itself, i.e. its ruler, embarked in grand style on an ambitious programme of economic and political activities and took on a number of national-economic functions direct.

As the principal instrument in this policy Mohammed Ali turned to the establishment of trade monopolies and State industries. The problem of securing the necessary experts was solved by engaging foreigners. Thus, he did not hesitate, for instance, to summon hundreds of foreign workers to Cairo and to take into his service at high salaries a vast number of European experts and officers as managers of factories, schools and institutes. Their gradual replacement by native personnel was envisaged, and several hundred young Egyptians were despatched to European schools and institutions. . . .

In keeping with Mohammed Ali's general policy aimed at making the Egyptian State as far as possible independent of external factors, even as regards the supply of important war materials, was his interest in the development of iron and metal works, quite unusual at that time. In 1820, in the Bulaq quarter of Cairo, a foundry was erected after the plans of an Englishman where practically every class of foundry goods could be executed. The works contained eight furnaces and could turn out 50 cwt. of castings per day, including machinery, looms, spinning machines, and even repairs to steam engines and essential parts of the arsenal. . . .

In order to convey some idea of the extent of Mohammed Ali's work, it will suffice to mention that the number of workers engaged in Egyptian factories during the years 1830-1840 amounted to over 30,000, the workers in the arsenals to 5,000, and that the capital invested in machinery and plant is estimated at no less than £12 million. In 1836, 95 per cent. of total exports came out of the Government's stores, whilst 40 per cent. of the total imports came into the country on the Government's account. . . .

In appraising this first large-scale plan for the inauguration of the industrial revolution in the Orient, our interest centres not merely in the fact that the originator was sorely disappointed in his expectations, but at least to an equal extent in the reasons for this lack of success. . . .

First, there is the problem of the bureaucratic management of such enterprises by officials of the State, and, allied thereto, comes the general question how to procure the entrepreneur personalities, to say nothing of the lower personnel who must possess the necessary qualifications for the modern production process. Egypt had neither the factory managers nor the skilled workers. Both categories were at that time lacking. The European experts often came too late to save a badly-run undertaking, or were inadequate in numbers to meet the demands on them. . . .

. . . Whatever these deficiencies were, they could have been overcome in the course of time, had not a political factor interfered in a decisive fashion with the industrial plans. This was the inevitable clash between foreign and local interests; for Mohammed Ali, who had already appropriated the whole of the agricultural land and its returns, was about to make himself the owner of non-agricultural production, and thus the sole regulator of the country's total circulation of goods. In this, however, he was encroaching on the sphere of interests of foreign powers who were interested in the sale of their goods and the purchase of certain raw materials from Egypt. Egypt represented an important market for the products of the new English and continental factories, and this position was seriously threatened by the Pasha's bold experiments. . . .

The result of this [British] intervention was the treaty of 1838, based on the Capitulations which guaranteed the foreign subject freedom of industry and shipping. It led to the abolition of most of the monopolies: in Turkey in 1839, in Egypt in 1840. [This meant the end of Egyptian industry since it was all a government "monopoly."] . . .

British intervention broke the Pasha's spirit of initiative in the industrial field once and for all. Even as early as 1840, two years before the final ratification of the treaty, a number of factories which could not show a profit were closed. When the treaty came into force, nearly all the other factories followed suit. A few years later the ruins of factories and rusted machinery were the sole indication of what was left of the first industrial revolution in Egypt.

The reasons for the collapse of the Pasha's programme of industrial-isations are to be found in various fields. They may be summed up as follows:

1. Shortcomings in the internal management, faulty economic calculation in the majority of undertakings, inadequate qualifications on the part of the personnel; lack of engineers and masters, lack of technical experience as regards the industrial production process in Egypt.
2. Difficulties of marketing and commercial policy; competition of cheap European goods. Political intervention on the part of export countries in favour of competition goods.
3. Sociological shortcomings: Absence of entrepreneur qualities in the Egyptians of that period. Arbitrary treatment of private trade interests by the State (inadequate protection of rights and property), clash between the liberal tendencies in industrial practice in Europe and the State-capitalistic planned economy of Mohammed Ali.

As long as these causes and deficiencies were effective, a development such as that witnessed in Europe was not possible. Mohammed Ali's attempt in itself proves that the more important prerequisites for a successful industrial-isation must be present simultaneously in order to achieve the desired result. As matters stood the most essential conditions were lacking. The only chance of success, in these circumstances, lay in an attempt by the head of the State himself to solve problems of industrialisation by a planning policy pursued along almost modern lines, and for this purpose to employ all material and personal means at his disposal.

80 WESTERN ECONOMIC IMPERIALISM IN EGYPT

Mehemet Ali's failure to industrialize Egypt was soon followed by that country's economic subjection to Europe, an occurrence brought about by the extravagance of Mehemet Ali's successors, who were quickly and unscrupulously exploited by European financiers. The following selection describes this process during the rule of Ismail (1863–1879). Ismail had ambitions and laudable plans for the moderni-

zation of his country, probably more so than the following account suggests. But he was ignorant of the ways of modern finance, so that he was quickly trapped in a mesh of ruinous debts contracted at usurious rates.*

251

Ismaīl's character, before he became Viceroy, had been that of a wealthy landed proprietor managing his large estates in Upper Egypt according to the most enlightened modern methods. He was praised by nearly all European travellers for the machinery he had introduced and the expenditure he had turned to profit, and it is certain that he possessed a more than usual share of that natural shrewdness and commercial aptitude which distinguishes the family of Mohammed Ali. His succession to the Viceroyalty had been more or less a surprise to him, for until within a few months of Saīd's death he had not been the immediate heir, and his prospects had been only those of an opulent private person. It was perhaps this unexpected stroke of fortune that from the beginning of his reign led him to extravagance. By nature a speculator and inordinately greedy of wealth, he seems to have looked upon his inheritance and the absolute power now suddenly placed in his hands, not as a public trust, but as the means above all things else of aggrandizing his private fortune. At the same time he was as inordinately vain and fond of pleasure, and his head was turned by his high position and the opportunity it gave him of figuring in the world as one of its most splendid princes. He was surrounded at once by flatterers of all kinds, native and European, who promised on the one hand to make him the richest of financiers, and on the other the greatest of Oriental sovereigns. In listening to these his own cleverness and commercial skill betrayed him, and made him only their more ready dupe. Ismaīl, before his accession, had been an astute money-maker according to the ways in which money was then made in Egypt, and he had had, too, a European education of the kind Orientals acquire on the Paris boulevards, superficial as regards all serious matters, but sufficient to convince him of his capacity to deal with the rogues of the Bourse with the weapons of their own roguery. In both directions he was led astray.

His first act of self-aggrandizement was simple and successful. The revenue, which rested chiefly on the land tax, was low, and he raised it by progressive enhancements from the 40 piastres where he found it, to 160, where it has ever since stood. The country under his hand was rich and at first could afford the extra burden. Men gave of their superfluity rather than of their necessity, and for some years did so without complaint. This enhancement, however, of the revenue was only part of his rapacious programme. His native flatterers reminded him that in the days of his grandfather the whole land had been regarded as the Viceroy's personal property, and that, moreover, Mohammed Ali had claimed and exercised for some years a monopoly of its foreign trade. Ismaīl schemed to revive these rights in his own person, and though he did not dare, in the face of European opinion, to commit any great acts of open confiscation in regard to the land, he gained to a large extent his ends by other means, and so rapidly that in a few years he managed to get into his own hands a fifth of the whole area of the cultivable land of Egypt. His method was by various means of intimidation and administrative pressure to make the possession of such lands as he desired to acquire a

* W. S. Blunt, *Secret History of the English Occupation of Egypt* (London: G. Allen, 1907), pp. 15-19.

burden to their owners, and to render their lives so vexatious that they should be constrained to sell at prices little more than nominal. In this way he had, as I have said, possessed himself of an enormous property in land, and he doubtless thought that this was to prove to him a correspondingly enormous source of personal income. But his very covetousness in the matter proved his ruin. It was found in practice that while under his personal management as a comparatively small owner his estates had been well worked, and had brought him wealth, his new gigantic ownership laid him open to losses in a hundred ways. In vain he laid out enormous sums on machinery. In vain he laid whole villages and districts under contribution to furnish him forced labour. In vain he started factories on his estates and employed managers from Europe at the highest salaries. He was robbed everywhere by his agents, and was unable to gather from his lands even a fraction of the revenue they had brought in taxation when not his own. This was the beginning of his financial difficulties, coinciding as it did with the sudden fall in agricultural prices, and especially of cotton, which soon after set in, and it was the beginning, too, of the ruin of the peasantry, whom, to supply his deficiency, he now loaded with irregular taxation of all kinds. . . .

It was not long, however, before Ismaïl fell into much more dangerous hands, and embarked in much more ruinous adventures than these early ones. To say nothing of the enormous sums which he poured out like water on his own private pleasures, of his follies of palace building, his follies with European women, and his follies of royal entertainment, there were schemes of ambition vast enough to drain the purse of any treasury. It is not known precisely how many millions he expended at Constantinople in procuring himself the Khedivial title, and in getting the order of the viceregal succession altered in favour of his son. But it must have been very many, while still more went in hare-brained schemes of speculation and in liabilities contracted towards European syndicates. Lastly, there was the conquest of the Upper Nile, and the attempted conquest of the kingdom of Abyssinia. To provide for all these immense expenditures loans had to be raised, at first on a small scale with local bankers and Greeks of Alexandria, and presently in more reckless fashion on the European Stock Exchange. Here his worst counsellor and evil genius had been Nubar Pasha, the Armenian financier, who, by a strange inversion of ideas, has come to be regarded by a certain class of Egyptian opinion ignorant of history as an "Egyptian patriot." Nubar was, however, in fact, the one man who, more than any other after Ismaïl himself, was responsible for Egypt's financial ruin. Commissioned by his master to find him money at any cost to meet his extravagant wants, he raised loan after loan for him in Europe on terms which realized for him hardly more than 10 per cent. of the capital sums he inscribed himself for as a debtor, while he, Nubar, pocketed as commission several millions sterling. Of the ninety-six millions nominally raised in this way, it has been calculated that only some fifty-four reached Ismaïl's hands.

81   REFORM AND REACTION IN PERSIA

To the east of the Arab world were the Persians, who also felt the impact of an aggressive and expanding West. Their country was not actually occupied, as *were the Arab provinces of North Africa, but the usual indirect, yet effective, control exerted by means of loans, concessions, advisers, and military missions was present. This foreign interference provoked a reform movement directed against the intruding powers and the corrupt and decrepit native Kajar dynasty. What chance the reformers might have had ended when Britain and Russia concluded their 1907 entente, which provided among other things, that Persia be divided into Russian and British spheres of influence, separated by a neutral buffer zone. The following selection is by an American financial expert, W. Morgan Shuster, who spent half a year in Persia in 1911 before being forced to leave by a Russian ultimatum. Shuster contrasts the hopeless obsolescence of the old regime in Persia with the forward-looking aspirations of the elected assembly, or* majlis (medjlis).*

253

... Imagine, if you will, a fast decaying government amid whose tottering ruins a heterogeneous collection of Belgian customs officers, Italian gendarmes, German artillery sergeants, French servants, doctors, professors and councilors of state, Austrian military instructors, English bank clerks, Turkish and Armenian courtiers, and last, but not least, a goodly sprinkling of Russian Cossack officers, tutors and drill instructors all go through their daily task of giving the Imperial Persian Government a strong shove toward bankruptcy, with a sly side push in the direction of their own particular political or personal interests. In this pleasant diversion the gentlemen and even the ladies of the foreign legations were somewhat peacefully engaged, when several unfortunate Americans landed on Persian soil with the truly extraordinary idea that they were to be employed under the orders of the Persian Government. Later, lest the gaiety of the scene should diminish, some ten or more Swedish officers were added to the list of those whom the *raiyat* [peasantry] of the provinces paid their tithe to maintain. ...

I might say that the Persian finances were tangled—very tangled—had there been any to tangle. There were no Persian finances in any ordinary sense of the word. The so-called Ministry of Finance, presided over by a succession of frequently changing Persian gentlemen whose sole claims to financial genius lay in their having run through their own money and thus become in need of pecuniary recuperation, was in reality an unorganized collection of under-officials who had charge of various bureaus or offices through which the internal taxes, called, generically, *maliat,* were supposed to be collected for the benefit of the Persian Government. There were no such things as civil service, or examinations or tests for fitness or integrity. The places were doled out by the different Ministers of Finance to those having sufficient family or political influence to obtain them. No official could be sure of retaining his post even over night ... There had never been any attempt made at centralizing the revenues in order that the Government might know just what it should receive from its various taxes and what it did not receive; nor was there any attempt to control the expenditure of such funds as did, in some mysterious manner, percolate into the coffers of the so-called treasury at Teheran. One of the first inquiries that I made was for the budget—the national budget—from which I hoped to gain some idea of the total gross

* W. Morgan Shuster, *The Strangling of Persia* (New York: Appleton, 1920), pp. 37-42, 239-46.

revenues or receipts of the Government from all sources and of the amounts which were supposed to be allotted to the different ministries and departments for their maintenance and upkeep. I soon learned that no budget existed. . . . The gentry of the Persian War Department claimed the time-honored privilege of disposing of about one-half of the total nominal revenues in exchange for conducting the commissariat, arsenals, general staff, medical corps, infantry, cavalry, and artillery divisions of the Persian regular army— a mythical corps worthy to take rank with the gnomes who disturbed the slumbers of Rip Van Winkle or with that most elusive of human conceptions, the Golden Fleece. During the eight months which I spent in Teheran . . . I never encountered the Persian regular army in appreciable quantities except upon the requisitions for their pay presented at the end of each month or in the form of bills for large orders of uniforms and other equipment which it was the privilege of the War Office to submit to the Treasurer-general for liquidation. . . .

The Cabinet ministers and other high executive officials with whom I came in contact during my stay in Persia, with few exceptions, did not impress me favorably. Many of them were men of good education and great intelligence, but they invariably lacked the ability to regard their power and office purely as a means of serving their country. I am aware that, tested by this standard, many public officials in other countries would leave something to be desired, but the defects of selfishness, of purely personal ambition, of seeking pecuniary profit at the expense of the Government, were more than usually prevalent among the so-called governing classes in Persia. These men were invariably chosen from the aristocracy—and a very degenerate aristocracy—and they were either unwilling or unable to oppose seriously corruption in the Government where it might even faintly affect themselves or their friends.

The deputies of the Persian Medjlis were a very different type of men. Among them were some few of the grandee element, of the wealthy land-owners and nobles. But as a rule they were nearer to the people; many had studied law or medicine; some had been clerks and inferior public officials. A number of the deputies were priests or *mullahs,* and, whatever their walk in life, they seemed to feel that the fact of their being chosen by a popular vote, instead of merely being appointed through some form of influence, made them the guardians of the rights of their countrymen. Most of these men sincerely believed that they embodied the dignity and ideals of the Persian people in their struggle to establish a representative form of government. . . .

The Medjlis in the main represented the new and just ideals and aspirations of the Persian people. Its members were men of more than average education; some displayed remarkable talent, character and courage. Nearly all believed that the salvation of their country depended upon their efforts to place the Constitutional Government upon a firm and lasting basis, and that by such means alone would they be able to restore peace, order and prosperity, and check both the sale of their country to foreigners and the future political encroachments of Russia and England. . . .

While the Medjlis was not ideally representative in the political sense, that is, only a small proportion of the population had participated in the election of its members, it more truly represented the best aspirations of the Persians than any other body that had ever existed in that country. It was as representative as it could be under the difficult circumstances which surrounded the institution of the Constitutional Government. It was loyally supported by the great mass of the Persians and that alone was sufficient justification for its existence. The Russian and British Governments, however, were constantly instructing their Ministers at Teheran to obtain this concession or to block that one, failing utterly to recognize that the days had passed in which the affairs, lives and interests of twelve millions of people were entirely in the hands of an easily intimidated and willingly bribed despot. With a popularly elected parliament in control of railroad, mining and other concessions, the old-time facility for getting certain things done for the time had disappeared. In other words, the Medjlis was inconvenient to the secret purposes, whatever they may have been, of the two powers which were so constantly proclaiming that their "interests" in Persia were in danger.

As to the Persian people themselves, it is difficult to generalize. The great mass of the population is composed of peasants and tribesmen, all densely ignorant. On the other hand, many thousands have been educated abroad, or have traveled after completing their education at home. The Persians are as a rule kind and hospitable. They have an undue respect for foreigners. French, and some English, is spoken among the wealthier classes. They, or at least certain elements among them which had had the support of the masses, proved their capacity to assimilate western civilization and ideas. They changed despotism into democracy in the face of untold obstacles. Opportunities were equalized to such a degree that any man of ability could occupy the highest official posts. As a race they showed during the past five years an unparalleled eagerness for education. Hundreds of schools were established during the Constitutional régime. A remarkable free press sprang up over night, and fearless writers came forward to denounce injustice and tyranny whether from within their country or without. The Persians were anxious to adopt wholesale the political, ethical and business codes of the most modern and progressive nations. They burned with that same spirit of Asiatic unrest which pervades India, which produced the "Young Turk" movement, and which has more recently manifested itself in the establishment of the Chinese Republic. The East has awakened.

Chapter Fifteen

Impact of dominance: India

82 INDIA'S TRADITIONAL SOCIETY

The basic feature of the pre-British traditional Indian society was the self-contained and self-perpetuating village, virtually a little world unto itself. Customary patterns and conventions of immemorial antiquity governed the social and economic relations of such a community. The following account, by an American authority on India, analyzes the nature and functioning of the typical village.*

When the Europeans arrived in India, they found an ancient civilization ruled by recent invaders from the North—the Moghuls. The Moghul Empire was an agrarian-based, semi-feudal society. Its Government was staffed by a bureaucracy, its revenues were primarily from the land, and its form of feudalism was that of rights to land revenues granted to nobles of the military or administrative hierarchy in return for their services in maintaining the Empire.

Underneath the Moghul state-system lay the myriad of ancient Indian villages. India lived in its villages, as it had from time immemorial, and the economic, political, social and religious life of the vast majority of the Indian people revolved around the individual village.

While generalizations are unsafe, one can say that most of the villages of India were organized on a self-sufficient and localistic

* R. I. Crane, "India: A Study of the Impact of Western Civilization," *Social Education,* XV (December, 1951), 365-66.

basis. Usually the village land was held in common by members of the village, being divided among the cultivating households at intervals by the traditional village *panchayat*—Council of Elders. Generally, the village paid its land tax to the Government in kind, as a percentage of its total crop. This percentage of the annual harvest passed into the hands of the Moghul administrators and moved up the line to support the various levels of the Moghul State. The basic contact of the village with the outside world was in the payment of a portion of its crop to the officials and in the irregular demands made on it for forced labor.

Within the tiny, self-sufficient village, economic life was generally of a non-commercial character. The residents of the village farmed their share of the village land, raised families, and died with almost no reference to commercial affairs or to matters outside the village.

In each village there were, in addition to the cultivating households, several families of secondary producers. These included the blacksmith, silversmith, carpenter, leather worker, scavenger, priest and astrologer. They served the rest of the village community on something akin to a barter basis. The carpenter or blacksmith produced for a known demand and was paid for his services by receiving grain from the cultivating households for whom he had performed such services, or by receiving a small portion of the village land for his own cultivation.

This intimate society, based on a face-to-face economy, was closely bound together by ancient tradition and by religious practice. The caste system usually indicated the hereditary occupation of each villager and fixed the relations between castes. The economic relations of exchange of goods and services were defined by the caste system and, at least in parts of India, by the closely-allied *jajmani* system.

The *jajmani* system provided that each caste family in the village had a fixed relationship in terms of duties, services and responsibilities with the other families of the village. Thus the shoemaker owed so many pairs of shoes a year to the other members of the village in terms of their status in the caste hierarchy and was paid or otherwise rewarded for the shoes as prescribed by the traditional regulations of the *jajmani* system. In this way the life of each of the villagers was intimately bound up with the life of the others.

In addition, the villager was supported and, in turn, controlled, by his caste council which supervised the social and religious life of the members of the caste residing in the village. The caste council also played what may be described as a legal role by representing its members in altercations with members of a different caste. The villager was also supported and controlled by the *joint-family* system. In the joint-family system, the family remains a social and economic unit, dwelling together under the paternalistic rule of the father or eldest male. As the sons marry they bring their wives home to the joint-family and continue as members of it, subject to its rulings. In economic affairs the joint-family takes precedence over its individual members and each is responsible for the welfare of the whole family while the family, in turn, shares what it has among all of its members.

The primary associations of joint-family, caste council, and village council thus provided control and direction over the activities of the villagers as well as support and integration for the individual. This close integration made for intellectual and emotional stability and for economic security. True enough, the economic security was generally at a very low level of subsistence. The village seldom produced much of a surplus and officialdom sometimes siphoned off most of the surplus to support the State. But, within the limits of a subsistence economy, each member of the village had an unquestioned right to some share in the total net produce of the family and of its village. Nor was this right conditioned in any significant way by non-local economic factors.

These hundreds of thousands of localistic, self-sufficient and non-commercial villages—virtually static as they were—comprised the base and bulk of Indian society. Kings might come and go, dynastic wars might rage and local bureaucrats might revolt, but the self-sufficient village held tenaciously to its piece of land, to its binding social interrelationships and to its traditional mores, beliefs and practices.

83 BRITISH IMPACT: ECONOMIC AND SOCIAL

The British Empire in India, begun after 1750, lasted almost two hundred years, thus enduring as long as the Mogul Empire which preceded it. But British rule had an incomparably greater impact on traditional Indian society than did the Mogul. Since the British originally arrived in India with economic objectives in mind, their control of that country had far-reaching repercussions on its economic and social structure. These are analyzed in the following selections, the first by Professor R. I. Crane, author of the preceding reading, and the second by E. Baines, an early nineteenth century English writer, who shows how India's initial superiority over England in textiles was gradually overcome and reversed with the assistance of discriminatory imposts.*

R. I. Crane

Into this rather static scene came the energetic entrepreneurs of Western commercial and trading organizations. Concerned, at first, with trade and profits, these roving merchants were anxious to obtain a monopoly of the rich trade with the Orient.

The representatives of the Great Trading Companies chartered by Britain, Holland, or France, confirmed believers in mercantilist theory, were anxious to exclude their rivals from the Orient trade and were similarly anxious to eliminate competition from the indigenous merchants of India or Southeast Asia. The key to their commercial thinking was monopoly, and the key to monopoly was power. The ultimate result was the consolidation of European political rule over non-European peoples of India and the East.

In India, between 1600 and 1763, the English East India Company contested with rivals from Portugal, Holland, and France, and finally emerged triumphant. In the process the Company became a political power in Bengal

---

* *Ibid.*, pp. 367-69; E. Baines, *History of the Cotton Manufactures in Great Britain* (London, 1835), pp. 56, 76-79, 81-82.

and, subsequently, in other parts of India. In becoming a political power, the Company added to its normal commercial activities the right to collect taxes in those areas given over to it by the Moghul Emperor or by his deputies. With the power to collect taxes went other forms of political control: judicial authority, the right to regulate trade, and so forth. Between 1763 and 1858 the Company extended its military and political power over ever larger areas of India.

The primary interest of the Company was in profitable trade and in the revenues to be gained from collecting the land tax. As a result it rapidly became involved in activities that struck at the core of the self-sufficient Indian village. The first great change was the introduction of a new land-tenure system based on English concepts of private ownership that differed from general Indian practice. Whereas formerly the tax-collectors, or *zamindars,* had been State officials charged with securing the State's portion of the crop from a number of villages assigned to them, the Permanent Settlement, established in 1793 by Lord Cornwallis, transformed the tax-collectors into English-style landlords, while most of the villagers, who had formerly held the land in common, were reduced to the status of tenants-at-will.

Accompanying this unprecedented change was the spread and dominance of other English legal concepts: individual ownership, contract law, mortgage, distraint, and forced sale. These legal concepts were mostly unknown or even repugnant to the traditional law of Indian society. Enforced as they were, in good part, by English judges in the English or Latin tongue, they disturbed the traditional economic and social polity of the Indian villager and caused him to suffer under a distinct disadvantage. Taken together, these new elements, introduced from outside, were the beginning of a fundamental "revolution" in Indian society. This revolution shook it at its very base—the village.

Moreover, the English revenue system was applied whereby each plot of land was assessed for value and paid a land-tax in cash to the Government.

In the *zamindari* areas the landlord paid the cash assessment and secured rent in cash or kind from his tenants. In other parts of India the arrangement was made by the Company directly with each separate peasant proprietor and in this instance the peasant proprietor had to pay the assessment in cash. The creation of a fixed cash land-tax payment struck directly at the old, localistic, non-commercial life of the village. The village land now belonged to a landlord or, in parts of India, to individual proprietors. Land could now be bought, sold, mortgaged, and lost. Communal rights in land had largely been wiped out and the land tax had, in most instances, to be paid in cash rather than in kind.

Even worse, the land tax was a fixed sum (though in many parts of India it could be revised periodically by English magistrates) and had to be paid on a certain day or the property would be put up for tax sale. In previous times the land-tax had been a percentage of the crop and if the crop failed the tax was not paid. Under the new system, until late nineteenth century reforms, the rigidity of the new cash tax was firmly maintained. The result, as the decades passed, was an increased loss of land.

Finally, all of this came to be administered by an alien bureaucracy, speaking an alien tongue and, generally, but poorly acquainted with local exigencies or ancient customs. These men were hardly conscious of the profound change they were working in the heart of Indian society and could not foresee its long-range, deleterious results. The process, however, continued.

Since the village members now had to pay taxes in cash they had to operate in terms of the cash-nexus. They had to sell their crop or their services to raise money with which to pay the tax. And, as time passed, English machine-made goods entered the Indian market, ousting the more costly handicraft products of the old society. When this process had extended its range throughout the countryside, the peasant had to find cash in order to purchase the simple necessities of life. Moreover, the establishment of a Government Salt Tax put an added monetary burden on the villager. The end result was, of course, that the Indian peasant was tied ever more firmly into a cash economy and into the world market with all of its fluctuations and uncertainties.

With this development much of the old security and stability passed away. The peasant no longer had a firm claim on a share of the village land; the *jajmani* system tended to become commercialized; the secondary producer lost his craft and turned to the land for a living; the binding integration of the old village society was increasingly disrupted by the new commercial and legal systems erected by the foreign rulers. The peasant now stood as a luckless tenant working for a grasping landlord, or tried to eke out an existence in an unfamiliar economic and legal world as a peasant proprietor selling in the world market and subject to world economic conditions of which he had little understanding.

When the village economy was thus transformed, the old social institutions tended to wither away, or at least to lose much of their *raison d'être*. As they moved toward loss of social utility, these institutions tended to lose their ability to support the individual and to define his value system for him. This involved a serious psychological disruption of which Landon says: "It is inevitable that the break-up of the traditional isolated social group, the decay of the usual ethical forms, should exert an influence on the psyche of the people . . . it tends to cause a feeling of distress, a notion of unfair suppression. . . ."

True, the joint-family system remained in force, but with its base in communal land eliminated, its power to give economic support to its members diminished and, as a matter of fact, under the new economic conditions the joint-family became in certain ways an economic hindrance to its members in a new setting of individual enterprise. True, the caste system remained as a religious and ritual institution but its support of the member tended to become minimal as the new world outside the village cast its shadow over his daily life.

The process, begun with a new land law and a new revenue system, was hastened by developments during the nineteenth century. These included the effective opening of India as a market for British goods, the development of a railway and road network which tied the village more firmly into the world market, and the rise of urban centers in which a way of life radically different from that rural India soon developed.

The old stability, the old security, the old supports were losing their vitality. Forced into commercial agriculture, deprived of communal supports, the peasant strove to keep his head above water. Statistics on land ownership, rural debt, expropriation, and famine, however, indicate that he fought a losing battle. A significant portion became landless agricultural laborers while an even larger number were reduced to the rank of sharecropper.

Another instance of European impact which has had deleterious results, would seem to be the rise of a parasitic entrepreneurial class in India. The character of the new land system, described above, created landlords and landlordism and caused Indians with wealth or with hopes of wealth to flock to the land, buying it up or securing it on mortgage-sale and making a handsome living by rack-renting their tenants.

As the East India Company strengthened its own monopoly on the India trade, a large number of the indigenous merchants found it impossible to compete. Abandoning an unprofitable business career they turned to land ownership and to living off rents. For a variety of reasons the easiest way to make an excellent return on investment was to push the level of rents up and live as absentee landlords whose position was reinforced and guaranteed by British law.

Moreover, as the full impact of commercialism broke upon the peasantry, the latter tended to sink ever deeper in debt. Under these circumstances it was apparent that rural money-lending would prove a profitable form of enterprise. Thus there arose a number of local money-lenders, almost unknown to India in pre-British days who advanced credit to the agriculturists at ruinous rates of interest. The landlord-money-lender, as time passed, tended to become the local grain and produce merchant, buying from the peasantry, transporting the crop to the seaports, and there selling to the European businessman who shipped goods to the West. In each case the Indian entrepreneur was to be found occupying the role of non-productive middleman, making a profit by buying and selling or by lending, mortgaging and rack-renting. These activities consisted in making money out of money and not in adding to the total net productive capacity.

Since it was in these essentially non-productive fields of activity that the Indian well-to-do found greatest scope for their energy, it was probably inevitable that an attitude toward capital would develop which has proven inimical to modern India. Today India needs large amounts of investment capital in order to modernize and expand her productive plant, but Indian businessmen, by and large, prefer to make their profits by speculation, rack-renting, money-lending and intermediary trade.

E. Baines

The Indians have in all ages maintained an unapproached and almost incredible perfection in their fabrics of cotton. Some of their muslins might be thought the work of fairies, or of insects, rather than of men; but these are produced in small quantities, and have seldom been exported. In the same province from which the ancient Greeks obtained the fines muslins then known, namely, the province of Bengal, these astonishing fabrics are manufactured to the present day.

We learn from two Arabian travellers of the ninth century, that "in this country (India) they make garments of such extraordinary perfection, that no where else are the like to be seen. These garments are for the most part round, and wove to that degree of fineness that they may be drawn through a ring of moderate size." Marco Polo, in the thirteenth century, mentions the coast of Coromandel, and especially Masulipatam, as producing "the finest and most beautiful cottons that are to be found in any part of the world";

and this is still the case as to the flowered and glazed cottons, called chintzes. . . .

The commerce of the Indians in these fabrics has been extensive, from the Christian era to the end of the last century. For many hundred years, Persia, Arabia, Syria, Egypt, Abyssinia, and all the eastern parts of Africa, were supplied with a considerable portion of their cottons and muslins, and with all which they consumed of the finest qualities, from the marts of India. . . .

Owing to the beauty and cheapness of Indian muslins, chintzes, and calicoes, there was a period when the manufacturers of all the countries of Europe were apprehensive of being ruined by their competition. In the seventeenth century, the Dutch and English East India Companies imported these goods in large quantities; they became highly fashionable for ladies' and children's dresses, as well as for drapery and furniture, and the coarse calicoes were used to line garments. To such an extent did this proceed, that as early as 1678 a loud outcry was made in England against the admission of Indian goods, which, it was maintained, were ruining our ancient woollen manufacture,—a branch of industry which for centuries was regarded with an almost superstitious veneration, as a kind of palladium of the national prosperity, and which was incomparably the most extensive branch of manufactures till the close of the eighteenth century. . . .

So sagacious and far-sighted an author as Daniel De Foe did not escape the general notion, that it was not merely injurious to our woollen and silk manufactures, but also a national evil, to have clothing cheap from abroad rather than to manufacture it dear at home. In his *Weekly Review,* [January 31, 1708] which contains so many opinions on trade, credit, and currency far beyond the age, he thus laments the large importations of Indian goods:—

> The general fansie of the people runs upon East India goods to that degree, that the *chints* and *painted calicoes,* which before were only made use of for carpets, quilts, &c., and to clothe children and ordinary people, become now the dress of our ladies; and such is the power of a mode as we saw our persons of quality dressed in Indian carpets, which but a few years before their chambermaids would have thought too ordinary for them: the chints was advanced from lying upon their floors to their backs, from the foot-cloth to the petticoat; and even the queen herself at this time was pleased to appear in China and Japan, I mean China silks and callico. Nor was this all, but it crept into our houses, our closets, and bed-chambers; curtains, cushions, chairs, and at last beds themselves, were nothing but callicoes or Indian stuffs; and in short, almost every thing that used to be made of wool or silk, relating either to the dress of the women or the furniture of our houses, was supplied by the Indian trade.
>
> Above half of the (woollen) manufacture was entirely lost, half of the people scattered and ruined, and all this by the intercourse of the East India trade.

. . . It appears, then, that not more than a century ago, the cotton fabrics of India were so beautiful and cheap, that nearly all the governments of Europe thought it necessary to prohibit them, or to load them with heavy duties, in order to protect their own manufactures. How surprising a revolution has since taken place! The Indians have not lost their former skill; but a power has arisen in England, which has robbed them of their ancient ascendancy, turned back the tide of commerce, and made it run more rapidly against the Oriental than it ever ran against the English. Not to dwell upon a point which will afterwards be illustrated, the following document furnishes superabundant proof how a manufacture which has existed without a rival for thousands of years, is withering under the competition of a power which is but of yesterday: it would be well if it did not also illustrate the very different measure of protection and justice which governments usually afford to their subjects at home, and to those of their remote dependencies:—

PETITION OF NATIVES OF BENGAL, RELATIVE TO DUTIES ON COTTON AND SILK.

Calcutta, 1st. Sept. 1831.

To The Right Honourable the Lords of His Majesty's Privy Council for Trade, &c.

The humble Petition of the undersigned Manufacturers and Dealers in Cotton and Silk Piece Goods, the fabrics of Bengal;

Sheweth—That of late years your Petitioners have found their business nearly superseded by the introduction of the fabrics of Great Britain into Bengal, the importation of which augments every year, to the great prejudice of the native manufactures.

That the fabrics of Great Britain are consumed in Bengal, without any duties being levied thereon to protect the native fabrics.

That the fabrics of Bengal are charged with the following duties when they are used in Great Britain—

On manufactured cottons, 10 per cent.

On manufactured silks, 24 per cent.

Your Petitioners most humbly implore your Lordships' consideration of these circumstances, and they feel confident that no disposition exists in England to shut the door against the industry of any part of the inhabitants of this great empire.

They therefore pray to be admitted to the privilege of British subjects, and humbly entreat your Lordships to allow the cotton and silk fabrics of Bengal to be used in Great Britain 'free of duty,' or at the same rate which may be charged on British fabrics consumed in Bengal.

Your Lordships must be aware of the immense advantages the British manufacturers derive from their skill in constructing and using machinery, which enables them to undersell the unscientific manufacturers of Bengal in their own country: and, although your Petitioners are not sanguine in expecting to derive any great advantage from having their prayer granted, their minds would feel gratified by such a manifestation of your Lordships' good will towards them; and such an instance of justice to the natives of India would not fail to endear the British government to them.

They therefore confidently trust, that your Lordships' righteous consideration will be extended to them as British subjects, without exception of sect, country, or colour.

And your Petitioners, as in duty bound, will ever pray.

[Signed by 117 natives of high respectability.]

*British rule in India affected the intellectual as much as the economic develop-
ment of that country, mainly because of the fateful British decision in 1835 to use
government funds to support an educational system based on the English language
and English type of curriculum. The effect of this decision was to greatly accelerate the diffusion of Western ideas among Indian intellectuals, which, in turn,
led to the development of an anti-British nationalist movement. The person most
responsible for the decision was Thomas Babington Macaulay, whose famous
"Minute on Education," given below, presented the reasoning behind his policy.**
*Macaulay grossly underestimated Indian literature when he stated that "a single
shelf of a good European library was worth the whole native literature of India
and Arabia." But he was proven fully justified in anticipating that his program
would lead to the regeneration of Indian thought and learning.*

How stands the case? We have to educate a people who can not at present
be educated by means of their mother tongue. We must teach them some
foreign language. The claims of our own language it is hardly necessary to
recapitulate. It stands pre-eminent even among the languages of the West.
It abounds with works of imagination not inferior to the noblest which
Greece has bequeathed to us; with models of every species of eloquence;
with historical compositions, which, considered merely as narratives, have
seldom been surpassed, and which, considered as vehicles of ethical and
political instruction, have never been equaled; with just and lively representa-
tions of human life and human nature; with the most profound speculations
on metaphysics, morals, government, jurisprudence, and trade; with full and
correct information respecting every experimental science which tends to
preserve the health, to increase the comfort, or to expand the intellect of man.
Whoever knows that language has ready access to all the vast intellectual
wealth which all the wisest nations of the earth have created and hoarded in
the course of ninety generations. It may safely be said that the literature
now extant in that language is of far greater value than all the literature
which three hundred years ago was extant in all the languages of the world
together. Nor is this all. In India, English is the language spoken by the
ruling class. It is spoken by the higher class of natives at the seats of government. It is likely to become the language of commerce throughout the seas
of the East. It is the language of two great European communities which are
rising, the one in the south of Africa, the other in Australasia; communities
which are every year becoming more important, and more closely connected
with our Indian empire. Whether we look at the intrinsic value of our literature, or at the particular situation of this country, we shall see the strongest
reason to think that, of all foreign tongues, the English tongue is that which
would be the most useful to our native subjects.

The question now before us is simply whether, when it is in our power to

* G. O. Trevelyan, *Life and Letters of Lord Macaulay* (New York: Harper, 1875), I,
353-55.

teach this language, we shall teach languages in which, by universal confession, there are no books on any subject which deserve to be compared to our own; whether, when we can teach European science, we shall teach systems which, by universal confession, whenever they differ from those of Europe, differ for the worse; and whether, when we can patronize sound philosophy and true history, we shall countenance, at the public expense, medical doctrines which would disgrace an English farrier—astronomy, which would move laughter in the girls at an English boarding-school—history, abounding with kings thirty feet high, and reigns thirty thousand years long—and geography, made up of seas of treacle and seas of butter.

We are not without experience to guide us. History furnishes several analogous cases, and they all teach the same lesson. There are in modern times, to go no further, two memorable instances of a great impulse given to the mind of a whole society—of prejudice overthrown—of knowledge diffused—of taste purified—of arts and sciences planted in countries which had recently been ignorant and barbarous.

The first instance to which I refer is the great revival of letters among the Western nations at the close of the fifteenth and the beginning of the sixteenth century. At that time almost every thing that was worth reading was contained in the writings of the ancient Greeks and Romans. Had our ancestors acted as the Committee of Public Instruction has hitherto acted; had they neglected the language of Cicero and Tacitus; had they confined their attention to the old dialects of our own island; had they printed nothing and taught nothing at the universities but chronicles in Anglo-Saxon and romances in Norman-French, would England have been what she now is? What the Greek and Latin were to the contemporaries of More and Ascham, our tongue is to the people of India. The literature of England is now more valuable than that of classical antiquity. I doubt whether the Sanscrit literature be as valuable as that of our Saxon and Norman progenitors. In some departments—in history, for example—I am certain that it is much less so.

Another instance may be said to be still before our eyes. Within the last hundred and twenty years, a nation which had previously been in a state as barbarous as that in which our ancestors were before the Crusades, has gradually emerged from the ignorance in which it was sunk, and has taken its place among civilized communities. I speak of Russia. There is now in that country a large educated class, abounding with persons fit to serve the state in the highest functions, and in no wise inferior to the most accomplished men who adorn the best circles of Paris and London. There is reason to hope that this vast empire, which in the time of our grandfathers was probably behind the Punjab, may, in the time of our grandchildren, be pressing close on France and Britain in the career of improvement. And how was this change effected? Not by flattering national prejudices; not by feeding the mind of the young Muscovite with the old woman's stories which his rude fathers had believed; not by filling his head with lying legends about St. Nicholas; not by encouraging him to study the great question, whether the world was or was not created on the 13th of September; not by calling him "a learned native" when he has mastered all these points of knowledge; but by teaching him those foreign languages in which the greatest mass of information had been laid up, and thus putting all that information within his reach. The languages of Western Europe civilized Russia. I can not doubt that they will do for the Hindoo what they have done for the Tartar.

When Macaulay recommended that the Indians be educated along English lines, he foresaw that "they may in some future age demand European institutions," a premonition that proved completely justified. At first, most Indian intellectuals who had contact with British schools and learning were greatly impressed and usually became champions of British rule, as was the case with Dadabhai Naoroji who, though criticizing the British on grounds of economic exploitation, considered their rule to be generally beneficial and therefore accepted it. This attitude is illustrated in the following excerpt from Naoroji's presidential address before the Second Congress in 1886.* But later Indian leaders, referred to as the "Extremists" in contrast to the earlier "Moderates," were more impressed by the exactions than the benefactions of British rule, and demanded self-government. A prominent leader of this group was B. G. Tilak, whose views are presented in the following selections from speeches he delivered in 1906 and 1907.**

Naoroji

The assemblage of such a Congress is *an event of the utmost importance in Indian History.* I ask whether in the most glorious days of Hindu rule, in the days of Rajahs like the great Vikram, you could imagine the possibility of a meeting of this kind, whether even Hindus of all different provinces of the kingdom could have collected and spoken as one nation. Coming down to the later Empire of our friends, the Mahomedans, who probably ruled over a larger territory at one time than any Hindu monarch, would it have been, even in the days of the great Akbar himself, possible for a meeting like this to assemble composed of all classes and communities, all speaking one language, and all having uniform and high aspirations of their own.

. . . Well, then, what is it for which we are now met on this occasion? We have assembled to consider questions upon which depend our future, whether glorious or inglorious. It is our good fortune that we are under a rule which makes it possible for us to meet in this manner. (*Cheers.*)

It is under the civilizing rule of the Queen and people of England that we meet here together, hindered by none, and are freely allowed to speak our minds without the least fear and without the least hesitation. Such a thing is possible under British rule and British rule only. (*Loud Cheers.*) Then I put the *question* plainly: Is this Congress a nursery for sedition and rebellion against the British Government (*cries of "No, no"*); or is it another stone in the foundation of the stability of that government? (*Cries of "Yes, yes."*) There could be but one answer, and that you have already given, because we are thoroughly sensible of the numberless blessings conferred upon us, of which the very existence of this Congress is a proof in a nutshell. (*Cheers.*) Were it not for these blessings of British rule, I could not have come here, as I have done, without the least hesitation and without the least fear that my children might be robbed and killed in my absence; nor could

---

* *Speeches and Writings of Dadabhai Naoroji,* 2nd ed. (Madras: G. Nateson, n. d.), pp. 2-4.
** B. G. Tilak, *His Writings and Speeches,* 3rd ed. (Madras: Ganesh, 1923), pp. 42-45, 55-56, 65.

you have come from every corner of the land, having performed, within a few days, journeys, which in former days would have occupied as many months. (*Cheers.*) These simple facts bring home to all of us at once some of those great and numberless blessings which British rule has conferred upon us. But there remain even greater blessings for which we have to be grateful. It is to British rule that we owe the education we possess; the people of England were sincere in the declarations made more than half a century ago that India was a sacred charge entrusted to their care by Providence, and that they were bound to administer it for the good of India, to the glory of their own name, and the satisfaction of God. (*Prolonged cheering.*) When we have to acknowledge so many blessings as flowing from British rule,— and I could descant on them for hours, because it would simply be recounting to you the history of the British Empire in India—is it possible that an assembly like this, every one of whose members is fully impressed with the knowledge of these blessings, could meet for any purpose inimical to that rule to which we owe so much? (*Cheers.*)

The thing is absurd. Let us speak out like men and proclaim that we are loyal to the backbone (*cheers*); that we understand the benefits English rule has conferred upon us; that we thoroughly appreciate the education that has been given to us, the new light which has been poured upon us, turning us from darkness into light and teaching us the new lesson that kings are made for the people, not peoples for their kings; and this new lesson we have learned amidst the darkness of Asiatic despotism only by the light of free English civilization. . . .

Tilak

. . . India is under a foreign rule and Indians welcomed the change at one time. Then many races were the masters and they had no sympathy and hence the change was welcomed and that was the cause why the English succeeded in establishing an empire in India. Men then thought that the change was for their good. The confusion which characterised native rule was in striking contrast with the constitutional laws of the British Government. The people had much hope in the British Government, but they were much disappointed in their anticipations. They hoped that their arts and industries would be fostered under British rule and they would gain much from their new rulers. But all those hopes had been falsified. The people were now compelled to adopt a new line, namely, to fight against the bureaucracy.

Hundred years ago it was said, and believed by the people, that they were socially inferior to their rulers and as soon as they were socially improved they would obtain liberties and privileges. But subsequent events have shown that this was not based on sound logic. Fifty years ago Mr. Dadabhai Naoroji, the greatest statesman of India, thought that Government would grant them rights and privileges when they were properly educated, but that hope is gone. Now it might be said that they were not fitted to take part in the administration of the country owing to their defective education. But, I ask, whose fault it is. The Government has been imparting education to the people and hence the fault is not theirs but of the Government. The Government is imparting an education to make the people fit for some subordinate appointments. . . .

Protests are of no avail. Mere protest, not backed by self-reliance, will not help the people. Days of protests and prayers have gone. ... Three P's—pray, please and protest—will not do unless backed by solid force. Look to the examples of Ireland, Japan and Russia and follow their methods. ...

Two new words have recently come into existence with regard to our politics, and they are *Moderates* and *Extremists*. These words have a specific relation to time, and they, therefore, will change with time. The Extremists of to-day will be Moderates to-morrow, just as the Moderates of to-day were Extremists yesterday. When the National Congress was first started and Mr. Dadabhai's views, which now go for Moderates, were given to the public, he was styled an Extremist, so that you will see that the term Extremist is an expression of progress. We are Extremists to-day and our sons will call themselves Extremists and us Moderates. Every new party begins as Extremists and ends as Moderates. The sphere of practical politics is not unlimited. We cannot say what will or will not happen 1,000 years hence—perhaps during that long period, the whole of the white race will be swept away in another glacial period. We must, therefore, study the present and work out a programme to meet the present condition.

It is impossible to go into details within the time at my disposal. One thing is granted, *viz.*, that this Government does not suit us. As has been said by an eminent statesman—the government of one country by another can never be a successful, and therefore, a permanent Government. There is no difference of opinion about this fundamental proposition between the Old and New schools. One fact is that this alien Government has ruined the country. In the beginning, all of us were taken by surprise. We were almost dazed. We thought that everything that the rulers did was for our good and that this English Government has descended from the clouds to save us from the invasions of Tamerlane and Chengis Khan, and, as they say, not only from foreign invasions but from internecine warfare, or the internal or external invasions, as they call it. We felt happy for a time, but it soon came to light that the peace which was established in this country did this, as Mr. Dadabhai has said in one place—that we were prevented from going at each other's throats, so that a foreigner might go at the throat of us all. Pax Britannica has been established in this country in order that a foreign Government may exploit the country. That this is the effect of this Pax Britannica is being gradually realised in these days. ...

Every Englishman knows that they are a mere handful in this country and it is the business of every one of them to befool you in believing that you are weak and they are strong. This is politics. We have been deceived by such policy so long. What the New Party wants you to do is to realise the fact that your future rests entirely in your own hands. If you mean to be free, you can be free; if you do not mean to be free, you will fall and be for ever fallen. So many of you need not like arms; but if you have not the power of active resistance, have you not the power of self-denial and self-abstinence in such a way as not to assist this foreign Government to rule over you? This is boycott and this is what is meant when we say, boycott is a political weapon. We shall not give them assistance to collect revenue and keep peace. We shall not assist them in fighting beyond the frontiers or outside India with Indian blood and money. We shall not assist them in carrying on the administration of justice. We shall have our own courts, and when time comes we shall not pay taxes. Can you do that by your united efforts? If you can, you are free from to-morrow.

Chapter Sixteen

Impact of dominance:
China and Japan

China's development during four millennia lead that country to have the world's most populous and, in certain respects, most cultivated society. This achievement, in turn, led to self-sufficiency and self-centeredness—to the feeling that China was indeed the Middle Kingdom, and the rest of the world was essentially subsidiary and inferior. Consequently, China's defeat by the West in the second half of the nineteenth century was a traumatic experience. It prompted soul-searching and eventually generated an intellectual revolution that has continued to the present day. At first the scholar bureaucracy that traditionally had ruled the country tried to cope with the barbarian intruders by making as few adjustments as possible. Typical was a certain Wei Yuan who published in 1842 a work entitled Record of the Imperial Military Exploits, *from which the following selection is taken.* Wei Yuan proposed to check the Westerners by discovering and imitating their "superior techniques." At this stage, the Chinese were not questioning the fundamentals of their civilization; they were merely trying out a few tricks to put the barbarians in their place.*

The Japanese barbarians (who raided China in the sixteenth century) were strong in land fighting and weak in water warfare,

---

* Ssu-yu Teng and J. K. Fairbank, *China's Response to the West: A Documentary Survey 1839-1923* (Cambridge: Harvard Univ., 1954), pp. 31, 33-35. Copyright 1954 by the President and Fellows of Harvard College. Reprinted by permission of the publishers.

because the pirates who came were all desperadoes from poor islands, who had no means to build large ships and big guns, but relied upon sheer courage to cross the ocean, and depended upon their swords and spears to invade China. Therefore, whenever they went ashore it was impossible to resist them. But when the Japanese ships met the junks of Fukien and Kwangtung, then they were like rice on a grindstone. If the Japanese ships met big cannons and firearms, they would be like goats chased by wolves. . . . In general, the strength of the Japanese was on the land. To attack them on the open ocean was to assail their weak point. The strength of the British barbarians is on the ocean. Wait for them in the inland rivers. Wait for them on the shore and they will lose their strength. Unfortunately, the Ming people, in warding off the Japanese, did not know how to oppose them on the ocean, and nowadays those who are guarding against the British do not lay ambushes in the interior.

The situation today is this: if there is a discussion about getting and using Western warships, then someone is sure to say that he fears borrowing aid from the outer barbarians would show our weaknesses. Yet when suddenly our weakness has been several times more fully exposed than this would have involved, they have been glad to do it without shrinking. If there is a discussion about building ships, making weapons, and learning the superior techniques of the barbarians, they say it is too expensive. But when suddenly the cost is ten times more than this, they again say it is a matter of exigency to meet an emergency and is not regrettable. If there is a discussion about the translation of barbarian books and prying into barbarian affairs, they are sure to say it would cause trouble. (Note: during the reign of Chia-ch'ing there was someone in Kwangtung who intended to publish a book giving transliterations of Chinese and barbarian characters, which would be very convenient for Chinese translating their characters. Yet it was forbidden by the Kwangtung authorities.) When suddenly something has happened, they ask, "What is the distance between the English capital and the Russian capital?" Or, "Via what route can the English barbarians communicate with the Mohammedan tribes? . . ."

It is proper for us to learn the barbarians' superior techniques in order to control them. The superior techniques of the barbarians are three: (1) warships, (2) firearms, and (3) methods of maintaining and training soldiers. . . .

The materials in their shipyards are piled up like hills and craftsmen congregate there like a cloud. Within twenty or thirty days a large warship can be completed. They can instantly spread the sails and adjust the tiller with a few shouted orders. Their craftsmen compete with each other in their talents and abilities. In construction they compete for speed and in navigation also. Construction goes on all year long, the fire illuminates the sky, and the noise shakes the earth. Thus, while the British ships and guns are regarded in China as due to extraordinary skill, in the various countries of Europe they are considered as quite ordinary. In Canton international trade has been carried on for two hundred years. At first the products of their strange skills and clever craftsmanship were received, and then their heterodox religions and poisonous opium. But in regard to their conduct of war and the effectiveness of their weapons, we are learning not a single one of their superior skills. That is, we are only willing to receive the harm and not . . . the benefit of foreign intercourse.

Let us establish a shipyard and an arsenal at two spots, Chuenpi and

Taikoktow outside of the Bogue in Kwangtung, and select one or two persons from among the foreign headmen who have come from France and America, respectively, to bring Western craftsmen to Canton to take charge of building ships and making arms. In addition, we should invite Western helmsmen to take charge of teaching the methods of navigating ships and of using cannon, following the precedent of the barbarian officials in the Imperial Board of Astronomy. We should select clever artisans and good soldiers from Fukien and Kwangtung to learn from them, the craftsmen to learn the casting of cannon and building of ships, and the good soldiers to learn their methods of navigation and attack. ... In Kwangtung there should be ten thousand soldiers; in Fukien, ten thousand; in Chekiang, six thousand; and in Kiangsu, four thousand. In assigning soldiers to the ships we must rely on selection and training. Eight out of ten should be taken from among the fishermen and smugglers along the sea coast. Two out of ten should be taken from the old encampments of the water forces. All the padded rations and extra rations of the water force should be ... used for the recruiting and maintenance of good soldiers. We must make the water forces of China able to navigate large ships overseas, and able to fight against foreign barbarians on the high seas.

CHINA'S RESPONSE TO THE WEST: INSTITUTIONAL PHASE   87

*Repeated defeats at the hands of the West forced China's leaders to reconsider their traditional values and policies. They were compelled to go beyond military technology and to consider institutional change. Outstanding in this respect was a gifted journalist, Wang T'ao, who wrote under the protection of British rule in Hong Kong, and boldly urged sweeping reforms. The following excerpts from a letter that he wrote between 1858 and 1860 * advocate reorganization of education, administration, and the armed forces, and also describe favorably and perceptively the nature of Britain's government.*

Formerly it was said, "The Europeans who have trade relations with China are more than one country; it is better to use them to attack each other, or to use them so that they make compromises with each other, or use them so as to separate them from each other." These three statements all seem to be calculations based on profound deliberation and far-reaching thought. And yet nowadays I am afraid that they are impracticable. Why? Because all European countries have the intention of keeping China on the outside. How can they be utilized by us? Even though there were one country which was willing to be utilized by us, all the other nations would undoubtedly ridicule her. As for two countries which engage in a prolonged struggle against each other, with the issue not yet decided, the practice in Western countries is to persuade them to make peace. If the advice is not taken, then assistance is given the weak party to attack the strong, just as England and France helped Turkey to attack Russia in recent years. ...

* *Ibid.*, pp. 137-40.

But the practice in the West is, after all, not a sufficient rule to be applied to China. The most tractable Western country is the United States of America. Nevertheless she still takes the victory or failure of England as her own glory or disgrace. ... Thus there has been occasions for her to assist England, but there has never been an occasion for her to assist us and attack England. As to her relations with us, though she has never made unreasonable demands on us, she has shared all the benefits gained by England and France. ... If she sincerely wants to give us support, how could she act in this way? ...

If, suddenly, the Westerners seized an opportunity to attack us, how could we resist them? Our soldiers are inferior to theirs, our finances are inferior to theirs, our weapons are inferior to theirs, and our military strategies are also inferior to theirs. They already thoroughly understand the hostile actions which we on our side may take, whereas we are as yet incapable of knowing what hostilities they may commit. We excuse ourselves by saying that it is because they are too far away from us. Yet with all the publication of daily newspapers and the spread of postal communications, can we not make some inquiries and obtain some information?

If Confucius were born today we may be certain that he would not stubbornly believe in antiquity and oppose making changes. ... First, the method of selecting civil servants should be reformed. The examination essays up to the present day have gone from bad to worse. ... And yet we are still using them to select scholars.

Secondly, the method of training soldiers should be reformed. Now our army camps and water forces have only names registered on books, but no actual persons. The authorities consider our troops unreliable, and then they recruit militia, who can be assembled but cannot be disbanded. ... This is called "using the untrained people to fight," which is no different from driving them to their deaths.

Thirdly, the empty show of our schools should be reformed. Now district directors of schools and sub-directors of schools are installed, one person for a small city, and two for a larger city. It is a sheer waste. ... Such people are usually degenerate, incompetent, and senile and have little sense of shame. They are unfit to set the example for scholars. ...

He who rules the empire should establish the foundation and not merely mend the superstructure. ... Formerly we thought that the foundation of our wealth and strength would be established if only Western methods were respected or adopted and that the result would be achieved immediately. ... Now in all the coastal provinces there have been established special factories to make guns, bullets, and ships. Young men have been selected and sent to study abroad. Seen from the outside, the effort is really great and fine. Unfortunately, however, we are still copying the superficialities of their methods, getting the terminology (of Western civilization) but little actual substance. The ships which were formerly built at Foochow were entirely based on old methods of Western countries, beneath contempt, to those who know. As to things made in other places, for the trick of moving a machine or valve we must rely on the instruction of Westerners. Yet, if we watch the bearing of the Chinese manufacturers, they already feel noisily pleased with themselves. They usually believe that their thinking and wisdom are sufficient to match those of the Westerners, or that they have even surpassed them.

In general (the advantage of) guns lies in the fine technique of discharging them, that of ships in the ability to navigate them ... The handling of effective weapons depends upon the people ... But the so-called able minds of our people are not necessarily able, and the so-called competent ones are not necessarily competent. They are merely mediocrities who accomplish something through the aid of others.

Therefore, the urgent problem of our nation today lies primarily in the governance of the people; next in the training of soldiers; and in these two matters the crucial thing to aim at is the accumulation of men of ability. Indeed, superficial imitation in practical matters is certainly not as effective as arousing genuine intellectual curiosity. The polishing and pounding in factories is definitely not as important as the machining of peoples' minds ...

Let us now talk about the conventional examination subjects. The themes on classics in the second examination ought to be replaced by some practical knowledge ... so that the candidates can understand the body politic and can transfer their knowledge into actual practice.

England is in a remote spot overseas, three islands which stand like mountains off the northwest of Europe. ... In view of the fine quality and strength of her armament and soldiers, the richness of her revenue and the abundance of her natural resources no European country dares to be stiff-necked with her. ... In recent years she has maintained her prosperity and preserved her state of peace and has been so cautious in resorting to arms that unless there is no other way out she never carelessly starts a military expedition. ...

The real strength of England, however, lies in the fact that there is a sympathetic understanding between the governing and the governed, a close relationship between the ruler and the people. ... My observation is that the daily domestic political life of England actually embodies the traditional ideals of our ancient Golden Age.

CHINA'S RESPONSE TO THE WEST: REVOLUTIONARY PHASE   88

By the end of the nineteenth century, some reformers in China were demanding not only institutional change but also outright revolution, a shift brought about by China's humiliating defeat at the hands of the Japanese in 1894–1895, and by the growth of a Chinese merchant class (within China and abroad) which felt little loyalty to the reigning Manchu dynasty. The leader of the revolutionists, Dr. Sun Yat-sen, who received a Western education in Honolulu and Hong Kong, founded in Tokyo in 1905 the T'ung-meng hui, or League of Common Alliance. Its program, from which the following selection is taken,* called not only for the overthrow of the Manchus, but also for the establishment of a republic and the distribution of land amongst the peasants.

We proclaim to the world in utmost sincerity the outline of the present revolution and the fundamental plan for the future administration of the nation.

---

* *Ibid.,* pp. 227-29.

1) *Drive Out the Tartars:* The Manchus of today were originally the eastern barbarians beyond the Great Wall. They frequently caused border troubles during the Ming dynasty; then when China was in a disturbed state they came inside Shanhaikuan, conquered China, and enslaved our Chinese people. Those who opposed them were killed by the hundreds of thousands, and our Chinese have been a people without a nation for two hundred and sixty years. The extreme cruelties and tyrannies of the Manchu government have now reached their limit. With the righteous army poised against them, we will overthrow the government, and restore our sovereign rights. Those Manchu and Chinese military men who have a change of heart and come over to us will be granted amnesty, while those who dare to resist will be slaughtered without mercy. Chinese who act as Chinese traitors in the cause of the Manchus will be treated in the same way.

2) *Restore China:* China is the China of the Chinese. The government of China should be in the hands of the Chinese. After driving out the Tartars we must restore our national state. Those who dare to act like Shih Ching-t'ang or Wu San-kuei will be attacked by the whole country.

3) *Establish the Republic:* Now our revolution is based on equality, in order to establish a republican government. All our people are equal and all enjoy political rights. The president will be publicly chosen by the people of the country. The parliament will be made up of members publicly chosen by the people of the country. A constitution of the Chinese Republic will be enacted, and every person must abide by it. Whoever dares to make himself a monarch shall be attacked by the whole country.

4) *Equalize land ownership:* The good fortune of civilization is to be shared equally by all the people of the nation. We should improve our social and economic organization, and assess the value of all the land in the country. Its present price shall be received by the owner, but all increases in value resulting from reform and social improvements after the revolution shall belong to the state, to be shared by all the people, in order to create a socialist state, where each family within the empire can be well supported, each person satisfied, and no one fail to secure employment. Those who dare to control the livelihood of the people through monopoly shall be ostracized.

The above four points will be carried out in three steps in due order. The first period is government by military law. When the righteous army has arisen, various places will join the cause. The common people of each locality will escape from the Manchu fetters. Those who come upon the enemy must unite in hatred of him, must join harmoniously with the compatriots within their ranks and suppress the enemy bandits. Both the armies and the people will be under the rule of military law. The armies will do their best in defeating the enemy on behalf of the people, and the people will supply the needs of the armies, and not do harm to their security. The local administration, in areas where the enemy has been either already defeated or not yet defeated, will be controlled in general by the Military Government, so that step by step the accumulated evils can be swept away. Evils like the oppression of the government, the greed and graft of officials, the squeeze of government clerks and runners, the cruelty of tortures and penalties, the tyranny of tax collections, the humiliation of the queue— shall all be exterminated together with the Manchu rule. Evils in social customs, such as the keeping of slaves, the cruelty of footbinding, the spread of the poison of opium, the obstructions of geomancy (feng-shui), should also all be prohibited. The time limit for each district (hsien) is three years. In those hsien where real results are achieved before the end of three years, the military law shall be lifted and a provisional constitution shall be en- acted.

The second period is that of government by a provisional constitution. When military law is lifted in each hsien, the Military Government shall return the right of self-government to the local people. The members of the local council and local officials shall all be elected by the people. All rights and duties of the Military Government toward the people and those of the people toward the Government shall be regulated by the provisional constitution, which shall be observed by the Military Government, the local councils, and the people. Those who violate the law shall be held responsible. Six years after the securing of peace in the nation the provisional constitution shall be annulled and the constitution shall be promulgated.

The third period will be government under the constitution. Six years after the provisional constitution has been enforced, a constitution shall be made. The administrative and military powers of the Military Government shall be annulled; the people shall elect the president, and elect the members of parliament to organize the parliament.

CHINESE INTELLECTUALS AND THE WEST 89

China's response to the West ended in revolution rather than in peaceful reorganization as had happened in Japan. One reason for this difference was the rigidity of the scholar bureaucracy that traditionally governed China. Committed to the tenets of Confucianism and unalterably convinced of the basic inferiority of Western civilization, these literati could not bring themselves to emulate something that they looked down upon. Thus China responded haltingly and inadequately to Western pressures until the resulting tensions generated a revolutionary wave that has persisted to the present. The following account * by an American scholar analyzes the role of the literati in determining the nature of China's response to the West.

The Chinese scholar-official had long constituted a special type of iron-clad intelligentsia, firmly based on the Confucian tradition and accustomed to rule China with unchallenged authority. This tradition was threatened for the first time in 1838 with the outbreak of the "Opium" or First Anglo-Chinese War. Outwardly, this was a simple military defeat by a "barbarian" force on one frontier of China, remote from the capital and court at Peking. As such it was nothing new in Chinese history. Hsiungnu, Toba Tartars, Mongols and Manchus had threatened and overrun Chinese borders through the centuries. To most articulate Chinese both this and successive assaults on China through the nineteenth century, were adequately explained by the traditional and reassuring *formula*.

---

* E. Swisher, "Chinese Intellectuals and the Western Impact, 1838-1900," *Comparative Studies in Society and History,* I (October, 1958), 27, 33-34, 37.

Some Chinese scholar-officials, however, saw in the European and American assault on China, a deeper significance—a challenge to the whole humanistic pattern of Confucian thought, which they represented. This was no mere nomadic horde riding rough-shod through China for plunder and conquest, but rather a sinister materialistic and mechanistic challenge to the Chinese way of life. . . .

In China, as distinguished from Japan and other "backward" countries, it was the intellectual who was called upon to face this challenge, which he regarded as both anti-intellectual and immoral, and to turn back the tide of materialism and militarism. In other countries, science and technology might be regarded as bulwarks of intellectualism, but to the Chinese intelligentsia, they represented at best diabolically clever but nonetheless barbaric devices which might be utilized to turn back the Confucian ethic from destruction. At no time throughout the nineteenth century did the entrenched intelligentsia of China acknowledge any western philosophy or ethical system as a legitimate rival to the Confucian system. Their response to the impact of the west was to borrow technological gadgets and organizational techniques and then to turn these against the materialistic barbarians themselves. They were confident that these superficial tricks could be easily mastered and improved upon by demonstrably superior Chinese minds and that China could thereby be saved.

The persons chosen to represent this nineteenth century response to the West are intellectuals—not technicians, or professional soldiers, or bankers. They are of the Chinese intelligentsia, steeped in the Confucian classics, disciplined by scholastic exercises in literary criticism and epigraphy, committed to an ethical and humanistic code of values, and skilled in the writing of succinct and brilliant essays in the classical form. All of them had collected libraries, written and published books, competed in scholarly debate and discussion, and held high public office in the tradition of China's government by sages. They differ from the large body of intellectuals constituting China's official and scholarly hierarchy only in one respect: they recognized the challenge of the West and attempted to formulate a response to it. In making this response, they stayed within the rigid framework of the Chinese intellectual tradition. . . .

In reviewing and reviving the evidence of Chinese response to the West in the 19th century, modern scholars both Chinese and Western have tended to allow their surprise and delight in finding Confucian intellectuals dabbling with gunpowder, steam, and ballot-boxes to distort their judgement and critical analysis. It is easy to visualize China eagerly embracing Western geographical knowledge in the 1840's and soberly instituting a Western political system in 1898. Complementing this rosy picture, there is necessarily assumed a readiness on the part of Chinese intellectuals to abandon the Confucian world view, including the moralistic idea of overcoming one's enemies by virtue, and the concept of government by precept and education.

Nothing could be further from the truth. Actually, as Teng Ssu-yu has aptly said, ". . . China's non-response to the West was a large part of her response." In other words, the more the Chinese intellectual saw of Western materialistic progress, the more convinced he became of China's intellectual and moral superiority. In the first place, what response there was was sporadic. After Lin Tse-hsu's feeble efforts to study enemy geography and toy with Western explosives at Canton, some effort was made by the Manchu

Ch'i-ying to continue the good work, but this was soon stifled by apathy on the part of fellow officials and the Chinese people and by a complete repudiation from Peking in 1850. Thereafter, little is heard about Westernization until a second European war and widespread civil war again threatened the Empire in the late fifties and early sixties. This "present danger" appeared to accomplish real gains for China in the form of arsenals, shipyards and Western military training. Indeed, through the following three decades, new style armies and a modern navy retained their popularity and much lip-service was done to Westernization of China. However, 1894 was to find China hopelessly weak against another oriental power, Japan. Actually, even in the simple, uncontroversial field of military Westernization, China's response to the West in the 19th century was both slight and superficial.

Not only was China's response sporadic and slight, it was also on a very small scale. Most of the country and most of the people did not respond at all. The only purely Chinese developments of any importance outside the treaty ports, were Chang Chih-tung's ventures in Canton and Wu-han. Here some factories and mines were developed, at least enough to make news-paper publicity—Chang was headlined as making Hankow into a "Chinese Chicago" and credited with the introduction of bicycles and loading cranes. Most of the other Westernization took place in or around Shanghai where the impetus was more foreign than Chinese. The other cities and provinces of China saw little or no Westernization in the 19th century. Nothing like a real "Industrial Revolution" was even projected in China before 1923 nor seriously attempted until 1949.

The fact of China's non-response to the West, on the material level, has been pointed out by critical modern scholars and can be amply documented by 19th century observers and 20th century compilations of statistics. Even more revealing, however, is the limited response of China on the philosophical or ideological level. . . .

It is perhaps not surprising that China's 19th century reformers did not probe to the bases of Western progress—the fundamental concept of human nature, the foundation of Roman law, the implementation of curiosity in the scientific method, or the development of a theory of progress—all of them categorically opposed to Confucian theory and apparently repugnant to the Chinese mind. Westernization appeared as a gadget, an easy trick, which would transform China in the twinkling of an eye, not into the like-ness of the West but into the image of the Golden Age created by the Chinese political philosophers of the Chou and Han.

It is surprising, however, that with the rapid deterioration of China and the acute awareness of the "present danger" felt by all the Chinese intellectuals of the 19th century, some of them did not turn to philosophies and experiments in China's own past, outside the Confucian pattern, which might have thrown a new light on the West and contributed useful precedents for reform or revolution. . . .

A few quotations from Wei Yang, 4th century B.C., will illustrate the point:

> The customs and laws of the ancients were good in their time. But times change. That which was good and useful at one time is no longer so in another. The first care of an intelligent government ought therefore to be to see to it that the customs and laws are exactly adapted to the uses of the present time. . . .

Nineteenth century China thus furnishes an example of an entrenched intelligentsia, too rigidly committed to a traditional pattern to make the basic ideological changes necessary to maintain its leadership. In the unswerving commitment of the Chinese intellectual to Confucius, perhaps 19th century China is most nearly analogous to Middle Age European commitment to Aristotle and scholasticism, before the intellectual revolution introduced by Bacon. The Chinese intellectual had many virtues and was frequently a man of brilliance and sound character, but he lacked flexibility and operated in too narrow a frame.

90 PIONEER JAPANESE ADVOCATE OF WESTERNIZATION

Japan led all other Asian countries in the nineteenth century in the speed and thoroughness of her modernization. Fukuzawa Yukichi (1834–1901), a pioneer in this modernization, learned Dutch and English, and traveled widely in the United States and Europe. On his return to Japan, he wrote books in which he enthusiastically described the advantages of certain aspects of Western civilization. Millions of copies were sold, making it possible for Fukuzawa to establish a newspaper through which he continued his campaign for change. In 1898, shortly before his death, Fukuzawa dictated his autobiography, from which the following passages have been selected. They reveal his opposition to the traditional Chinese learning, his keen interest in Western science, his reactions and difficulties while traveling in Europe, and his reflections on his life's work.*

The true reason of my opposing the Chinese culture with such a vigor is my belief that as long as the old retrogressive doctrine of the Chinese school remains at all in our young men's minds, our country can never enter the rank of civilized nations of the world. In my determination to save our coming generation from this detrimental influence, I was prepared even to face, single-handed, the Chinese scholars of the country as a whole.

Gradually the new education was showing its results among the younger generation; yet men of middle age or past, who held responsible positions, were for the most part uninformed as to the true spirit of the Western culture, and so whenever they had to make decisions, they turned invariably to their Chinese sources for guidance. And so again and again I had to rise up and denounce the all-important Chinese influence before this weighty opposition. It was not altogether a very safe road for my reckless spirit to follow. . . .

Of course at that time there were no examples of industrial machinery. A steam engine could not be seen anywhere in the whole of Japan. Nor was there any kind of apparatus for chemical experiments. However, learning something of the theories of chemistry and machinery in our books, we of the Ogata household gave much effort in trying out what we had learned, or trying to make a thing that was illustrated in the books.

---

* *The Autobiography of Fukuzawa Yukichi* (Tokyo: Hokuseido Press, 1947), pp. 90-92, 94-95, 135-38, 230-31, 357-59.

I had known since my residence in Nagasaki that iron could be tin-plated if we had zinc chloride for applying the tin metal. In Japan the art of plating copper with tin by the use of pine pitch had been known, for all the copper or bronze cooking vessels were tin-plated. We students decided that we would plate iron by the modern method. There was no standard chloric acid to be purchased in a store, so we had to find out a way of preparing it ourselves. After laboring over it from the description in the text, we finally made the acid, and obtaining the necessary zinc chloride, we succeeded in plating iron with tin—a feat beyond the practice of any tin craftsman in the land. Such was the irresistible fascination of our new knowledge.

. . . . .

Then we tried ammonium chloride. The first requisite for this experiment was bone, but we learned that horse-hoof would serve as well. So we went to a store where they sold tortoise-shell ware to get some fragments of horse-hoof. It was quite cheap; we could have it for the asking. I had heard that horse-hoof was used for fertilizing, but that was of no concern to us. We took a large quantity of the hoof and covered it in an earthenware jar with a layer of clay; then placed it on a charcoal fire in a large bowl. As we fanned the fire vigorously, a smelly vapor came out; this we condensed in an earthenware pipe.

Our experiment was going very well, and the condensed vapor was dripping freely from the pipe, but the disadvantage proved to be the awful stench of the vapor. It can easily be imagined what the result of heating bones and horse-hoof would be, especially in the small back yard of the dormitory. Our clothing became so saturated with the gas that when we went to the bath house in the evening, the street dogs howled at us. Then we tried the experiment naked; our skins absorbed the smell. The young men were so keen on their experiment that they stood the smelly ordeal without complaint. But all the neighbors objected and the servants in the Ogata household wailed that they could not eat their dinner on account of the sickening gas.

After all our hardships and the complaints and apologies, a strange powdery thing was the result—not very pure, nor the correct crystals of ammonium chloride. At this stage most of the young men, including myself, decided they had had enough. But others, more stouthearted, would not give up the search; they insisted that to give up a work unfinished was a disgrace to their profession. And so ammonium chloride was pursued.

They hired a cheap boat on the Yodo River, and placing their brazier and utensils on board, continued the odorous experiment in midstream. Still the vapor penetrated the nearby shores, and the people would come out and yell to them to get out of the way. Then the young men would have the boat rowed upstream, keeping on with the experiment until they were urged to move again downstream. So up and down from Tenjin Bridge to Tamae Bridge they went on for many days. The chief of these determined students was Nakamura Kyoan from Konpira in Sanuki province.

Besides such experiments in chemistry, the Ogata students were interested in dissecting animals, stray dogs and cats, and sometimes even the corpses of decapitated criminals. They were a hardened, rather reckless crowd, these aspirants for Western learning.

. . . . .

There were about forty men in the party, (travelling in Europe) including the three envoys, various secretaries, doctors, interpreters, and the personal attendants of the ambassadors, cooks and general servants. . . . We all wore our Japanese dress with a pair of swords in our girdles, and appeared on the streets of London and Paris in such attire. A sight indeed it must have been!

· · · · ·

When we reached Paris and had been formally received by the welcoming French officials, the first request we had to make was that as many of our party as possible be accommodated near the chief envoy's "camp" because of our number and the amount of our baggage. The heads of the mission were evidently anxious, because if different members of the party were scattered in remote hotels, it might be inconvenient and unsafe in the strange land. The host of the welcoming committee understood, nodded his approval and asked the number of our party. When he was told it was forty, he replied, "If you are only forty, why, one of our hotels could accommodate ten or twenty times that number." We did not comprehend what he meant, but on reaching the hotel assigned to us, we found that he was not jesting.

Our headquarters were the Hotel du Louvre, opposite the entrance to the imperial palace. It was really a huge edifice of five stories with six hundred rooms and over five hundred employees. More than a thousand guests could be accommodated at one time. So the large party of our Japanese envoys was lost in it. Instead of our anxiety lest the party might have to be separated in distant hostelries, our real anxiety became the possibility of losing our way in the maze of halls and corridors in the one hotel.

No stove or steam radiators were necessary in our rooms, for heated air circulated through them. Numerous gaslights served to illuminate the rooms and halls so that we could not distinguish at all the coming of darkness outside. In the dining hall there was such a spread of food, delicacies of "both the woods and the sea," that even those in the mission who professed their dislike of "foreign objects" could not maintain this aversion in the choice of food. The joke was in the stock of Japanese supplies brought along in our baggage. We could not cook our rice in the kitchen of the hotel; nor was it possible within reason to use the oil-wick lamps in the halls. Finally, disgusted with all this useless impedimenta, we piled it all up in an apartment and offered the entire store of rice, oil-lamps, and all to one of the lesser members of the welcoming committee, M. Lambert (?), and asked him to take it gratis.

As we were unfamiliar with Western life and customs, there was naturally no end of farcical situations occurring among our party. A servant brought *sugar* when ordered to go for *cigars*. Our doctor of Chinese medicine had intended to buy some powdered carrot, but instead he had come away with *ginger,* as he found later.

When one of the lord-envoys had occasion to use the toilet, he was followed to the doorway by one of his personal attendants who carried the lighted paper lantern, as is the custom in the homeland. The attendant in his most formal dress was to be seen squatting patiently outside the open door, holding his master's removed sword. This happened to be in the bustling corridor of the hotel where people were passing constantly, and the gas was burning as bright as day. But unperturbed sat the faithful guardian. I happened to come along and see the incident which I ended by shutting the doors. Then turning to the man, I told him quietly of the etiquette of Eu-

ropeans on such occasions, but my heart was fluttering with consterna-
tion. . . .

Sixty odd years is the length of life I have now come through. It is often
the part of an old man to say that life on looking back seems like a dream.
But for me the "dream" has been a particularly interesting one, full of
changes and surprises.

. . . . .

Were I to dwell on difficulties and hardships, I might easily describe this
life of mine as a pretty hard one. The old proverb reminds us, "Once past
the throat, the burn (of the food) is forgotten." Of course poverty and
other hardships were hard to bear. But looking backward now, they seem
dear among the old glowing memories which remain.

When I first began my studies, all that I hoped for was to acquire some
knowledge of the Western culture and then so manage my living that I should
not become a burden upon other men. That was my first ambition. Unex-
pectedly came the Restoration, and to my delight Japan was opened to the
world.

Seiyo Jijo (Things Western) and other books of mine published during
the old shogunate regime were written with no real expectation that they
would interest the public at all. Even if they were to have some attention,
I had no idea that the contents of the books would ever be applied to our
own social conditions. In short, I was writing my books simply as stories
of the West or as curious tales of a dream-land. Then contrary to all my
expectations these books were read widely and were even taken for guidance
by the people of the day. Moreover, the government of the new age proved
itself most courageous in applying the new thoughts. It went far beyond
what was advocated in my Seiyo Jijo, and began to surprise even the author
of the book himself.

In this unexpected turn of events I found that I could not be satisfied with
my former ambition. I must take advantage of the moment to bring in more
of the Western civilization and revolutionize our people's ideas from the
roots. Then perhaps it would not be impossible to form a great nation in
this far Orient, which would stand counter to Great Britain of the West and
take an active part in the progress of the whole world. So I was led on to
form my second and greater ambition.

Consequently I renewed activities with "tongue and brush," my two cherished instruments. On one side I was teaching in my school and making
occasional public speeches, while on the other I was constantly writing on
all subjects. And these comprise my books subsequent to Seiyo Jijo. It was
a pretty busy life, but no more than doing my bit or "doing the ten thou-
sandth part" as we often put it.

As I consider things today, while there are still many things to be regretted, on the whole I see the country well on the road to improvement and
advancement. One of the tangible results was to be seen a few years ago
in our victorious war with China (1894-1895). The victory certainly was
the result of the combined efforts of government and people.

The second half of the nineteenth century was a period of unprecedented change in Japan because the opponents of reform in that country, in contrast to those in China, were overruled and disregarded. The modernization of the economy, administration, army, and educational system inevitably affected the social life of Japan. In the following essay,* Professor Sakutaro Fujioka surveys the extent and nature of the social changes. His findings are of more than local significance because other peoples, as they became modernized, also experienced the changes in dress, the social mobility, and the cultural integration which the author describes.

Supposing that a man born fifty years ago returned to Japan after a wandering life in a foreign country without any news from his fatherland, how many of the scenes before him would resemble those of his childhood? Very few indeed. To commence with: he would find no trace of the Shōgun, the real ruler of his childhood, and no *daimyō,* except as peers, and these of little higher standing than the commoners, except in name. The castles of the *daimyō,* once so magnificent, would now show themselves to him as a mass of crumbling ruins; the spears, swords, and other implements of warfare, which he regarded with awe as a child, he would only find preserved by amateurs as objects of historic interest. What were then poor seashore hamlets, with only a few fishermen's cottages lying scattered about, would now be transformed into great naval ports or prosperous towns, such as Yokosuka, Sasébo, and the like. . . .

That Occidentalism was the main cause of the recent changes we need hardly say. Up to half a century ago, the nation, avoiding all intercourse with foreigners, indulged in the happy dream that the Japanese were the mightiest nation under the sun. What was their surprise, then, when they were brought face to face with the civilization of the West? . . . As a reaction from their former pride, they now passed to the other extreme, namely, a sense of humiliation, and they became keenly anxious to take in everything Western. Thus politics, economics, natural science, and art— everything was taken from the West with insatiable avidity, and the customs and usages of the people underwent a complete change, so complete that those alone who witnessed it can believe it.

Naturally most of these changes originated in Government offices, companies, and other public concerns, and then gradually found their way to the people at large. To cite some instances of the change: European clothes were at first used by officials as ceremonial costumes; then they were found very convenient to work in, and consequently came into popular use. Formerly holidays were limited to the five *sékku* festivals and a few other occasions, but now Sunday has been made a day of universal rest. To-day even private people, who can afford it, live in large European houses, and many in the middle class furnish one or more rooms of their Japanese houses in European style and use them as studies or drawing-rooms. Foreign restaurants are met with almost everywhere, and often the tourist finds Euro-

---

* S. Okuma, *Fifty Years of New Japan* (London: Smith, Elder, 1909), II, 443, 445-50. Reprinted by permission of J. Murray (Publishers) Ltd.

pean dishes served in a Japanese hotel. Indeed, there is no Japanese homestead wherein one does not find some marks of Western influence.

What determines the mode of women's dress is, in all countries, beauty of appearance rather than practical convenience; and since each nation has its own fancy, any change in female costume is naturally not so rapid as in that of men's. Nevertheless, the now popular use of the European style of hairdressing cannot fail to strike any observer, as also the prevalence of the *hakama* or skirts among the school-girls, though doubtless this is an imitation of the man's skirt, and supported by ancient usage, but it must have been encouraged by the dress worn by the fair sex of the West.

Until fifty years ago people did not know that the flesh of pigs and cows was eatable, or that coal was combustible; they had no petroleum lamps and no wagons drawn by horses. They had only black-and-white drawings and paintings in light colours, and they pleased their ears with the *koto* (harp) and *samisén* (three-stringed guitar). But to-day foreign oil paintings and water colours have many admirers, and the piano and the violin are more fashionable than the native instruments. Formerly novelists and dramatists received no honour, while actors were despised as an inferior class of men, but now the drama is recognized as the highest form of art.

To go into further examples would be only tedious and unduly swell the present article; so I shall confine myself to a general statement, and will proceed to consider the spirit which has governed and directed all these changes. . . .

The first of the series of social changes in modern Japan was the destruction of social rank. Before the Restoration it was necessary, for the maintenance of peace and order, to attach great importance to classes and ranks. . . . The *daimyō* were placed at the head of the aristocrats, and such was their authority that, if a merchant or a farmer met a *daimyō's* procession, he was bound to take off his shoes and prostrate himself on the road. Should a commoner offend a *samurai,* the latter was at liberty to slay him with his sword. . . .

This gulf between the two classes finally brought on a difference between them in literary and other tastes. Thus the *samurai* composed Chinese and Japanese poems, while commoners expressed their sentiment in less dignified forms of poetry, *kyoka* and *haikai.* The former class took delight in the paintings of the Tosa and Kanō schools, but the latter's favourites were the *Ukioyé,* which were more gorgeously coloured, and appealed to the popular taste. . . . The former played *go* (checkers), but the latter diverted themselves with *shōgi* (chess).

The upper class was conservative, and adhered to old traditions with fidelity; the lower class was progressive and inclined to novelties, though their tastes were vulgar and their manners unrefined. Yet this system of classes, strict as it was, was shattered by the reformation as completely as if it had been a piece of glass struck by an iron hammer. There exists, it is true, a distinction between the *samurai* class (*shizoku*) and commoners (*héimin*), but the distinction is entirely nominal. Now every one is perfectly free to use any style of dress that pleases his fancy, except at court or on ceremonial occasions. . . . The sharp difference in tastes between the two classes has been toned down to a considerable extent, and equality is gaining ground day by day.

The strict class system of former days was necessarily attended by the attachment of great importance to genealogy. From time immemorial people took fond delight in inquiring into the genealogy of one another, and the class system itself was to a great extent encouraged by this fancy. The mighty Hideyoshi, having no ancestors to be proud of, found it necessary to conceal his humble origin by assuming the family name of Toyotomi. . . .

Since genealogy was so important, people were in mortal fear lest their houses should come to an end, and thought themselves bound by duty to see that such a disaster did not happen in their generation. In their eyes the family was everything, and the individual nothing. A man was worth regarding only in the capacity of a member of a family. He worshipped the guardian gods of his house, but none of his own. . . . Should a man have no male issue, he adopted some one to continue the house; and should his son—even a real son—prove unworthy of maintaining the family honour, he was liable to be disowned and expelled. This family system, so strict and so important, began to die away with the collapse of the social classes, and now few would listen with reverence to any boast of heraldry or of the exalted names of ancestors. People have been converted to the new notion that man should create his status by his own capacity, and that self-made dignity alone adorns him.

When the class system was preserved with so much strictness, people naturally pursued the avocations of the house rather than their own choice. For instance, the carpenter's son became himself a carpenter, and a farmer's children were all brought up to follow the plough. A son who departed from his father's business was despised, and it was taken for granted that he would fail. Consequently, each man had a peculiar appearance which his respective family occupation conferred on him, so that on sight of him even a stranger could tell whether he was an artist, carpenter, or mason.

Another institution which grew up side by side with this hereditary succession of occupations was the strict custom of revering and following one's teacher. A pupil was taught to walk 'seven feet in the rear of his instructor, lest he should tread on the latter's shadow'. The teacher showed the way and the pupil had only to follow it. Hence the pupil was not allowed to depart a step from the teacher's instructions: he was permitted to reproduce but forbidden to improve. It is not surprising, therefore, that the teacher should have become more sparing of his teaching as the pupil advanced, or that he should have tried to sanctify his art by surrounding it with all manner of mythical traditions. If the pupil happened to be of a free and ungovernable turn of mind, and attempted to add his own devices to what was imparted to him, he was certain to provoke his instructor's wrath, and even became liable to be 'excommunicated.' With the advent of the Meiji era, however, everything became free, and every individual was set at liberty to do anything or follow any course. In the choice of occupations, there is no longer now any restriction to fetter the ambition of young people, and the son of a statesman may become an engineer, and a farmer's boy may join the army. At the same time, the teacher's word has ceased to be immutable law, and a school-boy regards his master as nothing more than a temporary guide along the pathway of practical business life.

Chapter Seventeen

Impact of dominance: Africa

THE SLAVE TRADE: EYEWITNESS REPORTS 92

Europe had an even greater impact upon Africa than upon Asia. One manifestation was the slave trade, by which the Europeans transported to the New World millions of Africans. It is estimated that for every 1,000 Africans kidnapped from their villages, only 300 lived to work on the plantations of the New World; the remainder perished either during the march to the coast or during the passage across the Atlantic. The following accounts by eyewitnesses make clear why the casualty rate was so high. The first is by Mungo Park, the famous Scottish explorer, who reached the Niger River. During his first trip he was allowed to travel with a slave caravan, and on his return he wrote the following firsthand account of how the slaves were herded to the coastal ports. The second selection, by a certain Falconbridge, who was a surgeon on one of the ships transporting the slaves across the ocean, reveals the horrors that decimated so many of the slaves during the passage to the Americas.*

Mungo Park

... The slaves which Karfa [the caravan leader] had brought with him were all of them prisoners of war; they had been taken by the Bambarran army in the kingdoms of Wassela and Kaarta, and carried to Sego [Segu], where some of them had remained three years in irons. ...

* M. Park, *Travels in the Interior Districts of Africa ... in 1795, 1796, 1797* (London, 1799), pp. 318-20, 331-34; H. Russell, *Human Cargoes* (London: Longmans, 1948), pp. 30-32.

They were all very inquisitive; but they viewed me at first with looks of horror, and repeatedly asked if my countrymen were cannibals. They were very desirous to know what became of the slaves after they had crossed the salt water. I told them, that they were employed in cultivating the land; but they would not believe me; and one of them putting his hand upon the ground, said with great simplicity, "have you really got such ground as this, to set your feet upon?" A deeply rooted idea, that the whites purchase Negroes for the purpose of devouring them, or of selling them to others, that they may be devoured hereafter, naturally makes the slaves contemplate a journey towards the Coast with great terror; insomuch that the Slatees [slave traders] are forced to keep them constantly in irons, and watch them very closely, to prevent their escape. . . .

In other respects, the treatment of the slaves during their stay at Kamalia, was far from being harsh or cruel. They were led out in their fetters, every morning, to the shade of the tamarind tree, where they were encouraged to play at games of hazard, and sing diverting songs, to keep up their spirits; for though some of them sustained the hardships of their situation with amazing fortitude, the greater part were very much dejected, and would sit all day in a sort of sullen melancholy, with their eyes fixed upon the ground.

April 24th. [1797] . . . As soon as day dawned we set out, and travelled the whole morning over a wild and rocky country, by which my feet were much bruised; and I was sadly apprehensive that I should not be able to keep up with the coffle [caravan] during the day; but I was, in a great measure, relieved from this anxiety, when I observed that others were more exhausted than myself. In particular, the woman slave, who had refused victuals in the morning, began now to lag behind, and complain dreadfully of pains in her legs. Her load was taken from her, and given to another slave, and she was ordered to keep in the front of the coffle. About eleven o'clock, as we were resting by a small rivulet, some of the people discovered a hive of bees in a hollow tree, and they were proceeding to obtain the honey, when the largest swarm I ever beheld, flew out, and attacking the people of the coffle, made us fly in all directions. . . . When our enemies thought fit to desist from pursuing us, and every person was employed in picking out the stings he had received, it was discovered that the poor woman abovementioned, whose name was Nealee, was not come up; and as many of the slaves in their retreat had left their bundles behind them, it became necessary for some persons to return, and bring them. . . . They . . . brought with them poor Nealee, whom they found lying by the rivulet. She was very much exhausted, and had crept to the stream, in hopes to defend herself from the bees by throwing water over her body; but this proved ineffectual; for she was stung in the most dreadful manner.

When the Slatees had picked out the stings as far as they could, she was washed with water, and then rubbed with bruised leaves, but the wretched woman obstinately refused to proceed any farther; declaring, that she would rather die than walk another step. As entreaties and threats were used in vain, the whip was at length applied; and after bearing patiently a few strokes, she started up, and walked with tolerable expedition for four or five hours longer, when she made an attempt to run away from the coffle, but was so very weak, that she fell down in the grass. Though she was unable to rise, the whip was a second time applied, but without effect; upon which Karfa desired two of the Slatees to place her upon the ass which carried our dry provisions; but she could not sit erect; and the ass being very refractory, it was found impossible to carry her forward in that manner. The Slatees however were unwilling to abandon her, the day's journey being nearly ended; they therefore made a sort of litter of bamboo canes, upon which she was placed, and tied on it with slips of bark; this litter was carried upon the heads of two slaves, one walking before the other, and they were followed by two others, who relieved them occasionally. In this manner, the woman was carried forward until it was dark, when we reached a stream of water, at the foot of a high hill called Gankaran-Kooro; and here we stopt for the night, and set about preparing our supper. . . .

April 25th. At daybreak poor Nealee was awakened; but her limbs were now become so stiff and painful, that she could neither walk nor stand; she was therefore lifted, like a corpse, upon the back of the ass; and the Slatees endeavoured to secure her in that situation, by fastening her hands together under the ass's neck, and her feet under the belly, with long slips of bark; but the ass was so very unruly, that no sort of treatment could enduce him to proceed with his load; and as Nealee made no exertion to prevent herself from falling, she was quickly thrown off, and had one of her legs much bruised. Every attempt to carry her forward being thus found ineffectual, the general cry of the coffle was *kang-tegi, kang-tegi,* "cut her throat, cut her throat"; an operation I did not wish to see performed, and therefore marched onwards with the foremost of the coffle. I had not walked above a mile, when one of Karfa's domestic slaves came up to me, with poor Nealee's garment upon the end of his bow, and exclaimed *Nealee affilita* (Nealee is lost). I asked him whether the Slatees had given him the garment, as a reward for cutting her throat; he replied, that Karfa and the schoolmaster would not consent to that measure, but had left her on the road; where undoubtedly she soon perished, and was probably devoured by wild beasts.

The sad fate of this wretched woman, notwithstanding the outcry before-mentioned, made a strong impression on the minds of the whole coffle, and the schoolmaster fasted the whole of the ensuing day, in consequence of it.

Falconbridge

... The men negroes on being brought aboard are immediately fastened two by two by handcuffs on their wrists and by irons riveted on their legs. They are frequently stowed so close as to admit of no other posture than lying on their sides. Neither will the height between decks, unless directly under the grating, permit them the indulgence of an erect posture, especially where there are platforms which is generally the case. These platforms are like shelves about eight or nine feet in breadth, extending from the side of the ship to the centre. They are placed nearly midway between the decks, at the distance of two or three feet from each deck. Upon these the negroes are stowed in the same manner as they are on the deck underneath. It often happens that those who are placed at a distance from the buckets, in endeavoring to get to them, tumble over their companions in consequence of their being shackled. These accidents, though unavoidable, cause continued quarrels in which some of them are always bruised. In this distressed situation they desist from the attempt and this results in a fresh source of disturbance which render the condition of the poor captives still more uncomfortable.

In favorable weather they are fed on deck, but in bad weather the food is given them below. Numberless quarrels take place amongst them during meals, more especially when they are put on short allowance which frequently happens. In that case the weak are obliged to be content with a very scanty portion. Their allowance of water is about half a pint at every meal.

When the negroes refused to take sustenance, I have seen coals of fire, glowing hot, put on a shovel and placed so near their lips as to scorch and burn them, and this has been accompanied with threats of forcing them to swallow coals if they any longer persisted in refusing to eat. These means have generally the desired effect.

I have been informed that a certain ship's captain in the slave trade poured melting lead on such of the negroes as obstinately refused their food.

The negroes are far more violently affected by seasickness than Europeans. It frequently ends in death, especially among the women. The exclusion of fresh air is amongst the most unbearable of their sufferings. Many ships have ventilators, but whenever the sea is rough and the rain heavy, it becomes necessary to shut these and every other means by which air is admitted. The fresh air being thus excluded, the negroes' rooms very soon become unbearably hot. The confined air being breathed repeatedly and the foul smells soon produce sickness and fevers which result in the death of a great number of the slaves. My profession as a doctor requiring it, I frequently went down among them till at length their rooms became so terribly hot as to be bearable only for a short time.

But the extreme heat was not the only suffering they had to endure. The deck, which is the floor of their rooms, was so covered with blood and mucous from their excreta that it resembled a slaughter-house. By only continuing among them for about a quarter of an hour, I was so overcome with the heat, stench and foul air, that I nearly fainted and it was not without help that I was able to get up on deck.

The slaves were so crowded that they had to lie one upon another. This causes such a death rate among them that, without meeting very stormy weather or having a longer voyage than usual, nearly half of them died before the ship arrived at the West Indies. The place allotted for sick negroes is under the half-deck, where they lie on the bare planks. Thus, those who are emaciated often have their skin and even their flesh rubbed off by the motion of the ship from their shoulders, elbows and hips so as to render the bones in those parts quite bare. The surgeon, going between decks in the morning, often finds several of the slaves dead, and sometimes a dead and a living negro fastened together by their irons.

93 LIVINGSTONE AND THE RAIN DOCTOR

The African explorers did not merely discover new lands and new rivers; they also found new peoples and learned about their religions, customs, and forms of political organization, as is illustrated in the following account by the most outstanding and best known of the explorers, David Livingstone. Between 1843 and 1846, he was stationed at Mabotsa, a little south of the Kalahari Desert. At this early stage Livingstone was a missionary first and an explorer second, so he *earnestly tried to convert the natives to Christianity. In the following selection he recorded with striking fairness and detachment the arguments he encountered in a conversation with a rain doctor.**

As the Bakwains believed that there must be some connection between the presence of "God's Word" in their town and these successive and distressing droughts, they looked with no good will at the church-bell, but still they invariably treated us with kindness and respect. I am not aware of ever having had an enemy in the tribe. The only avowed cause of dislike was expressed by a very influential and sensible man, the uncle of Sechele. "We like you as well as if you had been born among us; you are the only white man we can become familiar with; but we wish you to give up that everlasting preaching and praying; we cannot become familiar with that at all. You see we never get rain, while those tribes who never pray as we do obtain abundance." This was a fact; and we often saw it raining on the hills, ten miles off, while it would not look at us "even with one eye." . . .

As for the rain-makers, they carried the sympathies of the people along with them, and not without reason. With the following arguments they were all acquainted, and in order to understand their force we must place ourselves in their position, and believe, as they do, that all medicines act by a mysterious charm. The term for cure may be translated "charm."

Medical Doctor.—Hail, friend! How very many medicines you have about you this morning! Why, you have every medicine in the country here.

Rain-Doctor.—Very true, my friend; and I ought; for the whole country needs the rain which I am making.

M.D.—So you really believe that you can command the clouds? I think that can be done by God alone.

R.D.—We both believe the very same thing. It is God that makes the rain, but I pray to him by means of these medicines, and, the rain coming, of course it is then mine. It was I who made it for the Bakwains for many years, when they were at Shokuane; through my wisdom, too, their women became fat and shining. Ask them; they will tell you the same as I do.

M.D.—But we are distinctly told in the parting words of our Saviour that we can pray to God acceptably in His name alone, and not by means of medicines.

R.D.—Truly, but God told *us* differently. He made black men first, and did not love us, as he did the white men. He made you beautiful, and gave you clothing, and guns, and gunpowder, and horses, and wagons, and many other things about which we know nothing. But toward us he had no heart. He gave us nothing, except the assegai, and cattle, and rain-making; and he did not give us hearts like yours. We never love each other. Other tribes place medicines about our country to prevent the rain, so that we may be dispersed by hunger, and go to them, and augment their power. We must dissolve their charms by our medicines. God has given us one little thing, which you know nothing of. He has given us the knowledge of certain medicines by which we can make rain. *We* do not despise those things which you possess, though we are ignorant of them. We don't understand your book, but we don't despise

* D. Livingstone, *Missionary Travels and Researches in South Africa* (London, 1857), pp. 22-25.

it. *You* ought not to despise our little knowledge, though you are ignorant of it.

M.D.—I don't despise what I am ignorant of; I only think you are mistaken in saying that you have medicines which can influence the rain at all.

R.D.—That's just the way people speak when they talk on a subject of which they have no knowledge. When we first opened our eyes, we found our forefathers making rain, and we follow in their footsteps. You, who send to Kuruman for corn, and irrigate your garden, may do without rain; *we* cannot manage in that way. If we had no rain, the cattle would have no pasture, the cows give no milk, our children become lean and die, our wives run away to other tribes who do make rain, and have corn, and the whole tribe become dispersed and lost; our fire would go out.

M.D.—I quite agree with you as to the value of the rain; but you cannot charm the clouds by medicines. You wait till you see the clouds come, then you use your medicines, and take the credit which belongs to God only.

R.D.—I use my medicines, and you employ yours; we are both doctors, and doctors are not deceivers. You give a patient medicine. Sometimes God is pleased to heal him by means of your medicine; sometimes not—he dies. When he is cured, you take the credit of what God does. I do the same. Sometimes God grants us rain, sometimes not. When he does, we take the credit of the charm. When a patient dies, you don't give up trust in your medicine, neither do I when rain fails. If you wish me to leave off my medicines, why continue your own?

M.D.—I give medicines to living creatures within my reach, and can see the effects though no cure follows; you pretend to charm the clouds which are so far above us that your medicines never reach them. The clouds usually lie in one direction, and your smoke goes in another. God alone can command the clouds. Only try and wait patiently; God will give us rain without your medicines.

R.D.—Mahala-ma-kapa-a-a! ! Well, I always thought white men were wise till this morning. Who ever thought of making trial of starvation? Is death pleasant then?

M.D.—Could you make it rain on one spot and not on another?

R.D.—I wouldn't think of trying. I like to see the whole country green, and all the people glad; the women clapping their hands and giving me their ornaments for thankfulness, and lullilooing for joy.

M.D.—I think you deceive both them and yourself.

R.D.—Well, then, there is a pair of us (meaning both are rogues).

The above is only a specimen of their way of reasoning, in which, when the language is well understood, they are perceived to be remarkably acute. These arguments are generally known, and I never succeeded in convincing a single individual of their fallacy, though I tried to do so in every way I could think of. Their faith in medicines as charms is unbounded. The general effect of argument is to produce the impression that you are not anxious for rain at all; and it is very undesirable to allow the idea to spread that you do not take a generous interest in their welfare.

The opening up of Africa by the explorers was followed by the partitioning of the entire continent amongst the European powers. By 1914 only Liberia and Ethiopia remained independent of European rule. The customary procedure in acquiring territory was for a European agent to induce native chieftains to sign documents accepting foreign suzerainty. In return, they received either some token payment or simply the assurance of protection by the mysterious, all-powerful sovereign in Europe. An exceptionally successful practitioner of this craft was the German Dr. Carl Peters, who in 1884 acquired in East Africa no less than 60,000 square miles in ten days. The following selection from his account of a later expedition describes how he concluded a "treaty" with Sultan Hugo of the Gallas.*

It was on September 28th [1889] at two in the afternoon, that I met the Sultan Hugo and the great men of the Gallas, under the before-mentioned tree on the further side of the Tana, at a great consultation, to bring the question to a definite conclusion. ... Besides Sultan Hugo, three sultans of the Wapokomo had made their appearance, to take part in the deliberations. From the Sultan Hugo, with whom I had discussed the affair beforehand, I had heard that there was among the Gallas a strong opposition to my proposals, and I therefore made up my mind for an interesting assembly. Beside and behind Hugo reclined the warriors of the Gallas, with whom my Somalis exchanged looks of defiance. The hatred between the two races was so strong, that several times I had the greatest trouble to prevent a sudden outbreak and bloodshed. Every moment the Gallas were starting up, brandishing their spears, to rush upon the Somalis, or my Somalis were bringing their musket stocks to their shoulders to shoot down the Gallas. ...

I opened the proceedings with a short address, in which I asked the Gallas if they wished to have peace or war with me. Thereupon Sultan Hugo and the elders of the Wapokomo expressed their opinion at great length something to the following effect: "We know that thou art a great man, and hast much power, and that thou mayst have still more. We have also heard that more Germans are following thee, and will soon arrive here. Thou art as God, compared with us, and we wish for peace with thee. There have been Englishmen here, too. But we know that the Englishmen are quite little, and thou art very great. Thou art as God. Give us peace, great Lord; we will do everything that thou desirest." To this I replied as follows, after the general sentiment of the peace party among the Gallas had been thus declared: "I have been sent hither by the great nation of the Germans ('Wadutschi'). We dwell in the middle of Europe, and are the strongest of all the nations of the earth. You know the English and you know us; you can judge for yourselves which of us is the greater. But we make war upon those who attack us first; we overthrow them and kill them; while we give peace to all those who wish to live peaceably together with the Germans. We protect the weak; we cast down the strong, if they rise up against us. I am now only passing through the country of the Gallas, and am going to march far to the west, through the Massais, to a great German who lives alone in the middle of Africa; and in this, if you

* C. Peters, *New Light on Dark Africa* (London: Ward, Lock, 1891), pp. 133-36.

wish to be our friends you must help me. Westward of this is a great mountain, which is white; to that I wish to go first, and what I want of you is, that you give me guides thither. That is the mountain Kenia, in the land of the Massais; thither I want guides from you. I know that on the way thither there is no food for us, therefore I want food from you, and boats to carry it up the river. If you will help me in these two things, I am ready here to hoist our flag, which the Somalis know very well, and which will prevent them from attacking you. Here is a writing of the Somalis, that I will leave here with you. It is from the Sheriff Hussein. In case the Somalis should come, show it to them, and they will be your friends."

Long discussions now arose, after the Gallas had declared themselves willing to grant my requests generally. Twelve boatmen were provided for me at once, whose names I entered, and who only asked permission to go to their homes and take leave of their families, before removing into my camp. Three guides were also brought before me, who were to show me the way over Hamege, and from thence to the Kenia. It was five o'clock when these matters were settled, and I laid before them the treaty, which, in pursuance of the unanimous decision of the popular assembly, Sultan Hugo signed next morning in the name of the Gallas. The treaty is worded thus:—

> The following treaty is this day concluded between Dr. Carl Peters and the Galla Sultan Hugo:
>
> Dr. Peters acknowledges as Sultan's territory the land on the Tana, from Massa to the Kenia.
>
> Sultan Hugo places himself, with all his territory, under the protection of Dr. Peters. Dr. Carl Peters will endeavor to obtain for the Galla sultanate the friendship of His Majesty the German Emperor.
>
> Nevertheless this treaty is not dependent upon the granting of the protection of the German Empire or upon its ratification by any European power.
>
> Sultan Hugo cedes to Dr. Carl Peters the right of working the country above and below the ground in every direction.
>
> This right especially includes the exclusive commercial monopoly, the right of establishing plantations, and the exclusive mining monopoly.
>
> If gold is found, Sultan Hugo is to have a quarter of the net profit from the production of it.
>
> Dr. Carl Peters is to be supreme lord in the country of the Gallas, to command the armed forces, and judge the people.
>
> This is done for the blessing and welfare of the Galla land.
>
> After several long conferences, and after its contents have been deliberated, and unanimously resolved upon, in a great public popular meeting by the Gallas in general, this treaty is formally concluded this day by Sultan Hugo and Dr. Peters.
>
> Dr. Peters.
Hugo's mark.
>
> Witnesses {
>
> Von Tiedemann.
>
> Mark of Hugo Valogalgal, brother and Prime Minister of the Sultan.
>
> The Interpreter's mark.

The Africans took a very different view of what was happening to their lands than did the Europeans. Traditionally the Africans had regarded their lands as inalienable and owned collectively by the tribe. It was inconceivable to them that their chief's signing a piece of paper meant the transference of rights to the white intruders. Accordingly, they never reconciled themselves to the loss of their lands, which resulted in repercussions that are all too evident today. The attitude of the Africans toward this European "expansion" is evident in the following story popular among the Kikuyu people of Kenya. It is worth noting that Dr. Peters visited the Kikuyu during his travels, and also that this story is taken from a book written by the present-day famous Kikuyu nationalist and Kenya leader, Jomo Kenyatta.*

. . . Once upon a time an elephant made a friendship with a man. One day a heavy thunderstorm broke out, the elephant went to his friend, who had a little hut at the edge of the forest, and said to him: "My dear good man, will you please let me put my trunk inside your hut to keep it out of this torrential rain?" The man, seeing what situation his friend was in, replied: "My dear good elephant, my hut is very small, but there is room for your trunk and myself. Please put your trunk in gently." The elephant thanked his friend, saying: "You have done me a good deed and one day I shall return your kindness." But what followed? As soon as the elephant put his trunk inside the hut, slowly he pushed his head inside, and finally flung the man out in the rain, and then lay down comfortably inside his friend's hut, saying: "My dear good friend, your skin is harder than mine, and as there is not enough room for both of us, you can afford to remain in the rain while I am protecting my delicate skin from the hailstorm."

The man, seeing what his friend had done to him, started to grumble, the animals in the nearby forest heard the noise and came to see what was the matter. All stood around listening to the heated argument between the man and his friend the elephant. In this turmoil the lion came along roaring, and said in a loud voice: "Don't you all know that I am the King of the Jungle! How dare anyone disturb the peace of my kingdom?" On hearing this the elephant, who was one of the high ministers in the jungle kingdom, replied in a soothing voice, and said: "My Lord, there is no disturbance of the peace in your kingdom. I have only been having a little discussion with my friend here as to the possession of this little hut which your lordship sees me occupying." The lion, who wanted to have "peace and tranquillity" in his kingdom, replied in a noble voice, saying: "I command my ministers to appoint a Commission of Enquiry to go thoroughly into this matter and report accordingly." He then turned to the man and said: "You have done well by establishing friendship with my people, especially with the elephant who is one of my honourable ministers of state. Do not grumble any more, your hut is not lost to you. Wait until the sitting of my Imperial Commission, and there you will be given plenty of opportunity to state your case. I am sure that you will be pleased with the findings of the Commission." The man was very pleased by

* J. Kenyatta, *Facing Mount Kenya* (London: M. Secker, 1953), pp. 47-52.

these sweet words from the King of the Jungle, and innocently waited for his opportunity, in the belief, that naturally, the hut would be returned to him.

The elephant, obeying the command of his master, got busy with other ministers to appoint the Commission of Enquiry. The following elders of the jungle were appointed to sit in the Commission: (1) Mr. Rhinoceros; (2) Mr. Buffalo; (3) Mr. Alligator; (4) The Rt. Hon. Mr. Fox to act as chairman; and (5) Mr. Leopard to act as Secretary to the Commission. On seeing the personnel, the man protested and asked if it was not necessary to include in this Commission a member from his side. But he was told that it was impossible, since no one from his side was well enough educated to understand the intricacy of jungle law. Further, that there was nothing to fear, for the members of the Commission were all men of repute for their impartiality in justice, and as they were gentlemen chosen by God to look after the interests of races less adequately endowed with teeth and claws, he might rest assured that they would investigate the matter with the greatest care and report impartially.

The Commission sat to take the evidence. The Rt. Hon. Mr. Elephant was first called. He came along with a superior air, brushing his tusks with a sapling which Mrs. Elephant had provided, and in an authoritative voice said: "Gentlemen of the Jungle, there is no need for me to waste your valuable time in relating a story which I am sure you all know. I have always regarded it as my duty to protect the interests of my friends, and this appears to have caused the misunderstanding between myself and my friend here. He invited me to save his hut from being blown away by a hurricane. As the hurricane had gained access owing to the unoccupied space in the hut, I considered it necessary, in my friend's own interests, to turn the undeveloped space to a more economic use by sitting in it myself; a duty which any of you would undoubtedly have performed with equal readiness in similar circumstances."

After hearing the Rt. Hon. Mr. Elephant's conclusive evidence, the Commission called Mr. Hyena and other elders of the jungle, who all supported what Mr. Elephant had said. They then called the man, who began to give his own account of the dispute. But the Commission cut him short, saying: "My good man, please confine yourself to relevant issues. We have already heard the circumstances from various unbiased sources; all we wish you to tell us is whether the undeveloped space in your hut was occupied by anyone else before Mr. Elephant assumed his position?" The man began to say: "No, but—" But at this point the Commission declared that they had heard sufficient evidence from both sides and retired to consider their decision. After enjoying a delicious meal at the expense of the Rt. Hon. Mr. Elephant, they reached their verdict, called the man, and declared as follows: "In our opinion this dispute has arisen through a regrettable misunderstanding due to the backwardness of your ideas. We consider that Mr. Elephant has fulfilled his sacred duty of protecting your interests. As it is clearly for your good that the space should be put to its most economic use, and as you yourself have not yet reached the stage of expansion which would enable you to fill it, we consider it necessary to arrange a compromise to suit both parties. Mr. Elephant shall continue his occupation of your hut, but we give you permission to look for a site where you can build another hut more suited to your needs, and we will see that you are well protected."

The man, having no alternative, and fearing that his refusal might expose him to the teeth and claws of members of the Commission, did as they suggested. But no sooner had he built another hut than Mr. Rhinoceros charged in with his horn lowered and ordered the man to quit. A Royal Commission was again appointed to look into the matter, and the same finding was given. This procedure was repeated until Mr. Buffalo, Mr. Leopard, Mr. Hyena and the rest were all accommodated with new huts. Then the man decided that he must adopt an effective method of protection, since Commissions of Enquiry did not seem to be of any use to him. He sat down and said: "Ng'enda thi ndeagaga motegi," which literally means "there is nothing that treads on the earth that cannot be trapped," or in other words, you can fool people for a time, but not for ever.

Early one morning, when the huts already occupied by the jungle lords were all beginning to decay and fall to pieces, he went out and built a bigger and better hut a little distance away. No sooner had Mr. Rhinoceros seen it than he came rushing in, only to find that Mr. Elephant was already inside, sound asleep. Mr. Leopard next came in at the window, Mr. Lion, Mr. Fox, and Mr. Buffalo entered the doors, while Mr. Hyena howled for a place in the shade and Mr. Alligator basked on the roof. Presently they all began disputing about their rights of penetration, and from disputing they came to fighting, and while they were all embroiled together the man set the hut on fire and burnt it to the ground, jungle lords and all. Then he went home, saying: "Peace is costly, but it's worth the expense," and lived happily ever after.

EUROPE'S IMPACT: ECONOMIC **96**

The partitioning of Africa brought with it far-reaching economic consequences. Mines were opened, roads and railways constructed; white settlers moved into the fertile and healthy uplands, and Africans everywhere were compelled by various means to work on plantations and in mines. For the first time, the African was involved in the worldwide money economy, and subordinated, directly or indirectly, to the white man who was everywhere the boss. Precisely what these changes meant is evident in the following reply of an Anang (Nigerian) chief when asked which were better, the "old days" or modern times.*

Things have changed very much during the last few years. The beginning of Native ["indirect"] Administration and taxation has not all been good. The old men and chiefs are much poorer than the young men today. Children were more obedient to their parents than at present. Strong-headed sons and daughters were mercilessly punished. The young men lived in their fathers' compounds and worked for them. They might work for others and have some money but they could not make use of it without the knowledge and consent of the old men. The Father of the House had to protect them and provide food

* "The Story of Udo Akpabio of the Anang Tribe, Southern Nigeria," recorded by the Rev. W. Groves, in M. F. Perham, ed., *Ten Africans* (London: Faber, 1936), pp. 57-59. Reprinted by permission of Northwestern University Press.

and clothing. He would marry wives for his sons and give them some yams to add with their own to maintain themselves with their wives. They had to continue helping the old men and the people of the compound. Now, they look after their own interests. Sometimes they will give assistance if there is any big trouble. But at present, it is very hard for some people to get a helping hand if they have no money, for every small piece of work needs payment.

Before taxation we were informed that the price of palm produce would be raised, but now, oil and palm kernels are very little valued by the Europeans. As palm produce is the chief means of living, I do not know what the life of the people will be in a few years' time as regards the payment of tax and the buying of food. It is a struggle to work out ways and means for maintenance and taxation.

Taxation has also increased the number of thieves. There are many whose names have been recorded as taxpayers, but they have no means of fulfilling this condition. They have no proper work and neither can they get any in these days. Men come to me for help, asking for work to save them from stealing. I do my best for them. When the time comes to pay the tax there seems to be a plague of thieving. Sometimes the young men run away to different parts of the country and do not return to their homes for a long time. Some will stay away for one and two years. During this long absence the Father of the Family has to find the money to pay the full assessment of the tax. He has to pay for the absent ones and can get no relief unless he can prove that they are dead.

The paying of tax has done another evil thing. Young men apply to the District Officer [British colonial official] for work as clerks, messengers or labourers. The officers refer them to the chiefs. If the applicants are disappointed in their request they put the blame on the chiefs. For this they find ways and means of killing their chiefs.

In the native courts there are many more disturbances than there used to be years ago. In judging cases many people stand up and give their own decision even though they are not the elected chiefs. The District Officers of this time differ very much from those we had formerly; whenever they go to some courts they tell the non-members [those who are not chiefs] that they all have right in everything just because they have paid the tax. . . .

On the other hand there are many advantages derived from this new fashion of government. There are many new and better roads throughout the district. We are not now compelled to make and look after them. There are special labourers who work every day to keep them in good condition. They are paid from taxation funds. We have no trouble about carrying loads. This is all done by motors bought from the tax money. When we are called to build any house or do any kind of work we are now paid for it. Many bridges have been built. In some places where the people have to walk many miles for their water, deep wells have been made in their towns.

The establishment of many courts has done good in keeping all the villages in closer touch with the Government. At the same time it is bad in some ways. It brings a separation, jealousy and enmity between one clan and another. At present, when a man from one clan sues a man of another clan and the case is tried in the defendant's area, the chiefs of that court may sometimes be partial and spoil the case. This was not so when we had the central court. . . . The people would deal with one another as brothers.

This new system has also done good in the way it is encouraging education. Several schools have been built for different clans. There is also a Training

College where our best young men can become teachers. These are all paid for and supported by our tax.

*Europe affected Africa's culture as well as its economy. The key role in this field was played by the missionary, the only European who came with the deliberate intention of changing the African's way of life. The earlier reading, "Livingstone and the Doctor," shows that the missionaries were not always successful, especially in the early days when the African villages were virtually unaffected by the white man. But gradually, and in various ways, the missionaries left their mark. How one of them did so is described in the following account from the autobiography of Prince Modupe, an African who came to the United States in 1922 and decided to remain here. The incident he describes occurred during his boyhood when he was living amongst his people, the So-So tribe, in the village of Dubricka in present-day Guinea.**

Everyone was abuzz about the expected arrival of the white man with the powerful juju. If his magic was more powerful than ours, then we must have it. That was Grandfather's decree. Grandfather wanted our people to have the best of everything. I doubt now that he had the slightest notion of the sweeping changes the new juju would bring with it. He probably thought of it as similar to the juju with which we were familiar, only more potent.

We believed in the existence of a demon who was said to be white in color. But of course this man we were expecting could not be an ogre or Grandfather would not receive him. There were a few other white, or nearly white things in our lives—cotton, white chickens, white cola, grubs in rotten stumps, white ants. These seemed natural and everyday enough but a white human was beyond simple imagining.

As I listened to the wild speculation among the villagers, the image which formed in my mind was that of a white ant or termite queen. After she has been fertilized, she is sealed in a clay cyst in the castellated termite mound and her abdomen becomes hugely distended, several inches long. If this cyst is dug out and cracked open, the amazing abdomen, egg-swollen, can be seen softly palpitating. I wondered whether white human skin was soft as a swollen termite belly and whether the coursing of blood and the processes of digestion could be seen through a milkily transparent outer covering, unpleasantly soft to the touch.

. . . . .

Finally, the white man arrived. My first sight of him was a delightful relief. He did not appear to have demon quality and although his belly was large, it was not out of proportion to his head like the termite queen's. The only part of him that was much out of scale was his feet which were encased in

* Abridged from Prince Modupe, *I Was a Savage* (New York: Harcourt, 1957), pp. 62-72. © 1957 by Harcourt, Brace & World, Inc., and reprinted with their permission.

leather. For some reason, I had believed from childhood that to be a real man one had to have a large belly and big feet. This fellow had both and he looked human besides. Furthermore, he was not really white as milk is white, not the portion of him which showed, at least; he was more the color of leather. Most of him was covered; the black coat hung down past his knees, and the short stocky neck was bound with a band of cloth which was really white. His lips seemed like nothing more than a faintly red slit in his face and his nose seemed bird-beakish long and thin. His wife and a little girl-child were with him, and they, too, were encased in clothing. The child had hair which hung to her shoulders and was the color of gold. It was in ringlets like shavings from the chisels of our wood carvers, not springy and crisp like mine. The three were led across the clearing to the royal stool where my grandfather sat waiting for them. The elders, the witch doctors, and the head warriors moved forward with them as they advanced to stand before the chief. The rest of us, out of custom, remained in the background, not pressing too close. ... Grandfather sat his stool with grave dignity. There was a waiting-to-see in his posture as the missionary placed gifts at his feet. ...

Finally, stools were brought for the man and his family. If the stools had not been fetched, it would have meant lack of approval of the missionary's manners and lack of further interest on Grandfather's part. The interview would have been over. ... All that interested me at the moment was getting closer to the heap of gifts at Grandfather's feet.

When I had wormed my way into view of them, the objects seemed to be new things and there was glitter among them. They did not have the earth quality of our own artifacts. I later came to know these things as a Bible, a camera, a mirror, a kaleidoscope, shoes, a high hat, cigarettes, matches, canned goods, shiny trinkets, and yard goods. There was something else which may need a bit of explanation to an American reader—a keg of whiskey. We had palm wine to drink, a mild fermented brew of palm sap, but we had never heard of distilled liquor. In time I was to learn that the particular missionary who visited us belonged to a denomination which makes a distinction between temperance and abstinence. Their ministers are allowed to drink and to smoke but not to excess. I suppose our visitor thought that mellowing our minds toward his words was a worthy use of whiskey.

The photographs which the man brought showing bridges and cities, trains, boats, big buildings, were not impressive to us even when we were allowed to view them at close range. Having had no experience with the diminished scale of things in a photograph, we gained no concept of magnitude. But there were other pictures which disturbed me deeply. They were bright depictions of heaven and hell, which I later learned were made expressly for mission use. In them all the bright angels hovering over the golden streets had white faces. The tortured creatures in hell with the orange-red flames licking over agonized contorted bodies all had black faces! ...

The missionary spoke to us through his interpreter. He denounced our old ceremonious life, the rituals, especially sacrifice. He said that we worshipped wood and stone and graven images. This was not accurate but no one was impolite enough to contradict him. Anyway, it would have been too difficult to make a stranger understand. For a moment there was a deep silence. Someone coughed. An old man shuffled his feet. An elder next to me rumbled in his throat. I turned my head and saw that it was Granduncle D'gba. I gave my attention back to the missionary, wondering why Grandfather allowed him to go on insulting everything we held sacred and valuable. I could see that

Grandfather was trying his best to follow the spirited ranting of the white man. His expression was puzzled and he was trying his best to understand. Perhaps the juju would be clearer to us than the speech.

The crowd became restless. All this talk-talk! Their politeness held up but they shifted their weight on their feet, squirmed a little, rustled quietly. Finally, the harangue ended.

The missionary picked up the mirror, made a few twists of his wrist as though gathering up the invisible power in the vicinity of it, and gazed into the glass. Grandfather leaned forward watching closely. The white man proffered the shiny handle to Grandfather. My grandfather, who had always been considered a brave man by his people, jerked back away from it. Then, warily, he accepted it. He did not gaze into it at once. It was plain that he feared the thing. The missionary spoke reassurance.

The crowd tensed. Grandfather had to go through with what he had started or forfeit pride. He looked into the mirror. A cry of surprise escaped from his throat. He turned the handle, looking at the back, and saw his reflection disappear. When he turned it to the front side, there he was again! He spoke to his brother D'gba. . . .

D'gba reluctantly approached, his face contorted with scorn. An order from the chief was an order, brother or not. Every muscle in his body spoke of his aversion to the command but he dared not speak against it. Grandfather handed D'gba the mirror, pointed at the image. D'gba howled and fell to the ground, the mirror in his hand. He laid the fearful thing in the dust and smashed it with his fist. Perhaps he thought to liberate his trapped self from it, to get his face back. The glass broke, cutting his hand. Blood dripped from him as he stood up.

Blood has mystic significance to an African: Blood is life-stuff; life drips away with blood. . . .

While an excited murmur ran through the crowd and D'gba examined his red-dripping hand, the missonary spoke quickly and emphatically to Grandfather. Grandfather nodded and gave us the verdict. What had happened was due to D'gba's resentment of the white man's god. D'gba had been punished as we had all seen. The white man's god was capable of punishments far beyond this. What was the loss of a little blood compared to having to spend all of the time not yet come, rolling in the hot flames of hell? A black devil with horns kept the fires tended. . . .

The missionary followed up his initial triumph with a can opener. With great flourishes he opened the can of beans and tasted some of the contents to show they were not poisoned. He offered some to Grandfather who tasted a small portion and then larger portions, approving the flavor of this wonderful *ewa,* beans not cooked, yet ready to eat, coming all together from a shining "pod" which was hard like iron. The other articles were shown, demonstrated, explained. Grandfather was enchanted with the kaleidoscope, reluctant to put it down.

The missionary preached while the portions of whiskey were doled out, first to the chief and the elders, then to each villager in turn as they formed in line. Grandfather jerked his head at the first taste and coughed, but after the second attempt he was smacking his lips and requesting more.

A long time was required for the end section of the queue to come abreast of the keg. The young men had to defer to the elder ones in this as in all things, and many of the elders, after downing their allotments, would slip back into line with their age group for second helpings. . . . As many as drank and drew away and returned found themselves mellowed and ready to give themselves up to the new faith.

I noticed that Grandfather's eyes became blood-shot. When he stood up to walk he no longer moved with slow dignified royal steps. Uncertainty swayed him from side to side but he wavered toward the diminishing keg. His purpose was certain even if his feet were not. Grandfather was drunk! I did not know what drunkenness was so I attributed Grandfather's condition to his body's being possessed with the power of the new juju. I saw him waving the Bible in the air as he announced that we accepted the new religion for our own. It was true, then, I concluded, that the white juju was superior to our own. Its power had caught D'gba and drawn blood, its power had transformed Grandfather, its power produced the wonderful objects the missionary had brought, its power warmed the belly, so the men said who had swallowed the sacred elixir from the keg. . . .

Grandfather invited the white man to stay to dinner and for the night. The invitation was accepted. The women and children retreated to start the cooking and evening chores. Great fires were lighted in the compound and the warriors gathered around them. Good food was brought, steaming hot. I stayed as close to the missionary and his family as I dared. My eyes lingered on the little girl with the golden curls. I reasoned that she must be immensely wealthy to have gold-stuff for hair. It was because of her father's juju, of course, that this wealth had come to her and to her family.

. . . for the first time in my life I felt doubt about the desirability of a brown skin and kinky hair. Why did gold grow above the faces of little white girls, who according to the pictures sprouted shining wings as soon as they went to live in the glorious compound of worthy Deads, a compound glowing with gold under their pale little feet? How could they smile with what seemed a mother love delight as they peered down over the edge of the golden compound into a fiery pit . . . filled with black people who might have been So-Sos? Why did the horned demon who fueled the fires of hell have a black face like us? Why did he tooth his mouth with wild laughter while he seared the flesh of small boys who were as black as himself?

Perhaps the real reason why my limbs trembled and my hands shook was that a little of the pride and glory which I had felt in being a So-So youth had gone out with the light of this eventful day!

98 EUROPE'S IMPACT: POLITICAL

The economic and cultural changes in Africa described in the above two selections inevitably had far-reaching political repercussions. The traditional authority of tribal chieftains was undermined first by the new European administrators and then by the Western-educated Africans, resulting in the spread of new political ideas and aspirations which led up to the triumphant nationalist movement. The sources and the nature of this political revolution are reflected in the first of the following selections, a brief autobiographical sketch by Dr. Hastings Banda, leader of the Nyasaland nationalist party, who became prime minister of the new state *of Malawi in 1964. The second selection, by English writer Elspeth Huxley, analyzes the effect of the political revolution on Africa's traditional tribalism.**

Dr. Hastings Banda

I was born in Kasunga, Nyasaland, the son of an aristocratic family in my tribe. I was educated in a Church of Scotland mission. I left Nyasaland as a boy of 13 in standard three because I desired to get the kind of education I couldn't get in Nyasaland.

I walked to Johannesburg—a total of 1,000 miles—but not in a single stretch; I walked and walked and walked. Then I worked in the Rand mines, first underground, but then on the surface for the compound manager because I spoke English. I refused to go to the Dutch Reform Church and went to an African Methodist Episcopal Church. The Church helped me go to Wilberforce Academy in Ohio.

I received a diploma in 1929. I had talked to the Kiwanis Club in Marion, Indiana, and Dr. Herald—a white man—said that he wanted me to go to his alma mater, the University of Indiana. He helped me attend that university at Bloomington and from there I transferred to the University of Chicago. I received my Bachelor of Philosophy degree, studying political science and history, on December 22, 1931. Then I went to Meharry Medical School in Nashville, where I graduated in 1937. I continued my medical studies in Edinburgh and was an assistant medical officer in Liverpool, and then practiced in London.

When Federation of the Rhodesias and Nyasaland was suggested, I led the opposition in London. The Colonial Office said Federation was for economic, defense, and communications reasons, but the Southern Rhodesian whites demanded it to make sure that Nyasaland and Northern Rhodesia would not become independent states. Federation is not "partnership"—a word dangled as bait before British liberals—but it is domination by the racial policies of Southern Rhodesia which differ in degree but not in essence from those of South Africa. After independence, there can be genuine partnership, even Federation—but only of equals, entered into freely. Then Nyasaland might turn to Tanganyika, Northern Rhodesia, and Congo.

When Federation was imposed on my people in 1952, I decided to leave London. I went to Ghana and practiced medicine from 1953 to 1958. At the annual meeting of the African National Congress of Nyasaland in 1957 two resolutions were adopted, one calling for self-government, the other asking for secession from Federation. I was asked by my people to return to Nyasaland after 40 years to help them attain these objectives.

I returned on July 6, 1958. I toured the whole country and within less than four months I had all of Nyasaland on fire—politically. Because I refused to compromise, the government devised a story [of] . . . the so-called massacre plot. . . .

On March 3, 1959, more than 1,000 of us were arrested. I remained in prison for 13 months, without charges and without trial. What did I do in prison? I taught other prisoners. I studied the constitutional history of Eng-

* H. K. Banda, "Return to Nyasaland," *Africa Today,* II (June, 1960), 9; E. Huxley, "Two Revolutions That Are Changing Africa," *The New York Times Magazine* (May 19, 1957), pp. 9, 69-70. © 1957 by The New York Times Company. Reprinted by permission.

land and read biographies—of Washington, Jefferson, Lincoln, Franklin. I began my own autobiography. I was released on April 1, 1960. The British are the only colonial people who send a man to prison today only to invite him to Westminster [Parliament] if not Buckingham Palace tomorrow.

Elspeth Huxley

. . . Everywhere colonialism, in its old form, is on the way out. In places it has gone altogether. . . . In other countries it will linger on, but no one supposes that the winds of independence can be halted at this or that international boundary. . . .

The second revolution is the breakdown of tribalism, under which Africans have lived, not for a century or two, but for untold thousands of years. Tribalism is a pattern of living ingrained into their very bones and blood. . . .

Unquestioning loyalty to the chief or tribal council, and a reverence for ancestral spirits who remain active members of the family circle, are the twin pillars of tribalism. It is a system that binds people together, usually with bonds of ritual and secrecy, into close-knit units based on what anthropologists call the extended family—distant cousins and half-brothers-in-law as well as one's own parents and children—and for centuries it enabled them to survive and even prosper in the primitive conditions of pre-colonial society.

It is this system that is going, swept away by a great tide of Western education and political change. Nationalists like Nkrumah, and others less famous but as powerful in their own countries—Dr. Azikiwe and Chief Awolowo in Nigeria, Dr. Enderley in the Cameroons, Tom Mboya of Kenya, M. Houphouet-Boigny of the Ivory Coast, M. Senghor of Senegal, Julius Nyerere, the trade unionist of Tanganyika; Harry Nkumbula of Northern Rhodesia, Wellington Chirwa of Nyasaland—these and other educated, Westernized leaders ride the crest of the wave that is carrying to remote bush villages and roadless plains not simply Western customs and techniques, but a whole new social order.

Away with chiefs, welcome democracy; down with ritual, up with schools; out with peasantry, in with industry and trade unions; abolish the village council, set up the ballot box. These are the current demands, that is the revolution that is shaking to its foundations the oldest and most baffling continent of them all.

No revolution as profound as this can be made without destroying good as well as bad, without creating doubts as well as hopes. Votes, universal suffrage, Cabinets, Assemblies, Prime Ministers—these things are as foreign to Africa as refrigerators and telephones. The question is how many of them Africans will really want to keep. When the last palefaced civil servant has handed over his files to his native successor, will the set-up begin to drift back into something more native to the old Africa?

That is one doubt: that people only one generation removed from tribalism, still fearful of magic and ancestral spirits, still (in the main) illiterate and ignorant of the larger world, may find themselves unable to resist the blandishments of demagogues, and the temptation to barter their votes for impossible promises, or sell them to the highest bidder. Difficulties of keeping order may be such that leaders of the new central governments may take unto themselves the powers of dictators in order to prevent disintegration. There is, in short, the danger that the West is trying to sell the tribesmen of Africa something they will be unable to use, like television sets before there is any electricity.

Not long ago I asked an African politician, an Oxford graduate and now a Cabinet Minister, what, in his opinion, would happen after the Europeans withdrew. What about the talk of bribery, of rigged elections, of politicians lining their pockets with public money? (An independent tribunal, for instance, recently found the Prime Minister of Eastern Nigeria guilty of dipping into the treasury to prop up an insolvent bank, of which he and several members of his family were the directors.)

He replied indirectly. The spirit of the English Puritans, he said, acclimatized in North America, doesn't thrive in Africa. "It needs a cold winter," he smiled. "You never find it in the sunny countries—Spain, Italy, South America." He waved his cigar in an expansive gesture. "It may be," he added, "that we shall revert to more *human* standards."

And it may be that these things do not matter. The right to abuse freedom is, after all, inherent in the right to exercise it. And who are we to cast the first stone?

Chapter Eighteen

The Americas
and the British Dominions

99   EUROPE'S GREAT MIGRATIONS

Although Europe had a profound impact upon Africa and Asia during the nineteenth century, even more far-reaching was the imprint left upon the Americas and the British dominions. The basic reason for this influence was the unprecedented mass emigration from Europe, which overwhelmed the native peoples in the overseas continents. This great emigration led to the Europeanization of the formerly underpopulated portions of the globe. Such Europeanization could not occur in Africa or Asia, where the indigenous populations were too numerous and too advanced to be displaced by the Europeans. The following selection by an American historian describes the origins, the nature and the significance of European emigration.*

Man's history is a story of movement, of the conquest of land from nature and from fellowman, of adaptation to new environments, of the blending of blood and the intermixture of cultures, of a constant restless striving for "something better." At least this is the history of the peoples who have pursued progress. Non-migratory peoples have remained static—for example, the Bushmen of South Africa or Australia. Civilization may have begun when our savage ancestors found caves, built permanent campfires, and settled down. Yet by sitting still men did not find new resources or develop new ideas.

---

* Franklin D. Scott, *Emigration and Immigration* (Washington: American Historical Association, 1963), pp. 1-5.

The spread of ideas and people began when disaster or overcrowding forced men to move, or when they were drawn on by the lure of greener pastures and the challenge of the unknown.

Migration takes many forms. Sometimes it is the individual probing into the woods beyond the clearing, across the swamp, or over the mountain. Sometimes it is the push of armed hosts such as the invasion of the Huns into Europe, or the infiltration of the Roman Empire by the Teutonic hordes. It may be an originally peaceful but co-ordinated movement such as the Great Trek in South Africa. Or it may be the search for fresh grasslands for their flocks as among the tribes of ancient Asia, or the seasonal herding of their reindeer by the Lapps. It can be also the sending out of colonies to hold the frontiers of empire, or the exile of political minorities which extended Greek culture around the Mediterranean. Migration may be internal from region to region, or from country to city, or it may be a seasonal or occupational flow of people within a country or between countries. The greatest of all the chapters in the history of migration . . . was different in numbers and extent and even in character: it was the accumulation of millions of individual and small group movements; it extended over a period of four centuries; it took some 68,000,000 people from Europe and scattered them literally over the earth; it gave birth to new nations and roused old nations from their torpor; it Europeanized the world so well that "the lesser breeds without the law" (to use the phrase of Kipling, poet of empire) have adopted Europe's methods to throw Europe back on her heels; and thus the remarkable epoch of European expansion, colonization, emigration, has come to an end.

This tremendous migratory surge began when Europe discovered the "great frontier" of America and the other sparsely peopled lands such as Australia and South Africa. It was associated with the decline of feudalism in Europe, and it has hastened the end of feudal society—for migration is a feature of a free society; bondage to the land cannot survive when man is free to move. The tempo of movement was accelerated with increasing freedom and with new developments in shipping and means of communication, and with a complex and cumulative host of factors repelling people from the Old World and attracting them to the New. But certain broad and fundamental causes underlay the entire phenomenon.

The most powerful factor impelling emigration was an extraordinary increase in population, *preceding* the ability of agriculture to feed it or of industry to give it jobs. In 1650 approximately 545,000,000 human beings lived on this planet; three hundred years later the number had grown to about 2,500,000,000—more than a four-fold increase. Europe's people increased from c. 100,000,000 to 560,000,000, and during the same period she was sending abroad *permanently* some 40,000,000. Without the safety valve of the "great frontier," would Europe have suffered the crowding and the famines and cultural slow-down of Asia? We cannot know. We do know that as the death rate declined, and before the birth rate responded to keep things in balance, emigration skimmed off a significant portion of the surplus. This not only relieved Europe's numbers, but in transoceanic fields the emigrants from Europe raised wheat to feed the people who stayed home.

The population problem went hand in hand with economic pressures— occasionally in the stark form of hunger. The potato blight of the 1840's hit western Europe hard, and it left many an Irishman with the simple choice between starvation and emigration. Fortunately the pressures of hunger and joblessness were usually less severe. More often they acted as on a young Swede, one of seven sons, who saw that the patrimony would be too small for seven new families; against his father's will he crossed the sea, and he was one of the happy ones who made a fortune. The general operation of economic causation is illustrated by the fluctuations in the stream of emigration: it was shallowest during periods of prosperity in Europe and depression in the United States, and it swelled to a flood when Europe faced hard times and America rode a crest of prosperity. But variations and contradictions arose, too, out of local conditions and the phenomena of individual sectors of the economy.

This phenomenon of the business cycle in relation to migration indicates also that the causes of migration were located both in the country of origin and in the country of destination. Neither the push nor the pull functioned alone. Reasons there had to be for disappointment and frustration at home, but also reasons for hope in the new country. ... Basic economic factors were also indicated by the fact that it was neither the wealthy nor the very poor who left their homelands. The wealthy had too much at stake to tear up roots; the extremely poor had neither the passage money nor the stamina nor the vision to undertake the great adventure. The vast majority of emigrants were therefore from the lower-middle economic strata, people who had a little but had an appetite for more.

Of the multitude of other causative forces, besides population and economics, the most important was probably religion. The Jews at repeated times, from the Diaspora to the return to Israel, illustrated the religious motivation. The motives of both Pilgrims and Puritans were fundamentally religious. Groups like these were exercising their rights to flee from oppression, to seek freedom. In other cases the demand was for political freedom, as with refugees from the 1848 revolutions, from Nazi Germany in the 1930's, from Communist Russia after 1917. Often migration was literally forced, as in the Greco-Turkish exchange of populations after World War I, and the great refugee movements after World War II. These and other general factors, such as the desire to escape military service, appeared as causes for large numbers of emigrants, but purely personal causes were also effective.

The great migration of the nineteenth and twentieth centuries was a movement of individuals. Each person had to make his own decision even if he came with a group. And millions came entirely alone. They were affected by the deep-seated social causes of migration, but they were more immediately driven by the circumstances of their own lives, by factors such as disappointment in love, a brush with the police, a dispute with the boss, an overbearing father, or an urge to adventure. Reasons and combinations of reasons had to be numbered to infinity. The only factors universally applicable were dissatisfaction with things as they were and hope in what might be elsewhere.

Most of these millions of emigrants were young—the bulk of them in the fifteen to thirty-five year old age bracket. And most were male (85 per cent in the case of the early Austrian emigration), especially in the late nineteenth century rush as new nationalities suddenly awoke to the call of the New World. The proportion of the sexes evened out after the first or second decade when the men of the advance guard had saved enough money to send for sweethearts or families, or when demand for domestic servants provided jobs for girls. Some of them were in their own countries rebels and misfits; practically all were the unhappy, the propertyless or dispossessed, the restless and frustrated. But for the most part these same people were also the virile, the industrious, the hopeful, men with vision and drive and a love of adventure, men who could look to the future, strong young men.

As they became immigrants in a new land, some, even of the strong, were broken by the magnitude of the task or by sheer ill fortune. Others less strong found themselves misfits and disappointed wherever they went; by migration they only exchanged one set of adversities for another. The new slums might be worse than the old, or the isolation of the frontier could be unbearable. Some suffered massacre by Indians, others died in malarial swamps, more were broken by the competitive struggle in factories and offices. Several millions returned more or less quietly to their homes, others kept moving on and moving on, searching and hoping until they died. The totality of disillusionments and calamities was at least a third of the immigrant flow. But these, like the casualties of an army, were sloughed off; these were not the men and women who left the lasting impact. Perhaps they should have a monument, but the successful survivors would have to build it.

The survivors of this creative movement were legion. They peopled the empty spaces of the earth. In America they pioneered the prairies or restored the farms abandoned by the westward-moving earlier settlers. They built railroads and stoked factory furnaces, did domestic chores. They set up shops that grew into stores, they made watches, and glass, and clothes, they built bridges and buildings, they mined coal and ores. They established churches and schools and newspapers. They brought with them muscles and skills and dreams and ideas. They made farms and towns and cities, not alone but in co-operation with the heirs of earlier-arrived immigrants. Together they built. The newcomers faced tensions and misunderstandings due to differences in language and background exacerbated by the rivalries of the struggle up from poverty. But they learned to work together, to tolerate if not to understand the differences among them. They developed new interests and new loyalties. They learned the English language and American ways. They intermarried. They grew in education and in wealth. They, in all their variety of generations and national origins, became the American nation.

The three and one half centuries of European-American migration constitutes in magnitude and significance one of the greatest, if not the greatest of all chapters in the entire annals of man's mobility.

PEOPLING OF NORTH AMERICA **100**

The great exodus from Europe led to the peopling of the overseas continents. In earlier centuries, only a thin line of European settlements had taken hold along the coasts; but during the nineteenth century, the interiors of the continents were rapidly settled by the newcomers from Europe. The first of the following selections describes the wild rush of 100,000 homesteaders into Oklahoma District on April 22, 1889, when President Benjamin Harrison declared this territory open for settlement. The second is an official report on the growing migration to the

Canadian prairies; the report was submitted in 1904 by the Deputy Minister of Canada's Department of the Interior.*

Oklahoma Rush

For several weeks before the opening, the country, then being ready for the reception of homesteaders, was cleared of all individuals except the soldiers stationed there to prevent the arrival of "sooners." The latter, however, ingeniously effaced themselves for the time only; for, when the signal gun was fired, they seemed to rise from the ground, as though Cadmus had been on earth again sowing the fabled dragon's teeth. Men who had herded cattle, and those who had traded with the Indians for years, were not to be outdone by the vigilance of soldiers ignorant of sheltering "draws," hidden "dug-outs," and obscuring fastnesses of scrub-oak and blue-stem. "A feller had to keep mighty quiet until the marshal's gun fired," said a successful "sooner," "every draw kept fillin' with men all night long; an' it was hard to keep from seein' and bein' seen."

With everything cleared for action, the crowd was lined up on the border of the new country awaiting the hour of noon, April 22, 1889. It was a crowd of determined, almost desperate, men and women, many of whom, having failed in the fight for prosperity, had gathered here for a fresh trial. Every man's hand was against his fellow. His neighbor on the right placed there by accident, might be the one who would beat him in the race. The men who stood in line were composed of two classes: (1) those who had failed in every undertaking, and (2) others so young that this was their first bout with fortune. Some were mounted on ponies, which they had ridden from distant states; others were in farm-wagons in which they had journeyed from Kansas, Missouri, and even from Tennessee. The failure of Western Kansas after its period of booming was accountable for a large part of the enormous crowd that gathered at the Oklahoma border. The opportunity to try again so near home could not be neglected.

It was with difficulty that the crowd was restrained by the marshals; and, when finally the signal was given, a mad race began the results of which make interesting history. All men started as enemies. The reward was to the selfish and to the bully; and greed and strength were the winners. The number of homesteaders exceeded the number of claims; and more than one man pitched upon the same quarter section. In some cases as many as four or five insisted on the right of possession. Thus on the very first day began the contests which have ever since been a harvest to the lawyers, and have produced an unhappy condition of society unknown elsewhere. As an example, two families built their rude homes simultaneously on opposite corners of the same quarter-section; each family being positive of its own right. The help of the law was sought; decisions and reversed decisions resulted, harassing the contestants, until one, more unscrupulous and desperate than the other, shot his enemy through the window or among the outbuildings at twilight. This is not an exception, but a common condition of things.

* H. C. Candee, "Social Conditions in our Newest Territory," *The Forum*, XXV (June, 1898), 427-29; *Annual Report of the Department of the Interior for the Year 1903-1904* (Ottawa, 1905), X, XXIX-XXX.

Canadian Immigration

The steady increase in the flow of immigration that has been directed towards this country, the interest aroused amongst United States capitalists as to its possibilities, the attention which the wealth of its agricultural and other natural resources commands to-day in Great Britain, in Europe, and even in some of the most important British colonies, clearly show that Canada has at last emerged from a state of semi-stagnation in which it had remained for so many years, and its future advance, as judged by the remarkable progress of the past few years, must henceforth be by leaps and bounds.

That Canada, however, should be a nation of fifteen or twenty million inhabitants within a comparatively few years—and there are strong grounds for such belief from present indications—is a consummation to be sincerely wished for, but the question of number, desirable as it may be, is not the chief result aimed at by the department. The social character of the people that are being added to our population, and their adaptability to become loyal, prosperous and contented Canadians, is considered to be a matter of far greater moment. In this endeavor, I am glad to say, the department has been highly successful, as a careful analysis of the result of the work, both as regards the number of new arrivals and the desirable classes to which they belong will amply testify. . . .

From the returns submitted, it will be seen that the result of the work has been highly satisfactory. The total arrivals in Canada during the twelve months ending June 30 last, numbered 130,330, or, on an average, over two thousand five hundred settlers have located in the country every week during that period, and are now engaged in the development of its resources. . . .

It is the largest immigration in the history of Canada.

IMMIGRANTS IN ARGENTINA **101**

In the second half of the nineteenth century, many Europeans emigrated to South America as well as to the United States and Canada. The newcomers— mostly Italians, Spaniards, French, Belgians, and English-Irish—made important contributions to the economic development of their adopted countries. This is made clear in the following account by a pioneer English sheep raiser in Argentina.*

After the War of Independence, many foreigners, chiefly British, found their way to these countries. After the notification of the treaty with Great Britain conceding to her subjects unrestricted trading rights, with protection for their lives, properties, stock, and merchandise, and exemption from military service, forced loans and all other exactions whatsoever, many British subjects settling in Buenos Ayres and the Banda Oriental purchased properties and live stock, entered into local trades and industries, or initiated new or improved systems of industry, mechanical trades, pastoral and agricul-

* W. Latham, *The States of the River Plate* (London, 1868), pp. 312-30.

tural pursuits, effecting great improvements in produce, and expanding the commerce between the two nations. . . .

Few natives ventured to make any improvement on their estates, and they were as slow to introduce the sheep industry on them as they were to improve their sheep stock when they had it. A universal feeling of mistrust pervaded all. They knew not when every peon on their establishments might be carried off for military service, or what contributions, exactions, or confiscations might be looked for. The protection which their treaties secured to foreigners, placed them under these circumstances at an advantage over the natives, inasmuch as the former were absolutely exempt from military service and from forced contributions, horses excepted, which were considered articles of war; and any injury to their properties, or the taking of their cattle to intestinal warfare, constituted claims for compensation under the existing treaties.

Induced by the low price of land and the greater security which they enjoyed, foreigners, more especially the British, purchased largely of the lands offered for sale, and devoted themselves to the sheep industry and the improvement of the almost valueless native or Creole sheep. Several large establishments were formed expressly for their improvement by crossing with Merino rams. . . .

Foremost among the actors in industrial undertakings were, as a matter of course, the foreign residents, and foreign capitalists cooperating from without. . . .

Moles and wharfs shot up, and a large extent of street surface was paved in the city of Buenos Ayres; the streets were lighted with gas; carriages, cabs, and omnibuses crowded them; houses—almost palaces—sprang up in every block; and the city increased rapidly in extent and population—the latter doubling itself in a single decade. Railways, canals, and telegraphs were projected, and are now in operation; steamers, in quick succession, coursed the rivers and connected every town of any importance with the commercial centres of Buenos Ayres and Montevideo; rural industries were prosecuted with eagerness, if with little skill, and men of all nationalities began to root themselves to the soil. . . .

Near the cities, the enclosure of lands for agricultural and horticultural purposes, scarcely before known, went on year by year to such an extent that today, around the city of Buenos Ayres, all the lands over a radius of 15 to 20 miles are subdivided and enclosed as farms or market-gardens, cultivated by Italians, Basques, French, British, and Germans. Mechanical trades kept pace with and contributed to, the general progress, these being, as a matter of course, almost monopolized by foreigners, as it was only from the immigrant ranks that the demand for skilled or other labour could be even partially supplied.

102 BRITISH CAPITAL IN THE AMERICAS AND THE DOMINIONS

Europe provided the overseas territories with capital as well as with manpower. Economic development in the Americas and the Dominions was financed in large part by European, and especially British, capital. Whatever the individual peculi-

arities of economic growth in Latin America, the United States, and the Dominions, the fact remains that Britain provided much of the capital essential for growth. The following selection describes how British investors turned from Europe to overseas countries in the late nineteenth century. The statistics in the table show how large a proportion of their investments were concentrated in the Americas and the Dominions.*

In 1870 British capital was already playing a lessening part in the financing of the countries on the European continent. All the governments of Europe had earlier sought its help. The governments of Spain, Portugal, and Greece had been among the earliest and most disappointing borrowers; the rulers of the many states which later formed the German Empire, Austria, Hungary, and the Scandinavian countries, had often found aid in London; Russian and Turkish bonds were widely held. In addition to this financing of governments, the British people had supplied, during the early and middle part of the century, the enterprise of the neighboring continent. Not only capital was sent out to the mainland, but industrial knowledge, directing experience, machinery, and skilled workmen as well. In Austria, Rhenish Germany, Italy, Spain, Roumania, and Belgium, British capital had helped to finance the early railroad building, and English contractors had carried through the construction. . . .

In the closing decades of the nineteenth century the British holdings of continental securities declined rather than the contrary. France attained financial sufficiency—became an important lending country, in fact—and Germany moved in the same direction; the yield on their securities fell, while the perilous possibilities of continental politics grew no less. The financial situation of the Russian Government did not give assurance, while throughout the Middle and Far East its forward thrust collided with the British. From the middle seventies on, British investors were selling their "Russians." The continuous borrowing of the Spanish Government, its partial default in 1872 and perpetual approach to a repetition of that necessity, caused its securities to be sold to the continental markets; in similar fashion the Portuguese Government likewise moved from one default to another and shook the British faith. After the Turkish bankruptcy in 1876, the London market tended to refrain from further reliance upon the credit of that country—despite the existence of an International Debt Administration. Of the loans of the Balkan governments it took only a small fractional share. The chastening influence of losses suffered, the risks and uncertainties from which the financial and political outlook of the continental governments were never free, make the British investor obdurate to their requests. Furthermore, while those circumstances which had invited and stimulated the operations of British capital and enterprise on the continent continued to diminish, French, German, Belgian, and Swiss capital accumulations grew more adequate and their industrial competence greater. In construction work, in industrial organization, in technical knowledge, the independent capabilities of these countries came to rival England's. Thus Paris and Berlin became the borrowing centers for sovereigns of eastern and southeastern Europe. It was left mainly to the French and German banks, industrialists, and engineers to carry the machine

* Reprinted from *Europe: The World's Banker 1870-1914* by Herbert Feis, pp. 17-23. By permission of W. W. Norton & Company, Inc. Copyright 1930 by Yale University Press. Copyright © 1965 by Herbert Feis.

equipment of the industrial age throughout those regions. The British contractors and their supporters took up new chances in British India, South America, the plains of Canada and Australia, the United States, and the reaches of Africa.

British capital was turning in greater measure to what seemed to computing minds more attractive opportunities, and to national sentiment more desirable employments. These lay, above all, in the young and agricultural countries largely peopled by the British race. The populations of these countries, their farmers, miners, and builders, were on the march, and impetuously following upon the fringe of settlement; railroads were being laid across vast areas. British capital entered into the movement, providing, in the late eighties especially, unprecedented sums for railroad building, land settlement schemes, construction and mine operation. The same eager breaking open of new areas was going on in Argentina, the same headlong pushing forward of the railroad tracks, and here too British capital was willing to risk itself in the new effort. Hardly smaller were the loan requirements of British India, chiefly for railroad construction. During this period, also, a multitude of enterprising companies were alluring the British investor with the glint of the riches of Africa. Within twenty years of the discovery of gold a full 100 millions of pounds were contributed by British savings to pursue the quest. Inland from a dozen points along the African coast railroad systems were headed toward the interior. Great chartered companies, and smaller promotion groups, found capital for the work of exploration, for cultivation, railroad building, mining.

These were the chief occupations of British capital during the last decades of the nineteenth century. For a while at the end of the period they came to a halt in temporary, balked disappointment. The rapid extension of agricultural production brought falling food prices and financial distress in the newly opened areas. The speculative land and mining booms ended in a violent smash, especially in Australia. Many of the railroad systems of the United States, financially mismanaged and plunged into headlong competition, ceased payment on their bonds. Economic and financial maladjustment in Argentina ended in default upon all the securities of that government; while revolution and currency troubles in Brazil seemed to make further losses of the same sort inevitable. Repeatedly throughout the century investors in South American lands had seen their calculations defeated by such defaults. . . .

For a time, prolonged almost to a decade by the Boer wars, British capital movements to these new lands were of much smaller proportions, until people and governments recuperated, improved the organization of their economic life, and European needs for foodstuffs and raw materials caught up to the new production.

Then in the succeeding years of the twentieth century when the outward flow of British capital grew greater than ever before, it was to these same countries that the largest volume went. The credit of the Argentine and Brazilian governments became firmly and completely restored. In these two countries alone the British in the seven years from 1907 to 1914 risked over a billion dollars. Canada and Australia between 1900 and 1914 almost doubled their railway mileage, calling upon British investors for most of the needed funds. British India did not lag behind. The firm establishment of the gold standard in the United States, the gradual emergence of its railways from bankruptcy and the passage of the improved railway legislation, its vast industrial growth, all invited the resumption of British investment. The formation of the South African Union ushered in a period of economic advancement there. . . .

The following table gives roughly the distribution of British foreign investment, as it was in December, 1913.

LONG-TERM PUBLICLY ISSUED BRITISH CAPITAL INVESTMENT IN OTHER LANDS

Within the empire	Millions of pounds	Outside the empire	Millions of pounds
Canada and Newfoundland	514.9	The United States	754.6
Australia and New Zealand	416.4	Latin-America	756.6
South Africa	370.2	Europe	218.6
India and Ceylon	378.8	Rest of foreign world	253.5
Other colonies	99.7	Total	1,983.3
	1,780.0		
		Grand Total	3,763.3

"WHAT THEN IS THE AMERICAN, THIS NEW MAN?" 103

Europe provided the overseas territories with much of their culture, as well as with manpower and capital; but this culture was adapted to the new environment. In the United States, for example, from Colonial days to the present, the question has been asked repeatedly: What is an American? Both European visitors and settlers in the Colonies soon realized that different ways of life were developing on the two sides of the Atlantic. No one better described this difference than St. John de Crèvecoeur, a Frenchman who worked as a surveyor in Pennsylvania and then, in 1769, settled on a farm in New York State. There he wrote his famous Letters from an American Farmer *(1782), in which he eloquently described the virtues of the American—"this new man" as he called him.**

This new man will commence as a hunter and learn in these woods how to pursue and overtake the game with which it abounds. He will in a short time become master of that necessary dexterity which this solitary life inspires. Husband, father, priest, principal governor,—he fills up all these stations, though in the humble vale of life. Are there any of his family taken sick, either he or his wife must recollect ancient directions received from aged people, from doctors, from a skilful grandmother, perhaps, who formerly learned of the Indians of her neighbourhood how to cure simple diseases by means of simple medicines. The swamps and woods are ransacked to find the plants, the bark, the roots prescribed. An ancient almanac, constituting perhaps all his library, with his Bible, may chance to direct him to some more learned ways.

Has he a cow or an ox sick, his anxiety is not less, for they constitute part

---

* St. John de Crèvecoeur, *Sketches of Eighteenth Century America,* ed. H. L. Bourdin, R. H. Gabriel, and S. T. Williams (New Haven: Yale Univ., 1925), pp. 70-73.

of his riches. He applies what recipes he possesses; he bleeds, he foments; he has no farrier at hand to assist him. Does either his plough or his cart break, he runs to his tools; he repairs them as well as he can. Be they finally break down, with reluctance he undertakes to rebuild them, though he doubts of his success. This was an occupation committed before to the mechanic of his neighbourhood, but necessity gives him invention, teaches him to imitate, to recollect what he has seen. Somehow or another 'tis done, and happily there is no traveller, no inquisitive eye to grin and criticize his work. It answers the purposes for the present. Next time he arrives nearer perfection. . . .

His ingenuity in the fields is not less remarkable in executing his rural work in the most expeditious manner. He naturally understands the use of levers, handspikes, etc. He studies how to catch the most favourable seasons for each task. This great field of action deters him not. But what [shall] he do for shoes? . . . He has, perhaps, a few lasts and some old tools; he tries to mend an old pair. Heaven be praised! The child can walk with them, and boast to the others of his new acquisition. A second pair is attempted; he succeeds as well. He ventures at last to make a new one. They are coarse, heavy, ponderous, and clumsy, but they are tight and strong, and answer all the intended purposes. What more can he want? If his gears break, he can easily repair them. Every man here understands how to spin his own yarn and to [make] his own ropes. He is a universal fabricator like Crusoe. With bark and splinters the oldest of the children amuse themselves by making little baskets. . . .

What then is the American, this new man? He is either an European, or the descendant of an European, hence that strange mixture of blood, which you will find in no other country. I could point out to you a family whose grandfather was an Englishman, whose wife was Dutch, whose son married a French woman, and whose present four sons have now four wives of different nations. . . . The Americans were once scattered all over Europe; here they are incorporated into one of the finest systems of population which has ever appeared, and which will hereafter become distinct by the power of the different climates they inhabit. The American ought therefore to love this country much better than that wherein either he or his forefathers were born. Here the rewards of his industry follow with equal steps the progress of his labour; his labour is founded on the basis of nature, *self-interest;* can it want a stronger allurement? Wives and children, who before in vain demanded of him a morsel of bread, now, fat and frolicsome, gladly help their father to clear those fields whence exuberant crops are to arise to feed and to clothe them all; without any part being claimed, either by a despotic prince, a rich abbot, or a mighty lord. Here religion demands but little of him; a small voluntary salary to the minister, and gratitude to God; can he refuse these? The American is a new man, who acts upon new principles; he must therefore entertain new ideas, and form new opinions. From involuntary idleness, servile dependence, penury, and useless labour, he has passed to toils of a very different nature, rewarded by ample subsistence. This is an American.

Although some Europeans had great admiration for the new American man and his way of life, this was certainly not the case with most European intellectuals. They looked down upon the United States as a land of vigorous and industrious but vulgar and boastful people, ignorant of the arts, letters, and finer things of life. Typical is the following estimate made by an English clergyman and critic, Sydney Smith, in 1820.*

Such is the land of Jonathan, and thus has it been governed. In his honest endeavours to better his condition and in his manly purpose of resisting injury and insult we most cordially sympathize. Thus far we are friends and admirers of Jonathan. But he must not grow vain and ambitious, or allow himself to be dazzled by that galaxy of epithets by which his orators and newspaper scribblers endeavour to persuade their supporters that they are the greatest, the most refined, the most enlightened, and the most moral people upon earth. The effect of this is unspeakably ludicrous on this side of the Atlantic. The Americans are a brave, industrious, and acute people, but they have hitherto given no indication of genius. . . . They are but a recent offset, indeed, from England, and should make it their chief boast for many generations to come that they are sprung from the same race with Bacon and Shakespeare and Newton. Considering their numbers, indeed, and the favorable circumstances in which they have been placed, they have done marvellously little to assert the boast of such a descent, or to show that their English blood has been exalted or refined by their republican training and institutions. . . . During the thirty or forty years of their independence they have done absolutely nothing for the sciences, for the arts, for literature, or even for the statesmanlike studies of politics of political economy. . . . In the four quarters of the globe, who reads an American book or goes to an American play or looks at an American picture or statue? What does the world yet owe to American physicians or surgeons? What new substances have their chemists discovered or what old ones have they analysed? What new constellations have been discovered by the telescopes of Americans? What have they done in the mathematics? Who drinks out of American glasses? or eats from American plates? or wears American coats or gowns? or sleeps in American blankets? Finally, under which of the old tyrannical governments of Europe is every sixth man a slave whom his fellow-creatures may bully and sell and torture?

THE ENGLISH LANGUAGE OVERSEAS **105**

The most striking example of the diffusion and adaptation of European culture is found in the field of language, such as French in Quebec, Portuguese in Brazil,

* Cited by J. B. MacMaster, *A History of the People of the United States* (New York: Appleton, 1901), V, 313-14.

Spanish in the rest of Latin America, and English in the United States and the British Dominions. The following selections show what has happened to the English language overseas, in Australia, Canada, and the United States. The third selection emphasizes that the differences can be exaggerated and that the European languages have been less affected by adaptation than is commonly assumed.*

Australia

"Ut's hard yacker, mate. I'm crook, and everything's up the spout."

In this manner, a particularly salty Australian bloke, a man who speaks some of the most vigorous and inventive slang on earth, might suggest that things could hardly be going worse.

The Australian peppers his speech with words that mean little to the uninformed: Yacker (work), crook (out of sorts), tucker (feed), sheila (girl), furphy (rumor), fair cow (anything that does not meet with one's unqualified approval), and 'owyergoin'mate orright? (hello).

But the great Australian adjective is bloody, a word that is avoided by polite company in England. On the continent down under, however, the word has become so commonplace that no one would hesitate to use it anywhere except the pulpit. In Aussie slang, it is just about the handiest little six-letter word available, and it would not be stretching things to give the time as, "One o'bloody clock, mate." . . .

Like the American, the Australian invented his slang out of time and circumstance in a raw, lusty country.

Going camping, an Australian might sleep in a wurley, gunyah, goondie, or humpy. All of these are aborigines' words for casual shelter.

He'd doubtless eat damper—bread baked in ashes. Things would certainly be fair cow if he couldn't find a billabong, or water hole. He'd boil water for tea in a tin that he'd call a billy.

If this particular Australian were traveling in the Outback, he might run across some provocatively named settlements—Hunchy Mama Creek, Venus Jump Up, Bust-My-Gall, or Broken Cart. However, the Aussie proved surprisingly sentimental in selecting place names, and the traveler would more likely encounter Anna Creek, Louisa Downs, or Alice Springs.

But you can bet your bottom dollar that the first thing a thirsty bloke would look for in Alice Springs would be a cruiser (very large glass of beer), schooner (next biggest), middy (10 ounces), or pony (the least).

In places where Australians come into contact with aborigines, they have developed a kind of pidgin patois. The result is not exactly the King's English or the Australian's English, but it does have stark, primitive dignity.

Consider this pidgin translation of the second verse of the 23rd Psalm: "Big Name makum camp alonga grass, takum blackfella walkabout longa, no fighten no more hurry watta." . . .

An indication of how far out Australian slang can go is the unofficial national song, "Waltzing Matilda." The expression's exact origin is obscure; it probably referred to a roaming man carrying his swag, or bundle. At any rate, the phrase had nothing to do with dancing or girls.

* *National Geographic News Bulletin* (Washington, D.C., May 12, 1961); *The New York Times* (November 29, 1959). © 1959 by The New York Times Company. Reprinted by permission; R. Quirk, "American English and English English," *The New York Times Magazine* (December 2, 1956), pp. 132, 140. © 1956 by The New York Times Company. Reprinted by permission.

Canada

Canadians are becoming aware that they speak and write English in a
distinctive way.

They are discovering what some go so far as to call the Canadian language—a unique conglomeration of spelling, pronunciation and vocabulary. . . .

The mainstreams are British and American, but there are colorful traces of Indian, Eskimo and French, plus words and phrases that are wholly Canadian.

The first big wave of American settlers that came north during and after the Revolution began a war of words with the entrenched British that is still going on today. Although many Anglicisms remain unshaken, modern communication facilities seem to be giving Americanisms the upper hand.

However, this tide has been somewhat offset by two factors: first, British immigration has far outstripped American, particularly in the post-war years; second, British English has traditionally enjoyed superior prestige.

The linguists report that the British pronunciation of schedules (shedule) is threatening to push the American (skedule) out of the dictionary.

However, the British newcomer soon finds that he gets blank stares when he talks of petrol, silencer, boot and demister so he switches to gas, muffler, trunk and windshield wiper.

There are other areas where a Briton will be quite at home, however. Most Canadians say blinds, tap and braces, rather than shades, faucet and suspenders.

In pronouncing "dance," most Canadians pronounce the "a" as in "dad"; the British pronounce it as in "father." Yet the Canadians pronounce lever like beaver and been like bean (not sever and bin, as do Americans). . . .

In spelling also the conflict between the main influences is evident. Many still prefer the British axe, catalogue, centre, colour, honour, jeweller, mediaeval, plough and programme. But the trend seems to favor American spelling, particularly where it is more compact.

Perhaps the most interesting field for the dictionary-makers is that of the true Canadianisms, some of which, like mountie, are widely used.

One of the best examples of distinctive pronunciation is the word khaki. In Canada it rhymes with car key, whereas in the States it rhymes with lackey and in Britain with hockey.

United States

British travelers in the New World since the eighteenth century have returned home with lurid tales of the "barbarous" English used there. This description was in fact used by an Englishman in the Seventeen Thirties of the word "bluff," which he had heard in the sense of "steep bank." A century later we find Dickens in "Martin Chuzzlewit" making sarcastic comments on words like "location" and pronunciations like "prod-ooce" and "terri-tory." During the same period American visitors to Britain returned with jeers about the Englishman's overfrequent use of "you know," his "wery" for "very," "anythink" for "anything" and his clipped words like "lib'ry" and "secret'ry." An early nineteenth-century American farce burlesqued British speech also with lines like "Halbert, did you 'ear 'im?" . . .

But, despite spirited American counterattacks of this kind, the undeniable historical priority of British English, as well as the still enduring prestige of the English Court, have left most Brittons and many Americans with the belief that British English is somehow purer, more refined, less slangy than the New World variety. A typically nineteenth-century British attitude is illustrated in the story of a visit to England about 1850 by a young American lady of high social standing. At a party she got talking to a British officer who could not disguise his admiration for the way she was able to make herself understood. Unconscious of the implied insult, he took it upon himself to compliment her on her English; he even asked her if she were not remarkable among her compatriots. The girl answered, "Oh, yes, but then I had unusual advantages; there was an English missionary stationed near my tribe."

It is hard to imagine a similar exchange today. The growth of American prestige and other factors, such as the development of more sophisticated and tolerant attitudes to variations in speech (probably more prominently displayed today in Britain than in the United States), have contributed to a recognition of the right of American English (together with Australian English and other varieties) to be different from British English and yet be equally acceptable socially.

As for the extent of actual differences, there still remain serious misconceptions. These can be largely attributed to sensationalism and over-simplification on the part of most writers who offer commentaries on the regional variations within English. It is much easier to attract attention by concentrating on the differences that exist than on the broad area of agreement. It is engaging to read of what outlandish names others give to familiar objects; it is amusing to hear quips like "divided by a common language" and to read the largely invented stories of how Britons and Americans can misunderstand each other. . . .

There are popular lists of British and American variants arranged in double mutually exclusive columns which give a truly frightening impression of the degree of divergence between the major members of the English-speaking family. The British say "car," Americans, "automobile," we are told. What we are not told is that American use "car" too, and more frequently than "automobile" at that, and that "automobile" is readily understood in England, being found in the titles of the two motoring organizations, the Royal Automobile Club and the Automobile Association.

The British word "tap," we are told, corresponds to the American "faucet." Again there is truth in this so far as it goes; but it is dangerously incomplete —unless we know that many Americans use "spigot" instead; that both "spigot" and "faucet" have some currency in British dialects, and that having filled a glass from his faucet or tap, the American is likely to call it "tap-water." What Americans call "quotation marks" the British call "inverted commas." But there are many Britons who call them "quotation marks," too.

When the American says "sick," he means what the Englishman calls "ill," but throughout the British armed forces one "reports sick" at the "sick bay," and if lucky goes sent home on "sick leave," and, needless to say, this is seldom on account of nausea. In fact there are parts of the United Kingdom where "sick" is the normal word and "ill" is regarded as highfalutin.

The American "mad" and British "angry" are another pair; people tend to ignore both the frequency of "mad" in this sense in Britain and also the substandard flavor attached to its usage in the United States. "Mail" and "post," "sidewalk" and "pavement" are not absolute divergences. "Pavement" is used in the sense of "sidewalk" not only in Britain but in Philadelphia and elsewhere. The "post" is often called "mail" in Britain and is carried in red mail vans, on mail trains, and on Royal Mail steamers; in America, mail is sorted at the post office, often takes the form of a postcard, bearing a stamp saying "United States Postage" and is delivered by a man who is often described as a postman.

And so one could go on. The long and imposing lists of so-called distinctively British and American words and usages are 75 per cent misleading: it turns out either that both the words so nearly separated are used in one or the other country, or that both are found in both countries but are used in slightly different contexts or in different proportions. At their best, such lists draw attention to differences in preferred usage in the two areas; they are certainly no index of mutual intelligibility. There is sufficient variety of speech on both sides of the Atlantic to familiarize us with most of the forms actually used by any native speaker of English.

Indeed, even in matters of pronunciation, it is difficult to find many absolute British and American distinctions. The broad "a" in the southern British "dance" is not unlike that heard in Boston. Nasalized vowels, so often regarded as solely American, are found in Liverpool and London; the Cockney, like the New Yorker, is apt to say "noo toon" for "new tune," and "lieutenant" is pronounced "lootenant" in the Royal Navy.

Noah Webster spent years trying, largely in vain, to create a linguistic gulf by encouraging Americans to say things like "ax" for "ask," "deef" and "heerd" for "deaf" and "heard." But in his maturity, he came to recognize that in all essentials Britons and Americans spoke the same language and that (as he said) it was highly "desirable to perpetuate the sameness." There is no reason to believe that history will prove false to his wish.

Chapter Nineteen

*Significance
of the period
for world history*

106 Europe Dominates the World

> *The great outburst of imperialist activity in the latter part of the nineteenth century brought the entire globe under the rule of a handful of European powers. Never before in past history had one small peninsula dominated the remainder of the globe. The following firsthand observation, written in the beginning of the twentieth century by Arminius Vambery, a well-known Hungarian Orientalist and traveler, describes vividly how crushing and all-pervasive Europe's grip was. He refers specifically to Asia, with which he was particularly familiar, but his comments are equally valid for Africa and other portions of the globe.**

When, comfortably seated in our well-upholstered railway-carriage, we gaze upon the Hyrkanian Steppe, upon the terrible deserts of Karakum and Kisilkum, we can scarcely realise the terrors, the sufferings, and the privations, to which travellers formerly were exposed. ... And great changes similar to those which have taken place in Central Asia may also be noticed in greater or less degree in other parts and regions of the Eastern world: Siberia, West and North China, Mongolia, Manchuria, and Japan were in the first half of the nineteenth century scarcely known to us, and ... we now find that the supreme power of the Western world is gradually making itself felt. The walls of seclusion are ruthlessly pulled down, and the resistance caused by the favoured superstitions,

---

* A. Vambery, *Western Culture in Eastern Lands* (London: J. Murray, 1906), pp. 1-4.

prejudices, and the ignorance of the sleepy and apathetic man in the East, is slowly being overcome . . . present-day Europe, in its restless, bustling activity will take good care not to let the East relapse again into its former indolence. We forcibly tear its eyes open; we push, jolt, toss, and shake it, and we compel it to exchange its world-worn, hereditary ideas and customs for our modern views of life; nay, we have even succeeded to some extent in convincing our Eastern neighbours that our civilisation, our faith, our customs, our philosophy, are the only means whereby the well-being, the progress, and the happiness, of the human race can be secured.

For well-nigh 300 years we have been carrying on this struggle with the Eastern world, and persist in our unsolicited interference, following in the wake of ancient Rome, which began the work with marked perseverance, but naturally never met with much success because of the inadequate means at its disposal. . . . We may admire the splendour, the might, and the glory of ancient Rome, we may allow that the glitter of its arms struck terror and alarm into the furthest corners of Asia; but in spite of all that, it would be difficult to admit that the civilising influence of Rome was ever more than an external varnish, a transitory glamour. Compared with the real earnest work done in our days by Western Powers, the efforts of Rome are as the flickering of an oil-lamp in comparison with the radiance of the sun in its full glory. It may be said without exaggeration that never in the world's history has one continent exercised such influence over another as has the Europe of our days over Asia.

EUROPE'S IMPACT: ECONOMIC AND SOCIAL 107

Europe's domination of the globe was most evident in the economic sphere. Hundreds of millions of peasants in villages on all continents were forced to abandon their traditional self-sufficient manner of earning their living. Inexorably they were involved in the new money economy, producing for national or international markets. This basic change affected all aspects of peasant life, including family organization, social relationships, and religious practices. Clearly illustrated in the following selection are changes that occurred in the village of Nayon, in Ecuador, following the building of a railway in 1908.*

. . . Whether it be in Latin America, Asia, Africa, or elsewhere, village communities untouched by the industrial world tend to have common characteristics in contrast with the city. Most economic life is organized about the production of food. Specialization of labor tends to be by age and sex, and within each family is to be found knowledge of the basic techniques to produce the minimal necessities for food and shelter.

The members of the village community are known to one another. Social relationships tend to be on a face-to-face basis. Chiefs or headmen often are mediators rather than figures of authority. Although conflicts and methods of

* R. L. Beals, "The Village in an Industrial World," *The Scientific Monthly,* LXXVII (August, 1953), 65-73.

adjudicating them are always found, social controls tend to be indirect and informal. There is less need for a judge when everyone knows the rules. Social status and prestige are related to family size and standing and individual abilities. The social system tends to be limited to the village, even though integrated into some larger system governing relationships between villages. Religion or ritual affects most aspects of culture. Even if specialists are found, each family head is on occasion his own priest.

The village world tends to be stable in its social structure and adequate in fulfilling its cultural functions. It maintains its membership and satisfies in tolerable measure its basic physiological needs. Both birth rates and death rates are high, but the population tends to be in balance with resources and technology. Demands upon the individual for adjustment are limited to changes in age and status. Child-rearing practices tend to prepare individuals for adult life and to shape personalities to fit the existing social and cultural demands. The way of life appears to the individuals in it, and conditioned by it, to be rational, stable, satisfying; for them it is a proper way of life.

The urban way of life is very different, especially now that industrialism creates even broader demands for markets and raw materials. Economic life involves far more than the production of food and raw materials. The family no longer is the economic unit, and shrinks toward the parents and dependent children. Labor grows increasingly more specialized and dependent on complex organization. No man can know or comprehend the sources of all the economic goods for which an industrialized society has created secondary needs; men grow increasingly interdependent.

Face-to-face social relationships of importance are no longer with relatives and neighbors, but with chance associates or in the many voluntary associations. Formality and impersonality mark social intercourse, just as formal controls, police, and judiciary replace the more informal machinery of village justice. When no man knows his neighbor, he tries to make him take an oath. . . .

I should like to describe an anthropologist's field trip to the exotically remote Ecuadorian village of Nayon. Here, scarcely six miles from the Equator, one can see in microcosm some of the problems that today face the industrial world and the yet uncounted millions of village dwellers.

THE VILLAGE OF NAYON. . . . The people of Nayon are Quechua-speaking Indians, as are their neighbors. Under missionary control after the Spanish conquest, Nayon was organized as a parish. . . .

Until about thirty years ago, the village seems to have been a self-sufficient agricultural community with a mixture of native and sixteenth century Spanish customs. Lands were abandoned when too badly eroded. The balance between population and resources provided a minimum subsistence. A few traders exchanged goods between Quito and the villages in the tropical barrancas, all within a radius of ten miles. Houses were dirt-floored, with thatched roofs, and pole walls, sometimes mud plastered. Guinea pigs ran freely about each house and were the main meat source. Most of the population spoke no Spanish. Men wore long hair and ponchos and concerned themselves chiefly with farming. Most formal controls and external relationships were managed by a resident parish priest, but informal leadership and familial controls governed social relationships. From the consolidation of the Spanish conquest until about 1920, no significant change occurred. In short, people lived within an integrated, internally consistent system of social relationships, habits, customs, values, and living techniques which were satisfactorily in balance with ecological conditions, and which supplied the necessary requirements for survival of the society. . . .

RECENT CHANGES IN NAYON. The completion of the Guayaquil-Quito railway in 1908 brought the first real contacts with industrial civilization to the high inter-Andean valley. From this event gradually flowed not only technological changes, but new ideas and social institutions. Feudal social relationships no longer seemed right and immutable; medicine and public health improved; elementary education became more common; urban Quito began to expand; and finally—and perhaps least important so far—modern industries began to appear, although even now upon a most modest scale.

In 1948-1949, the date of our visit, only two men wore long hair, and only two old-style houses remain. If guinea pigs are kept, they are penned; their flesh is now a luxury food, and beef is the most common meat. Houses are of adobe or fired brick, usually with tile roofs and often containing five or six rooms, some of which have plank or brick floors. Most of the population speaks Spanish. There is no resident priest, but an appointed government official who, with a policeman, represents authority. A six-teacher school provides education. Clothing is becoming city-like; for men it often includes overalls for work, and a tailored suit, white shirt, necktie, and felt hat for trips to Quito. Attendance at church is low and many festivals have been abandoned. Volley ball or soccer is played weekly in the plaza by young men who sometimes wear shorts, blazers, and berets. There are few shops, for most purchases are made in Quito, and from there comes most of the food, so that there is a far more varied diet than twenty-five years ago. There are piped water and sporadic health services; in addition, most families patronize Quito doctors in emergencies. Since 1949 the road has been paved, and bus service is more regular. There is one reputed millionaire (in sucres, the national currency, and the equivalent of about $150,000 U.S.), and several are classed as wealthy.

Thus, although to the casual observer Nayon still seems a timeless, sleepy farm village, in little more than a quarter of a century the changes in the direction of what North Americans call progress have been enormous. Let us examine the meaning of these changes in terms of the pattern of living. . . .

LOSS OF SELF-SUFFICIENCY. The changes in housing and clothing mean greater dependence upon the outside world. Masons must be hired to lay adobe or brick or stone walls, and so a new kind of specialist has come into being, one who works for wages. For fine work, outside craftsmen are imported along with such materials as cement and tile. Sewing machines are now considered necessary, although much clothing is purchased.

Except for some new specializations, tools for the primary occupation of farming have undergone little change. The wooden beam plow drawn by oxen, and the dibble, hoe, shovel, mattock, and machete are the universal tools. But the crops and their use have undergone notable change. Maize or Indian corn is still the primary crop, but very little is harvested as grain. Almost all is sold in Quito as green corn to eat boiled on the cob, and a considerable amount of the corn eaten as grain in Nayon is imported. Beans, which do poorly here, are grown on a small scale for household consumption. Though some squash is eaten, most is exported. Sweet potatoes, tomatoes, cabbage, onions, capsicum peppers, and, at lower elevations, sweet yucca or arrowroot are grown extensively for export; indeed, so export-minded is the community that it is almost impossible to buy locally grown produce in the village. People cannot be bothered with retail sales. Although areas devoted to fruit are small, quantities in excess of household needs are sold in Quito. Oxen are kept for plowing, but there is no dairying; milk, if used, is brought from Quito. Donkeys, mules, and horses are kept by some as pack animals. A few people buy shoats and fatten them, but not many pigs are butchered locally; again they are sold in Quito. A few others do the same with cattle, buying in Otavalo to the north, fattening, and then selling in Quito.

Clearly, then, Nayon is no longer a self-sufficient village. It is now deeply enmeshed in the money economy of a larger region, and especially with the city of Quito. . . .

CHANGING SOCIAL RELATIONSHIPS. A characteristic of the village is its homogeneity; there are few specialists and most people share the same skills and knowledge. Nayon, once primarily agricultural, is today a village of traders. . . . Some traders handle single transactions of $6,000 or more. Others travel from Peru to Colombia. In addition, we find scattered individuals who are oil-well riggers, construction workers of at least medium skills, and mechanics. There are also two school teachers. No Nayon youth has yet reached the University, but half a dozen are in advanced technical schools and one is in the Ecuadorian naval academy. And, to keep the picture in some sort of balance, mention should be made of the persistence of older kinds of specialists such as blanket and belt weavers, and the development of a small, essentially landless class which survives as unskilled laborers, mainly on construction jobs in Quito.

The nature of Nayon religious life and participation has likewise changed. Nayon is still Catholic in the main, and the few who have become Protestants are disliked and distrusted. Indeed, despite the intelligent and wholehearted assistance of the parish priest, the greatest obstacle to securing cooperation for the Nayon study was the persistent suspicion that we were Protestant missionaries. Nevertheless, religious influence is declining in Nayon, especially among the younger people. The parish priest today must care for half a dozen parishes and no longer resides in Nayon. Few, indeed, wish him to. Although mass is held every Sunday, attendance is usually small. Young men rarely participate, although they do not start their Sunday games of volleyball, soccer, or pitching coins until mass is concluded. On occasion though, they have spoken rudely to the priest. Most religious festivals have been abandoned or reduced to celebration of the mass. Those still retained become increasingly secular, with emphasis upon social aspects, drinking, and dancing. Even the festival of the patron saint is a poor thing, shorn of most of its color and traditional folk dances. Religion in Nayon is essentially as formal and as restricted in its function and meaning as in any city.

PENALTIES OF SUCCESS. So far, perhaps, this account sounds like a success story entitled, "Indian Village Adapts Rapidly to Modern Life." Many members of the group have accepted major shifts in the socio-cultural system with little difficulty and look forward to additional changes. Most people in Nayon are conscious of change and of its attendant difficulties, and believe they have met the situation well.

But a major finding of modern anthropology is that culturally established technologies, behavior patterns, value systems, and social structures tend to form closely integrated socio-cultural systems. If this be true, have Nayon people understood all the ramifications of change? Has all the population adapted equally well? Let us look for some entries on the debit side. What are the problems Nayon faces, and what are the forces released by its abandonment of a way of life that has been moderately successful for four hundred years? And what has impelled Nayon citizens to make this change? These are questions Nayon shares with the thousands of villages on every continent.

One characteristic of the village world is the existence of a balance between resources and population. Birth rates and death rates are in balance unless nearby cities absorb surplus population. Living standards tend to be relatively unchanging. In Nayon improved health conditions, erosion, and new living standards have between them destroyed this resources-population balance.

On the surface, it seems difficult to maintain that health conditions in Nayon have improved. Inadequate surveys of school children indicate that at least sixty to eighty per cent of the population is infested with one or more intestinal parasites. Goiter, avitaminoses, and other forms of malnutrition are prevalent. Measles, mumps, and chicken pox are considered normal for all children. Tuberculosis, malaria, and venereal disease are increasing. On the other hand, smallpox and whooping cough are fairly well controlled.

Unsatisfactory as the health situation may appear by our standards, the best test of it is the relationship between births and deaths. From the beginning of the registration of vital statistics in Nayon in 1936 through 1948, there were 287 more births than deaths. This is a population increase of nearly thirty per cent in thirteen years.

MAN AND THE LAND.   Natural resources have diminished as population has increased. Great gullies are destroying the most fertile land. Sheet erosion has removed all the top soil from large areas, exposing a hard and infertile clay subsoil. In areas under cultivation each torrential tropical rain removes top soil with frightening rapidity; streets are becoming gullies. Consequently, much land has been abandoned, and even the forested areas have been planted recently with the alien eucalyptus.

Diminishing resources and expanding population have caused excessive fragmentation of land holdings. . . .

Another measure of pressures on land is the changing price structure. Land prices increased from 3,000 to 11,700 per cent between 1918 and 1948.

These few data make it clear that the traditional balance with the environment has been destroyed at Nayon. Even if improved agricultural techniques and erosion control are introduced, approximately one-half of the Nayon children who reach adulthood must emigrate if the village is to maintain its present relatively low living standards on the basis of agriculture. Moreover, the Nayon standard of living is rising, and aspirations for a continued betterment are strong. Any further improvement of health conditions must mean an even greater emigration rate. Alternatively, other sources of livelihood must be found.

To some degree both of these solutions are already in operation. A few families have emigrated, mostly to the coastal lowland areas now being developed in Ecuador. Others have purchased land elsewhere and may soon emigrate. This trend probably will be accelerated. Many have resorted to more extensive trading and entrepreneurial activities. Others work for wages in the nearby city.

The economic problems created in Nayon by increasing population, diminishing land base, and demands for a rising living standard are world-wide in scope. Whether on Pacific islands, in Africa, or in Asia—wherever modern public health has begun to penetrate, or where outside agencies have put a stop to such population-limiting devices as war, famine, and infanticide—population is pressing hard upon resources and native technology. Everywhere, too, the solutions being tried are creating new social problems, for the fabric of any society and its culture is composed of functionally interrelated parts; alteration of any significant part must affect all the others.

108 EUROPE'S IMPACT: CULTURAL

Nineteenth century Europe left its mark on the world in the cultural as well as the economic sphere. The Europeans, in their first period of expansion, did not particularly impress the peoples in the ancient centers of Asian civilization. In fact, the Moslems, Hindus, and Confucians tended to look down upon the Western sea captains and merchants as uncouth and crassly materialistic. By the beginning of the twentieth century, however, this attitude was for the most part reversed. More and more, Eastern spokesmen were conceding, albeit grudgingly, the superiority not only of Western technology but also of the European way of life in general. The first selection, from a Young Turk newspaper published in Cairo at the turn of the century, refers to "the light of civilization" emanating from the West. The second selection, written shortly after World War I by a distinguished Chinese scholar, states flatly that "real spirituality" is to be found not in the teachings of Eastern religions but in the labor-saving and life-saving inventions of Western science.*

Young Turk Newspaper

Five-and-twenty years ago, Sophia was full of crooked and dirty streets, such as we still see in Adrianople, Yanina, Monastir, etc., without any features to commend itself either for beauty or convenience, and with the exception of several places of worship, barracks, and prisons, there was nothing to denote any degree of culture. Since Sophia has been under Bulgarian government, one would scarcely recognize the place on account of the many improvements and changes which have been made. It now possesses straight wide streets, public squares, theatres, museums, zoological and botanical gardens, electric light, tramways, telephone, etc. And not only Sophia, but also Varna, Philippopolis, and other towns, have been Euro-

---

* A. Vambery, *Western Culture in Eastern Lands* (London: J. Murray, 1906), pp. 343, 344; Hu Shih, "The Civilizations of the East and the West," in C. A. Beard, ed., *Whither Mankind* (New York: Longmans, 1928), pp. 28-31. Used by permission of David McKay Co., Inc.

peanized. Roumania, Servia, and Greece, as well as Bulgaria, have been illumined by the light of civilisation since they have become independent States. Crete will soon follow suit. When we look round in our own land and see how Adrianople, Brussa, Aleppo, Damascus, and Bagdad, all once centres of the empire, have failed to maintain their former glory and beauty, and have become desolate through utter neglect of the spirit of modernization, we pity them for the darkness and ignorance into which they have sunk. At Brussa and Adrianople, situated at very short distances from the capital, we still find the primitive waggons pulled by oxen, and omnibuses, even, are an unknown convenience. But why quote instances from provincial towns? Let us take Constantinople itself, with its million inhabitants, and in point of natural beauty excelling all other capitals. On the roughly paved streets dirt and filth lie deep, and dogs prowl about. Barracks abound, but the military are only there to suppress revolts; for personal safety little or no provision is made. Stamboul has no theatres, no botanical or zoological gardens—modern institutions which have found their way even into Australia and Siberia. ... For God's sake, let us have done with this slowness, this negligence. Let us not turn our eyes away from the light of culture.

Chinese Scholar

In July, 1926, I arrived at Harbin, in Northern Manchuria, on my way to Europe. The modern city of Harbin was formerly a Russian Concession which grew up from a small trading centre into what is now called the "Shanghai of North China." With the development of the Russian Concession, there has grown up, a few miles away, the native city of Harbin which was once only a group of peasant villages. While I was touring through the city, I was struck by one interesting fact: whereas practically all the vehicles of locomotion in the native city were jinrickshas, or carriages pulled by human power, no 'ricksha was allowed to operate in the former Russian City which, though now under Chinese administration, still retained much of Russian influence and tradition. Transportation and travelling in the modern city of Harbin were by tramways and taxicabs; 'rickshas carrying passengers from the native city must leave without a fare.

Here I made my great discovery in modern geography—I discovered the borderline between the Eastern and Western civilizations. The city of Harbin separates the East from the West by separating the jinricksha (man-power-carriage) civilization from the motor-car civilization!

Let all apologists for the spiritual civilization of the East reflect on this. What spirituality is there in a civilization which tolerates such a terrible form of human slavery as the 'ricksha coolie? Do we seriously believe that there can be any spiritual life left in those poor human beasts of burden who run and toil and sweat under that peculiar bondage of slavery which knows neither the minimum wage nor any limit of working hours? Do we really believe that the life of a 'ricksha coolie is more spiritual or more moral than that of the American workman who rides to and from his work in his own motor-car, who takes his whole family outing and picnicking on Sundays in distant parks and woods, who listens to the best music of the land on the radio almost for no cost, and whose children are educated in schools equipped with the most modern library and laboratory facilities?

It is only when one has fully realized what misery and acute suffering the life of 'ricksha-pulling entails and what effects it produces on the bodily health of those human beasts of burden—it is only then that one will be truly and religiously moved to bless the Hargreaveses, the Cartwrights, the Watts, the Fultons, the Stephensons, and the Fords who have devised machines to do the work for man an relieve him from much of the brutal suffering to which his Oriental neighbor is still subject.

Herein, therefore, lies the real spirituality of the material civilization, of mechanical progress *per se*. Mechanical progress means the use of human intelligence to devise tools and machines to multiply the working ability and productivity of man so that he may be relieved from the fate of toiling incessantly with his unaided hands, feet, and back without being able to earn a bare subsistence, and so that he may have enough time and energy left to seek and enjoy the higher values which civilization can offer him. Where man has to sweat blood in order to earn the lowest kind of livelihood, there is little *life* left, letting alone civilization. A civilization to be worthy of its name must be built upon the foundation of material progress. As one of China's statesmen said twenty-six centuries ago, "when food and clothing are sufficiently provided for, honor and disgrace can be distinguished; and when granaries are full, the people will know good manners." This is not to drag in the so-called economic interpretation of history: it is simple commonsense. Picture a civilization where boys and girls and old women with bamboo baskets tied to their backs and with pointed sticks in hand, flock to every dumping place of garbage and search every heap of refuse for a possible torn piece of rag or a half-burnt piece of coal. How can we expect a moral and spiritual civilization to grow up in such an atmosphere?

Then people may point to the religious life in those regions where the material civilization is low. I shall not discuss those Oriental religions whose highest deities appear on roadsides in the shape of human sex-organs. I shall only ask: "What spirituality is there, let us say, in the old beggar-woman who dies in the direst destitution, but who dies while still mumbling, *Nama Amita Buddha!* and in the clear conviction that she will surely enter that blissful paradise presided over by the Amita Buddha? Do we earnestly think it moral or spiritual to inculcate in that beggar-woman a false belief which shall so hypnotize her as to make her willingly live and die in such dire conditions where she ought not to have been had she been born in a different civilization?"

No! A thousand times No! All those hypnotic religions belong to an age when man had reached senility and felt himself impotent in coping with the forces of nature. Therefore he gave up the fight in despair and, like the disappointed fox in the ancient fable who declared the grapes sour because he could not reach them, began to console himself and teach the world that wealth and comfort are contemptible and that poverty and misery are something to be proud of. From this it was only a step to the idea that life itself was not worth living and that the only desirable thing was the blissful existence in the world beyond. And when wise men calmly taught these ideas, fanatics went further and practiced self-denial, self-torture, and even suicide. . . .

How is it that the outlook upon life has so radically changed? The change has come because in the last two centuries men have hit upon a few key-inventions out of which a vast number of tools and machines have been constructed for the control of the resources and powers in nature. By means of these machines men have been able to save labor and reduce distance, to fly in the air, tunnel the mountains and sail underneath the deep seas, to enslave lightning to pull our carriages and employ "ether" to deliver our messages throughout the world. Science and machinery seem to meet no resistance from nature. Life has become easier and happier, and man's confidence in his own powers has greatly increased. Man has become the master of himself and of his own destiny.

WHITE MAN'S BURDEN **109**

Europe's overwhelming mastery of the globe in the nineteenth century led to the doctrine of the "White Man's Burden"—a doctrine stating that the Europeans were dominant because they were superior, and that this superiority obliged them to assume the duty of ruling the inferior peoples and guiding them along the path of civilization. The classic expression of this concept is the poem by Rudyard Kipling,* given below. John Strachey, a British official in India, in 1888 gave further expression to this concept by stating bluntly that he and his fellow officials knew what was best for India, and that that country must remain under British rule for its own good.**

From The White Man's Burden

Take up the White Man's burden—
Send forth the best ye breed—
Go bind your sons to exile
To serve your captives' need;
To wait in heavy harness,
On fluttered folk and wild—
Your new-caught, sullen peoples,
Half-devil and half-child.

Take up the White Man's burden—
In patience to abide,
To veil the threat of terror
And check the show of pride;
By open speech and simple,
An hundred times made plain
To seek another's profit,
And work another's gain.

Take up the White Man's burden—
The savage wars of peace—
Fill full the mouth of Famine
And bid the sickness cease;

---

* From "The White Man's Burden" by Rudyard Kipling, from *The Five Nations*. Reprinted by permission of Mrs. George Bambridge, Doubleday & Company, Inc., Methuen & Co., Ltd., and Macmillan Co. of Canada, Ltd.
** J. Strachey, *India*, 3rd ed. (London: Macmillan, 1903), pp. 501–6.

And when your goal is nearest
The end for other sought,
Watch sloth and heathen Folly
Bring all your hopes to nought.

Take up the White Man's burden—
No tawdry rule of kings,
But toil of serf and sweeper—
The tale of common things.
The ports ye shall not enter,
The roads ye shall not tread,
Go make them with your living,
And mark them with your dead.

John Strachey

... No reasonable man can doubt the answer that we must give to the question whether the 300,000,000 of people inhabiting the numerous countries of India have benefited by our government.

The first great and obvious fact, overshadowing all other facts in significance, is this, that in place of a condition of society given up, as it was immediately before our time, to anarchy and to the liability to every conceivable form of violence and oppression, we have now absolute peace. Let not this unspeakable blessing of the Pax Britannica be forgotten. There are not many European countries where protection to life and property is so complete. ... Except when not unfrequently the fanaticism and intolerance of rival sects of Mohammedans and Hindus burst into violent conflict, and show what would instantly follow if the strong hand of our Government were withdrawn, unbroken tranquillity prevails. Justice is administered under laws of unequalled excellence and simplicity. There is hardly any country possessing a civilised administration where the public burdens are so light. ...

Whether all this makes our Government really popular is another question. ...

I never heard of a great measure of improvement that was popular in India, even among the classes that have received the largest share of education. No one who has lived, as I have done for the better part of my life, among the people can have towards them feelings other than those of sympathy and affection and respect. They have qualities which deserve all admiration, but they are intensely conservative and intensely ignorant, wedded, to an extent difficult for Europeans to understand, to every ancient custom, and between their customs and religion no line of distinction can be drawn. We often deceive ourselves in regard to the changes that are taking place. We believe that our Western knowledge, our railways, and our telegraphs must be breaking up the whole fabric of Hinduism, but these things, as I have said before, have touched only the merest fringe of the ideas and beliefs of the population of India. The vast masses of the people remain in a different world from ours. They dislike everything new, they dislike almost everything that we look upon as progress, and they live, for the most part, in blind ignorance of the aims and ideas of their rulers. ...

It would thus be an error to suppose that the British Government is administered in a manner that altogether commends itself to the majority of the

Indian population. This we cannot help. Considerations of political prudence compel us to tolerate much that we should wish to alter, and to abstain from much that we might desire to see accomplished, but, subject to this most essential condition, our duty is plain. It is to govern India with unflinching determination on the principles which our superior knowledge tells us are right, although they may be unpopular.

First Challenges to Europe's Domination 110

Europe's domination of the globe seemed, in 1914, to be permanent and irresistible. Yet, it was beginning to be challenged in many parts of the colonial world. This was especially true after the 1904–1905 Russo-Japanese War, which excited colonial peoples everywhere with its spectacle of a small Asian kingdom defeating a great European power, and the contemporaneous Russian Revolution, equally inflammatory, which inspired corresponding revolutions against decrepit Oriental dynasties that had proven incapable of resisting European imperialism. Consequently, the decade after 1905 witnessed growing opposition to Europe's hegemony. Outright revolution upset the Manchu dynasty in China, the Kajar dynasty in Persia, and the Ottoman dynasty in Turkey; and agitation and disturbances were leveled against the British in India and the Russians in Central Asia. This was pre-1914 awakening is significant as marking the beginning of the great colonial nationalist movements that were later to undermine and sweep away those European empires that were so impressive before World War I. The following selections describe this early awakening of peoples in several colonial areas.

Persia

This nationalistic verse was written by a Persian reformer in 1896, shortly before suffering death in prison.

> Ne'er may that evil-omened day befall
> When Iran shall become the stranger's thrall!
> Ne'er may I see that virgin fair and pure
> Fall victim to some Russian gallant's lure!
> And ne'er may Fate this angel-bride award
> As serving-maiden to some English lord!*

India

In the following selection, Jawaharlal Nehru describes his reaction, as a boy of thirteen, to the news of Japan's victory over Russia.

* Cited in E. G. Browne, *The Persian Revolution of 1905-1909* (London: Cambridge Univ., 1910), p. XI.

Japanese victories stirred up my enthusiasm, and I waited eagerly for the papers for fresh news daily. I invested in a large number of books on Japan and tried to read some of them. I felt rather lost in Japanese history, but I liked the knightly tales of old Japan and the pleasant prose of Lafcadio Hearn. Nationalistic ideas filled my mind. I mused of Indian freedom and Asiatic freedom from the thralldom of Europe. I dreamed of brave deeds, of how, sword in hand, I would fight for India and help in freeing her.*

British Empire

A competent British observer, Maurice Baring, was in the Near East in 1909, and reported the impact of the Russo-Japanese War in these terms:

The British Empire includes large dominions inhabited by Muslims, and ever since the Russo-Japanese War, in all the Moslim countries which are under British sway, there have been movements and agitations in favour of Western methods of government, constitutionalism, and self-government. There has been a cry of "Egypt for the Egyptians," and of "India for the Indians," and in some cases this cry has been supported and punctuated by bombs and assassinations.**

Indochina

Following the Russo-Japanese War, numerous Annamite students left Indochina for Japan in order to learn the secret of the success of the victorious nation. In the following letter written in December, 1905, one of these students calls on his fellow-countrymen to prepare themselves for the struggle against their French masters.

. . . All powers, all profits are in the hands of the masters with the blue eyes, the red barbarians. And we, the yellow race, we are subjected by force to demoralization, to complete degradation. In order to obtain allies, it is necessary that we have recourse to representatives of our own race. I, your humble servant, an obscure student, having had occasion to study new books, and new doctrines, have discovered in a recent history of Japan how they have been able to conquer the impotent Europeans. This is the reason why we have formed an organization. . . . We have selected from among the young Annamites those most energetic, with great capacities for courage, and are sending them to Japan for study. . . . Several years have passed without the French being aware of this movement. This is why we have been able to increase our forces. At the present time there are about six hundred students from Indochina in Japan. Our only aim is to prepare the population for the

* *Toward Freedom. The Autobiography of Jawaharlal Nehru* (New York: Day, 1941), pp. 29-30. Copyright © 1941 by The John Day Company. Reprinted by permission of The John Day Company, Inc.
** M. Baring, *Letters from the Near East 1909 and 1912* (London, 1913), pp. 12-13.

future. ... Have you created any organization for this purpose in your region? *

Russian Central Asia

The stirring events of 1904–1905 contributed greatly to the political awakening of the subject Moslem peoples in Russian Central Asia, as described in the following analysis by an American scholar.

The defeat of Russia in the Russo-Japanese War and the Revolution of 1905 called forth an unprecedented upsurge of activity among Russia's Muslims, especially among the Turco-Tatars. This political and national awakening resulted in the holding of three all Turkish congresses in Russia, 1905-06. The first, held in Nizhny-Novgorod in August 1905, proclaimed the need for Tatar or Muslim unity in order to deal effectively with social, cultural, and political problems. The second, convened in the Russian capital, St. Petersburg, January 13-23, 1906, prepared for Muslim participation in the first Russian Duma, and decided in favor of backing the Russian Constitutional Democrats (Kadets), headed by Paul Miliukov. The fact—and important one for the Muslims—that they won twenty-five seats in the first Duma led to a third All-Muslim Congress on August 16, 1906, at Makariev, near Nizhny-Novgorod, for the purpose of organizing a Muslim Party in Russia and inaugurating a Turkic cultural and social program with a strong Pan-Turkic bent. The organization of a Muslim faction in the Russian Duma also demonstrated the active role of the Turco-Tatars in the new Russian constitutional regime. The second Duma included thirty-five Muslim deputies, and even after the revision of the electoral law, there were ten in the Third Duma of 1907.

After the Revolution of 1905 and the October Manifesto, about forty Tatar periodicals came into existence, an important medium for the spread of Muslim political activity inside Russia and abroad. In Azerbaijan, the Revolution led to the organization of new schools, theaters, and newspapers. Two outstanding news organs, *Hayat* and *Irshad,* were established in 1905. Not only did they report news about Muslims inside Russia, but they also reprinted much about Young Turk revolutionary activity in the Ottoman Empire.**

All Asia

The Chinese nationalist leader, Dr. Sun Yat-sen, delivered a speech in Japan in 1924 in which he analyzed the effect of Japan's victory over Russia as follows: ***

Thirty years ago ... men thought and believed that European civilization was a progressive one—in science, industry, manufacture, and armament—

* Cited in T. E. Ennis, *French Policy and Developments in Indochina* (Chicago: Univ. of Chicago, 1936), p. 178.
** I. Spector, *The First Russian Revolution. Its Impact on Asia* (Englewood Cliffs: Prentice-Hall, 1962; A Spectrum Book), pp. 63-64.
*** Sun Yat-sen, *China and Japan* (Shanghai: China United Press, 1941), pp. 142-43.

and that Asia had nothing to compare with it. Consequently, they assumed that Asia could never resist Europe, that European oppression could never be shaken off. Such was the idea prevailing thirty years ago. It was a pessimistic idea. Even after Japan abolished the Unequal Treaties and attained the status of an independent country, Asia, with the exception of a few countries situated near Japan, was little influenced. Ten years later, however, the Russo-Japanese war broke out and Russia was defeated by Japan. For the first time in the history of the last several hundred years, an Asiatic country has defeated a European Power. The effect of this victory immediately spread over the whole Asia, and gave a new hope to all Asiatic peoples. In the year of the outbreak of the Russo-Japanese war I was in Europe. One day news came that Admiral Togo had defeated the Russian navy, annihilating in the Japan Sea the fleet newly despatched from Europe to Vladivostock. The population of the whole continent was taken aback. Britain was Japan's Ally, yet most of the British people were painfully surprised, for in their eyes Japan's victory over Russia was certainly not a blessing for the White peoples. "Blood," after all, "is thicker than water." Later on I sailed for Asia. When the steamer passed the Suez Canal a number of natives came to see me. All of them wore smiling faces, and asked me whether I was a Japanese. I replied that I was a Chinese, and inquired what was in their minds, and why they were so happy. They said they had just heard the news that Japan had completely destroyed the Russian fleet recently despatched from Europe, and were wondering how true the story was. Some of them, living on both banks of the Canal had witnessed Russian hospital ships, with wounded on board, passing through the Canal from time to time. That was surely a proof of the Russian defeat, they added.

In former days, the coloured races in Asia, suffering from the oppression of the Western peoples, thought that emancipation was impossible. We regarded that Russian defeat by Japan as the defeat of the West by the East. We regarded the Japanese victory as our own victory. It was indeed a happy event. Did not therefore this news of Russia's defeat by Japan affect the peoples of the whole of Asia? Was not its effect tremendous?

PART IV

WORLD OF
WESTERN DECLINE
AND TRIUMPH, 1914-

Chapter Twenty

World War I:
global repercussions

BACKGROUND TO SARAJEVO $\quad$ 111

World War I represents a great turning point in world history be- *cause it began Europe's decline as master of the globe. The war was* *triggered by the assassination of the Archduke Francis Ferdinand at* *Sarajevo on June 28, 1914. Behind his assassination was the growth of* *nationalism among the subject peoples of Eastern Europe, who turned* *against the empires that held them in bondage. This was especially true* *of the Serbs in the Austro-Hungarian Empire, who wished to break away* *and join the small independent state of Serbia. To accomplish their aim* *they organized a secret, terrorist society named* Ujedinjenje ili smrt *(Union* *or Death), popularly known as the Black Hand. It was an agent of this* *society, Gavrilo Princip, who committed the murder at Sarajevo. The* *first of the following selections consists of excerpts from the constitution* *of the society, showing that the Black Hand planned to use force to lib-* *erate the Serbian provinces of Austria-Hungary. The second selection,* *from a letter sent by the Austrian Emperor to the German Emperor im-* *mediately after the murder, shows that Austria was determined to take* *strong action against Serbia because she regarded Serbian nationalist* *agitation a threat to her very existence. Thus, one of the basic causes* *for World War I was the clash between the multinational empires and* *their awakening subject peoples.* It should be noted that despite the Aus-*

---

* *Die Kriegsschuldfrage,* IV (September, 1926), 681-85; and *Outbreak of the* *World War: German Documents Collected by Karl Kautsky,* Carnegie En- dowment for International Peace (New York: Oxford Univ., 1924), pp. 68-69.

trian Emperor's suspicions, the Serbian government did not plan the murder. Certain Serbian officials were involved, but the Belgrade government itself was not in collusion with the Black Hand. Actually, it feared the secret society and opposed it as much as it dared.

Black Hand Constitution

Article 1. This organisation has been created with the object of realising the national ideal: The union of all the Serbs. . . .

Article 2. This organisation prefers terrorist action to intellectual propaganda and for this reason must be kept absolutely secret from persons who do not belong to it.

Article 3. The organisation bears the name "Union or Death."

Article 4. To accomplish its task, the organisation:

1. Brings influence to bear on Government circles, on the various social classes and on the whole social life of the Kingdom of Serbia, regarded as Piémont.
2. Organises revolutionary action in all the territories inhabited by Serbs. . . .

Article 5. A Central Committee having its headquarters at Belgrade is at the head of this organisation and exercises executive authority. . . .

Article 7. The Central Committee of Belgrade includes besides the members representing the Kingdom of Serbia a delegate from each of the Serbian territories abroad (Pokraine): 1. Bosnia and Herzogovina; 2. Montenegro; 3. Old Serbia and Macedonia; 4. Croatia, Slavonia and Syrmia; 5. Voivodina; 6. the coastal districts (Primorje). . . .

Article 30. Every member on entering the organisation must realize that by this act he forfeits his own personality, that he can expect within it neither glory nor personal profit, either moral or material. Consequently, any member attempting to make use of the organisation for personal or party motives will be punished. If by his acts he injures the organisation he will be punished with death.

Article 31. Anyone who once enters the organisation may never withdraw from it. Nor can anybody accept his resignation.

Article 33. When the Central Committee at Belgrade has pronounced penalty of death, the only matter of importance is that the execution take place without fail. The method of execution employed is a matter of indifference.

Article 34. The organisation has the following seal: In the middle of the signet a muscular hand with fingers bent, grasping an unfurled flag. On the flag as escutcheon, a death's head with crossbones and beside the flag a dagger, a bomb and poison. Around the outside of the seal runs the inscription, from right to left, *Ujedinjenje ili Smrt* (Union or Death) and beneath it the title of the Central Committee in Belgrade: *Vrhovna Centralna Uptrava* (Supreme Central Committee).

Article 35. On becoming a member one takes the following oath: I, N.N., on becoming a member of the organisation Union or Death, swear by the Sun that warms me, by the Earth that nourishes me, before God, by the blood of my ancestors, on my honour and on my life, that I will from this moment till my death be faithful to the laws of this organisation, that I will always be ready to make any sacrifice for it. I swear before God on my honour and on my life that I will take all the secrets of the organisation with me into my grave. May God confound me and may my comrades in this organisation judge me if I trespass against or either consciously or unconsciously fail to keep my oath.

Austrian Emperor to German Emperor

... The perpetration of the assassination of my poor nephew is the direct result of the agitations carried on by the Russian and Serbian Panslavists, the sole object of which is the weakening of the triple Alliance and the destruction of my realm.

According to all the evidence so far brought to light, the Sarajevo affair was not merely the bloody deed of a single individual, but was the result of a well-organised conspiracy, the threads of which can be traced to Belgrade; and even though it will probably prove impossible to get evidence of the complicity of the Serbian Government, there can be no doubt that its policy, directed toward the unification of all the southern-Slav countries under the Serbian flag, is responsible for such crimes, and that the continuation of such a state of affairs constitutes an enduring peril for my house and my possessions. ...

You, too, must be convinced, after the recent frightful occurrence in Bosnia, that a reconciliation of the antagonism that now divides Serbia and ourselves is no more to be thought of, and that the continuance of the peace policy of all European monarchs is threatened as long as this hearth of criminal agitation at Belgrade is left unquenched.

COMING OF WAR **112**

Another basic cause for the outbreak of World War I, in addition to nationalistic aspirations, was the conflict of the rival alliance blocs, the Triple Alliance (Germany, Austria-Hungary, and Italy) and the Triple Entente (France, Russia, and Britain). For some years prior to 1914, every dispute tended to become a major crisis because the members of each alliance fearfully supported each other, lest their allies drift away, a pattern evident in the following selections concerning the diplomacy after Sarajevo. The first selection is the German reply to the Austrian emperor, assuring him the full support of Berlin. This "blank check" did not mean that Germany wanted war; rather, it meant that she did not dare turn her back on her only reliable ally. Certain of Germany's support, Austria then sent an ultimatum to Serbia on July 23. The texts of this ultimatum and of Serbia's reply are given below. Austria rejected Serbia's studiedly evasive response as unsatisfactory, and declared war on July 28, as indicated in the fourth selection.*

* *Outbreak of the World War: German Documents Collected by Karl Kautsky,* Carnegie Endowment for International Peace (New York: Oxford Univ., 1924), pp. 78-79, 604-5; *International Conciliation,* No. 89 (April, 1915), pp. 69-77.

340   THE IMPERIAL CHANCELOR TO THE AMBASSADOR AT VIENNA. *Berlin, July 6, 1914.* The Austro-Hungarian Ambassador yesterday delivered to the Emperor a confidential personal letter from the Emperor Franz Joseph, which depicts the present situation from the Austro-Hungarian point of view, and describes the measures which Vienna has in view. A copy is now being forwarded to Your Excellency.

I replied to Count Szögyeny today on behalf of His Majesty that His Majesty sends his thanks to the Emperor Franz Joseph for his letter and would soon answer it personally. In the meantime His Majesty desires to say that he is not blind to the danger which threatens Austria-Hungary and thus the Triple Alliance as a result of the Russian and Serbian Panslavic agitation. . . .

As far as concerns Serbia, His Majesty, of course, can not interfere in the dispute now going on between Austria-Hungary and that country, as it is a matter not within his competence. The Emperor Franz Joseph may, however, rest assured that His Majesty will faithfully stand by Austria-Hungary, as is required by the obligations of his alliance and of his ancient friendship.

BETHMANN-HOLLWEG

Austro-Hungarian Ultimatum to Serbia, July 23, 1914

. . . The Imperial and Royal Government finds itself compelled to demand that the Serbian Government give official assurance that it will condemn the propaganda directed against Austria-Hungary, that is to say, the whole body of the efforts whose ultimate object it is to separate from the Monarchy territories that belong to it; and that it will obligate itself to suppress with the means at its command this criminal and terroristic propaganda. . . .

The Royal Serbian Government will furthermore pledge itself:

1. to suppress every publication which shall incite to hatred and contempt of the Monarchy, and the general tendency of which shall be directed against the territorial integrity of the latter;

2. to proceed at once to the dissolution of the *Narodna Odbrana* [anti-Austrian nationalist society], to confiscate all of its means of propaganda, and in the same manner to proceed against the other unions and associations in Serbia which occupy themselves with propaganda against Austria-Hungary . . . ;

3. to eliminate without delay from public instruction in Serbia, everything, whether connected with the teaching corps or with the methods of teaching, that serves or may serve to nourish the propaganda against Austria-Hungary;

4. to remove from the military and administrative service in general all officers and officials who have been guilty of carrying on the propoganda against Austria-Hungary . . . ;

5. to agree to the cooperation in Serbia of the organs of the Imperial and Royal Government in the suppression of the subversive movement directed against the integrity of the Monarchy;

6. to institute a judicial inquiry against every participant in the conspiracy

of the twenty-eighth of June who may be found in Serbian territory; the organs of the Imperial and Royal Government delegated for this purpose will take part in the proceedings held for this purpose;

7. to undertake with all haste the arrest of Major Voislav Tankositch and of one Milan Ciganovitch, a Serbian official, who have been compromised by the results of the inquiry;

8. by efficient measures to prevent the participation of Serbian authorities in the smuggling of weapons and explosives across the frontier . . . ;

9. to make explanations to the Imperial and Royal Government concerning the unjustifiable utterances of high Serbian functionaries in Serbia and abroad, who, without regard for their official position, have not hesitated to express themselves in a manner hostile toward Austria-Hungary since the assassination of the twenty-eighth of June;

10. to inform the Imperial and Royal Government without delay of the execution of the measures comprised in the foregoing points. . . .

Serbian Reply to Austria-Hungary, July 25, 1914

The Royal Servian Government has received the communication of the Royal Government of the 10th instant [old style date], and is convinced that its reply will remove any misunderstanding which may threaten to impair the good neighborly relations between the Austro-Hungarian Monarchy and the Kingdom of Servia. . . .

The Royal Government cannot be held responsible for manifestations of a private character, such as articles in the press and the peaceable work of societies—manifestations which take place in nearly all countries in the ordinary course of events, and which as a general rule are beyond official control. . . .

For these reasons the Royal Government has been painfully surprised at the allegations that citizens of the Kingdom of Servia have participated in the preparations for the crime committed at Serajevo; the Royal Government had expected to be invited to collaborate in an investigation of all that concerns this crime. . . .

Complying with the desire of the Imperial and Royal Government, it is prepared to commit for trial any Servian subject, regardless of his station or rank, of whose complicity in the crime of Serajevo proofs shall be produced. . . .

The Royal Government further undertakes:

1. To insert, at the first ordinary convocation of the Skuptchina [legislature], a provision into the press law for the most severe punishment of incitement to hatred and contempt of the Austro-Hungarian Monarchy, and for taking action against any publication the general tendency of which is directed against the territorial integrity of Austria-Hungary.

The Government engages at the impending revision of the Constitution an amendment permitting that such publications be confiscated, a proceeding at present impossible according to the clear provisions of Article 22 of the Constitution.

2. The Government possesses no proof, nor does the note of the Imperial and Royal Government furnish it with any, that the "Narodna Odbrana" and other similar societies have committed up to the present any

criminal act of this nature through the proceedings of any of their members. Nevertheless, the Royal Government will accept the demands of the Imperial and Royal Government and will dissolve the "Narodna Odbrana" Society and every other association which may be directing its efforts against Austria-Hungary.

3. The Royal Servian Government undertakes to remove without delay from the system of public instruction in Servia all that serves or could serve to foment propaganda against Austria-Hungary, whenever the Imperial and Royal Government shall furnish it with facts and proofs of such propaganda.

4. The Royal Government also agrees to remove from the military and the civil service all such persons as the judicial inquiry may have proved to be guilty of acts directed against the territorial integrity of the Austro-Hungarian Monarchy. . . .

5. The Royal Government must confess that it does not clearly understand the meaning or the scope of the demand made by the Imperial and Royal Government that Servia shall undertake to accept the collaboration of officials of the Imperial and Royal Government upon Servian territory, but it declares that it will admit such collaboration as agrees with the principle of international law, with criminal procedure, and with good neighborly relations.

6. It goes without saying that the Royal Government considers it a duty to begin an inquiry against all such persons as are, or possibly may be, implicated in the plot of the 15/28 June, and who may happen to be within the territory of the kingdom. As regards the participation in this inquiry of Austro-Hungarian agents or authorities appointed for this purpose by the Imperial and Royal Government, the Royal Government cannot accept such an arrangement, as it would constitute a violation of the Constitution and of the law of criminal procedure; nevertheless, in concrete cases communications as to the results of the investigation in question might be given to the Austro-Hungarian agents.

7. The Royal Government proceeded on the very evening of the delivery of the note, to arrest Commandant Foija Tankositch.

As regards Milan Ciganovitch, who is a subject of the Austro-Hungarian Monarchy and who up to the 15th June was employed (on probation) by the directorate of railways, it has not yet been possible to find out his whereabouts. Notices for his apprehension have been published in the press. . . .

8. The Servian Government will reinforce and extend the measures which have been taken for suppressing the illicit traffic in arms and explosives across the frontier. . . .

9. The Royal Government will gladly furnish explanations of the remarks made by its officials, whether in Servia or abroad, in interviews after the crime, and which, according to the statement of the Imperial and Royal Government, were hostile to the Monarchy, as soon as the Imperial and Royal Government shall have communicated to it the passages in question in these remarks, and as soon as it shall have shown that the remarks were actually made by the said officials, in connection with which the Royal Government itself will take steps to collect evidence.

10. The Royal Government will inform the Imperial and Royal Government of the execution of the measures comprised under the above heads, in-so-far as this has not already been done by the present note, as soon as each measure shall have been ordered and carried out. . . .

Austro-Hungarian Declaration of War, July 28, 1914

COUNT BERCHTOLD TO THE ROYAL SERVIAN FOREIGN OFFICE, BELGRADE. *(Telegram.) Vienna, July 28, 1914.* The Royal Servian Government having failed to give a satisfactory reply to the note which was handed to it by the Austro-Hungarian Minister in Belgrade on July 23rd, 1914, the Imperial and Royal Government is compelled to protect its own rights and interests, by a recourse to armed force.

Austria-Hungary, therefore, considers herself from now on to be in state of war with Servia.

TRENCH FIGHTING 113

When Austria attacked Serbia, Russia ordered mobilization. Germany replied by attacking Russia and France, and Britain then intervened on the side of her allies. Thus, the system of rival alliance blocs escalated the Sarajevo crisis to World War I. When the fighting began in early August, many expected that it would be over by Christmas. Instead, the superiority of defensive over offensive weapons dragged it on until the end of 1918. The following selection from a United States military handbook shows how the combination of trenches, machine guns, field artillery, and barbed wire entanglements effectively stopped the traditional infantry charges. The last paragraph contrasts casualties in World War I with those suffered in World War II. (This contrast is analyzed in detail in Reading 157, "Blitzkrieg.")*

Before World War I was barely three months old, open warfare between maneuvering armies had given way to static warfare in western Europe. No more flanks were left to turn, for the rival armies stretched some five hundred miles from the North Sea to Switzerland in two solid lines of trenches. Since the armies could no longer get around each other, they tried to smash through. For the next four years fighting on the Western Front consisted of rival attempts to break through the opposing lines. Occasionally, after terrific losses, the lines might bend a few miles but they never broke decisively until the last months of the war. Germany, England, France, Belgium, and later the United States, spent their major military efforts in holding or attacking those trench lines.

A new and unaccustomed type of fighting developed, dominated by the machine gun, the field artillery and barbed wire. The war on this front might, in fact, be called a gigantic siege. Even in the American Civil War the deadly power of the rifle had forced troops to "dig in" for protection. Now that had become an absolute necessity and, as rapid movements ceased and the armies faced each other for a long time, the trench systems became increasingly more elaborate. ... The average trench position was about a mile in depth, with four parallel trenches connected by so-called "communicating trenches."

* United States Marine Corps, *A Guide for the Study of the Evolution of the Art of War* (1954), pp. 87-89.

Out in front was a tangle of barbed wire to impede an infantry assault. Behind that, the closest of the four trenches to the enemy, was the outpost line. Then, in the center, came the main line of resistance and its supports; finally the reserves occupied the fourth line in the rear. Artillery was stationed behind the lines. This system was the so-called "rigid" defense designed to keep the enemy from getting past the second or third line.

The attack on such a position assumed a fairly conventional form during the early years of the war. Even before the fighting had settled down to trench warfare, the machine gun had revealed its deadly effect upon a skirmish line of infantry. With the added hazard of barbed wire the chances of reaching the enemy lines intact were still further reduced. Consequently, artillery was called upon to pave the way. An infantry attack was normally preceded by hours, and sometimes days, of bombardment by light, medium and heavy guns. The intention was not only to smash the barbed wire but to ensure that the defenders of the opposing trenches would be in no shape to resist the infantry attack. Finally, just before the infantry was ready to go "over the top," the light artillery would lay down a "rolling barrage," with a curtain of shells which was kept moving ahead just in front of the advancing infantry lines; the accurate features of the "75" made this possible. Even that tremendous artillery preparation was not enough; somehow, some of the enemy always managed to survive the inferno and to cut loose with the deadly rattle of machine guns as the infantry approached. Also other enemy troops were often able to emerge from their dugouts in time to engage in a melee with rifles, bayonets, or grenades.

Every such carefully prepared major attack by Allies or Germans was confidently hoped to be the coveted break-through; reserves of fresh infantry, and sometimes cavalry, were ready to exploit the anticipated opening in the trench line. But such opportunities failed to materialize for either side; even when the front lines were carried, enemy resistance invariably tightened in the rear. The attack, too, was always handicapped by having to advance over ground torn up by the artillery preparation. The net result was usually a few hundred yards or perhaps a few square miles gained at the expense of heavy infantry losses on both sides. The contest degenerated into a "war of attrition" in which the most to be expected was that the enemy's manpower would be used up more rapidly than one's own.

This deadly but futile type of warfare reached its climax in 1916 at Verdun, and on the Somme. The Germans in February of that year launched a major attack, preceded by a terrific artillery bombardment, against Verdun, the key position of the Allied right flank, where the French had completed the trench system with their prewar concrete fortifications. The defenders managed to prevent a breakthrough. Weathering the initial storm they rallied to the cry of "They shall not pass" and mowed down wave after wave of advancing Germans, who still kept coming even after all reasonable prospects of victory were gone. In five months of this fighting the Germans and the French each lost about 350,000 men.

Even before the bitter Verdun fighting ended, the British and French on July 1 had loosed a tremendous assault along the Somme near Amiens, preceded by a whole week of artillery preparation that had used up two million shells. Again the infantry advanced in close lines only to be mowed down by machine guns. In the first day of the attack the British suffered 60,000 casualties, killed, wounded or missing—which meant about 60 per cent of the officers and 40 per cent of the men in the infantry attack. Yet they doggedly kept on until the October rains turned the low country into a sea of mud and made further advance impossible. At the Somme the Allies suffered 600,000 casualties and the Germans about 500,000.

Altogether, those two 1916 drives had cost about 850,000 German casualties and about 950,000 British and French, yet neither side had broken through. Only a few square miles had changed hands and the Western Front still ran pretty much as it had at the beginning of the year. In amazing contrast of costs and results, the Germans overthrew Poland in their "Blitzkrieg" attack of 1939 with only 44,300 casualties, including 10,500 killed; and in the following year overran the whole of France with 156,500 casualties, including 27,000 killed—less than half of what they had paid for the meagre gains at Verdun.

WAR WEARINESS **114**

As the war dragged on year after year with mounting casualties and with no end in sight, the early confidence and enthusiasm gave way to weariness and defeatism. Demands for an end to the bloody holocaust were raised in both camps. Typical were the following appeals for peace, the first by Pope Benedict XV, and the second by Lord Lansdowne, former British foreign secretary.*

Pope Benedict XV, August 17, 1917

... About the end of the first year of the war we addressed to the contending nations the most earnest exhortations and in addition pointed to the path that would lead to a stable peace honorable to all. Unfortunately our appeal was not heeded and the war was fiercely carried on for two years more with all its horrors. It became even more cruel and spread over land and sea and even to the air, and desolation and death were seen to fall upon defenseless cities, peaceful villages, and their innocent populations. And now no one can imagine how much the general suffering would increase and become worse if other months or, still worse, other years were added to this sanguinary triennium. Is this civilized world to be turned into a field of death, and is Europe, so glorious and flourishing, to rush, as carried by a universal folly, to the abyss and take a hand in its own suicide? ...

In so distressing a situation, in the presence of so grave a menace ... we again call for peace and we renew a pressing appeal to those who have in their hands the destinies of the nations. ...

... Everybody acknowledges ... that on both sides the honor of arms is safe. Do not, then, turn a deaf ear to our prayer, accept the paternal invitation which we extend to you in the name of the Divine Redeemer, Prince of Peace. Bear in mind your very grave responsibility to God and man; on your decision depend the quiet and joy of numberless families, the lives of thousands of young man, the happiness, in a word, of the peoples to whom it is your imperative duty to secure this boon.

* *International Conciliation,* No. 119 (October, 1917), pp. 5-7; No. 122 (January, 1918), pp. 5, 8-10.

346   To the Editor of "The Daily Telegraph"

Sir:

We are now in the fourth year of the most dreadful war the world has ever known. ...

We are not going to lose this war, but its prolongation will spell ruin for the civilised world, and an infinite addition to the load of human suffering which already weighs upon it. Security will be invaluable to a world which has the vitality to profit by it, but what will be the value of the blessings of peace to nations so exhausted that they can scarcely stretch out a hand with which to grasp them?

In my belief, if the war is to be brought to a close in time to avert a world-wide catastrophe, it will be brought to a close because on both sides the peoples of the countries involved realise that it has already lasted too long.

There can be no question that this feeling prevails extensively in Germany, Austria, and Turkey. We know beyond doubt that the economic pressure in those countries far exceeds any to which we are subject here. ...

An immense stimulus would probably be given to the peace party in Germany if it were understood:

1. That we do not desire the annihilation of Germany as a great power.

2. That we do not seek to impose upon her people any form of government other than that of their own choice.

3. That, except as a legitimate war measure, we have no desire to deny to Germany her place among the great commercial communities of the world.

4. That we are prepared, when the war is over, to examine in concert with other Powers, the group of international problems, some of them of recent origin, which are connected with the question of "the freedom of the seas."

5. That we are prepared to enter into an international pact under which ample opportunities would be afforded for the settlement of international disputes by peaceful means. ...

If it be once established that there are no insurmountable difficulties in the way of agreement upon these points, the political horizon might perhaps be scanned with better hope by those who pray, but can at this moment hardly venture to expect, that the New Year may bring us a lasting and honourable peace. I am, Sir,

Your obedient servant,
LANSDOWNE.

115   ROOTS OF RUSSIAN REVOLUTION

War weariness and defeatism were most widespread in Russia, where deplorable conditions existed both for workers and soldiers. Excerpts from the minutes of meetings of the Council of Ministers reflect the grievances and growing disaffection of the Moscow and Petrograd workers. The second selection is from the letters of the Tsar to his Tsarina, in which he describes the tragic shortage of *guns and munitions. This deficiency contributed largely to the disastrous defeats suffered by the Russians, which in turn further stimulated defeatism and revolutionary agitation.**

Council of Ministers

August 24, 1915

... In conclusion, General Ruzski [who had been called in for consultation] touched upon the condition of labor in the Petrograd factories. He emphasized the fact that labor is carrying an exceedingly heavy load and is bending under the weight of the high cost of the necessaries of life. At the same time the employers have not adjusted wages to the new conditions. In order not to starve, the laborer is obliged to work overtime, which exhausts him. He [Gen. Ruzski] suggested that serious attention should be paid to this question and that something should be done quickly; otherwise there may be strikes and disorders. If that should take place "the war situation would be hopeless." ...

SCHERBATOV. The Council of Ministers knows that there were disturbances in Moscow which ended in bloodshed. ... There were even more serious disorders at Ivanovo-Voznesensk when it was necessary to fire on the crowd with the result that sixteen were killed and thirty wounded. There was a critical moment when it was uncertain what the garrison would do. ...

SHAKHOVSKOI. I have information ... that the workmen are quite aroused. Any kind of spark may start a fire. ...

GOREMYKIN. ... I should like to ask the Minister of the Interior what measures he is taking to put an end to the lawlessness ... going on everywhere. His principal function is to protect the State from disorder and danger.

SCHERBATOV. The Minister of the Interior is taking all the measures which his duty and present circumstances permit. ... How can you expect me to fight the growing revolutionary movement when I am refused the support of the troops on the ground that they are unreliable, that one can not be certain that they will fire on the mob? You can not quiet the whole of Russia by the police alone, especially now when the ranks of the police are being thinned out ... and the population is growing daily more excited by the speeches in the Duma, by newspaper stories, by continuous defeats, and rumors of disorders in the rear. ... Among the workmen, as among the population in general, there are terrible reports of graft in connection with war orders.

Letters of Tsar to Tsarina

Headquarters, December 2, 1914

... The only great and serious difficulty for our army is again the lack of ammunition. Because of that our troops are obliged, while fighting, to be cautious and to economize. This means that the burden of fighting falls on the infantry. As a result our losses are enormous. Some army corps have been reduced to divisions, brigades to companies, et cetera.

* F. A. Golder, ed., *Documents of Russian History 1914-1917* (New York: Appleton, 1927), pp. 179, 184-85, 192-96.

348 ... Again that cursed question of shortage of artillery and rifle ammunition—it stands in the way of an energetic advance. If we should have three days of serious fighting we might run out of ammunition altogether. Without new rifles, it is impossible to fill up the gaps. The army is now almost stronger than in peace time; it should be (and was at the beginning) three times as strong. This is the situation in which we find ourselves at present.

If we had a rest from fighting for about a month our condition would greatly improve. It is understood, of course, that what I say is strictly for you only. Please do not say a word of this to anyone.

July 2, 1915

... Owing to the heat we take long rides in automobiles and go very little on foot. We selected new districts and explored the surrounding country, being guided by our maps. Often we made mistakes because the maps we have were made eighteen years ago and since then some of the forests have disappeared while new woods and new villages have appeared.

Imperial Headquarters, June 24, 1916

... He [Sturmer, Prime Minister] is an excellent, honest man, but, it seems to me, unable to make up his mind to do what is needed. The most important and immediate question is fuel and metal,—iron and copper for ammunition. Without metals the mills can not supply a sufficient amount of bullets and bombs. The same is true [lack of fuel] in regard to the railways. Trepov [Minister of Transportation] assures me that the railways work better this year than last and produces proof, but nevertheless every one complains that they are not doing as well as they might. These cursed affairs. They confound me so much that I do not know where the truth lies. ... I usually go to bed after 1:30 A.M., spending all my time in hurried writing, reading, and receiving!!! It's terrible!

116 First Russian Revolution: March 1917

*The conditions described above undermined the Tsarist regime and brought about its collapse in March, 1917, when disaffected workers staged riots in Petrograd. Soldiers were ordered to crush the rioters, but instead they mutinied and fraternized in the streets. The Tsar abdicated a few days later, and a Provisional Government was formed to administer the country until a Constituent Assembly could be elected. The Provisional Government consisted of liberal Duma leaders who promptly proclaimed a reform program, which is reproduced below.**

Citizens, the Provisional Executive Committee of the members of the Duma, with the aid and support of the garrison of the capital and its inhabitants, has triumphed over the dark forces of the Old Régime to such an extent as to enable it to organize a more stable executive power. With this

* *Ibid.,* pp. 308, 309.

idea in mind, the Provisional Committee has appointed as ministers of the first Cabinet representing the public, men whose past political and public life assures them the confidence of the country. . . .

The Cabinet will be guided in its actions by the following principles:

1. An immediate general amnesty for all political and religious offenses, including terrorist acts, military revolts, agrarian offenses, etc.

2. Freedom of speech and press; freedom to form labor unions and to strike. These political liberties should be extended to the army in so far as war conditions permit.

3. The abolition of all socal, religious and national restrictions.

4. Immediate preparation for the calling of a Constituent Assembly, elected by universal and secret vote, which shall determine the form of government and draw up the Constitution for the country.

5. In place of the police, to organize a national militia with elective officers, and subject to the local self-governing body.

6. Elections to be carried out on the basis of universal, direct, equal, and secret suffrage.

7. The troops that have taken part in the revolutionary movement shall not be disarmed or removed from Petrograd.

8. On duty and in war service, strict military discipline should be maintained, but when off duty, soldiers should have the same public rights as are enjoyed by other citizens.

The Provisional Government wishes to add that it has no intention of taking advantage of the existence of war conditions to delay the realization of the above-mentioned measures of reform.

PROVISIONAL GOVERNMENT VERSUS SOVIETS 117

*Despite its reform program, the Provisional Government never was able to sink roots and consolidate its position, chiefly because it refused to satisfy two popular demands: to end the war and to divide land amongst the peasants. The Provisional Government insisted that such basic matters should wait for the election of the Constituent Assembly, which then would be able to act as the indisputable representative of the people. This position became increasingly unpopular as time passed, especially as the rapidly spreading Soviets were clamoring for "Land, Peace, and Bread." The Soviets, or councils, were soon appearing in villages and in army units, as well as in the cities. Eventually they constituted almost a rival or shadow government, paralleling the legal Provisional Government and continually challenging it. The following two selections show how peasants were seizing land without waiting for elections, and also how the army Soviets were usurping the authority of the regular army officers.**

Peasants Seize Land

VILLAGE OF TELIAZH, ORLOV GUBERNIIA.   Each year the peasants rented their land from the landholder. This year they went to him as usual and he

* *Ibid.,* pp. 382-83, 386-87.

asked the usual rent. The peasants refused to pay it, and without much bargaining went home. There they called a meeting and decided to take up the land without paying. They put the plows and harrows on their carts and started for the field. When they arrived, they got into an argument as to the division of the land because it was not all the same quality. When they had quarreled for a time, one of the party proposed that they proceed to the landholder's warehouse, where some good alcohol was kept. They broke into the place, where they found fifty barrels. They drank and drank, but could not drink it all. They became so drunk that they did not know what they were doing and carelessly set the place on fire. Four burned to death; the ninety others escaped. ...

On June 7 there was a village meeting. There were present two students (from Malo-Archangel) and thirteen soldiers. The soldiers and students were quite friendly. At the gathering one of the church readers made a speech, calling on those present to plunder the landholders and rich peasants. He was applauded and carried around. When quiet was restored, one of the students took the floor and pleaded, especially with the old men, not to believe what the psalm reader said. He reminded his hearers of what had come out of the last attempt at plundering. He was not allowed to finish, for from the crowd shouts came, "Kick him out. He is a burzhui." The student continued, but the audience left him.

Soviet Control in the Army

ORDER NO. 1, MARCH 14, 1917

To the garrison of the Petrograd District, to all the soldiers of the guard, army, artillery, and navy, for immediate and strict execution, and to the workers of Petrograd for their information:—

The Soviet of Workers' and Soldiers' Deputies has resolved:

1. In all companies, battalions, regiments, parks, batteries, squadrons, in the special services of the various military administrations, and on the vessels of the navy, committees from the elected representatives of the lower ranks of the above-mentioned military units shall be chosen immediately.

2. In all those military units which have not yet chosen their representatives to the Soviet of Workers' Deputies, one representative from each company shall be selected, to report with written credentials at the building of the State Duma by ten o'clock on the morning of the fifteenth of this March.

3. In all its political actions, the military branch is subordinated to the Soviet of Workers' and Soldiers' Deputies and to its own committees.

4. The orders of the military commission of the State Duma shall be executed only in such cases as do not conflict with the orders and resolutions of the Soviet of Workers' and Soldiers' Deputies.

5. All kinds of arms, such as rifles, machine guns, armored automobiles, and others, must be kept at the disposal and under the control of the company and battalion committees, and in no case be turned over to officers, even at their demand.

6. In the ranks and during their performance of the duties of the service, soldiers must observe the strictest military discipline, but outside the service and the ranks, in their political, general civic, and private life, soldiers cannot in any way be deprived of those rights which all citizens enjoy. In par-

ticular, standing at attention and compulsory saluting, when not on duty, is abolished.

7. Also, the addressing of the officers with the title, "Your Excellency," "Your Honor," etc., is abolished, and these titles are replaced by the address of "Mister General," "Mister Colonel," etc. Rudeness towards soldiers of any rank, and, especially, addressing them as "Thou," is prohibited, and soldiers are required to bring to the attention of the company committees every infraction of this rule, as well as all misunderstandings occurring between officers and privates.

The present order is to be read to all companies, battalions, regiments, ships' crews batteries, and other combatant and non-combatant commands.

SECOND RUSSIAN REVOLUTION: NOVEMBER 1917 **118**

The delegates elected to the rapidly spreading Soviets at first consisted mostly of Mensheviks and Socialist Revolutionaries; but as time passed, the Bolsheviks won increasing support with their slogans for immediate peace and immediate distribution of the land. By October, 1917, a majority of the Bolsheviks were elected to the Moscow and Petrograd Soviets. As soon as this happened, the Bolshevik leader, Lenin, made preparations to overthrow the Provisional Government. The first of the following selections is an appeal by the Provisional Government to the people for support against the Bolsheviks. The second is a statement by the Military Revolutionary Committee, which was established by the Bolsheviks to seize power, and which did so with very little resistance.*

Appeal of the Provisional Government, November 7, 1917

Citizens! Save the fatherland, the republic, and freedom! Maniacs have raised a revolt against the only governmental power chosen by the people—the Provisional Government.

The members of the Provisional Government, faithful to duty, will remain at their posts and continue to work for the good of the fatherland, the re-establishment of order, and the convocation of the Constituent Assembly, the future sovereign of Russia and of the peoples inhabiting it.

Citizens, you must help the Provisional Government. You must strengthen its authority. You must oppose these maniacs, with whom are joined all enemies of liberty and order including the followers of the old regime whose purpose is to destroy all conquests of the revolution and the future of our dear fatherland.

Citizens, rally around the Provisional Government for the defense of its provisional authority in the name of order and the welfare of every people of our great fatherland.

---

* J. Bunyan and H. H. Fisher, *The Bolshevik Revolution 1917-1918,* Hoover War Library Publications, No. 3 (Stanford: Stanford Univ., 1934), pp. 100-102.

Proclamation of the Military Revolutionary Committee, November 7, 1917

All railroad stations and the telephone, post, and telegraph offices are occupied. The telephones of the Winter Palace and the [District Military] Staff Headquarters are disconnected. The State Bank is in our hands. The Winter Palace and the [military] Staff have surrendered. The shock troops are dispersed, the cadets paralyzed. The armored cars have sided with the Revolutionary Committee. The Cossacks refused to obey the government. The Provisional Government is deposed. Power is in the hands of the Revolutionary Committee of the Petrograd Soviet of Workers' and Soldiers' Deputies.

119 LENIN PROCLAIMS THE NEW ORDER

The day after the overthrow of the Provisional Government, Lenin appeared before the Petrograd Soviet and delivered a speech defining the general objectives of his new regime. The text of this speech, given below, reveals the basic difference between the former Provisional Government and the new Bolshevik rulers, with their aims for a "world-wide socialistic revolution" and for "building up a proletarian socialist state." *

Comrades, the workmen's and peasants' revolution, the need of which the Bolsheviks have emphasized many times, has come to pass.

What is the significance of this revolution? Its significance is, in the first place, that we shall have a soviet government, without the participation of bourgeoisie of any kind. The oppressed masses will of themselves form a government. The old state machinery will be smashed into bits and in its place will be created a new machinery of government by the soviet organizations. From now on there is a new page in the history of Russia, and the present, third Russian revolution shall in its final result lead to the victory of Socialism.

One of our immediate tasks is to put an end to the war at once. But in order to end the war, which is closely bound up with the present capitalistic system, it is necessary to overthrow capitalism which has already begun to develop in Italy, England, and Germany.

A just and immediate offer of peace by us to the international democracy will find everywhere a warm response among the international proletariat masses. In order to secure the confidence of the proletariat, it is necessary to publish at once all secret treaties.

In the interior of Russia a very large part of the peasantry has said: Enough playing with the capitalists; we will go with the workers. We shall secure the confidence of the peasants by one decree, which will wipe out the private property of the landowners. The peasants will understand that their only salvation is in union with the workers.

* F. A. Golder, ed., *Documents of Russian History 1914-1917* (New York: Appleton, 1927), pp. 618, 619.

We will establish a real labor control on production.

We have now learned to work together in a friendly manner, as is evident from this revolution. We have the force of mass organization which has conquered all and which will lead the proletariat to world revolution.

We should now occupy ourselves in Russia in building up a proletarian socialist state.

Long live the world-wide socialistic revolution.

UNITED STATES ENTERS WORLD WAR I **120**

*Germany began unrestricted submarine warfare in 1917. By that time, the Germans had built enough submarines so that they were confident they could force England to surrender and thus end the war. They realized the United States would almost certainly intervene, but they believed it would all be over before American strength could be mobilized and used. On April 2, 1917, President Wilson read the following "War Message" to Congress. His request for a declaration of war was also an eloquent disclaimer of national gain and an appeal for "a concert of free peoples" and "peace and safety to all nations." ***

With a profound sense of the solemn and even tragical character of the step I am taking and of the grave responsibilities which it involves, but in unhesitating obedience to what I deem my constitutional duty, I advise that the Congress declare the recent course of the Imperial German Government to be in fact nothing less than war against the Government and people of the United States; that it formally accept the status of belligerent which has thus been thrust upon it; and that it take immediate steps not only to put the country in a more thorough state of defense, but also to exert all its power and employ all its resources to bring the Government of the German Empire to terms and end the war. . . .

We have no quarrel with the German people. We have no feeling toward them but one of sympathy and friendship. It was not upon their impulse that their Government acted in entering this war. It was not with their previous knowledge or approval. It was a war determined upon as wars used to be determined upon in the old, unhappy days, when peoples were nowhere consulted by their rulers and wars were provoked and waged in the interest of dynasties or of little groups of ambitious men who were accustomed to use their fellowmen as pawns and tools.

A steadfast concert for peace can never be maintained except by a partnership of democratic nations. No autocratic Government could be trusted to keep faith within it or observe its covenants. It must be a league of honor, a partnership of opinion. Intrigue would eat its vitals away; the plottings of inner circles who could plan what they would and render account to no one would be a corruption seated at its very heart. Only free peoples can hold their purpose and their honor steady to a common end and prefer the interests of mankind to any narrow interest of their own.

* *Congressional Record*, 65th Congress, 1st session, pp. 102-4.

We have no selfish ends to serve. We desire no conquest, no dominion. We seek no indemnities for ourselves, no material compensation for the sacrifices we shall freely make. We are but one of the champions of the rights of mankind. We shall be satisfied when those rights have been made as secure as the faith and the freedom of nations can make them.

Just because we fight without rancor and without selfish object, seeking nothing for ourselves but what we shall wish to share with all free peoples, we shall, I feel confident, conduct our operations as belligerents without passion and ourselves observe with proud punctilio the principles of right and of fair play we profess to be fighting for.

It is a distressing and oppressive duty, gentlemen of the Congress, which I have performed in thus addressing you. There are, it may be, many months of fiery trial and sacrifice ahead of us. It is a fearful thing to lead this great, peaceful people into war, into the most terrible and disastrous of all wars, civilization itself seeming to be in the balance. But the right is more precious than peace, and we shall fight for the things which we have always carried nearest our hearts—for democracy, for the right of those who submit to authority to have a voice in their own Governments, for the rights and liberties of small nations, for a universal dominion of right by such a concert of free peoples as shall bring peace and safety to all nations and make the world itself at last free.

121 World War I in World History

From the viewpoint of world, rather than European, history, the significance of World War I is that it marks the beginning of the end of Europe's domination of the globe. Why this domination was now effectively challenged for the first time is made clear in the following analysis by K. M. Panikkar, an Indian historian and diplomat.*

The Great War of 1914-8 was from the Asian point of view a civil war within the European community of nations. The direct participation of Asian countries, during some stages of this conflict, was at the invitation and by the encouragement of one of the parties, the *entente* Powers, and was greatly resented by the Germans. It is necessary to emphasize this internal character of the European conflict to realize its full significance on the development of events in Asia.

We have already noticed that at the beginning of the twentieth century the European nations, in the enjoyment of unprecedented economic prosperity and political prestige, remained unshakably convinced that they had inherited the earth, and that their supremacy in Asia was permanent and was something in the nature of a predetermined Divine Order. It was the age of Kipling and the white man's burden, and it seemed the manifest destiny of the white race to hold the East in fee.

* K. M. Panikkar, *Asia and Western Dominance* (London: G. Allen; New York: Day, 1953), pp. 259-66. Reprinted by permission of The John Day Company, Inc.

In 1914, when the German invaders had reached the Marne, divisions of the Indian Army under British officers had been rushed to France and had helped at the critical moment to stem the German tide. Later, they were extensively used in the defence of the Suez Canal and the Middle East and in campaigns elsewhere in Africa. In 1917, Siam declared war on Germany. An Indo-Chinese labour force had been recruited and was working in France. On August 14, 1917, China also joined the Allies. Thus all the nations of Asia were brought into the European civil war. However, opinion in India, China and even in Japan was at the time more pro-German than pro-Ally. In India, except among the ruling princes, there was no pro-British feeling, and public opinion rejoiced at every report of German victory and felt depressed when the Allies were winning. China declared war only with the greatest reluctance and for the express purpose of checkmating Japanese plans of aggression. In Japan itself, after the Shantung campaign, feeling against the Allies was most marked, and a Press campaign of great virulence was conducted against Britain at the end of 1916. Actually, though the Asian countries fought on the side of the Allies, public opinion in the East looked upon the conflict as a civil war in which neither party had a claim to the friendship of the peoples of Asia, and if any party could appeal to the sympathy of Asians it was the Germanic alliance which had no tradition of Asian conquest and was allied with the chief Muslim Power, Turkey.

But the participation of Asian people in the war had far-reaching consequences. The Indian soldier who fought on the Marne came back to India with other ideas of the *Sahib* than those he was taught to believe by decades of official propaganda. Indo-Chinese Labour Corps in the South of France returned to Annam with notions of democracy and republicanism which they had not entertained before. Among the Chinese who went to France at the time was a young man named Chou En-lai, who stayed on to become a Communist and had to be expelled for activities among the members of the Chinese Labour Corps.

More important than these influences was the fact that the French and British administrations in Asia had to appeal to their subjects for moral support. To ask Indians and Indo-Chinese to subscribe to war loans for the defence of democracy and to prevert the world being overwhelmed by German *Kultur,* would have sounded as strange and callous irony unless accompanied by promises of democracy for themselves and freedom for their own cultures. When, besides subscriptions for war loans, Indians and Indo-Chinese were pressed to join up and fight to save democracy, the contradictions of the position became too obvious even for the colonial administrators. In India the demand was made openly by the nationalist leaders that prior agreement on political problems was necessary before support of the war could be considered a national programme.

Politically, a further weakening of the colonial and imperialist position came about as a result of President Wilson's declaration of fourteen points. In 1917, the doctrine of the "self-determination of peoples" had the ring of a new revelation. Whatever its effect was on the suppressed nationalities of Europe, in Asia it was acclaimed as a doctrine of liberation. As every Allied Power hastened to declare its faith in the new formula of Wilson (and it was soon raised to the position of an accepted "war aim" in the propaganda campaign against the Germans), the colonial Powers found it difficult to oppose openly or resist publicly the claims of Asian nations based on this formula. It became difficult to proclaim self-determination of peoples as a great ideal for the establishment of which Asian peoples should co-operate with Europeans and fight and lose their lives in distant battle-fields, but which, however excellent, could not be applied to themselves. Self-government for colonial countries had thus to be accepted, and the claim to it could no longer be brushed aside as premature or stigmatized as sedition.

Apart from these political considerations economic forces generated by the war were also helping to undermine the supremacy of the West. Japan utilized the four years of war for a planned expansion of her trade in the East. German competition had been eliminated. Britain and France, engaged in a mortal struggle when their entire resources of production had to be directed towards victory, had also left the field fairly open. India gained her first major start on the industrial road and, with the strain on British economy, Indian national capital was placed in a position of some advantage. In fact the full results of the weakening of European capitalism became evident only after the war when the pre-eminence of London was challenged by America, and British capital, though still powerful, began to be on the defensive in India. The growth of capitalist enterprise in India, and the development of industries and participation by Indian capital in spheres so far monopolistically held by Britain, like jute, resulted directly from the weakening of the economic position of Britain.

Two other results of a general character may be indicated. The first, the growth of a powerful left-wing movement in the countries of Western Europe had a direct effect on shaping events in the Eastern Empire. The labour Party in England during the days of its growth had been closely associated with the nationalist movement in India. In fact, Ramsay MacDonald, the leader of the Socialist Party after the war, had been one of its champions from the earliest days. Similarly, Annamite nationalism had worked hand in hand with left-wing parties in France. In the period that immediately followed the war these parties had come to possess considerable influence in national affairs and, as we shall see, were instrumental in giving effect to policies which loosened the old bonds of political domination.

The second factor was, of course, the influence of the Russian Revolution. Imperialism meant something totally different after Lenin's definition of it as the last phase of capitalism and his insistence that the liberation of subject peoples from colonial domination was a part of the struggle against capitalism. Also, Russia's call for and practice of racial equality, abolition of the special privileges that Tsarist Russia had acquired in Persia and China, and her acceptance, in the first flush of revolutionary enthusiasm, of the independence of countries which had been previously annexed to Russia, made it difficult for Western nations which had so long claimed to stand for liberty and progress to deny the claims of Eastern nations.

Finally, the war had accelerated the pace of movements everywhere. For example, in India, the movement for independence which was confined to the intelligentsia in 1914 became a mass movement of immense proportions in 1919. Everywhere the case was similar. The *tempo* of events had acquired a momentum which few had foreseen and none had forecast in 1918. The war, on the world scale it was conducted in 1914-18, was in itself a great world revolution, and an impenetrable chasm has been created between the days preceding August 1914 and those following November 11, 1918.

One fact which stands out clear and illustrates this chasm in thought is the lack of faith in imperialist ideals in the period that followed the war. With the solitary exception of Churchill, there was not one major figure in any of the British parties who confessed to a faith in the white man's mission to rule. Successive Viceroys of India, Liberal, Conservative and non-party, professed publicly their adherence to the cause of Indian freedom. Secretaries of State from Edwin Montagu (1917-22) to Pethick Lawrence, including such stalwarts of Conservatism as Sir Samuel Hoare (Lord Templewood), claimed that they were working for the freedom of the Indian people and not for the maintenance of British rule. The French were no doubt more brave in their words, but the faith had gone out of them also.

Nowhere did this come out more clearly than in the treatment of China. Incidents which previously would have been dealt with sternly and for which territories and indemnities would have been exacted, were now only the subjects of a mild protest. Chiang Kai-shek's armies occupied the concessions at Hankow, and for months Hong Kong was subjected to an intensive trade boycott; these events would earlier have immediately led to a display of overwhelming naval strength. Britain in 1926 was prepared patiently to negotiate. Even the "old China hands," who had watched with regret the sudden eclipse of European prestige, though they acted the Blimps in their clubs, never seriously felt that Western authority could be re-established over China by the use of gunboats. There was no conviction left of the European's superiority or sense of vision.

Chapter Twenty-one

Nationalist uprisings
in the colonial world

122 Turkish National Pact, January 28, 1920

The peace settlement arranged at the end of World War I ignored the nationalist aspirations of the colonial peoples, with the result that a wave of revolts broke out in the overseas lands. The most successful of these uprisings was that of the Turks. They appeared to be helpless at the outset, having been compelled to accept the Sèvres Treaty, which deprived them of their Arab provinces as well as Eastern Thrace and certain Aegean islands. In addition, the Greeks were given a foothold in Smyrna, while Allied warships were anchored in the capital, Constantinople, where the Sultan had become a puppet of the western powers. Yet, in the face of these odds, the Turks managed to stage a comeback with the inspired leadership of Mustafa Kemal. He took the initiative in defying the Sultan and the Allies, in organizing a nationalist resistance movement in the interior of Asia Minor, and in preparing a National Pact which was adopted by the lower chamber of the Ottoman legislature on January 28, 1920. The following excerpts from the pact show that although the Nationalists were realistic enough to surrender their Arab provinces, they were insistent that the remaining Turkish lands be fully independent.*

The Members of the Ottoman Chamber of Deputies recognise and affirm that the independence of the State and the future of the Nation can be assured by complete respect for the following principles, which represent the maximum of sacrifice which can be undertaken in order to achieve a just and lasting peace, and that the con-

* A. J. Toynbee, *The Western Question in Greece and Turkey* (London: Constable, 1922), pp. 209-10.

tinued existence of a stable Ottoman Sultanate and society is impossible outside of the said principles:

Art. 1. Inasmuch as it is necessary that the destinies of the portions of the Turkish Empire which are populated exclusively by an Arab majority, and which on the conclusion of the armistice of the 30th October, 1918, were in the occupation of enemy forces, should be determined in accordance with the votes which shall be freely given by the inhabitants, the whole of those parts whether within or outside the said armistice line which are inhabited by an Ottoman Moslem majority, united in religion, in race and in aim, imbued with sentiments of mutual respect for each other and of sacrifice, and wholly respectful of each other's racial and social rights and surrounding conditions, form a whole which does not admit of division for any reason in truth or in ordinance. . . .

Art. 4. The security of the city of Constantinople, which is the seat of the Caliphate of Islam, the capital of the Sultanate, and the headquarters of the Ottoman Government, and of the Sea of Marmora must be protected from every danger. Provided this principle is maintained, whatever decision may be arrived at jointly by us and all other Governments concerned, regarding the opening of the Bosphorus to the commerce and traffic of the world, is valid. . . .

Art. 6. It is a fundamental condition of our life and continued existence that we, like every country, should enjoy complete independence and liberty in the matter of assuring the means of our development, in order that our national and economic development should be rendered possible and that it should be possible to conduct affairs in the form of a more up-to-date regular administration.

For this reason we are opposed to restrictions inimical to our development in political, judicial, financial, and other matters.

The conditions of settlement of our proved debts shall likewise not be contrary to these principles.

ABOLITION OF THE CALIPHATE AND BANISHMENT OF THE OTTOMAN IMPERIAL FAMILY, MARCH 3, 1924

123

Having divided the Allies—and enjoying the support of Russia and especially of his own people—Kemal was able to drive the Greeks out of Smyrna and to negotiate the Lausanne Treaty (July 24, 1923), replacing the onerous Sèvres Treaty. His country freed from foreign control, Kemal now proceeded with a comprehensive program of secularization, for he considered Ottoman theocratic institutions to have been largely responsible for the Turkish disasters. As part of his secularization drive he passed a law eliminating the Caliph, or viceregent of God, and also the Ottoman Imperial family, which had intermittently assumed the title of Caliph.*

* A. J. Toynbee, *Survey of International Affairs, 1925, I, The Islamic World Since the Peace Settlement* (London: Oxford Univ., under the auspices of the Royal Institute of International Affairs, 1927), 575.

Article 1: The Caliph is deposed. The office of the Caliphate is abolished, since the Caliphate is essentially comprised in the meaning and signification of [the words] Government and Republic.

Article 2: The deposed Caliph and all male and female members of the Imperial Family of the now extinguished Ottoman Sultanate, including the husbands of Imperial princesses, are deprived in perpetuity of the right to reside within the boundaries of the territories of the Republic of Turkey. The issue of ladies related to this Imperial Family are subject to the terms of this article.

Article 3: The individuals mentioned in Article 2 are required to leave the dominions of the Republic of Turkey within a maximum period of ten days as from the date of proclamation of the present law.

Article 4: The individuals mentioned in Article 2 are deprived of the status and rights of Turkish nationality.

Article 5: From now onwards the individuals mentioned in Article 2 may not enjoy the disposal of real property within the boundaries of the Republic of Turkey. For the winding-up of their affairs they may have recourse, by proxy, to the public courts of law during a period of one year.

124 CONSTITUTION OF THE TURKISH REPUBLIC, APRIL 20, 1924

Kemal also strove to modernize the new Turkish republic. Accordingly, he adopted a Western-type constitution, the first section of which is given below. Although the articles seem standard and innocuous, actually, they were revolutionary for a Moslem country. Prior to Kemal's secularization drive, Turkey would have been defined as a theocratic community rather than as a republic, and there would have been reference to the Holy Places of Mecca and Medina as well as to Angora (later, Ankara).*

Article 1: The Turkish State is a Republic.

Article 2: The religion of the Turkish State is Islam; the official language is Turkish; the seat of government is Angora.

Article 3: Sovereignty belongs without restriction to the nation.

Article 4: The Great National Assembly of Turkey is the sole lawful representative of the nation, and exercises sovereignty in the name of the nation.

Article 5: The legislative and executive powers are vested and centred in the Great National Assembly, which concentrates these two powers in itself.

Article 6: The Great National Assembly of Turkey exercises the legislative power directly.

Article 7: The Assembly exercises the executive power through the intermediary of the President of the Republic, whom it elects, and through a Cabinet chosen by him. The Assembly controls the acts of the Government and may at any time withdraw power from it.

Article 8: The judicial power is exercised in the name of the Assembly by independent tribunals constituted in accordance with the law.

* E. M. Earle and H. Y. Hussein Bey, "The New Constitution of Turkey," *Political Science Quarterly,* Vol. 40, No. 1 (March, 1925), p. 89. Reprinted with permission.

The Arab world also became a center of violence in the postwar years, in part, because of the gross discrepancy between the Allied promises of independence made during the war and the mandate system that was imposed at the end of the war. The most important agreement reached was that between Sir Henry McMahon, British High Commissioner in Egypt, and Emir Hussein, prominent in the Arab world as the Keeper of the Holy Places and Prince of Mecca. In return for an Arab revolt against the Turks, McMahon agreed to recognize the postwar independence of the Arab lands south of the 37th latitude. The following selections, taken from the ten letters exchanged by the two men from July 14, 1915 to March 10, 1916, reveal the roots of future trouble: the vague British reference to "the interests of her ally, France," and Hussein's warning that all concessions to France would be reclaimed at the first opportunity.*

From Sherif Hussein, 14 July 1915

Whereas the whole of the Arab nation without any exception have decided in these last years to live, and to accomplish their freedom, and grasp the reins of their administration both in theory and practice; and whereas they have found and felt that it is to the interest of the Government of Great Britain to support them and aid them to the attainment of their firm and lawful intentions (which are based upon the maintenance of the honour and dignity of their life) without any ulterior motives whatsoever unconnected with this object;

And whereas it is to their [the Arabs'] interest also to prefer the assistance of the Government of Great Britain in consideration of their geographical position and economic interests, and also of the attitude of the above-mentioned Government, which is known to both nations and therefore need not be emphasized;

For these reasons the Arab nation sees fit to limit themselves, as time is short, to asking the Government of Great Britain, if it should think fit, for the approval, through her deputy or representative, of the following fundamental propositions, leaving out all things considered secondary in comparison with these, so that it may prepare all means necessary for attaining this noble purpose, until such time as it finds occasion for making the actual negotiations:

Firstly. England to acknowledge the independence of the Arab countries, bounded on the north by Mersina and Adana up to the 37th of latitude. . . . England to approve of the proclamation of an Arab Khalifate of Islam.

Secondly. The Arab Government of the Sherif to acknowledge that England shall have the preference in all economic enterprises in the Arab countries whenever conditions of enterprises are otherwise equal.

Thirdly. For the security of this Arab independence and the certainty of such preference of economic enterprises, both high contracting parties to offer mutual assistance, to the best ability of their military and naval forces, to face any foreign Power which may attack either party. Peace not to be decided without agreement of both parties.

Fourthly. If one of the parties enters upon an aggressive conflict, the other

* Great Britain, *Parliamentary Papers, 1939,* Misc. No. 3, Cmd. 5957.

party to assume a neutral attitude, and in case of such party wishing the other to join forces, both to meet and discuss the conditions.

Fifthly. England to acknowledge the abolition of foreign privileges in the Arab countries, and to assist the Government of the Sherif in an International Convention for confirming such abolition.

From Sir Henry McMahon, 24 October 1915

I have received your letter of the 29th Shawal, 1333, with much pleasure and your expressions of friendliness and sincerity have given me the greatest satisfaction. . . .

I have, therefore, lost no time in informing the Government of Great Britain of the contents of your letter, and it is with great pleasure that I communicate to you on their behalf the following statement, which I am confident you will receive with satisfaction:

The two districts of Mersina and Alexandretta and portions of Syria lying to the west of the districts of Damascus, Homs, Hama and Aleppo cannot be said to be purely Arab, and should be excluded from the limits demanded.

With the above modification, and without prejudice of our existing treaties with Arab chiefs, we accept those limits.

As for those regions lying within those frontiers wherein Great Britain is free to act without detriment to the interests of her ally, France, I am empowered in the name of the Government of Great Britain to give the following assurances and make the following reply to your letter:

(1) Subject to the above modifications, Great Britain is prepared to recognise and support the independence of the Arabs in all the regions within the limits demanded by the Sherif of Mecca.

(2) Great Britain will guarantee the Holy Places against all external aggression and will recognise their inviolability.

(3) When the situation admits, Great Britain will give to the Arabs her advice and will assist them to establish what may appear to be the most suitable forms of government in those various territories.

(4) On the other hand, it is understood that the Arabs have decided to seek the advice and guidance of Great Britain only, and that such European advisers and officials as may be required for the formation of a sound form of administration will be British.

(5) With regard to the *vilayets* of Bagdad and Basra, the Arabs will recognise that the established position and interests of Great Britain necessitate special administrative arrangements in order to secure these territories from foreign aggression, to promote the welfare of the local populations and to safeguard our mutual economic interests.

I am convinced that this declaration will assure you beyond all possible doubt of the sympathy of Great Britain towards the aspirations of her friends the Arabs and will result in a firm and lasting alliance, the immediate results of which will be the expulsion of the Turks from the Arab countries and the freeing of the Arab peoples from the Turkish yoke, which for so many years has pressed heavily upon them.

The McMahon commitment to Hussein was contradicted almost immediately by several other agreements concluded by the British, one being with another Arab leader, Ibn Saud, who was recognized (December 26, 1915) as the independent ruler of the Nejd. Another was the Balfour Declaration of November 2, 1917, in which the British government placed itself on record as favoring the establishment in Palestine of "a national home for the Jewish people. . . . it being clearly understood that nothing shall be done which may prejudice the civil and religious rights of existing non-Jewish communities. . . ." Most serious were the secret treaties between Britain and her allies, France, Russia, and Italy. These powers agreed (Sykes-Picot Agreement, April 26, 1916, and St. Jean de Maurienne Treaty, April, 1917) to divide the Arab lands amongst themselves: Mesopotamia and the Haifa-Acre region to Britain, Syria-Lebanon to France, and Palestine under international administration. Thus, although the Arabs rose in revolt as scheduled, there was little likelihood that they would be able to organize the large independent state envisaged by Hussein and McMahon. For this reason, the British officer T. E. Lawrence, who fought with the Arabs in their revolt, later wrote of his uneasiness and disillusionment in doing so.*

The Cabinet raised the Arabs to fight for us by definite promises of self-government afterwards. Arabs believe in persons, not in institutions. They saw in me a free agent of the British Government, and demanded from me an endorsement of its written promises. So I had to join the conspiracy, and, for what my word was worth, assured the men of their reward. In our two years' partnership under fire they grew accustomed to believing me and to think my Government, like myself, sincere. In this hope they performed some fine things, but, of course, instead of being proud of what we did together, I was continually and bitterly ashamed.

It was evident from the beginning that if we won the war these promises would be dead paper, and had I been an honest adviser of the Arabs I would have advised them to go home and not risk their lives fighting for such stuff; but I salved myself with the hope that, by leading these Arabs madly in the final victory I would establish them, with arms in their hands, in a position so assured (if not dominant) that expediency would counsel to the Great Powers a fair settlement of their claims. In other words, I presumed (seeing no other leader with the will and power) that I would survive the campaigns, and be able to defeat not merely the Turks on the battlefield, but my own country and its allies in the council-chamber. It was an immodest presumption; it is not yet clear if I succeeded; but it is clear that I had no shadow of leave to engage the Arabs, unknowing, in such hazard. I risked the fraud, on my conviction that Arab help was necessary to our cheap and speedy victory in the East, and that better we win and break our word than lose.

* T. E. Lawrence, *Oriental Assembly* (London: Williams and Norgate, 1939), pp. 144-46. By permission of A. W. Lawrence.

Despite the many differences dividing the Arabs, they were virtually all united in opposing the substitution of Western rule for Ottoman government, under the guise of mandates. The following memorandum presented on July 2, 1919, by the General Syrian Congress to the King-Crane Commission is evidence of this. The latter was a commission of inquiry sent out by the Supreme Council in Paris. Originally the Commission was to have included representatives of all the Allied Powers, but in the end, all except the United States refused to participate.*

We the undersigned members of the General Syrian Congress, meeting in Damascus on Wednesday, July 2nd, 1919, made up of representatives from the three Zones, viz., the Southern, Eastern, and Western, provided with credentials and authorizations by the inhabitants of our various districts, Moslems, Christians, and Jews, have agreed upon the following statement of the desires of the people of the country who have elected us. . . .

1. We ask absolutely complete political independence for Syria. . . .

2. We ask that the Government of this Syrian country should be a democratic civil constitutional Monarchy on broad decentralization principles, safeguarding the rights of minorities, and that the King be the Emir Feisal, who carried on a glorious struggle in the cause of our liberation and merited our full confidence and entire reliance.

3. Considering the fact that the Arabs inhabiting the Syrian area are not naturally less gifted than other more advanced races and that they are by no means less developed than the Bulgarians, Serbians, Greeks, and Roumanians at the beginning of their independence, we protest against Article 22 of the Covenant of the League of Nations, placing us among the nations in their middle stage of development which stand in need of a mandatory power.

4. In the event of the rejection by the Peace Conference of this just protest for certain considerations that we may not understand, we, relying on the declarations of President Wilson that his object in waging war was to put an end to the ambition of conquest and colonization, can only regard the mandate mentioned in the Covenant of the League of Nations as equivalent to the rendering of economical and technical assistance that does not prejudice our complete independence. And desiring that our country should not fall a prey to colonization and believing that the American Nation is farthest from any thought of colonization and has no political ambition in our country, we will seek the technical and economical assistance from the United States of America, provided that such assistance does not exceed 20 years.

5. In the event of America not finding herself in a position to accept our desire for assistance, we will seek this assistance from Great Britain, also provided that such assistance does not infringe the complete independence and unity of our country and that the duration of such assistance does not exceed that mentioned in the previous article.

6. We do not acknowledge any right claimed by the French Government in any part whatever of our Syrian country and refuse that she should assist us or have a hand in our country under any circumstances and in any place.

---

* *Foreign Relations of the United States: Paris Peace Conference, 1919,* Vol. 12, pp. 780-81.

7. We oppose the pretensions of the Zionists to create a Jewish common-wealth in the southern part of Syria, known as Palestine, and oppose Zionist migration to any part of our country; for we do not acknowledge their title but consider them a grave peril to our people from the national, economical, and political points of view. Our Jewish compatriots shall enjoy our common rights and assume the common responsibilities.

8. We ask that there should be no separation of the southern part of Syria, known as Palestine, nor of the littoral western zone, which includes Lebanon, from the Syrian country. We desire that the unity of the country should be guaranteed against partition under whatever circumstances.

9. We ask complete independence for emancipated Mesopotamia and that there should be no economical barriers between the two countries.

10. The fundamental principles laid down by President Wilson in condemnation of secret treaties impel us to protest most emphatically against any treaty that stipulates the partition of our Syrian country and against any private engagement aiming at the establishment of Zionism in the southern part of Syria; therefore we ask the complete annulment of these conventions and agreements.

The noble principles enunciated by President Wilson strengthen our confidence that our desires emanating from the depths of our hearts, shall be the decisive factor in determining our future; and that President Wilson and the free American people will be our supporters for the realization of our hopes, thereby proving their sincerity and noble sympathy with the aspiration of the weaker nations in general and our Arab people in particular.

We also have the fullest confidence that the Peace Conference will realize that we would not have risen against the Turks, with whom we had participated in all civil, political, and representative privileges, but for their violation of our national rights, and so will grant us our desires in full in order that our political rights may not be less after the war than they were before, since we have shed so much blood in the cause of our liberty and independence.

We request to be allowed to send a delegation to represent us at the Peace Conference to defend our rights and secure the realization of our aspirations.

GUERRILLA TACTICS OF THE RIF IN MOROCCO 128

The Arabs of North Africa were as restless under European domination as those of the Middle East. Most spectacular was the resistance of the Rif tribesmen of Morocco, led by Abd-el-Krim. Between 1921 and 1926, Krim waged a remarkably successful struggle against both Spanish and French forces. The following analysis of the terrain and of guerrilla tactics explains why the Rif were able to hold their ground for so long against greatly superior forces.*

The prospective scene of operations, like the adjoining parts of the Spanish Zone, was an arid treeless country, covered with a thorny undergrowth, broken

---

* A. J. Toynbee, *Survey of International Affairs, 1925*, I, *The Islamic World Since the Peace Settlement* (London: Oxford Univ., under the auspices of the Royal Institute of International Affairs, 1927), 135-36.

up by ravines, and cursed with a scanty water-supply; and this was almost an ideal *terrain* for the Rifi forces, who were thoroughly at home in their native environment and at the same time had adopted such elements in the Western art of war as could be employed there to good purpose. Every Rifi fighting-man was adept at taking cover and, notwithstanding the brokenness of the country, he was disconcertingly mobile, since he lived in the open and carried no impedimenta except a handful of food, in the hood of his cloak, and his rifle and ammunition. With rifles, machine-guns, and small-arms ammunition the Rifis had supplied themselves abundantly at the Spaniards' expense; and, although the captured Spanish artillery was clumsily served and there was no air force on the Rifi side, these were luxuries and not necessities under the local conditions. On the other hand, the Rifi High Command had not only captured but learnt to utilize field telephones, and by means of these they were able to keep in touch with their widely scattered and constantly moving units, and to execute concerted manoeuvres over as wide a field as their opponents. They appear to have established district depots of rifles and ammunition, to which the tribesmen could be called up at short notice, fitted out, and then dispatched to any point where they were needed. The bulk of their forces was extremely fluid—the men being perpetually called up in relays and perpetually released (as far as the course of the campaign allowed) to work in the fields. Every tribe, however, appears to have been required to supply a permanent contingent, and the tribal levies were stiffened by a small standing army of regulars (mostly drawn from 'Abdu'l-Karim's [Abd-el-Krim's] own tribe, the Banu Wuryaghal of Ajdir) who were uniformly trained and equipped and were in receipt of pay and rations—in consideration of which they had to hand over their booty to the Government.

The Rifi tactics (which were directed by 'Abdu'l-Karim's brother, Mahammad, the mining engineer, as Commander-in-Chief) were to send forward a screen of irregulars who filtered through the enemy's line and raised the tribes in his rear—if necessary by coercion. By this means the Rifi army grew like a snowball as it advanced, each tribe whose territory became the scene of fighting being called out *en masse*. The tendency towards desultoriness and incoherence, which was to be looked for in an army recruited in this way, was guarded against by placing all the tribal contingents under the command of regulars, but the main body of the regular troops was carefully husbanded and kept in reserve. Advancing behind the screen of tribesmen they dug themselves in, provided a support upon which the skirmishers could fall back, and resisted enemy counter-attacks in hand-to-hand fighting, with a tenacity which reminded their French adversaries of European warfare.

129 OLD REGIME IN PERSIA

Postwar developments in Persia resembled those in Turkey in several respects, one being the increasingly apparent obsoleteness of the old regime. Although Persia had escaped Turkey's misfortune of being involved in the War as a defeated belligerent, the country was so helpless that it had been occupied at will by Russian, Turkish, and British armies. The ravages of these forces, together with

a disastrous drought, resulted in a famine that decimated the countryside in 1918.
The following description of Persia during this period is by a British officer who
*was hired by a Persian landowner to manage his estates.**

Persia was in a sorry state of famine. From 1915 to 1917 the Turkish and Russian armies had fought backwards and forwards through the country, from the western coast of the Caspian Sea to the borders of Mesopotamia.

The invasion had very seriously depleted this part of the country of its stocks of grain, and many of the farmers had been drained by the armies to such an extent that they had been obliged to eat their seed corn in order to avoid starvation. In the year 1917 they had nothing left to sow. To add to their misery, in the winter of 1916-1917 there was an exceptionally light snowfall and the resultant spring drought. This caused the breakdown of their irrigation system and in consequence most of the crops on the line of march failed.

The country was in a terrible state, and the peasantry was in the last stages of starvation. Every time I was forced to stop my car, I was surrounded by hundreds of near-skeletons who screamed and fought for such scraps as I was able to spare. In a single day's journey of fifty-six miles between the towns of Kirind and Kermanshah, I counted twenty-seven corpses by the roadside, most of them those of women and children, and the general condition of life amongst the peasants was so frightful that I was ashamed to eat my simple rations in their presence. . . .

At the death of his father in 1916, Sardar Akram inherited a vast agricultural estate, which covered an area of about 500 square miles.

On it were ninety-six villages, each of which contained from one hundred and fifty to two thousand inhabitants. . . .

To attend properly to this wonderful property, and to do his duty to his subjects was an insufferable bore to the Sardar. . . .

The high life at Teheran, the capital, where he could satisfy his favourite passion of card playing for high stakes, was preferable to him to the duty of looking after his property and his people. The result was that all of his affairs were in the hands of a parasitic crowd of underlings, who were growing rich by robbing their master, and also by bleeding the poor farmers whom they could oppress without interference in his absence. . . .

In addition to the tax levied on his grain, many others are imposed on the wretched peasant. Of everything he produces he must pay his feudal master a proportion, varying from a fifth to a third part. For the privilege of living in a mud hut which he has probably built himself, he must pay an annual sum in cash. For every horse, cow, ox, sheep, or donkey that he possesses, he must do likewise.

He must also give the use of his donkeys without payment, to carry the grain of the landowner to the nearest market, and for fourteen days each year he must labour without pay for his master, or as an alternative he must find a substitute to do this work for him.

* F. A. C. Forbes-Leith, *Checkmate: Fighting Tradition in Central Persia* (London: Harrap, 1927), pp. 20-21, 37, 43-44, 50.

In Persia, as in Turkey, a strong man arose in response to the domestic diffi-culties and foreign pressures. Reza Khan, an army officer like Kemal, was not as radical as his Turkish counterpart; he did rid Persia of the decrepit Kajar dynasty, but he ensconced himself in its place rather than establishing a republic. With extraordinary energy and ruthlessness, Reza Shah left his mark on almost all aspects of Persian life, though with results that were by no means an unmixed blessing. This is made clear in the following analysis by the head of an American mission that reorganized Persian finances between 1922 and 1927.*

A restrained or a constitutional role was not to be expected of Reza Shah. He was a creature of primitive instincts, undisciplined by education or expe-rience, surrounded by servile flatterers, advised by the timid and the selfish. He was sincerely and deeply moved by the sorry condition of his country, con-scious of his own strength, and supremely self-confident. . . .

He was in some respects a great man and, in the sum of his qualities and achievements, an extraordinary phenomenon. Big, erect, roughhewn, eagle-beaked, he remained to the end a soldier. Endowed with enormous energy, he worked without end or fatigue and drove others mercilessly. In the ancient way of oriental monarchs, he attended personally to the affairs of state from the highest policy to the minutest detail. In the later years of his reign he seems to have become insane with power. The story is told that he wished to plant some trees in a certain spot. His forestry expert said: "Your Majesty, they will not grow there." The reply was: "They will if I order them to. . . ."

Reza was first of all a militarist. He introduced universal military service, enlarged the Army from about 40,000 to over 90,000 men; joined the gen-darmerie to the Army; bought some Italian gunboats for a Navy; and purchased airplanes and tanks.

The Shah was an extreme nationalist. Already before my departure, the government, driven on by him, had ended the extraterritorial privileges of foreigners. . . . Under Reza's leadership, Persia won the tariff autonomy that had been anticipated by the American Mission. As soon as I had left, Reza gave the Caspian fisheries to the Soviets, though in form this important and strategically located industry was to be operated by a joint Soviet-Persian com-pany. After this act, which had apparently already been promised, the Shah seems to have given no more ground to the Soviets and no indulgence at all to pro-Russian Persians. He canceled the British oil concession, but renewed it on more advantageous terms for Persia. The British bank lost its monopoly of note issues. . . .

Reza's dislike of foreigners went to such extremes that he forbade his people to visit the embassies and legations and practically terminated social contacts between Persians and the foreign diplomats. The government continued to em-ploy experts from other countries, chiefly from Germany and Switzerland, but only for factory management and technical services and never with authority. The Belgian customs mission was dispensed with. Books imported from foreign countries were censored, in some cases banned, in many cases burned. . . .

* A. C. Millspaugh, *Americans in Persia* (Washington, D.C.: The Brookings Institution, 1946), pp. 26-30, 34-36.

Nationalism asserted itself in other directions. Before I left, the calendar was reformed and the names of the months changed from Arabic to Persian. Shortly the name of the country itself was changed to "Iran." The government propagandized the ancient glories and culture of the land and encouraged the printing of books in Persian.

While nationalism often took a reactionary form, Reza aimed to modernize his country. Before my departure, the *kola,* picturesque headdress of the men, had taken on an unbecoming visor, and later gave way entirely to the western felt hat. Reza's male subjects likewise discarded the dignified flowing *abbas.* Beards followed in this process of elimination; smoothshaven faces, formerly suggestive of eunuchs, became the rule. Finally in 1936 an order went out that the women should put off their veils. . . .

Education received the Shah's patronage, and to young Persians seemed the golden key to a golden world. The government sent numbers of young men to be educated in Europe. A university, proposed in my time, was founded at Teheran. Sports flourished at the command of the Shah and with the financial assistance of the government.

In the economic sphere, the Shah aimed at the development and self-sufficiency of his country and his own profit. He improved cultivation on the lands that he had appropriated for himself. His Ministry of Agriculture enlarged the agricultural school, increased the usefulness of the demonstration farms, imported agricultural machinery, set up a laboratory for the making of serums, combated animal diseases and plant pests, and created two or three well-planned villages with reasonably attractive and healthful houses and with intelligent attention to the community water supply. New crops were promoted; and marked increases occurred in the production of tobacco, cotton, tea, sugar beets, and silk cocoons. An agricultural bank assisted in this development. . . .

The Shah's efforts, for the most part, seem to have been concentrated on a program of government-owned industries. This program he co-ordinated fairly well with the development of agriculture and the mines; and it was carried out with astonishing speed. At the end of Reza's reign, the government owned and was operating a tobacco factory, a glycerine and soap factory, five sugar mills, a cottonseed oil plant, cotton, silk, and jute mills, a sulphuric acid plant, cement plants, an establishment for impregnating railroad ties, a lumber mill, an iron foundry, a gas mask factory, munitions factories, an airplane assembly plant, cotton gins, canning factories, and plants for cleaning rice and tea. Some of these were large and all were equipped with modern machinery. A government corporation supervised carpet manufacturing, handled the commercial side of the industry, and made progress in the rehabilitation of this ancient craft.

Reza Shah made some monumental additions to the country's transportation facilities. He completed the Trans-Persian Railway, one of the world's outstanding engineering feats, and partly completed three ambitious branch lines. He built new roads, improved old ones, and started paving. He widened the main streets in most of the cities, tore down walls, laid out boulevards, opened vistas. . . .

The Shah's taxation policy was highly regressive, raising the cost of living and bearing heavily on the poor. He exempted the landlords from direct taxation and restored the medieval duties collected at the gates of cities. Various services he procured for little or nothing because suppliers learned to be afraid of presenting bills to him. He used forced labor on roads and buildings, requisitioned trucks, and doubtless had other devices for getting things done cheaply. His private accumulations came from the produce of the agricultural lands that he appropriated, from a consistent looting of the rich and well-to-do, from the shares that he had in certain private enterprises, from gifts and bribes, from tribute paid by tribal chiefs, and from the rakeoff that he had from others' grafting. Altogether he thoroughly milked the country, grinding down the peasants, tribesmen, and laborers, and taking heavy toll from the landlords. While his activities enriched a new class of "capitalists"—merchants, monopolists, contractors, and politician-favorites—inflation, heavy taxation, and other measures lowered the standard of living of the masses. . . .

Some of Reza's public acts were statesmanlike and long overdue. Others were sound in conception and would have been beneficial at the right time and in the right place and relationship. A large part of his construction program, in the light of the country's fundamental needs, was premature and wasteful. Not much of what he did contributed to the practical enlightenment, the basic strengthening, or the long-run progress of his country. . . .

Agriculture, public health, and education are basic to the development and progress of the country. Agriculture depends upon water, and in Persia water depends upon irrigation. Yet, Reza's prodigious construction activities did not produce a single major irrigation project. Famines, caused by crop failures and maldistribution of grain production, have figured among Persia's most tragic visitations. No step was taken to cure this malady. . . .

In the field of public health, he started with hospitals, but largely overlooked preventive medicine and community hygiene. Nowhere did he build a city water system. Food and drink remained contaminated. . . .

However one may appraise the program, it is evident that Reza's most damaging failure lay in the means that he employed: dictatorship, corruption, and terror.

131   GANDHI AND NEHRU

The two outstanding leaders of the nationalist movement in India in the postwar years were Gandhi and Nehru, both of whom attracted worldwide attention, some highly critical and some almost idolatrous. Gandhi was denounced as a fraud and worshipped as a saint, while Nehru analyzed himself as "a queer mixture of the East and the West, out of place everywhere, at home nowhere." The following comments on Gandhi, taken from Nehru's autobiography, are as revealing of Nehru as of his subject.*

I imagine that Gandhiji is not so vague about the objective as he sometimes appears to be. He is passionately desirous of going in a certain direction, but this is wholly at variance with modern ideas and conditions, and he has so far been unable to fit the two, or to chalk out all the intermediate steps leading to his goal. Hence the appearance of vagueness and avoidance of clarity. But his general inclination has been clear enough for a quarter of a century, ever since

* *Toward Freedom. The Autobiography of Jawaharlal Nehru* (New York: Day, 1941), pp. 314-16. Copyright © 1941 by The John Day Company. Reprinted by permission of The John Day Company, Inc.

he started formulating his philosophy in South Africa. I do not know if those early writings still represent his views. I doubt if they do so in their entirety, but they do help us to understand the background of his thought.

"India's salvation consists," he wrote in 1909, "in unlearning what she has learned during the last fifty years. The railways, telegraphs, hospitals, lawyers, doctors, and suchlike have all to go; and the so-called upper classes have to learn consciously, religiously, and deliberately the simple peasant life, knowing it to be a life giving true happiness." And again: "Every time I get into a railway car or use a motor bus I know that I am doing violence to my sense of what is right"; "to attempt to reform the world by means of highly artficial and speedy locomotion is to attempt the impossible."

All this seems to me utterly wrong and harmful doctrine, and impossible of achievement. Behind it lies Gandhiji's love and praise of poverty and suffering and the ascetic life. For him progress and civilization consist not in the multiplication of wants, of higher standards of living, "but in the deliberate and voluntary restriction of wants, which promotes real happiness and contentment, and increases the capacity for service." If these premises are once accepted, it becomes easy to follow the rest of Gandhiji's thought and to have a better understanding of his activities. But most of us do not accept those premises, and yet we complain later on when we find that his activities are not to our liking.

Personally I dislike the praise of poverty and suffering. I do not think they are at all desirable, and they ought to be abolished. Nor do I appreciate the ascetic life as a social ideal, though it may suit individuals. I understand and appreciate simplicity, equality, self-control; but not the mortification of the flesh. Just as an athlete requires to train his body, I believe that the mind and habits have also to be trained and brought under control. It would be absurd to expect that a person who is given to too much self-indulgence can endure much suffering or show unusual self-control or behave like a hero when the crisis comes. To be in good moral condition requires at least as much training as to be in good physical condition. But that certainly does not mean asceticism or self-mortification.

Nor do I appreciate in the least the idealization of the "simple peasant life." I have almost a horror of it, and instead of submitting to it myself I want to drag out even the peasantry from it, not to urbanization, but to the spread of urban cultural facilities to rural areas. Far from this life's giving me true happiness, it would be almost as bad as imprisonment for me. What is there in "The Man with the Hoe" to idealize over? Crushed and exploited for innumerable generations, he is only little removed from the animals who keep him company.

> *Who made him dead to rapture and despair,*
> *A thing that grieves not and that never hopes,*
> *Stolid and stunned, a brother to the ox?*

This desire to get away from the mind of man to primitive conditions where mind does not count, seems to me quite incomprehensible. The very thing that is the glory and triumph of man is decried and discouraged, and a physical environment which will oppress the mind and prevent its growth is considered desirable. Present-day civilization is full of evils, but it is also full of good; and it has the capacity in it to rid itself of those evils. To destroy it root and branch is to remove that capacity from it and revert to a dull, sunless, and miserable existence. But even if that were desirable it is an impossible undertaking. We cannot stop the river of change or cut ourselves adrift from it, and psychologically we who have eaten of the apple of Eden cannot forget that taste and go back to primitiveness.

It is difficult to argue this, for the two standpoints are utterly different. Gandhiji is always thinking in terms of personal salvation and of sin, while most of us have society's welfare uppermost in our minds. I find it difficult to grasp the idea of sin, and perhaps it is because of this that I cannot appreciate Gandhiji's general outlook.

132   Non-cooperation Campaign

Gandhi preached to his followers that Britain's domination of India was possible only because of the cooperation of all classes of the population. Accordingly, he called for peaceful non-cooperation, a weapon that proved extraordinarily effective against the British rulers. The following selection describes the nature and results of Gandhi's first non-cooperation campaign, launched in 1920.*

At the time of my arrival in India, reports as to the success Gandhi had achieved in winning national support for his ideas were curiously conflicting. The strength of the movement was debated hotly on both sides. I set out to discover as far as I could the actual results of non-violent non-cooperation in the year in which it had been in existence.

To begin with, the Tilak Swarajya Memorial Fund of a *crore* of rupees, an amount not far from $3,000,000, had been easily subscribed in less than the allotted time. Thus the leaders found themselves in possession of plenty of money. Besides the sums spent in creating and maintaining a party organization which spread like a vast network over all the villages of India, large amounts were appropriated for publicity at home and abroad. Further immense sums were used to buy and distribute *charkas,* or spinning-wheels, in support of the economic aspect of the program, and the Congress organization had also undertaken to employ weavers and to dispose of *swadeshi* cloth that they or private individuals were able to produce.

Indians had not, apparently, shown much inclination to begin non-cooperation by surrendering their titles. Out of an approximate total of 5,000 holders of honorary titles, some 21 only, including Rabindranath Tagore, had resigned their titles. ... The movement for the secession of lawyers from the courts had met with more marked success, but the administration of the law was by no means paralyzed. It is still functioning, and recently the courts have done a thriving business in the prosecution and sentencing of political prisoners, including a large number of the "resigned" lawyers. With regard to the boycotting of elections to the newly created Legislative Councils ... the non-cooperators made strenuous efforts to render the elections of November, 1920, abortive by breaking up meetings, picketing the booths and intimidating candidates who had refused to recognize the Nationalist appeal to withdraw their

---

* Gertrude Emerson, "Non-Violent Non-Cooperation in India," *Asia,* XXII (August, 1922), 607, 608, 610.

candidature. As a result, only about 20 per cent of the total number of those exercising the privilege of the franchise made use of it. . . .

The part of the Gandhi program which involved the withdrawal of students from government institutions succeeded in introducing considerable disturbance into the educational system of India. Bengal has long been the cultural center of India and, as one might expect, showed the greatest sensitiveness in its immediate response to this appeal. In a report on the situation issued by the Vice-Chancellor of Calcutta University in September, 1921, it was stated that 42 per cent of the students below college grade had left the recognized schools of Bengal between September and March, a number equal to between forty and fifty thousand, and that by August, 1921, only 14 per cent had returned. . . .

The second phase of the swadeshi movement, the boycotting and burning of English goods, stirred up an immense amount of bitter feeling in India. . . .

I did not happen to be present at any of these bonfires, but the newspapers frequently described them in vivid terms. Among my clippings I find the following, from the *Servant of India,* October 14: "At the bonfire near the Elphinstone Mills on Sunday night the crowd was as large as on the last occasion. It could be counted only in *lakhs* [100,000's]. The enthusiasm of the people was very great. From early afternoon people were moving toward Elphinstone Bridge, clothed in Khaddar and later in the evening it was impossible to pass along the Elphinstone Bridge and its precincts. . . . In the middle of the arena a large platform was erected for the leaders and near it the foreign clothes which had been collected during the past few days were arranged in the shape of a pyramid. All sorts of clothes of foreign make were there—costly silks, costly coats, shirts, hats and in fact everything that was considered necessary up to this time, was there thrown in a heap all well arranged, soaked in kerosene and mixed with crackers. . . . Mahatma Gandhi, whose speech was full of pathos, moved his hearers very much and he spoke with a great deal of feeling of sorrow. Some tears were to be seen in his eyes, so moved he was by sorrow at the failure on the part of the people in doing their duty towards their country. . . . The Mahatma lighted the heap of foreign clothing. The sight was extremely impressive; the vast audience, the burning clothes, and the passionate speakers, under God's sky in the growing night." With even a remote understanding of impressionable Indian psychology, and of the incalculable power of Gandhi's personality, it is easy to perceive the far-reaching influence of meetings such as the one described, which took place in Bombay.

SUN YAT-SEN SEEKS FOREIGN AID **133**

China, like other non-Western countries, experienced violent change during the postwar years. The outstanding figure during its period of turmoil was a fiery nationalist from Canton, Dr. Sun Yat-sen. Trained in Western schools as a physician, he never practiced medicine; instead, he devoted his life to politics. Although the Manchu dynasty was overthrown in 1911, the republic that took its place was a government in name only. Warlords ruled the provinces, paying no attention to the central administration. Sun Yat-sen sought foreign aid in reorganizing his Kuomintang party in order to restore order. The following account by George E. Sokolsky, who was in China at the time, describes how Sun finally turned to the Soviet Union after being rejected by the West.*

It is an error to assume that Dr. Sun Yat-sen was essentially anti-foreign. If his activities previous to 1924 are studied, the influences of the West, particularly Great Britain and the United States are always evident. The Government which he organized was based upon American models; his political party was made to resemble an American political party; his emphasis on a written constitution was American. The years of futile argumentation over constitutionalism, the lack of organization within the *Kuomintang* and in the Government, the inability to achieve success, the constant betrayals by military men, led Dr. Sun Yat-sen in 1923, to seek a reorganization of the entire mechanism. In 1923, he sent his A.D.C., Mr. Morris A. Cohen, to Canada and the United States to recruit World War veterans who would reorganize his army on a modern basis. He also utilized his then English secretary and soon, his Minister of Aviation, Mr. Eugene Chen, to confer with the British authorities at Hongkong and in London for assistance. Both missions failed. Dr. Sun then applied to the Germans, but they were unable to offer what he needed. He thereupon wrote to Mr. Karakhan in Peking requesting him to send a representative with whom he might discuss mutual relations. Michael Borodin was sent. With characteristic ability he saw that the basic problem was one of organization. He immediately promised to obtain from Soviet Russia arms and munitions on easy terms; he also agreed to provide a corps of military and civilian experts who would help to reorganize the party and the Government along Soviet lines. Borodin was appointed High Adviser to the *Kuomintang*. His first task then was to propose unity of principle, unity of party organization, and a strict party discipline.

134 THE THREE PEOPLE'S PRINCIPLES

*With the help of Russian advisers, Sun Yat-sen built up a modern army and reorganized his Kuomintang party along authoritarian lines. The ideology of the party was summarized in his Three People's Principles, which were broadcast throughout the country. The following brief summary of the Three Principles is from an official Chinese government source.***

The Three People's Principles have guided the building of the nation; they are also the principles to be observed by the Kuomintang. They are Nationalism, Democracy, and People's Livelihood, an integrated whole. The aim of the Principle of Nationalism is to liberate the Chinese nation from foreign invasion and oppression and make it permanently free and independent, to attain full equality of all races within the country, and to render assistance to all weak

* *China Year Book, 1928* (Tientsin, 1929), pp. 1320-21.
** *China Yearbook, 1957-58* (Taipei, 1958), pp. 50-51.

races in the world with a view to realizing complete equality in the whole world.

The aim of the Principle of Democracy is to do away with political inequalities so that the nation belongs to every citizen. To carry out this Principle, the people enjoy the four political rights, i.e., election, recall, initiative, and referendum. The Government has five powers, i.e., executive, legislative, judicial, examination, and control. Such division of *rights* and *powers* is an ideal and progressive system under democracy.

The aim of the Principle of People's Livelihood is to help people solve the economic problems so that all persons may attain economic equality and enjoy a life of freedom and happiness. The methods for realizing this Principle are: (1) equalization of land ownership, and (2) control of private capital.

SUN YAT-SEN'S MESSAGE TO THE SOVIET UNION **135**

Russian assistance enabled Sun Yat-sen to become once more a power in Chinese affairs. His new army and reorganized party were the instruments needed to realize his hopes for China; but before he could use these instruments, Sun fell mortally ill. From his death bed he sent in March, 1925 a letter to the Central Executive Committee of the Soviet government in which he specifically called on his Kuomintang party to cooperate closely with the Soviet Union.*

Dear Comrades:

While I lie here in a malady against which men are powerless, my thoughts are turned towards you and towards the fates of my Party and my country.

You are at the head of the union of free republics—that heritage left to the oppressed peoples of the world by the immortal Lenin. With the aid of that heritage the victims of imperialism will inevitably achieve emancipation from that international regime whose foundations have been rooted for ages in slavery, wars, and injustice.

I leave behind me a Party which, as I always hoped, will be bound up with you in the historic work of the final liberation of China and other exploited countries from the yoke of imperialism. By the will of fate I must leave my work unfinished, and hand it over to those who, remaining faithful to the principles and teachings of the Party, will thereby be my true followers.

Therefore I charge the Kuomintang to continue the work of the revolutionary nationalist movement, so that China, reduced by the imperialists to the position of a semi-colonial country, shall become free.

With this object I have instructed the Party to be in contact with you. I firmly believe in the continuance of the support which you have hitherto accorded to my country.

Taking my leave of you, dear comrades, I want to express the hope that the day will soon come when the U.S.S.R. will welcome a friend and ally in a mighty, free China, and that in the great struggle for the liberation of the op-

---

pressed peoples of the world both those allies will go forward to victory hand in hand.

With fraternal greetings,
SUN YAT-SEN.

136 SUN YAT-SEN ON THE COLONIAL REVOLTS

The above selections indicate the nature and scope of the colonial revolts following World War I. Sun Yat-sen was very much aware of these, and emphasized their significance in a speech delivered in Japan on November 28, 1924. The following selections from this speech reflect the attitudes of many politically-conscious non-Westerners at this time toward the West and toward the new Soviet regime.*

Since the day of Japan's victory over Russia, the peoples of Asia have cherished the hope of shaking off the yoke of European oppression, a hope which has given rise to a series of independence movements—in Egypt, Persia, Turkey, Afghanistan, and finally in India. Therefore, Japan's defeat of Russia gave rise to a great hope for the independence of Asia. From the inception of this hope to the present day only 20 years have elapsed. The Egyptian, Turkish, Persian, Afghan, and Arabian independence movements have already materialized, and even the independence movement in India, has, with the passage of time, been gaining ground. . . . At present Asia has only two independent countries, Japan in the East and Turkey in the West. In other words, Japan and Turkey are the Eastern and Western barricades of Asia. Now Persia, Afghanistan, and Arabia are also following the European example in arming themselves, with the result that the Western peoples dare not look down on them. China at present also possesses considerable armaments, and when her unification is accomplished she too will become a great Power. We advocate Pan-Asianism in order to restore the status of Asia. Only by the unification of all the peoples in Asia on the foundation of benevolence and virtue can they become strong and powerful.

But to rely on benevolence alone to influence the Europeans in Asia to relinquish the privileges they have acquired in China would be an impossible dream. If we want to regain our rights, we must resort to force. In the matter of armaments, Japan has already accomplished her aims, while Turkey has recently also completely armed herself. The other Asiatic races, such as the peoples of Persia, Afghanistan, and Arabia are all war-like peoples. China has a population of four hundred millions, and although she needs to modernize her armament and other equipment, and her people are a peace-loving people, yet when the destiny of their country is at stake the Chinese people will also fight with courage and determination. Should all Asiatic peoples thus unite together and present a united front against the Occidentals, they will win the final victory. Compare the populations of Europe and Asia: China has a popu-

---

* T'ang Leang-li, *China and Japan: Natural Friends, Unnatural Enemies* (Shanghai: China United Press, 1941), pp. 145, 149, 150.

lation of four hundred millions, India three hundred and fifty millions, Japan several scores of millions, totalling, together with other peoples, no less than nine hundred millions. The population in Europe is somewhere around four hundred millions. For the four hundred millions to oppress the nine hundred millions is an intolerable injustice, and in the long run the latter will be defeated. . . .

At present there is a new country in Europe which has been looked down upon and expelled from the Family of Nations by the White races of the whole of Europe. Europeans consider it as a poisonous snake or some brutal animal, and dare not approach it. Such a view is also shared by some countries in Asia. This country is Russia. At present, Russia is attempting to separate from the White peoples in Europe. Why? Because she insists on the rule of Right and denounces the rule of Might. She advocates the principle of benevolence and justice, and refuses to accept the principles of utilitarianism and force. She maintains Right and opposes the oppression of the majority by the minority. From this point of view, recent Russian civilization is similar to that of our ancient civilization. Therefore, she joins with the Orient and separates from the West. The new principles of Russia were considered as intolerable by Europeans. They are afraid that these principles, when put into effect, would overthrow their rule of Might. Therefore they do not accept the Russian way, which is in accord with the principles of benevolence and justice, but denounce it as contrary to world principles.

Chapter Twenty-two

*Revolution
and settlement
in Europe to 1929*

137 ALLIED INTERVENTION IN RUSSIA

While the colonial world was experiencing nationalist uprisings, Europe itself was in the grip of social revolution. The history of Europe in the immediate postwar period was, to a large degree, the history of a struggle between revolutionary and counterrevolutionary forces. In Russia, the Bolsheviks were opposed by the White Russians and by Allied interventionist forces. The Allies began their intervention after the Brest-Litovsk Treaty which the Bolsheviks signed with the Germans on March 3, 1918. The motives of the Allies were partly fear that bolshevism might spread westward, and partly desire to have a new Russian government that would renew the war against Germany. When World War I ended with the German armistice, the question arose whether the intervention in Russia should be continued; it was debated in Paris by the Allied leaders in January, 1919. The following selections from these discussions reveal the complex combination of fears, hopes, and calculations that motivated the leaders and led them to conflicting positions.*

NOTES ON CONVERSATIONS HELD IN THE OFFICE OF M. PICHON AT THE QUAI D'ORSAY, ON JANUARY 16, 1919. *Preliminary discussion regarding the situation in Russia. . . .*

Mr. Lloyd George stated that there seemed to be three possible policies:

* U.S. Serial 7605, Doc. No. 106, pp. 1235 ff.

1. Military intervention. It is true ... the Bolsheviki movement is as dangerous to civilization as German militarism, but as to putting it down by the sword, is there anyone who proposes it? It would mean holding a certain number of vast provinces in Russia. The Germans with one million men on their Eastern Front only held the fringe of this territory. If he now proposed to send a thousand British troops to Russia for that purpose, the armies would mutiny. The same applies to U. S. troops in Siberia; also to Canadians and French as well. The mere idea of crushing Bolshevism by a military force is pure madness. Even admitting that it is done, who is to occupy Russia? No one can conceive or understand to bring about order by force.

2. A cordon. The second suggestion is to besiege Bolshevik Russia. Mr. Lloyd George wondered if those present realized what this would mean. From the information furnished him Bolshevik Russia has no corn, but within this territory there are 150,000,000 men, women, and children. There is now starvation in Petrograd and Moscow. This is not an health cordon, it is a death cordon. Moreover, as a matter of fact, the people who would die are just the people that the Allies desire to protect. It would not result in the starvation of the Bolsheviki; it would simply mean the death of our friends. The cordon policy is a policy which, as humane people, those present could not consider. . . .

3. The third alternative was contained in the British proposal, which was to summon these people to Paris to appear before those present. . . .

Mr. Lloyd George referred to the objection that had been raised to permitting Bolshevik delegates to come to Paris. It had been claimed that they would convert France and England to Bolshevism. If England becomes Bolshevist, it will not be because a single Bolshevist representative is permitted to enter England. On the other hand, if a military enterprise were started against the Bolsheviki, that would make England Bolshevist, and there would be a Soviet in London. For his part, Mr. Lloyd George was not afraid of Bolshevism if the facts are known in England and the United States. The same applied to Germany. He was convinced that an educated democracy can be always trusted to turn down Bolshevism.

Under all circumstances, Mr. Lloyd George saw no better way out than to follow the third alternative. Let the Great Powers impose their conditions and summon these people to Paris to give an account of themselves to the Great Powers, not to the Peace Conference. . . .

SECRETARIES' NOTES OF A CONVENTION HELD IN M. PICHON'S ROOM AT THE QUAI D'ORSAY ON TUESDAY, JANUARY 21, 1919, AT 15 HOURS.　　M. Sonnino explained that all the Russian parties had some representatives here, except the Soviets, whom they did not wish to hear. . . .

The Allies were now fighting against the Bolshevists who were their enemies, and therefore they were not obliged to hear them with the others. . . .

Mr. Lloyd George expressed the view that the acceptance of M. Sonnino's proposals would amount to their hearing a string of people, all of whom held the same opinion, and all of whom would strike the same note. But they would not hear the people who at the present moment were actually controlling European Russia. . . .

President Wilson asked to be permitted to urge one aspect of the case. As M. Sonnino had implied, they were all repelled by Bolshevism, and for that reason they had placed armed men in opposition to them. One of the things that was clear in the Russian situation was that by opposing Bolshevism with arms, they were in reality serving the cause of Bolshevism. The Allies were making it possible for the Bolsheviks to argue that Imperialistic and Capitalistic Governments were endeavouring to exploit the country and to give the land back to the landlords, and so bring about a re-action. If it could be shown that this was not true, and that the Allies were prepared to deal with the rulers of Russia, much of the moral force of this argument would disappear. The allegation that the Allies were against the people and wanted to control their affairs provided the argument which enabled them to raise armies. If, on the other hand, the Allies could swallow their pride and the natural repulsion which they felt for the Bolshevists and see the representatives of all organized groups in one place, he thought it would bring about a marked reaction against Bolshevism.

M. Clemenceau said that, in principle, he did not favour conversation with the Bolshevists; not because they were criminals, but because we would be raising them to our level by saying that they were worthy of entering into conversation with us. The Bolshevist danger was very great at the present moment. Bolshevism was spreading. It had invaded the Baltic Provinces and Poland, and that very morning they received very bad news regarding its spread to Budapest and Vienna. Italy, also, was in danger. The danger was probably greater there than in France. If Bolshevism, after spreading in Germany, were to traverse Austria and Hungary and so reach Italy, Europe would be faced with a very great danger. Therefore, something must be done against Bolshevism. . . .

M. Sonnino said that he . . . would remind his colleagues that, before the Peace of Brest-Litovsk was signed, the Bolshevists promised all sorts of things, such as to refrain from propaganda, but since that peace had been concluded they had broken all their promises, their one idea being to spread revolution in other countries. His idea was to collect together all the anti-Bolshevik parties and help them to make a strong Government, provided they pledged themselves not to serve the forces of re-action and especially not to touch the land question, thereby depriving the Bolshevists of their strongest argument. Should they take these pledges, he would be prepared to help them. . . .

Mr. Lloyd George said he wished to put one or two practical questions to M. Sonnino. The British Empire now had some 15,000 to 20,000 men in Russia. M. de Scavenius had estimated that some 150,000 additional men would be required, in order to keep the anti-Bolshevist Governments from dissolution. And General Franchet d'Esperey also insisted on the necessity of Allied assistance. Now Canada had decided to withdraw her troops, because the Canadian soldiers would not agree to stay and fight against the Russians. Similar trouble had also occurred amongst the other Allied troops. And he felt certain that, if the British tried to send any more troops there, there would be mutiny.

M. Sonnino suggested that volunteers might be called for.

Mr. Lloyd George, continuing, said that it would be impossible to raise 150,000 men in that way. He asked, however, what contributions America, Italy and France would make towards the raising of this Army.

President Wilson and M. Clemenceau each said none.

M. Orlando agreed that Italy could make no further contributions.

Mr. Lloyd George said that the Bolshevists had an army of 300,000 men who would, before long, be good soldiers, and to fight them at least 400,000 Russian soldiers would be required. Who would feed, equip and pay them?

Would Italy, or America, or France, do so? If they were unable to do that, what would be the good of fighting Bolshevism? It could not be crushed by speeches.

H. G. Wells on the Bolshevik Victory   138

Despite the opposition of Lloyd George and Wilson, the Allied intervention continued, only to prove futile in the end. The Bolsheviks emerged with a triumph that was partially due to the Allies' sending few troops, although their supply of money and war material was generous. Also, the various White Russian forces were weakened by dissension and by self-defeating policies that antagonized many peasants, besides which the Bolsheviks possessed certain advantages that eventually proved decisive. One advantage was the role of the highly disciplined Communist party, described in a firsthand account by the well-known English writer H. G. Wells.*

From end to end of Russia, and in the Russian-speaking community throughout the world, there existed only one sort of people who had common general ideas upon which to work, a common faith and a common will, and that was the Communist Party. While all the rest of Russia was either apathetic like the peasantry, or garrulously at sixes and sevens, or given over to violence and fear, the Communists believed and were prepared to act. Numerically they were and are a very small part of the Russian population. . . . Nevertheless, because it was in those terrible days the only organisation which gave men a common idea of action, common formulas and mutual confidences, it was able to seize and retain control of the smashed Empire. It was and it is the only sort of administrative solidarity possible in Russia. These ambiguous adventurers who have been and are afflicting Russia, with the support of the Western Powers, Denikin, Kolchak, Wrangel and the like, stand for no guiding principle and offer no security of any sort upon which men's confidence can crystallize. . . . The Communist Party, however one may criticise it, does embody an idea, and can be relied on to stand by its idea. So far it is a thing morally higher than anything that has yet been brought against it. It at once secured the passive support of the peasant mass by permitting them to take land from the estates and by making peace with Germany. It restored order—after a frightful lot of shooting—in the great towns. For a time everybody found carrying arms without authority was shot. This action was clumsy and brutal but effective. To retain its power the Communist Government organised Extraordinary Commissions with practically unlimited powers, and crushed out all opposition by a Red Terror. Much that that Red Terror did was cruel and frightful, it was largely controlled by narrow-minded men, and many of its officials were inspired by social hatred and the fear of counter-revolution, but if it was fanatical it was honest. Apart from individual atrocities, it did on the whole kill for a reason and to an end.

* H. G. Wells, *Russia in the Shadows* (London: Hodder, 1920), pp. 61-64. By permission of the Executors of H. G. Wells.

The main factor explaining the Bolshevik success is to be found in the attitude of the Russian peasants, the great majority of whom were apolitical and preferred to be rid of both the Reds and the Whites. On the other hand, many of them had seized land from the large estates during the course of the revolution, and their primary concern was to retain this land. Most of them believed they had a better chance of doing so under the Reds than under the Whites, and gave the Bolsheviks enough popular support to tip the balance in their favor. The following firsthand account is by the Secretary to the British Labor Delegation, which visited Russia in June, 1920. The author took advantage of the opportunity to live for some weeks in the village of Ozero, between the Volga and the Urals.*

My host's name was Alexander Petrovich Emilianov. He was of the "middle" type of peasant, which formed the great majority of the village. About one-fifth of its people were considered "poor" peasants. Of "rich" peasants there were only four or five, I was told.

Tall, upstanding and vigorous, with short, brown beard, in a much-worn cloth suit and top-boots, Emilianov reminded me of a Scots gamekeeper in East Lothian, one of my earliest and best friends. I soon found that he was a man of shrewd intelligence. He could read with ease. At church, which I attended on the following Sunday, it was his function to read the Epistle; he stepped out from the standing crowd and read it in a loud and sonorous voice, facing the priest (who had just read the Gospel). He was evidently well versed in the Bible, and could hold his own in theological argument. . . .

Before the Revolution my host had had eight acres—about the average holding in that region. He had now no less than eighty-five. This was the tremendous fact that I had turned over and over in my mind as we bumped along. Tremendous, surely; for my host's case was a type, not only of thousands, but of millions of others. . . .

"Look there," said Emilianov, pointing out from the edge of the village field over the limitless rolling steppe. "All that was the land of the landlords (*barin*). You may drive forty *versts* in a straight line from here and see nothing else." I came to realise that, in effect, the villages and their "fields," large as they seemed, were but islands in an ocean of large properties. On all sides they had been hemmed in by the estates of the great landlords.

"Who owned all this land?" I asked.

"All sorts of landlords. One was a Cossack. Two were Samara merchants. One was a German, Schmidt, who bought his from the Crown. Some was held by the Monks. One was an estate of Maria Feodorovna, the Tsaritsa."

"What has happened to them?"

"They are mostly gone," he replied in a matter-of-fact tone. "Some are in Samara. Most of them have left Russia, I suppose." . . .

The landlords' land was seized in Ozero in the summer of 1917—that is, during the Kerenski *regime,* and before the Communists came into power. I was told afterwards that by October of that year there was not a single great

* C. R. Buxton, *In a Russian Village* (London: Labour Publishing Co., 1922), pp. 14-15, 19, 21, 26-27, 47-48.

estate left in the Samara "Government." But it appears that the formal allocation of the land did not take place until after the October (i.e., Communist)
Revolution. With the land, the stock and implements were distributed also.

The Soviet of the *Uyezd,* Pugachev, allotted a certain quantity of land to
each village in its area, Ozero among others. The Soviet of Ozero was
specially elected for the purpose of dividing up the land, all the villagers
having the right to vote. The Soviet then distributed the land according to
an absolutely fixed principle, namely, five *desiatin* per "soul." No one was
to have more than he and his family could work. Emilianov's family, including wife and children, amounted to seven, and that is why he had thirty-five
desiatin, or approximately eighty acres. Appeals could be made to the Volost
(or District) Soviet, and on one occasion I heard such an appeal being tried.

"And what do the peasants think of it all now?" I asked Emilianov.

"It's a fine thing, the Revolution. Every one is in favour of it. They don't
like the Communist Party, but they like the Revolution."

"Why don't they like the Communist Party?"

"Because they are always worrying us. They are people from the towns
and don't understand the country. Commissars—powerful persons—are continually coming. We don't know what to do with them. New orders (*prikazi*)
are always coming out. People are puzzled. As soon as you understand one
of them, a different one comes along."

"What party do most people belong to here?"

"None at all. They are non-party (*bezpartini*)." . . .

The general attitude of the peasants, so far as I could judge, was that
they owed much to the Soviet Government in the matter of the land; they
approved of the "principle of everybody being equal"; they often talked of the
"true" Communist as being an ideal sort of person. But they complained
bitterly of the absence of necessities, of the compulsory contributions, and
the worry of perpetual orders and appeals, often hard to understand. They
considered that the Government was responsible for all these evils alike, and
that the peasant was somehow in a position of inferiority to the townsman.

And yet, in spite of all these complaints, when the opportunity was offered
them to choose between Kolchak on the one side and the Soviet Government
on the other, the peasants do not seem to have had much hesitation. . . .

They were for the Revolution; and for the moment the Soviet power was
the embodiment of the Revolution. They grumbled and cursed at it; but
when the opportunity was offered to overthrow it, they said "No."

DISCIPLINE OF THE GERMAN ARMY 140

*With the triumph of bolshevism in Russia, the crucial question for Germany
and the rest of Europe was whether or not the Spartacists (the German equivalent
of the Bolsheviks) would prevail over the moderate Socialists, as Lenin, in Russia,
had overthrown Kerensky. In the end, the moderate Socialists won out because
of a combination of factors. Since the war already was over, the Spartacists could
not use antiwar slogans as the Bolsheviks had done so effectively. Also, German
society was more healthy and prosperous than the Russian, with the result that
the peasants and workers were not as discontented and revolution-minded as their*

counterparts in Russia. Finally, the German army was not as demoralized and mutinous as the Russian, so that it heeded to a considerable degree the following appeal for military discipline made by the moderate Socialist government that took office following the Kaiser's abdication.*

The People's Government is inspired by the wish to see each of our soldiers return to his home as quickly as possible after his unspeakable sufferings and unheard-of deprivations. But this goal can only be reached if the demobilization is carried out according to an orderly plan. If single troops stream back at their own pleasure, they place themselves, their comrades, and their homes in the greatest danger. The consequences would necessarily be chaos, famine, and want. The People's Government expects of you the strictest self-discipline in order to avoid immeasurable calamity. We desire the High Command to inform the army in the field of this declaration of the People's Government, and to issue the following orders:

1. The relations between officer and rank and file are to be built up on mutual confidence. Prerequisites to this are willing submission of the ranks to the officer, and comradely treatment by the officer of the ranks.

2. The officer's superiority in rank remains. Unqualified obedience in service is of prime importance for the success of the return home to Germany. Military discipline and army order must, therefore, be maintained under all circumstances.

3. The Soldiers' Councils have an advisory voice in maintaining confidence between officer and rank and file in questions of food, leave, the infliction of disciplinary punishments. Their highest duty is to try to prevent disorder and mutiny.

4. The same food for officers, officials, and rank and file.

5. The same bonuses to be added to the pay, and the same allowances for service in the field for officers and rank and file.

6. Arms are to be used against members of our own people only in cases of self-defense and to prevent robberies.

141 THE "EBERT–GROENER DEAL"

In contrast to the Russian army, the regular army in Germany was used to crush the Communist revolution rather than to further it. Friedrich Ebert, leader of the Majority Socialists and Chancellor of the Republic, concluded an alliance for this purpose with General Wilhelm Groener, Chief of the General Staff. A secret and private telephone line was set up between the Reich Chancellery in Berlin and Supreme Headquarters at Spa. On this line, the so-called "Ebert–Groener Deal" was reached, calling for the cooperation of the army and the Majority Socialists against the extreme Left. This fateful alliance explains in large part why Germany emerged as the Weimar Republic rather than as a Soviet republic.**

---

* "The German Revolution," *International Conciliation*, No. 137 (April, 1919), p. 548.
** R. G. L. Waite, *Vanguard of Nazism* (Cambridge: Harvard Univ., 1952), pp. 4-5.

On the evening of November 9, 1918, the harried Chancellor, his coat removed and his shirt stained with sweat, was pacing the offices of the Reichs-chancellery. The problem of the return of the field armies and a dozen others demanded immediate solution. He had put in a grueling day— a day that had seen him first fighting to preserve the monarchy and now trying desperately to save the Republic from extremism. Even his title of Chancellor rested on the legal fiction that Prince Max in conferring it was acting as Regent. He was exhausted and he was alarmed—not so much for himself but for the Germany his simple soul loved. The restless, milling crowds beneath his window did nothing to reassure him. In the gathering twilight, the signs that screamed "Down with the Traitors of the Revolution," "Down with Ebert-Scheidemann" were still plainly visible. He winced as the strident strains of the *Internationale* crowded up from the Wilhelmstrasse below. Suddenly the telephone rang. It was the secret line which connected the Chancellery with Army headquarters at Spa. Ebert's hand trembled as he lifted the receiver. Then he breathed more easily. It was all right after all! It was only his old friend General Groener. After exchanging nervous amenities, Ebert requested that the OHL [Supreme Command] supervise the withdrawal of the field armies. That was agreed to. The conversation continued:

EBERT.   What do you expect from us?

GROENER.   The Field Marshal expects that the government will support the Officers' Corps, maintain discipline, and preserve the punishment regulations of the Army. He expects that satisfactory provisions will be made for the complete maintenance of the Army.

EBERT.   What else?

GROENER.   The Officers' Corps expects that the government will fight against Bolshevism, and places itself at the disposal of the government for such a purpose.

EBERT.   (after a slight pause) Convey the thanks of the government to the Field Marshal.

MUSSOLINI'S "AUTHORIZED LAWLESSNESS"   142

*Italy's postwar difficulties produced a strong left-wing upsurge that culminated in the occupation of factories by Socialist workers in 1920. The factories were soon evacuated and the Socialist movement declined after 1920. Nevertheless, the experience so frightened the propertied classes that they turned to Mussolini's new fascism as a bulwark against the Red menace. They supported Mussolini financially, while the organs of state assumed a benevolent neutrality. The result, an "authorized lawlessness," is described by Gaetano Salvemini.**

The Italian industrial class is of recent formation. It owes its wealth primarily to protective duties and government contracts, and has not yet

---

* G. Salvemini, *The Fascist Dictatorship in Italy* (New York: Holt, 1927), pp. 55-58. Copyright 1927 by Holt, Rinehart & Winston, Inc. Copyright © 1955 by Gaetano Salvemini. Reprinted bv permission of Holt, Rinehart & Winston, Inc.

acquired by a long political and economic experience a consciousness of its social dignity, of its rights and obligations. In particular the "new rich" of the war—the *pescicani* or "sharks" as we call them in Italy—are people of scant intellectual or moral refinement. Having achieved wealth and power more often by luck than merit, they are incapable of holding their ground in a system of free competition and political liberty. These profiteers, who form the bulk of the capitalist classes in Italy today, when their terror of "Bolshevism" had turned to anger, were not content to lead the workers back to a more reasonable frame of mind. On the contrary they purposed to exploit their victory to the uttermost and to destroy the workers' organization. Even more savage than the industrialists were the landowners, accustomed by secular tradition to consider themselves absolute masters of their lands and to treat the peasants as beasts of burden with no civil rights and no sense of human dignity. They, too, were not content to defend their own liberty and property: what they wanted was revenge on the serfs who had dreamed of becoming masters. "We will put you to draw the plough with the oxen!" said the farmers of Cremona to their labourers, and they set off to enroll themselves among the Fascists.

At the end of 1920, Giolitti, a "Liberal," was Prime Minister; Bonomi, a "Reformist Socialist," Minister for War; and Fera, a "Democrat," was Minister of Justice. These are the men who are chiefly responsible for the situation in Italy today. They saw in the Fascist counter-offensive a convenient means of diminishing the strength of the Christian-Democratic and Socialist Parties in the country and the Chamber. They therefore allowed the chiefs of the army to equip the Fascists with rifles and lorries and authorized retired officers and officers-on-leave to command them. The Carabineers, the Royal Guard, the police, and the magistrates received hints to take no notice of disturbances started by the Fascists, and to intervene only when it was a question of disarming, trying, and sentencing people who attempted to resist.

Italy thus entered upon a new phase of political life, that of "authorized lawlessness."

The Fascists, armed and officered, provided with funds and sure of impunity, rapidly increased in numbers and in strength during the first half of 1921.

In this new phase of their activity, they no longer confined themselves to fighting the "Bolshevists" in elections, in the press and at public meetings. ...

Soon their offensive was directed even against the Christian-Democrats. ...

Thousand of Fascists, in organized parties, with free passes on the railways, swarmed into the towns, sacked houses, looted Trade Union quarters, beat and maltreated, banished or murdered the organizers. The country was terrorized by "punitive expeditions" which set out openly from Fascist offices in the town. The Town Councils in the hands of the "Bolshevists" or the Christian-Democrats, were forced to resign under threats that the Mayor and Councillors would be murdered. For two years a terrible man-hunt was carried on, organized by the military authorities with the connivance of the magistrates and of the police.

With the support of the propertied classes and the organs of state, Mussolini was able in October, 1922 to stage his march on Rome and to seize power. He remained the dictator of Italy until his death during World War II. Although his Fascist movement was essentially anti-intellectual, Mussolini gradually evolved a supporting ideology with the aid of a philosopher, Giovanni Gentile. The following selection is taken from an article on fascism published in 1932 in the 14th edition of the Enciclopedia Italiana. *The article was published under Mussolini's name but was written by Gentile. It reflects, however, Mussolini's conviction that socialism, democracy, and liberalism were nineteenth-century creeds, and that fascism was the "wave of the future."* *

Fascism, the more it considers and observes the future and the development of humanity quite apart from political considerations of the moment, believes neither in the possibility nor the utility of perpetual peace. It thus repudiates the doctrine of Pacifism—born of a renunciation of the struggle and an act of cowardice in the face of sacrifice. War alone brings up to its highest tension all human energy and puts the stamp of nobility upon the peoples who have the courage to meet it. All other trials are substitutes, which never really put men into the position where they have to make the great decision—the alternative of life or death. Thus a doctrine which is founded upon this harmful postulate of peace is hostile to Fascism. And thus hostile to the spirit of Fascism, though accepted for what use they can be in dealing with particular political situations, are all the international leagues and societies which, as history will show, can be scattered to the winds when once strong national feeling is aroused by any motive—sentimental, ideal, or practical. This anti-Pacifist spirit is carried by Fascism even into the life of the individual; the proud motto of the *Squadrista,* "Me ne frego," ["I don't give a damn"] written on the bandage of a wound, is an act of philosophy not only stoic, the summary of a doctrine not only political—it is the education to combat, the acceptation of the risks which combat implies, and a new way of life for Italy. . . .

Such a conception of life makes Fascism the complete opposite of that doctrine, the base of so-called scientific and Marxian Socialism, the materialist conception of history; according to which the history of human civilisation can be explained simply through the conflict of interests among the various social groups and by the change and development in the means and instruments of production. That the changes in the economic field—new discoveries of raw materials, new methods of working them, and the inventions of science —have their importance no one can deny; but that these factors are sufficient to explain the history of humanity excluding all others is an absurd delusion. . . . And above all Fascism denies that class-war can be the preponderant force in the transformation of society. These two fundamental concepts of Socialism being thus refuted, nothing is left of it but the sentimental aspira-

* B. Mussolini, "The Political and Social Doctrine of Fascism," *Political Quarterly,* IV (July-September, 1933), 341-56.

tion—as old as humanity itself—towards a social convention in which the sorrows and sufferings of the humblest shall be alleviated. . . .

After Socialism, Fascism combats the whole complex system of democratic ideology, and repudiates it, whether in its theoretical premises or in its practical application. Fascism denies that the majority, by the simple fact that it is a majority, can direct human society; it denies that numbers alone can govern by means of a periodical consultation, and it affirms the immutable, beneficial, and fruitful inequality of mankind, which can never be permanently levelled through the mere operation of a mechanical process such as universal suffrage. The democratic regime may be defined as from time to time giving the people the illusion of sovereignty, while the real effective sovereignty lies in the hands of other concealed and irresponsible forces. Democracy is a regime nominally without a king, but it is ruled by many kings—more absolute, tyrannical and ruinous than one sole king, even though a tyrant. . . .

But the Fascist negation of Socialism, Democracy, and Liberalism must not be taken to mean that Fascism desires to lead the world back to the state of affairs before 1789. . . .

Fascism uses in its construction whatever elements in the Liberal, Social, or Democratic doctrines still have a living value; it maintains what may be called the certainties which we owe to history, but it rejects all the rest—that is to say, the conception that there can be any doctrine of unquestioned efficacy for all times and all peoples. Given that the nineteenth century was the century of Socialism, of Liberalism, and of Democracy, it does not necessarily follow that the twentieth century must also be a century of Socialism, Liberalism and Democracy: political doctrines pass, but humanity remains, and it may rather be expected that this will be a century of authority, a century of the Left, a century of Fascism; for if the nineteenth century was a century of individualism (Liberalism always signifying individualism) it may be expected that this will be the century of collectivism, and hence the century of the State. . . .

The foundation of Fascism is the conception of the State, its character, its duty, and its aim. Fascism conceives of the State as an absolute, in comparison with which all individuals or groups are relative, only to be conceived of in their relation to the State. The conception of the Liberal State is not that of a directing force, guiding the play and development, both material and spiritual, of a collective body, but merely a force limited to the function of recording results; on the other hand, the Fascist State is itself conscious, and has itself a will and a personality—thus it may be called the "ethic" State.

· · · · ·

It is not reactionary, but revolutionary, in that it anticipates the solution of the universal political problems which elsewhere have to be settled in the political field by the rivalry of parties, the excessive power of the Parliamentary regime and the irresponsibility of political assemblies; while it meets the problems of the economic field by a system of syndicalism which is continually increasing in importance, as much in the sphere of labour as of industry. . . .

The Fascist State is an embodied will to power and government; the Roman tradition is here an ideal of force in action. According to Fascism, government is not so much a thing to be expressed in territorial or military terms

as in terms of morality and the spirit. It must be thought of as an Empire—
that is to say a nation which directly or indirectly rules other nations, without
the need for conquering a single square yard of territory. For Fascism the
growth of Empire, that is to say the expansion of the nation, is an essential
manifestation of vitality, and its opposite a sign of decadence. Peoples which
are rising, or rising again after a period of decadence, are always imperialist;
any renunciation is a sign of decay and of death. Fascism is the doctrine best
adapted to represent the tendencies and the aspirations of a people, like the
people of Italy, who are rising again after many centuries of abasement and
foreign servitude. But Empire demands discipline, the co-ordination of all
forces and a deeply-felt sense of duty and sacrifice; this fact explains many
aspects of the practical working of the regime, the character of many forces
in the State, and the necessarily severe measures which must be taken against
those who would oppose this spontaneous and inevitable movement of Italy
in the twentieth century, and would oppose it by recalling the outworn ideology
of the nineteenth century.

Britain's Postwar Problems **144**

*The countries of Western Europe did not experience in the postwar years the
violent conflicts that convulsed Russia, Germany, and Italy, although their course
was by no means all smooth sailing. The main problem they faced was economic
dislocation, which resulted in chronic, large-scale unemployment. This was particularly true of Great Britain, owing to a combination of domestic and foreign
conditions which are analyzed here by a distinguished French economist.**

Obviously Old England has been living in a fool's paradise, fondly imagining that she could still rely on the spirit and methods of the nineteenth
century. Such reforms as have been attempted are insignificant; at any rate,
up to the War no serious efforts were made to transform coal mining, the metal
industry, or textiles—the three bases on which exports and prosperity were
founded. England is like a venerable mansion which, though well and solidly
built, has for years lacked repairs both inside and out. . . .

The crisis can be most easily gauged by the serious fall in exports. The figures take their full significance when they are amended in conformity with
the 1913 price level.

BRITISH EXPORTS

	Millions of Pounds Sterling	Percentage Reduced to 1913 Price Level
1913	525	100
1920	1,334	71
1921	703	50
1927	709	79
1929	730	82

* A. Siegfried, *England's Crisis* (London: Cape, 1931), pp. 24-25, 31, 33-34, 48-50,
58-60, 65-66, 69-73.

If the chief indication of the economic crisis is the falling off in exports, the most apparent social consequence is the agonising amount of unemployment. . . .

The phenomenon of unemployment has constantly recurred in England at regular intervals. . . . Throughout the nineteenth century and until the Great War, however, the depressions never lasted any length of time in an acute form, as they were only symptoms of congestion. The gravest feature of the present phase, which began in 1920-21, and of which the end is not yet in sight, is its permancy rather than its intensity.

UNEMPLOYMENT (in January of each year)

	Total Number Unemployed	Percentage of Insured Workers
1921	1,010,000	6.4
1922	2,003,000	14.2
1923	1,511,000	13.3
1924	1,268,000	11.9
1925	1,307,000	11.2
1926	1,252,000	11.1
1927	1,496,000	12.1
1928	1,336,000	10.7
1929	1,453,000	12.1
1930	1,479,000	12.6

The causes of British depression seem to be clearly divisible into two categories: first, those due to external factors and beyond Britain's control; and second, those originating within the country itself and capable of eventual correction by her own efforts. Each class can also be subdivided into temporary and permanent factors.

First let us consider the external causes. We have the world-wide impoverishment and confusion caused by the Great War, with its aftermath of turmoil, revolution, and civil wars. There is no longer any adjustment between consumption and production, for distribution is not normal. Capital does not flow easily—here it is totally lacking, there it is uselessly accumulating. In short, the economic exploitation of the globe is disorganised, with the result that there is a reduction of purchasing power in various international markets. England as a great exporting nation is naturally the first to suffer; in fact, it is her foreign trade that has borne the full shock of the War. No country has felt the War more directly or more brutally, even admitting that English territory was not violated and that none of her factories were destroyed.

Such causes, however, are temporary, and cannot continue to account for Britain's anaemia. By unduly stressing these factors immediately after the War, the English gave themselves a dangerous excuse for their failure to replace the out-of-date sections of their economic system. No doubt it is better to sail with the tide, but one should not altogether rely upon it.

The trouble lies deeper, and in order to discover the real source we evidently must go back earlier than 1914, perhaps as I have already said, even back to 1875 or 1880. What has really changed to the detriment of England is the economic interrelationship of the continents of the world. Since the beginning of the present century, and even earlier, there has been a tendency for distant countries to contest the industrial monopoly of Western Europe, of which England was the leader. Each country now hopes to convert its own raw materials and export them in manufactured form. Although the War did not originate this movement towards widespread industrialism, it undoubtedly accelerated the pace. At the same time, in spite of the Liberal school, which considers it madness, the doctrine that every State should be economically self-supporting is now generally adopted. This is a definite form of contemporary nationalism, which tends to lay stress on old-fashioned protectionist ideas, so dangerous to British exports. We used to be content with protective duties, which allowed local industries to fight on equal terms with foreign competitors for the home market. Customs duties were then considered a weapon of protection rather than prohibition. Now, however, our neo-protectionism has new aims and new methods, beginning with the principle that the home market should be reserved exclusively for national industries. These are given so great a priority that their profits, thus assured, serve as an export bonus, and permit systematic international dumping.

The widespread decentralisation of industry has produced new conditions throughout the world, depriving England of her century-old position. The reduction in the export trade, arising from these causes, must be accepted as permanent. . . .

Britain's difficulties are aggravated by the old-fashioned conditions existing in certain industries. The principal nations of Western Europe, as well as the United States, have renewed their equipment to a great extent since the War. France was more or less forced to do so owing to the necessity of reconstructing her devastated areas; under other circumstances, possibly, she might not have done so. However that may be, Continental industry emerged rejuvenated, while England continues to congratulate herself on her thousand years of unbroken tradition. Perhaps she is wrong, for under certain circumstances it is better to pull everything up by the roots and start afresh.

In this respect British industry is like a virgin forest, where old decaying trees are surrounded by young saplings. Certain branches of industry have made remarkable technical progress during and since the War, but in others one still finds machines for which the proper place is a science museum. These machines are obsolete, almost useless, but they are kept, because in England they like to preserve everything.

The heavy industries, especially coal, iron, and steel, continue to use equipment which is frankly out of date. The coal industry works many pits which, technically, must be classed amongst the most antiquated in Europe. There is comparatively little mechanical extraction: wooden pit-props are still used, and the utilisation of by-products, so important today, has progressed very slowly. Antediluvian coke ovens still function, and at most only about 25 per cent of the coal is washed mechanically, whereas in Germany the figure is 80 per cent and in France 85 per cent.

We find the same obsolete methods in entire branches of the iron and steel industry. Apart from certain ultra-modern works constructed during the War, the majority of the blast furnaces are still of very mediocre capacity in comparison with up-to-date practice; while the steel mills require decided remodelling if they are to be run on modern lines. One receives a general impression of worn-out equipment, in spite of certain remarkable exceptions. In the nineteenth century the engineers of the world came to England to learn the latest technical methods, but today they go to America or Germany, never to Durham, Northumberland, or South Wales.

Why this decadence? It cannot be lack of technical ability, for English engineers, taken individually, are certainly efficient. They often have decided mechanical genius, and so have many of the foremen and workmen. They draw up plans for remodelling the machinery, and reorganising the works, but only too often the owners will not listen. In times of prosperity the owners, who were accustomed to making money easily with their old equipment, could see no reason to change. They would always be prosperous, they thought, for is there not a special Providence that looks after the English? Now that things are going wrong, plant renovation is again postponed, but this time for different reasons. Confidence in the future of British industry has partially disappeared, and the boards of directors, inspired and often cohtrolled by the banks, are tempted to declare that their capital would bring in a greater return if invested abroad. As a result, capital is turning away from certain industries, and it is difficult to raise sufficient funds for even the most urgently needed equipment. . . .

British prestige in the last century was built up by an aristocracy of business men and statesmen, the former drawn from the middle, and the latter from the upper classes. The co-operation of these two groups overcame all obstacles. Unfortunately, once the industrialists became wealthy, they wished to penetrate into society, so instead of putting their sons into the business, they sent them to the schools and universities where the statesmen had been trained. Shorn of its leaders, industry eventually rested on its laurels, and its progressive spirit died down to mere conservatism.

The outlook of the average industrialist has changed little during the past few generations; suffice it to say that he is simply a middle-class Englishman, insular and imbued with all the prejudices of his class. He clings to the old British idea that discipline and practical experience are better than technique. Talk with any of the English schoolmasters and you will invariably find that their aim is summed up in the formula: "We wish to turn out gentlemen." In other words, in their scale of values, they put character before business ability, and certainly before science. . . .

Finally, there has been a decided decline in the output of labour. There is no doubt about the excellent qualities of honesty, loyalty, and decent living, as well as the skill of the British workman, but the fact remains that he has been accustomed to and still clings to a wage level which is no longer compatible with the depressed state of industry. . . .

Actually, instead of remaining stationary or declining, real wages have increased above the maximum of 1920, because wholesale prices have dropped from 325 to 122, and retail prices from 275 to 154. . . .

All workers are not equally favoured, for unskilled labour has benefited more than skilled, while the sheltered domestic trades, not being subjected to international competition, have profited. The export trades have had to adjust themselves more to foreign levels, and therefore their workers have not entirely maintained the increases acquired between 1914 and 1920. . . .

The average improvement in real wages between 1914 and 1929 was 17 per cent. . . .

High wages do not necessarily mean high costs of production, since it is quite possible for output to increase as rapidly as the rate of wages. In England, however, neither equipment nor organisation have progressed in proportion to real wages, while the workers themselves, imbued with old ca'-canny prejudices, are stolidly opposed to mechanical progress. Under such conditions the cost of wages per unit of production has increased instead of being reduced. This is not only true of the sheltered industries where no sacrifice has been asked from the workers, but also of the exporting industries, where wages have been greatly reduced. . . .

In the United States although costs are even higher this obstacle is overcome by superior methods of mass production, against which England competes with difficulty. But in certain other countries, as for example Continental Europe and Asia, everything is cheaper, including wages. Here again England cannot compete, especially against those whose equipment has been renewed.

The late 1920's were years of relative prosperity as well as seeming security. The most pressing problems seemed to have been settled by the Dawes Plan, the Locarno Pact, and the Kellogg–Briand Pact. Stabilization was especially evident in France, where the currency was no longer fluctuating, and in Germany, where there was a mellow "Indian summer." Compared to the disastrous thirties, these were comfortable and hopeful years.*

France

Nineteen twenty-six to 1929 were the happiest and most prosperous years of post-War France. The one unhealthy element—the falling currency—had been eliminated; and the hectic years of the currency crisis were succeeded by four years of economic and financial stability. Trade was brisk; French exports reached record figures in 1928-9, and tourism during these years represented an annual item of invisible exports of over ten milliard francs. Hundreds of thousands of British and American tourists swarmed to France; the Norman and the Breton Coast became almost English-speaking during the summer months; there was a boom in the Paris de-luxe trades, and the years were marked by an unprecedented development in the new French industries such as motor-cars. Between 1919 and 1929 the number of cars in France had increased tenfold. The bourgeois youth of Paris became motor-mad; the Salon d'Automobile, every October, attracting innumerable provincials to Paris, was an orgy of buying; motoring, jazz, cinema, and cocktail bars became the chief interest of a large part of their lives, and older Parisians shook their heads at this Americanization of Paris. The Champs-Élysées became a centre of shopping and night life; vast new cafés with nickel-tubed furniture sprang up all over the West End; hundreds of luxuriously office buildings and blocks of expensive flats were built in the Centre and West End; and thousands of *confort moderne* houses with running h. and c. water, and lifts, and thin walls, with the neighbours' inevitable wireless behind them, and high rents, sprang up in the less select quarters. The Loucheur Building Act started an unprecedented building boom all over France, and transformed much of the country round Paris into a mass—an incoherent mass—of ugly red-roofed suburban houses and villas. Transport facilities were improved and on the

* Alexander Werth, *The Destiny of France* (London: Hamilton, 1937), pp. 28-31; American title *Which Way France* (New York: Harper). Reprinted by permission of Harper & Row, Publishers. R. A. Brady, *The Spirit and Structure of German Fascism* (London: Gollancz, 1937), pp. 17-20. Copyright 1937 by Robert A. Brady. Reprinted by permission of The Viking Press, Inc.

suburban lines smart electric trains replaced the ancient, sooty two-storey carriages, which had not changed since Monet painted his Gare St. Lazare in the "seventies." The old ring of fortifications built in 1840 was razed to the ground, and blocks of flats were built in their place, and the old boundary between Paris and its surroundings became largely a fiction. Paris, the town of three million people, now surrounded by a ring of industrial suburbs full of active new industries, became a vast conglomeration of nearly six million people. . . .

The finances of the State had never been more prosperous than during 1926-9. The enormously fat "Papa" Cheron was M. Poincaré's Minister of Finance; and the thrifty old Norman managed to pile up in three years a surplus of something like nineteen milliard francs.

Germany

For most there was now [in the late 1920's] a certain freedom from actual hunger, a freedom to go and come at will, to speak and think more or less at ease. For a short stay of time it was not necessary to behave like a human robot. For the moment, one need not gear one's actions to the pattern of the stiff command, and for a while no one preached openly that servility and meekness to arbitrary authority were the only roads to virtue.

In this somewhat relaxed atmosphere Germany passed through a sort of "Indian Summer," a kind of late autumnal warming before the harshness of another bitter northern winter could set in. The German university once again became the intellectual leader of the world. The brief flowering of German science was so rich in content and varied in scope as to constitute, even in a country with such a glorious scientific past, a renaissance in achievements of the mind. The music and opera of the great German masters were revived on a new and richer level. The German theatre became for a short time the pride of western Europe. German scholars and men of letters began to turn out what seemed almost a tidal wave of books, brochures, and periodicals on every conceivable subject. For a period of time German new-book listings were as great as those of England, France, and the United States combined.

For the bulk of the population much of old German *Gemütlichkeit*— "easy-going-ness"—revived. The German term has a special meaning. It reflects the picture of the ordinary citizen who, after his day in the factory or in the office, returns home to play with his children on the floor, or to work, gently and with loving care, amongst his flowers in the little back-yard garden. In the evening he goes to a near-by park. There are tables, waiters, and an orchestra. He sips his beer, makes love to the waitress or his wife of thirty years, listens to the music, dances a little, and talks—talks about politics, the threatened wage cut, the music of Beethoven, or the decline of the Roman Empire.

Rich and poor alike, *Gemütlichkeit* in some degree or other was a fact of daily experience. In the poorest villages or the most scabrous quarters of the great industrial cities, some measure of the *feeling* for "good living," for enjoyment of food and music, for the slight float of mind that comes with a stein of Bock or—on occasion—a glass of wine, was regarded as the due need of all. In the poorest districts of Berlin or Cologne, Hamburg or Essen, one would see everywhere window-boxes of gaily coloured flowers, and *Bierstuben* where workmen sat of an evening with their wives.

.   .   .   .   .

More marked than this, however, was the mounting stream of men, women, and children who trekked to the country on every possible occasion. By train or river boat, by car or bicycle, alone or in especially arranged tours, and by the multiplied thousands they poured out of the cities in the evenings, on holidays and week-ends. Those who could not go far into the country, flocked to the parks, lakes, and near-by forests. The degree of mass participation in the enjoyment of the public facilities and the natural beauties of city and countryside was without parallel in any other European country.

The visitor was welcome in the counting-house or the workman's quarter. There was no embarrassed laughing at mistakes made in German, and no sneers for strange ways and thoughts. Everywhere there was a lively interest in America, in England and France, in Africa and the Orient. Books and tales on adventures in the most distant lands were paced by the almost unbelievable out-pourings of travel books and guides. An increasing number of the children in the lower common schools were learning French, English, Italian, or some other foreign language. There was, amongst the great rank and file, no hatred of the Jews, no hatred of the French, no hatred for the Russians or any other people. It was as easy to talk to a workman or a peasant on almost any conceivable subject as it was to get travel information from a professional guide.

There was, likewise, an almost unbelievable mass participation in the cultural side of life. Nowhere else in Europe could one find either the crowds or the complete representation of all social classes one would meet in the Kaiser Wilhelm Museum of Berlin, the Pinakothek of Munich, or the Zwinger of Dresden. At times the number of visitors to the gigantic industrial arts museum of Munich, the Deutsches Museum, were so great as to resemble organised pilgrimages. The same was true for the theatres and the opera houses. Anyone who has sat or stood in the galleries through the long performances of Wagnerian opera in Berlin or Munich during these years has some idea of the cross section of the population which such audiences represented. Entire galleries would at times have scarcely anyone in them who was not a student or a workman.

The percentage of the German population able to play some musical instrument or other must have been three or four times that of any other nation. Nowhere else were so many concerts given, so much singing and choral music, so much interest in the music of the past and of all other lands. Little theatres, local player troupes, folk dance ensembles and numerous other art forms were to be found in great profusion in the large cities, and represented in nearly every village and hamlet.

Chapter Twenty-three

The Five Year Plans and the Great Depression

146 THE MOTIVE

In 1928, the Soviet government, under the leadership of Joseph Stalin, launched the first of a series of Five Year Plans that have been continued to the present day. These were pressed forward, with the authority of the government, using all the human and material resources of the country. The reason for Stalin's ruthless insistence on maximum effort and speed is evident in the following excerpt from a speech he delivered in the midst of the first Plan.*

It is sometimes asked whether it is possible to slow down the tempo, to put a check on the movement. No, Comrades, it is not possible! The tempo must not be reduced! On the contrary, we must increase it as much as is within our powers and possibilities. To slacken the tempo would mean falling behind. Those who fall behind get beaten. But we do not want to be beaten. No, we refuse to be beaten! One feature of the history of old Russia was the continual beatings she suffered for falling behind, for her backwardness. Old Russia was beaten by the Mongol Khans. She was beaten by the Turkish beys. She was beaten by the Swedish feudal lords. She was beaten by the Polish and Lithuanian gentry. She was beaten by the British and French capitalists. She was beaten by the Japanese barons. All beat her—for her backwardness, for military back-

---

* Address to First All-Union Conference of Managers of Socialist Industry (February 4, 1931).

wardness, for cultural backwardness, for political backwardness, for industrial backwardness, for agricultural backwardness. She was beaten because it was profitable and could be done with impunity. Do you remember the words of the pre-revolutionary poet: "You are poor and abundant, mighty and impotent, Mother Russia." These words of the old poet were well learned by those gentlemen. They beat her. ... Such is the law of the exploiters—to beat the backward and the weak. ... That is why we must no longer lag behind. ... You must put an end to backwardness in the shortest possible time and develop genuine Bolshevik tempo in building up the socialist system of economy. There is no other way. ... Either we do it, or they crush us. That is why Lenin said during the October Revolution: "Either perish, or overtake and outstrip the advanced capitalist countries."

THE CARROT AND THE STICK **147**

The goals of the first Five Year Plan were grandiose—to treble the output of heavy industry, quadruple the output of kilowatt hours of electricity, and transform six million peasant holdings into mechanized collective farms. To reach these goals the Communist rulers used both "the carrot and the stick." The carrot, illustrated in the first selection, consisted of a massive propaganda drive designed to persuade the citizens to work and to sacrifice for the sake of creating a successful and prosperous socialist society. The stick, illustrated in the second selection, represented the force that was ruthlessly used to crush all opposition to the Plan, and was especially evident in the case of the rich peasants, or kulaks, who resisted joining the collective farms. The selection is from a novel by the distinguished Soviet author, Mikhail Sholokhov, and describes an episode in the class war which the government fomented in the villages against the kulaks.*

The Carrot

If we pick up, at random, any Russian newspaper of the period of the first Five-Year Plan when the strain was at its greatest, we receive an impression of ardent hopes, and of immense and general excitement, in which the sacrifices of individuals are forgotten by themselves as well as by others. The workers speak with their own voices and write with their own pens; on four pages of very poor paper, with very poor print, the vocal soldiers of industry shout themselves hoarse, with boasting, with exhortation, with criticism of failures, with challenges to Socialist competition, with offers of "tow-ropes" to less forward enterprises, with promises, with indignation. It happens to be an anniversary of the newspaper. Here is the Lenin factory of electrical apparatus, proclaiming itself the first-born of October, the giant of electro-technical industry, the strength of Bolshevik tempos, twice honoured with the order of Lenin, the active fighter for the Socialist reconstruction of

---

* Sir John Maynard, *Russia in Flux* (New York: Macmillan, 1949), pp. 341-42, 345; used with the permission of The Macmillan Company. Mikhail Sholokhov, *Virgin Soil Upturned* (Moscow: Foreign Languages Publishing House, n.d.), pp. 66-68, 71-72.

rural economy, the sharpshooter of the undertakings for Government grain-farms, the initiator of Lenin's great idea of mass workers' control from below over Soviet bureaucracy. We seem to see the giant slapping his bulging muscles, and challenging his rivals to competition.

. . . . .

More coal, more pig-iron, more steel, more machines, more oil, more paper! Such are the headlines which take the place of the murders, divorces, betting odds, and greyhound races, of our own [British] newspapers. The Boiler gang is short by fourteen boilers, and the quality of boilers has deteriorated. There is plenty of seed but it hasn't yet reached the farms, though the sowing season is upon us. The new beet-root regions are very ill supplied with beet-seed. There are plenty of tractors, but no spare parts. The workers have proclaimed an all-union muster roll of their own for the supply of spare parts. Cabbages and potatoes for the factory! We have planted our own vegetable garden, and challenge all others to Socialist competition to do the same. We, the workers, guarantee Soviet fire-bricks for metallurgical work.

. . . . .

No attacks upon Government; no sex; no financial article, except the quotation of the loans and of rates of exchange; no reference to religion, churches, or clergy. Japan is very much in the news. Otherwise there is nothing "patriotic" or "Russian" or "national" in the paper; and no scandals, or crossword-puzzles. The sport is all in the Socialist competition for more output, and the heroes are all shock-workers. The beautiful ladies have shed their beautiful smiles, and are busy planting beet-root, or helping in the supply of deficit commodities.

Such was the pabulum of the newspaper reader in the final year of the first Five-Year-Plan: and so eagerly was it sought after that queues were formed at the newspaper kiosks. The Soviet Government carried the masses on a wave of enthusiasm, and made them forget that their belts sometimes needed tightening. But the strain had been enormous. When it was over, not much less than a third of the national income for four years had been put into compulsory savings—in other words, had been expended upon providing the instruments of future production, to the detriment of the present standard of living. . . .

The Stick

Andrei Razmyotnov and his party arrived at Frol Damaskov's during the family's midday meal. Seated at the table were Frol himself, a little frail old man with a wedge-shaped beard and a torn left nostril (he had disfigured himself in childhood, falling from an apple-tree, hence his nickname Frol the Torn); his wife, a portly majestic old woman; his son Timofei, a young fellow of about twenty-two; and his daughter, a girl of marriageable age.

Handsome and well set up like his mother, Timofei rose from the table. He wiped his vivid lips under their youthfully soft moustache, narrowed his insolent, protruding eyes and with the jauntiness of the best accordion-player in the village and favourite of all the girls, made a sweeping gesture with his hand, "Come in and sit down, dear authorities!"

"We haven't time to sit down," Andrei took a paper out of his folder. "The assembled poor peasants of the village have laid it down that you, citizen

Frol Damaskov, are to be evicted from your house and have all your property and cattle confiscated. So finish up with your meal now and take yourselves out of the house. We are going to make a list of your property."

"What's all this for?" Frol threw down his spoon and rose to his feet.

"We are destroying you as the kulak class," Dyomka Ushakov explained.

Frol went into the parlour in his squeaking leather-soled felt boots and returned with a piece of paper.

"Here's the receipt, you signed it yourself, Razmyotnov."

"What receipt?"

"To say that I gave in the full amount of grain."

"This has nothing to do with grain."

"Then why should I be turned out of house and home?"

"The poor peasants have laid it down, I've told you."

"There's no such law!" Timofei shouted harshly. "This is just robbery! I'll go to the District Committee at once, Dad. Where's the saddle?"

"You will go to the District Committee on foot, if you want to. I won't give you a horse." Andrei sat down at the table and took out pencil and paper.

Frol's torn nose turned blue and his head began to shake. Suddenly he fell flat on the floor, scarcely able to move his swollen blackened tongue.

"S-s-sons-of-bitches! ... Rob me! Kill me!"

"Get up, Daddy, for Lord's sake!" The daughter cried, bursting into tears and grasping her father under the armpits.

Frol recovered himself, got up and dragged himself to a bench, where he lay listening indifferently while Dyomka Ushakov and the tall shy Mikhail Ignatyonok dictated to Razmyotnov:

"One bedstead, iron, with white knobs, one featherbed, three pillows, two wooden bedsteads ..."

"Cabinet and crockery. Have I got to mention all the crockery? Damn the lot!"

"Twelve chairs, one long chair with a back. A full-size accordion."

"You can't have that!" Timofei snatched the accordion out of Dyomka's hands. "Keep your distance, cross-eye, or I'll break your head."

"I'll break yours so your mother will never wash it up."

"Give me the keys of the chest, woman."

"Don't give them to him, Ma! Let them break it open if they've got the right to." ...

The list of the property that the house contained was almost complete.

"The keys to the barn," Andrei demanded.

Frol, black as a charred tree-stump, made a hopeless gesture.

"There aren't any!"

"Break it open," Andrei ordered Demid.

Demid went out to the barn pulling the pintle out of a cart as he passed. The massive five-pound lock had to be forced open with an axe.

"Don't hack the door-post! It's our barn now, go steady there!" Ushakov advised the panting Demid.

They began weighing up the grain.

"Mebbe we'll sow it straight away? There's a seeder over there in the bay," suggested Ignatyonok, who was quite drunk with joy.

They laughed at him, and many more jokes followed while they poured the good heavy grain into the measures.

"We can put by two hundred poods out of this for the grain delivery," said Ushakov, up to his knees in wheat. He shovelled the grain to the edge of the bin, scooped it up in handfuls and let it flow through his fingers.

"This is the stuff!"

"Not half! Worth its weight in gold, only some of it looks as if it'd been buried. See, it's sprouting."

Arkashka the Bargainer and another lad in the party were busy in the yard. Stroking his fair beard, Arkashka was pointing to a pile of ox dung with maize seeds in it.

"No wonder they can work! Eating solid grain! In the association we never had enough hay to go round."

From the barn came animated voices, laughter, the fragrant smell of wheat dust, and from time to time a strong salty oath. Andrei returned to the house. Mother and daughter had put their pots and pans together in a sack. Frol, his hands folded on his chest like a corpse, was lying on the bench in his socks. The subdued Timofei looked up with hatred in his eyes, then turned away to the window.

148 THE RESULTS

The use of the carrot and the stick proved effective: the goals of the various Five Year Plans were generally reached. By the end of the first Plan in 1932, Russia jumped from the fifth to the second industrial power of the world. In terms of repression and privation, however, the cost was heavy, as the following statistics reveal, showing extraordinary industrial growth but a relatively modest increase in the output of consumer goods.*

GROSS PRODUCTION, ALL INDUSTRY

[In milliard rubles in fixed prices at 1926-27]

1928	15.7
1932	34.3
1937	95.5
1938	106.8
1939	123.9

PER CAPITA PRODUCTION OF ARTICLES OF MASS CONSUMPTION

Products	Unit	1913	1928	1932	1937
Wheat and rye	Kilogram	2.9	2.5	2.6	4.5
Potatoes	Kilogram	160.0	300.0	329.0	386.0
Meat and fats	Kilogram	—	27.7	9.2	21.1
Milk	Kilogram	—	195.0	202.0	170.0
Sugar	Kilogram	9.4	7.7	5.0	14.0
Soap	Kilogram	.86	.94	2.1	3.0
Cotton fabrics	Square meter	15.3	15.2	15.8	16.0
Woolen fabrics	Square meter	.7	.5	.5	.6
Leather shoes	Pairs	—	.4	.5	1.0
Paper	Kilogram	1.4	1.8	3.9	5.0

* *Communism in Action. A Documented Study and Analysis of Communism in Operation in the Soviet Union*, 79th Congress, 2nd session, House Doc. No. 754 (Washington, D.C.: Government Printing Office, 1946), pp. 18, 65.

The success of the Five Year Plans attracted much attention in the West, which was suffering during the 1930's from the effects of the Great Depression. Even more interested were the peoples of the underdeveloped countries, who wanted, almost above anything else, the same rapid economic development attained by the Soviets. They were particularly impressed by the Moslem Central Asian republics of the Soviet Union, which were industrialized along with the rest of the country. The significance of this Central Asian showcase is made clear in the following reports by American correspondents, W. W. Lawrence and Harrison E. Salisbury.*

W. W. Lawrence (Samarkand, 1945)

Here in ancient, glamorous Samarkand it is possible to get the full flavor of the great experiment in industrial, agricultural and cultural uplift being carried out among the peoples of Uzbekistan and Kazakhstan at a pace that has been spurred rather than retarded by the impact of the greatest war in the world's history.

After five days' intensive touring in these two central Asiatic republics it is the considered judgment of this correspondent that more progress has been made in the twenty-one years since Soviet rule was firmly established here in 1923 than in all the other years since Alexander the Great first captured Samarkand in 329 B.C.

It is no exaggeration to say that conditions here at present are far superior to those in near-by Iran, which has been under the influence of Western civilization for a much longer period. It cannot be denied by any visitor here that results evident to the naked eye and obtainable from conversations with the highest officials that these republics are an impressive testimonial to what can be accomplished under the centralized Soviet system, which decides what is best for the natives and then sees to it that they conform.

Industry is being introduced, though it is not possible, for reasons of military censorship, to indicate the full scope or amount of production being turned out for the Red Army. Agriculture has been put on an advanced scientific basis with intensive use of fertilizers and continuing development of irrigation systems on a scale so large that the famed "starvation steppes" known to travelers from all parts of the world have lost their identity.

More and more schools are being built, and officials told us that a 90 per cent illiteracy condition had now been exactly reversed. The native theatre, preserving the folk lore and customs of these ancient people, receives the fullest encouragement and productions we saw in Alma Ata and Tashkent were eye-pleasing, soul-satisfying performances.

It is not the purpose of this report to give the impression that all defects have been eliminated. Officials frankly admit that housing and sanitary conditions for the natives, especially in the "old towns," are far from satisfactory. They know their distributive machinery must be improved vastly.

---

* *The New York Times* (July 14, 1945; W. W. Lawrence); (November 27, 1961; Harrison E. Salisbury). © 1945, 1961 by The New York Times Company. Reprinted by permission.

But, looking upon what has been done thus far as only the beginning, these officials, in making it possible for us to see everything we requested, asked only that we measured both the evident accomplishments and defects against an imagined background of thirty years ago, which was possible because we had seen the present-day Middle East.

Harrison E. Salisbury (Tashkent, 1961)

The Soviet Union is easily outdistancing all of its neighbors, with the possible exception of Communist China, in the race for Asian industrial and social leadership.

Tashkent, a bustling Soviet metropolis of more than 1,000,000, is in the center of Asia's heartland and the showplace of the Soviet challenge. Nowhere in Asia except China is basic development proceeding so swiftly.

Bursting with new heavy industry and growing light industry, Tashkent's factory-studded landscape bristles with new plants and mass housing projects. It contrasts sharply with its nearest Asian rival, flashy Teheran.

Teheran is nearly twice as large and has invested almost as much money in the last seven or eight years. But most of the Iranian money has gone into Hollywood-style villas, skyscrapers and neon lighting. Most of Tashkent's money has gone into factories, factories, and more factories.

Teheran's boom has created a kind of Persian Sunset Strip in the midst of Asia. Tashkent's spending has laid the foundation for an Asian Akron or Cleveland.

Daily delegations from the lesser developed lands of Africa and Asia are brought to Tashkent to see the fruits of Soviet development policy. The city lacks the vivid colors of Teheran, but in terms of economic and social progress it is superior to anything in adjacent Iran, backward Afghanistan or even progress-minded India and Pakistan.

This is the challenge that Shah Mohammed Riza Pahlevi of Iran says must be met within twenty years if Communist competition is to be matched.

150 SOCIAL REPERCUSSIONS

The Great Depression was unprecedented in its intensity, scope, and longevity. One out of every four workers was unemployed in Britain and the United States; two of every five in Germany. What these figures meant in terms of human lives is suggested by the following selections. The first describes the poverty amidst plenty in the United States, as related to a congressional committee in February, 1932; the second is from an article in Business Week *reporting the emigration of unemployed American workers to the Soviet Union.**

* Unemployment in the United States ... Hearings before a Subcommittee of the Com- mittee on Labor, *House of Representatives, 72nd Congress, 1st session, on H.R.206, H.R.6011, H.R.8088 (Washington, D.C.: Government Printing Office, 1932), pp. 98-99;* Business Week *(October 7, 1931), pp. 32-33.*

Poverty Amidst Plenty in the United States

During the last three months I [Oscar Ameringer of Oklahoma City] have visited, as I have said, some 20 states of this wonderfully rich and beautiful country. Here are some of the things I heard and saw: In the State of Washington I was told that the forest fires raging in that region all summer and fall were eased by unemployed timber workers and bankrupt farmers in an endeavor to earn a few honest dollars as fire fighters. The last thing I saw on the night I left Seattle was numbers of women searching for scraps of food in the refuse piles of the principal market of that city. A number of Montana citizens told me of thousands of bushels of wheat left in the fields uncut on account of its low price that hardly paid for the harvesting. In Oregon I saw thousands of bushels of apples rotting in the orchards. Only absolutely flawless apples were still salable, at from 40 to 50 cents a box containing 200 apples. At the same time, there are millions of children who, on account of the poverty of their parents, will not eat one apple this winter.

While I was in Oregon the *Portland Oregonian* bemoaned the fact that thousands of ewes were killed by the sheep raisers because they did not bring enough in the market to pay the freight on them. And while Oregon sheep raisers fed mutton to the buzzards, I saw men picking for meat scraps in the garbage cans in the cities of New York and Chicago. I talked to one man in a restaurant in Chicago. He told me of his experience in raising sheep. He said that he had killed 3,000 sheep this fall and thrown them down the canyon, because it cost $1.10 to ship a sheep, and then he would get less than a dollar for it. He said he could not afford to feed the sheep, and he would not let them starve, so he just cut their throats and threw them down the canyon.

The roads of the West and Southwest teem with hungry hitchhikers. The camp fires of the homeless are seen along every railroad track. I saw men, women, and children walking over the hard roads. Most of them were tenant farmers who had lost their all in the late slump in wheat and cotton. Between Clarksville and Russellville, Ark., I picked up a family. The woman was hugging a dead chicken under a ragged coat. When I asked her where she had procured the fowl, first she told me she had found it dead in the road, and then added in grim humor, "They promised me a chicken in the pot, and now I got mine." . . .

The farmers are being pauperized by the poverty of industrial populations and the industrial populations are being pauperized by the poverty of the farmers. Neither has the money to buy the product of the other; hence we have overproduction and underconsumption at the same time and in the same country.

American Emigrants to the Soviet Union

New Yorkers dominate the flow of Americans who have decided, at least for the time being, to cast their lot with the Russians. Pennsylvania, New Jersey, and Illinois show heavy quotas of recruits under the new call for "6,000 skilled workers," and Michigan, Ohio, California, and Massachusetts are well represented.

More than 100,000 applications have been received at the Amtorg's [official Soviet organization] New York office for the 6,000 jobs. One morning's grist of applications last week totaled 280. All but 10 states were represented. Both Alaska and Panama furnished an applicant, and 18 Canadians wanted to "try their luck in Russia."

Industrial states naturally supply the largest number of applicants, but others are represented. Iowa, Texas, and Idaho each offered some kind of skilled worker.

Because of the general knowledge that Russia is "industrializing," applicants usually are skilled workers at machine construction, on the railroads, in steel mills, automobile factories, or the building industries. A glance at the qualifications of some of the 280 applicants on this "typical" morning showed that experts in all lines were after work, even if it meant going to Russia and accepting pay in rubles. There were 2 barbers, 1 funeral director, 2 plumbers, 5 painters, 2 cooks, 36 "clerical" workers, 1 service station operator, 9 carpenters, 1 aviator, 58 engineers, 14 electricians, 5 salesmen, 2 printers, 2 chemists, 1 shoemaker, 1 librarian, 2 teachers, 1 cleaner & dyer, 11 automobile mechanics, 1 dentist.

About 85% of the applicants are citizens of the United States, though only 40% are native born. The 60% foreign born are largely from Eastern Europe. A few Negroes have applied but the number is small because the majority are unskilled laborers.

Women form only a small percentage of the applicants, though many wives have decided to accompany their husbands on the new venture. The majority of workers who apply are married and have children.

Three principal reasons are advanced for wanting the position: (1) unemployment; (2) disgust with conditions here; (3) interest in the Soviet experiment. Foreign-born workers practically all state that they intend to remain in the U.S.S.R. Of the engineers, only 10% to 20% plan to stay.

151 POLITICAL REPERCUSSIONS

Social dislocation of the magnitude depicted in the preceding selections inevitably had profound political repercussions. In the United States, Franklin Roosevelt and his New Deal replaced Herbert Hoover's Republican administration, while in Britain and France "national" governments were formed in order to cope with the new problems of unprecedented magnitude. Most dramatic and fateful was the advent of the Nazi regime in Germany. That Hitler's success was made possible by the Depression, though not inevitable, is indicated by the direct relationship between the number of unemployed and the number of Nazi votes. In years of prosperity the German voters had ignored Hitler; with the advent of the Depression they flocked to him as the savior who would rescue them from their misery and despair. Hitler himself was well aware of the effect of the Depression upon his political fortunes, as is evident in the following excerpts from two speeches: the first on January 27, 1932 (one year before he assumed office), when he emphasized the political dangers of unemployment; the second, on December 10, 1940, when he boasted of his success in eliminating unemployment.*

* N. H. Baynes, ed., *The Speeches of Adolf Hitler* (London: Oxford Univ., under the auspices of the Royal Institute of International Affairs, 1942), I, 802-3, 824-25.

Hitler Speech, January 27, 1932

In my judgement, at the present moment the worst evil, an evil which I would characterize as not merely economic but in the highest sense of the word a national—"volkic"—evil, is unemployment. Always people see only six or seven million men who take no part in the process of production: they regard these men only from the economic standpoint and regret the decline in production which this unemployment causes. But, gentlemen, people fail to see the mental, moral, and psychological results of this fact. Do they really believe that such a percentage of the nation's strength can be idle if it be only for ten, twenty, or thirty years without exercising any mental effect; must it not have as its consequence a complete change of spirit?—and do people believe that that can remain without significance for the future?

Gentlemen, we know from our own experience that, through a mental aberration whose consequences you can in practice trace on every hand, Germany lost the War. Do you believe that when seven or eight million men have found themselves for ten or twenty years excluded from the national process of production, that for these masses Bolshevism could appear as anything else than the logical theoretical complement of their actual, practical, economic situation? . . .

To-day we stand at the turning-point of Germany's destiny. If the present development continues, Germany will one day of necessity land in Bolshevist chaos, but if this development is broken, then our people must be taken into a school of iron discipline.

Hitler Speech, December 10, 1940

My dear friends, if I had stated publicly eight or nine years ago: "In seven or eight years the problem of how to provide work for the unemployed will be solved, and the problem then will be where to find workers," I should have harmed my cause. Every one would have declared: "The man is mad. It is useless to talk to him, much less to support him. Nobody should vote for him. He is a fantastic creature." Today, however, all this has come true. Today, the only question for us is where to find workers. That, my fellow countrymen, is the blessing which work brings. . . .

We have incorporated seven million unemployed into our economic system; we have transformed another six millions from part-time into full-time workers; we are even working over-time. And all this is paid for in cash in Reichsmarks which maintained their value in peacetime. In wartime we had to ration its purchasing capacity, not in order to devalue it, but simply to earmark a portion of our industry for war production to guide us to victory in the struggle for the future of Germany. . . .

I wish to put before you a few facts: The first is that in the capitalistic democratic world the most important principle of economy is that the people exist for trade and industry, and that these in turn exist for capital. We have reversed this principle by making capital exist for trade and industry, and trade and industry exist for the people. *In other words, the people come first.* Everything else is but a means to this end.

The Depression profoundly affected international relations as well as domestic politics. It forced governments to adopt restrictive and exclusive economic measures which created friction between countries; it goaded governments to abandon disarmament for rearmament which provided jobs as well as imagined security; and it prompted certain national leaders to demand territorial expansion as the solution for their countries' ills. The following selections illustrate Hitler's doctrine of lebensraum, *or living space. The first is an article by Hitler's Minister of Economics, Dr. Hjalmar Schacht, demanding the return of Germany's colonies; the second is from a speech made by Hitler during World War II.**

Schacht, January 1937

A particularly ridiculous charge to which Germany has often to listen in connection with her colonial demands is that colonies in general and her former colonies in particular are valueless, and that it would not do Germany any good if her colonies were returned to her. This immediately prompts the retort: If the colonies are so bad, why do you keep them? It is also misleading to refer to the minor part played by the colonies in Germany's pre-war foreign trade. I have already pointed out that before the war free trade prevailed on a large scale and that Germany had valuable resources in the form of foreign investments. Consequently, it was not necessary before the war for Germany to develop her colonies with particular energy. It nevertheless is astonishing what Germany did with her colonies before the war without any great effort. They had been in her possession, on the average, for only some twenty-five years, from the end of the eighties and the beginning of the nineties. But during those twenty-five years Germany did more with her colonies than other countries had done in two hundred and fifty years.

At the outbreak of the World War, that is, after two decades of German administration, the German colonies had ceased to be a burden on the mother country. In fact, the financial balance was so well established that even the colonial railway loans had been paid for by the earnings of the colonies. Only the seven thousand police troops were supported by the mother country. During the fifteen years before the war, the external trade of the German colonies had increased seven-fold. That happened in a time when Germany did not experience a scarcity of raw materials and foreign currency, in a time when world trade had not been interrupted by political and economic mistrust, in a time when the struggles of different currency systems were not being fought out, in a time, therefore, when Germany had no particular need to intensify her trade with her colonies. Today, when there no longer is free trade in the world, when Germany is crushed by foreign debt and harassed by the lack of raw materials and valuta, if her colonies were returned to her she would proceed to develop them with far greater intensity. A large part of the food supplies and raw materials which we now lack could be furnished by them.

---

* H. Schacht, "Germany's Colonial Demands," *Foreign Affairs* (January, 1937), pp. 230-34; *Foreign Affairs* articles are copyrighted by the Council on Foreign Relations, Inc., New York. *Voelkischer Beobachter* (December 11, 1940).

Of course there are short-sighted people who declare that if Germany got back her colonies they would compete with the other countries which supply raw materials, to the disadvantage of these latter. This is simply the eternally recurring, short-sighted, unbusinesslike attitude of all those people who are constantly afraid of any new development. It was this attitude which found expression in England in the nineties, when it was said that every Englishman would be the richer if only Germany were crushed.

.   .   .   .   .

I therefore wish to name two conditions essential to the solution of Germany's raw material problem. First, Germany must produce her raw materials on territory under her own management. Second, this colonial territory must form part of her own monetary system. Colonial raw materials cannot be developed without considerable investments. Colonial markets are not of the kind. that can live by the personal needs of the population. Shirts and hats for the negroes and ornaments for their wives do not constitute an adequate market. Colonial territories are developed by the building of railways and roads, by automobile traffic, radio and electric power, by huge plantations, etc. From the moment that the German colonies came under the Mandate Powers, Germany was cut off from the delivery of goods required for such investments. In 1913, for example, Germany's exports to Tanganyika formed 52.6 per cent of that area's imports. In 1935 they formed 10.7 per cent. The British Mandate Power as a matter of course places its orders in England and not in Germany or elsewhere. That is the reason why Germany needs colonial territories which she herself administers. Since, however, the development of colonies depends upon long term investments, and these investments cannot be made by the native negro population, the German currency system must prevail in the colonial territories, so that the required investments may be made with German credits. These, then, are Germany's two basic demands in the colonial field: that she have territories under German management and included in the German monetary system.

All the other questions involved—sovereignty, army, police, law, the churches, international collaboration—are open to discussion. They can all be solved by means of international co-operation so long as nothing unworthy is imputed against the honor of Germany. The German colonial problem is not a problem of imperialism. It is not a mere problem of prestige. It is simply and solely a problem of economic existence. Precisely for that reason the future of European peace depends upon it.

Hitler, December 10, 1940

We are involved in a conflict in which more than the victory of only one country or the other is at stake; it is rather a war of two opposing worlds. I shall try to give you . . . an insight into the essential reasons underlying this conflict. I shall, however, confine myself to Western Europe only. The peoples who are primarily affected—85,000,000 Germans, 46,000,000 Britishers, 45,000,000 Italians, and about 37,000,000 Frenchmen—are the cores of the states which were or are still opposed in war. If I make a comparison between the living conditions of these peoples the following facts become evident. Forty-six million Britishers dominate and govern approximately 16,000,000 square miles of the surface of the earth. Thirty-seven million Frenchmen dominate and govern a combined area of approximately 4,000,000 square miles. Forty-five million Italians possess, taking into consideration only those territories in any way capable of being utilized, an area scarcely 190,000 square miles. Eighty-five million Germans possess as their living space scarcely 232,000 miles on which they must live their lives and 46,000,000 Britishers possess 16,000,000 square miles. . . .

This world has not been so divided up by Providence or Almighty God. This allocation has been made by man himself. The land was parcelled out for the most part during the last 300 years, that is, during the period in which, unfortunately, the German people were helpless and torn by internal dissension. . . .

The second people that failed to receive their fair share in this distribution, namely the Italians, experienced and suffered a similar fate. Torn by internal conflicts, devoid of unity, split up into numerous small states, this people also dissipated all their energy in internal strife. Nor was Italy able to obtain even the natural position in the Mediterranean which was her due. Thus in comparison with others, these two powerful peoples have received much less than their fair share. The objection might be raised: Is this really of decisive importance?

Man does not exist on theories and phrases, on declarations or on systems of political philosophy. He lives on what he can gain from the soil by his own labor in the form of food and raw materials. This is what he can eat, this is what he can use for manufacture and production. If a man's own living conditions offer him too little, his life will be wretched. We see that within the countries themselves, fruitful areas afford better living conditions than poor barren lands. In the one case there are flourishing villages; in the other poverty-stricken communities. A man may live on a stony desert or in a fruitful land of plenty. This handicap can never be fully overcome by theories nor even by the will to work.

We see that the primary cause for the existing tensions lies in the unfair distribution of the riches of the earth. . . .

Providence did not place man on earth with the idea that one should claim for himself fifty or eighty times his neighbor's portion. Either he is reasonable and agrees to an equitable settlement, or the one who is oppressed and crushed by misfortune will sooner or later seize that to which he is entitled. That holds good for individuals as well as for nations. . . .

The right to live, therefore, is at the same time a just claim to the soil which alone is the source of life. When unreasonableness threatened to choke their development, nations fought for this sacred claim. No other course was open to them and they realized that even bloodshed and sacrifice are better than the gradual extinction of a nation. . . .

In Canada, for example, there are 2.6 persons per square mile; in other countries perhaps 16, 18, 20 or 26 persons. Well, no matter how stupidly one managed one's affairs in such a country, a decent living would still be possible. Here in Germany, however, there are 360 persons per square mile. The others cannot manage with twenty-six persons per square mile, but we must manage with 360. This is the task we face. That is why I expressed this view in 1933. We must solve these problems and, therefore, we will solve them.

In view of the leading role played by Hitler's Germany in European and world affairs during the 1930's and 1940's, it is worth noting the essential characteristics of the Nazi regime, particularly the führer *principle, which Hitler followed in running first his party and then the entire state. Selections from his speeches reveal the nature of this principle in theory and in practice.**

Speech of February 15, 1933

These parties [of the Weimar Republic] cannot deny that in fourteen years they have destroyed the economic life of Germany. The German peasant has been brought to ruin and to-day we have seven or eight million unemployed. When these parties now say: we want to govern for a few more years in order that we can improve the situation, then we say:

No! now it is too late for that! Besides, you had your fourteen years and you have failed.

In fourteen years you have proved your incapacity—from the Treaty of Versailles by way of the various agreements down to the Dawes and Young plans.

Speech of March 23, 1933

The splitting up of the nation into groups with irreconcilable views, systematically brought about by the false doctrines of Marxism, means the destruction of the basis of a possible communal life. The disintegration attacks all the foundations of social order. The completely irreconcilable views of different individuals with regard to the terms State, society, religion, morals, family, and economy give rise to differences that lead to internecine war. Starting from the liberalism of the last century, this development is bound by natural laws to end in communistic chaos. . . .

It is only the creation of a real national community, rising above the interests and differences of rank and class, that can permanently remove the source of nourishment of these aberrations of the human mind.

Proclamation of July 14, 1933

1. In Germany the only political party is the National Socialist German Workers' Party.

2. Whoever undertakes to maintain the organization of another political party or to form a new political party will be punished by penal servitude for a period up to three years or by imprisonment for a period of from six months up to three years so far as the act is not punishable with a more severe penalty under other regulations.

* N. H. Baynes, ed., *The Speeches of Adolf Hitler* (London: Oxford Univ., under the auspices of the Royal Institute of International Affairs, 1942), I, 241, 264, 265.

As basic as the führer *principle in Nazi Germany, was the concept of race. In all Hitler's thinking and actions, he held the firm conviction that there were superior and inferior races, that the progress of nations and of mankind rested on the achievements of the "master" Nordic race. In the following selection from Hitler's conversation with one of his lieutenants, Otto Strasser, on May 21, 1930, it is apparent that the concept of race was predominant in Hitler's thinking about both domestic and international affairs: the master Nordics must prevail over the Slavs, just as within Germany, the superior racial strains must rule the inferior.**

What you understand by socialism is sheer Marxism. Now look: the great mass of working men want only bread and circuses: they have no understanding for ideals of any sort whatever, and we can never hope to win the workers to any large extent by an appeal to ideals. We want to make a selection from the new dominating caste which is not moved, as you are, by any ethic of pity, but is quite clear in its own mind that it has the right to dominate others because it represents a better race: this caste ruthlessly maintains and assures its dominance over the masses. . . .

There are no revolutions except racial revolutions: there cannot be a political, economic, or social revolution—always and only it is the struggle of the lower stratum of inferior race against the dominant higher race, and if this higher race has forgotten the law of its existence, then it loses the day. All revolutions in world history—and I have studied them in detail—are nothing save racial struggles. . . .

You have spoken in favour of the so-called Indian "Freedom Movement," but it is clear that this is a rebellion of the lower Indian race against the superior English-Nordic race. The Nordic race has a right to rule the world and we must take this racial right as the guiding star of our foreign policy. It is for this reason that for us any co-operation with Russia is out of the question for there on a Slav-Tartar body is set a Jewish head. I know the Slavs from my home country! Formerly when on this Slav body there was set a German head, then one could co-operate with Russia, as Bismarck did. But to-day it would be simply a crime. . . .

The interest of Germany demands co-operation with England since it is a question of establishing a Nordic-Germanic supremacy over Europe and, in conjunction with Nordic-Germanic America, over the world.

155 Two Appraisals: Toynbee and Nehru

The combination of the Five Year Plans and the Great Depression had a shattering impact on the Western world. The supreme self-confidence of the nineteenth century had been undermined by World War I, but had been partially restored

* *Ibid.,* II, 988-89.

during the late twenties. Now the disasters of the thirties led to a failure of nerve that was reminiscent of the last days of the Roman Empire, a point specifically made in the following selection by the distinguished British historian, Arnold J. Toynbee. At the same time, some colonial leaders, impressed by the contrast between the Five Year Plans and the Great Depression, were turning from the West and looking more toward the Soviet Union. This attitude is evident in the selection below by the Indian nationalist and democratic socialist, Jawaharlal Nehru.*

Arnold J. Toynbee

The year 1931 was distinguished from previous years—in the "post-war" and in the "pre-war" age alike—by one outstanding feature. In 1931, men and women all over the world were seriously contemplating and frankly discussing the possibility that the Western system of Society might break down and cease to work. By the time when this possibility thus presented itself, Western Society had come to embrace all the habitable lands and navigable seas on the face of the planet and the entire living generation of Mankind; and, within narrower geographical limits, it had been in existence as "a going concern," without any breach of continuity, for some twelve or thirteen centuries. Western Civilization had been living and growing continuously, with only occasional and never more than temporary checks and set-backs, ever since the end of the interregnum which had followed the breakdown of the antecedent "Classical" Civilization and the break-up of the "Classical" super-state, the Roman Empire. In the West, that interregnum had closed, at the turn of the seventh and eighth centuries of the Christian Era, with the emergence of a new order of society embodied in Western Christendom; and this small and rudimentary society—the world of Bede and the world of Charlemagne—was the geographical nucleus and the historical embryo of "the Great Society" of 1931. During the intervening centuries, Western Civilization had gone from strength to strength; and, while it had never been dispensed from the struggle for existence, or been deprived of the perpetual stimulus of repeated challenges, it had always responded victoriously, and the Gates of Hell had not prevailed against it. In 1931, the members of this great and ancient and hitherto triumphant society were asking themselves whether the secular process of Western life and growth might conceivably be coming to an end in their day. ...

Among the generation living in 1931, every man and woman of forty years of age and upwards had grown to maturity, before the outbreak of the General War of 1914-18, in a mental atmosphere in which the prospect of Western Society breaking down was virtually inconceivable. In this "pre-war" age, the sense of power and security in Western minds was actually enhanced and not diminished by the disinterment of the material remains of ancient civilizations which were so utterly extinct that even their names had been forgotten. When the discovery of the buried civilizations of Egypt and Mesopotamia was followed by similar discoveries in Crete and Asia Minor and the Indus Valley and Central America, the pictures of these "finds" in

* A. J. Toynbee, *Survey of International Affairs, 1931* (London: Oxford Univ., for Royal Institute of International Affairs, 1932), pp. 1-6; *Toward Freedom: The Autobiography of Jawaharlal Nehru* (New York: Day, 1941), pp. 229-32. Copyright © 1941 by The John Day Company. Reprinted by permission of The John Day Company, Inc.

the illustrated papers evoked a feeling of pride in the enterprise and acumen and technical skill of Western archaeologists (akin to the pride in the conquest of the ether or the air) and a sense of satisfaction in the inference that the children of Western Civilization in these latter days were not as other men had been. So far from serving as a *memento mori,* like the mummy which was carried round with the last course at an Egyptian banquet, these disinterred corpses of extinct civilizations encouraged the "pre-war" generation of modern Western Society to "acquiesce," with the historian of the decline and fall of the Roman Empire, "in the pleasing conclusion that every age of the world has increased, and still increases, the real wealth, the happiness, the knowledge, and perhaps the virtue, of the human race."

This dogmatic belief in an automatic, invincible and interminable progress had been inherited intact, by the "pre-war" generation, from Gibbon and his contemporaries; and the potency of eighteenth-century optimism is demonstrated by the robust declaration of faith in the dogma of his age which Gibbon made—in the celebrated phrases just quoted—at the crisis of the American Revolutionary War and in spite of the historian's own sceptical temperament and affectation. In Gibbon's day, the dogma of progress had already been fortified by a hundred-years' currency in which the new faith had not been contradicted by experience. In 1781, Western Society had not been threatened with destruction by attack from a human enemy since the Osmanlis had raised their second and last siege of Vienna in A.D. 1683.

. . . . .

The catastrophe, however, which Western minds were contemplating in 1931 was not the destructive impact of any external force but a spontaneous disintegration of society from within; and this prospect was much more formidable than the other.

In the face of an external menace, the human spirit can find relief in either endurance or action. The onslaught of an overwhelmingly stronger human enemy can be resisted to the death; an act of God can be accepted with resignation; but when we feel that "we are betrayed by what is false within," we are apt to find ourselves spiritually paralysed in face of the most deadly peril with which humanity is ever confronted. "Do not ye understand that whatsoever entereth in at the mouth goeth into the belly and is cast out into the draught? But those things which proceed out of the mouth come forth from the heart, and they defile the man." Like human beings, human societies are apt to perish—when they do perish—from internal ills. A historian surveying the past in 1931 might doubt whether any of the civilizations which were known to have become extinct by that date had been done to death by external blows; and Western Civilization, at any rate, was still alive to testify that it had succeeded in surviving all the external menaces—human or divine, actual or imaginary—with which it had been confronted so far during the twelve or thirteen centuries that had elapsed since its birth. To find an historical precedent for the threat of spontaneous internal disintegration—the incipient failure of will and wisdom and vitality—with which Western Society felt itself threatened in 1931 for the first time in its history, the historian would have to cast his mind back behind the birth of Western Society to the death of the Society which had preceded it. In the breakdown of the "Classical" Civilization and break-up of the Roman Empire which occurred after the death of Marcus Aurelius, and in the fatal and final relapse, after the death of Theodosius, from a temporary rally, we have the appalling spectacle of a society which did disintegrate spontaneously from within through self-betrayal and self-defilement. In the third century and in the fifth century of the Christian Era, men and women must have been confronted in full view, as their inexorable doom, with that outlook of which other men and women were catching a terrifying glimpse in 1931.

. . . . .

Jawaharlal Nehru

With all her blunders, Soviet Russia had triumphed over enormous difficulties and taken great strides. . . . While the rest of the world was in the grip of the depression and going backward in some ways, in the Soviet country a great new world was being built up before our eyes. Russia, following the great Lenin, looked into the future and thought only of what was to be, while other countries lay numbed under the dead hand of the past and spent their energy in preserving the useless relics of a bygone age. In particular, I was impressed by the reports of the great progress made by the backward regions of Central Asia under the Soviet regime. In the balance, therefore, I was all in favor of Russia, and the presence and example of the Soviets was a bright and heartening phenomenon in a dark and dismal world. . . .

Russia apart, the theory and philosophy of Marxism lightened up many a dark corner of my mind. History came to have a new meaning for me. The Marxist interpretation threw a flood of light on it, and it became an unfolding drama with some order and purpose, howsoever unconscious, behind it. In spite of the appalling waste and misery of the past and the present, the future was bright with hope, though many dangers intervened. It was the essential freedom from dogma and the scientific outlook of Marxism that appealed to me. It was true that there was plenty of dogma in official communism in Russia and elsewhere, and frequently heresy hunts were organized. That seemed to be deplorable, though it was not difficult to understand in view of the tremendous changes taking place rapidly in the Soviet countries when effective opposition might have resulted in catastrophic failure.

The great world crisis and slump seemed to justify the Marxist analysis. While all other systems and theories were groping about in the dark, Marxism alone explained it more or less satisfactorily and offered a real solution. . . .

Vague communistic and socialistic ideas had spread among the intelligentsia, even among intelligent Government officials. The younger men and women of the Congress, who used to read Bryce on democracies and Morley and Keith and Mazzini, were now reading, when they could get them, books on socialism and communism and Russia. . . . Everywhere there was in evidence a new spirit of inquiry, a questioning and a challenge to existing institutions.

Chapter Twenty-four

Drift to war, 1929-1939

156 THE ORIGINS OF THE SECOND WORLD WAR

Whereas the late 1920's were years of stabilization and settlement, the 1930's, by contrast, were years of recurring crises, and eventually of war. The settlement of the twenties was challenged in the following decade by aggressive revisionist powers: Germany and Italy in Europe, and Japan in the Far East. For a variety of reasons, this challenge was not met by the status quo *powers, with the result that aggression followed aggression until the showdown in 1939. In the following selection, an American authority on diplomatic history analyzes the combination of factors culminating in the outbreak of World War II.**

Scholarly histories of the origins of the First World War began to appear within a few years of the close of hostilities. A dozen years later, the magisterial studies by Sidney B. Fay and Bernadotte E. Schmitt had appeared in this country, and comparable works had been completed by European scholars. It is now eighteen years since V-E Day, but no studies comparable to Fay or Schmitt have appeared. In part this contrast is explained by the slowness with which the diplomatic papers concerning the years from 1919 to 1939 are being made available. Far more important, however, is the fact that scholars do not believe that a history of the origins of the Second World War can be written with substantial completeness

---

* Raymond J. Sontag, "The Origins of the Second World War," *Review of Politics*, XXV (1963), 497-508.

from diplomatic records. In their studies of the years before 1914, Fay and Schmitt did consider subjects like nationalism and imperialism, but the thread that holds their story together is the history of negotiations between governments, and in particular the history of the European alliance system.

No such single thread suffices to give unity to European diplomatic history between the wars. For understanding of the events which culminated in the catastrophe of the Second World War, the historian must leave the foreign offices and explore the totality of the tumultuous history of those years. The magnitude of the task explains the fact that no even moderately satisfactory telling of the whole story has been attempted. However, excellent studies have been made of parts of the story, and every student working in the field has in his mind a working sketch of the story as a whole. Here, not even such a sketch will be attempted, but merely a statement of those aspects of the interwar period which, to one observer, are central to an understanding of the origins of the Second World War.

I

Before the Treaty of Versailles came into force on January 20, 1920, conditions had been created which made the prevention of a second war difficult. On the continent of Europe, the still not completely drawn new frontiers were made possible only by the collapse of three great empires—Germany, Russia, and Austria-Hungary. The Habsburg Monarchy was dead, although fear of its revival continued to haunt central Europe. Germany and Russia, however, were only temporarily weakened. When the giants revived, what would happen to the new map, particularly to the smaller states of central and southeastern Europe? These states had a total population equal to that of the United States but a population divided among a dozen weak and often antagonistic states. Unaided they could not hope to survive when Germany and Russia revived.

The peacemakers had sought to protect the new map by the Anglo-American treaty of guarantee to France, by providing for a continuation of the Supreme Council of the victors to stand guard over the treaties, and by the guarantees against aggression contained in the Covenant of the League of Nations. In January 1920, however, it was evident that the United States, the power which had determined the outcome of the war, would accept no responsibility for the protection of the treaty settlement. During the years that followed, our country was more often an obstacle than an asset to efforts to achieve stability in Europe. As for the British, they could not withdraw completely from participation in European affairs, but what support they did give was wavering, and they flatly refused to promise any support for the map of central and southeastern Europe.

Our defection, and the partial withdrawal of the British, left France to defend the Treaty of Versailles. The result was disastrous. Acutely conscious that their primacy rested on the artificial weakness of Germany, the French set out to keep Germany weak by enforcing every provision of the Treaty of Versailles. Even Briand was obliged to retreat when he attempted a reconciliation with Germany at Thoiry, and as late as 1931 the French compelled the abandonment of the Austro-German customs union, even though the cost was the financial collapse of Europe. Throughout, the policy of France was dominated by fear of what would follow German resurgence.

Conversely, the defection of the United States and Britain inevitably encouraged the Germans to believe that they need not accept the treaty. German resistance might rise to actual revolt, as during the Ruhr invasion, or it might wane, as during the Stresemann years. But the resistance never ceased, and Germans never lost the belief that the territorial settlement in central Europe was temporary, to be changed when German power revived.

No one, of course, can demonstrate that, if there had been effective force behind the Treaty of Versailles, the map would have become stabilized, and the peoples of Europe would have settled down to the tasks of peacetime existence. The lack of effective force behind the treaty, however, did make certain French intransigence, German resistance, and the fearful, precarious, Kafka-like history of Central Europe in the interwar years.

II

The second circumstance which made difficult the prevention of war was economic dislocation, chronic dislocation throughout, threatening complete disintegration in the catastrophe of the great depression. Even economists found the theory in which they had been trained before 1914 of little use in solving the problems of the interwar years; it is not strange, therefore, that statesmen were baffled to understand abstruse matters like terms of trade, balance of payments, productivity of labor, and the relation of production to consumption. The consequences of economic dislocation were momentous. Without the financial chaos in Italy after 1918, the triumph of fascism would have been unlikely. The German social structure cracked under the strain of inflation, rationalization, and depression, and social disintegration provided the opportunity for Hitler to attain power. The memory of the inflation of the twenties paralyzed successive French ministries in the thirties. Desire to cut loose from economic storms sweeping over the world after 1931 in part explains the triumph of isolationism in this country and the reluctance of Britain in the Baldwin era to assume the leadership of Europe. Everywhere, the feeling of being in the grip of problems for which the wisdom of the past offered no solution prepared men to accept new and desperate remedies.

Finally, the surge of Soviet industrial production, in exactly the years when industrial indices elsewhere were plummeting, helps to explain the growing conviction among the younger generation in western Europe that Russia was the land of youth and promise, the hope for the future. Actually, of course, Marxism in these years did not provide the key to unlock the secrets of history; it is an easy game to list the wrong guesses of Soviet theorists and statesmen. The experience of these years did not vindicate Marxism as a science, but that experience certainly did discredit orthodox classical economic theory. Probably of greater importance than any contribution of John Maynard Keynes to economic theory was the confidence which he imparted to young intellectuals, and to some statesmen in Britain and America, that there was a way out of the depression without the sacrifice of human freedom, without accepting either fascist or communist totalitarianism.

III

Intimately connected with economic dislocation were two other disturbing characteristics of the interwar years, the pressure of the lower classes for social change, and the pressure of subject peoples for freedom from imperial rule.

The pressure for social change reaches far back, of course, in European history, and that pressure had produced substantial results by 1914. After 1918, resistance to social change, already growing in the early years of the century, became much stronger as the vast formless lower middle classes, and the peasants also, found themselves being pressed down by economic changes which few understood. From these classes came the mass support for Mussolini's Black Shirts and Hitler's Brown Shirts, and for the other fascist movements. In France, the middle-class Radical Socialists shifted unhappily between alliance with the left and alliance with the right, and by these shifts contributed greatly to the instability of French political life. In central and southeastern Europe where the middle classes were weak, it was the Green International of the peasants which expressed a type of radicalism hostile both to the old ruling classes and the city workers. Because, after 1933, Hitler turned away from the socialism promised in his earlier program, it is likely to be forgotten that he was brought to power by a mass desire, not just for nationalism, but also by passionate and widespread desire for a socialism which was non-Marxian and representative of the lower middle class, but still revolutionary.

The demand of the city workers for social change was, therefore, weakened by the increasing difficulty, or the impossibility, of continuing the old alliance with large segments of the middle class. The strength of the city workers was even more seriously impaired by the split on the left, the split between socialists and communists. The fatal consequences of that split in Germany were shown in the first weeks of the revolution in 1918 when, to ward off communist efforts to force a second revolution, the leaders of the Weimar Republic entered into alliance with the old military, industrial, and administrative leaders of Germany. In the last years of the Weimar Republic, the communists tacitly cooperated with the Nazis, confident that "in order to grasp the bourgeoisie by the throat, it is necessary to step across the corpse of social democracy." The decisive importance of the split on the left is not as obvious in other countries, but it had its effects everywhere, and everywhere the effects were evident in foreign as well as domestic policy. When there was alliance between the parties of the left, as during the Popular Front in France in 1936, another weakness appeared. Because the Communist Party of France was a partner in the Popular Front, and because the obedience of the Communist Party to orders from Moscow had been repeatedly demonstrated, it was easy for the parties of the right to attack the Popular Front as a tool of the Soviet Union, and to denounce the French alliance with Russia as support for international communism. The split on the left, therefore, not only slowed, or even reversed, the movement towards social change; that split, together with Soviet control over communist parties in other countries, is of great importance in international affairs.

Between 1914 and 1939 the history of every great power of Europe, and most of the lesser powers, was decisively influenced by the struggle for social change—except Britain. In Britain there was social change, change of almost revolutionary proportions, but (unlike Russia, Italy, and Germany) Britain had no revolution, and (unlike France) British policy was not paralyzed by social strife. Rather, as a Scottish labor leader pointed out, Britain entered the Second World War more united than in 1914. Many circumstances of British history and British social life enter into any explanation of this singular good fortune. In part, however, and again as the Scottish labor leader maintained, some of the credit must go to Stanley Baldwin. Baldwin's fumbling foreign policy is partly responsible for the fact that there was a second world war. But Baldwin's ability both to win the support of labor, and to force the Conservative Party into the path of social reform, must form part of any explanation of British strength and unity when the war came.

IV

The revolt of dependent peoples against their masters played a less obvious role in the origins of the Second World War than it had in precipitating the first: the murders at Sarajevo on June 28, 1914, like the Young Turk revolution, the Bosnian crisis, and the Balkan wars, were all related to this revolt. Between the wars, the revolt was global in extent, and the rise of Chinese nationalism provided at least the occasion for the explosion of Japanese imperialism which did materially affect international politics from the Manchurian adventure in 1931 to Pearl Harbor a decade later. But Japanese expansion, like the conquest of Ethiopia by Italy, represented the effort of a second-class power to take advantage of the preoccupation of the stronger powers with more pressing problems. Similarly, no major results flowed from the efforts of the Soviet Union to execute a flank attack on the capitalist powers by allying with colonial nationalist movements. So far as the origins of the Second World War are concerned, these efforts had their greatest importance as one element in the reluctance of Britain and France to ally with the Soviet Union. Popular sympathy in Britain for the revolt of the colonial peoples did, however, in part explain the inability of the British government to make the concessions necessary to hold Italy and Japan away from alliance with Germany. It is also true that the preoccupation of Britain with the task of meeting the demands of the subject peoples of the Empire was one of the ingredients of the appeasement policy. In these ways the revolt of the colonial peoples did contribute indirectly to the coming of war in 1939.

V

The condemnation of imperialism, dominant in the United States, strong in Britain, and a force to be reckoned with in France, is part of the intangible but vitally important moral temper prevailing in the West. It is, I suppose, universally accepted that the moral consequences of the First World War were much greater than those of the Second World War. In part the contrast is explained by the fact that the First World War shattered the dominant illusion that man was progressing towards the solution of differences through discussion between reasonable men, while by 1939 few cherished illusions about the reasonableness, much less the gentleness, of man. Much more important was the cumulative effect over the years from 1914 to 1918 of all that is concealed in the words "war of attrition." In the trenches and on the barbed wire, spirit as well as flesh rotted. The result was summed up in the title of a British book on the war, C. E. Montague's *Disenchantment,* disenchantment with many things, but disenchantment above all with war itself.

At the end of 1918, the disenchantment was probably as general and as complete in Germany as in England. A change came in Germany with the announcement of the terms of the Treaty of Versailles, and especially as Germans pondered the indictment implied in Article 231, the so-called war guilt clause. Whatever those who drafted that article intended, it could be interpreted as an accusation that the German people were responsible for all the horror inflicted on the world by the war. To the Germans this meant that their sons, nearly two millions of them, had died in an ignoble, a base cause. Against that charge, the German people revolted. Revulsion against war did persist. Some of the most effective antiwar tracts, books like *All Quiet on the Western Front,* appeared much later. But from the spring of 1919 the German mind was becoming prepared to believe myths like the charge of the stab in the back.

Under the stress of the years that followed, Germans came to hate each other, and to fight each other over most things, but they were united in a nationalism which included determination to overthrow the Treaty of Versailles. By 1932, walking among the trees of the Hofgarten in Munich, one might have come suddenly on a sunken stone court. On the walls were inscribed the names of the thirteen thousand men of Munich who had been killed in the First World War. Standing there in the silence, looking up from this hole in the ground to the encircling trees, one could think that this was the Germany left by the war and the years since the war, a hole in the ground, a stone foundation of frustrated, outraged nationalism. In the next six years, on that foundation Hitler was to build, with the aid of the German people, aid given gladly for the most part, a prison house for Germans, for every German. On that foundation he also built the fortress from which the German people moved in perfectly disciplined formation to attempt the subjugation of Europe and the extermination of the "inferior" peoples who occupied ground needed as living space for the master German race.

In the years after 1919, the German people convinced themselves that their young men, fighting in a noble cause, had almost achieved victory when traitors at home stabbed them in the back. In Britain and France, and also in the United States, the conviction grew that their young men had died in an unnecessary war which had shaken the foundations of European civilization, and that another war would complete the ruin of European civilization. In December, 1918, the Allied governments could confidently assert that "the responsibility of Germany for the war has been incontestably proved." Two years later Lloyd George was saying that all governments, including the German government, "staggered and stumbled" into war, and the more scholars studied the origins of the war, the more mixed was the verdict they returned. The war itself, which had seemed so noble an effort while it was being fought, became in Keynes' phrase "a nightmare interlude" even when described with the enthusiasm of Winston Churchill. The attack on the Treaty of Versailles began immediately. Keynes' *Economic Consequences of the Peace,* certainly one of the most influential books of this century, appeared at the end of 1919. With the fervor of an Old Testament prophet, Keynes attacked the moral foundation of the treaty; much of the argument of those in Britain who supported Hitler's demand for "justice" in the thirties is a paraphrase of Keynes.

By 1926, Stanley Baldwin was asking, "who in Europe does not know that one more war in the West, and the civilization of the ages will fall with as great a shock as that of Rome?" Three years later, Winston Churchill, at the end of *The Aftermath,* warned that the advance of military technology was so rapid that in another war mankind itself might be exterminated. By 1937, Aldous Huxley's *Encyclopedia of Pacifism* stated as a demonstrated fact that, after aerial bombardment with new weapons, "the chief use of the army will be, not to fight an enemy, but to try to keep order among the panic-stricken population at home." In that year, Bertrand Russell said the obvious conclusion was that if Hitler invaded England, the Nazis should be welcomed like tourists: "Whatever damage the Germans could do us would not be worse than the damage done in fighting them, even if we won." He believed the damage would not, in fact, be great: "The Nazis would find some interest in our way of living, I think, and the starch would be taken out of them." [1]

Statesmen responsible for the security of their country could not, of course, accept the possibility of invasion as lightheartedly as Bertrand Russell. However, determination not to repeat the mass slaughter of 1914-18, and dread of the consequences of another world war, entered the thought and the action of French and British statesmen. Back of French military doctrine, which, proceeding from the axiom that "fire kills," ended with faith that the fixed fortifications of the Maginot Line would permit successful defense with a minimum sacrifice of life, there was the memory of Verdun and the other battles of the war of attrition. When the British ceaselessly repeated Liddell Hart's dictum, "defense is paramount," and when they chilled their French allies by repeated declarations that Britain would never again send a mass army to the continent, their thinking was undoubtedly overshadowed by the fear "taking grisly shape in the twilight," as Stanley Baldwin put it, "that the Great War, by the destruction of our best lives in such numbers, has not left enough of the breed to carry on the work of Empire." [2]

Baffling economic shifts, social strife, the problems of empire, the realization that Germany had been beaten by force in 1918 and held down by the threat of use of force from 1918 to 1933 without breaking the German will to resist, and above all the dread of another holocaust like that of 1914-18 —all these paralyzed the will of French leaders by 1936. After that, France followed passively in the tow of Britain.

VI

Those who supported Neville Chamberlain in his policy of appeasement, and most Englishmen did support that policy until March, 1939, were influenced but not dominated by these same problems and fears. The difference lay partly in the more real British confidence in the superiority of the defense over the offense in modern warfare. The difference lay partly also in confidence resulting from lack of acquaintance with defeat. Chiefly, however, Chamberlain and his followers were sustained by the entirely erroneous conviction that Germans and Italians would, if their grievances were removed, appreciate the ruinous folly of war. In his more pessimistic moods, Chamberlain feared Hitler was insane, and therefore might not recognize that resort to war was madness. Until the end, however, Chamberlain seemed to hold firmly to the belief that only a madman could fail to see what he saw so clearly, that by peace men could attain all those things which made life desirable, while by war men would be engulfed in a common ruin. One of the greatest forces making for war was the British conviction, implicit through the interwar years, explicit after Chamberlain became Prime Minister in April, 1937, that human nature was everywhere the same, that under modern conditions no sane man could hope for real victory in war, and that bellicose sentiments such as those evident in Germany and Italy resulted from grievances which must be removed so that the necessity for peace would be evident, even to Germans and Italians.

There was one other related element which helps to an understanding of British and French reluctance to use force: fear of what would follow the

[1] *The New York Times,* April 2, 1937, p. 9.
[2] Stanley Baldwin, *On England,* Penguin ed. (London 1938), p. 113.

defeat of Fascist Italy or Nazi Germany. Now, clearly, now obscurely, the fear obtrudes that if Mussolini or Hitler suffered military defeat, he would be overthrown and replaced by a communist regime. Here again the Soviet Union enters as a negative force in the drift towards war. The weight of the evidence is very much against those who argue that Chamberlain was working to promote war between Nazi Germany and the Soviet Union. The evidence is strong, however, that he, and French statesmen, dreaded a clash with Mussolini or Hitler partly because of fear that communism would fill the vacuum left by the collapse of the Fascist or Nazi regime.

Appeasement had precisely the opposite effect from that intended by Chamberlain. Hitler was borne to power by a popular movement which demanded both social change at home and freedom from the restraints of the Treaty of Versailles. From his first days in power, Hitler showed clearly that he had no intention of bringing about revolutionary social change within Germany; his regime would stand, or fall, on his ability to achieve success abroad. At least through his militarization of the Rhineland in March, 1936, he would undoubtedly have been forced to retreat without a serious fight if confronted with military force. Whether, once he embarked on territorial expansion two years later, he would have retreated without full-scale war is doubtful. However, unless one is prepared to distort or disregard clear and conclusive evidence, there can be no escape from the conclusion that appeasement had exactly the opposite effect from the one intended. Appeasement convinced Hitler, and Mussolini also, that they could move ahead with less risk and more speed. Appeasement did not induce them to be "reasonable"; appeasement convinced them only that their opponents were cowards, afraid to fight. Whatever stress one places in the nobility of Chamberlain's aspiration, and his policy did embody some of mankind's most noble aspirations, the consequences of his policy, and of French policy, were disastrous.

VII

At the same time, the direct and overwhelming responsibility of the Nazi regime for the coming of the war is clear and incontestable—unless again one is prepared to distort or ignore the evidence. By 1937 the British and French governments were willing, indeed eager, to give Germany not only freedom from the restraints of the Treaty of Versailles; they were willing to give Germany preponderance in central and southeastern Europe. In his conscious thought, Hitler would have been temporarily content if the countries of central Europe accepted a dependent status: even after his stormy interview with Schuschnigg in February, 1938, Hitler spoke of the necessity for an "evolutionary" solution of the Austrian problem. In practice, however, the kind of dependence he was willing to accept was unobtainable without actual conquest. The government of what was left of Czechoslovakia after Munich showed a desperate eagerness to make concessions which would anticipate Hitler's every whim, yet he was driven by his impatience for total control to the fatal step of annexing Bohemia and Moravia. If he had displayed, even after the annexation of Austria, the extraordinary ability to wait which he had shown in the decade before 1933, or even the patience he had shown in foreign affairs before 1938, it is probable that Germany could have won a position of leadership in Europe far higher than that achieved by Bismarck. Unlike Bismarck, however, in success Hitler had no consciousness of the limits of the possible. By driving beyond those limits, he brought his country, and Europe, to ruin. And the German people, after making all allowance for the difficulty not only of dissent but even of clear vision under a totalitarian regime, share the responsibility of the Nazi regime for the tragedy of the Second World War.

At this point the task of the historian ends, and the task of the citizen begins. In his great speech after V-E Day, Winston Churchill admonished his countrymen to study the past because "it is only from the past that one can judge the future." Just because the history of the interwar years is so important a part of the human experience upon which citizen and statesman alike must build their understanding of the present age, it is the duty of the historian to make certain that the record of those years is examined with scholarly detachment and presented without distortion.

Chapter Twenty-five

World War II:
global repercussions

BLITZKRIEG 157

Because the offense proved superior to the defense, World War II was much more a war of movement than World War I had been. During the first war, the opposite situation prevailed. At that time, the combination of trenches, barbed wire entanglements, machine guns, and field artillery had stopped all infantry charges and precipitated a bloody stalemate on the western front (see Reading No. 113, "Trench Fighting"). A stalemate was avoided during World War II by the development of a new type of military operation known as Blitzkrieg, or lightning war. This was based on the intensive use of planes and tanks, as described in the following account from a United States military handbook.*

The war started in September 1939, with a whirlwind demonstration of the new Blitzkrieg methods devised by the Germans to overcome the static conditions of the previous war. In overrunning Poland that fall, and a good part of western Europe the following spring, they demonstrated an effective, well-integrated utilization of large armored forces and air power, followed by the conventional ground forces in large scale infiltration tactics. Instead of butting in full force against the main line of enemy resistance they often bypassed the toughest points to penetrate the weaker ones. Tanks had developed enough speed and power to become the basic arm of entire armored divisions. By using many of these divisions in their

---

* United States Marine Corps: *A Guide for the Study of the Evolution of the Art of War* (1954), pp. 95-96.

highly mobile armies, and by supporting the tank units with combat aviation as well as with all the other arms, the Germans were able to break through weak places in the hostile defenses and thus dash deep into enemy territory. Once there, they were able to paralyze the opposing forces by seizing headquarters and disrupting communications, supply and reinforcement. After the tide turned in favor of the Allies in 1942, when they finally gained superior armor and air power, they too used similar tactics to overwhelm the strongest German defenses. Throughout the war offensive tactics were predominant.

The armored forces had thus gone far beyond the original mission of the slow tanks of World War I. . . . Now, organized in self-sustaining units which included infantry and artillery, and with the assistance of combat aviation, the armored forces took over the old cavalry role of piercing or encircling enemy positions. Then, fanning out through the hostile rear areas at great speed, these armored forces struck at enemy command and communication installations, supply centers and transportation lines, until the enemy was paralyzed. . . .

Air superiority proved itself to be a vital element in victory. Developed tremendously from its initial roles in World War I, aviation now had two distinct spheres of activity. It operated alone in the strategic bombing of distant enemy industrial and other important objectives. In tactical or combat aviation, on the other hand, it worked in and behind the battlefield in close air-ground cooperation for a common end. . . .

It was by this method that German aviation gave material support to the Blitzkrieg by overwhelming the defending air forces of Poland and France at the outset of hostilities. The British saved their trapped forces at Dunkirk by achieving temporary air superiority at that spot. Later, the Allies wrested general air superiority from the Germans and perfected their air-ground teamwork to a point which contributed greatly to their eventual victory. Late in 1941 Japanese air squadrons achieved surprise against defending aviation at Pearl Harbor and crippled the American fleet and air arm there. Like the Germans, the Japanese eventually lost air superiority and received severe lessons in the effectiveness of joint air-ground tactics.

158 FALL OF FRANCE

The Germans first demonstrated the effectiveness of Blitzkrieg *in Poland, where they won the campaign, for all practical purposes, within ten days. Much more astonishing was their victory over France in a whirlwind offensive of seven weeks. The fall of what was considered to be the strongest Allied power in so humiliating a fashion was a great shock to the Western world. Hitler took advantage of his great victory by compelling the French to sign the armistice in the same Compiègne Forest where the defeated Germans had signed the World War I armistice on November 11, 1918. This dramatic episode was described in an eyewitness report by the well-known American correspondent William L. Shirer.**

* CBS (June 21, 1940). Reprinted by permission of William L. Shirer.

ANNOUNCER. At this time, as the French government considers Germany's terms for an armistice, Columbia takes you to Berlin for a special broadcast by William Shirer in Germany. We take you now to Berlin. Go ahead, Berlin.

SHIRER. Hello, America! CBS! William L. Shirer calling CBS in New York.

William L. Shirer calling CBS in New York, calling CBS from Compiègne, France. This is William L. Shirer of CBS. We've got a microphone at the edge of a little clearing in the Forest of Compiègne, four miles to the north of the town of Compiègne and about forty-five miles north of Paris. Here, a few feet from where we're standing, in the very same old railroad coach where the Armistice was signed on that chilly morning of November 11, 1918, negotiations for another armistice—the one to end the present war between France and Germany—began at three-thirty P.M., German summer time, this afternoon. What a turning back of the clock, what a reversing of history we've been watching here in this beautiful Compiègne Forest this afternoon! What a contrast to that day twenty-two years ago! Yes, even the weather, for we have one of those lovely warm June days which you get in this part of France close to Paris about this time of year.

As we stood here, watching Adolf Hitler and Field Marshal Göring and the other German leaders laying down the terms of the armistice to the French plenipotentiaries here this afternoon, it was difficult to comprehend that in this rustic little clearing in the midst of the Forest of Compiègne, from where we're talking to you now, that an armistice was signed here on the cold, cold morning at five A.M. on November 11, 1918. The railroad coach—it was Marshal Foch's private car—stands a few feet away from us here in exactly the same spot where it stood on that gray morning twenty-two years ago, only—and what an "only" it is, too—Adolf Hitler sat in the seat occupied that day by Marshal Foch. Hitler at that time was only an unknown corporal in the German army, and in that quaint old wartime car another armistice is being drawn up as I speak to you now, an armistice designed like the other that was signed on this spot to bring armed hostilities to halt between those ancient enemies—Germany and France. Only everything that we've been seeing here this afternoon in Compiègne Forest has been so reversed. The last time the representatives of France sat in that car dictating the terms of the armistice. This afternoon we peered through the windows of the car and saw Adolf Hitler laying down the terms. That's how history reversed itself, but seldom has it done so as today on the very same spot. The German leader in the preamble of the conditions which were read to the French delegates by Colonel General von Keitel, Chief of the German Supreme Command, told the French that he had not chosen this spot at Compiègne out of revenge but merely to right a wrong. . . .

A warm June sun beat down on the great elm and pine trees and cast purple shadows on the hooded avenues as Herr Hitler with the German plenipotentiaries at his side appeared. He alighted from his car in front of the French monument to Alsace-Lorraine which stands at the end of an avenue about two hundred yards from the clearing here in front of us where the armistice car stands. That famous Alsace-Lorraine statue was covered with German war flags, so that you cannot see its sculptured works or read its inscriptions. I had seen it many times in the postwar years, and doubtless many of you have seen it—the large sword representing the sword of the Allies, with its point sticking into a large, limp eagle, representing the old empire of the Kaiser, and the inscription underneath in front saying, "To the heroic soldiers of France, defenders of the country and of the right, glorious liberators of Alsace-Lorraine."

Through our glasses, we saw the Führer stop, glance at the statue, observe the Reich war flags with their big swastikas in the center. Then he strolled slowly toward us, toward the little clearing where the famous armistice car stood. I thought he looked very solemn; his face was grave. But there was a certain spring in his step, as he walked for the first time toward the spot where Germany's fate was sealed on that November day of 1918, a fate which, by reason of his own being, is now being radically changed here on this spot.

And now, if I may sort of go over my notes—I made from moment to moment this afternoon—now Hitler reaches a little opening in the Compiègne woods where the Armistice was signed and where another is about to be drawn up. He pauses and slowly looks around. The opening here is in the form of a circle about two hundred yards in diameter and laid out like a park. Cypress trees line it all around, and behind them the great elms and oaks of the forest. This has been one of France's national shrines for twenty-two years. Hitler pauses and gazes slowly around. In the group just behind him are the other German plenipotentiaries—Field Marshal Göring, grasping his Field Marshal baton in one hand. He wears the blue uniform of the air force. All the Germans are in uniform. Hitler in a double-breasted gray uniform with the Iron Cross hanging from his left breast pocket. Next to Göring are the two German army chiefs, Colonel General von Keitel, Chief of the Supreme Command, and Colonel General von Brauchitsch, Commander-in-Chief of the German Army. Both are just approaching sixty, but look younger, especially General von Keitel, who has a dapper appearance, with his cap lightly cocked on one side. Then we see there Dr. Raeder, Grand Admiral of the German Fleet. He has on a blue naval uniform and the invariable upturned stiff collar which German naval officers usually wear. We see two nonmilitary men in Hitler's suite—his Foreign Minister, Joachim von Ribbentrop, in the field-gray uniform of the Foreign Office, and Rudolph Hess, Hitler's deputy, in a gray party uniform.

The time's now, I see by my notes, three-eighteen P.M. in the Forest of Compiègne. Hitler's personal standard is run up on a small post in the center of the circular opening in the woods. Also in the center, is a great granite block which stands some three feet above the ground. Hitler, followed by the others, walks slowly over to it, steps up, and reads the inscription engraved in great high letters on that block. Many of you will remember the words of the inscription. The Führer slowly reads them, and the inscription says, "Here on the eleventh of November, 1918, succumbed the criminal pride of the German Empire, vanquished by the free peoples which it tried to enslave." Hitler reads it, standing there in the June sun and the silence. We look for the expression on Hitler's face, but it does not change. Finally he leads his party over to another granite stone, a small one some fifty yards to one side. Here it was that the railroad car in which the German plenipotentiary stayed during the 1918 armistice negotiations stood from November 8 to 11. Hitler looks down and reads the inscription, which merely says: "The German plenipotentiary." The stone itself, I notice, is set between a pair of rusty old railroad tracks, the very ones that were there twenty-two years ago.

It is now three twenty-three P.M., and the German leaders stride over to the armistice car. This car, of course, was not standing on this spot yesterday. It was standing seventy-five yards down the rusty track in the shelter of a tiny museum built to house it by an American citizen, Mr. Arthur Henry Fleming of Pasadena, California. Yesterday the car was removed from the museum by the German army engineers and rolled back those seventy-five yards to the spot where it stood on the morning of November 11, 1918. The Germans stand outside the car, chatting in the sunlight. This goes on for two minutes. Then Hitler steps up into the car, followed by Göring and the others. We watch them entering the drawing room of Marshal Foch's car. We can see nicely now through the car windows.

Hitler enters first and takes the place occupied by Marshal Foch the morning the first armistice was signed. At his sides are Göring and General Keitel. To his right and left at the ends of the table we see General von Brauchitsch and Herr Hess at the one end, at the other end Grand Admiral Raeder and Herr von Ribbentrop. The opposite side of the table is still empty, and we see there four vacant chairs. The French have not yet appeared, but we do not wait long. Exactly at three-thirty P.M. the French alight from a car. They have flown up from Bordeaux to a nearby landing field and then have driven here in an auto.

They glance at the Alsace-Lorraine memorial, now draped with swastikas, but it's a swift glance. Then they walk down the avenue flanked by three German army officers. We see them now as they come into the sunlight of the clearing—General Huntziger, wearing a brief khaki uniform; General Bergeret and Vice-Admiral Le Luc, both in their respective dark-blue uniforms; and then, almost buried in the uniforms, the one single civilian of the day, Mr. Noël, French Ambassador to Poland when the present war broke out there. The French plenipotentiaries passed the guard of honor drawn up at the entrance of the clearing. The Frenchmen keep their eyes straight ahead. It's grave hour in the life of France, and their faces today show what a burden they feel on their shoulders. Their faces are solemn, drawn, but bear the expression of tragic dignity. They walked quickly to the car and were met by two German officers, Lieutenant Colonel Tippelskirch, Quartermaster General, and Colonel Thomas, Chief of the Paris Headquarters. The Germans salute; the French salute; the atmosphere is what Europeans call "correct"; but you'll get the picture when I say that we see no handshakes—not on occasions like this. The historic moment is now approaching. It is three thirty-two by my watch. The Frenchmen enter Marshal Foch's Pullman car, standing there a few feet from us in Compiègne Forest. Now we get our picture through the dusty windows of the historic old *wagonlit* car. Hitler and the other German leaders rise from their seats as the French enter the drawing room. Hitler, we see, gives the Nazi salute, the arm raised. The German officers give a military salute; the French do the same. I cannot see Mr. Noël to see whether he salutes or how. Hitler, so far as we can see through the windows just in front of here, does not say anything. He nods to General Keitel adjusting his papers, and then he starts to read. He is reading the preamble of the German armistice terms. The French sit there with marble-like faces and listen intently. Hitler and Göring glance at the green table top. This part of the historic act lasts but a few moments. I note in my notebook here this—three forty-three P.M.—that is, twelve minutes after the French arrived—three forty-three—we see Hitler stand up, salute the three with hand upraised. Then he strides out of the room, followed by Göring, General von Brauchitsch, Grand Admiral Raeder is there, Herr Hess, and, at the end, von Ribbentrop. The French remain at the green-topped table in the old Pullman car, and we see General Keitel remains with them. He is going to read them the detailed conditions of the armistice. Hitler goes, and the others do not wait for this. They walk down the avenue back towards the Alsace-Lorraine monument. As they pass the guard of honor, a German band strikes up the two national anthems *Deutschland über Alles* and the *Horst Wessel Song.*

The whole thing has taken but a quarter of an hour—this great reversal of a historical armistice of only a few years ago.

ANNOUNCER. You have just heard a special broadcast from the Compiègne Forest in France, where on the historic morning of November 11, 1918, representatives of the German army received from the Allies the terms of the armistice which ended the First World War, and where today, June 21, 1940, representatives of the French government received from Führer Adolf Hitler the terms under which a cessation of hostilities between Germany and France may be reached. As you know, the actual terms presented to the French plenipotentiaries have not yet been made public.

Music—*Organ*

ANNOUNCER. This is the Columbia Broadcasting System.

159 BATTLE OF BRITAIN

After his conquest of France, Hitler turned upon Britain. He planned an invasion of the island, but recognized that it would not be feasible without command of the skies. Accordingly, the German air force was turned loose upon Britain, and there ensued the fateful struggle between the Royal Air Force (RAF) and the Luftwaffe. The RAF emerged triumphant, partly because the British planes were superior in performance, though inferior in numbers, and partly because of the assistance of the newly-invented radar which helped to track down the German planes. The following account is from Prime Minister Churchill's report of August 20, 1940 to the House of Commons on the course of the air battle.*

The great air battle which has been in progress over this island for the last few weeks has recently attained a high intensity. It is too soon to attempt to assign limits either to its scale or to its duration. We must certainly expect that greater efforts will be made by the enemy than any he has so far put forth. Hostile airfields are still being developed in France and the Low Countries. It is quite plain that Herr Hitler could not admit defeat in his air attack on Great Britain without sustaining most serious injury. ...

On the other hand, the conditions and course of the fighting have so far been favourable to us. I told the House two months ago that whereas in France our fighter aircraft were wont to inflict a loss of two or three to one upon the Germans and in the fighting at Dunkirk, which was a kind of no-man's-land, a loss of about three or four to one, we expected that in an

---

* Parliamentary Debates, 5th ser., House of Commons, Vol. 364 (August 20, 1940), Col. 1165-71.

attack on this island we should achieve a larger ratio. This has certainly come true. (Cheers.)

It must also be remembered that all the enemy machines and pilots which are shot down over our island, or over the seas which surround it, are either destroyed or captured, whereas a considerable proportion of our machines and also of our pilots are saved, and many of them soon again come into action. A vast and admirable system of salvage, directed by the Ministry of Aircraft Production, ensures the speediest return to the fighting line of damaged machines, At the same time the splendid, nay, astounding, increase in the output and repair of British aircraft and engines which Lord Beaverbrook has achieved by a genius for organisation and drive which looks like magic —(cheers)—has given us overflowing reserves of every type of aircraft and an ever mounting stream of production in quantity and in quality. (Cheers.)

The enemy is, of course, far more numerous than we are, but our new production already, as I am advised, largely exceeds his, and the American production is only just beginning to flow in. It is a fact that after all this fighting our bombing and fighter strengths are larger than they have ever been. (Cheers.)

We hope and believe that we shall be able to continue the struggle indefinitely and as long as the enemy pleases, and the longer it continues the more rapid will be our approach first towards that parity and then into that superiority in the air upon which in a large measure the decision of the war depends.

The gratitude of every home in our island, in our Empire, and indeed throughout the world except in the abodes of the guilty goes out to the British airmen who, undaunted by odds, unwearied by their constant challenge and mortal danger, are turning the tide of world war by their prowess and their devotion.

Never in the field of human conflict was so much owed by so many to so few. (Prolonged cheers.) All hearts go out to the fighter pilots, whose brilliant actions we see with our own eyes day after day, but we must never forget that all the time, night after night, month after month, our bomber squadrons travel far into Germany, find their targets in the darkness by the highest navigational skill, aim their attacks, often under the heaviest fire, often at serious loss, with deliberate, careful precision and inflict shattering blows upon the whole of the technical and war-making structure of the Nazi power. (Cheers.)

HITLER ATTACKS RUSSIA **160**

The failure of the Luftwaffe *to gain control of the skies over Britain spelled the end of any possibility of a cross-Channel invasion. Frustrated in the West, Hitler turned eastward and ordered his armies to attack the Soviet Union, despite the Nonaggression Pact signed in Moscow in 1939. Stalin was caught by surprise, and his Red army suffered extremely heavy losses in the early stages of the fighting. The attack began on June 22, 1941; on July 3, Stalin made a radio appeal to his people calling for united and unyielding resistance to the German invaders. The* *following selection from his speech reflects embarrassment over his past dealings with Hitler, as well as a determination to fight to the end.**

Comrades! Citizens! Brothers and Sisters! Men of our Army and Navy! I am addressing you, my friends!

The perfidious military attack on our motherland begun on June 22 by Hitler Germany is continuing. In spite of the heroic resistance of the Red Army, and although the enemy's finest divisions and finest air-force units have already been smashed and have met their doom on the field of battle, the enemy continues to push forward, hurling fresh forces into the attack. Hitler's troops have succeeded in capturing Lithuania, a considerable part of Latvia, the western part of Byelorussia, and part of the Western Ukraine. The fascist air force is extending the range of operations of its bombers, and is bombing Murmansk, Orsha, Mogilev, Smolensk, Kiev, Odessa and Sevastopol. A grave danger hangs over our country.

How could it have happened that our glorious Red Army surrendered a number of our cities and districts to the fascist armies? Is it really true that the German-fascist troops are invincible, as is ceaselessly trumpeted by boastful fascist propagandists? Of course not! History shows that there are no invincible armies and never have been. ...

As to part of our territory having nevertheless been seized by German-fascist troops, this is chiefly due to the fact that the war of fascist Germany on the USSR began under conditions favorable for the German forces and unfavorable for the Soviet forces. The fact of the matter is that the troops of Germany, as a country at war, were already fully mobilized, and the 170 divisions hurled by Germany against the USSR and brought up to the Soviet frontiers were in a state of complete readiness, only awaiting the signal to move into action, whereas the Soviet troops had still to effect mobilization and to move up to the frontiers.

Of no little importance in this respect is the fact that fascist Germany suddenly and treacherously violated the non-aggression pact she concluded in 1939 with the USSR, disregarding the fact that she would be regarded as the aggressor by the whole world. Naturally, our peace-loving country, not wishing to take the initiative in breaking the pact, could not have resorted to perfidy. It may be asked: how could the Soviet Government have consented to conclude a non-aggression pact with such treacherous fiends as Hitler and Ribbentrop? Was this not an error on the part of the Soviet Government? Of course not! Non-aggression pacts are pacts of peace between two states. It was such a pact that Germany proposed to us in 1939. Could the Soviet Government have declined such a proposal? I think that not a single peace-loving state could decline a peace treaty with a neighboring state, even though the latter was headed by such fiends and cannibals as Hitler and Ribbentrop. But that, of course, only on one indispensable condition, namely, that this peace treaty does not infringe either directly or indirectly on the territorial integrity, independence, and honor of the peace-loving state. As is well known, the non-aggression pact between Germany and the USSR was precisely such a pact.

---

* "Radio Address of Joseph V. Stalin, July 3, 1941," *Soviet War Documents* (Washington, D.C.: Information Bulletin, Embassy of the U.S.S.R.), special supplement (December, 1944), pp. 3-7.

What did we gain by concluding the non-aggression pact with Germany? We secured our country peace for a year and a half and the opportunity of preparing its forces to repulse fascist Germany should she risk an attack on our country despite the pact. This was a definite advantage for us and a disadvantage for fascist Germany. What has fascist Germany gained and what has she lost by treacherously tearing up the pact and attacking the USSR? She has gained certain advantageous positions for her troops for a short period, but she has lost politically by exposing herself in the eyes of the entire world as a bloodthirsty aggressor. There can be no doubt that this short-lived military gain for Germany is only an episode.

. . . . .

All our industries must be put to work with greater intensity to produce more rifles, machine guns, artillery, bullets, shells, airplanes; we must organize the guarding of factories, power stations, telephone and telegraph communications, and arrange effective air-raid protection in all localities. . . .

In case of forced retreat of Red Army units, all rolling stock must be evacuated, the enemy must not be left a single engine, a single railway car, not a single pound of grain or gallon of fuel. . . .

In this connection, the historic utterance of the British Prime Minister, Mr. Churchill, regarding aid to the Soviet Union, and the declaration of the United States Government signifying its readiness to render aid to our country, which can only evoke a feeling of gratitude in the hearts of the peoples of the Soviet Union, are full, comprehensible and symptomatic. . . .

All our forces—for the support of our heroic Red Army and our glorious Red Navy!

All forces of the people—for the demolition of the enemy!

Forward, to our victory!

RESPONSIBILITY FOR PEARL HARBOR **161**

*The catastrophe at Pearl Harbor had the immediate effect of uniting an overwhelming majority of the American people to face the ordeal that lay ahead. But troublesome questions remained unanswered, and in the postwar period they became political issues and aroused partisan debates. Had President Roosevelt exceeded his authority in his undeclared naval war against Germany in the Atlantic? Had he deliberately provoked the Japanese to aggression in order to "enter the European war through the backdoor of Asia"? And who was responsible for the disastrous unpreparedness of the American forces at Pearl Harbor, despite the secret information made available to Washington with the cracking of the Japanese radio code? These questions are judiciously considered in the following analysis by Professor Richard W. Leopold, a distinguished authority on American foreign policy.**

* R. W. Leopold, "The President and Foreign Policy: The Two Roosevelts," *Tri-Quarterly, Northwestern University*, VI (Fall, 1963), 6-8. Copyright 1963.

Franklin D. Roosevelt possessed a temperament and talents well suited to exploit the potential of the presidency. Even more than Al Smith, he was the Happy Warrior. Sanguine and gay, he was instinctively a leader. Despite his privileged upbringing, he had the common touch. He coined phrases that inspired his fellow men. He could say "My friends" in ten different ways. A superb speaker with a mellifluous voice, he developed the medium of radio with effective fireside chats. A skilled actor with a flair for the dramatic, he gave the impression of moving forward even when he stood still. He travelled constantly through the land, perhaps to compensate for his inability to walk unaided. He revolutionized the press conference and endeared himself to correspondents whose newspapers excoriated him. He enjoyed personal diplomacy, corresponding not only with his own ambassadors abroad but also with the heads of other states or governments. Like the first Roosevelt, he understood the need to correlate foreign policy with military capability. He, too, loved the sea and the ships that sailed it. Most important of all, he viewed the presidency as a place to exercise both political and moral leadership.

On taking office, Roosevelt did not institute a new deal in foreign policy. His immediate goals differed little from those of the Hoover administration. Although the depression was global in its ramifications, he concentrated on domestic problems and gave priority to relief, recovery, and reform. The world, of course, did not stand still as he tried to build a new America. His first years saw the collapse of the Versailles settlement and the American compromise between traditional principles and Wilsonian precepts. So spectacular were Roosevelt's initial triumphs at home that we forget his many setbacks abroad. In July 1933 the World Economic Conference broke up in failure, partly because he refused to stabilize the dollar. In June 1934 the World Disarmament Conference reached a deadlock because no one could reconcile Germany's demand for rearmament with France's insistence on security. More revealing were his defeats on Capitol Hill where the Democrats enjoyed large majorities in both houses. In May 1933 he lost his bid for a discriminatory arms embargo designed to discourage revolution and aggression. In January 1935 he was beaten on the World Court Protocol. In August 1935 he signed a neutrality law he did not like. With many of his staunchest supporters on domestic matters disagreeing with him on foreign affairs, Roosevelt shrank from showdowns. Certainly he cannot be accused in these years of exceeding his constitutional authority or stretching the limits of the presidency in foreign affairs.

The real controversy over whether Franklin Roosevelt usurped the powers of Congress in foreign policy began as Europe careened toward war. The President was appalled by his inability to awaken the people to the dangers which, he felt, beset them. "It's a terrible thing," he said later, "to look over your shoulder when you are trying to lead—and to find no one there." He did try to secure a change in the existing neutrality laws, a change which would allow the executive discretion in applying the arms embargo, a discretion that might be used against the aggressors. Though he had wanted this discretion since 1933, and had sought it openly and by constitutional means, he was unsuccessful. Then the outbreak of war in September 1939 persuaded Congress to give him half a loaf.

With the fall of France, Roosevelt took the first of several steps for which he has been severely criticized. This was the Destroyers-Bases Agreement of September 1940 by which the United States transferred to Britain fifty overage and decommissioned destroyers in exchange for ninety-nine year leases on six Caribbean sites, suitable for naval and air bases, and the outright gift of two additional facilities in Bermuda and Newfoundland. Little fault could be found with the provisions. They amounted to the most advantageous acquisition for defense since the purchase of Louisiana. To be sure, the agreement was not consonant with traditional neutrality, but after the Nazi invasion of Holland most Americans realized that traditional concepts afforded no protection for the neutrals. What bothered many citizens was the method used, an executive agreement instead of a treaty. The Senate had been bypassed. Why? Not because he feared publicity—the text was published immediately. Not because he feared defeat—he could have mustered a two-thirds majority eventually. Rather he feared delay, a long debate during which Germany might invade England. The tempo of war had quickened; the air age had made obsolete the leisurely processes established in 1787. Modern planes, Roosevelt had warned four months earlier, had eliminated oceans as defensive moats; modern bombers could hit the United States from Greenland in a six-hour flight.

The Lend-Lease Act of March 1941 was the next step in an unprecedented response to what Roosevelt believed were unprecedented dangers. Note the word "Act." Lend-Lease was a law, a statute passed by Congress. It may have been un-neutral; by nineteenth century standards it was. It may have been unwise; I do not think it was. It may have delegated extraordinary powers to the president, and it did. But it was not usurpation by the executive. It was openly debated after full hearings in both houses; it was passed by substantial majorities. It conformed to the democratic process and was flawed only by premature assurances, implied rather than explicit, that American warships would not be needed to insure the safe delivery of Lend-Lease goods.

We come now to the climax of Roosevelt's pre-war diplomacy—the undeclared naval war with Germany in the Atlantic and the Japanese attack on Pearl Harbor. Did the President exceed his powers? Did he so maneuver the situation that he robbed Congress of the right to decide whether war should be declared? There is much about his course in the Atlantic that may be criticized, even if you agree—as I do—with his basic assumption that American security required that Lend-Lease goods reach England. On occasion he was not candid, even devious. He seemed afraid to tell the people bluntly what must be done. In this connection Secretary of War Stimson, a Republican who had served the first Roosevelt, Taft, and Hoover, later expressed the opinion that in 1941 Theodore would have done a better job than Franklin. "TR's advantage," Stimson said in 1947, was "his natural boldness, his firm conviction that where he led, men would follow. . . . Franklin Roosevelt was not made that way. With unequalled political skill he could pave the way for any given specific step, but in so doing he was likely to tie his own hands for the future, using honeyed and consoling words that would return to plague him later."

On September 11, 1941, Roosevelt ordered all American warships to "shoot on sight" any Axis naval vessel encountered in waters which the United States deemed essential to its defense—roughly the western half of the Atlantic. Five days later he put into effect an order, frequently canceled and long delayed, permitting belligerent and neutral merchant craft to join convoys destined for Iceland and escorted by the American navy. Both steps were taken publicly, but without congressional consent. Since the President was acting as commander-in-chief, such consent was not required, though he might have been wise to seek it. A month later Roosevelt did ask Congress to repeal certain outdated clauses in the neutrality laws, and by a close vote (close because of extraneous issues) that body went farther than he had requested. Paradoxically, in late

1941 Congress and the people would have opposed a flat declaration of war against Germany, yet a sizable majority favored a course that at any moment could precipitate full-scale hostilities. This confusion persisted until Japan struck in the Pacific.

The events leading to Pearl Harbor were diplomatic and military in character and thus, constitutionally, the concern of the executive. The deployment of ships and planes was the responsibility of the commander-in-chief; the dialogue with Tokyo to resolve Japanese-American differences fell to "the chief organ of the nation in its external relations." There was more secrecy surrounding developments in the Pacific than in the Atlantic, but then publicity is not customary during tense diplomatic negotiations or frantic military preparations. Certainly Congress could not be given the intercepts of secret Japanese dispatches which we were able to read after breaking the diplomatic code. The legislature could have acted, if it had wished, on perhaps the most decisive move in the long drama—the freezing of Japanese assets and the beginnings of an oil embargo. This step was taken by an executive order, but it was done openly and dealt with something within congressional jurisdiction. There was, however, no protest on Capitol Hill where a "get tough with Japan policy" was more popular than in the White House or the War and Navy Departments.

Roosevelt has often been accused of wanting to enter the European war through the backdoor of Asia. He is charged with provoking Japan to strike first (thus insuring united support at home) by presenting her with impossible demands. This premise and this charge I believe are false. Roosevelt had no desire to enlarge the war. His main aim was to help England contain and defeat Germany. America was unready to fight a two-front war. His military chiefs in November 1941 were begging for time, beseeching him to avoid a showdown, at least until April 1942 when they would have enough flying fortresses in the Philippines to make those islands safe from a Japanese invasion, or so they thought. The President concurred, but he also knew there were concessions beyond which he could not go to avoid war and there was a deadline beyond which the Japanese would not talk lest the season for amphibious operations pass. One can legitimately argue that a more flexible American policy might have postponed the clash with Japan—I do not think anything could have eliminated it—but that is not the same as saying that the president usurped the powers of Congress and insured war by compelling Japan to fire the first shot.

Roosevelt has also been charged with exceeding his authority by promising England and the Netherlands to come to their aid in event of a Japanese attack in Asia. This assurance the President consistently refused to give, at least down to December 6 when any such promise could not possibly affect Japanese policy. He was, to be sure, worried lest Japan weaken Hitler's foes by invading Malaya and the East Indies. His military advisers told him that a Japanese conquest of parts of Southeast Asia would imperil our own security. The dilemma was what to do if Japan did so invade without attacking American soil. That was a tough one. On November 28 the President and his cabinet agreed that he must go before Congress and request authority to use force to defend certain non-American territory. He planned to do so on December 8 or 9. Obviously he never had to go because the attack on Pearl and the Philippines removed the necessity. But here Roosevelt recognized the limits of his power and was ready to request Congress to supplement them. This was not usurpation.

The question of blame for the military disaster at Pearl Harbor does not properly belong in a discussion of the powers of the president in foreign affairs;

but since it continues to arouse controversy, I shall offer a few observations. Few Americans, it seems to me, save those under fire, showed to best advantage in that tragedy. The failure was universal. At every level, from the White House to the destroyer patrolling the harbor entrance, there were mistaken judgments and errors of omission. Not everyone was later judged by the same standards, but sympathy for those who were made the scapegoats must not lead us to accept their charges that a military defeat was staged in order to escape from a diplomatic impasse. Similarly, the refusal of officials in Washington to assume some of the blame must not cause us to conclude that they had a despicable plot to hide. There was no treason in high quarters in 1941, there is no unsolved mystery of Pearl Harbor. The true explanation of the debacle lies in the realm of human frailty; and since no one saw the portent clearly at the time, it behooves a later generation not to be omniscient after the event.

Vacuum in Southeast Asia 162

Within six months after the attack on Pearl Harbor, the Japanese had conquered a vast empire stretching from the Aleutian Islands to the borders of India. Prime Minister Churchill was forced to admit to Commons that ". . . the violence, fury, skill and might of Japan had far exceeded anything that we had been led to expect." The reason for the astounding success of the Japanese is that the whole of Southeast Asia was, for all practical purposes, a vast power vacuum. The following account by two American correspondents analyzes the various factors that combined to produce this vacuum.*

America was totally unprepared for the war that she had accepted on the far side of the globe. The chief armament of the Allies was an innocent faith in the superiority of the white man over the colored man, or at least of the white man's culture over any other. Defense preparations were more pitiful than imposing. In the Philippines we had the skeleton of an air force—thirty-five B-17's, lumbering early types of the Flying Fortress, undergunned and underarmored, of which seventeen were destroyed on the ground in the first day of action; twenty P-35's, serviceable but slow, built for the Swedish government and diverted to the Philippines; sixty early models of the P-40's; no medium bombers at all; and a mongrel assortment of A-27's, P-26's, and 90-mile-per-hour observation planes. After the first weeks of war this air force was reduced to thirty fighters and no bombers. Our ground forces consisted of the Philippine Scouts, excellent jungle fighters; several thousand National Guardsmen fresh from the States; and a hodgepodge mass of hastily trained Filipino reservists drawn from the rice paddies and farms of the islands.

The other Allies were weak, too. The Dutch in the Indies had 300 planes, but most of these were obsolete. They had 30,000 regular troops, of which six or seven thousand were Europeans and the rest natives. They had rifles, machine guns, some old field pieces, and little else. Supplementary levies of 40,000 were quickly called together, but they were untrained. The British in

* T. H. White and A. Jacoby, *Thunder Out of China* (New York: W. Sloane Associates, 1946), pp. 82-85. Copyright 1946. By permission of William Sloane Associates, Inc.

Malaya were guarded by the jungles, their own pride, and the traditions of empire. Their air force was almost entirely obsolete. They had built a huge naval base at Singapore at an estimated cost of $300,000,000, but it was prepared to defend itself only against attack from the sea; the Japanese attack, of course, came overland. Theoretically the British should have been the bastion of strength in the South Seas—they had an Australian division, thousands of British troops, and a heavy high-seas battle fleet; but the British command was incompetent and irresolute.

All the Western Allies in the Pacific—the Americans, British, and Dutch—were as ill prepared psychologically to face the Japanese as the French chivalry had been to face the crossbowmen of England at Agincourt. With the exception of Douglas MacArthur the commanders of the war against Japan in December 1941 were men blinded by an enormous and overweening arrogance. One of the generals of the United States Air Corps at Pearl Harbor had delivered himself of a profound statement at a party five months before the attack: "Hitler is our real worry," said he. "As soon as we take care of the Germans, we can turn to these Japs and say, 'There, there, little brothers, just behave yourselves,' and they'll behave."

In the mythology of the white-skinned warrior darker-skinned people were just not fighting men. Everybody knew that all Japanese were near-sighted and couldn't shoot, that their bombing was inaccurate, that they were mimics, that they could not build or maintain real machinery. Remember that story about how they copied a British ship, patches and all—or the one about how they built a ship from phony plans, which turned turtle as soon as it left the dry dock? Japanese planes were no good—remember how they cracked up the first model of the DC-4? In spite of all this full specifications of the Japanese Zero had been forwarded by military intelligence from China to Washington as early as March 1941; its maneuverability, range, and engine power were on record—filed away and ignored. The master minds of the West had watched the Japanese fight the Chinese for four years, and they were unimpressed. Although they could not understand the war in China and made little effort to find out more than the bare bones of military fact, they were serene in their conclusions; the war in China had proved to them that the Japanese were a fourth-rate military power, possessing neither the resources nor the skill necessary to fight a modern war.

If the Allies were unprepared militarily and psychologically to face the Japanese in field of battle, they were even more inadequately prepared to face the Japanese in a contest for the loyalty of the people in the lands under attack. An era in world history was coming to an end, but no one understood this until too late; even after victory many failed to grasp it. Japan's plunge into the South Seas was a turning point in the history of subject Asia, so portentous a phase in a revolution of hundreds of millions of men that the war itself was reduced almost to a detail. For four hundred years, since the galleons of Don Alfonso de Albuquerque threaded the Straits of Malacca in 1511, to be followed by Saint Francis Xavier a few decades later, the white man had trampled roughshod over the dignity and culture of the dark-skinned peoples of Asia. The white man in his military arrogance had looted the Orient of its wealth and thrust his faith down the gullet of the heathen at bayonet's point. For four hundred years the bitternesses of the people of Asia had been gradually accumulating against this system, and the pressure was volcanic. Now a dark-skinned people undertook to humiliate the white man within sight of his slaves.

The Filipinos have an ancient legend about how God made the world's first man. God fashioned a man tenderly until every detail was perfect, they say, and then put the image into the oven to bake. But He opened the oven too late; the man had burned black. This was, after all, the first man God had ever created. Breathing life into the figure, He determined to try again. He put the same material into a second man, shaped with the same care, and waited eagerly; but He grew impatient with waiting and opened the oven too soon, and the man was underdone, a sickly, pasty white. God was not satisfied and reproached Himself for this second mistake. So He made a third man; He looked into the oven every now and then, and when He took the figure out, this man was baked neither too much nor too little. He was a smooth golden brown, and God was satisfied.

The story could be Malay or Burmese or Indonesian; it could be told of China or Japan; it could be the story of any brown- or yellow-skinned people, who' had been made defensively aware of their color by the coming of the white man. The consciousness of color that had been imposed with stress on the superiority and dominance of the pale and on the humble subjection of the dark was the strongest weapon in Japan's arsenal. Japan's tempestuous assault on the empires of the South Seas in the winter and spring of 1942 seemed like an overwhelming, dynamic parade of military might; in actual fact it was not. It was the annihilation of a handful of white men and their decrepit military establishments trapped between the apathy and hatred of their subject peoples on the one hand and the storming advance wave of what some of those peoples thought was a crusade.

STALINGRAD 163

*While the Japanese were winning spectacular victories in the Pacific, the Germans were doing likewise in Russia. Thus, 1942 was a year of almost unbroken Axis triumphs. The turning point, however, came in the following year. In Russia, the shift in the balance of power was marked by the catastrophic German defeat at Stalingrad. When his armies reached that city on the Volga River, Hitler determined to hold on at all cost. But Stalin was resolved that the city should not fall, and ordered its defenders to fight to the end. At the same time, Stalin organized new armies in the East, and in mid-November, 1942, they counterattacked across the Volga and surrounded the German siege forces. The latter refused to surrender on orders from Berlin, and during the next three months they suffered the agonies of starvation, cold, and disease. Their ordeal, before they finally surrendered on February 2, 1943, is described below by a United States Marine Corps officer.**

It was now December. The blizzards of the steppe arose, viciously cutting at all forms of life on the barren, treeless steppe. Temperatures were steadily

* Second Lieut. Hans W. Henzel, "The Stalingrad Offensive," *Marine Corps Gazette* (September, 1951), pp. 52-56.

dropping until they had reached a constant nightly average of between 20 to 30 degrees below zero. . . .

Christmas came and passed; the only thing of note to happen was that the German death list had risen to 180,000. Near the railhead at Grumak, German dead, frozen stiff, were used as steps for the living to crawl into a stalled hospital train, where small stoves were surrounded by prone, motionless bodies clinging tenaciously to life in a vain attempt to prolong their unmitigated suffering. At Otorvonovkaa, what remained of a divisional medical unit, two doctors and six medics, sawed, hacked, and cut gangrenous flesh and rotten limbs from depraved and dissolute human wrecks during their 48-hour shifts. There was no more room for the stream of wounded which kept coming in from all sectors of the battered, shrinking front. No more anesthesia, no more bandages, no more medicines. German field doctors humanely ordered the most seriously wounded cases to be placed outside in exposed areas where they might slowly and painlessly freeze to death. There was no food whatsoever. Field rations were unavailable. The troops had had nothing for days. When rations arrived every man was doled his slice and a half of hardtack, seven peas, and a sliver of horse meat of the last animal in the unit's supply train. . . .

Army Headquarters was unaware of this and the flexibility of the front; Berlin was oblivious to it. The orders were to dig in. The orders were obeyed. Infantrymen, with frostbitten feet wrapped in rags, and frostbitten ears and noses, hacked away with frostbitten fingers at the soil of the steppe, frozen solid as marble, until their hands bled. The Russian attack came. Positions were overrun. A mad, insane rush by any means available toward Stalingrad took place. . . . Why Stalingrad? There was no other place to go. . . .

Thus, on 8 January two Soviet emissaries were sent to the German lines with a surrender ultimatum. They were met by fire. On the 9th, Russian planes dropped leaflets on the German lines. The Russian representatives attempted again on the 10th to make liaison with the German commander von Paulus. They failed; von Paulus would not see them. The Fuehrer had ordered it. The text of the ultimatum, for history's sake, should be included as part of the story of the struggle.

ULTIMATUM. To Colonel General von Paulus, commander of the German 6th Army, or his assistant, and to all the officers and men of the German forces surrounded at Stalingrad: The German 6th Army, formations of the 4th Tank Army and units sent to them as reinforcements have been completely surrounded since November 23, 1942.

The Red Army forces have surrounded this grouping of German troops in a solid ring. All hopes that your troops might be saved by a German offensive from the south and southwest have collapsed; the German troops rushed to your assistance have been routed by the Red Army and their remnants are now retreating towards Rostov.

Owing to the successful, swift advance of the Red Army, the German air transport force which kept you supplied with starvation rations of food, ammunition, and fuel is being compelled to shift its bases frequently and to fly long distances to reach you. Moreover, the German air transport force is suffering tremendous losses in planes and crews at the hands of the Russian air force. Its help to the surrounded forces is becoming ineffective.

Your surrounded troops are in a grave position. They are suffering from hunger, disease, and cold. The severe Russian winter is only beginning. The hard frosts, cold winds, and blizzards are still to come, and your soldiers are not protected by warm uniforms and live in extremely unhygienic conditions.

You, as the commander, and all the officers of the surrounded troops, must fully realize that you have no possibility of breaking through the ring that surrounds you. Your position is hopeless and further resistance is useless.

In view of the hopeless position in which you are placed, and in order to avoid unnecessary bloodshed, we offer you the following terms of capitulation:

All the surrounded German forces under the command of yourself and your staff are to cease hostilities.

All the troops, arms, equipment and war supplies are to be turned over to us by you in an organized manner and in good condition.

We guarantee life and safety to all officers and soldiers who cease hostilities and upon termination of the war their return to Germany or to any country to which the prisoners of war may choose to go.

All troops who surrender will retain their uniforms, insignia and orders, personal belongings, valuables and in the case of higher officers, their side-arms.

All officers, non-commissioned officers and soldiers who surrender will be provided normal food.

All wounded, sick and those suffering from frostbite will be given medical treatment.

Your reply is expected by 10 a.m. Moscow time on January 9, 1943 in written form, to be delivered by your personal representative who is to travel by passenger car, flying a white flag, along the road from Konny siding to the station of Kotluban. Your representative will be met by authorized Russian commanders in the district of B, one-half kilometer southeast of siding 564 at 10 a.m. on January 9, 1943.

In the event that you reject our proposal for capitulation, we warn you that the Red Army troops and the Red Air Force will be compelled to take steps to wipe out the surrounded German troops and that you will be responsible for their annihilation.

> COLONEL GENERAL OF ARTILLERY VORONOV—representative of the general headquarters of supreme command of the Red Army.
> LIEUTENANT GENERAL ROKOSSOVSKY—commander of troops of the Don Front.

The ultimatum rejected, Rokossovsky struck. It was 10 January, 1943, exactly six months to the day after the Germans had launched their original offensive. The attack came from the west and smashed into the German positions as a scalpel into a pus-filled ulcer. . . .

On 14 January the Russians launched another attack from the south. This was the blow that completely broke the Germans' back. The two columns, one from the south and one from the west, met and drove the Germans into the twisted wreckage of the city itself. . . .

Von Paulus and the southern group of defenders capitulated on 1 February, 1943. The northern group surrendered the next day. The siege was over. The battle for Stalingrad had been fought and lost. It culminated in the most staggering defeat of German arms since the defeat of the Teutonic Knights. The German Sixth Army had been annihilated. Of the 330,000 troops who were under von Paulus' command in September only some 90,000 survived.

One reason for the success of the Russians in turning back the German invaders is to be found in the large-scale aid received from the United States. By this time the American economy had been converted from a peace to a war basis, and the flood of military materials was so great that it not only bolstered the Soviet Union, but also made possible the invasion of the Continent on D-day, as well as the trouncing of the Japanese in the Pacific. The following report of a congressional investigating committee headed by Harry S. Truman, then senator, reveals the magnitude of American war production.*

War production is now firmly established on a successful working basis. Our armies are active on every fighting front, equipped with American-made weapons and secure in the knowledge that an uninterrupted flow of materials is assured. In contrast to the First World War, in which our own troops abroad obtained from our allies many of the most important items of equipment, including substantially all of their artillery and aircraft, we are supplying in this war substantially all of our own needs and an important portion of the needs of all of the other United Nations. . . .

Industry, labor, and Government deserve credit for the job of providing war matériel of excellent quality and quantity worthy of the use which the fighting forces are giving it.

The figures on production have properly been made public. In addition to guns, tanks, and regular equipment and clothing of all sorts for more than 10,000,000 men, we produced in 1941, 1942, and 1943, 153,061 airplanes, 746 combatant naval vessels, 1,899 Liberty ships with a total deadweight capacity of 20,450,800 tons, 702 commercial ships of other types, 1,567,940 military trucks, and 28,286 subsidiary naval vessels, including 23,867 landing craft.

We have constructed housing and training facilities for more than 10,000,000 men, and airfields and bases in all quarters of the world.

We have constructed nearly 20 billion dollars worth of the best and most modern plant facilities in the world equipped with the finest machine tools that can be designed. These plants are producing vast quantities of new materials, such as butadiene, synthetic rubber, and 100-octane gasoline, and have greatly increased our former capacity to produce basic commodities such as alloy steels, aluminum and magnesium. With them we can make fabulous quantities of engines, gears, turbines, valves, bearings and all the other articles necessary for mass production of the most complicated engines of destruction that man can devise.

To make all this possible our workers engaged in manufacturing, mining, and agriculture contributed nearly 45 percent more man-days of work in 1943 than in 1939, despite the fact that more than 10,000,000 men were withdrawn from the labor pool for the armed forces. In manufacturing alone, our workmen contributed 89.6 percent more man-days in 1943 than in 1939.

This astounding performance exceeds anything of its kind ever achieved in the history of the world. The results obtained are the best answer to the critics

* *Senate Reports,* 78th Congress, 2nd session, No. 10, Pt. 16 (1944), pp. 2-4.

of the home front. They do not indicate perfection, but they do evidence accomplishment of a high order.

All Americans who have participated can be justly proud, because the success is due to the accumulated efforts of the millions of people who have each done their share rather than to any miraculous planning of a few experts at the top. Women in particular deserve credit for filling the huge gap created by manpower requirements of the armed services. Older men who had retired from active work have returned to their jobs and because of their experience are among the most valuable of workers. The job that has been done not only assures that victory will be won, but it assures that it will be won more quickly and with fewer casualties. Our armed forces have more and better equipment than our foes.

D-DAY 165

Throughout 1942 and 1943, the Russians had been clamoring for the opening of a second front in France that would relieve them of the full weight of the German attack. Finally, the Anglo-American preparations for the greatest amphibious operation in history ended on D-Day, June 6, 1944. Prime Minister Churchill kept Marshal Stalin informed of the course of the operations; the following exchange of letters between the two men is as revealing of the close relations existing between them at the time as it is of the campaign itself.

6 June 44

PRIME MINISTER TO MARSHAL STALIN. Everything has started well. The mines, obstacles and land batteries have been largely overcome. The air landings were very successful, and on a large scale. Infantry landings are proceeding rapidly, and many tanks and self-propelled guns are already ashore. Weather outlook moderate to good.

His answer was prompt, and contained welcome news of the highest importance.

6 June 44

I have received your communication about the success of the beginning of the "Overlord" operations. It gives joy to us all and hope of further successes.

The summer offensive of the Soviet forces, organised in accordance with the agreement at the Teheran Conference, will begin towards the middle of June on one of the important sectors of the front. The general offensive of the Soviet forces will develop by stages by means of the successive bringing of armies into offensive operations. At the end of June and during July offensive operations will become a general offensive of the Soviet forces.

I shall not fail to inform you in due course of the progress of the offensive operations.

* Winston S. Churchill, *The Second World War: Triumph and Tragedy* (Boston: Houghton, 1953), pp. 6-9. Copyright 1953 by Houghton Mifflin Company. Reprinted by permission of the publisher.

I was actually sending Stalin a fuller account of our progress when his telegram arrived.

7 June 44

PRIME MINISTER TO MARSHAL STALIN.   I am well satisfied with the situation up to noon today, 7th. Only at one American beach has there been serious difficulty, and that has now been cleared up. Twenty thousand airborne troops are safely landed behind the flanks of the enemy's lines, and have made contact in each case with the American and British seaborne forces. We got across with small losses. We had expected to lose about 10,000 men. By tonight we hope to have the best part of a quarter of a million men ashore, including a considerable quantity of armour (tanks), all landed from special ships or swimming ashore by themselves. In this latter class of tanks there have been a good many casualties, especially on the American front, owing to the waves overturning the swimming tanks. We must now expect heavy counter-attacks, but we expect to be stronger in armour, and of course overwhelming in the air whenever the clouds lift.

2. There was a tank engagement of our newly landed armour with fifty enemy tanks of the 21st Panzer-Grenadier Division late last night towards Caen, as the result of which the enemy quitted the field. The British 7th Armoured Division is now going in, and should give us superiority for a few days. The question is, how many can they bring against us in the next week? The weather outlook in the Channel does not seem to impose any prohibition on our continued landings. Indeed, it seems more promising than before. All the commanders are satisfied that in the actual landing things have gone better than we expected.

3. Most especially secret. We are planning to construct very quickly two large synthetic harbours on the beaches of this wide, sandy bay of the Seine estuary. Nothing like these has ever been seen before. Great ocean liners will be able to discharge and run by numerous piers supplies to the fighting troops. This must be quite unexpected by the enemy, and will enable the build-up to proceed with very great independence of weather conditions. We hope to get Cherbourg at an early point in the operations.

4. On the other hand, the enemy will concentrate rapidly and heavily and the fighting will be continuous and increasing in scale. Still, we hope to have by D plus 30 about twenty-five divisions deployed, with all their corps troops, with both flanks of the second front resting on the sea and possessed of at least three good harbours—Cherbourg and the two synthetic harbours. This front will be constantly nourished and expanded, and we hope to include later the Brest peninsula. But all this waits on the hazards of war, which, Marshal Stalin, you know so well.

5. We hope that this successful landing and the victory of Rome, of which the fruits have still to be gathered from the cut-off Hun divisions, will cheer your valiant soldiers after all the weight they have had to bear, which no one outside your country has felt more definitely than I.

6. Since dictating the above I have received your message about the successful beginning of "Overlord," in which you speak of the summer offensive of the Soviet forces. I thank you cordially for this. I hope you will observe that we have never asked you a single question, because of our full confidence in you, your nation, and your armies.

Stalin replied:

MARSHAL STALIN TO PRIME MINISTER.   I have received your message of June 7 with the information of the successful development of the operation "Overlord." We all greet you and the valiant British and American armies and warmly wish you further successes.

The preparation of the summer offensive of the Soviet armies is concluding. Tomorrow, June 10, the first stage will open in our summer offensive on the Leningrad front.

I repeated this at once to Roosevelt.
Stalin telegraphed again on June 11:

As is evident, the landing, conceived on a grandiose scale, has succeeded completely. My colleagues and I cannot but admit that the history of warfare knows no other like undertaking from the point of view of its scale, its vast conception, and its masterly execution. As is well known, Napoleon in his time failed ignominiously in his plan to force the Channel. The hysterical Hitler, who boasted for two years that he would effect a forcing of the Channel, was unable to make up his mind even to hint at attempting to carry out his threat. Only our Allies have succeeded in realising with honour the grandiose plan of the forcing of the Channel. History will record this deed as an achievement of the highest order.

OKINAWA **166**

At the same time that Russia and the western powers were defeating the Axis in Europe, the United States was steadily regaining the Pacific islands that had fallen to Japan in the early months of the war. The closer the fighting came to the Japanese home islands, the more fanatic became the resistance of the defending garrisons. The island of Okinawa, only 350 miles from Tokyo, was taken in June, 1944 after a savage struggle, described in the following selection by a New York Times *correspondent.**

Day after day and night after night, there were alerts unending; for more than 40 continuous days—until foul weather brought a brief but blessed break —there were air raids every night and every day. Sleep became a long-forgotten thing; yearned for, dreamed about; heads drooped over gunsights; nerves frazzled, tempers snapped; skippers were red-eyed and haggard. Tension was palpable, tangible; never before had the Navy experienced so many cases of combat fatigue. . . .

* Hanson W. Baldwin, "Okinawa: Victory at the Threshold," *Marine Corps Gazette* (January, 1951), pp. 44-49. Reprinted by permission of the copyright holder, the Marine Corps Association, publishers of the Marine Corps Gazette, professional journal for Marine Officers. Copyright © January, 1951 by Marine Corps Association.

That saving American trait—a sense of humor—kept some from the brink of horror. On one picket station a tiny gunboat, its crew fed up with constant attacks, near misses, suiciders and close brushes with death, rigged up a huge sign with a pointing arrow: "To Jap pilot—This Way to Task Force 58."

"After a couple of months of action," recorded Lt. Stuart D. Cowan, Jr., USNR, "you can guess pretty well what kind of a night it will be. Sometimes you take off only your shoes and flop down in dirty, sweaty khakis. If it looks quiet, you sleep in your shorts—nobody ever wears pajamas. The searing heat makes you break out with heat rash all over your body and sweat soaks the sheets. . . . The pounding of the main battery on a tin can (destroyer) makes living extremely uncomfortable. Fiber glass particles, from the insulation material, sift down like fine snow and fill your bunk—you feel as if you'd been sleeping on needles—and your arms and legs break out with red splotches. The damn stuff gets in your clothes, hair and eyes. Cork and dirt are blown out of the ventilating system into your food, dishes are smashed, pipes break, rivets pop out; fixtures dangle drunkenly, and the ship shudders from stem to stern each time the guns fire."

Ashore, the bloody, slogging progress inches into the Shuri Line, but the Japs' defenses are still intact, and on 22 May, the commanding general of the III Amphibious Corps reports that the Marines are encountering the most effective artillery fire yet encountered in the Pacific. The "plum rains" of Okinawa come in a deluge in late May; fields become swamps, tanks are mired, mud is king; ammunition and fuel are moved to the front in amphibious vehicles. From 22 to 29 May, the enemy line holds "with hardly a dent against every attack."

Back in the rear areas, the gyrenes (nickname for Marines), huddled in the dripping tents, raised their cans of beer, and let forth with the famous MacArthur parodies:

> "Now the greatest of generals is Douglas, the proud,
> Writer of fine flowing prose
> He paces the floor as his orders ring out
> Down through his aquiline nose. . . .
> With the help of God
> And a few Marines
> MacArthur retook the Philippines. . . ."

Afloat, as ashore, the "no-quarter" fight goes on. Enemy submarines, midget submarines, and suicide boats join the Kamikaze planes in harassment of the fleet. Submarine contacts are reported on May 18, 20, 22, 24, 25, 26, 27, and 28. . . .

The Japs try a new twist. They bomb the American airstrips ashore at Yontan and Kadena, and then follow up with an airborne landing. Five bombers try to make it; four are shot down in the air; the fifth makes a wheels-up belly landing on a Yontan runway and 10 or 11 Japs jump out and commence to shoot up the neighborhood. Before their riddled bodies line the strip they have destroyed seven American planes, damaged 26 others, ignited 70,000 gallons of gasoline and in general raised "pluperfect hell." In the darkness and the melee wild-shooting Americans kill and wound some of their own people. . . .

The battle for Okinawa can be described only in the grim superlatives of war. Churchill correctly characterized it as among "the most intense and famous of military history." . . .

It was a no-quarter struggle, fought on, under, and over the sea and land. ... More than 110,000 Japanese died, 12,281 Americans were killed; more than 36,000 wounded.

More significant than any other episode in World War II was the dropping of an atomic bomb by the United States on the Japanese city of Hiroshima, a fateful event that began a new era in the history of warfare and of mankind. On August 15, 1945, five days after Japan sued for peace, President Truman ordered a study of the effects of all types of air attack that had been used against Japan. The study was made by the United States Strategic Bombing Survey, and the following selection is taken from its report concerning the Hiroshima bombing.*

A single atomic bomb, the first weapon of its type ever used against a target, exploded over the city of Hiroshima at 0815 on the morning of 6 August, 1945. Most of the industrial workers had already reported to work, but many workers were enroute and nearly all the school children and some industrial employees were at work in the open on the program of building removal to provide fire-breaks and disperse valuables to the country. The attack came 45 minutes after the "all clear" had been sounded from a previous alert. Because of the lack of warning and the populace's indifference to small groups of planes, the explosion came as an almost complete surprise, and the people had not taken shelter. Many were caught in the open, and most of the rest in flimsily constructed homes or commercial establishments.

The bomb exploded slightly northwest of the center of the city. Because of this accuracy and the flat terrain and circular shape of the city, Hiroshima was uniformly and extensively devastated. Practically the entire densely or moderately built-up portion of the city was leveled by blast and swept by fire. ...

The surprise, the collapse of many buildings, and the conflagration contributed to an unprecedented casualty rate. Seventy to eighty thousand people were killed, or missing and presumed dead, and an equal number were injured. The magnitude of casualties is set in relief by a comparison with the Tokyo fire raid of 9-10 March, 1945, in which, though nearly 16 square miles were destroyed, the number killed was no larger, and fewer people were injured. ...

When the atomic bomb exploded, an intense flash was observed first, as though a large amount of magnesium had been ignited, and the scene grew hazy with white smoke. At the same time at the center of the explosion, and a short while later in other areas, a tremendous roaring sound was heard and a crushing blast wave and intense heat were felt. The people, even those who lived on the outer edge of the blast, all felt as though they had sustained a direct hit,

---

* The United States Strategic Bombing Survey, *The Effects of the Atomic Bombs on Hiroshima and Nagasaki* (Washington, D.C.: Government Printing Office, 1946), pp. 3-5, 8-9.

and the whole city suffered damage such as would have resulted from direct hits everywhere by ordinary bombs. . . .

The impact of the atomic bomb [on Hiroshima] shattered the normal fabric of community life and disrupted the organizations for handling the disaster. In the 30 percent of the population killed and the additional 30 percent seriously injured were included corresponding proportions of the civic authorities and rescue groups. A mass flight from the city took place, as persons sought safety from the conflagration and a place for shelter and food. . . .

By 1 November, the population of Hiroshima was back to 137,000. The city required complete rebuilding. The entire heart, the main administrative and commercial as well as residential section was gone. In this area only about 50 buildings, all of reinforced concrete, remained standing. All of these suffered blast damage and all save about a dozen were almost completely gutted by fire; only 5 could be used without major repairs. . . .

Such a shattering event could not fail to have its impact on people's ways of thinking. . . .

Typical comments of survivors were:

"If the enemy has this type of bomb, everyone is going to die, and we wish the war would hurry and finish."

"I did not expect that it was that powerful. I thought we have no defense against such a bomb."

"One of my children was killed by it, and I didn't care what happened after that."

Other reactions were found. In view of their experiences, it is not remarkable that some of the survivors (nearly one-fifth) hated the Americans for using the bomb or expressed their anger in such terms as "cruel," "inhuman," and "barbarous."

". . . they really despise the Americans for it, the people all say that if there are such things as ghosts, why don't they haunt the Americans? . . ."

"After the atomic bomb exploded, I felt that now I must go to work in a munitions plant. . . . My sons told me that they wouldn't forget the atomic bomb even when they grow up."

The reaction of hate and anger is not surprising, and it is likely that in fact it was a more extensive sentiment than the figures indicate, since unquestionably many respondents, out of fear or politeness, did not reveal their sentiments with complete candor.

Chapter Twenty-six

Grand alliance to cold war

ROOTS OF THE GRAND ALLIANCE **168**

The Grand Alliance against the Axis powers developed more out of force of circumstances than because of ideological affinities. Britain had been left alone to face the Axis following the collapse of France, and in June, 1941, was joined by the Soviet Union following Hitler's attack on that country. In December, 1941, after the attack on Pearl Harbor, the United States also joined the ranks. The following speech broadcast by Prime Minister Churchill on the very day of the German invasion of Russia reveals the pragmatic basis of the Grand Alliance.*

The Nazi regime is indistinguishable from the worst features of Communism. It is devoid of all theme and principle except appetite and racial domination. It excels all forms of human wickedness in the efficiency of its cruelty and ferocious aggression. No one has been a more consistent opponent of Communism than I have for the last twenty-five years. I will unsay no word that I have spoken about it. But all this fades away before the spectacle which is now unfolding. The past, with its crime, its follies, and its tragedies, flashes away. I see the Russian soldiers standing on the threshold of their native land, guarding the fields which their fathers have tilled from time immemorial. I see them guarding their homes where mothers and wives pray —ah, yes, for there are times when all pray—for the safety of their loved ones, the return of the bread-winner, of their champion, of their protector. I see the ten thousand villages of Russia where the means of existence is wrung so hardly from the soil, but where there are still primordial human joys, where maidens laugh and children play. I see

---

* Winston S. Churchill, *The Second World War: The Grand Alliance* (Boston: Houghton, 1950), pp. 371-73. Copyright 1950 by Houghton Mifflin Company. Reprinted by permission.

advancing upon all this in hideous onslaught the Nazi war machine, with its clanking, heel-clicking, dandified Prussian officers, its crafty expert agents fresh from the cowing and tying-down of a dozen countries. I see also the dull, drilled, docile, brutish masses of the Hun soldiery plodding on like a swarm of crawling locusts. I see the German bombers and fighters in the sky, still smarting from many a British whipping, delighted to find what they believe is an easier and a safer prey.

Behind all this glare, behind all this storm, I see that small group of villainous men who plan, organise, and launch this cataract of horrors upon mankind. . . .

I have to declare the decision of His Majesty's Government—and I feel sure it is a decision in which the great Dominions will in due course concur—for we must speak out now at once, without a day's delay. I have to make the declaration, but can you doubt what our policy will be? We have but one aim and one single, irrevocable purpose. We are resolved to destroy Hitler and every vestige of the Nazi regime. From this nothing will turn us—nothing. We will never parley, we will never negotiate with Hitler or any of his gang. We shall fight him by land, we shall fight him by sea, we shall fight him in the air, until, with God's help, we have rid the earth of his shadow and liberated its peoples from his yoke. Any man or state who fights on against Nazidom will have our aid. Any man or state who marches with Hitler is our foe. . . . That is our policy and that is our declaration. It follows, therefore, that we shall give whatever help we can to Russia and the Russian people. We shall appeal to all our friends and allies in every part of the world to take the same course and pursue it, as we shall faithfully and steadfastly to the end. . . .

This is no class war, but a war in which the whole British Empire and Commonwealth of Nations is engaged, without distinction of race, creed, or party. It is not for me to speak of the action of the United States, but this I will say, if Hitler imagines that his attack on Soviet Russia will cause the slightest divergence of aims or slackening of effort in the great democracies who are resolved upon his doom, he is woefully mistaken. On the contrary, we shall be fortified and encouraged in our efforts to rescue mankind from his tyranny. We shall be strengthened and not weakened in determination and in resources.

This is no time to moralise on the follies of countries and Governments which have allowed themselves to be struck down one by one, when by united action they could have saved themselves and saved the world from this catastrophe. But when I spoke a few minutes ago of Hitler's blood-lust and the hateful appetites which have impelled or lured him on his Russian adventure, I said there was one deeper motive behind his outrage. He wished to destroy the Russian power because he hopes that if he succeeds in this he will be able to bring back the main strength of his army and air force from the East and hurl it upon this island, which he knows he must conquer or suffer the penalty of his crimes. His invasion of Russia is no more than a prelude to an attempted invasion of the British Isles. He hopes, no doubt, that all this may be accomplished before the winter comes, and that he can overwhelm Great Britain before the Fleet and air power of the United States may intervene. He hopes that he may once again repeat, upon a greater scale than ever before, that process of destroying his enemies one by one by which he has so long thrived and prospered, and that then the scene will be clear for the final act, without which all his conquests would be in vain—namely, the subjugation of the Western Hemisphere to his will and to his system.

The Russian danger is, therefore, our danger, and the danger of the United States, just as the cause of any Russian fighting for his hearth and home is the cause of free men and free peoples in every quarter of the globe. Let us learn the lessons already taught by such cruel experience. Let us redouble our exertions, and strike with united strength while life and power remain.

CHURCHILL AND STALIN DIVIDE THE BALKANS 169

One of the most striking examples of British–Russian cooperation during World War II occurred when Churchill and Stalin met in Moscow in October, 1944. As the Red army advanced into the Danube Valley, the Germans began to evacuate the Balkans, raising the question of how the resulting vacuum was to be filled. The following account by Churchill describes the agreement he reached with Stalin.*

The moment was apt for business, so I said, "Let us settle about our affairs in the Balkans. Your armies are in Rumania and Bulgaria. We have interests, missions and agents there. Don't let us get at cross-purposes in small ways. So far as Britain and Russia are concerned, how would it do for you to have ninety percent predominance in Rumania, for us to have ninety percent of the say in Greece, and go fifty-fifty about Yugoslavia?" While this was being translated I wrote out on a half-sheet of paper:

Rumania	
Russia	90%
The others	10%
Greece	
Great Britain	90%
(in accord with U.S.A.)	
Russia	10%
Yugoslavia	50-50%
Hungary	50-50%
Bulgaria	
Russia	75%
The others	25%

I pushed this across to Stalin, who had by then heard the translation. There was a slight pause. Then he took his blue pencil and made a large tick upon it, and passed it back to us. It was all settled in no more time than it takes to set down. . . .

After this there was a long silence. The pencilled paper lay in the centre of the table. At length I said, "Might it not be thought rather cynical if it seemed we had disposed of these issues, so fateful to millions of people, in such an offhand manner? Let us burn the paper." "No, you keep it," said Stalin.

---

* Winston S. Churchill, *The Second World War: Triumph and Tragedy* (Boston: Houghton, 1953), p. 227. Copyright 1953 by Houghton Mifflin Company. Reprinted by permission.

In February, 1945, as the war was drawing to a close, Roosevelt, Churchill, and Stalin attended a conference at Yalta. It represented the first substantial attempt to deal with specific postwar issues. At the time, the agreements reached were hailed in both the United States and abroad as "a great hope to the world" (Herbert Hoover) and as "one of the most important steps ever taken to promote peace and happiness in the world" (Senator Barkley). With the onset of the Cold War, a popular opinion changed, and Yalta was widely criticized and even branded as a "sellout" and a "Munich." W. Averell Harriman, who was present at the secret talks as American ambassador to Russia, gave the following interpretation in 1951 to the Committees on Armed Services and Foreign Relations of the Senate.*

I am submitting this statement for use in connection with the hearings on the Far Eastern situation. My objective is to clarify the confusion that has arisen regarding the understandings reached at Yalta by President Roosevelt and Prime Minister Churchill with Premier Stalin.

Much has been said and written about Yalta and its effect on the postwar course of events. Some people have shown a lack of understanding of our objectives in the conduct of the war and our efforts during the war to lay a foundation for a peaceful postwar world. Others appear to have profited from hindsight. Still others—for reasons best known to themselves—have distorted and perverted the facts to a point where their statements have little or no basis in reality. As a result, a myth has grown up that what President Roosevelt and Prime Minister Churchill did at Yalta has led to our postwar difficulties with the Soviet Union. This myth is without foundation in fact. . . .

President Roosevelt and Prime Minister Churchill met with Stalin at Yalta in early February 1945. The question of Roosevelt's physical condition at the time of Yalta has been the subject of considerable discussion. Unquestionably, he was not in good health and the long conferences tired him. Nevertheless, for many months he had given much thought to the matters to be discussed and, in consultation with many officials of the Government, he had blocked out definite objectives which he had clearly in mind. He came to Yalta determined to do his utmost to achieve these objectives and he carried on the negotiations to this end with his usual skill and perception.

The discussions at Yalta covered a wide range of topics, including final plans for the defeat of Hitler, the occupation and control of Germany, reparations, the United Nations Conference to meet at San Francisco on April 25th, the restoration of sovereign rights and self-government to the liberated peoples of Europe, and the establishment of a free, independent, and democratic Poland through the holding of free and unfettered elections. By the Declaration on Liberated Europe, Roosevelt and Churchill obtained the pledge of Stalin for joint action to secure the fundamental freedoms for the people in territories overrun by the Red Army. . . .

Had Stalin honored these commitments taken at Yalta, Eastern Europe

---

* *Hearings on the Military Situation in the Far East,* U.S. Senate, 82nd Congress, 1st session (1951), pp. 3328ff.

would be free today and the United Nations would be a truly effective organization for world security.

The last understanding to be reached was that relating to the Far East. The crucial issue was not whether the Soviet Union would enter the Pacific War, but whether it would do so in time to be of help in the carrying out of the plans of the Joint Chiefs of Staff for an invasion of the Japanese home islands. The great danger existed that the Soviet Union would stand by until we had brought Japan to her knees at great cost in American lives, and then the Red Army could march into Manchuria and large areas of Northern China. It would then have been a simple matter for the Soviets to give expression to "popular demand" by establishing People's Republics of Manchuria and Inner Mongolia. President Roosevelt sought to reduce the general assurances which Stalin had previously given to specific undertakings for the early entry of Russia in the Pacific War, to limit Soviet expansion in the East and to gain Soviet support for the Nationalist Government of China.

It should be recalled that it was only on the second day of the Yalta Confernece that General MacArthur entered Manila. The bloody battles of Iwo Jima and Okinawa still lay ahead. It was not until more than five months later that the first and only experimental explosion of the atomic bomb was successfully concluded at Alamogordo. The military authorities estimated that it would take 18 months after the surrender of Germany to defeat Japan, and that Soviet participation would greatly reduce the heavy American casualties which could otherwise be expected. The Joint Chiefs of Staff were planning an invasion of the Japanese home islands, and were anxious for the early entry of Russia in the war to defeat the Japanese Kwantung Army in Manchuria and in order that our bombers could operate from bases in Eastern Siberia. . . .

President Roosevelt felt that he had achieved his principal objectives. He had obtained the agreement of the Soviet Union to enter the war against Japan within three months after the defeat of Germany. This was the period required to move Soviet troops from the European front to Siberia. It was considered to be in good time, and conformed to the plans of the Joint Chiefs of Staff which involved the redeployment of our forces from Europe to the Pacific. Roosevelt had also obtained Stalin's pledge of support for Chiang Kai-shek and recognition of the sovereignty of the Chinese National Government over Manchuria.

In recent years several objections have been leveled at the terms of the Yalta understanding on the Far East and the circumstances under which it was concluded.

It has been asserted that the understanding was a mistake because, as it turned out, Russian participation had no influence on the defeat of Japan. To President Roosevelt at Yalta, the lives of American fighting men were at stake. He had been advised by the Joint Chiefs of Staff that the defeat of Japan would take many months after VE-day and that if the Soviet Union came in soon enough countless American lives would be saved. Furthermore, up to that time, Stalin had carried out vital military undertakings. Roosevelt, therefore, considered that a definite commitment from Stalin was of supreme importance and would be of great value.

Another criticism is that Chiang Kai-shek was not consulted before the understanding was signed and that the understanding was kept secret. The question of consulting Chiang was a difficult one. Secrecy was a military necessity. Experience had shown that whatever was known in Chungking got to the Japanese. Stalin was unwilling to risk Japanese knowledge of his plans until he had been able to strengthen his forces in Siberia. . . .

Some people claim that we "sold out" to the Soviet Union at Yalta. If this were true, it is difficult to understand why the Soviet Union has gone to such lengths to violate the Yalta understandings. The fact is that these violations have been the basis of our protests against Soviet actions since the end of the war. There would have been a sell-out if Roosevelt and Churchill had failed to bend every effort to come to an understanding with the Soviet Union and had permitted the Red Army to occupy vast areas, without attempting to protect the interests of people in those areas.

Only by keeping our military forces in being after Germany and Japan surrendered could we have attempted to compel the Soviet Union to withdraw from the territory which it controlled and to live up to its commitments. The people of the United States and the war-weary people of Europe were in no mood to support such an undertaking. This country certainly erred in its rapid demobilization in 1945, but this is an error for which the entire American people must share the responsibility. I cannot believe that anyone seriously thinks that the move to bring the boys home could have been stopped. I still recall my grave concern when I was in Moscow at the cold reception the Congress gave to President Truman's recommendation for universal military training in the fall of 1945.

The most difficult question to answer is why Stalin took so many commitments which he subsequently failed to honor. There can be no clear answer to this question. I believe that the Kremlin had two approaches to their postwar policies, and in my many talks with Stalin I felt that he himself was of two minds. One approach emphasized reconstruction and development of Russia, and the other external expansion. . . .

The Kremlin chose the second course. It is my belief that Stalin was influenced by the hostile attitude of the peoples of Eastern Europe toward the Red Army, and that he recognized that governments established by free elections would not be "friendly" to the Soviet Union. In addition, I believe he became increasingly aware of the great opportunities for Soviet expansion in the postwar economic chaos. After our rapid demobilization, I do not think that he conceived that the United States would take the firm stand against Soviet aggression that we have taken in the past five years.

171 APPROACH OF THE COLD WAR

As soon as the fighting ended in Europe, the latent differences within the Grand Alliance began to come to the fore. In place of democratically elected governments in Eastern Europe, as provided for at Yalta, there appeared the "people's democracies," thinly disguised instruments of Soviet control. More serious was the clash among the Allies over the treatment of Germany. One of the first to warn the West publicly of the nature and significance of the growing East–West rift was Churchill, who did so in a famous speech at Westminster College in Fulton, Missouri, on March 5, 1946, from which the following portion is taken.*

A shadow has fallen upon the scenes so lately lighted by the Allied victory. Nobody knows what Soviet Russia and its Communist international organisation intends to do in the immediate future, or what are the limits, if any, to their expansive and proselytising tendencies. I have a strong admiration and regard for the valiant Russian people and for my wartime comrade, Marshal Stalin. There is deep sympathy and goodwill in Britain—and I doubt not here also—towards the peoples of all the Russias and a resolve to persevere through many differences and rebuffs in establishing lasting friendships. We understand the Russian need to be secure on her western frontiers by the removal of all possibility of German aggression. We welcome Russia to her rightful place among the leading nations of the world. We welcome her flag upon the seas. Above all, we welcome constant, frequent and growing contacts between the Russian people and our own people on both sides of the Atlantic. It is my duty however, for I am sure you would wish me to state the facts as I see them to you, to place before you certain facts about the present position in Europe.

From Stettin in the Baltic to Trieste in the Adriatic, an iron curtain has descended across the Continent. Behind that line lie all the capitals of the ancient states of Central and Eastern Europe. Warsaw, Berlin, Prague, Vienna, Budapest, Belgrade, Bucharest and Sofia, all these famous cities and the populations around them lie in what I must call the Soviet sphere, and all are subject in one form or another, not only to Soviet influence but to a very high and, in many cases, increasing measure of control from Moscow. Athens alone—Greece with its immortal glories—is free to decide its future at an election under British, American and French observation. The Russian-dominated Polish Government has been encouraged to make enormous and wrongful inroads from Germany, and mass expulsions of millions of Germans on a scale grievous and undreamed-of are now taking place. The Communist parties, which were very small in all these Eastern States of Europe, have been raised to preeminence and power far beyond their numbers and are seeking everywhere to obtain totalitarian control. Police governments are prevailing in nearly every case, and so far, except in Czechoslovakia, there is no true democracy.

Turkey and Persia are both profoundly alarmed and disturbed at the claims which are being made upon them and at the pressure being exerted by the Moscow Government. An attempt is being made by the Russians in Berlin to build up a quasi-Communist party in their zone of Occupied Germany by showing special favours to groups of left-wing German leaders. At the end of the fighting last June, the American and British Armies withdrew westwards, in accordance with an earlier agreement, to a depth at some points of 150 miles upon a front of nearly four hundred miles, in order to allow our Russian allies to occupy this vast expanse of territory which the Western Democracies had conquered.

If now the Soviet Government tries, by separate action, to build up a pro-Communist Germany in their areas, this will cause new serious difficulties in the British and American zones, and will give the defeated Germans the power of putting themselves up to auction between the Soviets and the Western Democracies. Whatever conclusions may be drawn from these facts—and facts they are—this is certainly not the Liberated Europe we fought to build up. Nor is it one which contains the essentials of permanent peace. . . .

These are sombre facts for anyone to have to recite on the morrow of a victory gained by so much splendid comradeship in arms and in the cause of freedom and democracy; but we should be most unwise not to face them squarely while time remains. . . .

On the other hand I repulse the idea that a new war is inevitable; still more that it is imminent. It is because I am sure that our fortunes are still in our own hands and that we hold the power to save the future, that I feel the duty to speak out now that I have the occasion and the opportunity to do so. I do not believe that Soviet Russia desires war. What they desire is the fruits of war and the indefinite expansion of their power and doctrines. . . .

If the Western Democracies stand together in strict adherence to the principles of the United Nations Charter, their influence for furthering those principles will be immense and no one is likely to molest them. If however they become divided or falter in their duty and if these all-important years are allowed to slip away then indeed catastrophe may overwhelm us all.

172 TRUMAN DOCTRINE

The most dramatic official recognition of the Cold War described by Churchill was President Truman's intervention in the Greek civil war. Communist-led guerrillas were threatening the existence of the British-supported government in Athens. When London decided that it no longer could afford the cost of bolstering the Athens regime, President Truman enunciated (March 12, 1947) the principles that subsequently became known as the Truman Doctrine.*

The gravity of the situation which confronts the world today necessitates my appearance before a joint session of the Congress.

The foreign policy and the national security of this country are involved. One aspect of the present situation, which I wish to present to you at this time for your consideration and decision, concerns Greece and Turkey. . . .

The very existence of the Greek state is today threatened by the terrorist activities of several thousand armed men, led by Communists, who defy the Government's authority at a number of points, particularly along the northern boundaries. A commission appointed by the United Nations Security Council is at present investigating disturbed conditions in northern Greece and alleged border violations along the frontier between Greece on the one hand and Albania, Bulgaria, and Yugoslavia on the other.

Meanwhile, the Greek Government is unable to cope with the situation. The Greek Army is small and poorly equipped. It needs supplies and equipment if it is to restore the authority of the Government throughout Greek territory.

Greece must have assistance if it is to become a self-supporting and self-respecting democracy.

The United States must supply this assistance. . . .

Greece's neighbor, Turkey, also deserves our attention.

The future of Turkey as an independent and economically sound state is clearly no less important to the freedom-loving peoples of the world than the

---

* U.S. Congress, *Congressional Record*, 80th Congress, 1st session (Washington, D.C.: Government Printing Office, 1947), XCIII, 1980-81.

future of Greece. The circumstances in which Turkey finds itself today are considerably different from those of Greece. Turkey has been spared the disasters that have beset Greece. And during the war, the United States and Great Britain furnished Turkey with material aid.

Nevertheless, Turkey now needs our support. . . .

I am fully aware of the broad implications involved if the United States extends assistance to Greece and Turkey, and I shall discuss these implications with you at this time.

One of the primary objectives of the foreign policy of the United States is the creation of conditions in which we and other nations will be able to work out a way of life free from coercion. This was a fundamental issue in the war with Germany and Japan. Our victory was won over countries which sought to impose their will, and their way of life, upon other nations. . . .

The peoples of a number of countries of the world have recently had totalitarian regimes forced upon them against their will. The Government of the United States has made frequent protests against coercion and intimidation, in violation of the Yalta agreement, in Poland, Rumania, and Bulgaria. I must also state that in a number of other countries there have been similar developments.

At the present moment in world history nearly every nation must choose between alternative ways of life. The choice is too often not a free one.

One way of life is based upon the will of the majority, and is distinguished by free institutions, representative government, free elections, guarantees of individual liberty, freedom of speech and religion, and freedom from political oppression.

The second way of life is based upon the will of a minority forcibly imposed upon the majority. It relies upon terror and oppression, a controlled press and radio, fixed elections, and the suppression of personal freedoms.

I believe that it must be the policy of the United States to support free peoples who are resisting attempted subjugation by armed minorities or by outside pressures. . . .

I therefore ask the Congress to provide authority for assistance to Greece and Turkey in the amount of $400,000,000 for the period ending June 30, 1948. . . .

In addition to funds, I ask the Congress to authorize the detail of American civilian and military personnel to Greece and Turkey, at the request of those countries, to assist in the tasks of reconstruction, and for the purpose of supervising the use of such financial and material assistance as may be furnished.

MARSHALL PLAN 173

The economic counterpart to the Truman Doctrine was the Marshall Plan. In a commencement address at Harvard University on June 5, 1947, Secretary of State George C. Marshall pointed out that for the time being, Europe's requirements far exceeded her ability to pay for them. Accordingly, he proposed that the United States finance a recovery program prepared by the European nations *themselves. Although aid was offered to all of Europe, the Communist countries on orders from Moscow refused to participate.**

I need not tell you gentlemen that the world situation is very serious. That must be apparent to all intelligent people. I think one difficulty is that the problem is one of such enormous complexity that the very mass of facts presented to the public by press and radio make it exceedingly difficult for the man in the street to reach a clear appraisement of the situation. Furthermore, the people of this country are distant from the troubled areas of the earth and it is hard for them to comprehend the plight and consequent reactions of the long-suffering peoples, and the effect of those reactions on their governments in connection with our efforts to promote peace in the world.

In considering the requirements for the rehabilitation of Europe, the physical loss of life, the visible destruction of cities, factories, mines, and railroads was correctly estimated, but it has become obvious during recent months that this visible destruction was probably less serious than the dislocation of the entire fabric of European economy. For the past 10 years conditions have been highly abnormal. The feverish preparation for war and the more feverish maintenance of the war effort engulfed all aspects of national economies. . . . Under the arbitrary and destructive Nazi rule, virtually every possible enterprise was geared into the German war machine. Long-standing commercial ties, private institutions, banks, insurance companies, and shipping companies disappeared, through loss of capital, absorption through nationalization, or by simple destruction. In many countries, confidence in the local currency has been severely shaken. The breakdown of the business structure of Europe during the war was complete. Recovery has been seriously retarded by the fact that two years after the close of hostilities a peace settlement with Germany and Austria has not been agreed upon. But even given a more prompt solution of these difficult problems, the rehabilitation of the economic structure of Europe quite evidently will require a much longer time and greater effort than had been foreseen.

There is a phase of this matter which is both interesting and serious. The farmer has always produced the foodstuffs to exchange with the city dweller for the other necessities of life. This division of labor is the basis of modern civilization. At the present time it is threatened with breakdown. The town and city industries are not producing adequate goods to exchange with the food-producing farmer. Raw materials and fuel are in short supply. Machinery is lacking or worn out. The farmer or the peasant cannot find the goods for sale which he desires to purchase. So the sale of his farm produce for money which he cannot use seems to him an unprofitable transaction. He, therefore, has withdrawn many fields from crop cultivation and is using them for grazing. He feeds more grain to stock and finds for himself and his family an ample supply of food, however short he may be on clothing and the other ordinary gadgets of civilization. Meanwhile people in the cities are short of food and fuel. So the governments are forced to use their foreign money and credits to procure these necessities abroad. This process exhausts funds which are urgently needed for reconstruction. Thus a very serious situation is rapidly

* *A Decade of American Foreign Policy: Basic Documents, 1941-49.* Senate Doc. 123, 81st Congress, 1st session (Washington, D.C.: Government Printing Office, 1950), pp. 1268-70.

developing which bodes no good for the world. The modern system of division of labor upon which the exchange of products is based is in danger of breaking down.

The truth of the matter is that Europe's requirements for the next three or four years of foreign food and other essential products—principally from America—are so much greater than her present ability to pay that she must have substantial additional help or face economic, social, and political deterioration of a very grave character.

The remedy lies in breaking the vicious circle and restoring the confidence of the European people in the economic future of their own countries and of Europe as a whole. The manufacturer and the farmer throughout wide areas must be able and willing to exchange their products for currencies, the continuing value of which is not open to question.

Aside from the demoralizing effect on the world at large and the possibilities of disturbances arising as a result of the desperation of the people concerned, the consequences to the economy of the United States should be apparent to all. It is logical that the United States should do whatever it is able to do to assist in the return of normal economic health in the world, without which there can be no political stability and no assured peace. Our policy is directed not against any country or doctrine but against hunger, poverty, desperation, and chaos. Its purpose should be the revival of a working economy in the world so as to permit the emergence of political and social conditions in which free institutions can exist. Such assistance, I am convinced, must not be on a piecemeal basis as various crises develop. Any assistance that this Government may render in the future should provide a cure rather than a mere palliative. Any government that is willing to assist in the task of recovery will find full cooperation, I am sure, on the part of the United States Government. Any government which maneuvers to block the recovery of other countries cannot expect help from us. Furthermore, governments, political parties, or groups which seek to perpetuate human misery in order to profit therefrom politically or otherwise will encounter the opposition of the United States.

It is already evident that, before the United States Government can proceed much further in its efforts to alleviate the situation and help start the European world on its way to recovery, there must be some agreement among the countries of Europe as to the requirements of the situation and the part those countries themselves will take in order to give proper effect to whatever action might be undertaken by this Government. It would be neither fitting nor efficacious for this Government to undertake to draw up unilaterally a program designed to place Europe on its feet economically. This is the business of the Europeans. The initiative, I think, must come from Europe. The role of this country should consist of friendly aid in the drafting of a European program and of later support of such a program so far as it may be practical for us to do so. The program should be a joint one, agreed to by a number [of], if not all, European nations.

An essential part of any successful action on the part of the United States is an understanding on the part of the people of America of the character of the problem and the remedies to be applied. Political passion and prejudice should have no part. With foresight, and a willingness on the part of our people to face up to the vast responsibility which history has clearly placed upon our country, the difficulties I have outlined can and will be overcome.

Just as the wartime unity of the Allies was reflected by the dissolution of the Communist International on May 22, 1943, so the onset of the Cold War was reflected by the establishment of the Communist Information Bureau (Cominform) at the end of September, 1947. Representatives of communist parties of France, Italy, and Eastern Europe, meeting in Poland, adopted the following resolution and accompanying manifesto.*

Resolution

The conference states that the absence of connections between Communist parties who have taken part in this conference is in the present situation a serious shortcoming. Experience has shown that such division between Communist parties is incorrect and harmful. The requirement for an exchange of experience and voluntary coordination of actions of the separate parties has become particularly necessary now in conditions of the complicated postwar international situation and when the disunity of Communist parties may lead to damage for the working class.

Because of this, members of the conference agreed on the following:

First, to set up an Information Bureau of representatives of the Communist party of Yugoslavia, the Bulgarian Workers party (of Communists) of Rumania, the Hungarian Communist party, the Polish Workers party, the All-Union Communist party (bolshevik), the Communist party of France, the Communist party of Czechoslovakia and the Communist party of Italy.

Second, the task given to the Information Bureau is to organize and exchange experience and, in case of necessity, coordinate the activity of Communist parties on foundations of mutual agreement.

Third, the Information Bureau will have in it representatives of the Central Committees—two from each Central Committee. Delegations of the Central Committees must be appointed and replaced by the Central Committees.

Fourth, the Information Bureau is to have printed an organ—fortnightly and, later on, weekly. The organ is to be published in French and Russian and, if possible, in other languages.

Fifth, the Information Bureau is to be in Belgrade.

Manifesto

As long as the war lasted the Allied states fighting against Germany and Japan marched in step and were one. Nevertheless, in the Allies' camp already during the war there existed differences regarding the aims of the war as well as the objectives of postwar and world organization. The Soviet Union and the democratic countries believed that the main objective of the war was the rebuilding and strengthening of democracy in Europe, the liquidation of fascism and the prevention of a possible aggression on the behalf of Germany, that its further aim was an achievement of an all around and lasting cooperation between the nations of Europe.

The United States of America and with them England placed as their war aim a different goal—the elimination of competition on the world market (Germany and Japan) and the consolidation of their dominant position. This difference in the definition of war aims and post-war objectives has begun to deepen in the post-war period.

Two opposite political lines have crystalized: on the one extreme the U.S.S.R. and the democratic countries aim at whittling down imperialism and the strengthening of democracy. On the other side the United States of America and England aim at the strenthening of imperialism and choking democracy. Because the U.S.S.R. and the democratic countries stand in the way of fulfilling imperialistic plans aiming at world domination and crushing democratic movements, a campaign against the Soviet Union and the countries of the new democracy was undertaken. . . .

In this way there arose two camps—the camp of imperialism and anti-democratic forces, whose chief aim is an establishment of a world-wide American imperialists' hegemony and the crushing of democracy; and an anti-imperialistic democratic camp whose chief aim is the elimination of imperialism, the strengthening of democracy and the liquidation of the remnants of fascism. . . .

In these conditions the anti-imperialistic democratic camp has to close its ranks and draw up and agree on a common platform to work out its tactics against the chief forces of the imperialist camp. . . .

In consequence the Communist parties should place themselves in the vanguard of the Opposition against the imperialistic plans of expansion and aggression . . . and they should at the same time . . . gather around themselves all democratic and patriotic forces in their respective nations.

NORTH ATLANTIC TREATY 175

Because of the growing seriousness of the Cold War, several West European countries, together with the United States and Canada, signed the North Atlantic Treaty on April 4, 1949. Its objectives and provisions are given in the following excerpts.*

Preamble

The parties to this treaty reaffirm their faith in the purposes and principles of the Charter of the United Nations and their desire to live in peace with all peoples and all governments.

They are determined to safeguard the freedom, common heritage, and civilization of their peoples, founded on the principles of democracy, individual liberty, and the rule of law.

They seek to promote stability and well-being in the North Atlantic area.

They are resolved to unite their efforts for collective defense and for the preservation of peace and security.

* *The New York Times* (March 20, 1949). © 1949 by The New York Times Company. Reprinted by permission.

They therefore agree to this North Atlantic Treaty:

Article 1. The parties undertake, as set forth in the Charter of the United Nations, to settle any international disputes in which they may be involved by peaceful means in such a manner that international peace and security, and justice, are not endangered, and to refrain in their international relations from the threat or use of force in any manner inconsistent with the purposes of the United Nations.

Article 2. The parties will contribute toward the further development of peaceful and friendly international relations by strengthening their free institutions, by bringing about a better understanding of the principles upon which these institutions are founded, and by promoting conditions of stability and well-being. They will seek to eliminate conflict in their international economic policies and will encourage economic collaboration between any or all of them.

Article 3. In order more effectively to achieve the objectives of this treaty, the parties separately and jointly, by means of continuous and effective self-help and mutual aid, will maintain and develop their individual and collective capacity to resist armed attack.

Article 4. The parties will consult together whenever, in the opinion of any of them, the territorial integrity, political independence, or security of any of the parties is threatened.

Article 5. The parties agree that an armed attack against one or more of them in Europe or North America shall be considered an attack against them all; and consequently they agree that, if such an armed attack occurs, each of them, in exercise of the right of individual or collective self-defense recognized by Article 51 of the Charter of the United Nations, will assist the party or parties so attacked by taking forthwith, individually and in concert with the other parties, such action as it deems necessary, including the use of armed force, to restore and maintain the security of the North Atlantic area.

Any such armed attack and all measures taken as a result thereof shall immediately be reported to the Security Council. Such measures shall be terminated when the Security Council has taken the measures necessary to restore and maintain international peace and security.

Article 6. For the purpose of Article 5 an armed attack on one or more of the parties is deemed to include an armed attack on the territory of any of the parties in Europe or North America, on the Algerian Departments of France, on the occupation forces of any party in Europe, on the islands under the jurisdiction of any party in the North Atlantic area north of the Tropic of Cancer or on the vessels or aircraft in this area of any of the parties. ...

Article 9. The parties hereby establish a Council, on which each of them shall be represented, to consider matters concerning the implementation of this treaty. The Council shall be so organized as to be able to meet promptly at any time. The Council shall set up such subsidiary bodies as may be necessary; in particular it shall establish immediately a defense committee which shall recommend measures for the implementation of Articles 3 and 5.

Article 10. The parties may, by unanimous agreement, invite any other European state in position to further the principles of this treaty and to contribute to the security of the North Atlantic area to accede to this treaty. Any state so invited may become a party to the treaty by depositing its instrument of accession with the Government of the United States of America. The Government of the United States of America will inform each of the parties of the deposit of each such instrument of accession.

An important turning point in world events following World War II was the victory of Mao Tse-tung's Communists over Chiang Kai-shek's Kuomintang Nationalist government. Chiang emerged in 1945 seriously weakened after eight years of resistance to the Japanese. Despite substantial supplies of war materials from the United States, he was unable to hold his own against the Communists. In the fall of 1948, his armies in Manchuria were forced to surrender; and by the end of 1949, he was fleeing to the island of Taiwan. Some light on the reasons for Chiang's defeat is shed by American Ambassador John L. Stuart's report to Washington, November 24, 1947, and an editorial, "Lose No Time in Winning the People's Confidence," in Chung Yang Jih Pao, *November 4, 1948.**

John L. Stuart

I have the honor to comment further on some of the spiritual or human factors in the civil war as they are revealing themselves more clearly in the midst of rapidly deteriorating military and fiscal trends. The Communist organizers have a fanatical faith in their cause and are able to inspire their workers and to a large extent their troops and the local population with belief in its rightness, practical benefits and ultimate triumph. As against this the Government employees are becoming ever more dispirited, defeatist, and consequently listless or unscrupulously self-seeking. This of course still further alienates the liberal elements who ought to be the Government's chief reliance. Even the higher officials are beginning to lose hope. The effect on military morale is disastrous. In this drift toward catastrophe they clutch at American aid as at least postponing the inevitable. This is all that such monetary aid can do unless there is also among the Kuomintang leaders a new sense of dominating purpose, of sacred mission, of national salvation, expressing itself in challenging slogans, arousing them to fresh enthusiasms, leading them to forget their personal fears, ambitions and jealousies in the larger, more absorbingly worthwhile cause. It seems to me that this idea can be urged upon them under two emphases.

(1) *Freedom.* There can be absolutely no freedom of thought or action under Communist rule. The contentment that comes from a measure of economic security is conditioned on mute acceptance of party dictation. The zeal is generated by what is in large measure false and malicious indoctrination. If the Kuomintang could appreciate the propagandist value of exposing this and go to the opposite extreme in guaranteeing freedom of speech, publication and assembly, at whatever seeming risk of subversive activities, it would win the loyalty of the intellectuals as nothing else could. The really harmful agitation of Communist agents in newspaper offices, schools or even in Government bureaus, could be safely left to the constructive elements in each unit concerned. An aggressive ideological warfare over this issue by the Kuomintang might be made tremendously effective. But the Government

---

* *United States Relations with China,* Department of State Publication 3573, Far Eastern Series 30 (Washington, D.C.: Government Printing Office, 1949), pp. 375-76; 880-82.

would have to take an adventurous leap and cease to rely upon its secret service and other suppressive agencies.

(2) *The People's Livelihood.* The third of the famous *Three Principles* [of Dr. Sun Yat-sen] is being constantly honored in speeches and published articles. The Communists have gone a long way toward its realization but the Government shows up lamentably in comparison. True, it has had incessant foreign and domestic conflicts, but making all allowance for its difficulties the record to date has been extremely discreditable. If, however, all who do not want China to be communized could be enlisted in a movement to support the Government in effecting better local administration, there might well be a resurgent revolutionary movement that would attack at once graft and the inefficiency among Government officials and the wantonly destructive policy of the Communists.

Chung Yang Jih Pao

Recent military reverses in the Northeast are facts which the Government no longer tries to hide and everybody is suffering terribly from the new high prices. The masses of people live under a feeling of fear and are pursued relentlessly by difficult living conditions. Such facts are so undeniably true that they can no longer be ignored just because some people find them unpleasant to the ear, nor can they be white-washed by beautiful words.

At this moment when the nation's fate is flickering, and when the people are suffering terribly, what comfort and hope is there for them? The special privileged classes still enjoy their privileges, and the people can do nothing to them. Those plutocrats who have made their money because of personal or political relations, are either having a nice time abroad, or keeping right on with their activities in fleecing the people. . . . Nobody even dares to touch them ever so slightly. Nepotism rides on just as it has always done and the masses of people have no right to say anything. . . .

China today is experiencing troubles unprecedented in seriousness since the Tai Ping Rebellion. Of course our present troubles are enhanced by international intrigue, but we must admit that fundamentally it is because of the many defects that exist in our social system. While the essential purpose of the Communists is to grasp political power, on the surface they capitalize on these social defects in order to attract the people to their banner. This explains why Communist eradication has been such a difficult task. . . .

Giving full allowance for the worst, the area that lies south of the Yangtze River is big enough to contain more than ten European nations and has a population of more than 200 million. There is easy access to the sea, there is an abundance of all kinds of products and adequate transportation facilities. Compared to the time of the Northern Expedition, conditions today are far more favorable. Why then should there be pessimism? This is because something is fundamentally wrong with ourselves. If we can gain full control and make full use of the manpower and material resources within this large tract of land, we have more than the strength we need in eliminating the Communists. However, the key to the full mobilization of this manpower and material resources lies in our winning of the people's confidence and we must realize that the people's confidence cannot be won by the mere issuance of an official order on a sheet of paper. . . . Facts must be used to prove absence of selfishness and that bandit [Communist] suppression is not for the purpose of protecting the interests of the privileged classes but for the protection of territorial integrity, freedom and democracy for the people. . . .

Waste no time in winning the people's confidence. This is our last chance.

WAR IN KOREA 177

In the Far East, in contrast to Europe, the Cold War became "hot" with the outbreak of the Korean war on June 24, 1950, when Communist North Korean troops crossed the frontier to "liberate" South Korea. A UN commission in South Korea reported that the country was the victim of aggression. The question now was what would be the response of the UN, and particularly of the United States, the responsible Western power in South Korea. In his memoirs, Harry S. Truman describes how he reached his decision to resist the aggression with armed force.*

As I discussed Korean policy with my advisers in the spring of 1948, we knew that this was one of the places where the Soviet-controlled Communist world might choose to attack. But we could say the same thing for every point of contact between East and West, from Norway through Berlin and Trieste to Greece, Turkey, and Iran; from the Kuriles in the North Pacific to Indo-China and Malaya.

Of course each commander believed that his area was in the greatest danger. It is obvious that the final decisions on the allocation of forces and materiel cannot be left to an area commander and must be made by the top-level command.

The intelligence reports from Korea in the spring of 1950 indicated that the North Koreans were steadily continuing their build-up of forces and that they were continuing to send guerrilla groups into South Korea. There were continuing incidents along the 38th parallel, where armed units faced each other.

Throughout the spring the Central Intelligence reports said that the North Koreans might at any time decide to change from isolated raids to a full-scale attack. The North Koreans were capable of such an attack at any time, according to intelligence, but there was no information to give any clue as to whether an attack was certain or when it was likely to come. But this did not apply alone to Korea. These same reports also told me repeatedly that there were any number of other spots in the world where the Russians "possessed the capability" to attack.

On Saturday, June 24, 1950, I was in Independence, Missouri, to spend the weekend with my family and to attend to some personal family business.

It was a little after ten in the evening, and we were sitting in the library of our home on North Delaware Street when the telephone rang. It was the Secretary of State calling from his home in Maryland.

"Mr. President," said Dean Acheson, "I have very serious news. The North Koreans have invaded South Korea."

* Harry S. Truman, *Years of Trial and Hope: Memoirs* (New York: Doubleday, 1956), II, pp. 331-33, 335-37. © 1956 Time Inc.

My first reaction was that I must get back to the capital, and I told Acheson so. He explained, however, that details were not yet available and that he thought I need not rush back until he called me again with further information. In the meantime, he suggested to me that we should ask the United Nations Security Council to hold a meeting at once and declare that an act of aggression had been committed against the Republic of Korea. I told him that I agreed and asked him to request immediately a special meeting of the Security Council, and he said he would call me to report again the following morning, or sooner if there was more information on the events in Korea.

Acheson's next call came through around eleven-thirty Sunday morning, just as we were getting ready to sit down to an early Sunday dinner. Acheson reported that the U.N. Security Council had been called into emergency session. Additional reports had been received from Korea, and there was no doubt that an all-out invasion was under way there. The Security Council, Acheson said, would probably call for a cease-fire, but in view of the complete disregard the North Koreans and their big allies had shown for the U.N. in the past, we had to expect that the U.N. order would be ignored. Some decision would have to be made at once as to the degree of aid or encouragement which our government was willing to extend to the Republic of Korea.

I asked Acheson to get working with the Service Secretaries and the Chiefs of Staff and start working on recommendations for me when I got back. Defense Secretary Louis Johnson and Chairman of the Chiefs of Staff Omar Bradley were on their way back from an inspection tour of the Far East. I informed the Secretary of State that I was returning to Washington at once. ...

When the *Independence* landed, Secretary of State Acheson was waiting for me at the airport, as was Secretary of Defense Johnson, who himself had arrived only a short while before. We hurried to Blair House, where we were joined by the other conferees. ...

It was late, and we went at once to the dining room for dinner. I asked that no discussion take place until dinner was served and over and the Blair House staff had withdrawn. ...

Earlier that Sunday evening, Acheson reported, the Security Council of the United Nations had, by a vote of 9 to 0, approved a resolution declaring that a breach of the peace had been committed by the North Korean action and ordering the North Koreans to cease their action and withdraw their forces. ...

As we continued our discussion, I stated that I did not expect the North Koreans to pay any attention to the United Nations. This, I said, would mean that the United Nations would have to apply force if it wanted its order obeyed.

General Bradley said we would have to draw the line somewhere. Russia, he thought, was not yet ready for war, but in Korea, they were obviously testing us, and the line ought to be drawn now.

I said that most empathically I thought the line would have to be drawn. General Collins reported that he had had a teletype conference with General MacArthur. The Far East Commander, he told us, was ready to ship ammunition and supplies to Korea as soon as he received the green light.

I expressed the opinion that the Russians were trying to get Korea by default, gambling that we would be afraid of starting a third world war and would offer no resistance. I thought that we were still holding the stronger hand, although how much stronger, it was hard to tell. ...

By Monday the reports from Korea began to sound dark and discouraging, and among the messages that arrived was one from Syngman Rhee asking for help. ...

There was now no doubt! The Republic of Korea needed help at once if it was not to be overrun. More seriously, a Communist success in Korea would put Red troops and planes within easy striking distance of Japan, and Okinawa and Formosa would be open to attack from two sides.

I told my advisers that what was developing in Korea seemed to me like a repetition on a larger scale of what had happened in Berlin. The Reds were probing for weaknesses in our armor; we had to meet their thrust without getting embroiled in a world-wide war.

I directed the Secretary of Defense to call General MacArthur on the scrambler phone and to tell him in person what my instructions were. He was to use air and naval forces to support the Republic of Korea with air and naval elements of his command, but only south of the 38th parallel. He was also instructed to dispatch the Seventh Fleet to the Formosa Strait. The purpose of this move was to prevent attacks by the Communists on Formosa as well as forays by Chiang Kai-shek against the mainland, this last to avoid reprisal actions by the Reds that might enlarge the area of conflict.

I also approved recommendations for the strengthening of our forces in the Philippines and for increased aid to the French in Indo-China. Meanwhile the Security Council of the United Nations met again and adopted on June 27 the resolution calling on all members of the U.N. to give assistance to South Korea.

Chapter Twenty-seven

End of empires

178 COLONIAL REVOLUTIONS AFTER WORLD WAR I
AND WORLD WAR II

*One of the chief trends in world history following World War II
was the great colonial revolution that swept the globe. During its first
decade, most of the Asian colonies won their independence, followed in
the next decade by most of the African possessions. The net result was
that by 1964, no less than fifty-three new states had arisen, comprising
almost one-third of the world population.*

*Although revolution had also swept the colonial world after World
War I, the outbreak after World War II differed from that of the earlier
period in certain basic respects. These differences explain why the current colonial upheaval is sweeping everything before it, in contrast to
the very limited success of the earlier uprisings. A distinguished American scholar analyzes the nature of these differences and their implications
for Western policy-makers.**

While the focus of attention has been on the conflict between
Russia and the West in Europe, another fateful clash has been joined
on the other side of the world. Communism is bidding, just as it did
after the first World War, for ascendancy in Asia and under conditions more favorable than after 1919.

There are revolts and, as after 1919, they are essentially revolts
for emancipation from Occidental rule, with social accompaniments

* Nathaniel Peffer, "Communism Bids for Dominance in Asia," *The New York
Times Magazine* (October 31, 1948), pp. 10, 50-52. © 1948 by The New
York Times Company. Reprinted by permission.

—the demand of the chronically underfed Asian masses for a decent livelihood. And, as after 1919, communism, originating in Moscow and skillfully directed from Moscow, acts as a goad on both counts. What Russia's motives are, whether ideological or imperialistically expansionist, is still unclear, but in either case it is still true that Russia is exploiting a historical situation rather than creating it.

The locale has shifted. In 1919 and immediately after, the centers of revolt lay in China and India, the two largest groups in Asia and those with the longest history and the most highly developed culture. Now both have won national independence, and, while they still suffer from internal conflict, it is conflict of a different order.

Now the center of revolt lies in areas where national consciousness was still nascent in 1919 but is now fully formed, with all the vitality of a new and heady impulse. In Indonesia, Malaya and Indo-China, all advanced by a long stage since 1919, there is open warfare on the direct issue of native peoples against foreign rule. In Burma the difficulties are mainly social but in part the aftermath of the period of British rule, and even in India the internal strife has nationalistic complications.

The variations from post-1919 are three in number. First, there is the sharper edge of the social issue, almost wholly lacking in the native revolts after 1919. Those were almost exclusively political, more nearly of the nineteenth century order of movements for national independence. The present movements are almost as much economic as political. They are efforts not only for freedom from alien rule but for the emancipation of the masses from economic oppression by native feudal masters.

Second is Russia's increased stature in international politics. After 1919 Russia was important in Asia for its nuisance value, its ability by propaganda and the manipulation of agents to create embarrassment for European empires on their outer edges. Today it is one of the two greatest powers and carries corresponding prestige. Now it can openly bulwark native movements, and the promise, tacit but none the less real, that it can defend them against efforts at suppression, carries weight. Whether it does so as a counter in the power struggle or in order to extend the social revolution is immaterial for political purposes. The effect is the same anywhere in Asia. And where its promise does not win adherents, fear can.

The third variation is the new role of America, now not just a spectator, as thirty years ago, distantly sympathetic to movements for colonial liberation, but potentially a participant by virtue of the new conflict of power politics. While there is nothing new in colonial possessions and movements for colonial independence serving as pawns in international politics, the Russian-American bi-polarization and the sharpening of the struggle between the two gives the pawns a higher value.

The various peoples of Asia can be assets, either in substantive use or as threats. In other words, America can hardly permit extension of Russian power and influence into the Asiatic areas that are now colonies, and Russia can use the actuality of threat of such extension for the acquisition of more power in its orbit or as a counter to America.

Russia's role in the Asiatic turmoil should not be misunderstood. Its aim to use native disaffection as a weapon against Western empires is not new. It goes back to the famous thesis of Lenin, enunciated at the second congress of the Third International in 1920. Lenin's argument was simple, and ran as follows:

The basis of capitalism is imperialism. Strike successfully at imperialism, and capitalism is undermined. The place to strike at imperialism is in the colonies where there is native discontent. Foment and encourage native uprisings and the empires can be undermined first at the outer edges and then nearer the center. Break up the empires and capitalism falls of its own weight.

On this reasoning the first scene of action was China, where moral and material assistance was given to anti-Western resentment. That this has borne fruit is starkly evident, with Chinese Communists making a formal and probably successful bid for ascendancy over the country.

The same strategy is being employed elsewhere in Asia now, though more indirectly. It is no longer necessary for Russia to intervene through its own agents. In the decades since 1919 native Communist groups have been formed and undergone discipline, some of their leaders having actually had training in Moscow. Russia can sit back and watch its graduates working on their own—an advantage since it absolves Russia of any charge of active interference.

All this is true, but one thing should be emphasized. Had there never been a Russian revolution, the difference in Asia now would be one of degree only. Chinese intellectuals were embittered by foreign domination long before the Russians came bearing gifts in 1923. Nationalism was taking root in southeastern Asia and had to grow anyway. The seed had fallen in the soil of the time. And no Russian was needed to inform the natives of the region that they were hewers of wood and drawers of water, eking out a bare existence in an age when there was production of fabulous wealth, as they could see by looking about them in the semi-modern cities planted in their midst. No Russian was needed to persuade them that it is better to live comfortably.

All that would have come anyway. What the Russians have done is to use it for their purpose. Again, it is immaterial, so far as the political effect is concerned, whether their purpose is to extend Russia as an empire or to extend the area of social revolution. And if Russia were to be expunged from the planet tomorrow, there would still be native revolts in Asia. . . .

In some ways the political question, the relation between the imperial rulers and the native people, is more simple than the social question. The discontent of the native people with their economic lot, their resentment against their own rulers, may not be so rancorous as their feelings against their alien rulers; feeling toward the outsider always takes on greater asperity, no matter what the cultural level. But economic grievances are sharp none the less, and the Communists, both Russian and native, can be relied on not to let them become dull.

There is ground for resentment and material for propaganda. The lot of the overwhelming majority in all the Asian lands is not easily recognized by Occidentals who have shared at least in some measure the increased productivity of the machine age and the higher standard it has made possible and who have benefited by the rise in social consciousness since the middle of the nineteenth century. The peasants in nearly all of Asia and most of the urban dwellers, for that matter, are not technically serfs, but their plight is no better. They do not live; they subsist. They do not starve—except in emergencies—but they live on the edge of starvation. Whether workers in the plantations owned by great Western corporations or on the lands of princes of their own race, they are things rather than persons.

So long as this seemed to be nature's dispensation—a kind of law of nature that decreed that some few should dwell in luxury and all others never have quite enough to eat—it was accepted. Fate cannot be challenged or defied. But submission does not come so easily when it is revealed that man, not fate or nature, has decreed. What man has decreed can be revoked by man. And in the technologically most backward parts of the world it has become visible to all men that there is more to be had for all, that demanding with sufficient force behind the demand is all that is necessary.

In the first place, as has already been said, the luxury of the modern cities, implanted by the white man on the shores of Asia, has acted as temptation and incitation. In the second place, some modern ideas penetrate even to the illiterate, and the idea of a more equitable distribution of the world's goods, the idea familiar to all modern Western man, has carried to the most backward. In the third place, Communist indoctrination and the effect of the Russian revolution itself, about which something has penetrated into the world's most remote fastnesses, have begun to tell. The Russians themselves have not obstructed the passage of their ideas, of course. And to those who have never had anything the prospect of having something is infectious.

One thing is certain. There will have to be economic amelioration for the masses of Asia or there will be turbulence in Asia, whatever flag flies over any part of it. This is true without regard to whether the colonies win independence or not. In fact, independence may mark a retrogression in this respect. There is no reason to assume that native princes or rajahs will be more generous in division of wealth or less oppressive than the Western plantation owners. In fact, there is reason to believe that they will exploit even more. They will not be inhibited by nineteenth century humanitarianism and social consciousness. Nor will they be restrained by the force of public opinion such as that which developed in liberal groups in the West to impose restraint on their own people operating in colonies.

It must be remembered that the excesses of colonial exploitation were exposed, not by native victims but by the indignant countrymen of the colonial exploiters. Native rulers, accustomed to absolutism and with no colonial offices to watch them, may be more rapacious than any Western plantation owner ever was. If so, with or without independence, there will be trouble.

Declaration of Independence in Vietnam 179

Japanese rule and propaganda during World War II left their marks on the people of Southeast Asia. The Japanese, before departing, deliberately recognized and armed various nationalist organizations in order to make the return of the Europeans as difficult as possible, and constant reiteration of the theme "Asia for the Asians" further inflamed the already aroused nationalist passions. All this, together with the postwar weakness of Britain, France, and Holland, contributed to the universal demand for independence at the end of the war, and to the eventual satisfaction of that demand. Typical was the following Declaration of Independence, dated September 2, 1945. Although referring explicitly to the American Declara-

tion of Independence, it was signed by the Communist leader, "President Ho Chi Minh." *

470

"All men are created equal. They are endowed by their Creator with certain inalienable rights, among these are Life, Liberty, and the Pursuit of Happiness."

This immortal statement was made in the Declaration of Independence of the United States of America in 1776. . . . The Declaration of the Rights of Man and the Citizen of the French Revolution in 1791 also states: "All men are born free and with equal rights, and must always be free and have equal rights." . . .

Nevertheless for more than eighty years, the French imperialists deceitfully raising the standard of Liberty, Equality, and Fraternity, have violated our fatherland and oppressed our fellow citizens. They have acted contrarily to the ideals of humanity and justice.

In the province of politics, they have deprived our people of every liberty.

They have enforced inhuman laws; to ruin our unity and national consciousness, they have carried out three different policies in the north, the center and the south of Vietnam.

They have founded more prisons than schools. They have mercilessly slain our patriots; they have deluged our revolutionary areas with innocent blood. They have fettered public opinion; they have promoted illiteracy.

To weaken our race they have forced us to use their manufactured opium and alcohol.

In the province of economics, they have stripped our fellow citizens of everything they possessed, impoverishing the individual and devastating the land.

They have robbed us of our rice fields, our mines, our forests, our raw materials. They have monopolized the printing of banknotes, the import and export trade; they have invented numbers of unlawful taxes, reducing our people, especially our country folk, to a state of extreme poverty.

They have stood in the way of our businessmen and stifled all their undertakings; they have extorted our working classes in a most savage way.

In the autumn of the year 1940, when the Japanese fascists violated Indochina's territory to get one more foothold in their fight against the Allies, the French imperialists fell on their knees and surrendered, handing over our country to the Japanese, adding Japanese fetters to the French ones. From that day on, the Vietnamese people suffered hardships yet unknown in the history of mankind. The result of this double oppression was terrific: from Quangtri to the northern border two million people were starved to death in the early months of 1945.

On the 9th of March, 1945, the French troops were disarmed by the Japanese. Once more the French either fled, or surrendered unconditionally, showing thus that not only were they incapable of "protecting" us, but that they twice sold us to the Japanese.

Yet, many times before the month of March, the Vietminh had urged the French to ally with them against the Japanese. The French colonists never

* A. B. Cole, *Conflict in Indo-China and International Repercussions. A Documentary History 1945-1955* (Ithaca: Cornell Univ., 1956), pp. 19-21. © 1956 by The Fletcher School of Law and Diplomacy. Used by permission of Cornell University Press.

answered. On the contrary, they intensified their terrorizing policy. Before taking to flight, they even killed a great number of our patriots who had been imprisoned at Yenbay and Cao-bang.

Nevertheless, towards the French people our fellow citizens have always manifested an attitude pervaded with toleration and humanity. . . .

The whole population of Vietnam is united in common allegiance to the republican government and is linked by a common will, which is to annihilate the dark aims of the French imperialists.

We are convinced that the Allied nations which have acknowledged at Teheran and San Francisco the principles of self-determination and equality of status will not refuse to acknowledge the independence of Vietnam.

A people that has courageously opposed French domination for more than eighty years, a people that has fought by the Allies' side these last years against the fascists, such a people must be free, such a people must be independent.

For these reasons, we, members of the provisional government of Vietnam, declare to the world that Vietnam has the right to be free and independent, and has in fact become a free and independent country. We also declare that the Vietnamese people are determined to make the heaviest sacrifices to maintain its independence and its liberty.

INDEPENDENCE FOR BURMA 180

*The Declaration of Independence for Burma was ignored by the French, who attempted to reimpose their authority in Indochina. The result was years of costly warfare, culminating in the forceful expulsion of the French in 1954. By contrast, the British in Burma read the handwriting on the wall and allowed the Burmese to decide freely their postwar status. When the decision was made for complete independence outside the Commonwealth, the British promptly granted independence. The following selection from the statement in the House of Lords (November 23, 1947) by the Earl of Listowel, Secretary of State for Burma, is a revealing analysis of the forces at work in Southeast Asia as well as of British accommodation to these forces.**

This Bill, for which I am asking your Lordships' approval this afternoon, brings to fruition the policy of full self-government for Burma which has been pursued by successive Governments in this country for many years. The whole period of Parliamentary responsibility for the welfare of Burma, which has now lasted sixty-two years, has been in retrospect a striking example of the broadening path of political freedom in one of the largest dependencies of the British Crown. Until the incursion of the Japanese into Burma in 1942, we had an equally good record in two other respects no less vital to the well-being of the population; for we had established and maintained peaceful and orderly conditions in a country with a turbulent history, and the enterprise of our business and commercial undertakings had secured a

* *House of Lords Debates* (November 23, 1947), Vol. 152, Col. 846-66.

much fuller utilization of its largely untapped resources of minerals, timber and rice. Burma had undoubtedly achieved a greater measure of security and prosperity during the years of British rule than she had ever experienced in the past. No longer decimated at regular intervals by outbreaks of war, famine or disease, her population had more than quadrupled between 1824 and 1947.

At the beginning of the last century the Irrawaddy Delta was high jungle and tall grass with an occasional lonely village in a clearing amid the trackless expanse of malarial swamp. Now it has become a fertile plain of green paddy-fields, larger in area than Wales. Its 5,000,000 inhabitants produce more rice than the whole country can consume, leaving a surplus that made Burma before the war the largest rice exporter in the world. When we came to Burma in 1824, Rangoon was a small town with a few thousand inhabitants built round its famous shrine, the Shwe Dagon, on the banks of the Irrawaddy. It is now one of the largest modern ports east of Suez with a population of 500,000 souls. History will not forget that these changes have all taken place since the British connexion with Burma.

The spirit that has informed our treatment of Burma throughout these years of Parliamentary control and responsibility will always remain, in spite of shortcomings we can readily admit, something of which we and the people of this country can be proud. Our attitude has been characterized by a peculiarly British conception of obligation and trusteeship quite unknown to the empires of the past. We started to associate the local inhabitants with the administration of Burma almost from the time that Upper as well as Lower Burma came under our rule. . . .

I should like to emphasize the fact that Burma was already, shortly before the war, so close to political maturity, because it has been suggested that the people of Burma are still unfitted for self-government and that we should, therefore, have waited somewhat longer to introduce this Bill. . . .

The entry of Japan into the conflict in 1941 was soon followed by the invasion of Burma, by the heroic retreat of Lord Alexander in face of overwhelming odds, and by the temporary suspension of Parliamentary rule on the withdrawal of the British administration from the country. In December, 1942, the Governor was obliged to resume the full powers of government and he continued to exercise these powers in exile from Simla until civil authority was restored in 1945. In the meantime, Burma had been liberated by the brilliant leadership of General Slim and Lord Mountbatten, in a campaign for ever memorable for the gallantry and endurance of our Forces. The seizure by the Japanese of the many territories within the future co-prosperity sphere of South East Asia stimulated everywhere the latent consciousness of nationality, provoking a new intensity of desire to cast off foreign rule. Japanese rapacity also brought into being throughout this area political organizations and military formations that became the spearhead of more vigorous and widespread national movements.

The general tendency prevalent in South East Asia was heightened in Burma by the Japanese promise of immediate independence which resulted in the acquisition by Burma in 1943 of the outward trappings of a sovereign State, including an *adipadi,* or Head of State, to replace the King, and a number of ambassadors in foreign capitals. I do beg any noble Lords who consider this Bill precipitate or untimely to reflect upon the rapid growth and increasing strength of national movements in South East Asia in the last six years, and to ask themselves this simple question: Is it not a wiser policy, and one more in keeping with our traditional championship of liberty, to assist in the direction of these popular forces into paths of constructive statesmanship, where they can benefit the people they represent and the rest of the world, rather than to divert them, by trying forcibly to stem their advance into sterile, dangerous, and even destructive opposition to us and to every influence emanating from the West? ...

It was at the final session of the Constituent Assembly in September [1947] that unanimous approval was given to the draft Constitution, which declared in its first clause that Burma is to become a sovereign, independent republic. There is no one here or elsewhere who will not profoundly regret this impending gap in the family circle formed by the nations of the British Commonwealth. But we have always maintained that the peoples of the Commonwealth must decide their own future. The choice could lie only with Burma, and it was freely made by the unanimous vote of a fully representative body. We here do not regard membership of the Commonwealth as something to be thrust by force upon a reluctant people, but as a priceless privilege granted only to those who deeply desire it and are conscious of its obligations as well as its advantages. The essence of the Commonwealth relationship is that it is a free association of nations with a common purpose, who belong together because they have decided of their own volition to give and to take their fair share in a world-wide partnership. Our willingness to accept the decision of Burma to withdraw is surely the best proof of the difference between the British Commonwealth and the older systems of Imperial rule. The critics of British Imperialism can no longer say, as they have so often said in the past and as some still say at the present, that we believe in freedom and equality for every nation save only for the weaker peoples in the British Empire.

It should not be supposed that the decision of Burma to leave the Commonwealth is due to a lack of good will towards us—the Treaty arrangements make this perfectly clear—or to any lessening of the affection and respect evinced by the people of Burma for the King and the members of our Royal Family. Your Lordships will probably have noticed that Burma has sent Princess Elizabeth a ruby necklace containing 96 rubies from the famous Mogok Mines, but you may not have seen the inscription on the ivory case which reads as follows:

From the people of Burma, in token of their affection and esteem.

NATIONALIST RIOTS IN INDIA **181**

Although the Japanese did not occupy India, that country also was seething with nationalist agitation during World War II. In August, 1942, the British made mass arrests of nationalist leaders because their Congress party passed a resolution demanding immediate independence. Although neither armed nor organized, the masses reacted with great demonstrations, described in the following account by Jawaharlal Nehru. After the war the British recognized the strength of this nationalist movement and granted independence to India and Pakistan in 1947.*

* Jawaharlal Nehru, *The Discovery of India* (New York: Day, 1946), pp. 494-98. Copyright © 1946 by The John Day Company. Reprinted by permission of The John Day Company, Inc.

In the early morning of August 9, 1942, numerous arrests were made all over India. What happened then? Only scraps of news trickled through after many weeks to us, and even now we can form only an incomplete picture of what took place. All the prominent leaders had been suddenly removed and no one seemed to know what should be done. Protests, of course, there had to be, and there were spontaneous demonstrations. These were broken up and fired upon and tear gas bombs were used, and all the usual channels of giving expression to public feeling were stopped. And then all these suppressed emotions broke out and crowds gathered in cities and rural areas and came in conflict with the police and the military. They attacked especially what seemed to them the symbols of British authority and power, the police stations, post offices, and railways stations; they cut the telegraph and telephone wires. These unarmed and leaderless mobs faced police and military firing, according to official statements, on 538 occasions, and they were also machine-gunned from low-flying aircraft. . . .

This reaction in the country was extraordinarily widespread, both in towns and villages. In almost all the provinces and in a large number of the Indian states there were innumerable demonstrations, in spite of official prohibition. There were hartals, closure of shops and markets, and a stoppage of business, everywhere, varying in duration from a number of days to some weeks and in a few cases to over a month. So also labor strikes. More organized and used to disciplined action, industrial workers in many important centers spontaneously declared strikes in protest against government action in arresting national leaders. A notable instance of this was at the vital steel city of Jamshedpur, where the skilled workers, drawn from all over India, kept away from work for a fortnight and only agreed to return on the management's promising that they would try their best to get the Congress leaders released and a national government formed. In the great textile center of Ahmadabad there was also a sudden and complete stoppage of work in all the numerous factories without any special call from the trade union. . . .

All over India the younger generation, especially university students, played an important part in both the violent and peaceful activities of 1942. Many universities were closed. Some of the local leaders attempted even then to pursue peaceful methods of action and civil disobedience, but this was difficult in the prevailing atmosphere. The people forgot the lesson of nonviolence which had been dinned into their ears for more than twenty years, and yet they were wholly unprepared, mentally or otherwise, for any effective violence. That very teaching of nonviolent methods produced doubt and hesitation and came in the way of violent action. If the Congress, forgetful of its creed, had previously given even a hint of violent action, there is no doubt that the violence that actually took place would have increased a hundredfold. But no such hint had been given, and indeed the last message of the Congress had again emphasized the importance of nonviolence in action. . . .

Official estimates of the number of people killed and wounded by police or military firing in the 1942 disturbances are: 1,028 killed and 3,200 wounded. These figures are certainly gross underestimates, for it has been officially stated that such firing took place on at least 538 occasions, and besides this, people were frequently shot at by the police or the military from moving lorries. It is very difficult to arrive at even an approximately correct figure. Popular estimates place the number of deaths at 25,000, but probably this is an exaggeration. Perhaps 10,000 may be nearer the mark. It was extraordinary how British authority ceased to function over many areas, both rural and urban, and it took many days and sometimes weeks for a "reconquest," as it was often termed.

LIBERATION STRUGGLES IN ALGERIA AND ANGOLA 182

Contrary to general expectations, African nationalism swept everything before it after World War II, the pace of liberation depending usually on the absence or presence of European settlers. West Africa, where the climate is not attractive to Europeans, had no permanent colonists and therefore no substantial diehard opposition to the granting of independence. There, as in Asia, the British took the lead in relinquishing their authority and were followed closely by the French.

In contrast to the peaceful political evolution in the British and French colonies of sub-Saharan Africa, a costly war was fought between 1954 and 1962 in Algeria, where one million European settlers had lived for many decades. An insurrection also began in 1961 in Angola, where the Portuguese government was rushing out settlers in order to build up a base for continued rule. The first of the following selections, by a British journalist, describes the guerrilla tactics successfully used by the Algerian nationalists. The second selection, by an American journalist, is a revealing firsthand account of the Angolan revolutionary movement in its infancy—its sources of support, its organization and tactics, and its objectives.*

Algeria

The war in Algeria is all over, bar the shouting, but Algerian independence—now certain—will have been won at an almost intolerable price. The Arabs of Algeria say that, out of a total population of 9 million, they have lost nearly a million dead, and that, of these, more than 90 per cent have been civilians.

Algeria has been devastated in a way perhaps unparalleled in any country since the Middle Ages. At least 20,000 villages have been destroyed.

The regroupment of civilians in French camps (1,000,000 have been subjected to this process) and the consequent abandonment of flocks to starvation have produced a diminution of livestock that it will take years to recover from.

In the south many oases have been engulfed by the sands of the Sahara. Vast tracts of valuable cork forest have been burned down as a matter of military policy—some of these conflagrations spreading across the frontier into Tunisia.

Across the war-desolated country a huge French army has been playing an ineffective game of military hide-and-seek with the guerrilla forces of the F.L.N. (National Liberation Front). It is a game that has gone on for more

* N. Lewis, "Men Who Cry: 'Algérie Algérienne!'" *The New York Times Magazine* (February 4, 1962), pp. 12, 54; and *The New York Times* (December 16, 1963; Lloyd Garrison). © 1962, 1963 by The New York Times Company. Reprinted by permission.

than seven years, and the French high command has clung to its hopes of victory until the very end.

But now General de Gaulle has announced the truth so bitter to many French ears—"Algeria is finished as a battleground"—and the withdrawal of French divisions has begun. . . .

The military leaders [of the Algerian nationalists] have no objection to discussing their tactics with a visiting journalist. A major, white-haired at 32, analyzed the reasons for the F.L.N.'s virtual defeat of an army at least eight times its numerical strength, an army, moreover, supported by abundant armor, and by an air force of 1,000 planes.

"We have the whole of our civilian population solidly behind us," the major said. "They keep track of the enemy's positions for us, so that we're never taken by surprise. And then, again, the French have to keep to the roads. We use the goat tracks and move three times as fast as they can.

"Take the celebrated Operation Brumaire in 1958; and there've been a dozen more like it.

"The French plan was to knock out the headquarters of our Third Wilaya. They threw in three divisions—tanks, heavy bombers, everything they had. Of course, we got word that they were on their way, and by the time they'd got their 105-mm. howitzers into position, we'd moved our headquarters ten miles. We ran rings around them, shot up their rear, ambushed their reinforcement columns as fast as they came up.

"Before they had enough of it and pulled out, they burned every village in the area. The fact is, we drive our people hard. A forced march in our army means sixteen hours at a stretch. The French are welcome to their tanks and howitzers. Light anti-aircraft, machine-guns, bazookas and mortars—that's all we need for our kind of war."

A European doctor, converted to the F.L.N. cause, who had fought in the mountains with the rebel army, described its war of nerves. "The object is to keep the whole country in a state of siege," he said. "We cut off the towns' water and electricity supplies, cut the telephone cables, sabotage the railway lines, ambush the convoys of food supplies.

"The enemy has to keep a permanent guard on every bridge and every tunnel, every important building in the country. In that way, half their manpower's tied down on guard duties.

"The French have thousands of small forts scattered all over the country and no post ever knows, from one minute to the next, when it's going to be attacked. We've worked out a perfect liaison system that makes it possible to synchronize a dozen attacks in different parts of the country, so that reinforcements have to be rushed off in all directions."

Angola

Almost every night a column of Angolan rebels slips across the border from the Congo. The rebels are bound for secret staging camps here in the north of Angola. They carry mines, mortars, bazookas and new automatic rifles.

The influx of men and weapons is a vital part of the rebels' first major drive against the Portuguese since the revolt for independence erupted more than two-and-a-half years ago.

The drive is being pressed by 7,500 disciplined troops of the Angolan Liberation Army with modern weapons received from abroad.

The rebel build-up bears not only on the future of Angola. It is directly linked with the struggle for independence throughout the white-dominated southern tier of Africa.

Holden Roberto, leader of the Angolan revolutionary government in exile, has pledged "unlimited" support for African underground movements in South Africa, South-West Africa and Southern Rhodesia. . . .

In fact, after interviewing scores of Africans in Portuguese-held Angola as well as in the rebel north, one is left with a single overwhelming impression: that black and white in Angola are separated by a gulf of suspicion so wide and deep it may never be bridged.

None of the Africans interviewed regarded themselves as "Portuguese" and none wanted to be "Portuguese." . . .

Ranged against the rebels are more than 40,000 Portuguese troops. Lisbon maintains that Angola is a province of Portugal and has vowed to defend it at all costs.

It is a bitter, frustrating war of ambush and counter-ambush, of mines planted along trails and beside water holes, of forays against Portuguese-held bridges and communication lines.

In March, 1961, when the revolt began, the rebels had only one advantage: the element of surprise.

Except for a few Angolan deserters from the Portuguese Army, none of the insurgents had any military training. There was no over-all strategy and only a trickle of supplies filtered through from Angolan exiles in the Congo.

Portuguese forces gradually squeezed the rebels into an area half as large as the territory they originally overran. The insurgents retreated into the mountains and the Portuguese reoccupied the towns and main roads. Lisbon began describing the war as a "mopping up" exercise.

In recent months, however, the entire character of the rebellion has changed.

Today the troops of the Angolan Liberation Army are soldiers who have passed through a rigorous basic training course at Camp Kinkuzu in the Congo.

The camp was started by 22 Angolan officers who little more than a year ago were undergoing basic training themselves in Algeria. Camp Kinkuzu is now turning out reinforcements for the Angolan rebels at a rate of 2,200 men every eight weeks.

In addition, 25 members of the banned Pan-African Congress in South Africa and 50 volunteers from South-West Africa are being trained in guerrilla warfare at Kinkuzu. Others are expected to follow them.

War material for the Angolans has come almost entirely from Algeria. A new, 100-ton Algerian arms shipment will probably contain enough weapons to arm 7,000 more men.

Arms, ammunition, bandages, even typewriter ribbons, are carried into Angola on the heads of bearers over narrow animal tracks. The bearers march at night to avoid enemy patrols and spotter planes, often covering 40 miles by daybreak.

It is a crude system of supply, but it works. Some columns of bearers trek as much as 200 miles southward to the "rotten triangle," a mountainous rebel stronghold where fighting is particularly intense.

Angolan military leaders like Antonio Muandazi, the 32-year-old commander here in the Serra de Canda, 65 miles in the interior, have no illusions about a clear-cut military victory.

"The war here is like Algeria," he said. "We can't beat the Portuguese in the field but we can wear them down until the politicians are ready to talk."

He added: "This is a war of the will. It took the Algerians seven years before the French gave in. We are just as determined."

Commander Muandazi spoke from behind a desk in the thatched-hut office of his Canda mountain headquarters. A clerk was typing carbons of orders of the day.

Outside, soldiers drilled on a parade ground camouflaged by giant singa-singa trees. Nearby were 25 barracks, three supply sheds and an eight-bed dispensary with two orderlies but no medicine except a bottle of iodine and some aspirin.

Antonio Muandazi commands more than 1,000 men. Yet his uniform is the same as a private's. No one in the Angolan Liberation Army wears any identifying insignia. Officers and men alike address each other as "Comrade," a term borrowed from the Algerians.

"The troops know who is who," Commander Muandazi said. "After independence we can have a regular army with bars and chevrons and no doubt someone will invent some medals. But not now."

His remark reflected a spirit that motivates this army; that all men share equally the hardships of war and that, while there must be sergeants and officers to command and lead, rank bestows no special privilege.

Every soldier is a volunteer. When a soldier signs up he swears to serve until independence is won. No one is paid.

Many of the insurgents speak only a few words of Portuguese and the language of their tribe—in this area, Kimongo. A large number are illiterate.

Because of the scarcity of medicine, a soldier knows that if he is wounded he will be treated only with local herbs. If he is severely wounded, he will probably die before reaching the Congo.

Many soldiers have been fighting in this area for almost a year without a day off. When they are not on patrol they spend most of their time washing clothes and cleaning their weapons.

Despite the hardships, morale is high. In 13 days of marching with the rebels, this correspondent never overheard a soldier complain about anything more serious than the load he was assigned to carry.

In the Serra de Canda, where the insurgents maintain tight control, the troops never seem to stop singing. A favorite marching song is "The Yellow Rose of Texas," and horas sung in Hebrew have caught on quickly since the return of 25 Angolan medical corpsmen from training in Israel.

Hunger is a constant companion, for the army lives entirely off the land. Soldiers frequently march for two or three days with only a few chunks of raw manioc root to eat.

Occasionally a patrol comes across bananas and pineapples growing wild. . . .

Why are these men fighting in the first place?

The ones who left Angola to live in the former Belgian Congo are perhaps the most articulate on this point. They went seeking not only higher wages but also a freer political climate.

"In Angola," said Pedro Pemo, a 24-year-old private, "if you complained about wages the local Portuguese chef de posto would probably send you away on contract labor to some Portuguese plantation. The Belgians were not all good, but Africans could have unions and they could strike."

Miguel Rana, 22, another private, remembers being conscripted as a 12-year-old to work on the roads near his Angolan village.

"I've seen freedom in the Congo," he said. "My boy is never going to have to do what I had to do." . . .

The Angolan revolutionary government in exile is dominated by one figure: Holden Roberto, 38, who also heads the National Front for the Liberation of Angola.

At first glance, he does not look like a man who commands a revolution.

Dressed always in a conservative gray suit and never without his gold-rimmed spectacles, he looks much more the accountant, which he once was, or perhaps the school teacher, which he once had ambitions to be.

In the Serra de Canda, the government in exile has an official in every refugee village and army encampment. As part mayor, part political commissar, he registers births, deaths and marriages, mediates civilian disputes and looks after a slow but operative postal system.

As yet the rebels have not defined their goals beyond the single aim of achieving independence.

And then? The government in exile speaks broadly about establishing a democratic regime, allowing free labor unions and initiating land reforms. How these things are to be accomplished is not spelled out.

BRITISH DEPARTURE AND EGYPTIAN REJOICING **183**

Although Egypt had become formally independent in 1936, Britain was still allowed to maintain a garrison along the Suez Canal and to administer the Sudan together with Egypt. The latter right was relinquished by treaty arrangement in 1953, but the Suez garrison remained; and this became the prime issue for Egyptian nationalists. It was settled in October, 1954, when Premier Gamal Abdel Nasser negotiated an agreement for the withdrawal of the British garrison under certain stipulated conditions—the final triumph over the unwelcome foreigners. Egyptians celebrated with unrestrained enthusiasm, evident in firsthand reports by an American correspondent. The first describes the British departure; the second, the Egyptian rejoicing. *

British Departure

Britain quietly ended today her seventy-four-year occupation of the Suez Canal Zone. She handed over to the Egyptians full responsibility for defending the great East-West shipping lane.

The last token force of eleven officers and eighty men sailed out of Port Said aboard a British tank landing ship early in the morning. They headed

* *The New York Times* (June 14, 19, 1956; Osgood Caruthers). © 1956 by The New York Times Company. Reprinted by permission.

for Famagusta, Cyprus, where the British established their main Middle East defense base after having agreed twenty months ago to leave Egypt.

Brig. John H. S. Lacey, who had been left behind as commander of this final contingent of the British forces in Egypt, handed over the keys of his headquarters at Navy House on what was known as the British Quay in Port Said harbor to Lieut. Col. Abdullah Azouni of the Egyptian Army.

As he stepped aboard a launch to join his officers and men aboard the departing Navy vessel, Brigadier Lacey looked back with a rather wistful smile and said: "I am the last British soldier to leave Egypt."

The Union Jack, which for years had flown over the yellow stucco Navy House, was lowered at retreat last night and was not raised again.

Following a brief ceremony at dawn, Egyptian guards took over control of the Navy House compound and raised the green flag of Egypt with its white crescent and three stars.

The British began the gradual evacuation of their Suez Base, which at its peak was manned by 80,000 men, soon after Britain bowed to Egypt's growing nationalist pressure and, in October, 1954, signed the agreement to leave.

The last British soldier left six days before the June 18 deadline set in the agreement. . . .

It was obvious by the daily declarations in the Cairo press that the Egyptians had hoped to make quite a flourish of the Britain departure.

The British, sensitive over seeing another vital link in their empire melt away, preferred not to take part in Egypt's spectacle.

"There were some even at home that had hoped we would march out with colors flying and pipes skirling as we did from India," said Col. John M. White, British Deputy Director of Public Relations in the Middle East. "But we decided we did not want to make a song and dance of our final departure."

Egyptian Rejoicing

Jubilant Egyptians virtually mobbed Premier Gamal Abdel Nasser at Port Said today as he formally proclaimed the end of the seventy-four years of British occupation of the Suez Canal.

The Premier flew to Port Said this morning to raise the Egyptian flag in front of Navy House, last British headquarters in the once vast Suez base. . . .

Colonel Nasser looked somewhat disheveled after having run a gamut of screaming, almost rioting rejoicers. As he raised the green Egyptian flag with its white crescent and three stars he declared "this is a memorable moment of a lifetime."

He drove through the streets of Port Said in an open car. Crowds swarmed around the Premier and threatened at one time to smother him as they fought with each other to get near enough to embrace and kiss him. . . .

Reporters who watched the swarming throngs brave policemen's clubs to try to kiss the Premier said at one time he had completely disappeared from sight under their weight.

Nine Soviet-built M.I.G. fighter planes flew in formation overhead during the flag-raising ceremony. A salute was fired from an Egyptian frigate that had been sold to Egypt by the British. Also in the harbor were five small torpedo boats that one Egyptian naval officer identified as of Yugoslav origin.

As he raised the flag Colonel Nasser told the crowd, "citizens we pray that

God may forbid any other flag to fly over our land." He kissed the flag before he raised it. . . .

There also were great celebrations in Alexandria and Cairo and in villages up and down the Nile.

Little more than one month after the departure of the British garrison, Premier Nasser startled the world by nationalizing the Suez Canal, hitherto owned and operated by the Suez Canal Company. In a speech on July 26, 1956, he proclaimed the act of nationalization; and in doing so he accused the company of unconscionable exploitation of Egypt. Passages from the speech reflect his bitterness toward the company and toward imperialism in general—a sentiment undoubtedly shared by most of his countrymen.

On November 7, 1854, Ferdinand de Lesseps arrived in Egypt. He went to Mohammed Said Pasha, the Khedive. He sat beside him and told him, "We want to dig the Suez Canal. This project will greatly benefit you. It is a great project and will bring excellent returns to Egypt." . . .

On November 30, 1854, he had already obtained the Concession for the Canal from [the Khedive]. The Concession said: "Our friend De Lesseps has drawn our attention to the benefits which will accrue to Egypt by joining the Mediterranean and the Red Sea by a waterway for the passage of ships. He informed us of the possibility of forming a company for this purpose to comprise the investors of capital. We have approved the idea and have authorised him to form and to operate a company for the digging of the Suez Canal and to exploit it between the two seas." . . .

The Suez Canal Company was formed, and Egypt got 44 per cent of the shares. Egypt undertook to supply labour to dig the Canal by corvee, of whom 120,000 died without getting paid. We also paid De Lesseps in order that he might give up some concession. We gave up the 15 per cent of the profits which we were supposed to get over and above the profits of our 44 per cent of the shares. Thus, contrary to the statements made by De Lesseps to the Khedive in which he said that the Canal was dug for Egypt, Egypt has become the property of the Canal. . . .

Egypt then borrowed money. What happened? Egypt was obliged, during the reign of Ismail, to sell its 44 per cent of the shares in the company. Immediately England sent out to purchase the shares. It bought them for 4 million pounds. Then, Ismail gave up his 5 per cent of the company's profits against the ceding of some concessions by the Company which were granted to it.

Then Ismail was obliged to pay to Britain the 5 per cent profit which he had relinquished. This amounted to over 4 million pounds. In other words, Britain got Egypt's 44 per cent of the Company's shares free. This was the history which took place a century ago.

Is history to repeat itself again with treachery and deceit? Will economic independence . . . or economic domination and control be the cause of the destruction of our political independence and freedom?

Brothers, it is impossible that history should repeat itself.

Today, we do not repeat what happened in the past. We are eradicating the traces of the past. We are building our country on strong and sound bases.

Whenever we turn backwards, we aim at the eradication of the past evils which brought about our domination, and the vestiges of the past which took place despite ourselves and which were caused by imperialism through treachery and deceit.

Today, the Suez Canal where 120,000 of our sons had lost their lives in digging it by corvee, and for the foundation of which we paid 8 million pounds, has become a state within the state. It has humiliated ministers and cabinets. . . .

Britain has forcibly grabbed our rights, our 44 per cent of its shares. Britain still collects the profits of these shares from the time of its inauguration until now. All countries and shareholders get their profits. A state within the state; an Egyptian Joint Stock Company.

The income of the Suez Canal Company in 1955 reached 35 million pounds, or 100 million dollars. Of this sum, we, who have lost 120,000 persons, who have died in digging the Canal, take only 1 million pounds or 3 million dollars! This is the Suez Canal Company, which was dug for the sake of Egypt and its benefit!

Do you know how much assistance America and Britain were going to offer us over five years? 70 million dollars. Do you know who takes the 100 million dollars, the Company's income, every year? They take it of course. . . .

We shall not repeat the past. We shall eradicate it by restoring our rights in the Suez Canal. This money is ours. This Canal is the property of Egypt because it is an Egyptian Joint Stock Company.

The Canal was dug by Egypt's sons and 120,000 of them died while working. The Suez Canal Company in Paris is an imposter company. It usurped our concessions. . . .

Therefore, I have signed today the following law which has been approved by the Cabinet: [Article 1 of the decree read, "The Universal Company of the Suez Maritime Canal (Egyptian Joint-Stock Company) is hereby nationalized. All its assets, rights and obligations are hereby transferred to the Nation. . . ."]

185 COLONIALISM IN RETROSPECT

Now that the world seems to be entering what might be called a postimperialism era, it is appropriate to take stock of the departing imperialism. Its numerous failings have been depicted at length in many of these readings. Its impact, however, was by no means altogether baneful. If newly independent countries such as Ghana and Nigeria are compared to states such as Liberia and Ethiopia, which never experienced extended foreign rule, it becomes evident that colonialism had its positive as well as negative aspects. An American authority presents the bal-

As practiced in its heyday by every European power, colonialism was a conceipt wrapped in a concern that was frequently less religious than sanctimonious and less charitable than mercenary. It proceeded on the premise that it was dealing with, as Kipling wrote, "lesser breeds without the Law," or, as a Southern Rhodesian administrator put it in 1925, that "we are in this country because . . . we are better men." It employed methods that were bossy, when not dictatorial, or worse. It was everlastingly telling people what was good for them, and what was bad. And all too often it failed to practice the good it looked for in others or to eschew the bad it abhorred in them.

Granted, there have been vast differences in the records of the various colonial powers. Not all of them have made the same mistakes. Thus, the French did not mistakenly classify people by the color of their skins and build separate and unequal schools, churches, park benches and washrooms for those not of their color.

On the other hand, the British did not presume to think that their wards wanted to speak English and to live like Englishmen, or that the chief end of man was to glorify the British Constitution and enjoy it forever. Of course, they did not stand in the path of those who wished to adopt British ways. Indeed, they eagerly helped them to attain this end, but the matter was not one on which they insisted. They assumed, almost from the start, that sooner or later most educated people want to be themselves and manage or mismanage their affairs in their own way.

And neither the French nor the British made the mistake of supposing that it was possible—in the words of a Governor General of the former Belgian Congo—"to live together with the African, while remaining ourselves," or, as the Portuguese did, that nobody should be allowed to remain himself but, rather, that every African should be exhorted (if need be, by methods more punitive than persuasive) to live in an orderly, regimented society purged of the old tribal excesses and hostilities.

. . . . .

Where all the colonial powers failed, it seems to me is in the following respects:

First, they failed to forecast the rising of the "winds of change." In a recent book, Margery Perham, one of Britain's most highly respected students of colonialism, confessed that she was "taken by surprise" by these winds, and that as late as 1939 the feeling about West Africa in the "official world," that is, the British Colonial Office, was pretty much that "we can be sure that we have unlimited time in which to work." As things turned out, the British had less than twenty years in which to work.

Many French people, we may assume, were taken even more by surprise, since down to the mid-Nineteen Fifties the common official view seems to have been that France would stretch from the Rhine to the Congo. As for the Belgians, as recently as 1958 they were still affirming their intention to

* G. H. T. Kimble, "Colonialism: The Good, the Bad, the Lessons," *The New York Times Magazine* (August 26, 1962), pp. 11, 62, 64. © 1962 by The New York Times Company. Reprinted by permission.

stay in the Congo—because "the Congo needs us even more than we need the Congo."

Yet, for those with eyes to see them, there had long been signs of the coming change. From World War I onward there had been international conventions devoted to the subject of "African liberation." From the Nineteen Twenties there had been African student organizations (notably in the United Kingdom) that served as seedbeds for the germination of nationalist ideas and programs.

From the Nineteen Thirties there had been political congresses, parties and undercover organizations that worked to the same end in several British and French territories. From about the same time there had been African newspapers which sought to form—and sometimes to inflame—public opinion. And for a generation or more there had been Africans who journeyed to Moscow and other unpatriotic places.

As the colonial powers now see, they failed to understand African nationalism—both the source of its strength and passion, and the reasons for its surging discontent with servitude in any guise.

In the second place, they failed to provide the African with sufficient "protection" when the winds did rise. None of the newly independent countries had enough skilled African administrators to run their own show; not infrequently, independence meant an increased, rather than decreased, reliance on outsiders. (As one wit put it, "It takes a lot of Europeans to Africanize a place.")

None of the countries had enough African technicians to keep their public utilities working smoothly, or enough African professional men to ensure that the health of their people would be protected and their economic and legal interests adequately served. Somalia had no indigenous doctors when it became independent; Nigeria less than one dentist for every million people; Tanganyika only two engineers; the Congo one engineer, and no doctors, dentists, lawyers or public accountants.

And no country had an electorate that knew what independence was all about or what the keeping of it would cost in self-discipline, or cold cash.

Third, the colonial powers failed either to understand the nature of the African's environment or to live up to their understanding of it. They underestimated the difficulty of getting the environment to "go to work" for the African, and so of establishing economies that were at once strong enough to take the strain of independence and durable enough to keep those who worked them independent.

All too frequently they regarded the African's land as a bank to be robbed for their profit rather than as a trust to be husbanded for him. Only belatedly did they come to perceive the delicacy of Africa's physical and biological balance: the hunger of its soils, the variability of its rainfall, the scourge of its heat and humidity, and its hostility to sustained effort and large-scale enterprise.

Today, roughly half the lands of Africa are in poorer shape than they were fifty years ago. In at least one-third of the continent wind and water are removing topsoil faster than it is being replaced, and ground water levels are receding because of the consequently increased evaporation and run-off. In at least one-half of the forest country timber is being cut for fuel, lumber, wood ash and a dozen other purposes faster than it is growing.

The agricultural picture is scarcely brighter. In many areas the rest period given to land that has been cropped—as most of it periodically is—

to the point of exhausation, is now shorter than it used to be. While this is partly because of growing population pressure on the cultivated land, it is also because in many areas the farmers are now restrained from following their traditional "bush fallowing" system of soil conservation, under which sections of land are allowed to return to "bush" for a number of years. The Government feels that this method removes too much acreage from cultivation.

Needless to say, there are ways of stabilizing the soil and of increasing its yield of water, wood and crops; but up to now these have been more often talked about than tried. When tried, they have more than once been on the wrong scale or in the wrong place.

Perhaps the colonizers' greatest failure of all was their failure to understand the African—his hopes and fears, his capacities, needs and sensibilities. True, they did much better by him in the Nineteen Fifties than in the days of H. M. Stanley and Joseph Conrad. But they (and, for that matter, we) have lost little of the old-time zeal to make over (if not to take over) his economy—to convert him to Western ways of running farms and ruining the soil, of making money and creating unemployment, and of arousing desires that cannot be satisfied.

Neither have they (or we) lost much of the old-time zeal to teach him Western ways of organizing academies and armies, of behaving toward God and neighbor, of marrying and raising a family, of dressing, drinking and dying. (Already in some territories the automobile kills more people than the anopheles mosquito.)

All this has quietly undermined, when it has not destroyed, the African's self-respect, his sense of being valued for what he is and not merely for what he can do. It has also forced him to do virtually all of the taking and none of the giving. If we are to believe Laurens van der Post, the writer-explorer, who has lived closer to the African than most, it is this denial of the African's creativeness that has embittered his spirit, inflamed his passion and been responsible for much of the continuing "darkness" of his continent.

This is not to say that the colonial powers are called upon to renounce their record, let alone to stand trial for it. As George F. Kennan observed in his Reith Lectures in England in 1957: "The establishment of the colonial relationship did not represent a moral action on somebody's part; it represented a natural and inevitable response to certain demands and stimuli of the age. It was simply a stage of history." To judge the colonial powers in the light of the standards of a later age is unfair.

Furthermore, some of the things to come out of the "colonial relationship" are cause more for praise than for shame. To begin with, independence came out of it. The fact that there are independent states in Africa today is very largely the result of the European "presence." Without this, it is hard to see how the people living there could have bridged the gap between tribaldom and nationhood, between anarchy and order in so short a time.

For all its faults, colonial government was a hundred times better than the unregulated dealings of men like Conrad's Kurtz, who were armed with power to destroy and corrupt and had no scruples about using it. It provided security of person and property in lands that had known little of either, and so, enlarged the borders of the world in which a man could wander and work, live and die. It also provided experience in the running of business, industry and civil services for people who had hitherto shown few signs of developing these for themselves.

Then, too, it provided education (little enough, to be sure) that enabled men to know of Jefferson and Burke, the Magna Carta, the Bill of Rights and the no less revolutionary doctrines of the New Testament. In other words, it provided the grain of opportunity on which the pearl of independence could be cultured.

It did more than this. It provided much of the sustenance for the growing pearl. For it was the colonial powers who were largely responsible for the opening of the region to the lumberman, miner, planter and other men of means without whom its wealth would have continued to lie fallow.

Before colonial times, almost the only tropical African "goods" to command an overseas market were slaves, ivory and gold. There was a little trade in hardwoods such as ebony, and in kola nuts, spices and incense, but none at all in cocoa, coffee, rubber, peanuts, sisal and a dozen other commodities that are now indispensable revenue-earners in as many countries.

The colonial powers were also responsible for a great deal of development that was not, and could not have been, financed from export revenues. The French Investment Funds for Economic and Social Development, the Belgian Funds for Native Welfare, the British Colonial Development and Welfare Grants and the Portuguese Colonial Development Fund—to name only four sources of such development money—provided the means, and often the ways, by which people could learn to overcome the handicaps imposed on them by a difficult environment and by centuries of isolation and apathy. In pre-colonial times there were no high schools or colleges in tropical Africa, nor any hospitals, clinics, dispensaries or other health services, and no roads or railways.

A number of uncovenanted gains also have come out of the colonial relationship. Among these is the mutual esteem—affection is not too strong a word—which has frequently developed between the colonial administrator and those he administered. Many Africans have been frank to admit that, if they have to be shoved around by somebody of another tribe, they would just as soon he was of a European "tribe."

Chapter Twenty-eight

End of bipolarism

COLD WAR THAW—PEACEFUL COEXISTENCE **186**

*The immediate post-World War II years had witnessed an un-
precedented decline of Europe in world affairs. The great colonial empires were breaking up, while at home the continent had become dependent upon, and to varying degrees dominated by, the United States
and the Soviet Union. After a decade, this situation began to change.
With growing prosperity, Europe became more independent in economic
and political matters. At the same time, China was asserting herself
against her ally and mentor, the Soviet Union. These trends produced
an entirely new configuration of world politics; the short-lived American–
Russian primacy gave way to a new pluralism.*

*One reason for the decline of the American–Russian primacy was
the thaw in the Cold War that had begun in the mid-1950's. So long as
the Cold War reigned, the countries of Western Europe felt constrained
to follow America's leadership, while those of Eastern Europe acquiesced
in Russia's domination. But in 1953, the Cold War began to wane, owing
to a combination of factors including the death of Stalin, the advent of
the new Eisenhower administration in Washington, the ending of the
Korean War, and the acquisition of the hydrogen bomb by Russia as well
as the United States—a development that pointed up the impossibility
of resorting to war to settle international disputes.*

*One manifestation of the thaw was Premier Khrushschev's cam-
paign for what he termed "peaceful coexistence," a concept that he explained and defended in an article published in the American quarterly,*
Foreign Affairs. *Excerpts from this article are given in the first of the*

following selections. The second is from an article in the same journal by a former American Ambassador to the Soviet Union, George Kennan, who points out various distortions in Khrushchev's arguments. Despite the sharp disagreements reflected in these selections, the mere fact that "peaceful coexistence" was being widely discussed at that time reflected the Cold War thaw.*

Premier Nikita Khrushchev

... Whether you like your neighbor or not, nothing can be done about it, you have to find some way of getting on with him, for you both live on one and the same planet. ...

From its very inception the Soviet state proclaimed peaceful coexistence as the basic principle of its foreign policy. It was no accident that the very first state act of the Soviet power was the decree on peace, the decree on the cessation of the bloody war.

What, then, is the policy of peaceful coexistence?

In its simplest expression it signifies the repudiation of war as a means of solving controversial issues. However, this does not cover the entire concept of peaceful coexistence. Apart from the commitment to nonaggression, it also presupposes an obligation on the part of all states to desist from violating each other's territorial integrity and sovereignty in any form and under any pretext whatsoever. The principle of peaceful coexistence signifies a renunciation of interference in the internal affairs of other countries with the object of altering their system of government or mode of life or for any other motives. The doctrine of peaceful coexistence also presupposes that political and economic relations between countries are to be based upon complete equality of the parties concerned, and on mutual benefit.

It is often said in the West that peaceful coexistence is nothing else than a tactical method of the Socialist states. ... They say: The Soviet leaders argue that they are for peaceful coexistence. At the same time they declare that they are fighting for communism and they even say that communism will be victorious in all countries. How can there be peaceful coexistence with the Soviet Union if it fights for communism?

·   ·   ·   ·   ·

But when we say that in the competition between the two systems, the capitalist and the Socialist, our system will win, this does not mean, of course, that we shall achieve victory by interfering in the internal affairs of the capitalist countries. Our confidence in the victory of communism is of a different kind. It is based on a knowledge of the laws governing the development of society. Just as in its time capitalism, as the more progressive system, took the place of feudalism, so will capitalism be inevitably superseded by communism—the more progressive and more equitable social system. We are confident of the victory of the Socialist system because it is a more progressive system than the capitalist system. Soviet power has been in existence for only a little more than forty years, and during these years we have gone

* Nikita S. Khrushchev, "On Peaceful Coexistence," *Foreign Affairs* (October, 1959), pp. 1-18; George F. Kennan, "Peaceful Coexistence: A Western View," *Foreign Affairs* (January, 1960), pp. 172-90. *Foreign Affairs* articles are copyrighted by the Council on Foreign Relations, Inc., New York.

through two of the worst wars, repulsing the attacks of the enemies who attempted to strangle us. Capitalism in the United States has been in existence for more than a century and a half, and the history of the United States has developed in such a way that never once have enemies landed on American territory.

Yet the dynamics of the development of the U.S.S.R. and the U.S.A. are such that the 42-year-old land of the Soviets is already able to challenge the 150-year-old capitalist state to economic competition; and the most far-sighted American leaders are admitting that the Soviet Union is fast catching up with the United States and will ultimately outstrip it. . . .

We are prepared now as before to do everything we possibly can in order that the relations between the Soviet Union and other countries, and, in particular, the relations between the U.S.S.R. and the U.S.A., should be built upon the foundation of friendship and that they should fully correspond to the principles of peaceful coexistence.

. . . . .

What, then, is preventing us from making the principles of peaceful coexistence an unshakable international standard and daily practice in the relations between the West and East?

Of course, different answers may be given to this question. But in order to be frank to the end, we should also say the following: It is necessary that everybody should understand the irrevocable fact that the historic process is irreversible. It is impossible to bring back yesterday. . . .

The existence of the Soviet Union and of the other socialist countries is a real fact. It is also a real fact that the United States of America and the other capitalist countries live in different social conditions, in the conditions of capitalism. Then let us recognize this real situation and proceed from it in order not to go against reality, against life itself. Let us not try to change this situation by interferences from without, by means of war on the part of some states against other states.

I repeat, there is only one way to peace, one way out of the existing tension; peaceful coexistence.

George F. Kennan

In the public debate that has marked the progress of what is called the cold war, no term has been used more loosely, and at times unscrupulously, than the word "coexistence." In the article under his name, published in the last issue of *Foreign Affairs,* Mr. Khrushchev has given us an interesting definition of what he understands by this term. Peaceful coexistence, he says, signifies in essence the repudiation of war as a means of solving controversial issues. It presupposes an obligation to refrain from every form of violation of the territorial integrity and sovereignty of another state. It implies renunciation of interference in the internal affairs of other countries. . . .

Not only has Mr. Khrushchev given us this definition but he has made it plain that he considers that the Soviet Union abides by these principles, has abided by them ever since the revolution of the autumn of 1917 and cannot help but abide by them in view of its social foundation; whereas there are still important elements in the Western countries who, in his view, do not abide by these principles, who "believe that war is to their benefit." . . .

There could be few propositions more amazing than the assertion that the Soviet state "from its very inception . . . proclaimed peaceful coexistence as the public principle of its foreign policy," and that the initial Communist leaders in Russia were strong partisans of the view that peaceful coexistence could and should prevail among states with different social systems.

.   .   .   .   .

One shudders to think what Lenin would have said to these preposterous distortions. Do the present leaders of the Russian Communist Party really profess to have forgotten that Lenin regarded himself outstandingly as an *international* socialist leader? Who was it wrote, on October 3, 1918, "The Bolshevik working class of Russia was always internationalist not only in words, but in deeds, in contrast to those villians—the heroes and leaders of the Second International. . . ."? Who was it said, in that same document, "The Russian proletariat will understand that the greatest sacrifices will now soon be demanded of it for the cause of internationalism. . . . Let us prepare ourselves at once. Let us prove that the Russian worker is capable of working much more energetically, and of struggling and dying in a much more self-sacrificing way, when it is a matter not of the Russian revolution alone but of the international workers' revolution.'"?

This is, as every good Communist in Russia knows, only a single quotation out of literally thousands that could be adduced to illustrate the devotion of the Bolsheviki in Lenin's time to socialism as an international cause —the devotion, that is, precisely to the duty of interfering in the internal affairs of other countries with the object of altering their system of government and mode of life.

The proposition that the political power dominant in the Soviet Union has always been on the side of coexistence, as defined by Mr. Khrushchev, also calls upon us to forget the long and sinister history of the relationship between Moscow and the foreign Communist Parties in the Stalin era. There is ample documentation to show for what purposes foreign Communist Parties were used during those years, by whom, and by what methods.

.   .   .   .   .

The cold war, let it be said most emphatically, does not exist because people in the West object to the Russian people having socialism or any other system they wish. If, in fact, it were only a matter of ideologies, and only a matter of the relationship between the West and Russia proper, there would be no reason why the Soviet demand for "peaceful coexistence" should not be accepted without reservation.

But the Soviet Union is not only an ideological phenomenon. It is also a great power, physically and militarily. Even if the prevailing ideology in Russia were not antagonistic to the concepts prevailing elsewhere, the behavior of the government of that country in its international relations, and particularly any considerable expansion of its power at the expense of the freedom of other peoples, would still be a matter of most serious interest to the world at large.

And it is, let us recall, precisely such an expansion that we have witnessed in recent years. So far as Europe is concerned, this expansion had its origin in the advance of Soviet armies into Eastern and Central Europe in 1945. This advance was not only accepted at the time—it was generally welcomed in the West as a very important part of the final phase of the struggle against Hitler. But it has had a consequence which few people in the West foresaw in 1945 and which fewer still desired: the quasi-permanent advancement of the effective boundaries of Moscow's political and military authority to the very center of Europe. . . .

The fact is that this extension of Russia's political and military power into the heart of Europe represents a major alteration in the world strategic and political balance, and one that was never discussed as such with Western statesmen, much less agreed to by them.

It is not just the *fact* of this situation which is of importance to the Western peoples; there is also the question as to *how* it came into existence and *how* it is being maintained. The truth is that it did not come into existence because the majority of the people in the region affected became convinced that Communism, as Mr. Khrushchev has put it, was "the more progressive and equitable system." This peaceful competition for the minds of men which the Communists today ask us to accept as the concomitant and condition of peaceful coexistence had precious little to do with the means by which socialist governments, on the pattern approved by Moscow, were established in the countries of Eastern Europe in 1944 and 1945 or with the means by which their rule was subsequently consolidated there. In the view of the West, formed on the strength of overwhelming historical evidence, these régimes were imposed by the skillful manipulations of highly disciplined Communist minorities, trained and inspired by Moscow, and supported by the presence or close proximity of units of the Soviet armed forces. They have been maintained in power by similar means.

. . . . .

It was indicated above that the existence of the Soviet brand of socialism in *Russia itself* may well be regarded in the West as Russia's own business and need not be a barrier to peaceful coexistence. The Soviet régime is, after all, an indigenous régime throughout the greater part of the area of the Soviet Union. The processes in which it had its origin were not democratic ones in the Western sense, but they were deeply Russian ones, reflecting some very basic realities of the Russian political life of that day. It is indeed not the business of Americans to interfere with such a régime.

But when it comes to the governments of the Communist bloc in Eastern and Central Europe, then the problem is inevitably more complicated. These governments are not, in the main, truly indigenous. All this is of course relative; for seldom, if ever, is there *no* area of identity between the interests and sentiments of a people and the régime, however despotic, that governs it. But these régimes represent, in Western eyes, the fruits of a species of conquest and subjugation which was not less real for the fact that it did not generally involve hostile military invasion in the usual sense. And the thought inevitably presents itself: if such a thing could be done to *these* peoples, by means short of overt military aggression, and if we are now asked to accept it as something not to be discussed in connection with peaceful coexistence, to how many other peoples could this also be done, within the very framework of coexistence we are being asked to adopt?

. . . . .

Mr. Khrushchev is right in viewing the weapons race of this day as inconsistent with any satisfactory form of coexistence. But the prospects for bettering this situation will not be promising so long as Moscow persists in viewing the military policies pursued in the Western coalition in recent years as solely the products of the lust of Western financiers and manufacturers thirsting for another war in the hopes of greater profits, and refuses to recognize that these policies, however misconceived or overdrawn, represent in large measure the natural and predictable reactions of great peoples to a situation which Moscow itself did much to create.

187 AFFLUENCE IN EUROPE

Parallel with the Cold War thaw was the burgeoning prosperity of Western Europe. In contrast to the immediate postwar years when the Continent lay prostrate, Europe now rose rapidly to the level of affluence. An American correspondent describes precisely the meaning of this prosperity in terms of everyday life and class relationships.*

Europe is in the chips. An affluence undreamed of a few years ago is filling European pockets with hard cash, European kitchens with new gadgets, and European highways with new cars. Rooftops have sprouted forests of antennas. Luxurious jet planes ferry busy men and women across the Alps, across the Rhine. People who used to ride the streetcar now drive to work. The stores are crammed with great quantities of the good things in life. Three hundred million human beings—the inhabitants of Europe on the sunny side of the Iron Curtain—are enjoying a prosperity that is unprecedented in the Old World's history.

Postwar reports of Europe's demise have since proved premature. That it was a narrow squeeze nobody here denies. "If we are still around at all," a ranking French official said, "it is most likely due to the forty-odd billion aid dollars the United States has lent or given Europe since the end of World War II. But we are now on our own. We've broken through. We have entered a new phase, and we are moving forward on our own momentum."

In my own little world, the nook of Paris where I make my home, things have crept up on me. Since when, I wonder, has Monsieur Louis who owns the *bistro* down the way—a favorite haunt of truck drivers and workmen— used an expensive station wagon for his marketing? The television antenna marring the view from my back window dates back—let's see—to last July. I seem to have a neighbor who gives cocktail parties. An expensive-looking candy store has recently opened its doors. The toy shop has taken on an extra salesgirl and put out a neon sign. The bank has had its face lifted. My friend the antique dealer and his wife spent their summer vacation driving all the way to the North Cape and back again.

· · · · ·

Project this picture post card on a vaster screen and what you get is Europe, 1962. While the United States has passed through at least two reces-

* Ernest O. Hauser, "Affluent Europe," *The Saturday Evening Post* (February 10, 1962).

sions since the Korean War, Europe has suffered nothing worse than a couple of mild dips. And while we have increased our national wealth since 1950 at the modest rate of 3.8 percent a year, France's annual rate of growth has averaged 7.1 percent; Italy's 8.4 percent; and finally, Western Germany's, a staggering 9.6 percent.

The rise from rags to riches, to be sure, must be seen in its proper perspective. In several European countries expansion has been so spectacular largely because they had suffered heavy damage during World War II. Starting at the bottom, they came up fast, while our own economy was merely clambering from an already high plateau to a still higher one. Even today the average European is still "poor" by our standards, his annual income being roughly half the income of the average American in terms of real purchasing power.

Moreover there remain some ugly holes in the bright picture of Europe's new prosperity. Greece, Portugal, Southern Italy and parts of Spain are still beset by their old incubus, mass poverty. Slums, even cave dwellings, exist in many cities. There are regions where such necessities of life as electricity and running water are still considered luxuries. Even in Britain, Western Germany, and France the electricity output per person is less than half our own. Housing, almost everywhere in Europe, is still distressingly inadequate, with many families living in one small room or sharing the homes of relatives. Last but not least, the distribution of wealth still leaves a lot to be desired, and abject misery frequently hides hard beneath the glittering surface.

Still, the great bulk of Western Europe's population is now immeasurably better off than in the recent past. . . .

A static continent has turned dynamic. Cities have outgrown their old forms and spilled into the countryside. (Look down on any European capital from the air, and you will see its venerable body dwarfed by a brood of modern surburbs.) The birth rate has been climbing merrily since World War II—even old France, stagnant and over-age for decades, has spawned some record crops of babies, increasing her population from a prewar 42,-000,000 to 45,800,000. The accent is on youth. Everywhere one goes in Western Europe one is impressed with the great number of young people, taller than their elders, and by the flocks of boisterously healthy children, dressed no longer like tiny adults but in dungarees and T shirts.

People are on the move. Farmers flock to the cities. Townsfolk become suburbanites. Touched by a magic wand, the great outdoors has come to life—long-silent forests swarm with campers, the lakes are white with sailboats, gingerbread mountain towns are packed with skiers. Anything that spells "hobby" and "outdoors"—from barbecue grills to records, stamps and movie cameras—is selling briskly. The money has come out of socks and mustard pots, and it circulates.

The most remarkable thing about this new prosperity in a notoriously class-ridden continent is that it is a mass phenomenon. "Exclusive" signs are coming down all over Europe. "I went to Capri last summer as I do every year," an Italian industrialist told me. "The first day on the island I met our maid with her husband. The next day I encountered my optician. And the day after that I bumped into my tailor, who promptly measured me for a new suit."

.   .   .   .   .

If supermarkets have begun to flourish in many European cities—France has nearly 100 of them and expects to build 3000 in the next four years—it is because more women work and can no longer spare the time to gossip with the butcher, the grocer and the pastry baker. If quick-lunch counters are besieged at midday by a throng of workers and employees, it is because more and more businesses are switching to the continuous working day, replacing the hallowed institution of the three-hour lunch with a quick break. Vending machines and jukeboxes have become part of Europe's scenery, along with plastics and synthetic fabrics, slacks for the ladies, frozen food, soft drinks and tranquilizer pills.

... Consumer credit, virtually unknown in many European countries before World War II, has been accepted, albeit cautiously, as a necessary feature of the market place. The average Englishman today owes $33 in installment debts on goods he has bought; the German, $22; and the Frenchman, $16—compared with $212 owed by the average American.

But it is the motorcar—catalyst of our own machine-age civilization—that has revolutionized the European way of life.

· · · · ·

True, Europe is still well behind us in mobility—where there is one passenger car for every three Americans, there still is only one every eight Frenchmen, every nine Britons, every eleven West Germans, every twenty-six Italians and every 200 Greeks! However, Western Europe's total number of automobiles has jumped from some 10,000,000 in 1950 to more than 30,000,000; Italy alone has multiplied her herd of passenger cars by six in the same period. An Italian friend of mine who works for a government agency in Rome reports: "In 1958 only one man besides me owned a car in my department. Today nine other people drive their own automobiles, including two girl secretaries and one of the ushers."

· · · · ·

Cooped up in his own bailiwick for many war and postwar years, the European yields to the exhilarating rush of a new freedom. Along hurriedly widened roads and brand-new superhighways, past gleaming service stations and motels that weren't there last year, through recently completed Alpine tunnels, he rumbles off to see the world. For the first time in history millions of Europeans cross their own borders and take a look at foreign lands which heretofore were well beyond their reach. Paris in springtime is overrun with Germans. Spain, Italy and Greece become, during the summer months, the happy hunting grounds of Frenchmen, Belgians, Germans, Britons, Scandinavians. ...

Alas, a shadow falls across this happy picture. Not weaned on the internal combustion engine, the European is still ill at ease with so much speed and power. The middle-aged apprentice driver perspiring at the side of his instructor as he stalls the car in heavy traffic is a common sight in European streets. Male fledglings, especially in Latin countries, find it hard to resist the urge to show off, with a mighty roar, to their admiring girl friends. As for the average woman driver, her turn at the wheel comes so infrequently—two-car families still being few and far between in Europe—that she is likely to remain a public hazard all her life. Add to all this the absence of a speed limit in many regions, and what you get is sudden death. Comparative statistics are appalling. The United States, with 74,000,000 motor vehicles on the road, registers nearly 38,000 traffic deaths a year; France, with 7,000,000 vehicles, kills 8000 people; Italy, with 2,500,000—also 8000; and Germany with 5,000,000 cars, holds the macabre record of 14,000 victims.

The second-biggest annual show in Paris, after the autumn Automobile *Salon,* is the *Salon des Arts Menagers*—a sample fair of household gadgets and appliances which, every spring, fills the French capital with eager visitors who come to ogle and to buy. Europe has gone appliance-happy. Refrigerators, washing machines, dishwashers, mixers, vacuum cleaners, record players and TV sets largely account for the fantastic rise in the turnover of consumer durables. While our own expenditure for this kind of hardware has increased by 20 per cent over the last decade, Europe's has doubled.

. . . . .

Beneath the surface ripples of Europe's golden age, one finds some basic changes which are beginning to affect the structure of society itself. Class hatred, for one thing, is disappearing fast as today's have-nots expect to be tomorrow's haves. A Fiat automobile representative with whom I talked in a small town in Italy smilingly pointed to a poster in his office. It was a slicked-up photograph showing six beaming persons—a blonde in slacks, a bronzed young man with gôlf clubs, and other stand-bys of the advertising trade—grouped casually around Fiat's latest ranch wagon on the luxurious lawn of a suburban house.

"Ten years ago," the dealer said, "we would not have dared put up a thing like that. A poster of this kind would have caused nothing but resentment. Today every Italian can visualize himself—or at any rate his children—as members of that happy group."

But Old World capitalism itself has come of age and is no longer the terrifying bogey it used to be. Gone is the penny-pinching, stiff-necked, ice-cold manufacturer who ran the business by his own lights, brooking no interference. In his place there has risen a managerial elite very much like our own. Board any of the continent's crack trains—the *Sette Bello* between Milan and Rome, or the Trans-Europe Express on its Cologne-to-Paris run—and you will find in it a cross section of the new business aristocracy. Well groomed, well tailored, full of vim and vigor, your fellow passengers closely resemble American executives as they talk shop over cigars and brandy.

. . . . .

The signs at this point read FULL SPEED AHEAD. Barring such unforeseeable calamities as war and *coups d'état,* the experts say that ten or twelve years hence our European cousins should be as prosperous as we are now.

PRESIDENT DE GAULLE'S INDEPENDENT COURSE 188

The combination of the Cold War thaw and economic prosperity enabled the countries of Western Europe to lessen their dependence upon the United States. The most striking example was President de Gaulle's vigorously independent *course in various areas, particularly evident in his recognition of Communist China in the face of strong American disapproval. In a news conference held on January 31, 1964, President de Gaulle gave the reasons for his policy of recognition.**

We are going to speak of China. China—a great people, the most numerous on earth. . . .

This country's entry into contact with the modern nations has been very hard and very costly. The many European, American, Japanese demands, interventions, expeditions, invasions, were for it so many humiliations and mutilations. Then many national upheavals, and also the will of the elite to transform the country at all costs so that it might reach the condition and the power of the people that oppressed it, led China to the revolution.

Certainly, Marshal Chiang Kai-shek, to whose valor, patriotism, spiritual elevation, I am duty bound to render homage, feeling certain that history and the Chinese people will one day do the same, Marshal Chiang Kai-shek, after leading China to the Allied victory that in the Pacific put the seal on the Second World War, tried to channel the torrent.

Since then an enormous effort, which was imperative anyway, concerning the development of natural riches, industrial development, agricultural production, education against the scourges inherent in this country, famine, epidemics, soil erosion, the overflowing of the rivers, etc., has been undertaken throughout the territory.

As always in a Communist system, what was achieved entailed terrible human suffering, an implacable constraint of the masses, immense losses and wasting of goods, the crushing and decimation of innumerable human values. However, results were achieved that are due in part to the action of the totalitarian machine and also to the ardor of a proud people who want to better themselves in all fields and who are capable of deploying treasures of courage and ingenuity whatever the circumstances.

It is true that Soviet Russia first of all provided China with quite considerable assistance: the opening of credits for the purchase of machinery and supplies, mining and industrial equipment, the installation of whole factories, the direct training of students and specialists, the sending of engineers, technicians and qualified workers, etc.

This was the time when the Kremlin planned to keep China under its control and thereby dominate Asia. But the illusions have been dissipated. Doubtless there remain between Moscow and Peking a certain doctrinal solidarity which can express itself in the world ideological competition. But under this mantle, more and more torn, there appears a difference of national policies.

The least one can say on this subject is that in Asia, where the frontier separating the two states, from the Hindu Kush to Vladivostok, is the longest in the world, the interest of Russia, which is one of conserving and maintaining, and that of China, which needs to grow and to take, cannot be confused.

Considering that for 15 years almost the whole of China has been gathered under a Government that rules it and that she shows herself abroad

* *The New York Times* (February 1, 1964). © 1964 by The New York Times Company. Reprinted by permission.

as an independent, sovereign power, France was disposed in principle, and for years now, to establish regular relations with Peking.

Moreover, certain economic and cultural exchanges were already taking place and, with America, Britain, the Soviet Union, India and other states, we were led in 1954, at the Geneva conference, when the fate of Indochina was settled, to negotiate with the Chinese representatives.

497

And it was the same in 1962, in the same form and in the same town, when the Laos situation was more or less defined.

But with the weight of evidence and reason making itself felt more and more every day, the French Republic decided to place its relations with the People's Republic of China on a normal, in other words diplomatic, basis.

We met in Peking an identical intention. It was then that the two countries agreed to accomplish the necessary. I spoke of the weight of evidence and reason and in fact in Asia there is no political reality concerning Cambodia, Laos, Vietnam, or India, Pakistan, Afghanistan, Burma, Korea, or Soviet Russia or Japan, etc., that does not interest or concern China.

On this Continent, there is no imaginable peace or war without her being implicated and it is inconceivable to suppose that it is possible ever to conclude a neutrality treaty concerning the states of Southeast Asia, to which we French show a very special and cordial attention, without China's being a party to it.

But also China's mass, its value and its present needs and the dimension of its future all lead her to manifest herself more and more in the interest and the concerns of the whole universe. Indeed it is clear that France must be able to hear China directly and also to make herself heard by China.

What is already being done, economically speaking, with regard to China, what is being done by us, and which can be improved, will no doubt for a long time be limited, and it is the same with regard to investments we are already making in Chinese industrial development.

In the case of technique, the situation is no doubt very different, as the sources of technique in France are more and more valuable and China represents for French technique an almost infinite field.

Then who knows whether the affinities that exist between the two nations regarding everything concerning spiritual matters, and taking also into account the fact that deep down they have always felt for each other sympathy and consideration, will not lead them to a growing cultural cooperation? In any case this is sincerely desired here.

So Peking and Paris have agreed to exchange ambassadors. Obviously on our part there is nothing in that implying any kind of approval of the regime that at present dominates China.

By establishing with this country, with this state, official relations as many other free nations have done before and as we have done with other countries which suffer similar regimes, France only recognizes the world as it is.

"POLYCENTRISM" IN THE COMMUNIST WORLD **189**

Just as de Gaulle pursued a policy independent from that of the United States, Rumania asserted herself in relations with the Soviet Union. The trend began in

Eastern Europe with Tito's heresy in 1948, burst forth again with the Polish and Hungarian outbreaks in 1956, and thereafter gained strength quietly but steadily. By April, 1964, it had developed to the point where the Rumanian Communist party issued a statement demanding complete equality and independence in the political and economic relations between Communist states and parties. This statement, from which excerpts are given below, defines forthrightly the principle of "polycentrism" toward which the Communist world is moving—a principle quite different from the monolithic unity imposed earlier by Stalin.*

The economic and technical-scientific progress of the socialist countries relies on the relations of co-operation and mutual assistance established between them. These fruitful relations have seen a steady development; they have proved their efficiency, making a particularly important contribution to the successes scored by the socialist countries.

With a view to the complete utilization of the advantages of these relations, the Council of Mutual Economic Assistance was set up. According to its Rules, its aim is to contribute, through the uniting and co-ordination of efforts, to the development of the national economy, to speeding up economic and technical progress, to raising the level of industrialization of the less developed countries, to the steady increase in labour productivity and to the ceaseless improvement in the welfare of the peoples in the member countries.

Co-operation within CMEA is achieved on the basis of the principles of fully equal rights, of observance of national sovereignty and interests, of mutual advantage and comradely assistance.

As concerns the method of economic co-operation, the socialist countries which are members of CMEA have established that the main means of achieving the international socialist division of labour, the main form of co-operation between their national economies is to co-ordinate plans on the basis of bilateral and multilateral agreements.

During the development of the relations of co-operation between the socialist countries which are members of CMEA, forms and measures have been suggested, such as a joint plan and a single planning body for all member countries, interstate technical-productive branch unions, enterprises jointly owned by several countries, inter-state economic complexes, etc.

Our Party has very clearly expressed its point of view, declaring that, since the essence of the suggested measures lies in shifting some functions of economic management from the competence of the respective state to the attribution of superstate bodies or organisms, these measures are not in keeping with the principles which underlie the relations between the socialist countries.

The idea of a single planning body for all CMEA countries has the most serious economic and political implications. The planned management of the national economy is one of the fundamental, essential and inalienable attributes of the sovereignty of the socialist state—the state plan being the chief means through which the socialist state achieves its political and socio-economic objectives, establishes the directions and rates of development of

* *Statement on the Stand of the Rumanian Workers' Party Concerning the Problems of the World Communist and Working-Class Movement . . . April 1964* (Agerpress: Rumanian News Agency, n.d.), pp. 28-33, 46, 49-51.

the national economy, its fundamental proportions, the accumulations, the measures for raising the people's living standard and cultural level. The sovereignty of the socialist state requires that it effectively and fully avails itself of the means for the practical implementation of these attributions, holding in its hands all the levers of managing economic and social life. Transmitting such levers to the competence of super-state or extra-state bodies would turn sovereignty into a notion without any contents.

All these are also fully valid as concerns inter-state technical-productive branch unions, as well as enterprises commonly owned by two or several states. The State Plan is one and indivisible, no parts or sections can be separated from it in order to be transferred outside the state. The management of the national economy as a whole is not possible if the questions of managing some branches or enterprises are taken away from the competence of the Party and government of the respective country and transferred to extra-state bodies. ...

Such is the viewpoint of the Rumanian Workers' Party as concerns the nature of the relations of economic co-operation between the socialist countries in the present stage of history.

Undoubtedly if some socialist countries deem it fit to adopt in the direct relations between them forms of co-operation different from those unanimously agreed upon within CMEA, that is a question which exclusively concerns those countries, and can be decided by them alone in a sovereign way. ...

At the same time, the socialist international division of labour cannot mean isolation of the socialist countries from the general framework of world economic relations. Standing consistently for normal, mutually advantageous economic relations, without political strings and without restrictions or discriminations, the Rumanian People's Republic, like the other socialist states, develops its economic links with all states irrespective of their social system. ...

The transformation of socialism into a world system, the winning of power by the working people in a number of states, has faced the communist and workers' parties with the task of radically changing not only social relations on a national level, in their own country, but also of organizing mutual relations between these countries, of working out the norms of co-operation in the framework of a great world community of states. This has arisen as an entirely new problem, for which there was no previous practical experience—and which was all the more complex as it concerned countries differing in size, might, degree of economic, political and social development, in addition to their national distinctions and historical peculiarities.

By promoting in the international arena a qualitatively new system of relations, unprecedented in history, the communist and workers' parties in the socialist countries have placed at the foundation of these relations the principles of national independence and sovereignty, equal rights, mutual advantage, comradely assistance, non-interference in internal affairs, observance of territorial integrity, the principles of socialist internationalism. ...

Of late, the divergencies in the international communist and working-class movement have deepened, and the public polemic has assumed particular sharpness. Instead of a debate imbued with the endeavour to bring standpoints closer to each other and to find solutions based on Marxist-Leninist ideology, forms and methods have been adopted in the course of the public polemic which considerably envenom relations between parties, and offensive judgements, as well as accusations and the ascribing of certain intentions are being resorted to.

Strict observance of the principle that all Marxist-Leninist parties enjoy equal rights, of the principle of non-interference in other parties' domestic affairs, of each Party's exclusive right to solve its own political and organizational problems, of appointing its leaders, of orienting its members in problems of internal and international politics—is an essential condition for the correct settlement of issues in which there are divergencies, as well as of all problems raised by their common struggle.

. . . . .

There does not and cannot exist a "parent" party and a "son-party," parties that are "superior" and parties that are "subordinate," but there exists the great family of communist and workers' parties, which have equal rights. No party has or can have a privileged place, or can impose its line and opinions on other parties. Each party makes its own contribution to the development of the common treasure store of Marxist-Leninist teaching, to enriching the forms and practical methods of revolutionary struggle for winning power and building the socialist society.

In discussing and confronting different points of view on problems concerning the revolutionary struggle or socialist construction, no party must label as anti-Marxist, anti-Leninist the fraternal party whose opinions it does not share. . . .

It is inconceivable that in relations between communist parties reciprocal and deeply offensive accusations be levelled against the leaders of a fraternal party as being "the biggest revisionists of our time," who are in "collusion with U.S. imperialism," and "throw wide open the gates for the restoration of capitalism," or that they are "trotzkyites" who "furiously attack world socialism," "partners on the right-flank of the American 'wild men.' "

190 The United States and the New Eastern Europe

Just as the United States supported Tito in his break with Stalin in 1948, so the United States supported Rumania's independent course by signing agreements in June, 1964 for a great expansion in trade, including credit arrangements. The rationale behind this move was spelled out by President Lyndon Johnson in a speech at the dedication of the George C. Marshall Research Library at Lexington, Virginia, on May 23, 1964.

When he [General Marshall] had helped guide us to victory he knew that peace, like victory, would go not just to the righteous but to the skillful, not just to the free but to the brave.

He followed Harry Truman's wise reminder that peace is not a reward that comes automatically to those who cherish it. It must be pursued unceasingly and unswervingly by every means at our command.

---

* *The New York Times* (May 24, 1964). © 1964 by The New York Times Company. Reprinted by permission.

To this end, under President Truman's direction, he proposed the Marshall Plan.

We know how much our freedom and the freedom of all Western Europe owes to that single stroke.

But that vision did not stop where Soviet conquest began. To General Marshall permanent peace depended upon rebuilding all European civilization within its historic boundaries. The Iron Curtain rang down upon that hope, but the correctness of his conviction has not changed.

Today we work to carry on the vision of the Marshall Plan.

First, to strengthen the ability of every European people to select and shape its own society.

Second, to bring every European nation closer to its neighbors in the relationships of peace. This will not be achieved by sudden settlement or by dramatic deed. But the nations of Eastern Europe are beginning to re-assert their own identity. There is no longer a single Iron Curtain. There are many. Each differs in strength and thickness, in the light that can pass through it and the hopes that can prosper behind it.

We do not know when all European nations will become part of a single civilization, but as President Eisenhower said in 1953, and I quote: "This we do know. A world that begins to witness the rebirth of trust among nations can find its way to peace that is neither partial nor punitive."

We will continue to build bridges across the gulf which has divided us from Eastern Europe. They will be bridges of increased trade, of ideas, of visitors and of humanitarian aid.

We do this for four reasons:

First, to open new relationships to countries seeking increased independence yet unable to risk isolation.

Second, to open the minds of a new generation to the values and the vision of the Western civilization from which they come and to which they belong.

Third, to give freer play to the powerful forces of legitimate national pride—the strongest barrier to the ambition of any country to dominate another.

Fourth, to demonstrate that identity of interest and the prospects of progress for Eastern Europe lie in a wider relationship with the West. . . .

We are pledged to use every peaceful means to work with friends and allies so that all Europe may be joined in a shared society of freedom.

SINO–SOVIET CONFLICT 191

The most dramatic, and perhaps the most significant, manifestation of the new pluralism in world affairs has been the conflict between the two Communist giants, the Soviet Union and China. In marked contrast to the thirty-year treaty of "friendship, alliance and mutual assistance" which they signed in 1950, the two powers have drifted apart to the point of engaging in unrestrained name-calling, ideological vituperation, and open rivalry all over the globe. The bitterness is re-flected in the following selections * from an article in the Peking People's Daily

(January 1, 1963) entitled "The Differences between Communist Togliatti and Us," and a point-by-point rebuttal carried in Pravda *(January 6, 1963) official organ of the Communist party of the Soviet Union. Later exchanges have been much more virulent, naming names in place of euphemisms such as "some people."*

Peking People's Daily

... What are the real differences between them [the Italian Communists] and us? They are manifested mainly in the following three questions:

1. The CCP [Communist Party of China] holds that the source of modern war is imperialism. The chief force for war and aggression is U.S. imperialism, the most vicious enemy of all the peoples of the world. In order to defend world peace, it is necessary to expose the imperialist policies of aggression and war unceasingly and thoroughly, and call on the people of the world to maintain a high degree of vigilance.

. . . . .

It will be recalled that three years ago, following the "Camp David talks," some persons in the international Communist movement made propaganda in a big way about Eisenhower's sincere desire for peace, saying that this ringleader of U.S. imperialism was just as concerned about peace as we.

Now we hear some people saying that Kennedy is even more concerned about world peace than Eisenhower was and that Kennedy showed his concern for the maintenance of peace during the Caribbean crisis. One would like to ask: Is this way of embellishing U.S. imperialism the correct policy for defending world peace?

The intrusion into the Soviet Union of spy planes sent by the Eisenhower administration, the aggression against Cuba by the Kennedy administration, and a hundred and one other acts of aggression around the world by U.S. imperialism, and its threats to world peace—have these not repeatedly confirmed the truth and shown that the ringleaders of U.S. imperialism are no angels of peace but monsters of war? And are not those people who try time and time again to prettify imperialism deliberately deceiving the peoples of the world? ...

2. The CCP holds that world peace can only be securely safeguarded in the resolute struggle against imperialism, headed by the U.S. by constantly strengthening the Socialist camp, and by constantly strengthening the national and democratic movements in Asia, Africa, and Latin America, the people's revolutionary struggles in various countries and the movement to defend world peace.

To achieve world peace it is necessary to rely mainly on the strength of the masses of the people of the world and on their struggles. In the course of the struggle to defend world peace, it is necessary to enter into negotiations on one issue or another with the governments of the imperialist countries, including the government of the U.S., for the purpose of easing international tension, reaching some kind of compromise and arriving at certain agreements subject to the principle that such compromises and agreements must not damage the fundamental interests of the people.

However, world peace can never be achieved by negotiations alone, and in

* *The Chicago Sun-Times* (January 20, 1963).

no circumstances must we pin our hopes on imperialism and divorce ourselves from the struggles of the masses.

3. The CCP holds that the struggle for the defense of world peace supports, is supported by, and indeed is inseparable from the national liberation movements and the people's revolutionary struggles in various countries. The national liberation movements and the peoples' revolutionary struggles are a powerful force weakening the imperialist forces of war and defending world peace.

. . . . .

It would simply result in a phony peace or bring about an actual war for the people of the whole world if you pin your hopes of peace on imperialism, and take a passive or negative attitude towards the national liberation movements, as advocated by those who attack the CCP. This policy is wrong and all Marxist-Leninists, all revolutionary people, all peace-loving people must resolutely oppose it.

On the question of war and peace, the differences with Togliatti find striking expressions in our respective attitudes to nuclear weapons and nuclear war. . . .

Togliatti and certain others talk volubly about "the suicide of mankind" and the "total destruction" of mankind. They believe that "it is in vain even to discuss what could be the orientation of these fragments of survivals regarding social order."

We are firmly opposed to such pessimistic and despairing tunes. We believe that it is possible to attain a complete ban on nuclear weapons in the following circumstances: the Socialist camp has a great nuclear superiority; the peoples' struggles in various countries against nuclear weapons become broader and deeper; having further forfeited their nuclear superiority, the imperialists are compelled to realize that their policy of nuclear blackmail is no longer effective and that their launching of a nuclear war would only accelerate their own extinction.

If, after we have done everything possible to prevent a nuclear war, imperialism should nevertheless unleash nuclear war, without regard to any of the consequences, it would result in the extinction of imperialism and definitely not in the extinction of mankind.

Comrade Togliatti and certain other comrades have strongly opposed the Marxist-Leninist proposition of the CCP that "imperialism and all reactionaries are paper tigers."

Comrade Togliatti said that it "was wrong to state that imperialism is simply a paper tiger which can be overthrown by a mere push of the shoulder." Then there are other persons who assert that today imperialism has nuclear teeth, so how can it be called a paper tiger?

Prejudice is farther from the truth than ignorance. In the case of Comrade Togliatti and certain other comrades, if they are not ignorant, then they are deliberately distorting the proposition of the CCP. In comparing imperialism and all reactionaries with paper tigers, Comrade Mao Tze-tung and the Chinese Communists are looking at the problem as a whole and from a long-term point of view and are looking at the essence of the problem. What is meant is that, in the final analysis, it is the people who are really powerful, not imperialism and the reactionaries.

Comrade Mao Tze-tung first put forward this proposition in August, 1946. With great lucidity he said:

"All reactionaries are paper tigers. In appearance, the reactionaries are terrifying, but in reality they are not so powerful. From a long-term point of view, it is not the reactionaries but the people who are really powerful. . . ."

Comrade Mao Tze-tung's analysis of imperialism and all reactionaries is completely in accord with Lenin's analysis. In 1919 Lenin compared the "universally mighty" Anglo-French imperialism to a "Colossus with feet of clay."

We ask, what is wrong with Lenin's position? Is this proposition of Lenin's "outmoded"?

. . . . .

On peaceful coexistence we have another difference with those who are attacking us. We hold that the question of peaceful coexistence between countries with different social systems and the question of revolution by oppressed nations or by oppressed classes are two different kinds of questions, and not questions of the same kind.

The principle of peaceful coexistence can apply only to relations between countries with different social systems, not to relations between oppressed and oppressor nations, nor to relations between oppressed and oppressing classes. For an oppressed nation of people the question is one of waging a revolutionary struggle to overthrow the rule of imperialism and the reactionaries; it is not, and cannot be, a question of peaceful coexistence with imperialism and the reactionaries.

. . . . .

Some people have repeatedly charged China with creating difficulties in the Caribbean situation and with wanting to plunge the world into a thermonuclear war. This slander against China is most malicious and most despicable.

How can one possibly interpret the resolute support which the Chinese people gave to the Cuban people in their struggle against international inspection and in defense of their sovereignty as meaning that China was opposed to peaceful coexistence or wanted to plunge others into a thermonuclear war?

Does this mean that China also should have applied pressure on Cuba to force her to accept international inspection, and that only by so doing would China have conformed to this so-called "peaceful coexistence"?

We neither called for the establishment of missile bases in Cuba nor obstructed the withdrawal of the so-called "offensive weapons" from Cuba. We have never considered that it was a Marxist-Leninist attitude to brandish nuclear weapons as a way of settling international disputes. Nor have we ever considered that the avoidance of the thermonuclear war in the Caribbean crisis was a "Munich."

What we did strongly oppose, still strongly oppose, and will strongly oppose in the future, is the sacrifice of another country's sovereignty as a means of reaching a compromise with imperialism. A compromise of this sort can only be regarded as 100 per cent appeasement, a "Munich" pure and simple.

Hitherto, history has not witnessed a single example of peaceful transition from capitalism to socialism. Communists should not pin all their hopes for the victory of the revolution on peaceful transition. The *bourgeoisie* will never step down from the stage of history of its own accord. This is a universal law of class struggle.

Communists must not in the slightest degree relax their preparedness for revolution.

Moscow Pravda

... The most important, the most vital problem of our time is the problem of war and peace. In real life the choice is: either peaceful coexistence between states with different social systems or a devastating war. There is no other alternative.

The question arises: What position should the Communists take? Only one—the position of peaceful coexistence.

The Socialist countries do not need war. They are successfully developing in peaceful conditions and will be victorious in the peaceful economic competition with capitalism, which fact will be of exceptional importance for making the peoples choose the socialist way as the only correct one.

The Albanian leaders—Enver Hoxha for instance—boast that they do not agree with those who "regard peaceful coexistence as the general line of the foreign policy of the Socialist countries."

But what then is the general line? War? If so, where is then the difference between such an approach to the solution of the question about the victory of communism or capitalism and the viewpoint of the adventurist circles of imperialism?

In point of fact, the only difference is that the frenzied imperialists have lost faith in the ability of capitalism to stand its own in the competition with socialism, while the dogmatists do not believe in the possibility of the victory of communism in the conditions of peaceful competition of states with different social systems.

But which Marxist-Leninist would agree that the way to the victory of communism lies through a thermonuclear war?

The most important thing in the struggle for peace is to curb the aggressors in time, to avert war, to prevent it from flaring up. This is particularly necessary in view of the unprecedented destructive force of modern weapons.

In contrast to these propositions, the dogmatists emphasize that nuclear war is not to be feared, that modern weapons are monstrous only "in the opinions of the imperialists and reactionaries," that "the atom bomb is a paper tiger." This is nothing but renunciation of the main goal in the struggle for peace indicated in the statement of the policy of peaceful coexistence.

The dogmatists present peaceful coexistence as "renunciation of the struggle for the exposure of imperialism," as "discontinuation of the struggle against imperialism."

They do not understand that competition in peaceful conditions is one of the most important battlegrounds between socialism and capitalism. As regards the struggle against imperialism proclaimed by the dogmatists, it boils down to mere high-sounding invective phrases and foul language.

Historically, it fell to the lot of the Soviet people to bear the brunt of the struggle against imperialist warmongers. It is not an easy task to bear such a burden. The Soviet people even not infrequently have to deny themselves things they need.

Who was it that extinguished the raging flames of war in the Suez Canal Zone in 1956 by compelling the British-French-Israel aggressors to beat a retreat? Who was it that in 1957 prevented the invasion of Syria prepared by the imperialists? Who was it that in 1958 prevented war in the Near East and in the area of Taiwan Strait from flaring up?

It was the Soviet Union, all countries of the Socialist camp, the peace forces. They, and above all the might and the vigorous actions of the U.S.S.R., compelled the imperialist warmongers to retreat. . . .

The postwar years have not witnessed a more acute international crisis, fraught with the danger of a world-wide thermonuclear conflagration, than the recent crisis created by American imperialism in the Caribbean area. . . .

Now that the crest of the crisis is behind, representatives of the "leftist phrasemongers" are striving slanderously to present the case as if the Soviet Union had capitulated to imperialism and even agreed to a "second Munich."

But everyone who unbiasedly analyzes the results of the liquidation of the crisis in the Caribbean area sees that there is not a grain of truth in the accusations of the dogmatists, that the phrases they utter are actually calculated to provoke war.

The crisis was settled on the basis of mutual concessions and sensible compromise. The solution of disputed questions between states without wars, by peaceful means—this is precisely the policy of peaceful coexistence in action. . . .

The beacon of freedom in the Western Hemisphere is burning still brighter. Is this a "Munich"? Is this a retreat? The authors of the term "second Munich" are obviously at odds with elementary history and know not what they are speaking about. . . .

A modern war cannot be approached with old yardsticks. A world war, if we fail to prevent it, will immediately become a thermonuclear conflict, will lead to the death of millions upon millions of people, to the destruction of tremendous material values, to the devastation of whole countries.

In their cynical gamble with human lives, certain people dare to scoff at those who defend the lives of hundreds of millions of people, accusing these fighters of "cowardice" and "spinelessness." But Communists, the more so Communist statesmen and political leaders, cannot act like these irresponsible penhacks. . . .

To impose on the Communist movement their definition of modern imperialism and to ignore its atomic fangs, some people claim that the "paper tiger" thesis is tantamount to Lenin's definition of imperialism as a "colossus on clay feet."

It is common knowledge, however, that the figurative expression does not cover or substitute all the substance of V.I. Lenin's all-round definition of imperialism. Moreover, this expression stresses that imperialism is still strong (colossus), but it stands (on clay feet) on an unstable basis and is rent by internal contradictions.

The "paper tiger" definition of imperialism speaks only of its weakness. The main point, however, is that what we need are not paper definitions, stubbornly thrust upon us, but a genuine analysis of contemporary imperialism: disclosure of its vices, weaknesses and laws, leading to its ruin; and at the same time a sober assessment of its forces, including the huge atomic and other military potential.

. . . . .

To believe that a recipe for a Socialist revolution can be invented to suit all times and all countries, and to thrust it upon the fraternal parties operating in the specific conditions of their countries, is to do a harmful thing, to display haughtiness alien to Communists, to set oneself as a teacher of all Communist parties, and a teacher divorced from life, at that, and therefore incapable of offering anything but dogmatic formulas. . . .

Communists cannot but feel gravely concerned over the thesis launched recently that there is a "temporary majority" in the international Communist movement which "persists in its mistakes," and a "temporary minority" which "boldly and resolutely upholds the truth."

This thesis only serves to justify a split of the Communist movement and renunciation of the common positions of the Marxist-Leninist parties.

This contention is especially harmful in that it is associated with an incredible pretension to proclaim one party the true heir of Lenin, and all other parties to be apostates from Marxism-Leninism. . . .

What the Communists need is not division into "majority" and "minority," but unity, unity, and once more unity.

Chapter Twenty-nine

Decline and triumph of the West

192 TRIUMPH OF EUROPE: ECONOMIC

The combination of polycentrism in the Communist world and of assertive independence in Western Europe represents the end of the short-lived American–Russian hegemony and the emergence of a new global pluralism. Paradoxically, the world at the same time was becoming increasingly homogeneous—even homogenized—because of the accelerating diffusion of Europe's three great revolutions: economic, scientific, and political. This diffusion is at the basis of the current process of modernization that is transforming the entire globe. It should be noted that today the stimuli toward modernization may come not only from Europe but also from the United States or the Soviet Union or even China. Yet the roots go back to Western Europe where the economic, scientific, and political revolutions originated. Consequently, the modernization of the globe—now proceeding at an accelerated pace—represents, directly and indirectly, the triumph of Europe.

This is particularly noticeable in the economic field, for the primary objective of the underdeveloped states, after attaining political independence, is to develop their economies as rapidly as possible. This objective is illustrated by an advertisement published in The New York Times *on January 20, 1964 by the government of Nigeria.*

I welcome this chance of addressing myself to the entrepreneur who is seeking investment opportunities. To that person I say: "Why not invest in my country, the Federal Republic of Nigeria?"

One African out of every six is a Nigerian. With over 40M people, Nigeria has a large population, therefore the largest potential market, compared with any other African nation. Among our agricultural resources are cotton, hard woods, rubber, hides and skins, cocoa and oil seeds. And the Republic's mineral resources include tin, coal, ceramic clays, iron, limestone and petroleum. Our exports and imports far exceed one billion dollars a year, and the Republic offers many investment opportunities which will provide at least 20% net return on investment per annum.

Progress, economic and political, has been our watchword. Our balance of trade deficit for 1961, during our first full year of Independence, was over $130M. This was reduced to $103M in 1962. For the first half of 1963, our Republic showed a favorable balance of trade of a little over a half million dollars. Our imports increasingly comprise capital goods which will help us generate economic activity and stimulate economic growth. When the country attained Independence on the 1st of October, 1960, planning for development in our widely divergent Federation seemed an insurmountable task. A comprehensive and realistic $1,895 billion National Six-Year Development Plan is however now getting into its stride. A cornerstone of the Plan is the $196M Kainji Dam Project on which construction is expected to start early in 1964.

Since Independence, over 150 manufacturing businesses with ten employees or over have been established. In 1963 alone 34 new manufacturing establishments worth over $65M came into production. At the present time 20 factories worth over $58M are under construction, and over $60M worth of projects are planned and are likely to go ahead in the immediate future. These projects exclude an $80M Iron and Steel complex which is under consideration. Compared with the advanced industrialized nations, as indices to achievement, some of these figures may not be staggering. But for a developing country, barely three years after independence, they are not unimpressive. Our energies are directed towards improving on those figures, and all they mean in terms of economic prosperity and higher standard of life for our people.

In common with all developing nations, we are having our growing pains. As with Government procedures in other parts of the world, ours may at times appear frustrating. But many of these procedures are designed to ensure the stability and co-ordinated progress which businessmen rightly demand. We are doing all we can to streamline the procedures in the light of experience, without sacrificing orderly progress in the process. Skilled labor is still scarce, and is not yet generally accustomed to modern industrial organization and processes. But it is very adaptable and demonstrably responsive both to training and to incentives. Our per capita income is only around $100 a year; but the country's economy is moving ahead steadily, and in some sectors rapidly.

You will therefore see that while, as a developing country, we are having our teething problems, we are doing everything we can to resolve those problems with as little pain as possible and within the shortest possible time. I would like to emphasize that private foreign investment forms an integral part of our Development Plan. We shall need overseas capital, and those managerial and technical skills which accompany overseas capital, for many years to come. We have a stable Government. We offer as many industrial incentives as our economy can bear, in order to ensure rapid, sustained, and balanced economic growth.

I would like to take this opportunity of assuring you once again that overseas capital under mutually satisfactory conditions is most welcome in the Federal Republic of Nigeria, and that the interest of investors will always be safeguarded. We invite you to come and help us build a strong, prosperous Federal Republic of Nigeria in the best and fruitful liberal traditions, and so help in removing that explosive gap between the rich and the poor nations of the world.

ABUBAKAR TAFAWA BALEWA,
Prime Minister of the Federal Republic of Nigeria

193 TRIUMPH OF EUROPE: SCIENTIFIC

*Scientific development, recognized as a prerequisite for both military and economic strength, is as much sought after as economic growth. The motives and objectives of this pursuit of science are clearly evident in the official description of the Five Year Plan for the Promotion of Science adopted by the United Arab Republic.**

The UAR government, conscious of the vital role of scientific discovery in raising the standard of living for both individuals and the nation as a whole, has conscientiously endeavored to establish a sound scientific foundation for the country's economic and social reawakening.

The world today is witnessing tremendous competition in the field of scientific research. Some of this research is aimed at the achievement of military superiority for a particular nation. But much of it, in any country, is a means to increase the production that affects other aspects of life in the society.

The situation with regard to the UAR is such that its leaders have been impressed by the necessity to give more and more attention to science, to regard it in fact as a safeguard for the country's political independence, as a means of circumventing the technical control that otherwise might be exercised by foreign powers over UAR use of its own resources.

Practically speaking, steps have thus been taken to develop the country's scientific capability, organize and mobilize it so as to be able to follow up closely the programs of economic development, sustaining them by scientific experiment and research.

Specifically, the government in 1956 promulgated its Law No. 5, establishing a Supreme Science Council on lines similar to groups set up for the same purpose in countries more advanced in scientific research.

The Council's central activity has been to design a five-year plan for the promotion of science in the UAR. This plan was put into effect in 1962. There were three essential considerations in formulating this plan: the individual, the equipment, and the subjects of study. In other words, to carry the plan through to fruition, first are needed the individuals with adequate efficiency

* "UAR Plans Growth Through Science," *Arab World* (July-August, 1963), pp. 14-15.

and experience; second, sufficient scientific instruments and physical facilities must be made available to equip the human element; finally it was necessary that the planners have a profound insight into the future scientific requirements in both the governmental and non-governmental sectors, in terms of both production and services.

The five-year plan was drawn up on just these bases, with just these goals in mind. It took twelve months to prepare and called into action the combined talents of more than 3,000 experts. The overall plan is divided into two sections, the first specifying necessary activity in the field of research science and the second dealing with applied science.

The section devoted to scientific research activity has in turn been divided into six main areas of application: 1) Mathematical and physical sciences; 2) Chemical sciences and industries; 3) Geological and metallurgical sciences; 4) Engineering and its auxiliary industries; 5) Agricultural and biological sciences; 6) Medical sciences.

For each of these categories, the plan further delineates proposed activity, setting forth (a) applied local problems which need solution through scientific research, (b) a plan organizing missions abroad and within the country, (c) a program for subsidizing experts who are to collaborate in the study of the problems of a geographic sector, and (d) proposed funds for the laboratory equipment and library services which make research possible.

The total amount of funds required for implementing these projects is about $56 million.

The specialized scientists and the basic research techniques produced and learned through the efforts of the primary phase of the science promotion plan will soon be in a position to be applied—to carry out projects more pertinent to the physical development of the UAR national economy. Projects now ready and awaiting the attention of the UAR's growing scientific potential are, for example:

1—The use of controlled supersonic waves to precipitate artificial rain to aid agriculture.
2—Study of uranium extraction methods.
3—The use of solar energy for power generation.
4—Research to develop petro-chemical industries.
5—Exploitation of plaster for new industries.
6—Production of artificial fibers from local materials.
7—The completion of a geological map of Egypt.
8—Developing methods of crystallizing and purifying the products of black sand.
9—Producing new varieties of cotton.
10—Study of water sources.
11—Research in engineering and production economics.
12—Improving export crops and their consumer qualities.
13—Studies in land reclamation.
14—Improving fisheries.
15—Studies of the rural communities.
16—Studies of medical subjects of vital importance; for instance, pharmaceutical and biochemical industries as well as the study of major diseases, such as tuberculosis, cancer and bilharzia . . .

In this whole endeavor, the Supreme Science Council has been following the advice of President Nasser when he said:

We have to keep up with the new world and new discoveries. We suffered so much in the past because we were left behind by the ages of steam and electricity. What suffering awaits those who fail to keep up with the new dawn will certainly be much greater than whatever we have experienced in the past. ... In this world of breathtaking discoveries, to be left behind is to forfeit one's right to existence.

194 TRIUMPH OF EUROPE: POLITICAL

The contemporary diffusion of Europe's political revolution is tangibly and dramatically manifested in more than fifty countries that have won their independence within two decades after World War II. Prime Minister Harold Macmillan of Great Britain recognized the force of this movement in a speech given before the Parliament of South Africa on February 3, 1960. After pointing out the European origins of the "wind of change" sweeping the colonial world, he warned his audience that they were failing to take it into account and that the consequences were likely to be felt throughout the globe.*

As I have traveled through the Union, I have found everywhere, as I expected, a deep preoccupation with what is happening in the rest of the African continent. I understand and sympathize with your interest in these events, and your anxiety about them.

Ever since the break-up of the Roman Empire, one of the constant facts of political life in Europe has been the emergence of independent nations.

They have come into existence over the centuries in different shapes with different forms of government. But all have been inspired with a keen feeling of nationalism, which has grown as nations have grown.

In the twentieth century, and especially since the end of the war [World War II], the processes which gave birth to the nation-states of Europe have been repeated all over the world. We have seen the awakening of national consciousness in peoples who have for centuries lived in dependence on some other power.

Fifteen years ago this movement spread through Asia. Many countries there, of different races and civilizations, pressed their claim to an independent national life.

Today the same thing is happening in Africa. The most striking of all the impressions I have formed since I left London a month ago is of the strength of African national consciousness.

In different places it may take different forms. But it is happening everywhere. The wind of change is blowing through the continent.

Whether we like it or not, this growth of national consciousness is a political fact. We must all accept it as a fact. Our national policies must take account of it.

* *The New York Times* (February 4, 1960).

Of course, you understand this as well as anyone. You are sprung from Europe, the home of nationalism.

And here, in Africa, you have yourselves created a full nation—a new nation. Indeed, in the history of our times, yours will be recorded as the first of the African nationalisms.

And this tide of national consciousness which is now rising in Africa is a fact for which you and we and the other nations of the Western world are ultimately responsible.

For its causes are to be found in the achievements of Western civilization in pushing forward the frontiers of knowledge, applying science in the service of human needs, expanding food production, speeding and multiplying means of communication, and, above all, spreading education.

As I have said, the growth of national consciousness in Africa is a political fact and we must accept it as such. I sincerely believe that if we cannot do so, we may imperil the precarious balance of East and West on which the peace of the world depends.

The world today is divided into three great groups.

First, there are what we call the Western powers. You in South Africa and we in Britain belong to this group, together with our friends and allies in other parts of the Commonwealth, in the United States of America, and in Europe.

Secondly, there are the Communists—Russia and her satellites in Europe and China, whose population will rise by 1970 to the staggering total of 800,000,000.

Thirdly, there are those parts of the world whose people are at present uncommitted either to communism or to our Western ideas. In this context, we think first of Asia and of Africa.

As I see it, the great issue in this second half of the twentieth century is whether the uncommitted peoples of Asia and Africa will swing to the East or the West.

Will they be drawn into the Communist camp? Or will the great experiments in self-government that are now being made in Asia and Africa, especially within the Commonwealth, prove so successful and by their example so compelling, that the balance will come down in favor of freedom and order and justice?

The struggle is joined and it is a struggle for the minds of men. What is now on trial is much more than our military strength or our diplomatic and administrative skill. It is our way of life.

The uncommitted nations want to see before they choose. What can we show them to help them choose right? Each of the independent members of the Commonwealth must answer that question for itself.

It is the basic principle for our modern Commonwealth that we respect each other's sovereignty in matters of internal policy. At the same time, we must recognize that in this shrinking world in which we live today, the internal policies of one nation may have effects outside it.

We may sometimes be tempted to say to each other, "Mind your own business." But in these days I would myself expand the old saying so that it runs: "Mind your own business, but mind how it affects my business, too."

Let me be very frank with you, my friends. What governments and parliaments in the United Kingdom have done since the war in according independence to India, Pakistan, Ceylon, Malaya and Ghana, and what they will do for Nigeria and the other countries now nearing independence—all this, though we take full and sole responsibility for it, we do in the belief that it is the only way to establish the future of the Commonwealth and of the free world on sound foundations.

All this, of course, is also of deep and close concern to you. For nothing we do in this small world can be done in a corner or remain hidden. . . .

It may well be that in trying to do our duty as we see it, we shall sometimes make difficulties for you. If this proves to be so, we shall regret it.

But I know that even so you would not ask us to flinch from doing our duty. You, too, will do your duty as you see it.

I am well aware of the peculiar nature of all the problems with which you are faced here in the Union of South Africa. I know the differences between your situation and that of most of the other states in Africa.

You have here some 3,000,000 people of European origin. This country is their home. It has been their home for many generations. They have no other. The same is true of the Europeans in Central and East Africa.

As a fellow member of the Commonwealth, it is our earnest desire to give South Africa our support and encouragement, but I hope you won't mind my saying frankly that there are some aspects of your policies which make it impossible for us to do this without being false to our own deep convictions about the political destinies of free men, to which in our own territories we are trying to give effect.

195 GLOBAL HOMOGENIZATION

The diffusion of Europe's three revolutions is creating a world that is becoming more and more homogenized, despite the growing pluralism in power relationships. This process of global homogenization is evident in the following reports by American correspondents in various parts of the globe. The final selection shows that homogenization is taking place within the United States itself, and for essentially the same reasons that it is occurring abroad.

New Guinea

A message in pidgin English is being carried through steaming rain forests, across snow-crested mountains and up crocodile-filled rivers throughout this territory. It says:

"Ol pipol belong Papua-New Guinea vote long bigfella No. 1 Council liklik time."

It means that all residents of the territory will vote for a new House of Assembly beginning Feb. 15.

Getting this message, and its implications, to the people has been a staggering task for the Australian administration. For months, hundreds of political-education teams have trekked to the remote corners of the land to tell the Papuans what the "elekson" is all about. [*The New York Times,* February 8, 1964.]

Mongolia

Outer Mongolia still lives by the social pattern carved across her terrain by the ruthless hand of Genghis Khan. But after nearly 700 years this remote Asian country stands on the brink of change. ... What is happening in Outer Mongolia is simply this: the nation's Communist rulers have embarked on a program designed to catapult the country from the thirteenth to the twentieth century within not more than ten years. ... The essence of the program is: full speed ahead in a plan to change a nation of nomads into a nation based on the agriculture of the plow and the industry of the production line. [*The New York Times,* August 3, 1959.]

Southern Rhodesia

African brides-to-be in Southern Rhodesia are rebelling against Lobola—the traditional marriage price that has been paid in cattle to parents for centuries.

Middle-class African girls who are abandoning in the cities and towns their beads and skins for European-style dresses, chic hats, and high-heeled shoes are protesting that the Lobola system has become "a humiliating, masculine racket."

Their outcry, "We are no longer mere goods and chattels," is symptomatic of the urge in modern Africa to snap the shackles of slavish tribal custom and to gain equality with the male in a country where the law of the kraal (village) is still deep-rooted and dies hard. [*The New York Times,* September 25, 1960.]

Borneo

A great awakening is taking place among the Dyaks, the former head-hunters of the vast and primitive island of Borneo.

These people, a bit weary of being described as charming savages, are increasingly discarding their loincloths and leaving their skull-decorated long houses, putting on sport shirts and long pants and migrating down river to the big cities.

"Teach us how to read and write, to be doctors, engineers, business men; give us typewriters, transistor radios, outboard motors for our dugouts"—these are the new battle cries of the Dyaks, who once told an inquisitive European, "You like books, we like heads." [*The New York Times,* November 26, 1960.]

Japan

At Tokyo's famed Nichigeki music hall screaming teenagers storm the stage to tug at Japan's latest rock-and-roll sensation. The putt-putt of tiny tractors echoes from a thousand valleys, shattering the pastoral quiet of centuries from Kanto to Kyushu. Billboards sprout like ugly mushrooms amid the green of the rice paddies. ...

Parking meters are installed. Supermarkets spring up almost overnight.

Small shopkeepers contend they are being driven out of business, which indeed many of them are. . . .

Japanese children have developed a taste for Western food through the school lunch programs, which include milk and often meat instead of fish. [*Chicago Daily News*, July 29, 1959.]

Pakistan

The women of Pakistan are on the verge of achieving the legal right to choose their husbands and to divorce them. . . .

Under old laws, a woman has virtually no rights. As a girl she may be sold or given away. Once wed, she is the servant of her husband. He may take a second wife or any number of wives.

The proposed code would bar marriage of girls under 16 years old and boys under 18. The presence and consent of both parties would be required. Divorce would be permitted only upon presentation of grounds in court. Furthermore, a husband seeking another wife would have to prove in court his ability to support all his wives and children in the manner to which they had been accustomed. [*The New York Times*, March 27, 1960.]

Bolivia

The Prado La Paz, a central boulevard (in La Paz, Bolivia) looks almost like the main street of a southwestern United States city when school lets out, except for Indian women in brown bowler hats and babies slung over their backs in colored ponchos. Bolivian girls wear their hair in pony-tails, dress in toreador pants or skirts, bobbysox or saddle shoes. Boys by preference wear blue jeans and black leather jackets. In an Indian market place an Aymara girl tending her mother's stand solemnly chews what turns out with a pink pop to be not the traditional coca leaves but bubble gum. [*The New York Times*, March 20, 1959.]

Egypt

The government is trying to get Egyptian men out of their flowing robes and into trousers. Within the last few weeks the Central Ministry of Social Affairs has launched a campaign to popularize a loose-fitting blouse and slacks combination that looks like the casual outfits some American men wear for lounging in their backyards. Hussein el-Shaffei, Social Affairs Minister, hopes this costume will eventually replace the gallibiya, a loose cotton robe that falls from the shoulders to the ankles like a nightshirt. [*The New York Times*, June 29, 1959.]

United States

The approach to every American city seems the same. The road widens and divides, traffic thickens, an intersection light appears—an outdoor movie, motels, a wrecked car dump with its most unbelievably flattened specimens next to the highroad. . . . Then, where through-route cement jolts into municipal maintenance macadam, spreads the new subdivision—cellar excavations going on at one end, baby carriages and ranch houses standing at the other. Then comes a city avenue in violent transition—gas stations, used car lots, down-at-heel mansions, the bankers' home of 80 years ago now the Aleppo Temple, the stately house where the cast-iron deer once stood now labeled "Tourists." Here are the older, maple-tree suburbs, a white church with many-paned windows, the new high school. ... At the center of town they have cut down the elms to widen Main Street. Here is the row of chains: Woolworth, Sears, A&P; the familiar drugstore; the local hotel (run from Chicago); the corner diner by the depot; the high office buildings; the green square and the war monument.

Here are the inevitable groups of teenagers, all in blue jeans, slouching around the entrance to the drugstore or the movie house, their poses, their gestures stylized like figures from a ballet. Boys and girls in jeans, chewing gum, smoking, hanging around the drugstore in a terrible effort to be casual until one of them gets his first car and it's zoom-zoom-zoom with everybody else.

Across town you reach the river, the factories, the poorer homes, the slums. ...

You can walk down the streets at night in the new suburban subdivisions and see six families to a block looking at the same picture after supper. How they ever passed the time before TV nobody can guess. Now they have everything, prize fights, religion, Westerns, breathless cash prizes. They have a tidal-wave of advertising, new desires and discontents—above all a feeling of identification, of belonging, and a common denominator of accent, clothes and viewpoint. [T.R.B. in *The New Republic,* September 19, 1955, © 1955, Harrison-Blaine of New Jersey, Inc.]

Chapter Thirty

Epilogue:
Our Golden Age?

196 RACE CONFLICT

The mid-twentieth century is above all an age of transition—an age in which change is taking place more rapidly than at any time in the past. Furthermore, this change is not confined to any one region; it is affecting the entire globe. The preceding readings show that the motive force behind this dynamism is the impact of the West and the response to that impact. The net result is an age of unprecedented promise and unprecedented problems. The following selections are designed to indicate the nature of both the promise and the problems.

In considering first the problems, there stands out prominently the conflict between races. Before the expansion of Europe this problem did not exist, at least in its present form, because the various races had little contact with each other. Today, however, they are mixed to a considerable degree, especially in North and South America and in parts of Africa. Since the white man was the master in these territories, as well as in the colonial world as a whole, the contemporary anticolonial movement inevitably has antiwhite overtones. A distinguished British scholar analyzes the nature and the implications of race conflict today.*

As anyone who has recently spent any length of time in Africa and Asia can testify, there have been three prevalent attitudes toward

* Barbara Ward, "Race Relations as a World Issue," *The New York Times Magazine* (November 11, 1956), pp. 12, 69-71. © 1956 by The New York Times Company. Reprinted by permission.

the white man. There has been, first of all, an uncritical acceptance of the white man at his own valuation and of white skin as a natural superiority. Europeans of liberal outlook in Africa have sometimes been surprised and shocked by their African servants' resistance to the entertainment of Africans in the house. Gloom descends on the kitchen. Dinner is served with less than usual efficiency. The steward will even demand inferior whisky to offer to non-white guests. "Master, you no give dat black man good whisky"—"dat black man" being a graduate of Cambridge and a barrister of the Middle Temple.

All over primitive Africa black men watched the coming of the white man with an awed and innocent eye and expected a new heaven and a new earth from his religion, his skills, his magic, his confidence and his power. Then the title "Bwana"—master—was not demanded. It was given freely and with hope.

Nor was this acceptance of the white man as inherently superior unknown in Asia. In spite of its ancient splendors and millennial philosophy, India in the nineteenth century contained many men who accepted without question the superiority of all things Western. Rising Arab nationalism in the nineteenth century looked to Western influence as a liberating force. To this day, in Malaya, some Chinese residents among the so-called "Queen's Chinese" still tend to regard the white man's standards, outlook and company as naturally superior.

Today, in some parts of Africa and among many groups in Asia, this early unsophisticated acceptance of white superiority has given way to more rational and self-respecting standards of judgment. In West Africa, for instance, where, thanks to the courage and devotion of a century of missionary effort, modern education has been available to some African families for over a hundred years, it is possible for the educated African and European to meet on a basis of unforced social equality and to experience a meeting of minds molded in comparable traditions.

In India, men sent to study in British universities and admitted, after 1920, to full equality in the Indian civil service, learned to work with white colleagues on a basis of mutual respect.

Even in the troubled Arab world, French education in such countries as Tunisia produced Arab leaders who until these last tragic events, were ready to work with France on a basis of equality. And between Englishmen such as Glubb Pasha and the late King Abdullah of Jordan, equality of feeling reached virtually a sense of blood brotherhood.

Yet the common denominator of this sense of equality and possible partnership wherever it has appeared in Asia or Africa tends to be education. For the mass of people, once the almost magical acceptance of white superiority had faded, the easiest emotion to excite is the opposite one—a xenophobic racialism, an irrational hatred of the white skin, an instinctive prejudice against all things Western.

In every recent crisis between Asia and the West, the area of dispute has been enlarged to cover racial antipathy. The Chinese Communists, drumming up anti-American feeling during the Korean crisis, denounced the Americans not only as imperialists and capitalists but also in traditional terms of Chinese xenophobia—as "red devils" or "red barbarians."

Colonel Nasser accompanied the mounting Suez crisis with ever more violent broadcasts to all his Arab and African neighbors—as far to the south as Mombasa or Dar es Salaam—urging them to throw out the white man.

At present, the three ways of looking at white-skinned peoples—veneration, equality, hatred—can still be found in Asia and Africa. Attitudes are still fluid, although they are changing with revolutionary speed. There is still time in which to work for peaceful and creative relationships. But there is not much time.

The two leading nations of world communism are not troubled by the racial issue. China is "colored" (in our old-fashioned Western use of the word). Russia has large Asiatic populations with whom Russians freely mix. They are therefore free in all their propaganda and diplomatic activity to whip up and exploit latent Asian and African resentment against the white man and his centuries of domination.

The racial clashes in Sophiatown, Johannesburg—or Clinton, Tenn.—are more than a news story in the local press. The French-Arab conflict in North Africa and the "white" attack upon Arab peoples in Egypt [Anglo-French-Israeli invasion of Egypt] make up more than a Middle East crisis. They are fuel for Communist propaganda in Asia and Africa. This propaganda paints a picture of the white man as the inexorable exploiter of men and women of Asian, Arab or African stock, as an unrepentant racialist and finally as an outsider with whom no relations are possible save those of violence and rejection.

That day is not reached yet. And some Westerners may argue that, for a strong, self-confident Atlantic world, it does not matter too much if it ever is. But the consequences of a world organized on an anti-white basis are not so easily dismissed. White men are outnumbered in the world by three to one and the disproportion is increasing. In all international organizations they would be outvoted and outmaneuvered. Their repulse by Asian nationalism would leave Asia's millions wide open to Communist infiltration. All growth of Western commerce would be checked. Present trading interests and investments would be in jeopardy. The white man's position in Africa would become untenable. And, as white influence receded, that of Russia and China would inexorably grow.

Above all, any hope of a cooperative world order, based on racial equality—the kind of world order which liberal opinion in the West sets as its ultimate goal—would be blocked by massive, relentless, irrational, anti-white prejudice. This outcome is not yet certain or necessary. Western imagination and generosity can check what drift and indifference are tending to create. But with each year lost, the potentially explosive force of anti-Western feeling is growing. At present, most Westerners think of the race problem as being primarily one of whether men and women of African stock—in Africa or the United States—can achieve full equality of status. But this definition is probably already outdated. The question is no longer whether Africans can achieve equality. It is becoming the wider query whether men and women of white color shall lose it. There is no certainty that mankind will, after three hundred years of white dominance, move safely to race equality.

Another basic problem of the mid-twentieth century is the global economic imbalance, becoming more serious as the gap between rich and poor lands widens. In statistical terms, this imbalance means an annual per capita income of more than $2,000 in contrast to less than $100. In human terms, the imbalance is described in the following selections, the first describing the fate of an Iranian peasant who lacked the money and social confidence to save his eyesight, and the second depicting what is termed "peticare" in the affluent American society.*

Iranian Peasant

Today the surgery is finished and Mahmad lies on his hospital bed staring at the ceiling, his thick, peasant hands slack at his sides. Next to him, sitting in rigid silence is his wife, her faded garments a blur of color against the antiseptic walls. About them flows the casual urgency of hospital life, a life far removed from the soil and the sky, from the acrid odor of dust, from the long shadows of a depleted sun setting over a brown plain—from the life that Mahmad has always known.

For Mahmad all that is familiar and secure lies in his village, a primitive agglomeration of mud huts fifty miles distant. He was born in this village (he isn't sure when), he was married there, and for at least thirty years one day has routinely followed another, each devoted to the incalculable, all-absorbing trivia of a simple life.

He has plowed the hard brown earth in the spring, he has sown the rice, he has helped to irrigate the fields; and in the fall he has harvested the crop, collecting his small percentage of it from the man who owns the earth he tills—his landlord. He has drunk his tea and eaten his bread and gossiped with his neighbors; and, if life had no more to offer, at least he could hope that it had no less.

Mahmad remembers now, as he lies in his bed, that it was fall. The leaves of the poplars were yellow and the harvest was gathered, piled on the ground in a huge golden heap. On a night like hundreds before it, he and his villager friends set off for the fields—a quiet, companionable little group that would pass the long night guarding the grain from the maraudings of men and of animals.

Out along their familiar way they went, and gradually Mahmad realized that the signposts he had known since childhood were all missing—the rocks at the side of the path, the bridge over the stream, the abandoned mud hut at the roadside—all were gone. Suddenly he realized that they were gone because he couldn't see, and a rush of horror engulfed him.

How does a man of the land of Iran guide a plow if he cannot see? How does a man whose vision is gone follow the sheep, seeking out those small, vital spots of green pasturage on a barren landscape? How can a blind man take his place among his fellows, replanting the little shoots of fresh, green

* Peggy and Pierre Streit, "For Want of $3.94," *The New York Times Magazine* (April 30, 1961), pp. 24, 42; © 1961 by The New York Times Company. Reprinted by permission. "Peticare," copyright *Newsweek*, Inc. (December 23, 1963), pp. 52-53.

rice in new beds? What is there for a sightless man in an Iranian village but to be led about by a small impatient boy or to go to the city to beg?

Mahmad held his hands before his eyes. There, standing in the stillness of the night, he knew that he was blind and he sank to the ground and cried.

Throughout the night he stayed where he fell, his tears finally spending themselves. But when dawn broke he wept afresh, but now with relief and gratitude, for he found that he could distinguish night from day and he knew that he wasn't completely blind. The sight of his right eye was gone but vision remained in the left, and as the day dawned, so did hope.

When the men came back from their vigil in the fields they led Mahmad home to the only man of the village with the knowledge or the power to help him—their landlord. Standing before him, his cap in his hand, his head humbly bowed, as befits an Iranian peasant, Mahmad asked for counsel.

Go to the city, said the landlord. Go to Shiraz. There was a modern hospital, staffed by Iranian and American doctors, and there he might find assistance. And so, next morning, Mahmad and Pari, his wife, set off, riding the fifty miles to the hospital atop a truck loaded with sacks of rice.

Mahmad's case fell to an American neurosurgeon to whom the medical history was urgently clear. The man suffered from a tumor of the brain that had already destroyed the sight of one eye and there was imminent danger that it might rob him of vision in the other. It was probable that an operation would save his life but his sight was suspended between the jumps of the minute hand of a clock; each hour brought Mahmad closer to total irrecoverable blindness.

Immediate surgery was indicated and Mahmad was given a note of admission to the hospital's clinic for indigents, some blocks down the street. At the admissions desk he was asked routinely for 50 toman—$6.57. But Mahmad and Pari didn't have $6.57. Tied in a knot in the end of a scarf was the raggle-taggle end of a few good harvests—a meager collection of coins and bills that represented their total negotiable wealth: $2.63.

Almost surely, had Mahmad protested the demand for the money—had he gone back to his doctor for help the fee would have been waived. But he didn't protest, for it isn't in the nature of a peasant to dispute the ruling of a superior. He never complained. He never said in desperation, "But I'm going blind, let me in," for he presumed as any other Iranian peasant would presume, that one doesn't get something for nothing in this world.

Fifty toman was fifty toman and that was that. He was losing his sight? But that was his affair, wasn't it? Didn't everyone have problems? Who was Mahmad? What claim had he on the services of a hospital or a doctor if he couldn't pay the fee?

And because he took for granted that he had none, he turned, unquestioning, from the admitting desk and, led by his wife, groped his halting way back to the street. There they found a truck that carried them back to the anonymity of their distant village.

On their way they nursed a last hope. One of the few times of the year that an Iranian peasant can hope to have cash in his hands is at harvest. When Mahmad and Pari had left their village for the hospital, the gathered crop was on the ground and by right of tradition and custom a fragment of it was Mahmad's—the reward of a year of his work.

The bulk of it, of course, belonged to the landlord—the man who owned the land Mahmad worked and the cattle Mahmad plowed with and the seed Mahmad sowed and the water Mahmad drank. But a bit of the grain was

Mahmad's and if this small fragment could be converted quickly to the $3.94 he needed, the hospital fee could be met.

But when they arrived back at the village they found that in their absence the division of the crop had been made among the peasants and Mahmad's share had found its way into the storeroom of the landlord. When they asked him for it he said, "You have been sick and away from your work during part of the harvest. You can't expect to be paid for something you haven't done, can you?"

Mahmad never protested. He showed no surprise, no resentment; for he knew as well as any other peasant that the man who left his gains unguarded, for whatever reason, stood in danger of losing them.

He knew the rules of survival and he knew they applied to all men—to landlord and to peasant alike. This was a pitiless world; a man took what he could get, protected himself as best he could, and one of the best protections on an earth abounding in misery were the blinders a man could don to shut the misery out. Deep in his tough peasant heart Mahmad knew that were he the landlord, he, too, would hold sway with ruthless self-interest. Without demur he turned back to his cottage and his private ordeal.

Mahmad needed $3.94. What of his family and friends and the people who share his life in their hamlet? Why didn't he seek the money from them? But who in a small village would dare part with $3.94 if he had it; for who knew when disaster might strike? How many in Iran, including the landlords, were confident enough of the future, secure enough in the present, to afford that great luxury—generosity?

For fourteen days Mahmad sat in the doorway of his cottage as day by day and hour by hour the sight in his left eye slipped away. Finally, on the fifteenth day, stirred from his apathy by the magnitude of his fear and horror, he went again to the landlord and asked, not for his share of the crop, but merely for $3.94. "I don't have it," said the landlord. "Go to the hospital." And because there was no other hope Mahmad and Pari left once again for the city.

This time, as they groped their way to the out-patient clinic, Mahmad was claimed by one of the hospital attendants, alerted to his disappearance by the deeply perturbed and baffled American neurosurgeon who had been searching and waiting, day after day, to operate. Where had Mahmad been? Why hadn't he come to the clinic as he had been told? Dull and frightened and uncomprehending, he told the simple truth: he had gone to find $3.94.

A week has passed since the tumor was removed from Mahmad's brain. The operation was successful; his life has been saved. But the days and the hours of wasting and waiting have taken their toll and what might have been, had Mahmad's world been different, can never be now. The operation was too late. Mahmad is blind.

What lies before him? No one knows better than the impoverished peasant who lies on a hospital bed and stares at the ceiling with all the desperate intensity of a sightless man—or the stolid woman sitting silently at his side. In another two weeks Mahmad will return to his village and there he will sit, like a lump of clay, for the rest of his life.

It was a busy morning for Dr. William Brunn. The first patient was given his fifth X-ray therapy treatment for a huge mammary tumor. Then Brunn and an assistant performed an operation on an eye ulcer. After his colleague administered the anesthetic, the surgeon delicately scraped the underside of the eyelid, bringing healing blood to the surface. Then the eyelid was pulled like a flap over the ulcer on the surface of the eyeball and sutured shut.

Minutes later, the patient was wheeled into the recovery room; in half an hour he was back on his feet—all four of them.

These exquisite operations, performed respectively on a small cocker spaniel and an eight-year-old boxer at the Ambassador Animal Hospital in suburban Washington, D.C., last week, underline the fact that, from womb to tomb, U.S. pets now receive nearly the same quality of medical care as their owners.

In thousands of veterinary clinics and hospitals, pets are undergoing operations for cancerous tumors, cataracts, Caesarean births, hysterectomies, gallstones, and even heart and brain defects. Some aging dogs have been fitted with false teeth and contact lenses, and comedian Jerry Lewis supposedly spent $15,000 for his springer spaniel's hearing aid. "Ninety per cent of the dogs in America," says San Francisco veterinarian Norman Freid, "probably get better medical treatment than half the people in the world."

The reasons for all the tender loving peticare are various. According to a Washington sociologist, "The American public, clutching at love and attention, has made the pet an accepted, almost necessary member of the family." Part of the change lies with the veterinarians themselves. Now numbering more than 22,000 to treat the estimated 50 million dogs and cats in the U.S., the veterinarians, like their M.D. counterparts, must graduate from a four-year veterinary medical school and pass a stiff, state-licensing exam. Most work in modern, well-equipped clinics that closely resemble the typical small hospital, with sterile, soundproof operating rooms and the latest X-ray, anesthetic, surgical, and other equipment—including sound waves to treat the back ailments of low-slung dogs. Some clinics even boast blood banks and 24-hour emergency service complete with ambulances; the convalescing pets languish in air-conditioned kennels, munching special dietary foods while listening to piped-in mood music.

Detroit's Gasow Veterinary Hospital, whose eighteen-member staff often handles 150 cases a day, has a complete lab that is able to check for diabetes, analyze spinal fluids and blood chemistry, and run more tests than the average physician's office. Dogs get most human ailments, Dr. Fred Gasow pointed out last week, plus a few humans avoid, such as rabies and distemper. Gasow and his colleagues also perform "cosmetic surgery"—tail-docking, claw-removal—and even silence a dog's bark. And at one New York City hospital, a large area is set aside for metabolism tests for pets with "that rundown feeling." Such care has doubled the life expectancy of dogs in the last twenty years and started the new field of "animal geriatrics."

Today's vet must also treat emotional problems. In New York, a worried cat owner informed a vet that his pet had turned nervous and sulky ever since the arrival of a new baby in the family. Suspecting a case of sibling rivalry, the vet advised the new father to lavish more attention on his cat, then prescribed tranquilizers for both. Dr. Chet Griffith of Seattle says: "The advent of tranquilizers has meant a great deal in treating pet problems."

Most vets, however, save their best kennel-side manner for the pet's owners. "We have to treat the owners more than the pets," says Chicago's Dr. Alvin Becker. One Chicago dog owner, lonely for her hospitalized pet, recently called her veterinarian to request that her dog be brought to the telephone so she might hear him bark. The understanding vet—unwilling to disturb his patient—walked away momentarily, then returned to the phone and began barking vigorously, while the owner cooed baby talk. At Boston's Angell Memorial Animal Hospital, it is not uncommon for dog owners to request a kennel with a view, send get-well greeting cards, and, on special occasions, to provide a Western Union boy to sing "Happy Birthday to Buster."

The new vets, of course, command higher fees; their average annual earnings are about $14,000 (vs. $10,000 in 1955). Many charge $5 for an office call and $10 for a house call, and a typical combination of diagnosis, major surgery, and convalescence can cost as much as $2,000. An Atlanta mother of two moaned last week: "I owe more to my vet than I do to my family doctor."

But the excesses continue—even unto The End. At "Pet Heaven" cemetery in Atlanta two weeks ago, a dozen shivering mourners stood around a casket containing the last remains of Inky, an eighteen-year-old cocker spaniel. A wreath had a rubber bone tied to it, and the silk-ruffled casket contained the pair of low-heeled shoes Inky loved to gnaw on.

Just before the casket was lowered into the grave, cemetery owner Mrs. Mabel Stovall read from Ecclesiastes 3:18-22 ("For the fate of the sons of men and the fate of beasts is the same; as one dies, so dies the other").

INCREASING PRODUCTION AND INCREASING UNEMPLOYMENT **198**

Affluent America also has serious economic problems in the mid-twentieth century, especially the problem of increasing unemployment at a time of increasing production. This phenomenon became noticeable for the first time in 1941, when business activity was 108 per cent of normal, but unemployment averaged 5,560,000, or nearly 10 per cent of the work force. Heretofore, large-scale unemployment had always been a product of "hard times" and had disappeared with the return of prosperity. But during the 1960's, a period of soaring productivity, the official rate of unemployment remained at over 5 per cent, and this official rate underestimates the true extent of the unemployment. On March 16, 1964, President Johnson recognized the gravity of this problem when he launched his "War on Poverty" program. The first of the following selections is from his special message to Congress concerning this program. The second reading consists of interviews with victims of chronic unemployment.*

President Johnson's "War on Poverty"

We are citizens of the richest and most fortunate nation in the history of the world.

* Text of President Johnson's Message in *The New York Times* (March 17, 1964); unemployed interviewed by A. H. Raskin, *The New York Times* (April 6, 7, 8, 1964). © 1964 by The New York Times Company. Reprinted by permission.

One hundred and eighty years ago we were a small country struggling for survival in the margin of a hostile land.

Today we have established a civilization of free men which spans an entire continent. . . .

The path forward has not been an easy one.

But we have never lost sight of our goal: an American in which every citizen shares all the opportunities of his society, in which every man has a chance to advance his welfare to the limit of his capacities.

We have come a long way toward this goal.

We still have a long way to go.

The distance which remains is the measure of the great unfinished work of our society.

To finish that work I have called for a national war on poverty. Our objective: total victory.

There are millions of Americans—one fifth of our people—who have not shared in the abundance which has been granted to most of us, and to whom the gates of opportunity have been closed.

What does this poverty mean to those who endure it?

It means a daily struggle to secure the necessities for even a meager existence. It means that the abundance, the comforts, the opportunities they see all around them are beyond their grasp.

Worst of all, it means hopelessness for the young.

The young man or woman who grows up without a decent education, in a broken home, in a hostile and squalid environment, in ill health or in the face of racial injustice—that young man or woman is often trapped in a life of poverty.

He does not have the skills demanded by a complex society. He does not know how to acquire those skills. He faces a mounting sense of despair which drains initiative and ambition and energy.

The Chronically Unemployed

The computers that are the brains of automation can perform a hundred thousand tasks, from rolling steel to deciding how many frankfurter rolls a bakery driver should leave at a Third Avenue delicatessen on a rainy summer Friday.

They design in an hour a new chemical plant that would take a platoon of engineers a year, monitor space vehicles on their way to the moon, coach baseball players, govern switches and signals on 35,000 miles of railroad track from a single remote-control center, collect eggs in electronic henhouses, refine oil, issue insurance policies, operate acres of industrial machinery and provide the guideposts for billions of dollars in corporate decisions. One thing the computers cannot do, however, is tell how many workers have been added to the nation's hard core of unemployment by the technological progress they so strikingly exemplify.

They are equally incapable of forecasting how fast future displacement of manpower will occur as our expanding work force moves toward pushbutton factories, robot-run marketing, communications and transport systems and what may become a cashless, checkless financial network, in which your thumb before a scanning machine will be as good as a bank draft or credit card. . . .

Unemployment wears many faces, all of them dour. In a surplus foods warehouse in Charleston, Va., a jobless truck driver tugs at a sack of dried beans and sighs: "Well, at least I won't have to pay any gas bill this month. The company shut it off."

In Detroit a laid-off Chevrolet worker winds up a futile job-hunting tour that has led him from the Metropolitan Airport through the Michigan Bell Telephone Company and United States Rubber to the Chrysler tank arsenal.

"I still think there is a future for me and my boy here," he says. "At least in Detroit I know what to expect. If I go someplace else, even if I had the money to do it, I wouldn't know anybody. I wouldn't have any background for getting a job."

In the town hall at Sanford, Me., a 57-year-old textile spinner, stranded when the community's only big mill moved to the South, paints a corridor in return for grocery credit slips.

"After 40 we're outcasts," he grumbles.

In Pittsburgh a furloughed steel worker, waiting to apply for extended unemployment insurance benefits under the emergency program just approved by Congress, says:

"Being out of work leaves a person with mental and spiritual frustration. It's painful, like living in a vacuum."

A jobless miner stood on a sere hillside near Scranton, staring down at the shell of an abandoned Pennsylvania colliery. "I'm one of the lucky ones," he said. "I only have to wait twelve years till I get my Social Security."

In Pittsburgh, a railroad brakeman, out of work for two years, scowled at a stockbroker's ad with the caption, "Buy a Share in America."

"I can't even buy a wheelbarrow," he muttered. "When is America going to buy a share in me."

PROBLEMS OF URBANIZATION 199

One of the most significant trends of the mid-twentieth century is the rush from the countryside to the city, a headlong urbanization that is creating serious problems for all countries, developed and underdeveloped. The nature and extent of these problems are analyzed by a well-known British economist.*

Most people in North America and Western Europe are probably aware that something fairly drastic is happening to their cities. They grow. They congest. One has the feeling that if it were possible to train some gigantic, extraterrestrial slow-motion camera on the whole process, one would see what looks like a strange, agitated, rugous membrane spreading densely and more and more rapidly over wider and wider areas of the planet's surface.

And the camera would not lie. Behind the average citizen's vague awareness of constant and possibly uncontrollable change lie some formidable facts.

* Barbara Ward, "The City May Be as Lethal as the Bomb," *The New York Times Magazine* (April 19, 1964), pp. 22, 23, 110. © 1964 by The New York Times Company. Reprinted by permission.

They spring from the three vast movements of revolutionary change in which the whole human race is involved. The first is the revolution of rising population; the second, the technological revolution; the third, "the revolution of rising expectations." All three have converged on the old static city and blown it to smithereens.

The modern economic system is overwhelmingly urban. Economic factors —patterns of transport, concentrated labor markets, quick communication, access to suppliers, minimum costs in getting goods to consumers—set the trend to large urban concentrations in motion and, once it has started, the apparent conveniences of largeness make the areas larger still. Then to these new cities stream the men and women stirred from rural stagnation by the bright lights and the "sidewalks paved with gold." And as the world's population has moved onward to a rate of growth of some 2 per cent a year, the stream of aspiring humanity has become a flood. Urban population grows at twice the general rate, and big cities grow faster still. Some of the largest are growing by 8 per cent a year. Sao Paulo, heading for the 5 million mark, receives 5,000 new inhabitants a day. If Bombay were to follow Japanese patterns, it could grow to 35 million within decades.

From one end of the world to the other, the countryside empties its people into the cities. Southern Italians to Turin and Milan, Southern Negroes to Chicago and New York, Ibos and Yorubas to Lagos, Puerto Ricans to San Juan, Soviet peasants to Moscow, Bantu into the purlieus of Johannesburg— year by year, the urban flood goes on until, some 80 years from now, the proportion of the human race depending wholly on farming may be no greater than the 4 or 5 per cent who live on the land in England. Irretrievably, inescapably we are heading toward an urban world. But, on present showing, it may not be a world worth living in.

Downright satisfaction with the present city is already scarce. Not many people in London today would echo Dr. Johnson's robust statement that "when a man is tired of London, he is tired of life." In fact, one can argue that much in the present pattern of urbanism has been created by dissatisfaction. The move to the suburbs is an escape from the city. When people can afford it, they move away and, as others catch up with them, move farther still. Meanwhile, in a city center deprived of leadership and wealth, people stay not because they will but because they must, and around them the rural migrants, arriving fresh from the countryside, fill in the gaps and, through ignorance, bewilderment and poverty, depress standards still further.

This pattern, naturally, is variable. In cities built before the industrial revolution, the center may still wear the magnificence of monarchical society. London, Madrid, and Rome have a certain ceremonial spaciousness that Manchester or Detroit never possessed. The genius of Baron Haussman is preserved in Paris. In these cities, meaner quarters are not a solid core but scattered through the city and out into the first ring of suburbs—the banlieue rouge of Paris, for instance. But even here, there is suburban sprawl and decline at the center.

This underlying pattern, created in large measure by the movements of people in search of something else, is not a happy model for mankind's urban future. Its economic costs are high. To give only a few examples, within the city itself, any abandonment of existing areas means enormous loss in the shape of expensive urban capital under-used while sewers, power lines, roads and so forth are duplicated elsewhere.

One has also to count the "dead time" absorbed in distant commuting and the cost of maintaining a vast web of public commuter transport. Private traffic, often absorbing for one driver the space of four travelers, swells uncontrollably the cost of road programs.

The word "uncontrollably" is not inaccurate since modern traffic, like flood water, tends to fill completely the channels opened for it, however often they are enlarged. Last summer, the British Government rejected a handsome scheme for redesigning the rather undistinguished heart of London at Piccadilly on the ground that it underestimated the future flow of traffic. The Government's critics pointed out that no plan can satisfy future flows since the size of the roads will itself determine the scale of the traffic flow which will choke them. Even Los Angeles has not solved this dilemma, although, in trying to do so, it has virtually ceased to be a city and is now a place where catering for the automobile takes up some 70 per cent of urban space.

But economic losses involved in the provision or duplication of expensive physical plant are only the tip of the iceberg. The social costs of the modern city spread out underneath the surface of urban life, not always fully visible below the ebb and flow of daily living but cold, hard, menacing and capable of producing deadly banks of intellectual fog.

The city, after all, is not just a collection of buildings and services. It is, or should be, a community in which human beings are civilized and enriched. "Civility," "urbanity" were once the words used to express the virtues and manners by which men could be raised above crude self-concern and the blind clash of competitive instinct. Throughout most of Western civilization, in time and space, the city has been the school of the nation in the sense that Athens claimed to be "the education of Hellas." At this highest level of function, what can we say of it today?

Its vast physical dispersal must lessen its cultural impact simply because meeting, learning and exchanging experience are at the core of culture. When the leaders in wealth and education leave the city, it is not only the tax revenues that dwindle, important as they are to civic standards. Stimulus, variety, experiment wane as well. Nor does the single-class, single-culture suburb, with its predominantly female occupancy over long stretches of time, seem to make for a very vigorous cultural achievement, in spite of sincere efforts in that direction.

If this were all, the matter might not be too disturbing. There has, after all, been some recovery of civic culture in many Western centers in the last two decades. The real crisis lies in the degree to which parts of the modern city produce the opposite of culture—brutality, delinquency, antisocial behavior of every sort.

The rural populations move in with more rapidity than any present program of urban construction can match. In Lagos, in Nigeria, for instance, the effect of almost universal primary education in the up-country villages has been to send a spate of 12-year-olds, barely literate, educated to little beyond distaste for country pursuits, into a city where even unskilled jobs are scarce and possibilities of further education scarcer still. By 1970, there may be half a million unemployed school leavers concentrated in Lagos. There are already 20,000 prowling around Nairobi, and perhaps 80,000—thieving, demonstrating, despairing—in the towns of the Copper Belt.

This combustible material is already the recruiting ground of the Congo's disruptive movements, and it is increasingly available for any form of violence. Thus the cities become the centers of irresponsible pressure, and aggravate enormously Africa's gravest risk—the breakdown of civil order.

Or take the bursting cities—every one ringed with barrios and *favellas,* filthy concentrations of grass and tin huts offering, without water or light, a pretense of shelter to migrant families. At times, these settlements reach fantasies of squalor. Outside San Juan in Puerto Rico, the huts are built on piles over water. The tide brings all the scum and excrement of the city to the doorstep. On a rough day, unsuspecting health visitors sometimes even become seasick as wave and wind rock the swaying houses.

Once arrived in the city, the migrant begins the search for work, for the "golden pavements." In developing countries, the stumbling block is usually the degree to which the economy is not growing fast enough to absorb so much raw new urban labor. In many developed cities, the decline of unskilled employment as automation moves in and businesses move out has a comparable effect of high urban worklessness. The plight of the unskilled American Negro in a dozen of America's big cities can be repeated in a hundred others around the globe. There is a difference, however—an explosive one: the degree to which in America the line of misfortune follows the line of race. But even this is not unique. The Malayan migrant resents the able Chinese city dweller, the East African laborer hates the Asian middle class.

It is at this point that the dispersal of the new city adds to the social pressures. Too often those with the means, the self-confidence and the influence to confront the despair and revolt at the cities' core grow up and live in tree-lined suburbs where, from nursery to maturity, they have face-to-face contact only with their own kind. Their imagination is little nourished by the sense of a "diversity of creatures." They know little directly about the plight of not-so-distant neighbors. And all too often lack of knowledge is the beginning of fear.

One sees this segregation by residence undermining political confidence in new African states. One sees it in New Delhi, where ministers and senior civil servants live coolly and spaciously in the old imperial enclave. It is a burning, searing element in the Negro struggle for emancipation in America, since the color bar takes away an important safety valve available in other cities—the ability of anyone to move out, once a leafy, lawn-girt villa is within his economic grasp.

Wherever it is found—in new countries or old, in developing continents or the wealthy West—it is dynamite in the foundations of any urban order. And if, in the next four or five decades of headlong urban expansion, no better models emerge, the world is condemning itself to go through the most socially unstable era it has ever had to face.

200 THE GOOD NONLIFE

The process of technological advance and conditioning is invading life to a degree that is so all-pervasive that it is largely unrecognized. Technology is creating a new environment for man that is as controlling as the traditional environment of nature. This is made uncomfortably clear in a devastating analysis by Newsweek.*

* "The Good Non-Life," copyright *Newsweek,* Inc. (March 30, 1964), p. 68.

For breakfast he has non-caffeine coffee, meatless sausage, and the day's first nicotine-free cigarette. At the office he sits behind his non-working desk —a drawerless, paper-free form intended to look like a coffee table. At home, his wife has her wig, her false eyelashes, and a suntan from a bottle. His children are in school echoing the newest homilies of the teacherless teaching machine. After class his daughter practices the current non-dance, an over-all tremor requiring no movement of the feet.

This is today's surrogate world, where man can have his cake substitute (made without butter) and eat it, too. Modern science, salesmanship, and ancient human laziness have now combined to produce the ultimate miracle products—indulgence without penalties, experience without risk, deprivation without deprival. Gluttony can now be non-fattening, lust can be non-procreative, and even thought can be reduced to a complex of magnetic tapes, transistors, and computer cards. "It's all part of our technology, our sterilized environment," says Dr. Sheldon Korchin, who is head of the Psychology Clinic at the University of California at Berkeley. "Partial or substitute satisfaction, thanks to technological advancements, allows the illusion of engaging with the world when you're not."

For the cholesterol-conscious lacking the discipline of deprivation, one food synthesizer produces 40 kinds of meatless burgers, cutlets, and sausages. And for vegetarians who yearn for meaty meals but want to adhere to their principles, Ohio's Worthington Foods, Inc., puts out cans of "beef-style slices with gravy, a quick and easy dish with beef-like flavor and texture." The yummy goodness of this non-beef comes from a soybean derivative called Fibrotein (U.S. patent 2,682,466). Diners who like garlic but dislike its antisocial effects can add flavor to Fibrotein with odorless Schiff garlic capsules, which are especially good on quasi-festive occasions when washed down with "Celebration," a non-alcoholic champagne.

To recover from the celebrating, there is the modern weight-reducing "studio" with its battery of electric and steam machines that probe, slap, pummel, and vibrate. But the benefits may also be surrogates. "Mechanical horses, vibrating belts, and Turkish baths may make you feel good for the moment," says Lloyd Crofoot, physical director of New York City's Health Roof, Inc., "but they're really a waste of time. To lose weight you've got to burn up flesh with regulated physical activity and diet control."

Still, the surrogate life is ideal for the impatient—the Sunday artist who paints by numbers, the non-musician who plucks instant chords from an Autoharp or sits with a proprietary grin before that least demanding of instruments, the player piano (now enjoying a resurgence of popularity). The nonreading culture snob can now tack strips of book backs along his empty bookshelves, and the Winter Lawn Sales Corp. in Augusta, Ga., puts out a green paint to spray on lawns in winter. "People are no longer interested in planting seeds," says one garden-store chain executive. "They want to take a rose blooming from our store straight to their yard and put it in the ground."

In the city, the illusory is all around. The prewar apartment room ceilings of 10 to 12 feet are now down to 8 feet and they are still sinking. (Apartments walls, of course, no longer wall out neighboring noise.) Smaller rooms have prompted the trend toward non-furniture. One designer has shrunk 18th-century American, Hepplewhite, Chippendale, Queen Anne, and French pieces to one-third their normal size. The future is clear: mini-meals served on toy tables and chairs that can't be sat in.

A number of U.S. motels are now offering "Magic Fingers" beds, where for 25 cents the weary dilettantes can receive a 15-minute jiggling without moving a muscle. ...

When the psychic complications become too messy, psychiatrists may now practice dry-run therapy on an IBM pseudo-patient, a systematically mixed-up robot at the Stanford University Computation Center. The machine can be programed with artificial complexes and taught to respond properly, to the extent of its 257-word vocabulary, under the probing of its interrogator. "If the machine reacts badly to a line of questioning, you merely erase those questions and start again with a new approach," Dr. Kenneth Mark Colby, a Stanford University psychologist, explained last week. "It's as if you had never asked the offending questions." Once the psychiatrist has placated the machine, he can apply his refined theories to humans.

But the ultimate pacification of the psyche, of course, now comes from those modern churches that offer courses in How to Succeed in Eternity Without Really Trying. The theme is that God is promising everything for nothing—just ask for it. As the Rev. William Sloane Coffin Jr., chaplain of Yale University, put it last week: "When churches succumb to the temptation to put forth soothing assurances that everything is all right, they blunt their true message. Samuel said: 'Speak, Lord, for thy servant heareth.' When the average man communes with God today he says: 'Listen, Lord, for thy servant speaketh'." In the surrogate world, The Maker may not be listening— but the fake-makers are.

201 THREAT OF NUCLEAR WAR

Ever since Hiroshima and Nagasaki, the world has lived in dread of nuclear war. In October, 1962, it appeared that this specter might become fearful reality. The world teetered on the brink of disaster as the United States and the Soviet Union confronted each other, "eyeball to eyeball," over Cuba. An account by Newsweek *reporter Lloyd H. Norman recreates the tense situation in the Pentagon War Room as American military might was put at the ready for war.**

Far down in the gray concrete vitals of the Pentagon, in the U.S. Air Force's "War Room," a handful of red-eyed, weary, uniformed men sat on a balcony, stared down into a plastic-trimmed nightmare of electronics, and pondered the fate of the world. Panoramic screens scanned U.S. outposts around the globe, bulb-clustered boxes showed troop movements, lighted maps flashed with blobs of color, each indicating a nuclear warplane or missile aimed and "cocked" at millions of human beings who lived on in ignorance of their peril.

The target: the Soviet Union. Detonation: hours away.

That was just one year ago this week. The U.S. and the U.S.S.R. stood frighteningly close to war, the world terrifyingly close to destruction, It was

* "The Cuba Crisis: Nuclear War Was Hours Away," copyright *Newsweek,* Inc. (October 28, 1963), pp. 24, 25.

the first all-out nuclear confrontation in history. From the perspective of a year later, it appears to have brought the world from deathbed to plausible hope for a peaceful future. And a year later, the handful of men who had their forefingers pointed at the ultimate buttons could relive—in hitherto undisclosed detail—the critical week when Russia mounted the missiles on Cuba, when President Kennedy ordered that island sealed off from the world, when Russia's Premier Nikita Khrushchev was told to order the rockets out—or clsc.

"When I went down to the command post, I had a feeling I never had before," an Air Force captain recalled. "I wondered if I would see my wife and kids again. I felt we were near to war."

The captain, in that dread week of Oct. 22, 1962, descended the escalator to the Pentagon's lowest level, walked down concrete steps, and wound through deep corridors to Room BD 927. He pushed a buzzer, spoke into the microphone in a two-way mirror, and, identified, pushed through the green door that leads to the War Room.

There, he found himself on the balcony overlooking the controls and five translucent screens. Each of them showed major commands in a state of DEFCON 2—the symbol for the last combat step short of DEFCON 1, or Defense Condition 1, which is war.* Among the officers who sat in the eighteen softly upholstered, beige cloth-covered chairs was Gen. Curtis E. LeMay, Air Force Chief of Staff, who usually stays in touch from a fourth-floor office. The captain's apprehensions, in short, were well based.

For the 30-odd officers, a general's star was the only sure ticket to a seat. They could see a small box which relayed radar readings of BMEWS (Ballistic Missile Early Warning System) from stations across the top of North America; flashing numbers would count Russian missiles fired at the U.S. and predict their toll. Nearby hung a U.S. map, where NUDETS (Nuclear Detection System) would show in red dots wherever a nuclear weapon might strike.

Down on the floor of the room itself, a team of seven officers and sergeants had control of the push buttons—the lines that carried the word from these world-wide detectors to the President, the Secretary of Defense, and the Joint Chiefs of Staff. They dressed the part.

One officer and one sergeant carried holstered .38-caliber pistols, bone-handled, snub-nosed weapons intended only to shoot any member of the team who might crumble under pressure and threaten to set off war on his own panicky impulse. Two officers wore keys around their necks, each affixed to plastic tags.

Should President Kennedy himself sound the Klaxon signal for DEFCON 1, they would remove the keys, unlock separate padlocks on a red box, 2 feet by 6 inches, take out 5-inch-square plastic bags, tear them open, and pull out the same typewritten message to all Strategic Air Commands from Alaska to Guam, Spain to England. The coded message: go to war.

"We came mighty near hearing the Klaxon horn," an officer caught up in the War Room nightmare said last week. "If Khrushchev had made the wrong move and fired any of his MRBM's [medium-range ballistic missiles] at this country, SAC would have gone in."

The controls in the War Room that week showed that 90 B-52s packed

---

* DEFCON 3 and 4, progressive states of combat readiness, retreat finally to DEFCON 5, which means putative peace and leave for combat men.

with 25- and 50-megaton bombs were constantly crisscrossing the Atlantic, awaiting the order to go. On the ground, 550 more loaded B-52s, 800 lighter B-47s, and 70 faster and newer B-58 Hustlers were standing by. Eight Polaris submarines in the North Atlantic had their 128 missiles trained on Russia. In the Mediterranean and China seas, Sixth and Seventh Fleet aircraft carriers had nuclear bombers poised for take-off. Across the U.S., 102 Atlas, 54 Titan, and twelve Minuteman ICBM's [intercontinental ballistic missiles] sat on their launching pads.

SAC bombers, while circling the seas, also watched for Soviet ships heading for Cuba. "We surprised hell out of the Navy by furnishing not only the longitude and latitude but the course and speed and the name of the ships," said an Air Force officer.

While this awesome nuclear air armada assembled, other services too were one step short of war at DEFCON 2. The Army had put together the biggest invasion force since World War II, rushing about 100,000 men to the Southeast, principally Florida, where they could be ferried the 90 miles to Cuba. Besides those 100,000, said Gen. Earle G. Wheeler, Army Chief of Staff, he had 10,000 to 20,000 more for backup support. The Florida buildup included the First Armored Division, rushed from Fort Hood, Texas, by rail and air; and the Peninsula Base Command collected from the Second Logistical Command; the 82nd and 101st Airborne Divisions, and two infantry divisions.

Even before President Kennedy spoke on Oct. 22, proclaiming the quarantine of Cuba, the Army had put on air defense the Hawk missile battalion and its launchers in Key West. The First Armored began moving the next day.

The Navy broke off exercises at sea, stationing 183 warships manned by 85,000 men along a 2,100-mile quarantine line to watch for Soviet ships. Marines, thousands-strong, also moved into Florida and the Fifth Marine Brigade, plus a battalion landing team, hastened to the defense of Guantanamo, the U.S. naval base on the flank of Cuba herself.

Nor was the Soviet Union unarmed. The medium-range (1,200 miles) missiles on Cuba were all but ready to go. The intermediate-range (2,200) missiles probably would have been ready in early December. U.S. military experts fully expected the Russian threat from Cuba before Christmas.

And then Khrushchev flinched. The drooping but still vigilant men in the War Room could draw a deep, shuddering breath; the world could live for yet a while. . . .

As McNamara put it: "We confronted the Soviet Union with nuclear war over the issue of the offensive weapons and forced them to remove the offensive weapons rather than engage in nuclear war. This was our purpose, it was our objective, we accomplished it."

·　·　·　·　·

In another crisis, it would still be perilously possible for one side to misread the intentions of the other. But the sobering escape from a doomsday that either side could have touched off suggested that only accommodation held out real hope for survival. And from that realization, no less than from Russia's internal economic strains and its growing friction with China, grew a new mood in U.S.–Russian relations. That mood produced such tentative but significant steps as the opening of "the hot line" between Washington and

Moscow, the nuclear test-ban treaty, and the outlawing of nuclear weapons in space.

PROMISE OF SCIENCE 202

That the mid-twentieth century is a period of unprecedented promise as well as peril, is particularly true of science. Frequently regarded as an uncontrollable Pandora's box, it may also be viewed as a beneficent Aladdin's lamp. A distinguished scientist explains why science, if used constructively, "promises a future truly worth living for." *

A writer who offers to forecast the future ought to begin by showing his credentials. My credentials are that I am an optimist and a scientist. I know that it is not usual for a prophet to be an optimist; most prophets prefer to play the part of Jeremiah and Cassandra. But then, that is because most prophets have not been scientists either; they have not really been in favor of progress.

We can see this in the most popular prophets of our own lifetime: in Aldous Huxley and George Orwell. Every reader must be struck by the revulsion against science and, joined with that, by the deep-seated fear of the future, which Huxley and Orwell share. "Brave New World" and "1984" are surely the most depressing societies that have ever been imagined, because their authors are so full of self-righteousness. They seem to me to be, not works of prophecy, but Puritan works of morality, preaching on every page a fire-and-brimstone sermon of foreboding. From the first page, the authors are sure that progress must be wrong—that everything that is good is already known to them.

I do not intend to follow the social and political preoccupations of Huxley and Orwell. Certainly the political world will be very different fifty years from now, when Asia and Africa will be immensely more developed and more vigorous in world affairs. But I shall not discuss politics, and I shall not even discuss social life in the future, except in one way—the way in which they will be shaped by the scientific discoveries and the inventions which can be foreseen now. I shall stick to predictions which are rooted in technical grounds.

There are three outstanding scientific changes which, I believe, will dominate the next fifty years. One is a change in the use of energy: this change has been set in motion by the discovery that men can tap the energy in the atomic nucleus. The second is a change in the control of energy: this change has been set in motion by the development of those electronic devices which go under the general name of automation. And the third is what I call the biological revolution: the discovery, which is still unfamiliar to us, that men can remake their biological environment, including parts of the human body and mind.

* J. Bronowski, " '1984' Could Be a Good Year," Address to the 69th Congress of the Royal Society of Health, *The New York Times Magazine* (July 15, 1962), pp. 12, 41-45. © 1962 by The New York Times Company. Reprinted by permission.

535

NUCLEAR ENERGY.   One result of the addition of nuclear power to our other resources of power is, of course, to increase the amount of energy at the command of men the world over. What I have to say on this subject is best said in strictly numerical terms; and since I have already made these calculations once before, I should like to quote them as I made them:

"Today the inhabitants of the United States command, every man, woman and child, the amount of mechanical energy each year that would be generated, roughly, by ten tons of coal. This is the backing that civilization provides now, and it is equal, again at a rough estimate, to the work that would be done by a hundred slaves. If we are no longer a slave civilization, it is because even a child in the United States has as much work done for it as would require the muscle of a hundred slaves. By contrast, Athens at her richest provided for the average member of a citizen's family—man, woman or child—no more than five slaves.

"In most parts of the world, people today still command only a fraction of the American standard. In India, for example, the average use of energy amounts to the equivalent of about half a ton of coal a year, or five slaves—the standard of Athens over 2,000 years ago. This is the figure that will rise most steeply in the next fifty years. It cannot rise to the standard of the United States in that time, but it can reach a fifth of that standard. We can expect that in the next fifty years the energy used in the poorest countries will reach at least the equivalent of twenty slaves a head each year.

"It may seem very cold to measure the lives of people by the mechanical equivalent of two tons of coal a year, or twenty slaves. But the figure is not at all cold. In the first place, it could not be achieved had nuclear energy not been discovered. All the resources of the traditional fuels in the world would not yield this figure; and the dreams of liberal minds, to raise the dark races to the standard of the white, were an illusion until nuclear energy was discovered. The standards of the West will become at least tangible to the backward countries in the next fifty years because nuclear energy can provide the power."

This is one important effect of the coming of nuclear energy; and yet, to my mind, it is not the most important. To my mind, what is most important is that energy will be more evenly distributed in the future. It will no longer be necessary to concentrate industry where either coal or oil is plentiful. We shall not need to take the industry to the fuel, but the other way about—the fuel, the nuclear fuel, to the industry. For a nuclear fuel is more than a million times as concentrated as a chemical fuel; and where we could not take a million tons of coal or oil, to South America, to the copperbelt, to the Australian desert, we shall be able to take a ton of uranium or of heavy hydrogen.

True, it will, for example, still be proportionately cheaper to build a large nuclear power station than a small one. But there is now no longer an inherent difficulty in siting any power station far from the line of supply of its fuel. In the past, the logic of concentrating the generation of electric power in a few large stations was that it was easier to carry the current from the station in a wire than to carry the coal to the station in a truck. But if the fuel is nuclear fuel, this is no longer so; a small nuclear station can become the center of a remote township as effectively as it already drives a submarine or keeps an army camp alive under the polar ice.

Over the next fifty years, nuclear energy is also essential to the growing of food on a world scale. It is, of course, clear that if energy is cheap, then it is possible to make a substitute for any material that we need, all the way from industrial diamonds to vitamins. In this sense, then, we can count on finding a decent standard of living, in food as well as in energy, for all the six billion people who will be alive fifty years from now. And in agriculture, we shall need nuclear energy above all for the irrigation and exploitation of marginal lands, including the brackish lands now poisoned by salt water.

If energy is cheap and transportable anywhere, then irrigation is possible anywhere. In agriculture, what energy will buy fifty years from now is water; and water will be the key to growing food for the world's population, which will be twice as large as today.

AUTOMATION.   Second, I want to discuss the future influence of automation. In one sense, an automatic machine is still a machine, and automation is no more than the logical use of machines. But, in fact, automation implies such a difference in outlook, such a change in the conception of the place of the machine itself, that I ought to discuss it quite fundamentally.

Two hundred years ago, the West discovered that a man's or a woman's output of work can be multiplied many times if the repetitive tasks which a handworker must do are done by a machine. Machines were invented, all the way from the power loom to the mechanical digger, that could mimic those actions of the human muscle which a man must carry out laboriously and monotonously, time and time again, in order to get a piece of work finished. The wealth of the West, and its high standard of living, derive directly from the revolution in manufacture—the Industrial Revolution—which these machines created.

Until recently, the machines of industry confined themselves to those mechanical tasks which need muscle and no more. Only in the last years have we come to see, what now seems obvious enough, that any repetitive task is really best handled by a machine. This is true, whether the repetitive task is muscular, like rolling steel sheets, or whether it demands more delicate skills of calculation and judgment, such as controlling the thickness of the steel and computing its price.

This is the real nature of automation: the discovery that repetition is a machine task, even if the repetition is in adding up a ledger or controlling the distillation of a chemical. Men and women thrive on variety, but machines thrive on monotony. Machines do not get bored (and they seldom get tired), their attention does not wander, they do not feel that their gifts are being wasted. They like nothing better than to repeat themselves.

Fifty years from now, the machine operator of any kind will be as much a fossil as the hand-weaver has been since 1830. Today we still distinguish between skilled and unskilled jobs of repetition, between office worker and factory worker, between white collar and no collar. In fifty years from now, all repetitive jobs will be unskilled.

The social implications of this change are profound, and I believe that they, more than anything else that I have forecast, will shape the community of the future. For their effect will be to change the social status of the different jobs in the community. The ability to handle a column of figures will become no more desirable than the ability to drive a rivet; and even the ability to write business letters may become less sought after than the ability to repair the machine that writes them by rote. As a result, the clerk will sink in social status, and the electrical technician will rise; and that in itself is a change as far-reaching as was once brought about by the dissolution of the monasteries.

A SOCIAL REVOLUTION. Here I want to turn boldly to make a social prophecy. I believe that the combined effect of nuclear energy and of automation will be to revolutionize the way in which men run their industries. Today industries are concentrated in large cities. The reasons for this are twofold: we find it convenient to generate energy on a large scale, and at the same time we have to have large labor forces.

I have already shown that nuclear energy will make it possible to generate electric power in quite small units, where it is wanted. One reason for working in large cities will therefore disappear. But industry has moved to (and has created) large cities for another reason also: in the search, above all, for people. A product, whether it is a car or a can of polish, goes through many stages, so that many hands are needed to process and pass it on step by step. Is there any reason to think that industry will be able to break away from the huge arrays of semi-skilled workers which have served it hitherto?

I think that industry *is* breaking away, and that the traditional mass of factory hands *is* shrinking. The new wind in industry is automation, and I believe that it can transform industrial life in the next fifty years. There has been a great deal of technical talk about automation in recent years, but once again its more remote but important social consequences seem to me to have been missed. Yet automation is likely to revolutionize the balance between work and leisure, and the size and structure of community life, in the next fifty years.

Our industrial civilization has gone on herding people together in huge complexes of cities. Now there is a hope that the next fifty years may reverse this trend, and may begin to dissolve the ugly concentrations of the Ruhr and the Clyde, of Pittsburgh and Tokyo. In automation, joined to nuclear energy, we have the means to run industries on the scale of a small country town—a scale which does not dwarf the human sense of community.

This shift in the pattern of working life is the most far-reaching change that I foresee. The fifty years ahead of us will provide the means to create a social revolution: to create lively and efficient small communities which can hold their own in the industrial world.

There are many things to be gained by leaving the large cities. For example, we shall gain the hours (about one eighth of our waking hours) which most workers now spend in the tedium and discomfort of travel. This is a great gain in leisure, and some people will think that it will create new problems of leisure. I do not think so; I think that leisure is only a problem today in those places where tedium and discomfort have reduced everyone to a dull indifference.

I am not the first prophet, or the first dreamer, to hope that the monstrous cities of today, like glaciers of an industrial ice age, will begin to melt away. But when social reformers in the past have longed for small communities which could be self-sufficient, they have usually wanted to found them on agriculture. They have wanted to go back to the land literally—to work on the land. This is quite unrealistic, now and in the future.

In short, it is not necessary to retreat from the disaster of the metropolis into the inertia of the village. The small town of the future can be as well-equipped, physically and intellectually, as the largest modern city. It will be served physically by the new forms of travel, and intellectually by the new links of communication which we can already foresee. My guess is that it will then need to be large enough only to support those unpractical but delightful luxuries which give life to a community—a baseball club and a theatre and places where people play chess or go bowling. I think that you can do all these things in a town of about thirty thousand strong, and this is my forecast of the size of the new industrial communities in the future.

But the small community that I have sketched has no room for dullness and indifference. If thirty thousand people make an industrial town which is physically and intellectually self-sufficient, they must all be skilled. The one unpractical luxury that they cannot afford is a man with no skill.

THE BIOLOGICAL REVOLUTION.   The third fundamental change which will, I think, shape the future is what I have called the biological revolution. We are just beginning to learn that we can mold our biological environment as well as our physical one. During the next fifty years, this will be the most exciting and, I believe, the most influential work in science.

Let me single out a few lines of work which seem to me especially interesting and promising.

There is, to begin with, the practical progress in the attack on organisms which damage us. They may be pests which damage our food supply, at one extreme, or microbes which invade our bodies at the other. Fine work has already been done in developing specific chemicals to tackle each specific enemy. I think this method of combat, the development of exact and specific chemicals, will play a growing part in making men healthier and richer.

Let me give one example. We used to think that a man could produce the antibodies which resist a virus infection (for example, smallpox) only if he were given a mild dose of the infection. Now we know that this is not necessary. We know that a virus consists of two parts—a living center of nucleic acid, and an outside covering of protein. And we know that the protein covering alone will suffice to stimulate the cells to produce the antibodies which fight the whole virus. This is how, for example, the protein in the killed polio vaccine works.

I believe in the future we shall go even further: we shall protect against a virus disease by making, in the chemical laboratory, the protein covering of that virus.

This leads me to the next outstanding field of study. We know that there are drugs which greatly sharpen a man's faculties, and others which help him to be at peace with himself. Each kind of drug helps a man to make better use of his natural (but often hidden) gifts. I am sure that there is a bright prospect here for the future and that, as a result, men and women will lead livelier and happier lives, in work and in leisure right into their old age.

Finally, I should pay tribute to the searching work that is being done in the study of biological processes on the smallest, molecular scale. This has already given us a new understanding of the nature and of the dynamics of life, and at this very moment it has opened a deep insight into the basis of all heredity. I believe that in the long run this fundamental knowledge, which still seems abstract and remote, will have the greatest effect of all in the practice of medicine.

SCIENCE FOR PEACE.   I began by saying that I am an optimist and a scientist, and you now see that the two go together. There is plenty of ground for pessimism in world affairs, and perhaps we shall not avoid the suicide of mankind. But can we not? Can we not prevent the leaders of nations from being proudest of those scientific inventions which make the loudest bang?

We *must,* exactly because science has so much better uses to offer for its fundamental discoveries. I have shown you the rich future that should grow out of the very discoveries that people dread most—out of nuclear energy, automation, and biological advance.

What people fear is the reach, the power of these discoveries. And there people are not foolish: they recognize that nuclear energy, automation, and biological advance are the most powerful social forces of this century. But that power can be as great in peace as in war; we can use it to create the future and not to murder it. Science promises a future in which men can lead intelligent and healthy lives in cities of a human size, and I think it is a future truly worth living for.

203 SECOND INDUSTRIAL REVOLUTION

The mid-twentieth century is witnessing also the fateful advent of the second industrial revolution. The first, which began in Britain in the late eighteenth century, replaced the handicraft worker with the machine operator; the second, characterized by automation, is replacing the machine operator with the supervisor of an automatically controlled operating system. The second industrial revolution, like the first, is responsible for considerable unemployment and dislocation in certain branches of the economy. But this should not obscure its potential for a tremendous increase in human productivity and, ultimately, a corresponding decrease in human want. The contrast between the two revolutions is depicted in the following selections, the first describing the evolution of the Ford conveyor belt at the beginning of the twentieth century, and the second, the operation of an automated Ford engine plant half a century later.*

Conveyor Belt

The idea of the belt was borrowed from the Chicago packers, who used an overhead trolley to swing carcasses of beef down a line of butchers. Ford tried the idea first in assembling a small unit in his motor, the fly-wheel magneto, then in assembling the motor itself, and then in assembling the chassis.

A chassis was hitched to a rope one day, and six workmen, picking up parts along the way and bolting them in place, travelled with it on an historic journey down a line two hundred and fifty feet in length as a windlass dragged it through the factory. The experiment worked, but developed one difficulty. God had not made men as accurately as Ford made piston rings. The line was too high for the short men and too low for the tall men, with a resultant waste in effort.

* Charles Merz, *And Then Came Ford* (Garden City: Doubleday, 1929), pp. 198-99. Copyright 1929 by Doubleday & Company, Inc. Reprinted by permission of the publisher. Robert Bendiner, "The Age of the Thinking Robot, and What It Will Mean to Us," *The Reporter,* XII (April 7, 1955), 13, 14. Copyright 1955 by The Reporter Magazine Company.

More experiments were tried. The line was raised; then lowered; then two lines were tried, to suit squads of different heights; the speed of the line was increased; then lessened; various tests were made to determine how many men to put on one assembly line, how far to subdivide the operations, whether to let one man who set a bolt in place put on the nut and the man who put on the nut to take time to tighten it. In the end, the time allotted for assembly on a chassis was cut from twelve hours and twenty-eight minutes to one hour and thirty-three minutes, the world was promised Model T's in new abundance, and mass production entered a new phase as men were made still more efficient cogs of their machines.

Engine Plant

Automation has made most headway in industries most readily reduced to a continuous-flow process—such as oil refining, flour milling, and chemical production. . . .

Solids are harder to handle, but some of the most complex problems were solved by the time the Ford Motor Company opened its much-publicized engine plant near Cleveland three years ago. Here six-cylinder engine blocks are turned out by the union of an electronic brain, fed by twenty-seven miles of wire, and forty-two mechanical hands in the form of automatic machine units. Through this giant complex, 1,545 feet long, rough castings are pushed, pulled, turned in every direction, conveyed, and subjected to cutting, drilling, honing, milling, boring, and broaching in more than five hundred manless operations, each one checked and inspected only by the "brain" itself for performance and accuracy. Thoroughly instructed in advance, it decides when a block is ready for the grinder, how fine it is to be ground, and where it is to move when it is done. A block that once took nine hours to complete is now sped through in fifteen minutes.

Where it once took thirty-nine men working twenty-nine machines just to drill the necessary oil holes in a crankshaft, only nine men are needed for that job at the new Ford plant. Most of the small crew lost in the acre of machinery stand by and watch, and replace worn tools whenever a "tool-meter" panel flashes the signal that some particular instrument is approaching the end of its usefulness. "Ours is the only foundry in the world," says the manager proudly, "where the molding sand used to make castings is never touched by human hands except maybe out of curiosity."

GLOBAL RESPONSIBILITY 204

A unique and promising feature of this age is a growing sense of global consciousness and global responsibility, the product in part, of the world's new physical unity through modern communication and transportation, and of the accelerating productivity that makes global welfare a feasible goal rather than a romantic notion. The nature and significance of this sense of global responsibility is analyzed by the well-known historian Arnold Toynbee. A concrete example of this

sense of responsibility is provided in President Johnson's eloquent appeal for
*foreign aid as an act of necessity and as a moral imperative.**

542

Arnold Toynbee

Can we guess what the outstanding feature of our twentieth century will appear to be in the perspective of 300 years? No doubt we shall not all guess alike. Some of us will guess that the present age will be looked back upon as the age of scientific discovery. Others will expect to see it branded as the age in which Fascist and Communist apostates from a Christian civilization harnessed science to the service of a neo-barbarism. My own guess is that our age will be remembered chiefly neither for its horrifying crimes nor for its astonishing inventions, but for its having been the first age since the dawn of civilization, some five or six thousand years back, in which people dared to think it practicable to make the benefits of civilization available for the whole human race.

By comparison with the significance of this common twentieth century new ideal, the differences between the conflicting ideologies will—so I should guess—come to look both less important and less interesting than will be easily credible to anyone alive today. In the easy wisdom that comes after the event, our successors will perhaps, be able to pronounce that this or that policy for achieving a common twentieth century ideal was more suitable than the rival policy was to the social conditions of this or that region in that antique and still unstandardized twentieth century world.

They may even judge one twentieth century ideology as better or worse than another in some absolute moral sense. But the common features of our century will, I fancy, be the features standing out the most prominently in perspective; and, among these, the new ideal and objective of extending the benefits of civilization to the common man will in future centuries tower above the rest.

Perhaps there are two points here that are worth underlining: This vision of a good life for all is a new one, and—whatever our success or our failure may be in the attempt to translate this vision into reality—this new social objective has probably come to stay. That the ideal of welfare for all is new is surely true; for, as far as I can see, it is no older than the seventeenth century West European settlements on the east coast of North America that have grown into the United States. And it has surely come to stay with us as long, at any rate, as our new invention of applying mechanical power to technology. Mankind's hope of better things lies in a permanent industrial revolution.

The outlook of the twentieth century world at large is governed, as I see it, by two facts. The first fact is that three-quarters of mankind are today still living the traditional life of an agricultural civilization in which there is no reserve of virgin soil and therefore no possibility of providing more than a tiny minority of the population with anything better than bare subsistence out of agricultural production.

But, in this old-fashioned starveling agrarian world, the Industrial Revolu-

---

* Arnold J. Toynbee, "Not an Age of Atoms but of Welfare for All," *The New York Times Magazine* (October 2, 1951), p. 15; *The New York Times* (April 22, 1964). © 1951, 1964 by The New York Times Company. Reprinted by permission.

tion has brought with it a hope for all mankind, from the prosperous American technician and farmer to the most miserable Chinese or Indian coolie, of breaking right through the iron limits to which the extension of the benefits of civilization has normally been subject in an agricultural society.

This hope is now rapidly dawning in the hearts of the depressed and ignorant peasantry that today still constitutes three-quarters of the living generation of mankind. They have begun to ask themselves how they are to attain those benefits of civilization which a mechanized technology has at last brought within the horizon of every man's hopes.

How is this depressed three-quarters of mankind going to set about the stupendously difficult task of gaining the benefits of civilization? Now that the hundreds of millions of peasants are aware of the relative well-being of the Western peoples, nothing is going to stop them from setting out to reach a goal which the West seems to them to have attained already. And no doubt only trial and error are going to make them aware of the difficulties in their path which are glaringly manifest to Western eyes.

President Lyndon Johnson

On three continents, in dozens of countries, hundreds of millions of people struggle to exist on incomes of little more than a dollar a week. In the 112 or more nations, only six of them have an income of as much as $80 a month, Sweden and Switzerland, Australia and New Zealand, Canada and the United States.

Here we ought to get down on our knees every night and thank the Good Lord for our blessings, that our income can be more than $200 a month, when more than two-thirds of the people of the world have less than $8 a month.

These people have less to spend each day on food and on shelter and on clothing, on medicine, on all of their needs, than the average American spends at his corner drug store for a package of cigarettes. They live in run-down country shacks of tar paper. They live in city slums. They live without heat, water or sanitation of any kind.

Their children have no schools to go to. They have no doctors or hospitals to attend. Their life expectancy is somewhere between 35 and 40 years of age. Worst of all, many of them live without any hope at all. They see no escape from the ancient cycle of misery and despair.

These are not new conditions. Poverty, hunger, and disease are afflictions as old as man himself. But in our time and in this age there has been a change. The change is not so much in the realities of life, but in the hopes and the expectations of the future. If a peaceful revolution in these areas is impossible a violent revolution is inevitable.

We who stand here in peace and security and prosperity must realize that we are greatly outnumbered in this world, more than 17 to 1 in population, in area, in race, in religion, in color. You take any criteria and measure yourself by that standard, and you will find that we are in a very small minority.

This knowledge has helped create the worldwide boom of vast portent which we know as the revolution of rising expectations. The meaning of this revolution is very simple.

It means that people in the rest of the world want for themselves the same things that you and I want for our loved ones, for our friends, and for our children, and that most of us already have.

They intend that their families shall live a decent life and that they have a job that gives them survival and dignity. They intend that their children shall be taught to read and to write. They intend that the hungry shall be fed and the sick shall be treated. They intend to take their place in the great movement of modern society, to take their share in the benefits of that society.

These just desires, once unleashed, can never again be stifled. The people of the developing world are on the march, and we want to be beside them on that march. . . .

Our gross national product in this, the richest of all nations, this quarter, is running at the rate of $608.6 billion. . . . We are asking to distribute in the form of help, aid, and military assistance to all the nations who want to have freedom less than one-half of 1 per cent of that amount—3 billion 400 million.

But because of what we call it, and because of how it has been administered, and because it is far away, we don't realize that this investment is not only one of the most Christian acts that this great, powerful, rich country could do, but it is an act of necessity if we are to preserve our image in the world and our leadership in the world, and most of all, our society.

We must help developing countries because our own welfare demands it. It takes no great gift of foresight to realize that unless there is progress and unless there is growing satisfaction of just desires, there will be discontent and there will be restlessness.

The developing world would soon become a cauldron of violence, hatred and revolution without some assistance. How would you feel if you were a member of a family whose total income was less than $80 per year? Yet a majority of the people of the world have incomes of less than $80 a year.

Under such conditions, Communism, with its false and easy promises of a magic formula, might well be able to transform these popular desires into an instrument of revolution. That is why every American who is concerned about the future of his country must also be concerned about the future of Africa, Asia and our old friends in Latin America. . . .

Every night when I go to bed I ask myself, "What did we do today that we can point to for generations to come, to say that we laid the foundation for a better and more peaceful and more prosperous world?"

205 ONE VOTE FOR THIS AGE OF ANXIETY

In this final reading, the anxieties of the mid-twentieth century are considered in a new perspective. For those who denigrate this "age of anxiety" and romanticize earlier periods as ages of bucolic bliss, this analysis by a distinguished American anthropologist affords a salutary corrective.*

* Margaret Mead, "One Vote for This Age of Anxiety," *The New York Times Magazine* (May 20, 1956), pp. 13, 56. © 1956 by The New York Times Company. Reprinted by permission.

When critics wish to repudiate the world in which we live today, one of their familiar ways of doing it is to castigate modern man because anxiety is his chief problem. This, they say, in W. H. Auden's phrase, is the age of anxiety. This is what we have arrived at with all our vaunted progress, our great technological advances, our great wealth—everyone goes about with a burden of anxiety so enormous that, in the end, our stomachs and our arteries and our skins express the tension under which we live. Americans who have lived in Europe come back to comment on our favorite farewell which, instead of the old goodbye (God be with you), is now "Take it easy," each American admonishing the other not to break down from the tension and strain of modern life.

Whenever an age is characterized by a phrase, it is presumably in contrast to other ages. If we are the age of anxiety, what were other ages? And here the critics and carpers do a very amusing thing. First, they give us lists of the opposites of anxiety: security, trust, self-confidence, self-direction. Then, without much further discussion, they let us assume that other ages, other periods of history, were somehow the ages of trust or confident direction.

The savage who, on his South Sea island, simply sat and let breadfruit fall into his lap, the simple peasant, at one with the fields he ploughed and the beasts he tended, the craftsman busy with his tools and lost in the fulfillment of the instinct of workmanship—these are the counter-images conjured up by descriptions of the strain under which men live today. But no one who lived in those days has returned to testify how paradisiacal they really were.

Certainly if we observe and question the savages or simple peasants in the world today, we find something quite different. The untouched savage in the middle of New Guinea isn't anxious; he is seriously and continually *frightened*—of black magic, of enemies with spears who may kill him or his wives and children at any moment, while they stoop to drink from a spring, or climb a palm tree for a coconut. He goes warily, day and night, taut and fearful.

As for the peasant populations of a great part of the world, they aren't so much anxious as hungry. They aren't anxious about whether they will get a salary raise, or which of the three colleges of their choice they will be admitted to, or whether to buy a Ford or Cadillac, or whether the kind of TV set they want is too expensive. They are hungry, cold and, in many parts of the world, they dread that local warfare, bandits, political coups may endanger their homes, their meager livehihoods and their lives. But surely they are not anxious.

For anxiety, as we have come to use it to describe our characteristic state of mind, can be contrasted with the active fear of hunger, loss, violence and death. Anxiety is the appropriate emotion when the immediate personal terror—or a volcano, an arrow, the sorcerer's spell, a stab in the back and other calamities, all directed against one's self—disappears.

This is not to say that there isn't plenty to worry about in our world of today. The explosion of a bomb in the streets of a city whose name no one had ever heard before may set in motion forces which end up by ruining one's carefully planned education in law school, half a world away. But there is still not the personal, immediate, active sense of impending disaster that the savage knows. There is rather the vague anxiety, the sense that the future is unmanageable.

The kind of world that produces anxiety is actually a world of relative safety, a world in which no one feels that he himself is facing sudden death. Possibly sudden death may strike a certain number of unidentified other people—but not him. The anxiety exists as an uneasy state of mind, in which one has a feeling that something unspecified and undeterminable may go wrong. If the world seems to be going well, this produces anxiety—for good times may end. If the world is going badly—it may get worse. Anxiety tends to be without locus; the anxious person doesn't know whether to blame himself or other people. He isn't sure whether it is 1956 or the Administration or a change in climate or the atom bomb that is to blame for this undefined sense of unease.

It is clear that we have developed a society which depends on having the *right* amount of anxiety to make it work. Psychiatrists have been heard to say, "He didn't have enough anxiety to get well," indicating that, while we agree that too much anxiety is inimical to mental health, we have come to rely on anxiety to push and prod us into seeing a doctor about a symptom which may indicate cancer, into checking up on that old life insurance policy which may have out-of-date clauses in it, into having a conference with Billy's teacher even though his report card looks all right.

People who are anxious enough keep their car insurance up, have the brakes checked, don't take a second drink when they have to drive, are careful where they go and with whom they drive on holidays. People who are too anxious either refuse to go into cars at all—and so complicate the ordinary course of life—or drive so tensely and overcautiously that they help cause accidents. People who aren't anxious enough take chance after chance, which increases the terrible death toll of the roads.

On balance, our age of anxiety represents a large advance over savage and peasant cultures. Out of a productive system of technology drawing upon enormous resources, we have created a nation in which anxiety has replaced terror and despair, for all except the severely disturbed. The specter of hunger means something only to those Americans who can identify themselves with the millions of hungry people on other continents. The specter of terror may still be roused in some by a knock at the door in a few parts of the South, or in those who have just escaped from a totalitarian regime or who have kin still behind the Curtains.

But in this twilight world which is neither at peace nor at war, and where there is insurance against certain immediate, downright, personal disasters, for most Americans there remains only anxiety over what may happen, might happen, could happen.

This is the world out of which grows the hope, for the first time in history, of a society where there will be freedom from want and freedom from fear. Our very anxiety is born of our knowledge of what is now possible for each and for all. The number of people who consult psychiatrists today is not, as is sometimes felt, a symptom of increasing mental ill health, but rather the precursor of a world in which the hope of genuine mental health will be open to everyone, a world in which no individual feels that he need be hopelessly brokenhearted, a failure, a menace to others or a traitor to himself.

INDEX